The Franks in the Aegean, 1204–1500

The Franks in the Aegean, 1204–1500

Peter Lock

Longman
London and New York

Longman Group Limited,
Longman House, Burnt Mill,
Harlow, Essex CM20 2JE, England
and Associated Companies throughout the world.

Published in the United States of America
by Longman Publishing, New York

First published 1995

ISBN 0 582 05140 1 CSD
ISBN 0 582 05139 8 PPR

British Library Cataloguing-in-Publication Data

A catalogue record for this book is
available from the British Library

Library of Congress Cataloging-in-Publication Data

Lock, Peter, 1949–
    The Franks in the Aegean, 1204-1500 / Peter Lock.
      p. cm.
    Includes bibliographical references and index.
    ISBN 0-582-05140-1 (CSD). -- ISBN 0-582-05139-8 (PPR)
    1. Franks--Aegean Sea Region--History. 2. Byzantine Empire-
  -History--1081-1453. 3. Crusades--Later, 13th, 14th, and 15th
  centuries. 4. Civilization, Aegean--Foreign influences. I. Title.
  DF609.L63 1995
  949.5'02--dc20
                                                94-39822
                                                    CIP

Set by 7.00 in 10/12 Sabon
Produced by Longman Singapore Publishers (Pte) Ltd.
Printed in Singapore

Contents

List of Genealogical Tables and Maps

Genealogical Tables

Maps

Acknowledgements

My debt to institutions and to individuals is enormous. All have contributed to the improvement of this work and none are responsible for any errors or infelicities which remain. In particular I would like to express my thanks to friends and colleagues in the Department of History at the University College of Ripon and York St John, the Department of History at the University of Nottingham, and the British School of Archaeology at Athens for help, criticism and support; to the various librarians at my own college, at the Hallward Library of the University of Nottingham, at the Cambridge University Library, at the British School in Athens, and at the London Library for unfailing help and courtesy in dealing with numerous obscure requests over the years; to the Institute for Medieval Studies at the University of Nottingham for awarding me a Visiting Fellowship in 1991/2 which permitted much of the research for this book to be undertaken; to John Bintliff and Anthony Snodgrass, co-directors of the Boeotia Survey, who fostered and encouraged my interest in the Franks; to Peter Burridge, Christine Hodgetts, Eric Ivison and Guy Sanders for informative and stimulating conversations on matters Frankish; to my parents Edgar and Eva Lock for their interest and support, and to Andrew MacLennan and Stephanie Cooke of Longman who must be two of the most courteous and enthusiastic editors any author could have. My especial thanks go to Bernard Hamilton, Ruth Macrides and Jonathan Phillips who read drafts of all or part of the book, made numerous valuable suggestions and saved me from many errors; those that remain are my personal contribution. Throughout I have relied heavily on the writings of others. I hope that I have given an accurate summary of their work and due acknowledgement to it in the appropriate places. If I have not, I tender my apologies unreservedly. Writing a book is very much a family affair and my love and thanks go to Joan, Sophie and Alexander who now know a lot about the Franks in the Aegean. I hope that they will enjoy the book and it is to them that it is dedicated.

Abbreviations

ABSA *Annual of the British School of Archaeology.*
Akropolites A. Heisenberg, ed., *Georgii Acropolitae Opera*, 2 vols (Leipzig, 1903), citation by page.
AFP *Archivum fratrum Praedicatorum.*
AHR *American Historical Review.*
AJA *American Journal of Archaeology.*
BCH *Bulletin de correspondance hellénique.*
BMF A. Bon, *La Morée Franque* (Paris, 1969).
ByzF *Byzantinische Forschungen.*
BZ *Byzantinische Zeitschrift.*
CGR C. Hopf, *Chroniques Gréco-romanes, inédites ou peu-connue* (Berlin, 1873; reprinted Bruxelles, 1966), citations by page.
Choniates J.A. Van Dieten, ed., *Nicetae Choniatae Historia* (Berlin, 1975), citations by page.
Choniates (Magoulias trans.) H.J. Magoulias, *O City of Byzantium, Annals of Niketas Choniates* (Detroit, 1984), citation by page.
Clari P. Lauer, ed., *Robert de Clari, La Conquête de Constantinople*, (Paris, 1924), citations by paragraph.
Clari (McNeal trans.) E.H. McNeal, *The Conquest of Constantinople Translated From the Old French of Robert of Clari* (New York, 1936), citation by page.
DOC Antoni Rubio I Lluch, ed., *Diplomatari de l'Orient Català (1301–1409)*, (Barcelona, 1947), citation by document number and page.
DOP *Dumbarton Oaks Papers.*
EHR *English Historical Review.*
JHS *Journal of Hellenic Studies.*
L de C J. Longnon, ed., *Livre de La Conqueste de la Princée de L'Amorée: Chronique de Morée* (Paris, 1911), citation by paragraph (French version).
L de F A. Morel-Fatio, ed., *Libro de los Fechos et Conquistas del*

Principado de la Morea (Geneva, 1885), cited by paragraph (Aragonese/Castilian version).

Longnon & Topping J. Longnon & P. Topping, eds, *Documents sur le Régime des Terres dans La Principauté de Morée au XIVe Siècle* (Paris, 1969), citation by page/line numbers.

MGH, SS *Monumenta Germaniae historica. Scriptores.*

Muntaner *Cronica* Karl Lanz, ed., *Chronik des edlin en Ramon Muntaner* (Stuttgart, 1844).

OCP *Orientalia christiana periodica.*

ODB A. Kazhdan et al., eds., *The Oxford Dictionary of Byzantium* 3 vols (New York, 1991), citation by page.

Pachymeres I. Bekker, ed., *De Michaele et Andronico Palaeologo, Libri XIII* 2 vols (Bonn, 1835), citation by page.

PBSR *Papers of the British School at Rome.*

Perrat & Longnon C. Perrat & J. Longnon, eds, *Actes Relatifs a la Principauté de Morée*, (Paris, 1967), citation by page and/or document.

PL J-P. Migne, *Patrologiae cursus completus. Series Latina* 217 vols (Paris, 1844–64), citation by volume and column number.

Pressutti P. Pressutti, ed., *Regesta Honorii papae III* 2 vols (Rome, 1888–95), citation by abstract number.

Register Clement V Benedictines of Monte Cassino, eds, *Registrum Clementis Papae V ex Vaticanis Archetypis* 9 vols, (Rome, 1885–92).

RHGF M. Bouquet et al., eds., *Recueil des Historiens des Gaules et de la France* 24 vols (Paris, 1738–1904).

Setton K. Setton, *The Papacy and the Levant (1204–1571)* I (Philadelphia, 1976).

Thiriet F. Thiriet, *Régestes des Délibérations du Sénat de Venise concernant La Romanie* 3 vols (Paris, 1958–61), citation by abstract number.

TM *Travaux et Mémoires du Centre de Recherche d'Histoire et Civilisation byzantines.*

TRHS *Transactions of the Royal Historical Society.*

Urkunden G.L.F. Tafel & G.M. Thomas, eds, *Urkunden zur Älteren Handels- und Staatsgeschichte Der Republik Venedig*, 3 vols (Vienna, 1856–57; reprinted Amsterdam, 1964), citation by volume and page.

Valenciennes J. Longnon, ed., *Henri de Valenciennes, Histoire de l'Empereur Henri de Constantinople* (Paris, 1948), citation by paragraph.

Villehardouin E. Faral, ed., *Villehardouin, La Conquête de Constantinople* 2 vols (Paris, 1938), citation by paragraph.

X t M. J. Schmitt, ed., *The Chronicle of Morea, To Chronikon Tou Moreos* (London, 1904; reprinted New York, 1979), citation by line number.

Currencies and Grain Measurement

1 hyperperon	=	20 sterlini or sterlings
1 hyperperoñ	=	80 deniers tournois or tornesi
1 hyperperon	=	96 Venetian billon torneselli
1 sterlino	=	4 deniers tournois
3 hyperpera	=	1 ducat = 1 livre d'Anjou
1 hyperperon	=	8 grossi
1 ducat	=	24 grossi
240 grossi	=	10 ducats = 1 livre de gros

The gold onza was a money of account (ie. not actually coined). It was equivalent to 3,600 denari.

The gold hyperperon had ceased to be minted by 1400 and became a money of account.

It is uncertain what these currencies were worth in the middle ages and impossible to give a modern value.

Grain, like some other agricultural products, was variously measured by the salma (seaume or seam) and the misura (measure).
These were measures of capacity not weight.
In Venice and its Aegean possessions wheat was sold in quantities of 100 measures. The misura was equivalent to about 80 litres.
In Naples and the Principality of Achaia grain transactions were carried on in terms of the salma which approximated to 275–300 litres.

The Frankish Aegean: Background, Context and Problems

The Frankish states in the Aegean were set up after the capture of Constantinople by French and Venetian crusaders in 1204. The world of the Frankish Aegean was small-scale and complex. It was politically fragmented and lacked any real focal point. The mountainous terrain fostered any impetus for regionalism and tended to accentuate the process of fragmentation. The external political influences with which the rulers of these states had to contend were also diverse, disunited and frequently opposed to one another. In brief they may be listed as the papacy, the royal courts in Paris, Naples, Palermo, and Barcelona, the Vlacho-Bulgarian kingdom centred on Tirnovo, the Serbs and Albanians, the Seljuks of Rum at Konya, and the various Greek successor states to Byzantium in Arta, Thessalonika, Nicaea and Trebizond. This world was only in small part a creation of the western crusaders. The Byzantine empire into which the Frankish conquerors moved was very old in 1204. Just as they needed guides to the towns and territories which they acquired, so the modern reader coming fresh to the medieval Aegean may well feel the need for an overview before venturing further. This chapter is for them. Those readers who are already familiar with medieval Byzantium may skip through this first chapter if they wish. Like many of the Venetian crusaders in 1204 they will already know what they are looking for. A full chronological summary of the principal political and military events of the period from 1204 to 1500 is provided in Appendix 1 and a list of rulers will be found in Appendix 2.

The Byzantine empire

In 330 the emperor Constantine refounded the city of Byzantium on the Bosphorus as Constantinople, the City of Constantine. It remained the

1

capital of the Byzantine empire until 1453.[1] The term Byzantine was a creation of French scholars in the seventeenth century. The people of the empire called themselves 'Rhomaioi', the inhabitants of the Roman empire (*basilieia ton Rhomaion*). They thus acknowledged that their territorial possessions and many of their political traditions were the legacy of the late Roman empire. At the same time they were not fossilised Romans. Their language was Greek and their religion Christianity. The empire was the first Christian state and its armies might be said to be always fighting for God in the defence of an empire which encompassed the civilised Christian world. Between the fourth and the seventh centuries there had been many cultural and perceptional changes which had turned the eastern Roman empire into medieval Byzantium. Precisely when it is appropriate to speak of the Byzantine rather than the late Roman empire is a matter of debate. Alexander Kazdhan and Ann Wharton Epstein have drawn attention to the importance of the seventh century in this process and have emphasised the organisation of space as an important marker. The urban culture of antiquity had given place to a society based in the countryside. Towns were fewer in number and the survivors enjoyed an enhanced status. In the Aegean the towns of Thessalonika, Thebes and Corinth retained commercial and administrative importance although they were dwarfed by Constantinople. This megalopolis monopolised the resources of the empire along with its political, cultural and official religious life. Within towns, street-scapes and buildings were becoming smaller in scale and introspective in design. The ancient forum (*agora*) was replaced by stalls in alleys and streets and the great public baths gave place to small privately-operated bathhouses. The theatres and the circuses were closed. The Aegean of late antiquity had become medieval.

The political history of Byzantium was one of peaks and troughs, in which the revivalist rhetoric of imperial renewal was important. It centred on the person of the emperor. Both Alexios I Komnenos (1081–1118) and his grandson Manuel I (1143–80) came out well in this respect from the political and military fluctuations of their reigns. Not so their successors Andronikos I Komnenos (1183–85) and Isaac II Angelos (1185–95) who were openly blamed for the plight of the empire in 1200. However, even if these men had not been so ineffectual as rulers they did not cause the malaise of the empire. In 1000 Byzantium was the richest and most cultured state in western Europe. Its artefacts influenced craftsmen from Venice to Winchester. Its religion had recently been adopted in Kiev and its missionaries ranged as far as Scandinavia. The frontiers of the empire

---

[1] Best accounts for this period are M. Angold, *The Byzantine Empire, 1025–1204* (London, 1984); A. Kazdhan and G. Constable, *People and Power in Byzantium* (Washington DC, 1982); A.P. Kazdhan and A.W. Epstein, *Change in Byzantine Culture in the Eleventh and Twelfth Centuries* (Berkeley, 1985) and P. Magdalino, *The Empire of Manuel I Komnenos, 1143–1180* (Cambridge, 1993), on all of which this section is based.

extended from the River Araxes in eastern Turkey to the River Volturno near Capua in southern Italy, and from the Crimea to the River Yarmuk in the Lebanon and included the islands of Crete and Cyprus. Two centuries later it has been aptly dubbed the 'Sick man of Europe'. Considerable tracts of territory had been lost. In 1071 the Normans captured Bari and Brindisi, the last Byzantine outposts in Italy. On 26 August in the same year the Byzantines were defeated at the battle of Manzikert in eastern Turkey. For reasons by no means clear this defeat was followed by the rapid occupation of Asia Minor by the Seljuk Turks. Effective Byzantine control in that area was confined to the coasts of the Aegean and the Sea of Marmora. Its northern frontiers in Macedonia and Thrace were disputed by Serbs and Bulgarians, eager to reassert their independence of Byzantium. Imperial control in Greece was insecure. The Normans from southern Italy had conducted unsuccessful but destructive invasions of Greece in 1082, 1147 and 1185. In the Aegean the disbandment of the fleet in 1182 had opened the sea-lanes to pirate attacks. In this atmosphere of instability and insecurity it is hardly surprising that local inhabitants looked to their own defence and turned for protection to powerful landowners and officials with territorial ambitions of their own, independent of the emperor in Constantinople.

Much of this might explain the separatist movements in the empire of the late twelfth century, a process in which the men of the Fourth Crusade were soon to participate. It does not explain the attack on Constantinople in 1204. The First Crusade (1096–99) brought large numbers of westerners to Constantinople for the first time. Even before that, about the middle of the eleventh century, western mercenaries were to be found serving in the ranks of the Byzantine army. Wealth and the rumours of wealth attracted the more ambitious and enterprising from the west into Byzantine service and commercial ventures. Some Latin nobles like the brothers Renier and Conrad de Montferrat rose to prominence at the imperial court and for the first time westerners meddled directly in the court politics of Byzantium. Less exalted westerners who had come east to grow rich by trade in Byzantine dominions received a rude shock in the 1180s when the emperors of the day sought to bolster their precarious positions by pandering to the xenophobic inclinations of the Constantinopolitan mob. There was no serious proposal to conquer Byzantium in order to protect western commercial interests in the 1180s. That possibility was first aired as the result of a crusade and the Byzantine part in the crusading enterprise. The Byzantines had taken on the role of protectors of the crusader states in the Holy Land and until the time of the Third Crusade in 1188–89 were generally seen in the west as reliable supporters of the crusades against Islam. In 1188 Isaac Anglos accepted a subsidy from Saladin to hold up the Third Crusade. His hostility towards Frederick Barbarossa almost provoked an attack on Constantinople in 1188, whilst rumours of Byzantine unreliability circulated in crusading circles in the west. Nothing happened on that occasion but the idea once formed would not go away.

The financial straits of the warriors proceeding on the Fourth Crusade, and the generous endowments promised by the exiled Alexios Angelos in return for crusader support to place him on the Byzantine throne, brought together the idea of capturing Constantinople, the opportunity to intervene in Byzantine political life and the military means to accomplish both. It was this combination of desperation, greed and idealism which was to lead to the assault on Constantinople in April 1204.

Conquest and newcomers

In the year following the capture of Constantinople, the French crusaders went on to capture Thessalonika and central Greece east of the Pindos Mountains and to begin the subjection of the Peloponnese, an enterprise that was still going on in the 1240s. The Latin emperor Baldwin I and his followers tried to subdue Thrace and the lands of Asia Minor opposite Constantinople. They achieved no conquest worth the name due to the fierce and determined opposition of the Bulgarians and the Greeks of Nicaea. It was only the hostility between their opponents which saved the Latins from being driven from Constantinople in the 1220s. Thessalonika was lost to the Greeks in 1224 and Constantinople followed in 1261. Shortly thereafter the restored Byzantine government in Constantinople gained possession of the strongholds of Mistra, Maina and the port of Monemvasia in the Peloponnese. From these bases a war of recovery was mounted against the Latins. The principality of Achaia was not completely recovered by the Greeks until 1430, just 30 years before the whole of the Aegean was incorporated into the Ottoman empire. The Latin lordships of central Greece held on despite almost continuous incursions by the Greeks from Epiros and Thessaly in the years from 1210 to 1236 until they too were extinguished by the Ottoman Turks in 1460. The Venetians concentrated upon securing harbours from which they could protect the sea-lanes essential to their Constantinopolitan and Black Sea trade. They left the conquest of the Aegean islands to the sons of Venetian noble families and only on Crete did they embark upon substantial colonial conquest in the name of the home government.

Not surprisingly it was military difficulties which led to the appearance of newcomers in the Aegean in the late thirteenth and fourteenth centuries. The Genoese appeared in 1260 enlisted by the Greeks of Nicaea to provide naval support for a planned assault on the Latins in Constantinople. The attack did not materialise in the form envisaged, but the Genoese stayed on to exploit the concessions they had gained as payment for their support. The

Angevins of Naples, a cadet branch of the French royal family, entered the politics of the Aegean in 1267 in response to an appeal from the Latin ruler of the Peloponnese for military support against the Greeks of Mistra, who in turn were the first to introduce the Turks into the warfare of the Aegean by using them as mercenaries in their armies sent to the Peloponnese in the mid-1260s. Finally, the Catalan mercenaries who were employed by the duke of Athens to campaign on his behalf against the Greeks of Thessaly in 1309, turned against him and killed him in 1311. They established themselves as rulers of the duchy of Athens and sought the political support of the king of Aragon, who in 1312 became yet another factor in the politics of the Aegean world.

The Frankish states in the Aegean

Even the seemingly straightforward task of listing the Frankish states in the Aegean which were established after the partition of the Byzantine empire in 1204 is not as easy as at first it might appear. For convenience I have enumerated the six territories which had some form of settled political organisation by 1210. They were the Latin empire of Constantinople, the kingdom of Thessalonika, the lordship or megaskyrate (later duchy) of Athens and Thebes, the duchy of the Archipelago, the triarchies of the island of Euboea or Negroponte, and the principality of Achaia. In addition to these six, there were numerous family holdings like the counties of Boudonitza and Salona, which were usually dependent upon the lords of Athens and Thebes, and a variety of Italian lords installed on islands in the Cyclades, Sporades and Ionian Group who were dependent on Venice or the duke of the Archipelago on Naxos. There were in excess of 30 different dynasties of such lordlings during the period of Frankish control in the Aegean. Finally, there were a few strictly colonial territories administered by officials sent out from Venice or Genoa for fixed annual or biennial tours of duty, and taking their direction from and responsible to the home government. In this group were the two castellans of Modon and Coron, the duke of Crete, and after 1346 the representatives of the Genoese chartered company or *mahona* on Chios.

No short account can be entirely satisfactory, especially in a subject which sits uneasily on the edge of two great historical fields of study, the history of Byzantium and the history of the crusades. Does it belong to both or neither? Was the cultural contribution and social reaction of the Franks in the Aegean entirely negative or can positive and original responses to unique problems be identified? My own approach is to see the Frankish states as both an important part of the war against Islam and the succouring of the Holy Land and as a unique experiment in the conquest and settlement

5

of lands which possessed their own rich cultural heritage. However, as archaeological and historical research proliferate, there is a need for an up-to-date account which provides the student with the developments and shifts in emphasis since William Miller produced his fine study, *The Latins in the Levant*, in 1908.

The Aegean world had an existence in the geographical terminology of the thirteenth century as '*Romania*' or the '*imperium Constantinopole*' and its component parts of *Graecia, la tere d'Ebire* (Epiros), *Vlachia* and *la Turkie* were identifiable if not precisely defined in the chronicles and letters of the time. Venetian writers of the fourteenth century frequently referred to Negroponte (Euboea), Crete, and the Peloponnese as forming part of '*Romania Bassa*'. There was apparently no equivalent reference to the lands between the Isthmus of Corinth and the Bosphorus as Upper Romania.[2]

The states founded by western Europeans in the Aegean began and ended with conquest. This gives some indication of the dogged and determined opposition of the Byzantines and of the lack of stability enjoyed by the Latin states. Their genesis was the conquest of Constantinople by the forces of the Fourth Crusade on 12 April 1204. Their end came at various points from the thirteenth to the seventeenth centuries – Thessalonika captured by Theodore Komnenos Doukas in December 1224, Constantinople retaken by the Byzantines on 25 July 1261, Patras, the last outpost of the Frankish Morea, recovered by the Greek despot of the Morea in 1430, and the duchy of Athens conquered by the Turks in 1450. The Venetian and Genoese colonies survived into the early modern period but these too were eventually conquered by the Turks – Negroponte in 1470, Modon and Coron in 1500, Chios in 1566 and Crete in 1669, after the 24-year siege of Candia. The ragged nature of these beginnings and endings not only reflects the fragmented nature of the Frankish Aegean but also demonstrates that if some of the new crusader states were politically and economically unviable from the outset, the majority clearly had a fair chance of survival.

The Latin empire claimed suzerainty over the whole of the Latin Aegean, known collectively as Romania. In practice it was seldom exercised outside Thrace and more usually confined to the city of Constantinople and its hinterland. The weakness of the empire was due to a variety of factors. The greatest of these was poverty. Militarily unable to expand its frontiers or to establish any lasting peace with its enemies, its rulers could not exploit the resources of their new realm and instead became dependent on financial and military support from the west. In particular this included that of the pope and the king of France, eked out with loans from Venice and a variety of stop-gap measures involving the sale of relics and even the lead from their palace roofs. In turn this meant that its rulers were never entirely masters in their own house and never attained that status in the west to which their

---

[2] R.L. Wolff, 'Romania: The Latin Empire of Constantinople' *Speculum* 23 (1948), 1–34.

rank of emperor might have entitled them. With the exception of the emperor Henry (1206–16), the Latin emperors were a poor lot celebrated more for incompetence than strong military leadership. Henry was the only emperor to campaign in Greece and to enforce his overlordship there. The final year of his reign has been dubbed the apogee of the Latin empire. For the rest, their suzerainty consisted in underpinning the Latin claim to the Aegean, a role which they could exercise as well in exile in Italy as they could in Constantinople. Their poverty was exacerbated by the needs of defence. In 1205–7 the Vlacho-Bulgarians under Kalojan came near to overwhelming them, and again in the 1230s the Bulgarians seemed set fair to dominate Thrace and take Constantinople. The Greeks in Epiros and in Nicaea maintained pressure on both Constantinople and Thessalonika, driven by their desire to recapture the ancient capital of Byzantium. Thessalonika fell to Theodore Doukas, the despot of Epiros, in 1224, although it was lost in turn to John III Vatatzes of Nicaea in 1246. Thereafter the Latins became resigned to the loss of Constantinople. When the city fell to the Greeks in July 1261 its loss was barely noted in western Europe.

In March 1204 the leadership of the French and Venetian crusaders had laid down guidelines for the disposal of the lands and offices of the Byzantine empire in the event that their attack on Constantinople should prove successful. By the act of partition of September 1204, some effect was given to this earlier arrangement. The Latin emperor Baldwin received one-quarter of the former Byzantine territory and the Venetians and the French three-eighths each. This land had to be conquered and in this process the neat demarcations of the partition became overridden. Boniface of Montferrat, the unsuccessful candidate for the imperial throne, gained lands around Thessalonika not registered in the partition and proceeded to direct the distribution of territory in Thrace and Boeotia which formed part of the French crusaders' condominium. The Venetians for their part received more territory than they could readily occupy. They had acquired the harbour towns of Modon and Coron in Messenia by 1209 and their colonisation of Crete began in 1211. These territories formed colonial possessions with officials sent out by and accountable to the Venetian senate. With regard to the Aegean islands, the Venetians sought to conquer and control these through the sons of their own wealthy families. One such nobleman, Marco Sanudo, conquered the Cycladic islands in 1207. Surprisingly he sought out the suzerainty of the emperor in order to establish his and his descendants claim to the Archipelago and to secure a measure of independence from Venice.

Of the French territories in Greece, the principality of the Morea was the best-documented, the richest and the most secure, cut off from the Greeks of Epiros by the Gulf of Corinth and shielded by the lordship of Athens. By 1210 the Frankish lords of Athens and Thebes had to cope with the Epirote reconquest of southern Thessaly and the temporary loss of Salona. From both these areas raids were launched on their lands culminating in a series of attacks on Thebes itself in the mid-1230s. In general until 1261 the leadership of the Franks in Greece was both active and competent. They clearly felt sufficiently secure to allow themselves to indulge in a destructive civil war in 1255–58. Thereafter, with the loss of Constantinople in 1261 and the recovery of the Peloponnesian towns of Mistra, Maina and Monemvasia by the Byzantines in 1262, the Latins in Greece lost both their security and the initiative. The defensive stance which they were now forced to adopt and which they maintained until their final loss of political control in the mid-fifteenth century involved them in seeking the military help from rulers of the west Mediterranean. The price to be paid was the acknowledgement of the suzerainty of these rulers, often expressed by marriage ties and the transfer of titles. The original Frankish ruling families had died out by 1314 and nominal rule now resided with kings in Naples, Trani and Barcelona. The able and the ambitious like the Fadriques, the Foucherolles, the Orsini and the Acciaioli could carve out substantial lands and positions for themselves as officials of these absentee rulers. In the Aegean Catalans, Turks, Hospitallers and Venetians now took a leading role fighting and intriguing against each other either on their own account or as part of some holy war. The Aegean had become a fully integrated part of the Mediterranean world and the frontier of Christendom against the Turk.[3]

Frank and Frankish?

The terms 'Frank' and 'Frankish' require some explanation since they are neither as chronologically nor as culturally discrete as they might at first appear to be. By the middle of the twelfth century in Greek lands the word '*Phrangoi*' had become a generic term for western Europeans. From an ethnic marker applied by early Byzantine writers such as Eusebius (263–339), Zosimus (late fifth century), Prokopios (mid-sixth century) and Theophanes (*c*. 752–818) to one of the groups of Germanic barbarians which had invaded the Roman province of Gaul in the fifth century, the term had lost all specificity by the time of the crusades and the first general exposure of Byzantines to western Europeans en masse. This late Greek

---

[3] Short basic accounts of the Latins in the Aegean are D.M. Nicol (ch.vii) and K.M. Setton (ch.ix) in *Cambridge Medieval History* IV, i (Cambridge, 1967), pp.275–330 and 389–430; R.L. Wolff (ch.vi) and J. Longnon (ch.vii) in R.L. Wolff and H.W. Hazard, eds, *A History of the Crusades* II (Madison, 1969), pp.187–276; C. Brand and G. Dennis in J.R. Strayer, ed., *Dictionary of the Middle Ages* VII (New York, 1968), pp.346–9 and 376–82; H.E. Mayer, *The Crusades* 2nd edn (Oxford, 1988), pp.201–13; J. Riley-Smith, *The Crusades* (London, 1987), pp.180–7.

usage perhaps implied a greater political and cultural homogeneity than the western settlers in the Aegean in the thirteenth century and after in fact possessed. Certainly they shared some presuppositions regarding religious belief, family bonds and personal honour which were not so different from those of their Greek hosts. Most saw land as the repository of wealth but not all. As David Jacoby has emphasised, some like the French, and to a lesser extent the Lombard, crusaders came from areas with highly-evolved structures of social subordination and vassalage, whilst others like the Venetians and Catalans came from homelands which lacked a feudal superstructure.[4]

The pejorative aspect of this terminology equated all Franks, that is west Europeans, with barbarians, that is with the subjective late antique assessment of the Franks proper. This was a survival of the cultural snobbery of late antiquity, which in the twelfth century brought about a reverse physical and moral snobbery on the part of western writers which equated the Greeks with weak and deceitful actions. Both these characterisations had their roots in the late Roman empire and regrettably are still to be found in the pages of some studies of Byzantium and the crusades. The Franks, like their historians, were not perfect and this book is no apologia for them, but to dismiss them and their history out-of-hand is to lose sight of a significant part of Aegean, Byzantine, and crusading history. The Frankish states of the Aegean were after all the last crusader states to be founded in the Levant.

The Franks of the Aegean have certainly had a bad press. For many Byzantinists and classicists they have fitted conveniently into the decline-and-fall model of the eastern Roman empire. According to extreme views, they pillaged and destroyed and contributed nothing to late medieval Aegean society.[5] Labelling them as instruments of colonial exploitation misreads both the nature of the states themselves and, more importantly, the reorientation that was going on amongst states and rulers in the Aegean, a process which linked that region ever after firmly to the west. For other commentators the Franks were hopelessly romantic and impractical, and as such they gained a place in Greek historical novels of the last century. As we shall see, this interpretation conceals their very real military and political accomplishments.

---

[4] D. Jacoby, 'Social evolution in Latin Greece', ch.vi in H.W. Hazard and N. Zacour, eds, *A History of the Crusades* VI (Madison, 1989), pp.175–221.
[5] F. Dolger, 'Die Kreuzfahrerstaaten auf dem Balkan und Byzanz' *Südost-Forschungen* 15 (1956), 141–59 for such a view.

Who were the Frankish settlers?

Five broad categories of western immigrants may be distinguished in the 300-year existence of the Frankish states in the Aegean. First the Venetians, Genoese and merchants of other Italian mercantile republics had been active in the Aegean trade throughout the twelfth century. The Venetians had formed a sizeable community in Constantinople and there were other communities in Thessalonika, Thebes and Corinth before the arrival of the Fourth Crusade. Just how long Venetian merchants expected to be resident in Constantinople in the twelfth century is unknown. Certainly the marriage of some of them with Greek women had not only occurred but actually received official encouragement from the Byzantine government. This would seem to suggest a growing number of Venetians with a permanent commitment in the Aegean. The Fourth Crusade increased official Venetian influence in the Aegean, with the colonisation of Crete and Messenia administered by officials appointed for two-year terms and sent out from Venice and a number of island dukedoms created by younger sons of the Venetian nobility and owing allegiance to Venice.

The influx of westerners associated with the Fourth Crusade and the Latin state-building in the Aegean in the early thirteenth century is that generally considered as the genesis of the Frankish Aegean, although the actual population transfer from the west and from the Latin states in Syria was really quite modest. In the main those men who were not Venetians came from Burgundy, Champagne, Flanders and Lombardy, and as such could be said to be eponymous Franks in that they came from lands once ruled by the emperor Charlemagne.

The third group, albeit very small, emerged after the 1260s and was associated with the loss of Constantinople and the turning of the Frankish states to the protection of the Angevin kings of Naples. Some families, like the de Toucy and the d'Aulnay (Aunoy), moved from Constantinople to the Morea. After the death of William of Achaia in 1278 there was a growth in Italian personnel in the Morea. At first these were temporary officials and soldiers involved in the Angevin administration, but the family of le Maure established itself at this time. There were also Florentine and Pisan banking families involved in the financing of the Angevin administration and tending to set up counters in Glarenza and Corinth. In just this way, the Acciaioli from Florence became established in Greece, first by way of a branch bank at Glarenza in 1331 and a decade later by the arrival of Niccolo Acciaioli in the suite of the princess of Achaia, Catherine de Valois. Bishoprics too were increasingly being given to Italian clerics in the fourteenth century as the policy of papal provision led to a better-educated episcopate but one that was increasingly Italian and absentee in character.

Arguably the greatest influx of westerners into the Aegean came in 1302 with the arrival of the Catalan Grand Company from the battlefields of Sicily and southern Italy, following the peace of Caltabellota which left them unemployed. Moving from Byzantine to Frankish service they quarrelled with their new masters and slaughtered the flower of Frankish chivalry at the battle of Halmyros in 1311. They took over the duchy of Athens in sufficient numbers to expand it territorially into Thessaly and to find the supply of Latin priests insufficient to their needs so that they turned in large numbers to the ministrations of the Orthodox clergy.

The Gascon and Navarrese mercenaries who arrived in the Aegean in the late 1370s were, like the Catalans before them, left without occupation due to peace in the west, and also like the Catalans their leadership was concerned to obtain lands and honours for themselves. Their numbers are unknown, but they proved an important catalyst in that last series of political changes in the 1380s that was to usher in the period of the Ottoman conquest of the Aegean.

The attraction of the Aegean

Why these groups settled in the Aegean can only be guessed. The Catalans and Navarrese were obvious adventurers with an eye to the main chance and a better opportunity in the destabilised environment of the Aegean than in the increasingly organised and stratified world of western Europe. The same enterprise culture might be discerned amongst those warriors of the Fourth Crusade when a chapter of accidents lead to their successful assault on Constantinople in April 1204. Out of those who were there because they were there, only the determined and the fortunate stayed on to participate in the establishment of permanent states in the Aegean, men who had nothing better or more challenging to await them at home. Such settlements were clearly not in the minds of the crusaders as they set out from their homes in 1201. None of the leaders appear to have brought their wives with them and only Baldwin of Flanders seems to have made advance plans for his wife to join him, not in Constantinople but in Acre, whither the crusade was heading. It is possible that he was considering a long stay in the east. Equally Boniface of Montferrat took a wife almost as soon as the conquest of Constantinople was completed. He kept touch with his marquisate in Montferrat but immersed himself in gaining lands in the east. Just so his supporters like Champlitte, Geoffrey de Villehardouin the younger and Otho de la Roche. The spirit of war and adventure possibly yielding high returns in land and status cannot be discounted in the psychology of these men.

The creation of the Frankish states in the Aegean area integrated that area into a wider Mediterranean world for the first time since the failure of the emperor Justinian's policy of reconquest in the mid-sixth century. Events in the Aegean now had direct repercussions in Avignon, Barcelona, Naples,

11

Palermo, Paris and Rome. At various times, as appropriate to their standing in the west, the rulers of the Frankish states turned to the papacy, the Angevins of Naples or the Aragonese rulers of Sicily for military and financial support when the military pressures of their neighbours in the Aegean became too intense. The quality and quantity of this support might be disappointing but western rulers felt that it entitled them to be heard and obeyed in the Aegean. There was, however, considerable latitude in applying the edicts of these west European potentates. Without actually biting the hands which threw them scraps, the rulers of the Frankish territories were both jealous of their status and independence and conscious that they knew local conditions better than their overlords in the west. This can best be seen in the disputes with the papacy over tithes and church property in the first 20 years of the thirteenth century, in the introduction of the earliest mortmain legislation in Europe (see pp.179–80), in the role played by women at the parliament of Nikli in 1262, and in the disputes between Guyot of Athens and the Angevins in the late 1280s (see p.95). It was a frontier society and to that extent different from the society at home in France and the society which it had replaced in the Frankish Aegean.

In the west the possession of the Aegean was perceived as one that was well worth having, not just in terms of the struggle against Islam but in terms of wealth. Traders came from as far afield as Catalonia, whilst the Venetians and the Genoese fought four considerable naval wars for commercial dominance in the area, an artery of the Black Sea. There were certainly fortunes to be made there in the commodities trade and substantial incomes to be derived from agriculture. Yet it is by no means clear in what actually lay the wealth of Greece. Was it a western perception with little backing in fact? Certainly the wild east, the last Christian frontier in the Levant, was a place for the young and the bold. Older heads might talk of fortunes to be made there, but they seldom ventured there themselves and advised others to go in their stead.

Mass immigration did not occur either from the west or from the crusader states in the Levant after 1291. Westerners remained unmoved by papal appeals for settlement and financial and military support, and the Frankish Aegean lacked the emotional and religious appeal of the kingdom of Jerusalem. For a large but unknown number of western knights and sergeants the Aegean remained an area where they gained occasional employment in the armies of the Latin states or of those of their Greek enemies, returning home when the money or the fighting ran out. I have concentrated in much of what follows on the establishment of the Frankish states. As the last crusader states to be established in Outremer, this emphasis, I believe, is justified. The Franks were not the ossified romantics which they are sometimes taken to have been, but creative, practical and at times highly original in their creation of states and in their dealings with their Greek neighbours. Knowledge of Greek amongst them and, indeed, in the west generally must have been more widespread than is usually believed. The writing of this study has certainly focused my own attention on the techniques and modes of language acquisition in the medieval Aegean, and to the prevalence of some knowledge of ancient Greek history amongst laymen in the thirteenth century.

Social and cultural implications

The fall of Constantinople in April 1204 and the subsequent Frankish penetration of the Aegean involved more than just territorial conquest and political control. The period of the Frankokratia had profound social and economic implications for the region, and it is precisely in these fields that most recent research has concentrated and wrought the most significant changes in perspective since the historical studies of Miller and Hopf in 1908 and 1868 respectively. In Constantinople and Rome in the the thirteenth century, the Latin empire of Romania was linked ideologically with the crusading east, but politically, culturally, and economically it looked west to Italy just a short voyage away.

With regard to the majority Greek population, a divergence between policy in Constantinople and that in the rest of the Aegean can be discerned on the part of the ruling Latin elite. In the latter, a policy of live and let live was followed with regard to religious and legal practices. Local Greek landowners were eager to salvage what they could of their lands and status. They were found a place in Latin social and commercial circles. This stopped far short of complete integration but it seems to have been acceptable to a majority of the provincial Greek landholding class who perhaps thought it a small price to pay for some sort of political stability. It was certainly far better than the situation in Constantinople where a strong Venetian interest, the presence of papal legates and the proximity of Bulgarian and Nicene troops tied the hands of the Latin emperors even should they wish to act in a more conciliatory fashion towards their Greek subjects. What the peasantry, that is those who actually did the farming for Greek and Latin lords, thought about the new dispensation was nowhere recorded or apparently thought worthy of enquiry.

It was in Constantinople in the first decade after the conquest that the westerners, who saw themselves and were still seen by the pope as crusaders, pilgrims and christians (*peregrini, crucesignati* and *christiani*), were referred to as 'pigs' and 'dogs' in certain Greek religious circles. This usage which so distressed Innocent III did not seem to extend into the captured Byzantine provinces in Greece. However, language, religion, and after 1204, their free status made the Franks distinct from the majority population, their Greek subjects. Their Byzantine neighbours called themselves '*Rhomaioi*' (Romans) and had coined the expression '*Romania*' for their empire. In the thirteenth century westerners purloined this term as a collective name for the Frankish territories in the Aegean. The Byzantine usage went back at least to the fourth century but was tending to be dropped during the thirteenth century, partly as a reaction to the western application of the term and partly in favour of a more specific terminology like Hellas, Asia, and so forth. National rather than cultural lines were being accentuated.[6]

In such a geographically, ethnically, politically and religiously fragmented world it is hardly surprising that family bonds and loyalties were of prime importance as a source of individual definition and mental stability. Marriage could transcend these lines of fragmentation by cementing political and commercial agreements and by transferring lands, titles and status. In this the westerners shared an important common perception with their Greek subjects and neighbours. Yet a family group need not be imported from Europe with the conquerors in 1204. Some men brought out their wives and children when conditions had stabilised, as did Otho de la Roche and Geoffrey de Villehardouin in 1209 and 1210 respectively. Others, like Boniface of Montferrat, acquired wives in the east. The extreme example here was the Catalans in 1311 who married the widows of the men whom they had slain at Halmyros. The history of Frankish Greece can be viewed through the family histories of the twelve great baronies of Achaia, in some ways the archetypal founding fathers of the new frontier. This is a valid framework for looking at the political history of Frankish Greece and the traditional nineteenth century approach. Yet such families were a minority within a minority grouping and such a genealogical approach tends to exclude the majority of Frankish settlers. Certainly a powerful and active man from a wealthy family like Nicholas III de St Omer exerted more influence than the family of a mounted sergeant, yet it was the personal ability to exercise that influence which counted, rather than the shadow of a great name, and as we shall see this distinction was not lost on the ladies of the Morea when discussing the choice of a partner for a second marriage. For those at the sergeant level, who often assumed the title 'miles', it was the family structure that was important for them in establishing their external relationships and ethnic identity. Biologically, the founding families of Frankish Greece were not fertile and the high attrition rates in this unstable society resulted in their extinction in the male line by the end of the thirteenth century. Their political successors, both Catalan and Florentine, operated the same familial structures. The genealogical tables produced by Charles Hopf more than a century ago in his *Chroniques Gréco-Romanes* contain numerous errors of the sort inherent in such work. However,

---

[6] P. Magdalino, 'Hellenism and nationalism in Byzantium', first published as essay XIV in idem, *Tradition and Transformation in Medieval Byzantium* (London, 1991); *ODB*, p.1805.

provided they are used with this caution in mind, they are a very useful guide to the wide range of complex family relationships in the Aegean.

Transliteration of names and titles

The transliteration of Greek names and institutions has raised the usual problems where no agreed system of transcription exists. The tendency in modern Greece to classicise the place names of the medieval and post-medieval period can also lead to confusion. In both cases I have generally sought to follow the modern majority practice and hope that I have managed to achieve consistency in this. Established English forms of names have been used where to do otherwise would be pedantic. At all events I trust that no awkwardness or confusion results and that the usages here are clearly identifiable in other indices and atlases.

Chapter 2 ....

Sources and Historiography

The Latin states of the Aegean existed in the main for some 250 years from 1204 until the mid-fifteenth century, when they ceased to have an independent existence and were incorporated in the Ottoman empire. The break-up of that empire in the nineteenth and early twentieth centuries fragmented the Aegean world which the Franks had known into national states with frontiers, anthems, and official histories. These new national states sought their historical identities in their ancient pasts.[1] Just as the Turks looked to Mesopotamia and named battleships after the sites and gods of Sumer and Babylon, so the Greeks, more plausibly, looked to their writers, artists and monuments of the fifth century BC. Not surprisingly, Greekness came to mean Pericles, Phidias, the Parthenon and the Elgin Marbles: a mirror of western philhellenism. It was not sought in the period of the 'Frankokratia' and the 'Turkokratia'. The ephemeral existence of these 'kratias' and their alien culture were seen as irrelevant to the national identity and led to their neglect by national schools of Greek and Turkish historiography. It is unfair to blame these nationals alone. In 1205 Innocent III had agreed that Greece was the well-spring of western culture, where the study of letters had its first beginning (*in Graeciam ... unde noscitur exordium habuisse*).[2] By the late eighteenth century the economic and technological resources available to a privileged section of western society led to a desire to discover and to imitate the material culture of classical Greece. The physical expressions of this enthusiasm were neo-classical buildings and furnishings, a certain amount of soft pornography, and a

---

[1] Nationalism in Slav lands was obscured by the idea of Pan-slavism, which saw all Slavs as forming one big family. Nonetheless studies of folk traditions and language flourished. See B. Jelavich, *History of the Balkans* I (Cambridge, 1981), pp.171–9, and H. Wilkinson, *Maps and Politics* (Liverpool, 1951), passim.
[2] PL, 215:637

preoccupation of western scholarship with the prehistoric and the classical past of Greece. In 1874 a group of western scholars, including Schliemann, had provided funding for the demolition of the Frankish tower on the Acropolis at Athens in order to reveal the Propylaea of Mnesikles.[3]

The historical study of the Frankish states also benefit, or suffer, twice over at the hands of a dual tradition. Established as they were in the wake of the Fourth Crusade and in the partition and conquest of parts of the former Byzantine empire, they are treated either as part of the history of the crusades or as an aspect of Byzantine history. This duality was present from the beginning in the surviving chronicles of Choniates, Villehardouin and Clari, but it also became implanted in the works of modern historians of the crusades and Byzantium. Byzantinists see the whole episode as regrettable, destructive and a major factor in the disintegration of Byzantium. Historians of the crusade see it as a symptom and a result of that disintegration rather than a cause. Whilst not spurning some of the original and constructive aspects of the Latin settlement, they have perhaps downgraded the whole enterprise as a side-show of the 'real' crusades. For all that, the crusader states in the Aegean were the last crusader states to be founded in the Levant and some existed into early modern times, like the Genoese on Chios down to 1566 and the Venetians on Naxos (1574) and Crete (1669). The other aspect of this duality is like the international aspirations of both the crusades and Byzantium: they have attracted the attention of international scholarship in the last century and this has brought its own problems to the student whose linguistic abilities extend to perhaps two or three modern European languages. The variety of linguistic skills required is beyond the scope of one individual and one life to master, and has inevitably lead to the overlooking of important contributions in the less accessible languages. Any view of the Latin states must therefore be provisional.

No archives which may once have been generated by the Latin states have come down to us. This is a terrible gap and may have been evident as early as the mid-fifteenth century when the Ottoman government instituted its own survey of the conquered lands in the Balkans without reference to any Frankish material that might be expected to have been to hand. There are contemporary references to the keeping of records of imperial grants, court judgements and the like. From the former, Dr Hendrickx has attempted to list the chrysobulls and charters of the Latin emperors, whilst no copy of any acts of the Latin emperors survives other than a few in the archives of Venice and Rome.[4] No episcopal registers survive for any Latin diocese in the Aegean, and very few estate documents survive except those which have come down in Italian archives for the fourteenth century or later. The

---

[3] O. Taplin, *Greek Fire* (London, 1989); R. Tomlinson, *The Athens of Alma Tadema* (Stroud, 1991); P. Lock, *ABSA* 82 (1987), 131–3.
[4] B. Hendrickx, 'Régestes des Empereurs Latins de Constantinople, (1204–1261/72)' *Byzantina* 14 (1988), 7–221.

Franks may not have been such enthusiastic generators of records as the Byzantines, who really did keep records in triplicate, but they did produce records and the loss of these together with the Byzantine archives is a testimony to the disturbed nature of Balkan politics in the medieval period.[5] Early in the nineteenth century this gap was appreciated and the importance of relevant administrative documents in the archives of Barcelona, Naples, Venice, Florence and Malta signalled by the French historian J.A.C. Buchon who published a selection of this archival material in 1848 in his *Nouvelles Recherches Historique*, an important work now long out-of-print and difficult to obtain.[6]

Western chronicles

The western immigrants to the Aegean had developed their own historical tradition from the start. This was much influenced by epic and the chansons de gestes. The chronicles of Geoffrey de Villehardouin (*c.* 1150 to *c.* 1212–18)[7] and Robert de Clari (d. after 1216), who were both participants in the Fourth Crusade, give dramatic and focused accounts of the capture of Constantinople and the early Latin settlement in the Aegean.[8] Villehardouin was a military commander, the marshal of Champagne and after 1204 the marshal of Romania too. Clari, on the other hand, was a poor knight and a vassal of Pierre d'Amiens. Both writers represent the crusade's diversion and capture of Constantinople as a chapter of accidents brought about by divine providence, and both authors have been accused of distorting the facts in order to justify this unholy crusade.[9] Clari may well have written the main part of his story up to 1205 in Constantinople and completed his account up

[5] R. Morris, 'Dispute settlement in the Byzantine provinces in the tenth century', in W. Davies & P. Fouracre, eds, *The Settlement of Disputes in Early Medieval Europe* (Cambridge, 1986), pp.125–47, esp. p.125.
[6] J.A.C. Buchon, *Nouvelles Recherches Historiques sur la Principauté Française de Morée et ses Hautes Baronnies a la suite de la Quatorzieme Croisade* (Paris, 1848).
[7] Not to be confused with his nephew and namesake the Prince of Achaia, who died sometime between 1218 and 1228.
[8] Geoffrey de Villehardouin, *La conquête de Constantinople*, ed. Edmond Faral, 2 vols (Paris, 1938–9) text and French translation. An older edition of the text by M. Natalis de Wailly (Paris, 1874) also publishes the text of Henri de Valenciennes as a continuation together with a modern French translation of both. The paragraph numbering is slightly different in the two editions. Faral's numbering is generally followed today. Modern English translations by Frank Marzials (Everyman, 1908) and M.R.B. Shaw (Penguin, 1963). Robert de Clari, *La Conquête de Constantinople*, ed. Philippe Lauer (Paris, 1924); modern translation Edgar McNeal (New York, 1936).
[9] A. Pauphilet, 'Robert de Clari et Villehardouin', in *Mélanges A. Jeanro* (Paris, 1928), p.564, and H. Gregoire in *Byzantion* 14 (1936), p.158.

to 1216 after his return to the west. He was clearly not so well-informed as Villehardouin about the deeds and decisions of the crusading leadership, but on many matters including the topography of Constantinople, past Byzantine history and, most importantly, the principles on which the division of the empire was made in September 1204, he provides better information. Clari's reputation and reliability as a source are thereby enhanced and he most certainly does not deserve the nineteenth-century epithet of 'simple knight' which implies that he was naive and unsophisticated. By contrast, Villehardouin, as marshal of Romania, must have had access to archives. However, his attempt to give almost day-to-day accounts of events depended much on memory and definite dates were lacking. Villehardouin's latest commentator has judged him sufficiently honest and careful, but like other memoir writers he omitted painful facts whilst remaining accurate on the main points.[10] Clari was much more diffuse and impressionistic in his writing and like most contemporary writers he made mistakes over figures, numbers and some dates.[11] While both concentrated on military events, incidentally they both contributed much information on the making of a Latin emperor, the division of the empire and the topography of Constantinople. Clari finished his detailed account with the partition of the empire in September 1204, although the last event he recorded was the death of the emperor Henry in June 1216. The events of 1205 to 1216 were summarily treated in an epilogue, sketched presumably from information heard from those returning from the Aegean, after his own departure late in 1204. Villehardouin ended his account with the death of Boniface of Montferrat on 4 September 1207.

Traditionally regarded as a continuation of Villehardouin, the *Histoire de L'Emperuer Henri de Constantinople* by Henri de Valenciennes shared many of the chronological vagaries of Villehardouin's chronicle and did not resume the latter's account until 25 May 1208. Valenciennes concentrated on the events of 1208–9 and he is the chief source for the so-called Lombard war in Thessalonika. Valenciennes was diffuse in his presentation and chose to present opposing issues in the form of speeches delivered by the principal contenders. His work is generally regarded as inferior to that of Villehardouin, but it is an exciting and full text and does add much topographical detail from outside Constantinople. The identity of the author is not securely known. Jean Longnon, his most recent editor, has established that he was a priest, possibly in the entourage of Baldwin of Flanders, and that he might be the same man as the Master Henry who was sent as a

---

[10] C. Morris, 'Geoffrey de Villehardouin and the conquest of Constantinople' *History* 53 (1968), 24–34.
[11] C.P. Bagley, 'Robert de Clari's *La Conquete de Constantinople*' *Medium Aevum* 40 (1971), 109–15.

messenger to Innocent III in 1205 and became a canon of Santa Sophia in 1210. He wrote before 1216 and the death of the emperor Henry.[12]

Circumstantial evidence is also contained in a number of chronicles concerned with wider issues than the Frankish entry and settlement of the Aegean. The most important are the various Old French continuations of William of Tyre and related works. They contain much detail on the deeds of John de Brienne in the Latin empire up to 1230, but their provenance and relationship is most obscure.[13] Two others, like the *Historia Constantinopolitana* by Gunther of Pairis in Alsace and the *Peregrinatio in Graeciam* in the Annals of Halberstadt, were written to authenticate relics brought from Constantinople in 1204.[14] The *Chronicon Flandrense* and the *Gesta Innocentii tertii* were a comital chronicle and a papal biography with obvious relevance.[15] A number of general chronicles of wide scope, like those written by Robert of Auxerre, Alberic of Trois-Fontaines, Ralph of Coggleshall, Roger of Wendover and Matthew Paris, have some useful observations on the conquest of Constantinople in 1204 and the fate of the Latin emperors in 1261. Finally, a number of important descriptions and allusions to the capture of Constantinople and the events of 1205 are contained in some of the poems of the Provencal troubadour Raimbaut de Vaqueiras (*c.* 1155–1207?).[16] Raimbaut participated in the Fourth Crusade in the contingent of his patron and lord Boniface of Montferrat and may have died with him in the Rhodope Mountains in September 1207. Not only did he depict Boniface as a perfect knight but he also gave insights into the marquis's character which were lacking in the chronicles of Villehardouin and Clari. For Raimbaut the Frankish conquests in the Aegean were an essential part of the war against Islam, whilst Boniface was the rightful if uncrowned king of Thessalonika.

All of this material, with the exception of paras 324 to 332 in Villehardouin and paras 667 to 688 in Valenciennes, deals directly with either the Fourth Crusade or the north Aegean states based in Constantinople and Thessalonika. Three works, however, deal specifically

---

[12] Henri de Valenciennes, *Histoire de L'Empereur Henri de Constantinople*, ed. J. Longnon (Paris, 1948). No translation available other than the modern French by N. de Wailley, *La conquete de Constantinople par Geoffroi de Villehardouin avec la continuation de Henri de Valenciennes* (Paris, 1882), pp.38–421. See articles by Longnon in *Journal des Savants* (1945), 134–43, and *Romania* 69 (1946), 198–218, and note 9 above.

[13] M.L. de Mas Latrie, ed., *Chronique d'Ernoul et de Bernard le Tresorier* (Paris, 1871), pp.339–472; M.R. Morgan, *The Chronicle of Ernoul and the Continuations of William of Tyre* (Oxford, 1973), pp.51–97.

[14] Paul Riant, ed., *Exuviae sacrae Constantinopolitanae* I (Paris, 1877), pp.10–21, 57–126, also in PL, 212:271–20 and CGR, pp. 82–96.

[15] *Urkunden* I, pp.293–304; PL, 214:xvii–ccxviii.

[16] Lyric poems XIX–XXIII and the Epic Letter in J. Linskill, *The Poems of the Troubadour Raimbaut de Vaqueiras* (Paris, 1964), pp.218–53, 301–44.

with areas of Frankish Greece proper. All were written in the first half of the fourteenth century, two in the tradition of epic and chanson de gestes, the other a proposed continuation of the chronicle of Geoffrey de Villehardouin, but with the epic and romance left out. They are the Catalan *Cronica* of Ramon Muntaner, the *Istoria del Regno di Romania* by Marino Sanudo Torsello, the Venetian merchant and crusade propagandist, and the *Chronicle of the Morea*, the most important chronicle source for the Frankish states in mainland Greece.

Ramon Muntaner (1265–c.1336) was the chancellor of the Catalan Grand Company in the Aegean from 1309 and a principal participant in many of the events which he described. He wrote down his *Cronica* in Catalan in the years 1325–28. His skill as a narrator often led him to sacrifice historical accuracy in order to emphasise the drama of an event. His pride in his countrymen's achievements comes through in his writing and the chronicle is one of the most exciting of a very exciting group.[17]

Marino Sanudo Torsello (c.1270–1343) travelled widely in the Levant. He was related to the dukes of Naxos and spent some time living in the Morea, where in 1312–13 he wrote part of his most famous work *Secreta Fidelium Crucis*. Between 1326 and 1333 he wrote a history of the Frankish states in the Aegean. The original was written in Latin but survives today only in a late Italian version.[18] Although Sanudo was generally better informed about the Morea than he was about the former Latin empire, his work does contain unique and interesting details about the latter. According to R.L. Wolff he is the only source which mentions the stripping of lead from the palaces of Constantinople by Baldwin II in order to raise cash. He does succeed in presenting a more analytical approach than most of his contemporaries and in relating the events taking place in Romania in a wider Mediterranean setting.[19]

The Chronicle of the Morea

The most important single source for the political history of the Frankish states in Greece in the thirteenth and fourteenth centuries is the *Chronicle of*

---

[17] Karl Lanz, ed., *Chronik des edlin En Ramon Muntaner* (Stuttgart, 1844). English translation by Lady Henrietta Goodenough, *The Chronicle of Muntaner* (London, 1920–21).

[18] CGR, pp.99–176. No modern edition or translation available.

[19] R-J. Loenertz, 'Pour une edition nouvelle de l'Historia del Regno de Romania de Marin Sanudo l'Ancien' *Studi veneziani* 16 (1974), 33–66; R.L. Wolff, 'Hopf's so-called "Fragmentum" of Marino Sanudo Torsello' *The Joshua Starr Memorial Volume* (New York, 1953), pp.1–10, reprinted in idem, *Studies in the Latin Empire of Constantinople* (London, 1975); ODM, p.1840.

the Morea. Not surprisingly, it has attracted more study and debate than that given to any other source of the Frankokratia. It survives in four versions: French, Greek, Aragonese and Italian in a total of eight manuscripts of which five are of the Greek version. The latter is in verse; the other three versions are in prose. The Italian version has been shown by Professor Jacoby to be a translation and an abridgement of the Greek version, and to belong to the sixteenth century and not to the fourteenth as was formerly believed by its editor Charles Hopf.[20] The Aragonese/Castilian version, or *Libro de los Fechos et Conquistas del Principado de la Morea*, is the only one that bears a date. It was commissioned by Juan Fernandez de Heredia, the grand-master of the Knights Hospitallers (1377–96). His scribe Bernard de Jaca completed the work of copying on Thursday 24 October 1393, presumably in Avignon where Heredia was then resident. In its 726 paragraphs it relates the history of the Latin empire and the principality of Achaia from 1200 to 1377. It contains additional information to the French version which it used as its prime source and is the most informative of all the four versions available.[21] This brings us to the Greek and French versions and to the debate whether the original was in French or in Greek or whether both were derived from a prototype now lost. The problem is succinctly explained by Harold Lurier in the introduction to his translation of the Greek chronicle.[22] It is still hotly debated, with protagonists dividing on crusader/Byzantine lines in their affiliations.

The French version survives in one manuscript only, Bibliotheque Royale de Bruxelles, no. 15702. In its 1,024 paragraphs it deals with the years 1099 to 1305, ending with the tournament and parliament at Corinth. There is a brief chronological table which recorded a few events down to 1333 and incidentally mentioned that Catherine de Valois-Courtenay (d.1346), the titular Latin empress of Constantinople and princess of Achaia, was still alive. The scribe specifically stated that this version was an abridgement of an original which formerly belonged to Bartolommeo Ghisi and was found in his castle at Thebes.[23] Ghisi was castellan there from 1327 to 1331. From this internal evidence it appears that the French version was written between 1333 and 1346 and depended on a French prototype. Its

---

[20] CGR, xlii, 414–68; D. Jacoby, 'Quelques considérations sur les version de la Chronique de Morée' *Journal des Savants* (1968), 133–89, reprinted in *Société et démographie à Byzance et en Romanie Latine* (London, 1975).

[21] Alfred Morel-Fatio, ed., *Libro de los Fechos et Conquistas del principado de la Morea* (Geneva, 1885), reprinted Otto Zeller (Osnabruck, 1968) with a French translation. A new edition and English translation by Anthony Luttrell is imminently expected.

[22] H.E. Lurier, *Crusaders as Conquerors* (New York, 1964), pp.32–59.

[23] J. Longnon, ed., *Livre de la Conqueste de la Princée de l'Amorée* (Paris, 1911) is the standard edition. No translation available. The earliest edition was produced by J. Buchon, *Recherches historique sur la Principauté Française de Morée et ses Hautes Baronnies* I (Paris, 1845).

editor Professor Longnon suggested that it may well have been written at Catherine's request during her stay in the Morea from November 1338 to June 1341.[24]

The Greek chronicle survives in five manuscripts of which two, Codex Havniensis 57 in Copenhagen (H) and Codex Parisiensus Grec 2898 (P), are the fullest texts. Schmitt published both in parallel in 1904 and Kalonaros published manuscript H in 1940.[25] In its 9,000 lines it covers the period 1095 to 1292, breaking off with Florent de Hainaut's campaign at Arta. Since pages are missing in H, the story probably came down to 1304 as in the French version. However, as in that version, later material was interpolated in the text, such as the slighting of Thebes castle by the Catalans in 1332. In line 8,469 of manuscript H, Erard III le Maure, lord of Arkadia, was mentioned as still alive, whilst in line 8,472 of manuscript P, it was suggested that he was dead. It would appear from this that the Copenhagen text was copied sometime before and that of Paris sometime after his death in 1388. It would also appear that the author was connected in some way with the family of le Maure, well-informed on matters of feudal and chivalric procedure and intensely pro-Frankish.

The French and Greek chronicles can clearly be shown to be copies and abridgements of earlier texts, but the language of the prototype is still in question, and here the preoccupations of historians and philologists diverge. Historians are less concerned with the evolution of demotic Greek, than the cross-cultural relations of Greeks and Latins. The praise heaped upon the Franks in the Greek chronicle is certainly evidence for cultural mix but also suggestive of contacts circumscribed by property interests and concomitant personal relationships. Such views may not have been shared outside a particular archontic family or group of families, whilst the existence of a putative Greek prototype which enshrined in some way folk tradition would suggest much wider multi-racial contacts contrary to the indications contained in other sources. Dr Michael Jeffreys has suggested that the formulaic repetitions of the Greek version may well indicate origins in oral tradition rather than the hesitations of a translator. For him, as for Schmitt, the original was written in Greek.[26] Buchon and Hopf plumped for a French original, as does Professor Jacoby in his closely argued article in the *Journal des Savants* 1968. For him the Greek text bears all the hallmarks of a translation, whilst it is inconceivable that the Greeks should sing the praises

---

[24] J. Longnon, *L'Empire latin due Constantinople et la Principauté de Morée* (Paris, 1949), p.325.

[25] J. Schmitt, ed., *The Chronicle of Morea* (London, 1904; reprinted New York, 1979); P. Kalonaros, ed., *To Chronikon Tou Moreos* (Athens, 1940; re-issued Athens nd=1985?). English translation, H.E. Lurier, *Crusaders as Conquerors, The Chronicle of Morea* (New York, 1964).

[26] M.J. Jeffreys, 'Formulas in the Chronicle of the Morea' *DOP* 27 (1973), 163–95, and 'The Chronicle of the Morea: priority of the Greek version' *BZ* 68 (1975), 304–50.

of the Franks before the latter did so themselves.[27] Whilst I am personally convinced by the latter, the case must remain open and await further debate.

The existence of the chronicle has served both to focus attention on the principality of Achaia and at the same time to provide a framework for the early historical studies of the Frankish Aegean. Its value as a source amidst the paucity of other evidence cannot be denied nor can its dominant and long-term influence on the study of the crusader states in the Aegean. The aura of romance in the chronicle, as well as in the writings of Villehardouin, Valenciennes, and Muntaner, was passed on by the historians of the late nineteenth century to their predominantly middle-class readership who were then beginning to visit the Aegean in increasing numbers. Whether it was conscious or not, this romanticising of the Frankish settlers in the Aegean has not served them well in the twentieth century.

Assizes of Romania

The 219 clauses of the Assizes of Romania represent the law code of the Latin Aegean: a fusion of feudal custom, Byzantine law and the tradition of the crusader kingdom of Jerusalem.[28] Although effectively the code which governed the relationship of the prince of Achaia with his feudatories at some stage, the Assizes were consciously identified with both the kingdom of Jerusalem and the empire of Romania as their validating bodies. The research of Professor Jacoby supersedes and complements all earlier work on the Assizes.[29] Like all feudal custom they were a developing body of law. Something of a law-code existed by 1276 and the claim of Margaret de Neuilly on the barony of Akova. In the course of that famous lawsuit the French chronicle quoted the prince as acting '... selonc que les usances et les coustumes du pays'.[30] Sometime between 1333 and 1346 an unknown French jurist collected the customs as they were known in his day and it is substantially in this form that they have come down to us. It is impossible to distinguish to any considerable degree what pre-dated 1276 and what was

---

[27] D. Jacoby, 'Quelques considérations sur les versions de la Chronique de Morée' *Journal des Savants* (1968), pp.133–89.

[28] The standard edition is that by Georges Recoura, *Les Assises de Romaniee. . .* (Paris, 1930). There is an English transation by Peter Topping, *Feudal Institutions as Revealed in the Assizes of Romania* (Pennsylvania, 1949), reprinted in idem, *Studies on Latin Greece* (London, 1975). The first text to be published was by P. Canciani, *Barbarorum leges antiquae cum notis et glossariis* III (Venice, 1785), pp.493–534.

[29] D. Jacoby, *La féodalité en Grèce médiévale: Les Assises de Romanie* (Paris, 1971); P. Topping, 'The formation of the Assizes of Romania' *Byzantion* 17 (1944–5), 304–14, reprinted in *Studies in Latin Greece* (London, 1975).

[30] L de C, 504

added by the Angevin suzerains to the Villehardouin compilation. The Assizes survive today in ten manuscripts, all in Italian. They owe this and indeed their very survival to a decision by the Venetian senate to commission an official translation for use in its Aegean possessions in 1452.

Byzantine historians

All these sources were produced either in the Aegean or concerning it under western inspiration. The Greeks too had their historic identity and their own tradition of historical writing. This material not only provides information on events in the Frankish Aegean from a different perspective but at the same time sheds light on the Byzantine perception of the westerner. The principal Greek historical writers in this period were Nicetas Choniates (*c*.1156–1217),[31] George Akropolites (1217–82),[32] George Pachymeres (1242–*c*.1310),[33] and Nikephoros Gregoras (1290–1360).[34] In addition to these, other lesser known authorities have been used in the last decade or so to illustrate cross-cultural contacts in both Epiros and the Peloponnese. In particular these are the writings of Demetrios Chomatianos, archbishop of Ochrid (*c*.1217–35), whose importance have been highlighted by Günter Prinzing and Paul Magdalino, and the chronicles of Ioannina and of the Tocco, used by both Donald Nicol and Aneta Ilieva to explore something of the *mentalité* behind the history of events.[35]

---

[31] J.L. van Dietan, ed., *Historia* (Berlin, 1975). English translation by H. Magoulias, *O City of Byzantium* (Detroit, 1984).
[32] A. Heisenberg, ed., *Georgii Acropolitae opera* 2 vols (Leipzig, 1903). No translation available.
[33] I. Bekker, ed., *Georgii Pachymeris De Michaele et Andronico Palaeologis* 2 vols (Bond, 1835). No translation available.
[34] L. Shopen and I. Bekker, eds, *Nicephori Gregorii Historia Bizantina* 3 vols (Bonn, 1829–55); J.L. van Dieten, ed., *Nikephoros Gregoras, Rhomaïsche Geschichte, Historia Rhomaïke* 3 vols (Stuttgart, 1973–88). No English translation available.
[35] P. Magdalino, 'A neglected authority for the history of the Peloponnese in the early thirteenth century: Demetrios Chomatianos, Archbishop of Bulgaria' *BZ* 70 (1977), 316–23; G. Prinzing, 'Studien zur Provinz- und zentral Verwaltung im Machberich der Epirotischen Herrscher Michael I und Theodoros Dukas' *Epeirotika Chronica* 24 (1982), 73–120 and 25 (1983), 37–112; D. Simon, 'Die Bußbescheide des Erzbischofs Chomatien von Ochrid' *Jahrbuch der Österreichischen Byzantinistik* 37 (1987), 235–76; D.M. Nicol, *The Despotate of Epiros, 1267–1479* (Cambridge, 1984), p.164ff; A. Ilieva, 'The image of the Morea in the mentality of a Giannotes' in *Praktika Diethous Symposiou Gia To Despotou Tis Epeirou* (Arta, 1992), pp.309–12. My thanks to Ruth Macrides for the references to the articles by Prinzing and Simon.

Printed primary sources

Since Buchon published a selection of documents relating to the Aegean from the archives of the west in 1848, they have not unnaturally received very unequal treatment, both as regards their availablity in published form and as regards their accessibility and even survival. With the exception of the letters of Pope Innocent III (1198–1216), which were published in full by J-P. Migne, all papal correspondence from this period has been edited and calendared: by Cardinal Pressutti for Honorius III (1216–27) and for the other popes of the thirteenth and fourteenth centuries by various editors for the Ecole d'Athenes et de Rome.[36] Material from the Venetian archives generated by the Senate and other assemblies of the city concerning Romania has been summarised by the late Freddy Thiriet.[37] Since the 1970s the wealth of Venetian notarial books as a source of information on language acquisition, cross-cultural, matrimonial and commercial alliances has come to be recognised and the material, particularly rich for Crete, is coming under scrutiny.[38] Other than Buchon's work and the twelve invaluable documents on estate exploitation edited by Jean Longnon and Peter Topping, the considerable Acciaioli archive in Florence remains unpublished and in part uncatalogued.[39] Catalan material in Barcelona was transcribed and published posthumously by Antoni Rubio I Lluch in *Diplomatari de L'Orient Català (1301–1409)* in 1947. The archives of the Knights Hospitallers on Malta has much material relevant to the Aegean, but at the moment it represents a very large vineyard with but one labourer, Anthony Luttrell. The Angevin archives in Naples fell a casualty of war in September 1943 and 378 registers of the Angevin kings were destroyed. Apart from the selection published by Buchon and the 240 or so documents including the Treaty of Viterbo of 1267 copied by Charles Perrat in the 1930s and published in 1967, nothing remains.[40] Charles Hopf worked in these archives in preparation for his *Geschichte Griechenlands vom Beginn des Mittelalters*. The numerous references therein contained have transformed the use of this work from that of an out-of-date secondary source to that of a quasi-primary source as regards the Angevin material. I am aware that this is an all-too-brief conspectus of the archival material but

---

[36] Listed H.E. Mayer, *Bibliographie zur Geschichte des Kreuzzüge* (Hanover, 1965), pp.71–4.
[37] F. Thiriet, *Régestes des Délibérations du Sénat de Venise concernant la Romanie* 3 vols (Paris, 1958–61), and *Délibérations des Assemblées Vénitiennes* (Paris, 1966).
[38] A.E. Laiou, 'Observations on the results of the Fourth Crusade' *Medievalia et Humanistica* 12 (1984), 43–60.
[39] J. Longnon and P. Topping, eds, *Documents sur le Régime des Terres dans la Principauté de Morée au XIVe siècle* (Paris, 1969); Sovrintendenza Archivistica per la Toscana, *Archivi Dell'Aristocrazia Fiorentina* (Firenze, 1989), pp.23–39.
[40] C. Perrat and J. Longnon, *Actes Relatifs a la Principauté de Morée, 1289–1300* (Paris, 1967).

I believe that its point – that there is still much to be done and that until it is done our view of the Frankish Aegean must be provisional – is a valid one.

Monuments and travellers

A quite different source from the muniments is provided by the monuments and artefacts of Frankish Greece. They have suffered from neglect in the scramble to explore the classical antiquity of the Aegean. An audit of those monuments surviving above-ground is badly needed. A magnificent example of a one-man survey of the archaeology of the Morea is Antoine Bon's *La Morée Franque*, which was published in Paris in 1969 complete with a useful album of maps, photographs and plans. It took over 30 years to produce and provides an excellent political history of the area to boot. The most obvious remains are those of the castles and towers, yet there is no complete listing of these either official or private nor anything like a corpus of plans and photographs. Even the castles mentioned in the *Chronicle of the Morea* have not all been located, nor their role in the conquest and defence of the Peloponnese in the thirteenth century assessed. Excavation is costly, but the sites of Modon and Glarenza (Clarence) are crying out for detailed study and excavation. They are discrete Frankish centres, built up and destroyed during the Frankokratia, Glarenza in 1429 and Modon in 1500. They would add much to the study of urbanism in the medieval Balkans as well as contributing significantly to the study of ceramics and the organisation of western trading and administrative centres. In the interpretation of rural settlement and towns, the work of various non-excavational surface surveys have much to add. The expeditions in the Argolid, Boeotia, Kea, Laconia and Messenia have raised many issues and pointed to some answers.[41] Their drawback for the medieval period is that they provide processual interpretation and this can be difficult to integrate into documentary interpretations and event-based history. They are also dependent for their chronology on the surface scatters of pottery. The geology of the Aegean makes these abundant but they lack the relationship which excavated material provides and are of course dependent on the current knowledge of ceramics. Here matters have improved dramatically in the last five years. Work on excavated material from Athens, Corinth and

---

41 W.A. McDonald and G.R. Rapp, eds, *The Minnesota Messenia Expedition* (Minneapolis, 1972); J.L. Bintliff and A.M. Snodgrass, 'The Cambridge/Bradford Boeotian expedition: the first four years' *Journal of Field Archaeology* 12 (1985), 147–9; idem, 'Mediterranean survey and the city' *Antiquity* 62 (1988), 57–71; J.F. Cherry, J.L. Davis and E. Mantzourani, *Landscape Archaeology as Long-Term History: Northern Keos in the Cyclades* (Los Angeles, 1991), pp.351–64.

Thebes is providing clear chronological markers for the pottery of the Frankokratia and at last a move is being made away from the misleading cultural label of 'Frankish' towards dating by century. This will pave the way for new interpretations of material within an historic context. Numismatists are breaking new ground in studying coins not just as artefacts but in terms of the monetary economy. Sadly they are hampered in their endeavours by the disappearance or non-declaration of coin hoards, many of which still seem to appear on western markets despite the Greek antiquity laws. Systematisation and the production of a database for the physical remains of the Frankish past should be the next step forward.

Finally, to return to documents but in an archaeological context, the memoirs of travellers and sojourners in Greek lands from Cyriac of Ancona and Cristofero Buondelmonti in the fifteenth century to the compilers of the tourist-orientated guidebooks of the 1990s can shed much light on the location and changing condition of the medieval monuments in the Aegean. Toponomy too benefits from their writings, as it does from map-bases compiled by the great powers in the nineteenth century and from the Catalan Portulans of the fifteenth.[42] To mention just a very few travellers by name, the accounts of Evilya Celebi (*c.* 1631), F.C.H.L. Pouqueville (travelled 1806–16), William Leake (1777–1860), Heinrich Lolling (1848–94) and Theodore Bent (1852–97) are particularly useful for the remains of Frankish Greece but all of the travellers are very readable and all repay reading or at least skipping. The definitive work on travellers up to 1821 is that by Kyriakos Simopoulos.[43]

Historiography

In 1639 Thomas Fuller in his *History of the Holy War* gave short shrift to the Latin conquest of Greece – 'one could not now see the Grecian empire for empires' – and suggested that this first diversification of crusading resources led to the eventual loss of the Holy Land.[44] That apart, western European academic interest in the history of crusader Greece may be said to have begun with the work of Charles du Fresne Ducange (1610–88) and the publication of his *Histoire de l'Empire de Constantinople sous les*

---

[42] A. Delatte, *Les Portulans Grecs* (Paris, 1947).

[43] Full lists of the travellers and their work may be found in K. Simopoulou, *Xenoi Taxidiotes stin Ellada* 3 vols (Athens, 1984). Shirley H. Weber, *Voyages and Travels in Greece ... Made Prior to the Year 1801* (Princeton, 1953) and J.P.A. Van Der Vin, *Travellers to Greece and Constantinople* 2 vols (Leiden, 1980) both have interesting discussion.

[44] T. Fuller, *The Holy War* (London, 1840), ch.xvii, p.145.

Empereurs Francais in Paris in 1657.[45] It was no accident that the France of Louis XIV should have produced research which served to commemorate the achievement of those noble French families which had participated in an early phase of French territorial expansion. A collection of documents gathered by Ducange and not published for another 200 years saw the light of day as *Les Familles d'Outremer*, published in 1869 at another period of French imperial interest under Napoleon III.[46] Whatever might be said of Louis XIV's reasons for encouraging the work of the Bollandist and Maurist fathers, the study of Byzantine palaeography and Frankish Greece were placed upon the academic agenda. A probable direct effect of this may be noted in the memoirs of Louis Spon and George Wheler, who travelled in the Balkans in 1675–76. They were, as far as I am aware, the first travellers to note some Frankish monuments as they passed, albeit as markers of their journey.[47]

The political history of the ruling elites of Romania was given form and publicity in the 60 years after 1840.[48] The moving spirits in this were Jean Alexandre Buchon (1791–1846) and George Finlay (1799–1876). Buchon's literary output and range of interest in a comparatively short writing life from the 1820s to 1840s is a lesson to all on application and diligence.[49] He had a developed consciousness of the French contribution to crusading which came through in his historical work, much of which was published posthumously. His great contribution, however, was his realisation of the importance of west Mediterranean archive sources as a supplement to the *Chronicle of the Morea* for the history of the Frankish Aegean and his publication of these sources for the first time in a useable and accessible form. In addition to documentary material, Buchon constructed the first genealogical tables for the French dynasties of the Aegean and produced illustrations of seals, coins and sites, many of which he drew himself on a visit to the Aegean in 1840 and 1841. Whilst visiting Euboea at this time he drew the Frankish tower on Mount Kandelion and aroused the interest of his host in medieval antiquities as well as engaging in

---

[45] Most accessible in J.A. Buchon, ed., *Collection des chroniques nationales francaises* II–III (Paris, 1826; reprinted New York, 1971).

[46] E.G. Rey, ed., *Collection des documents inédits sur l'histoire de France* 18 (Paris, 1869; reprinted New York, 1971) deals almost exclusively with Jerusalem and Cyprus.

[47] Sir George Wheler, *A Journey into Greece* ... (London, 1682).

[48] The first publication in the field was *Geschichte der Halbinsel Morea Während des Mittelalters* 2 vols (Stuttgart, 1830–36; reprinted Hildesheim, 1965) by Jacob Fallermayer (1790–1861). The book is more famous for its racial and linguistic views than for its history. These are contained in I, pp.iii–xlv. He maintained that modern Greeks were mainly of Slav extract and that the Greek language was a conscious revival of the Orthodox church. His views became almost heretical in the newly independent Greece, but the study of medieval Greece had certainly started with a bang!

[49] Bibliography compiled by Jean Longnon in his edition of Buchon's *Voyage dans L'Eubée, les Îles Ioniennes et les Cyclades en 1841* (Paris, 1911), pp.lix–lxiii.

public debate in newspapers on the significance of medieval armour found at Chalkis. Finlay, on the other hand, approached the subject from an interest in Greece where he had gone in 1823 and remained for the rest of his life. Becoming disillusioned with the life of a share-cropping landlord in Attica, he moved to Athens and turned to the writing of the history of Greece since the Roman occupation. Between 1843 and 1864 he brought out a series of monographs on Byzantium, medieval and modern Greece, which appeared after his death under the title *A History of Greece from its Conquest by the Romans to the Present Time* edited by H.F. Tozer (7 vols, Oxford, 1877) and some of which were subsequently reprinted in the Everyman series. Where Buchon's books had been expensively produced in a very small print run, Finlay's work was accesible. Nonetheless, his material on Frankish Greece in volumes III to V of the Tozer edition relied heavily on the sources published by Buchon and on the reliable Byzantine texts then appearing in the Bonn Corpus begun by Barthold Georg Niebuhr in 1828.[50] Western interest in the history of Greece, stimulated as a result of the War of Independence, was given form and substance by Finlay's work which was compared to that of Gibbon in its range and went some way to undo the damage done by the latter to western perceptions of Byzantine studies. Finlay's approach gave play to the great variety of influences, conscious and unconscious, on Aegean culture. His work most certainly does not deserve the neglect into which it has fallen in the latter part of the twentieth century. In 1867–8 Karl Hopf (1832–73) brought out his heavily annotated study *Geschichte Griechenlands vom Beginn des Mittelalters*, curiously buried away as volumes 85 and 86 of the 167 volume series *Allegemeine Encyklopädie des Wissenschaften und Kunste*, edited by J.S. Ersch and J.G. Gruber between 1818 and 1889.[51] This work was undoubtedly the most detailed study of Frankish Greece ever undertaken but it does not have an index and as such is very difficult to use for reference purposes. In the historiography of Frankish Greece Karl Hopf is the second daunting example of a short working life which left so much of such quality as its memorial. This publication, together with Wilhelm Heyd's *Geschichte des Levantehandels im Mittelalter* which had appered in installments between 1858 and 1862, firmly established the ascendancy of German scholarship in medieval Greek history.[52]

By the 1880s interest in the history of the Aegean had passed outside the walls of academe where scholars had the leisure to peruse these large

---

[50] *Corpus Scriptorum Historiae Byzantinae* (Bonn, 1828–97).

[51] The two volumes were reprinted in New York in 1960. For a bibliography of Hopf's works see Ernst Gerland, *BZ* 8 (1899), 347–68.

[52] W. Heyd in *Zeitschrift fur die gesamte Staatswissenschaft* 14 (1858) – 18 (1862). References today are to the French translation by Furcy Raymond, *Histoire du commerce du Levant au moyen age* 2 vols (Leipzig, 1885/6 and Paris, 1936; reprinted Amsterdam, 1959).

tomes. There was a demand for shorter studies, all of which to a greater or lesser extent passed on the aura of romance contained in the chansons de geste tradition of the chronicle sources. In order of publication, but not of influence, the monographs that now appeared were: Charles Beving, *La principauté d'Achaïe et de Morée, 1204–1430* (Brussels, 1879); Diane de Guldecrone, *L'Achaïe Féodale. Études sur le Moyen Âge en Grèce* (Paris, 1886); Ferdinand Gregorovius, *Geschichte der Stadt Athen im Mittelalter* (Munich, 1889); Rennell Rodd, *The Princes of Achaia and the Chronicles of Morea* (2 vols, London, 1907) and William Miller, *The Latins in the Levant* (London, 1908), which was translated into Greek and enlarged by Spiros Lambros in seven fascicules between 1909 and 1910. For the nineteenth century, true history was political history and these publications reflected this preoccupation. Be that as it may, it could be said that by the onset of the First World War the history of Frankish Greece had been relatively well-served.

The collection and publication of medieval source material, often as an expression of national pride and identity, was another prominent feature of historical studies in the nineteenth century. Individual and national enterprises like the editions of papal correspondence, the work of J-P Migne, Buchon, Hopf, Tafel and Thomas, and Miklosich and Muller all contained material with a direct bearing on the medieval history of the Aegean. Between 1880 and 1890 K.N. Sathas published his nine volumes of *Monumenta Hellenicae Historiae*. Although the bulk of this material came from Venetian sources, the new Greek kingdom very consciously had its own form of Pertz's *Monumenta*. By the onset of the First World War, the history and sources of Frankish Greece had been selectively covered and the work fitted in well with the mainstream of historical practice of the day.[53]

From say the 1930s, as noted by Christopher Dyer, a shift of emphasis is discernable amongst western medievalists away from chronicles to a closer analysis of official records. By the 1960s stress was being laid on the lives of ordinary people, and during the 1970s not only were these concerns becoming academically respectable, but the combined effect of the Annales school and the emergence of feminist historiography was making itself felt and bringing non-elitist areas like childhood, longevity and *mentalité* to the attention of medievalists.[54]

For students of medieval Greece, these trends seemed to be working their way through in the 1980s and are perhaps best seen in the journal *Byzantinische Forschungen*. Miller is clearly out-dated, yet his lucid pages still cast a long shadow. His *Latins in the Levant* was re-issued, unrevised, in 1964 and is still the main reference for undergraduates in search of information on medieval Greece. Indeed the relevant chapters in the new

---

[53] G.P. Gooch, *History and Historians in the Nineteenth Century* 2nd edn, (London, 1952), pp. 454–8; D. Knowles, *Great Historical Enterprises* (London, 1963), pp.1–62.
[54] C. Dyer, *Standards of Living in the Later Middle Ages* (Cambridge, 1989), pp.1–4.

edition of the *Cambridge Medieval History* IV (1967) and Nicolas Cheetham's *Medieval Greece* (Yale, 1981) are both directly in the mould first cast by Miller in 1908.

Medieval studies since the 1980s, particularly in Britain, have seen a return to political and military history and a revival of narrative. However, it is no longer a tale of dynasties and battles, but a political history concerned as much with popular culture, economic realities, and the role of the family – in short, a political history that has learned much from the aims and methods of historians working in the 1960s and 1970s.[55] The fruits of this in terms of the Frankish Aegean may be seen in the contributions to a joint meeting of the XXII Spring Symposium of Byzantine Studies and of the Society for the Study of the Crusades and the Latin East held at the University of Nottingham in 1988, and most recently in the work of Aneta Ilieva of the University of Sofia.[56]

The work of the 1960s and 1970s has been eloquently and conveniently summarised and reviewed in two articles by Charles Brand and Angeliki Laiou.[57] It is perhaps invidious to single out scholars from what is after all a cumulative and cooperative effort, but tribute should be paid to the contributions made by Peter Charanis, David Jacoby, Raymond-Joseph Loenertz, Jean Longnon, Kenneth Setton, Peter Topping and Robert Wolff. It was they among others who focused attention on problems of government, demography, colonialism, and social organisation in the Frankish states. All have added very substantially to our knowledge and interpretation of the Frankish Aegean, all figure prominently in the notes and bibliography of the present work, and most have enjoyed the distinction of having their work collected and re-issued.

Finally, what of archaeology and the medieval Aegean? In 1914 it too reflected the interests and preoccupations of the western scholarly world and was almost totally focused on classical antiquity and prehistory. The researches into the prehistoric Aegean conducted by Heinrich Schliemann and Sir Arthur Evans were very much in the popular mind and on the agendas of the various foreign schools of archaeology in Athens. There were of course notable exceptions, usually scholars interested in a site or an historical event and comprehending Frankish remains as a point in their wider interest. Thus in Constantinople Dr Paspates, Alexander van Millingen and Sir Edwin Pears noted presumed Frankish structures as did

---

[55] N. Stone, 'The revival of narrative: reflections on a new old history' *Past and Present* 85 (1979), 1–23; C.T. Wood, 'The return of Medieval politics' *AHR* 94 (1989), 391–404.
[56] B. Arbel, B. Hamilton and D. Jacoby, eds, *Latins and Greeks in the Eastern Mediterranean After 1204* (London, 1989); A. Ilieva, *Frankish Morea (1205–1262), Socio-cultural Interaction Between the Franks and the Local Population* (Athens, 1991).
[57] C. Brand, 'The Fourth crusade: some recent interpretations' *Medievali et Humanistica* 12 (1984), 33–41; A.E. Laiou, 'Observations on the results of the Fourth Crusade: Greeks and Latins in ports and markets' *Medievalia et Humanistica*, 12 (1984), 43–56.

Tafrali in Thessalonika, Hasluck on the Cyzicus peninsula and Heinrich Lolling in his notes for the proposed Baedeker guide to Greece. The same was true for those like Tozer, Bury and Miller who were engaged upon writing aspects of the history of Frankish Greece. Their occasional reference to its monuments took the form of incidental asides.[58] These were very much subsidiary to other concerns and lacked the single-mindedness which had been displayed by Buchon in 1841 and certainly did not amount to an accurate archaeological record or structural analysis. Only three articles, which come in this latter category and were specifically dedicated to Frankish remains, appeared in these years. They were Alan Wace's study of sculpture at Paroria and Geraki, Richard Dawkin's and J.P. Droop's note on glazed pottery found at Sparta, and Ramsay Traquair's paper on Frankish architecture in Greece which appeared in 1924.[59]

In the 1930s and 1940s considerable fieldwork was undertaken by individuals like Antoine Bon, Kevin Andrews, and A.K. Orlandos, who made significant inroads into the neglect of the standing Frankish remains of the Greek countryside.[60] Alongside their efforts, the American School of Classical Archaeology in Athens began its excavations at Athens and Corinth. By 1940 these had produced fundamental studies of Byzantine pottery and a detailed study of the fortifications on Akrocorinth.[61] This work laid the foundations for the dating of medieval pottery and had a profound effect on the both the chronology and the development of archaeology in Greece. The implications and refinement of this work is still going on and may be seen in the pages of current archaeological publications.[62] The momentous discovery of a long plateia of the Frankish

---

[58] E. Pears, *Forty Years in Constantinople* (London, 1916; reprinted New York, 1971); F.W. Hasluck, *Cyzicus* (Cambridge, 1910); O. Tafrali, *Thessalonique des origines au xive siecle* (Paris, 1919); H.G. Lolling, *Reisenotizen aus Griechenland, 1876 und 1877* (Berlin, 1989); W. Miller review in *EHR* 22 (1907), 572; H.F. Tozer, 'The Franks in the Peloponnese' *JHS* 4 (1883), 165–236; J. Bury, 'The Lombards and Venetians in Euboia' *JHS* 7 (1886) – 9 (1888).

[59] A. Wace, 'Frankish sculpture at Paroria and Geraki' *ABSA* 11 (1904–5), 130–45; R. Dawkins and J.P. Droop, 'Byzantine pottery from Sparta' *ABSA* 17 (1910–11), 23–8; R. Traquair, 'Frankish architecture in Greece' *Journal of the Royal Institute of British Architects* 31 (1923–4), 33–48, 73–86.

[60] A. Bon, 'Fortresses médiévales de la Grèce centrale' *BCH* 61 (1937), 136–208; idem, *La Morée franque 1204–1430* (Paris, 1969) and K. Andrews, *Castles of the Morea* (Princeton, 1953; reprinted Amsterdam, 1978). The work of the Vienna-based *Tabula Imperii Byzantini*, although firmly based in Byzantine monuments, should not be overlooked, especially J. Koder and F. Hild, *TIB 1: Hellas Und Thessalia* (Vienna, 1976).

[61] C. Morgan, *Corinth XI: The Byzantine Pottery* (Harvard, 1942); Alison Frantz, 'Middle Byzantine pottery in Athens' *Hesperia* 7 (1938), 429–67; idem 'Turkish pottery from the Agora' *Hesperia* 11 (1942), 1–28; R. Carpenter and A. Bon, *Corinth III, ii: The Defences of Akrocorinth ...* (Harvard, 1936), pp.128–281.

[62] For example see work by P. Armstrong, E. Ivison, P. Lock and G. Sanders in *ABSA* 80 (1985) – 88 (1992), and in P. Lock and G. Sanders, eds, *Essays in the Archaeology of Medieval Greece* (Oxford, forthcoming).

period and of a Latin church and burial ground on the high ground south of the Archaeological Museum of Ancient Corinth in 1989 and 1990 for the first time provides stratified remains containing much coin evidence and seems set to revise all existing knowledge of the ceramics of the Frankish period and of the position of Corinth in the Frankish Morea.[63] Like modern developments in historical studies, archaeologists too have turned to *mentalité* and the perception of time measurement and burial practices in the Frankokratia, whilst the survey work noted above is adding numerous sites belonging to this period and throwing up problems of Greco–Latin co-existence not yet worked out, let alone that of historical and archaeological approaches to the past.[64] One important point which has emerged from recent work is that there was a considerable gap between the material culture of the Frankish Aegean and contemporary western perceptions of the wealth of that area, a gap explicable by a selective knowledge of classical writers without the benefit of visits to the lands in question by medieval western commentators.

One aim of this book is to remove that aura of romanticism which has attached itself to the Frankish settlers in former Byzantine territory in the thirteenth century. The other is to add to William Miller's study of 1908 something of the results of the historical and archaeological research of the last 80 years and to show how that work has changed and modified attitudes and perceptions of the Franks in the Aegean area.

---

[63] See the interim reports by C.K. Williams II and Orestes Zervos in *Hesperia* 59 (1990), 325–69; 60 (1991), 1–58; 61 (1992), 133–91 and 62 (1993), 1–52.
[64] S. Tabaczynski, 'The relationship between history and archaeology: elements of the present debate' *Medieval Archaeology* 37 (1993), 1–14.

Chapter 3 ....

The Crusader States of the North Aegean

Of the six crusader states which grew up after the conquest of Constantinople by the men of the Fourth Crusade the two in the north Aegean, the Latin Empire of Constantinople and the Kingdom of Thessalonika, were the first established and the first lost.

By the evening of Monday 12 April 1204 the soldiers of the Fourth Crusade had established themselves within the walls of Constantinople. At dawn the next day it became apparent to them that Byzantine resistance had collapsed and that that '*magna urbs*' and '*regia civitas*' was in their hands.[1] Of course appearances were deceptive – the crusading army had not decisively crushed Greek resistance. This was in the process of relocating and new leaders were coming to the fore.

Geographically, the two kingdoms shielded the other Aegean states from the principal aggressors of the region in the early thirteenth century. As the first and second cities of Byzantium, they attracted not just trade and wealth but also the full force of their Greek and Bulgarian rivals, eager to add the 'queen city' and the second city to their own territories. Both Baldwin of Flanders, the first Latin emperor (d. July 1206), and Boniface of Montferrat, the uncrowned king of Thessalonika (d. September 1207), were killed defending the hinterlands of their cities from the Bulgarian tsar Kalojan. In 1224 the city of Thessalonika was recaptured by the Greeks of Epiros and thereby the Latin emperor in Constantinople was cut off from land communication with his subjects in the Greek peninsula. In 1261 the city of Constantinople fell to the Greeks of Nicaea, who since the 1220s had effectively confined the Latins to the city and its suburbs. In 1246 they had taken Thessalonika from their Epirote Greek rivals and thus effectively established themselves as the true heirs of Constantine.

---

[1] PL, 216:452; P. Lock, 'Latin emperors as heirs to Byzantium', in P. Magdalino, ed., *New Constantines* (London, 1994), pp.295–304.

The Latin rulers of these two northern states were unable to establish clearly defined territories or to develop the resources and revenues which a prolonged period of peace might have permitted. As a result they were able neither to attract and retain settlers nor compete with their Greek opponents in the recruitment of the mercenaries necessary for defence and for the collection of booty, an essential income supplement to rulers who lacked more settled sources of revenue.[2] However, by absorbing the attention of the Greeks and Bulgars in the opening decades of the thirteenth century, they contributed substantially to the development of their vassal states in Greece, further to the south and west.

After 1261 and the recovery of Constantinople by the Byzantine emperor Michael VIII Palaeologos, Greek attention was turned to the Latin states of mainland Greece. However, for the Byzantines Hellas did not enjoy the same symbolic significance as the two major cities of the empire and a sustained campaign of rural reconquest was to prove beyond their immediate resources. During the first half-century of their existence, the Latin states in Greece and the islands had enjoyed a modicum of stability: rulers had not had their lives cut short on the battlefield, a power structure had had time to evolve, resources exploited, and above all a modus vivendi with Greek landed interests had been worked out. The price for this stability had been paid by the two states in the north Aegean. It has become commonplace to paint a negative and destructive picture of the Latin Empire and the Kingdom of Salonika. However understandable this might be, these ephemeral states did display some innovative features and the picture of sterility is by no means a fair one.

The heirs of Byzantium

In a very real sense these two northern states were the heirs of Byzantium. An emperor was elected by the victorious crusaders because that was the political system which they found in place in Constantinople in 1204. The man chosen as the first Latin emperor, Baldwin count of Flanders, adopted the titles of his Greek predecessors and used this imperial formulary in both its Greek and Latin versions. Furthermore, he was at pains to stress continuity by reference to the good laws of the ancient Greeks.[3] Baldwin's

---

[2] Villehardouin, 376; see PL, 215:636–7 and *Urkunden* I, p.302 for attempts by Baldwin to attract settlers and ibid., II, pp.37–42 for appeals by Henry for troops. See PL, 216:354 for uncompetitive rates of pay offered by the emperor Henry in 1210. In the late 1250s according to the anonymous minstrel of Reims, knights and sergants were returning west because Baldwin II could not pay them, cited by Malcolm Barber in 'Western attitudes to Frankish Greece in the thirteenth century', in B. Arbel et al., eds, *Latins and Greeks in the Eastern Mediterranean after 1204* (London, 1989), p.123.
[3] See chapter 7.

rival for the imperial throne also emphasised precedent and continuity in the kingdom which he received. Boniface of Montferrat, who failed to secure election as the first Latin emperor, seemed consciously to hark back to the supposed 'Kingdom of Thessalonika' thought to have been bestowed on his brother Renier de Montferrat by Manuel I Komnenos at the time of Renier's marriage to the emperor's daughter, Maria Porphyrogenita, in 1180.[4] Boniface's own marriage in May/June 1204 (certainly after Baldwin's coronation on 16 May) with Margaret of Hungary, the widow of the Byzantine emperor Isaac II Angelos, must have had more to do with his expectations in Thessalonika and Greece than with any belated hope of gaining the imperial throne. He certainly used his wife's former position and her children by Isaac to bolster his own position with the Greeks and to exploit his new kingdom. It was through her that he enlisted the support of Michael Komnenos Doukas for a short time in late 1204. Michael was the illegitimate son of the sebastokrator John Doukas and a cousin of the emperors Isaac II Angelos and Alexios III. Boniface failed to retain Michael in his service for long. Either despairing of advancement or disillusioned by Boniface's rapacity, Michael went to Epiros and set himself up as the leader of the Greek opposition there. In this atmosphere of conquest might meant right, but Boniface clearly felt some need to justify his new regal estate, both to Latins and to Greeks alike.

In late 1204 the strong centrifugal tendencies which had been operating within the Byzantine empire since the 1180s now aided the Greeks in their hour of need, just as in a few months' time it was to assist the Latins in their initial sweep through Thessaly and Greece. Political instability had encouraged localism in the provinces. Powerful and persuasive local notables in Bulgaria, Cyprus, Rhodes, central Greece and the theme of Thrakesion in Asia Minor had persuaded the politically important groups of those areas to look to them for protection and to place their own interests before those of the centralised empire.[5] Localism was not a new phenomenon to the western crusaders, who had been exploiting it for as long as any of them could remember in their own counties and marquisates at home. Indeed, both Frederick Barbarossa and Richard the Lionheart had treated with separatist governors at Philadelphia and on Cyprus in their journies east in 1190 and 1191.[6] Then, and again in 1204–5, it was the personality of these local

---

[4] *Urkunden* I, p.513; C. Brand, *Byzantium Confronts the West* (Harvard, 1968), p.19; P. Magdalino, *The Empire of Manuel I Komnenos* (Cambridge, 1993), pp.100, 235 and 245. Our only source for this supposed connection is Robert de Clari (Clari, XXXIII–XXXVIII, McNeal trans., pp.60–6). See Raimbaut de Vaqueiras, epic letter I/4 and lyric poem XX/7–10 for Boniface's moral right in J. Linskill, *The Poems of the Troubador Raimbaut de Vaqueiras* (Paris, 1964), pp.227, 309.
[5] C. Brand, *Byzantium Confronts the West* (Cambridge, Mass., 1968), pp.9–14, 44–55.
[6] R.L. Wolff and H.W. Hazard, eds, *A History of the Crusades* II (Wisconsin, 1969), pp.45–125.

potentates, and not the political process of which they were a part, which had held the attention of the crusaders. In one sense the Franks after 1204 were just joining the ranks of the jostlers for power and not defeating them or bringing them to heel. What the crusaders had gained with their conquest of Constantinople was not a territorial empire but a repository of political and religious traditions, many of which were alien to them. The Latins had been beguiled by Constantinople as the icon of empire, but in 1204 this delusion appeared to be appreciated only by the Greek historian and civil servant Nicetas Choniates.[7]

Choniates realised that the Frankish victory on the 12/13 April had been gained by default. A small army estimated at some 20,000 combatants had captured the largest city in Christendom, which over the last five centuries had withstood sieges by much larger armies of Arabs, Russians and Bulgarians. The sudden collapse of Greek resistance in the city required some explanation, at least for the defeated side. The jubilant crusaders were content to attribute their victory to the just judgement of God on the proud and sinful Greeks and this view was endorsed by Pope Innocent III. Divine intervention in human history was accepted by both sides, as was the connection between sinfulness and defeat. Much to the Pope's displeasure, his legate, Peter Capuano, had reacted to the conquest by lifting the ban of excommunication which had been passed on the doge and the Venetian contingent since the seizure of Zara in November 1203.[8] Nicetas Choniates took a more analytical view based on the recent history of Byzantium. In the last 20 years there had been five coups – 1182, 1185, 1195, 1203 and 1204 – all extending outside the immediate court and involving the populace of Constantinople. The result was a lack of commitment to the emperor for the time being and, perhaps more important, a loss of faith in the mission of the Eastern Roman Empire. Thus on the evening of 12 April the emperor of some 100 days, Alexios V Murtzouphlos, although not lacking in personal courage, failed utterly to rally a defence force and had to flee the city. The very fact that he could escape shows how ineffective was the crusader investiture of the city. Indeed, in November when he was captured and brought back to Constantinople for execution, there does not seem to have been any notable outcry or outrage from the remaining Greek inhabitants. The Latin conquerors might be able to ignore popular feeling in Constantinople but they had not decisively defeated the Greeks nor indeed acquired an empire. Both Choniates and the Russian Novgorod chronicler saw it as an event in Byzantine history.[9]

---

[7] Choniates, 595.

[8] PL, 215:521.

[9] *Chronicle of Novgorod*, where the conquest is merely noted with no hints that Moscow should become the Third Rome in 1204. This perhaps indicates both the great confidence of the Latins and the relative insignificance of Moscow at this period soon to face the Mongol onslaught.

The western vision of Constantinople was a material one of a rich and sophisticated city, steeped in imperial and religious tradition and containing many of the prime religious relics of Christendom. Its monuments and relics had impressed western visitors since the days of the First Crusade and during the twelfth century it had become part of the pilgrim itinerary to the Holy Land. For all this increased familiarity with the region, the Franks of 1204 did not take on much of the Greek ideology surrounding the city of Constantinople. Of the Byzantine epithets for the city only that of the 'queen city' or '*regia civitas*' was regularly used by western writers. This terminology did not spring into use in 1204. It had been employed in the west since the 1140s, most notably in the chronicle of Otto of Freising, and was used to emphasise the size and amenities of Constantinople compared to those of west European cities. There was no connotation of Constantinople as the symbol of universal rule in any twelfth century western writer.[10] Indeed it was the size of Constantinople which so impressed the crusaders in 1204. Both Geoffrey de Villehardouin and Robert de Clari made this point many times in their chronicles. There was certainly no echo of the image of the God-protected city, an urban icon, which they might pollute by their very presence and which would require official acts of purification in 1261 such as Nikephoros Gregoras delighted to describe.[11]

For the Greeks the metaphorical descriptions and significance of Constantinople were elaborated and took on new force in the years of the Latin occupation. This is evident in the court rhetoric and the episcopal correspondence in the 'free territories', most notably in the Silention of Theodore I Laskaris in Nicaea (1205–22), the letters of John Apokaukos, metropolitan of Naupaktos (*c*.1223), and in the correspondence of John Vatatzes and Pope Gregory IX in May 1237.[12] The God-protected city rightly belonged to the ruler of the Byzantine empire, who must be a Greek. For their part, the Latins naturally downgraded this ethnic qualification for imperial rule and emphasised the role of the unction bestowed at coronation.[13] It would appear from Robert de Clari's record of the incident that much publicity was given in the crusader ranks to the reported views of a certain Greek from Adrianople to this effect, expressed in an exchange with Boniface of Montferrat.[14] The Greek rulers of Epiros and Nicaea would exert pressure for as long as they would to gain control of the city and thus legitimise their claim to leadership of the Greek world. This clash

---

[10] PL, 216:452. Baldwin seems to have been the only westerner after Otto of Friesing to use the epithet. It was not much used after 1204.
[11] Gregoras, *Bizantina Historia* I, L. Schopen and I. Bekker, eds (Bonn, 1830), pp.86–8.
[12] M. Angold, *Byzantine Government in Exile* (Oxford, 1975), pp.29–33; H. Ahrweiler, 'L'experience nicéenne' *DOP* 29 (1975), 21–40.
[13] See chapter 7.
[14] Clari, CI. (McNeal trans., p.119).

between the spiritual and the material the Latins ignored at their peril, especially if they failed to destroy the Greek resistance in Arta and Nicaea.

About the turn of the century Constantinople was seen by both Christians and Moslems as a vital base for the recovery and sustenance of the Crusader states in Outremer. This was to form a consistent theme in papal correspondence from 1204 until the end of the century, particularly in the 1230s when the Latin Empire seemed about to succumb to Greek attack and a crusade for its defence was preached in the west. For the first three years of the Latin occupation of Constantinople, the Pope continued to address the Latins there as '*crucesignati*' or '*peregrini*' and lost no opportunity to encourage the Latin leadership to fulfil their mission to liberate the Holy Land.[15] This sort of vocabulary should be taken at face value and not cynically dismissed. No less a leader than Saladin had also been concerned about the substantial aid which Byzantium could give to crusaders and in 1185–88 had tried to break up the crusade of Frederick I by treaty arrangements with Isaac Angelos. The decision by the French and English kings to take a sea passage to Syria in 1190 may have been influenced by rumours of the suspect loyalty of the Greeks.[16] The high barons of the Fourth Crusade, both in parliament at Zara and again at Corfu, were in no doubt of the value of Byzantium in the war against Islam and that the proposed diversion was well within the bounds of practical crusading.[17]

The Pact of March, 1204

The actual setting up of the Latin Empire was an ad hoc affair. There was no firm commitment to place a westerner on the throne of Byzantium until the Pact of March 1204. About that time Marie of Champagne, the wife of the future emperor-elect, was setting out from Marseilles to join her husband, as she thought, at Acre. Before January 1204 the crusaders were concerned to re-finance their expedition and maintain unity in its ranks. The decision to divert the crusade to Constantinople had been agreed upon at Zara in early 1203 and confirmed in May when Alexios Angelos, the son of the deposed emperor Isaac II Angelos, joined the army at Corfu. The arrangement was a reasonable one in that in return for placing Alexios on the throne, the difficulties of which were minimised in conference, the

---

[15] PL, 215:710, 1036, 1131, 1395 and PL, 216:353–4, which is an important letter referring to Saladin's links with Constantinople including his building of a mosque (*meskittam*). It re-states the crusading purpose behind the Latin empire in 1210.
[16] C. Brand, 'The Byzantines and Saladin, 1185–1192: opponents of the Third Crusade' *Speculum* 37 (1962), 167–81.
[17] Villehardouin, 96, 114–15.

crusade would be substantially re-endowed. For the onward progress of the crusade Alexios had promised a sum of 200,000 marks, a Byzantine reinforcement of 10,000 men for one year and thereafter, for the term of his life, a garrison of 500 men to bolster the defence of the Holy Land. In addition, on ascending the throne he would acknowledge the papal overlordship of the church and bring the Greek church into canonical obedience.[18] Despite the generosity of these terms, there was disagreement over the use of a crusade to change the political dispensations of Christians, but the group that prevailed were those who stressed the supreme importance of a new crusading strategy that would involve Egypt and Constantinople.[19]

The siege and capture of Constantinople need not concern us. However, the preliminaries to that assault as enshrined in the Pact of March 1204 are instructive, for it was then that the Latin empire was conceived.[20] It is, however, far from clear whether the planning at this stage extended to a federation of Latin states under the suzerainty of the Emperor of Constantinople or just concerned the city itself. The pact was drafted in an atmosphere of crisis and desperation in the crusader camp which does not fit well with the confident assumptions of the drafters of the pact that the Byzantine empire would be conquered.

Towards the end of 1203 Greco–Latin relations in Constantinople had deteriorated markedly. Repeated requests had failed to gain fulfilment of his promises from Alexios IV and in November 1203 he was formally defied by a deputation composed of Conon de Bethune, Villehardouin and Miles le Brabant. Street violence erupted between Greeks and Latins. In one of these incidents a fire directed at the mosque built in 1183 near the church of St Irene destroyed property in the Pergama district of the city. This was the second serious fire caused by such incidents since August 1203.[21] Racial tensions were high. Western residents in the city no longer felt safe and, according to Villehardouin, some 15,000 now sought refuge in the crusader camp. In January 1204 the ardently anti-Latin courtier Alexios Doukas Murtzouphlos seized power from Alexios IV and his father and sought to gain support for his usurpation by bringing pressure on the Latins to leave.[22] The gates of the city were closed to the crusaders, markets denied them and

---

[18] Villehardouin, 93; PL, 214:cxxx–i and 1123–5; D. Queller, *The Fourth Crusade* (Pennsylvannia, 1977), pp.67–84; Brand, op.cit., 234–6; J. Folda, 'The Fourth Crusade, 1201–1203' *Byzantinoslavica* 26 (1965), 277–90; C. Brand, 'The Fourth Crusade: some recent interpretations' *Medievalia et Humanistica* 12 (1984), 33–41.

[19] Villehardouin, 96.

[20] *Urkunden* I, 444–52.

[21] T.F. Madden, 'The fires of the Fourth Crusade in Constantinople 1203–1204: a damage assessment' *BZ* 84/85 (1991–2), 72–93.

[22] B. Hendrickx and C. Matzukis, 'Alexios V Doukas Mourtzouphlos: his life, reign and death (?–1204)' *Hellenika* 31 (1979), 108–32.

fire-ships sent against their fleet. Without funds, supplies and support not only could the crusaders not leave the city but the demands on their resources had been increased by the refugees in their midst. Their plight was becoming desperate and their response had been to raid and forage in Thrace right up to the Black Sea and to burn the country houses of Constantinopolitans. Another month was to pass before it was decided that the best hope lay in an attack on Constantinople.[23].

Unity was essential in the crusading ranks as they prepared for their first real test of siege warfare. At Zara certain crusaders had urged the defenders to hold out, whilst the new hardline Byzantine leadership might well succeed in galvanizing the defence. Disputes and secession had dogged the crusade since it assembled in Venice in 1202, and on a number of occasions where assaults on Christians had been involved, the crusade had been in danger of disintegrating. The crusading army of some 20,000 combatants was too small to invest the city but large enough to concentrate on forcing some of the gates.[24] The Pact of 1204 was in fact a series of identical contracts between the various crusade leaders. Its prime aim was to establish '... *unitas et firma concordia et fecit utraque unam*'. It was essentially a document of the moment and not a considered attempt to lay the foundations for a new state.[25]

After the conquest, the pact acquired surprising significance with regard to the Latin empire, evident in the retrospective observations of Villehardouin and Clari. It never received papal confirmation. The emperor Baldwin was to request this in January 1205. By that time Pope Innocent III had already acknowledged him as emperor in a letter dated 7 November 1204, but he resolutely refused to confirm the pact because of its implications for lay control of the patriarchate and church property in Constantinople.[26] Whatever its shortcomings in the eyes of the pope, its confirmation by every subsequent Latin emperor on his accession gave the pact the status of law within the new empire. It has been called the constitution of the Latin Empire, yet beyond establishing Latin property rights in the imperial and patriarchal offices of the former Byzantine empire, it had nothing to contribute on the organisation of the Latin state and society. Its fundamental principle was the limitation of executive functions in all but name. Rather it was concerned with the protection of sectional interests, that is the rights of the Venetian commercial community which were specifically mentioned and given a legal existence in chrysobulls and

---

[23] Queller, op.cit., pp.119–37; Clari, LIX–LX (McNeal trans., 84–5); Villehardouin, 206–20.

[24] B. Hendrickx, 'A propos du nombre des troupes de la quatrieme croisade et de l'empereur Badouin I' *Byzantina* 3 (1971), 29–40 and Queller, op.cit., pp.139, 212, n.12 for comments.

[25] *Urkunden* I, 445; Villehardouin, 234; Clari, LXIX (McNeal trans., 91).

[26] PL, 215:447–454, 510, 524. See p.199.

the memory of man, and the rights of conquerors to possess what they could acquire and hold in those parts of the city or the empire which were to be assigned to them. These rights were created by the pact and were both conditional and immaterial. It was essentially a document produced by a committee with their eyes on the immediate future. One of its effects was to ensure that Franco–Byzantine rulership would be stillborn.

The drafters of the pact had to address themselves to the crisis in which the crusading army found itself. Confidence, even over-confidence, was justifiable. The city was to be attacked and if captured, an emperor and a patriarch were to be elected by committees chosen for the purpose. Possession of Constantinople if not of the persons of the Greek emperor and patriarch was considered sufficient justification for these actions. The army was to be kept in being for a year till March 1205 after which soldiers would be free to stay, proceed to the Holy Land or go home. The proposals dealing with Venetian commercial privileges were the most specific clauses in the document. The future emperor's freedom of action as regards the Venetians was curtailed in advance by the consenting parties to the pact. Unlike the vague territorial ambitions of the western soldiery, these were a matter of fact dating back to 992. All such concessions, whether in writing or not, were to be had henceforth as of right and were not to be dependent on the whims of a ruler. All enemies of the Venetians were to be excluded from the empire, whilst the doge and the Venetians were exempted from performing homage to the emperor. Just as the Byzantine emperors had learned to their cost of the dangers and difficulties of dealing with such an autarkic entity, so the new Latin emperor would have no option but to accept the Venetian position. A committee would be appointed to apportion fiefs and honours, whilst those who might not aspire to such status would be allowed three days of pillaging and the prospect of urban property to which they might stake a claim. There was much that was vague here and which could only be addressed once the condition of victory had been fulfilled.

The first Latin emperor

The election of Baldwin of Flanders as emperor on 9 May 1204 was not the triumph of mediocrity which it is often purported to be, nor the passing over of Boniface because of his unacceptability to the Venetians alone. Choniates hinted at a packed electoral college and suggested that Boniface was dumbfounded when he was not selected. Yet it was important that the new emperor should be able to work well with all sides of the crusading partnership. Boniface had been the leading soldier of the crusade but Baldwin was no mean warrior and possibly displayed a resourcefulness lacking in Boniface. Whereas Boniface has left behind a reputation for rapacity, Baldwin from the start took on something of the traditional imperial role in religious life, writing to the pope to supply missals, monks and scholars for his new empire. He had a wife on her way to join him and the prospect of sons to complement the two daughters left behind in Flanders. Failing sons, there was always his brother Henry. He stood as well with the pope as any layman on the crusade and supported Otto IV, the Welf candidate for the German throne. He was thought well of by both Latins and Greeks and could reconcile those opposed to him. Equally he could take a determined line. Although he was prevented from imposing his suzerainty on Boniface by resort to arms in 1204, the actions of his successor in 1207 and 1209 showed that his assessment of the situation was accurate even if his reaction was intemperate. It also demonstrated that he had the wisdom to realise this and to give way when necessary. Temperamental differences might well have influenced the twelve electors in May 1204, just as much as any hidden Venetian agenda. Baldwin was no pious booby or compromise candidate. No Latin in Constantinople had any interest in selecting a weak emperor. The Chronicon Flandrense presented Baldwin as a model of medieval kingship: active and accessible, righting wrongs and giving just judgements. Whilst this might not be a totally objective source, Choniates from a different perspective described Baldwin as devout, steadfast and temperate.[27]

In March 1204 more attention had been paid to the election of a Latin emperor than to his actual role and powers.[28] These were to be worked out in the year or so after the conquest. First, the coronation in Hagia Sophia on Sunday 16 May 1204 brought Baldwin a great increase in status and influence among his Greek subjects. That there was no long-established royal tradition in his family would have been of more concern to westerners than to Greeks. The coronation, albeit conducted by a Latin bishop, Nivelon de Cherissy from Soissons, was sufficiently splendid to impress the Greek onlookers and courtiers that an emperor had indeed been made. Choniates, Clari and Villehardouin all agree that this provided some legitimisation of Latin rule in Greek eyes. Clari, in particular, contrasted the ease with which Baldwin received the submission of the towns of Thrace in 1204 with the difficulties encountered by Boniface, who tried to induce the inhabitants of Adrianople to receive his step-son, the son of Isaac Angelos, as their ruler. He was told that once the child had been crowned in Constantinople then they would know their duty. Baldwin on the other hand was met by

---

[27] J. Longnon, *Les Compagnons de Villehardouin* (Paris, Geneva, 1978), pp.137–40; PL, 214:585, 1179; 216:636–7; Corpus Chronicorum Flandriae in *Urkunden* I, 302; Choniates, 595–9, 643. Vaqueiras in lyric poem XX/41–60, in J. Linskill, op.cit., pp. 226, 228, suggests that should the new emperor fail to succour the Holy Sepulchre his guilt will be great as will that of the electoral college headed by Nivelon de Cherissy for choosing Baldwin and not Boniface.

[28] See chapter 7.

deputations of priests and clerks '… and all the Greeks worshipped him as the sacred emperor'. Baldwin's imperial status was recognised. In late September Baldwin hosted a banquet for Greek nobles at which they witnessed the dubbing of 600 western knights and listened to a speech which made flattering references to the Greek past as an inspiration for both Latin knights and Greek archons.[29]

Whether it was the coronation or the act of anointing which had conferred imperial status upon Baldwin in the eyes of his Greek subjects cannot be known in this context. For his fellow Franks it was probably the act of anointing which set him apart in a way which election could not. So ingrained was the idea of sacral kingship that in Rome at this time Innocent III was trying to draw a distinction between the significance of the anointment of kings and that of bishops, and was attempting to downgrade its implications of a Christ-like and Christ-centred kingship which had developed in the west since the eighth century. In a letter to the Bulgarian archbishop of Tirnovo written at the end of February 1204, Innocent set out his current thinking on unction: monarchs were to be anointed on the arm or the hand with ordinary holy oil (the oil of the catachumens) whilst bishops were to be anointed with a special oil mixed with balm (oil of chrism) upon their heads.[30] For him anointing was not a source of royal priesthood and neither Baldwin nor his followers acted as if it was. However, Innocent's teaching, later enshrined in the decretal 'On Holy Unction', had little influence outside Rome. The kings of France and England continued to be anointed with chrism and saw such anointment as conferring a special status. In Constantinople, Clari, who was an eye-witness of the coronation of 16 May, gave a detailed description of Baldwin's robes and procession, but sadly did not describe the manner of his anointment. However, he did remark upon the reclothing of Baldwin with the imperial pall and mantle after his anointment and immediately before his crowning. Possibly he saw this act as one which set Baldwin apart from other men as one now worthy to be crowned emperor, but in truth we shall never know the significance of this act for either Greeks or Latins in Constantinople.[31]

The partition of the empire, September 1204

If one imperial role was to conciliate the Greeks, another was to conquer land. In October 1205 in the confirmation of the pact by the new emperor

---

[29] Corpus Chronicorum Flandriae, *Urkunden* I, 302.
[30] PL, 215:282–287; M. Bloch, *The Royal Touch*, English edn (London, 1961), pp.116–17 for discussion. The letter was later included in the Decretals headed 'De sacra unctione'.
[31] Clari, XCVI–XCVII (McNeal trans., 115–17); E.H. Kantorowicz, *The King's Two Bodies* (Princeton, 1957), pp.319–23.

Henry, this duty was spelt out, '*ad expeditionem, ad acquisitionem et defensionem Imperii*'.[32] Here lay one opportunity for the emperor to extend his own influence. Between October 1204 and March 1205 Baldwin had sent two armies of some 100 knights apiece into Asia Minor to occupy territory allotted to him in the partition. Late in October he created three dukedoms to be carved out of territory not officially distributed.[33] These marcher lordships were put into the hands of men who could put retinues of the order of 120 knights in the field and so stood some chance of increasing imperial territory, which they would hold as imperial vassals. Louis de Blois obtained the Duchy of Nicaea, Renier de Trit that of Philippopolis and Etienne du Perche that of Philadelphia. Villehardouin suggested that such grants were imperial policy whilst Clari thought the initiative came from the greater barons themselves. All these places were deep in enemy territory and in the event none of these lordships was ever established. The only dukedom to come into existence at this time was the Duchy of the Archipelago which was not conceived by Baldwin nor apparently discussed with him. It was created in 1207 by Marco Sanudo, a Venetian present on the Fourth Crusade and a nephew of the doge Enrico Dandolo. Later in that year Sanudo regularised his position with regard to the emperor by becoming an imperial vassal rather than acknowledge the suzerainty of his native Venice.[34]

Just what made these dukedoms different from the other grants of lands, other than their potential size and vague definition, is not at all clear and is nowhere stated. Of the three noblemen granted dukedoms by the emperor Baldwin, Louis of Blois was the only one who was a count in his own right. Indeed the tally of counts and marquises which made up the crusader leadership as a whole could be numbered in single figures. Counties and duchies were forms of hereditary public authority which could only be created by kings and emperors. Duchies were a rarity in western Europe at this time and there the social gulf between a duke and a count was considerable. Possibly in the case of these new creations, as with the Norman dukes of Apulia in the eleventh century, a duchy was given to a leader who was to conquer land and oversee its settlement. In Greece, much of Thrace, and in Bithynia, conquest was directed by Boniface of Montferrat and by the emperor Baldwin. Nobles with large retinues deemed capable of extending the empire beyond these territories were accorded a status above that of their followers, marked by the title of duke. In so far as these duchies represented the command of a large district, the three new titles may have been influenced by the Byzantine office of doux and its control of a doukaton, but this can only remain a possibility and is impossible to prove or disprove.

---

[32] *Urkunden* I, 537.
[33] Villehardouin, 304–5, 310–11, 316.
[34] See chapter 7.

The title of count and marquis were used in the Aegean for those who bore these titles in their own right in the west. Thus Count Louis of Blois, Count Umberto di Biandrate, Berthold von Katzenellenbogen, known as 'Le comte', and the marquis Guido Pallavicino did not derive their comital authority from the Latin emperor. Just when the lordships of Boudonitsa and Salona in central Greece were elevated to the status of counties is unclear. If they were the creations of Boniface of Montferrat in his role as king, this was not mentioned by the troubadour Raimbaut de Vaqueiras, who was a member of Boniface's court in Thessalonika. In 1205, in stanzas 7 and 8 of an important but often overlooked poem, Raimbaut saw the partition of the empire in terms of dukedoms and kingdoms and in terms of the war against Islam:

> ... Never did Alexander or Charlemagne or King Louis lead such a glorious expedition, nor could the valiant lord Aimeri or Roland with his warriors win by might, in such noble fashion, such a powerful empire as we have won, whereby our Faith is in the ascendant; for we have created emperors and dukes and kings, and have manned strongholds near the Turks and Arabs (prop dels Turcs e dels Arabitz), and opened up the roads and ports from Brindisi to St George's Straits.
>
> By us will Damascus be assaulted, and Jerusalem conquered, and the kingdom of Syria liberated for the Turks find this in their prophecies.[35]

The Pact of 1204 made provision for the setting up of a partition committee of 24 men: 12 Venetians and 12 Franks. This was working away by September 1204 with one of the commissioners apparently being the chronicler Villehardouin.[36] These men were to audit the land resources of the empire and make a broad tripartite division of territory amongst the emperor, crusaders and Venetians in the proportion of one-quarter to the former and three-eighths to each of the latter. At some stage there was an attempt to define a standard fief producing a revenue of 300 livres d'Anjou for its holder, the equivalent, Professor Longnon has estimated, to 1,000 hyperpera.[37]

The logistics of the partition are unknown beyond that it was a daunting task speedily completed. With the exception of the Marshal of Champagne, Geoffrey de Villehardouin, the names of the 24 commissioners responsible for the work are lost. The research that went on into Byzantine

---

[35] Lyric poem XXII/74–88, in J. Linskill, op.cit., pp. 241–6, whose translation is quoted here.
[36] *Urkunden* I, 447, 451; J. Longnon, *Recherches sur la vie de Geoffrey de Villehardouin* (Paris, 1939), pp.88, 192.
[37] J. Longnon, *L'Empire Latin de Constantinople ...* (Paris, 1949), p.62.

archives and the task of converting all this information into livre d'Anjou was impressive, even if, as Nicholas Oikonomides has convincingly suggested, the 'Partitio Romaniae' was a copy of Byzantine cadasters (tax registers) compiled in 1203 for Alexios IV. Certainly omissions in the partitio corresponded to areas where control from Constantinople had lapsed either before the arrival of the crusaders or in some cases as a result of it. The area of Philadelphia had thrown off central control in the late twelfth century whilst no tax returns were made for the estates of the empress Euphrosyne in Thessaly since they were controlled by her husband Alexios III, who had fled from Constantinople in July 1203. Oikonomides's hypothesis gains further support from the emphasis which both Clari and Choniates placed on tax valuations as forming the basis for the Latin land distribution.[38] Greek translators and revenue officials were essential to unravel and explain Greek fiscal terminology like 'katapanikia', 'episkepseis' and 'proasteia'. Baldwin might have snubbed the upper echelons of the Greek civil service but clerks and translators were necessary and often seem to have been forcibly kept at their posts. The father of the historian George Akropolites, who may have been a fiscal clerk, wanted to slip away from the Latins secretly ('lathro') whilst the corps of translators under Theodore Tornikes seem to have had less opportunity for such stealthy escape. Theodore was killed by the Bulgarians in April 1205 when he sought asylum with them as the only alternative to continued service with the Latins.[39]

Both Robert de Clari and Nicetas Choniates wrote summary accounts of the partition process from the point of view of those not closely involved. Both stressed the importance of valuation as the basis for distribution and the role of lords in determining who was going to stay on after March 1205 and who was to receive what fiefs from their own block grant. The two commentaries are given here. First, Choniates on the background research.

> As though they have been installed as king of kings and held the whole terrestial globe in their hands, they [the Latins] commissioned tax assessors to register the taxable Roman lands, wishing first to ascertain their annual value before apportioning these by lot ...[40]

---

[38] N. Oikonomides, 'La décomposition de l'empire byzantin à la veille de 1204 et les origines de l'empire de Nicée: à propos de la Partitio Romaniae' *XVe Congrés international d'Etudes Byzantines, Rapports et Co-rapports, 1/1*, Athènes, 1976 3–28, reprinted idem, *Byzantium from the Ninth Century to the Fourth Crusade* (London, 1992). For texts of the Partitio Romaniae see A. Carile, 'Partitio Terrarum Imperii Romanii' *Studi Veneziani* 7 (1968), 125–305, and 'Partitio regni Graeci' in *Urkunden* I, 452–501, together with a Greek translation of the Latin text by Tafel and Thomas.
[39] Choniates, 598 and 643 (Magoulias trans., pp.328, 353); Akropolites, *Chronike syngraphe*, c. 30 ed. Heisenberg (II, 46).
[40] Choniates, 595 (Magoulias trans., p.327).

Second, Clari on the distribution itself,

> ... first to the counts and then afterwards to the other high men. And they considered who was the richest man and the highest and who had the most people of his own following in the host and to him they gave the most land. And so to one was given two hundred knights' fees, to another a hundred, to another seventy ... to another twenty, and to another ten; and to those who had the least had seven or six of them, and the fief was worth three hundred livres of Anjou.[41]

The link between the arrangements of the partitio and lands which were assigned and conquered outside that framework is not easy to comprehend, firstly because the land division was made in blocks or condominia to the emperor, the Venetians or the crusaders rather than to named individual grantees. Constantinople was divided between the emperor and the Venetians in the proportion of 3:5. Asia Minor together with the islands of Samos, Chios and Lesbos went to the emperor. In Thrace the emperor received territory between Agathapolis on the Black Sea and Tzurulum (mod. Tchorlu) virtually on the Sea of Marmora, the Venetian lands formed a triangle with apices at Tzurulum, Adrianople and Gallipoli, whilst the crusaders had the remainder up to Mosynopolis. From thence to the river Aliakmon west of Thessalonika the territory was unassigned. In Thessaly and central Greece the Venetians received all lands to the west of the Pindos mountains and the crusaders those to the east, whilst much of the Peloponnese went to the Venetians together with rights to Aegina and the ports of Oreos, Negroponte (mod. Chalkis) and Karystos in Euboea.[42] All of these allotments were areas to be conquered and occupied in the true frontier spirit. The interest which had the right to a particular territory could grant it away to a potential conqueror who would then hold his conquests as a vassal of the grantor. Imperial and Venetian interests could be identified in the persons of the emperor and the doge, but what of the crusaders? Allotments by some form of standarised fief suggests individual grantees, but if so this stage is missing from the records, and we must assume that the fief with an annual value of 300 livres d'Anjou was a notional one for the guidance of grantors only.

In practice, in Thrace and Asia Minor the emperor organised the conquest and in Greece the task fell to Boniface, as the highest and most powerful lord. Possession and effective defence were critical. Where these were absent the apparently clear lines of the partitio became blurred. The

---

[41] Clari, CVII/8–19 (McNeal trans., 123).
[42] See note 38 above for texts of the partitio. For summaries see J. Longnon, *L'Empire latin de Constantinople* ..., pp.49–50; Setton, pp. 18–19, and D. Nicol, *Byzantium and Venice* (Cambridge, 1988), pp.148–50.

Venetians were slow to occupy most of their concessions, not really getting underway until 1207–10. This resulted in the granting of Adrianople, a town in the Venetian condominium, together with the imperial town of Demotika, to Theodore Branas by the emperor Henry in 1206, on the grounds of a more effective defence against the Bulgarians.[43] About the same time the rapid advance of the crusaders in the Peloponnese led to the seizure of Modon and Coron by the forces of William de Champlitte.

Boniface of Montferrat acquired lands not listed in the partitio. His claim to Crete rested upon a grant allegedly made to him personally by Alexios IV in 1203. This claim he sold to the Venetians in August 1204 in return for support of his claim to Thessalonika. According to Clari, sometime in May or June 1204 when Boniface asked the emperor Baldwin to grant him the Kingdom of Salonika, the emperor replied '... that it was not his to give, for the barons of the host and the Venetians had the larger part of it. As far as it rested with him he would give it to him very gladly ... but the part belonging to the barons of the host and the Venetians he could not give him'.[44] This suggests that lands not assigned by the partitio were available for grant by the emperor, as was the case with all or parts of the three new duchies, or were up for grabs by any interested party, such as the lands of the empress Euphrosyne in Thessaly. Baldwin proceeded to march on Thessalonika and to seize the towns west of Mosynopolis. In September 1204 with Baldwin and Boniface on the brink of civil war it was agreed that imperial officials should hand over these towns to Boniface, whose dependence on the emperor was thus asserted. Thereafter Boniface campaigned in eastern Greece effectively setting himself up as the suzerain of the crusader interest in the peninsula. The neat divisions of the partitio had thus given way before military and political events.

The work of the commissioners may have reminded Choniates of Christ Geometer, but he was aware that this was paperwork and that what was needed to give reality to their researches was war work and sufficient men on the ground.

The campaigns of October 1204 to March 1205 were well described by Villehardouin and show the Latins taking advantage of Greek confusion and disorganisation.[45] By September 1204 the area between Constantinople and Thessalonika south of the Rhodope range was reported subdued. Between then and March 1205 war was waged on three fronts. In central Greece resistance was light and the crusading army led by Boniface had little trouble in taking Thebes, Athens and Euboea and tying down Greek

---

[43] Villehardouin, 423, 441. Branas's possession of Demotika seems to have recommended it as a place of retirement to the former Greek Patriarch John Kamateros, see p.201.
[44] Clari, XCIX/16–21 (McNeal trans., p.118, quoted here).
[45] Villehardouin, 300–42.

resistance in the fortresses of Akrocorinth, Argos, and Nauplion, where the first campaign came to a halt.[46]

In northern Turkey Henry, the emperor's brother, aided by a group of Latin settlers from Espigal (modern Spiga, just west of the Cyzikos Peninsula) and local Armenians from the Troad, captured the towns of Abydos, Lopadeion, Apollonia and Adramyttion. They drove off two Greek armies sent out from Brusa and this tightened their hold on the region. Further east, the town of Nicomedia (mod. Izmit) was secured for the emperor and its principal church, Hagia Sophia, fortified as a base.

In Thrace several small expeditions were mounted towards specific goals – Renier de Trit and his relatives occupied Philippopolis and fortified Stenimaka as an outpost against the Bulgarians, Hugues of St Pol sent knights to Demotika, the Venetians occupied Adrianople and the emperor sent William de Blanvel to garrison Tchorlu. A great deal of territory had been acquired, Greek resistance either tied down or bases constructed for further advance. The problem posed by the dispersal of the crusading army in March 1205 seemed to be less acute with the arrival of reinforcements from Syria. One of these newcomers, Etienne du Perche, was granted Philadelphia in the Kaganos valley well to the east of Ephesos; further advance was clearly contemplated.

The Vlacho-Bulgars

From April 1205 the initiative passed from the crusaders to their enemies in Thrace and the Troad. First, these enemies soon reorganised and then coordinated their attacks on the Latins, whose numbers were too small to sustain fighting on two fronts for even a short time. Now the crusaders lost not only battles but also an emperor. Confidence in the new settlement foundered and over 7,000 Latins left the area in April. The most fearsome of their foes were the Vlacho-Bulgars lead by Kalojan, also known as Johanitsa or Joanicius.

The Bulgars had arrived in the Balkan peninsula in the seventh century and established hegemony over the Slav settlers there. Despite occasional defeats, after one of which in 811 Khan Krum was reputed to have acquired the skull of Nikephoros I as a drinking vessel, Byzantine forces generally contained Bulgarian aspirations and in 1014 inflicted a crushing defeat on the army of Tsar Samuel at Kleidion. It was after this battle that the emperor Basil II is alleged to have ordered the blinding of the 14,000 Bulgarian prisoners leaving every hundredth man with one eye to lead the

---

[46] See chapter 4.

defeated army home. Be that as it may, for nearly 180 years thereafter Byzantium dominated Bulgaria. In 1186 the unreasonable demands of a weak Byzantine government again encouraged the Bulgarians to revolt under the leadership of the brothers Peter and Asen. This time imperial control was not reasserted and in 1202 territory north of the Rhodope mountains was abandoned to the Bulgarians. Two years later Kalojan, who had succeeded his brothers in 1197, successfully petitioned the Pope for a Bulgarian primate in Tirnovo and a crown and a papal banner for himself. The Bulgarian kingdom was thus recognised by the papal curia and its imperial ambitions revived in Thrace if given no wider credence in either Rome or Constantinople.[47]

Kalojan's ambitions were Balkan ones but he had a certain fascination with Latin culture and was not fundamentally opposed to the Latin presence south of the Rhodope. In the spring of 1204 he sent ambassadors to the Latins offering substantial military assistance in return for the recognition of his empire. The Latin leadership gave a haughty and dismissive reply and conversations in the crusader ranks spoke of Kalojan as the somewhat impertinent manager of a stud farm of the former Greek emperor.[48] In late 1204 Kalojan found the Latins laying claim to the Maritsa valley from their bases at Adrianople and Philippopolis. The Latin threat must have seemed very real indeed. They had quickly established themselves in Thrace and enjoyed the support of the Greeks of the region. They might well establish links with Emeric I, King of Hungary (1196–1204), who was wont to raid into Bulgarian territory, had himself taken the cross in 1201, and had family ties through his sister Margaret with Boniface of Montferrat. Kalojan wrote to the pope in early 1205 asking him to warn the Hungarians, now ruled by Emeric's brother Andrew, and the Latins not to invade his territory. Innocent took no action and Latin involvement in the Maritsa valley was disastrous.[49]

The loyalty of the Greeks seemed to have been a critical factor for the Latin position in Thrace.[50] It was their abandonment of the Latins and the seeking of accommodation with Kalojan that tipped the scale. Villehardouin thought it was due to the small numbers of Franks in the area and he was probably right since the Greeks had originally capitulated to the Latins in return for protection from the Bulgarians. This protection may have been as much ideological as physical and perhaps pointed to an early acceptance by the Greeks of the Latins as heirs to the Byzantine tradition, at least by

---

[47] R. Browning, *Byzantium and Bulgaria* (London, 1975); R.L. Wolff, 'The second Bulgarian Empire' *Speculum* 24 (1949), 167–203, reprinted in idem, *Studies in the Latin Empire of Constantinople* (London, 1976); PL, 215:155–8, 277–95.

[48] Clari, LXIV (McNeal trans., 86).

[49] PL, 215:551–4, 710.

[50] Villehardouin, 404–500 covers the campaigns in Thrace between January 1206 and September 1207.

contrast with the claims of Kalojan. Villehardouin also suggests a division in interests between rural and urban Greeks. The former were pastoralists and horses formed a substantial part of the plunder taken by the Bulgarians; an end to Cuman raids could clearly be in their interest. There can be no doubt that French resistance collapsed and panic set in. At Stenimaka Renier de Trit was abandoned by his son, brother and nephew and left with just fifteen household knights. This disgraceful behaviour was excused only by the death of the deserters at the hands of the Greeks of the countryside. Thrace was abandoned and the Franks withdrew to Tchorlu on the southern edge of the region. In April 1205 Baldwin was captured trying to regain control of Adrianople and the Frankish forces in the area only saved from extinction by the rapid transfer of troops from Asia Minor. One year on from the capture of Constantinople only the coastal towns of Rodosto and Selymbria remained in Frankish hands, whilst in the Troad all conquests had been abandoned in order to bolster the Latin position in Thrace and to preserve the landward approaches to Constantinople. Only the original Latin settlers in Spigal remained on the Asiatic side of the Marmara. They had been settled there before 1204 but now required a small garrison to ensure their safety.

The Latin empire had failed to expand and within a year had lost even the small conquests it had made. Its resources were being wasted by war and pillage. There were just not enough men to occupy the land and in June 1205 barely enough to defend Constantinople. The crusading army had largely dispersed in March 1205, most discouraged by the catalogue of military disasters. Villehardouin witnessed the departure of 7,000 men in five large Venetian ships. On board were a number of knights who were deaf to the appeals that they should delay their departure in this hour of need. The former pilgrims had had enough. Count Henry brought back some 20,000 Armenians when he withdrew from the Troad in April. However, the pressing needs of the Franks in Thrace forced him to hurry ahead and left them exposed to Greek attack. They were all either killed or captured somewhere between Sestos and Rodosto. Latin control extended just a bow-shot from the dwindling Frankish army, which was scattered between the capital, the ports of Rodosto, Roussion and Aspros, and Tchorlu, a town on the Via Egnatia. In desperation the council in Constantinople sent a deputation to the pope to ask for support. Henry was accepted as regent or moderator of the empire until the fate of his brother, the emperor, should become clear.

Aware of the shortage of Latin troops, Kalojan began a campaign of extermination. Massacres of Latins and any Greek supporters took place at Serres, Roussion, Aspros and Athyra, which was just fifteen miles from Constantinople. The abandonment of Renier de Trit by his kinsmen had provoked scorn in March 1205; one year later the flight of Latin garrisons from the Thracian towns of Arcadiopolis, Daonum, Heraklea, Panedon and

Rodosto provoked barely a comment. The Latin perimeter was contracting and in June 1206 only Bizoe (Vizye) and Selymbria remained in Latin hands. Kalojan's policy of terror had worked. He now overreached himself and began to devastate the towns of those Greeks who had surrendered to him, starting with Tchorlu, Demotika and Adrianople. By thus attempting to destroy the material resources of the Latins, he gave them the support of the Greeks.

There was a breathing space for the Latins between June and November 1206 as Kalojan sought to transport plunder and prisoners back across the Rhodope mountains. He was concerned to build up the resources of his kingdom at the expense of the Thracian countryside rather than to extend his frontiers southwards. Villehardouin noted that the Bulgarian ruler had been planting settlements in the foothills of the Wallachian mountains around a place called Eului, and that some 20,000 Greeks complete with their belongings in carts from the Adrianople region were liberated from Kalojan's camp by the emperor Henry in September 1206.[51] Rural depopulation was a Balkan problem, and one that lack of western immigration and constant petty warfare was not going to solve.

The emperor Henry, 1206–16

The lull in the fighting in Thrace allowed the Latins to mount two limited campaigns in Turkey, one aimed at garrisoning the Cyzikos peninsula and the other to acquire territory between Nicomedia and Kibotos. The impetus to make conquests was very strong even though it would result in the Latins being thinly spread. In March 1207 Theodore Laskaris urged Kalojan to raid into Thrace since the bulk of the Latin forces were now concentrated in Turkey. He responded by raiding right up to the walls of Constantinople and most Latin troops were ferried back to defend the capital. Laskaris mopped up the small Latin garrisons left behind and then negotiated a two-year truce by which the Latins formally relinquished all their conquests in Asia Minor for the time being in return for the release of all western prisoners. Meanwhile raid and counter-raid continued in Thrace. In one of these incidents near Mosynopolis on 4 September 1207, the formidable Boniface of Montferrat was killed by an arrow. On this low psychological note for the Latins, Villehardouin chose to finish his account of the Fourth Crusade. However, the resolve of the Latins to fight on was not impaired.

---

[51] Villehardouin, 448, 491–2. The presence of carts demonstrates that these armies were moving by road rather than across country and emphasises the importance of nodal communication centres like Adrianople, Lopadeion and Adramytteion in the campaigns of these years.

The Latins now entered into a series of negotiations and alliances which showed that they had adapted quickly and creatively to their new circumstances.[52] If they had been influenced by Byzantine attitudes to the Bulgarians in 1204, they had dropped these pretensions by 1208. The death of Kalojan on 8 October 1207 resulted in the division of his kingdom between two relatives, Boril and Strez. After defeating a raid by the former into Thrace near Phillippopolis in July 1208, the emperor Henry, now a widower, married Boril's cousin, a daughter of Kalojan. He secured the quiescence of Strez by giving him an illegitimate daughter of his own to wife.[53] What a change from the reserved attitude to Kalojan's overtures in 1204! Meanwhile, Theodore Laskaris had extended his influence southwards from Nicaea by defeating various rivals who had set up in Philadelphia (Theodore Mankaphas), Miletus (Sabas Asidenos) and the Maeander Valley (Manuel Mavrozomes). In order to preoccupy him, the Latins formed alliances first with the Grand Komnenoi, David and Alexios, of Trebizond whose sphere of influence extended as far west as Pontic Heraklea but who could not maintain their independence of Nicaea without Latin help, and with the Seljuk sultan of Iconium (Konya), Kai-Khusrai, who had first approached the Latins for military help in a dynastic dispute sometime in late 1203 or 1204.

Eight years after the capture of Constantinople the Latins had not gained a dominant position in the Aegean and became an additional element in the regional mosaic of princelings. In addition to the various Latin states, the Epirote, Nicene and Trapezuntine Greeks, Serbs, Vlacho-Bulgars and Turks of Konya all lacked that edge that would give any one of them an outright victory. In these circumstances much depended upon temporary truces and alliances and the personality and judgement of a leader stood for much. Should he be unfortunate enough to be killed or captured, his whole cause might experience a temporary decline such as that which followed the deaths of Baldwin I in 1205, Kalojan in 1207, Kai-Khusrai in 1211, Peter de Courtenay in 1217 and the capture of Theodore Angelos in 1230. Equally one victory could lead to significant changes of fortune and tactical direction. Latin military assistance to Kai-Khusrai had encouraged him to dispute possession of the Maeander valley with Laskaris and to deflect that ruler's attention from Latin ambitions in Bithynia. Kai-Khusrai's death in 1211, apparently in single combat with Laskaris at Antioch-on-the-Maeander, lead to a truce with his successor and the concentration of Greek attention on the Latins in Constantinople.

The emperor Henry took the offensive in 1211 and on 15 October defeated a Greek army near Brusa. He followed up this victory by marching to Pergamum on the borders with the Seljuks and from there on 13 January

---

[52] J. Longnon, *L'Empire Latin de Constantinople ...*, pp.102–10.
[53] Clari, CXIX, (McNeal trans., 127); Valenciennes, 533–49.

1212 he addressed his open letter to western Christendom announcing his triumph over the four enemies of his empire, namely Boril and Strez of Bulgaria, Michael of Epiros and Theodore Laskaris of Nicaea. He appealed for more settlers to consolidate the gains he had made. Although he then exercised a loose control over most of north-west Turkey from Pergamum to Lake Apollonia, he had to admit that without reinforcements he could not hold on to the gains that had been made ('... *nisi Latinorum copiam, quibus possimus praebere terram quam acquirimus*').[54] In the short term Henry's forebodings were proved correct. The historian Akropolites recorded the making of a truce between Henry and Theodore Laskaris around December 1214, in which the Latins were confirmed in possession of a much smaller area in Asia Minor, namely Adramyttion, Achiraos and the Marmara coast.[55] In the long term such a situation, exacerbated by the attrition of war and by some backflow of population to the west, would naturally favour natives over incomers.

Immigration and reinforcements from the west were fitful and disappointing. Direct appeals for reinforcements were made in 1204, 1205, 1206 and 1212, but with little or no effect.[56] In the west the attitude to the Aegean settlements was ambivalent. In 1204–5 Innocent III had focused upon lay control of the church rather than the possession of the eastern empire by a Latin lord, and had chosen to stress the continuation of the crusade to the Holy Land at least up to 1207 rather than the extension of Christendom in the Aegean.[57] The scholars and masters of the University of Paris had not been enticed by job opportunities in Constantinople and the emperor Henry's brother, Philip of Namur, could not be coaxed from his comital lands in 1206; instead he sent Pierre de Douai with an unknown number of reinforcements which arrived in 1208 and stayed for about a year.[58] Over one-third of the army had left Constantinople in one sailing alone in April 1205 and even many of the great men of the crusade who had gained lands and offices in the east chose to return to the west. William de Champlitte, the first prince of Achaia, left in 1209. Umberto II de Biandrate, baili of Thessalonika, returned to Italy in 1211 and Manasser de l'Isle left for Champagne between 1210 and 1214. He left relatives behind him in the Aegean, as did Berthold (Dietrich) von Katzenellenbogen, the lord of Velestino, who joined the Fifth Crusade in 1217, and Otho de la Roche, lord of Athens and Thebes, who retired to Burgundy around 1226. Even those who spent the remainder of their days in the Aegean never severed their

---

[54] *RHGF* XVIII, pp.532–3; G. Prinzing, 'Der Brief Kaiser Heinrichs von Konstantinopel vom 13 Januar 1212' *Byzantion* 43 (1973), 395–431.
[55] Akropolites, cc.15–16 (I, pp.27–9).
[56] PL, 215:452, 706–10; *Urkunden* II, 37–42.
[57] See chapter 7.
[58] PL, 215:637; Valenciennes, 512–18, 529–30, 574–91; J. Longnon, *Les Compagnons de Villehardouin* ... (Paris, 1978), pp.182–3.

links with the west, maintaining titles, property interests, affiliations with religious houses and even wives in their home regions. The most notable of this latter group were Henry of Flanders (d. 1216) and his brother Eustace (d. 1217?), the chronicler Villehardouin (d. 1218) and his nephew Geoffrey of Achaia (d. 1227/8), Conom de Bethune (d. 1219), and Milon le Brabant (d. 1224).[59]

The kingdom of Thessalonika

In mainland Greece and the islands the vague suzerainty of the Latin emperor had turned to sovereignty by 1212. This state of affairs might be seen as implicit in the Pact of 1204, but its realisation was the result of active imperial policy without which the position of the new territorial blocks within the empire would have remained vague and theoretical. The creation of the lordship, later Kingdom, of Thessalonika, was the occasion for this resolution.

The hiving off of Thessalonika, the second city of the empire and an important communication centre on the Via Egnatia where it crossed the Strymon delta, was not envisaged in 1204. The unsuccessful candidate in the imperial election was to receive '... *tote la terre d'autre part del Braz, devers la Turkie, et l'isle de Grece*'.[60] In the week following the election on 9 May Boniface persuaded the emperor-elect and the crusading leadership to exchange Thessalonika for Asia Minor. This deal was not popular with the rank and file, but Thessalonika had been excluded from the formal partitio. Boniface insisted on conquering it himself, but this might well compromise the position of the emperor who decided to receive the surrender of the city and re-grant it to Boniface. This dispute brought the two parties to the brink of war in August 1204 and Boniface attacked the city of Demotika, which contained a garrison placed there by the emperor Baldwin. Boniface appealed to the crusading council and in the interest of unity Baldwin had to submit to arbitration. It was clear from all these proceedings that the Thessalonika region was deemed to start at Mosynopolis, but where did it extend to on the west and what were the isles of Greece? This last expression has been variously interpreted to refer to Crete, the Archipelago or even the Peloponnese on the analogy with Alberic of Trois-Fontaines's reference to that peninsula as '*insula Montionis*', the isle of Modon.[61] Certainly Boniface led the 1205 campaign into Greece and assigned lordships in Thessaly, Euboea and central Greece. It was he who gave

[59] J. Longnon, op.cit.
[60] Villehardouin, 258.
[61] Oikonomides, art.cit., 5–9.

permission to William de Champlitte to leave the siege of Akrocorinth and join with Geoffrey de Villehardouin, although it is not known what conditions if any he stipulated with regard to this enterprise. Was he acting as a vassal of the Latin empire or a de facto monarch?

Boniface never called himself king of Thessalonika nor was he addressed as such by others. In his dispute with Baldwin in September 1205 he had neither impugned the legitimacy of Baldwin's coronation nor claimed himself to be the rightful emperor. He had, however, offered his step-son to the inhabitants of Adrianople as a possible ruler. Just how seriously this was meant is difficult to know but Boniface had performed homage at Baldwin's coronation and his behaviour at Adrianople was a matter of comment amongst Robert de Clari and other crusaders at Constantinople. The position of the lord of Thessalonika would have to be regularised.

After September 1204 Baldwin's short reign was occupied with fighting and the task fell to his successor Henry.[62] In 1206 it was arranged that Henry would marry Boniface's daughter Agnes. It is unclear when and upon whose initiative these negotiations took place, but the wedding was celebrated in Hagia Sophia on 4 February 1207 and cordial relations between the two men ensued. In August they met at Kypsella near Mosynopolis where Boniface did homage to Henry for his lands and granted a fief to Geoffrey de Villehardouin, the Marshal of Romania. The relationship of the two rulers was a personal one and could be disrupted by death. When Boniface was killed in September 1207 he left an infant son Demetrius with his widow Margaret of Hungary as regent. By means which are not at all clear, a group of north Italian lords formed the regency council and the old companions of Boniface found it prudent to busy themselves with the affairs of their new lordships in Thessaly and Boeotia. The new councillors were Umberto II de Biandrate, the baili, Amedée de Pofoy, the constable, Albertino and Rolandino da Canossa, the joint lords of Thebes, Guido Pallavicino, the lord of Bodonitsa and Ravano dalle Carceri, the leading lord of Euboea. The Templars in Thessaly also supported these Lombard lords and were to lose their estates at Ravennika as a result. These lords sought to regularise Montferratine rule in the 'isles of Greece', now defined as the whole of Greece with apices at Makri in Thrace, Durazzo in Epiros, and Modon in the south of the Peloponnese. They also wished to replace the infant Demetrius with his half-brother William IV, marquis of Montferrat.

The Venetian reaction to these claims is unknown, but they did encompass territory west of the Pindos mountains which had been assigned to the Venetians in 1204. Henry reacted to this challenge with vigour and presumably with the backing of his council. In December 1208 he marched

---

[62] Valenciennes, 560–679 records the events of the following paragraphs. J. Longnon, *L'Empire Latin de Constantinople* ..., pp.81–152, Setton, pp.27–43, and D. Nicol, *The Despotate of Epiros* (Oxford, 1957), pp.24–75 all provide detailed discussion.

to Thessalonika and won over the support of the regent Margaret, who feared for the fate of her infant son. On 6 January 1209 Henry crowned Demetrius the first king of Thessalonika and thereby exercised the right of a universal authority to create a kingdom. His action was endorsed by Innocent III in March 1209 when he recognised Demetrius as king and took him under papal protection. It is totally unclear why both Henry and Innocent III considered it so wrong for William IV to inherit Thessalonika. After all, William was the eldest son of Boniface and Boniface could claim his kingdom by right of conquest.

Henry then summoned a parliament to meet on 1 May at Ravennika, a place now unknown somewhere near modern Lamia, where those prepared to acknowledge the overlordship of the Latin emperor could renew their homage and regularise their position. At that gathering Amedée de Pofoy was pardoned and confirmed in his office of constable of the Empire, Otho de la Roche was apparently promised possession of Thebes, and the younger Geoffrey de Villehardouin travelled from Achaia to acknowledge Henry as overlord and to receive from him confirmation of is principality and the office of seneschal of Romania. Those lords who had not appeared were now to be warred down in a campaign which lasted a fortnight. Both William of Larissa and Guido Pallavicino at Boudonitza near Thermopylae submitted as the imperial army approached their strongholds. Both were pardoned and allowed to retain their lands. Thebes was besieged and quickly taken, and an imperial progress made into Attica and Euboea. Henry had exerted imperial authority in the Greek peninsula.

In March 1209 Henry had sent his brother Eustace into the Maritsa valley with two squadrons, one French and one Greek, to cover the Bulgarian and Epirote movements while he campaigned in Greece. He then took up the claims which the Lombards had extended over Epiros. These claims may well have gone back to the days of Boniface when Michael Doukas had attached himself to the Latin army then beginning its movement into Thessaly and central Greece. Perhaps despairing of adequate reward from Boniface, Michael had taken himself off to Arta and installed himself as governor of the Byzantine theme or province of Nikopolis. Henry demanded that Michael should hold these lands as a fief of the empire. Such a request did not appeal to one who was soon to claim rule of the theme of Peloponnesos. Instead Michael offered a marriage alliance and promised one-third of his domains as the dowry. Henry and his advisors accepted this offer as the best on the table and the marriage took place between his younger brother Eustace and Michael's eldest daughter in the summer of 1209.

If Lombard claims to Epiros had been unpalatable to the Venetians, as is surmised, then those of the emperor Henry were certainly no less so. Relieved at the withdrawal of the emperor from Thessaly, Michael Doukas sought an alliance with the Venetians. In June 1210 he swore, as despot of

Arta, to hold Epiros as a vassal of the doge Peitro Ziani.[63] The Venetian claim to the lands west of Pindos was thus acknowledged and in return Michael received access to the Venetian armament and mercenary market. Before 1209 Epiros and the Latin Empire had not impinged upon each other, but thereafter, with both blocks consolidating their hold east and west of the Pindos, a clash could not be long postponed.

Michael attacked the kingdom of Thessalonika in the summer of 1210. He was joined by Henry's other relative by marriage, the Bulgarian Strez. This coalition shows both the effectiveness of the imperial army in 1209 and Henry's wisdom in occupying the Maritsa valley. It also shows the effect of the military build-up and recruitment of Latin mercenaries that had taken place in Epiros in the intervening year. There was an air of holy war about this assault, marked by the nature and the extent of the violence meted out to Latin prisoners. Latin priests were reported to have been executed wherever they were found, whilst Amedée de Pofoy, together with his Latin chaplain and three companions, were crucified.[64] The Latin defence of Thessalonika was determined and a lightning expedition by Henry from Constantinople relieved the city in 1210. However, the Epirotes could not be prevented from capturing lands in Thessaly. By 1212 the main towns of the region – Larissa, Halmyros, Valestino, Domokos and Pharsala – were in Greek hands and any Latins in them forced to flee. It also appears from the Chronicle of Galaxidhi that the Latins were temporarily thrown out of Salona in 1210.[65] The Epirotes clearly appreciated that control of the Via Egnatia was essential to prevent any assistance coming from the west. In 1213 Durazzo at its western end was captured, and in 1216 Ochrid and Pelagonia, important stations on its route, surrendered to Michael's successor, Theodore Angelos. In that same year the emperor Henry died of natural causes in Thessalonika while superintending the repair of the city's defences.

The north Aegean, 1216–61

Henry's successor was his brother-in-law Peter de Courtenay, who took advantage of his journey from Flanders to Constantinople to obtain coronation at the hands of the pope in Rome. In May 1217, with a force of 160 knights and 5,500 foot-soldiers, he sought to regain control of the Via Egnatia by attacking from the west. Thereby he might relieve Epirote pressure on Thessaly and Thessalonika, open the land-route from the

---

[63] *Urkunden* II, 120–3.
[64] PL, 216:353–4.
[65] K.N. Sathas, ed., *To Chronikon Tou Galaxeidiou* (Athens, 1895), pp.134, 201.

Aegean to the Adriatic, and reassert imperial authority in Macedonia and Greece. His instincts were sound even if his military intelligence was defective. He failed to recapture Durazzo but continued with the second stage of his bold plan to march to Thessalonika. He, together with the archbishop of Salona and the papal legate John Colonna, was captured by Theodore Angelos somewhere in Epiros and his army disintegrated. In 1218, as a result of papal pressure, Colonna was released and proceeded to Constantinople but the other prisoners were not heard of again. The regency was in the hands of the empress Yolande who died in September 1219. The de Courtenay heirs were in Flanders. The regency council remained in being while the throne was offered first to Philip de Courtenay, marquis of Namur, who refused the honour and then to his younger brother Robert who did not arrive in Constantinople until 1221. Both Thessalonika and Constantinople now lacked military rulers able to provide a firm lead by example. The military situation was to deteriorate further when the Latins became involved in war in Asia Minor.

Early in 1219 Peter's consort, the empress Yolande, had arranged the marriage of one of her daughters to Theodore Laskaris. Relations with Nicaea continued on a cordial footing until Theordore's death in August 1222, when the Latins were drawn into the succession dispute. They put their weight behind Theodore's brothers and when his son-in-law John Vatatzes secured the succession, they were once again faced with hostile elements on two fronts, a commitment which they could not sustain. Their defeat at Poimanenon in Asia Minor in 1224 prevented them from sending assistance to Thessalonika and was thus a major factor in that City's fall to the Epirotes in December 1224. Meanwhile, the loss of Serres and Platamonas in 1221 tightened the Epirote cordon around Thessalonika. Demetrius went to Italy in 1222 to seek aid in person for his kingdom, the first of a succession of north Aegean rulers soon to do the same, and in 1223 his mother sought refuge in her native Hungary.[66]

The first crusade which actually arrived in the Aegean in support of the crusader states there was preached in defence of Thessalonika, at least in the diocese of Arles in May 1223.[67] It was lead by those with some interest or family connection with Thessalonika. In the summer of 1222 an advanced force was lead by Umberto II de Biandrate who had been baili of Thessalonika before his enforced departure for Italy in 1211. In March 1224 the crusade proper under William IV de Montferrat began to assemble in Brindisi, and Nicholas, bishop of Reggio, appointed as papal legate with the army.[68] The Latin emperor Robert was instructed to coordinate an advance from Constantinople with William's arrival in Thessaly and similar

---

[66] Pressutti, 4269.
[67] Ibid., 4355, 4360.
[68] Ibid., 5132–3.

instructions were sent by the pope to the rulers of Achaia and central Greece.[69] Illness delayed William's departure until 1225 and warfare in north Turkey preoccupied Robert. In December 1224 the garrison at Thessalonika surrendered. When William eventually arrived, his army was weakened by dysentery, of which he died. The crusade collapsed. Demetrius fled to Italy and the court of Frederick II. According to Richard of San Germano, he died at Amalfi in 1230 and bequeathed the rights in his kingdom to Frederick. His involvement with the east did not end in 1224. He accompanied Frederick on crusade in 1227 and Philip of Novara listed him as one of the kings present at a banquet in Limassol in 1228.[70]

Right from the foundation of the Latin empire, its rulers and the papacy had seen the retention of Constantinople in Latin hands as a stepping-stone to the recovery of the Hold Land.[71] The logistics of this idea were never clearly worked out and were apparently unconvincing to most contemporaries in western Europe, whose crusading aspirations were emotionally bound up with the Holy Land. Lords like Pierre de Dreux, count of Brittany, and Richard, duke of Cornwall, who were preparing expeditions to the east in the 1230s, were urged to go to the Aegean instead. These appeals demonstrate that the Aegean was linked with the Holy Land in papal circles, although the efforts of Gregory IX in this respect in 1237–39 had produced little or no response. The one crusade which actually reached the Aegean in these years had been the Montferratan crusade in 1225. This expedition had been built around family interests. On 16 April 1217 Peter de Courtenay had invested both Demetrius and William IV with all the rights of their father Boniface. In June 1222 and May 1223 Pope Honorius had granted indulgences to those prepared to join William's army, but for the rest William was left to make shift for himself. Such an expedition proved beyond the resources of one family. In March 1224 when the expedition should have been well underway, William was still trying to raise the necessary finance and for a loan of 9,000 marks he pledged all his possessions to the emperor Frederick.

The death of the emperor Robert in January 1228 left the succession to the Latin throne to the ten-year-old Baldwin, who had been born in Constantinople in 1217 while his father Peter de Courtenay was campaigning in Epiros. Once again another regency council took control at a desperate juncture in the military affairs of the empire. A warrior was clearly needed and the regency and co-emperorship was offered to one of the foremost soldiers of the day, John de Brienne (*c.* 1170–1237), who was then marshal of the papal armies in Apulia. John had been King of Jerusalem

---

[69] Ibid., 4754, 4758.

[70] Philip de Novare, *Frederick the Second and the Ibelins*, trans. La Monte and Hubert (New York, 1936), p. 77; San Germano, 'Historia Montisferratis', in A. Muratori, ed., *Rerum Italicarum Scriptores* XXIII, pp. 381–2.

[71] See note 17 above.

(1210–25) and an active participant in the Fifth Crusade. In April 1229 the terms for his co-emperorship were agreed at Perugia by Vilain I d'Aulnay and Pons de Lyons for the regency council. Clearly much was expected of John and this was reflected in the territorial arrangements of the agreement which bear comparison in their optimism at least to the terms of the partitio of 1204. John was to be co-emperor and senior partner in the Latin principate for life. Baldwin was to marry John's daughter Mary immediately and on reaching the age of twenty was to be invested with the kingdom of Nicaea (*de regno Niceno*) in as full a measure as in the days of the emperor Henry. On John's own death, Baldwin would become sole emperor but was bound in advance to grant to John's heirs the lands of Theodore Doukas in Epiros and Macedonia. All of these territories had yet to be conquered or re-conquered and John, who arrived in Constantinople in July 1231, only achieved very modest success.[72]

The fate of the Latin empire and its rulers failed to impress itself on the courts of western Europe.[73] Honorius's attempt to interest the French royal family in the fate of '*Nova Francia*', as he had dubbed the Aegean states in May 1224, did not appeal on francophone lines nor influenced in any way their own political and crusading agendas. Fifteen years later Henry III's brother, Richard of Cornwall, refused either to commute his crusading vow into cash for Constantinople or to shed Christian blood in Greece. The account given by Matthew Paris of the oath taken at Northampton by the crusading barons on 12 November 1239 reflected a certain distaste for expeditions to help the Latin empire and a general disillusion with the Latin settlements in the Aegean.[74] This perception was not appreciated in Constantinople where hope and belief in widespread European concern for the Latins of the Aegean persisted. In 1236 Baldwin II, backed by his father-in-law and co-emperor John de Brienne, began his tours of the courts of Europe which continued until 1248, when his wife made the rounds in his stead. The interest in relics, the polite receptions and the exiguous gifts and empty promises revealed that the problems of his empire's survival were of marginal concern to western rulers.

Little is known of the actual revenues and resources of the Latin emperors. When Baldwin II began his peregrinations in Europe the imperial finances were in turmoil. Alberic de Trois-Fontaines recorded that Geoffrey II de Villehardouin assigned an annual subsidy of 22,000 hyperpera to John de Brienne in 1231 for the hire of mercenary troops. De Brienne's economies with regard to mercenary pay were well-known in the traditional recruiting

---

[72] *Urkunden* II, 265–70; J. Longnon, *L'Empire Latin de Constantinople ...*, pp. 169–77; J.M. Buckley, 'The problematical octogenarianism of John of Brienne' *Speculum* 32 (1957), 315–22.
[73] M. Barber, op.cit., pp.111–28.
[74] H.R. Luard, ed., *Matthaei Parisiesis: Chronica majora* IV (London, 1877), p.1.

areas, whilst in 1239 Gregory IX advised Pierre de Dreux not to take too many soldiers to Constantinople because of the lack of cash available there for their maintenance. Desperate circumstances required desperate remedies and rulers like Louis IX of France were not adverse to exploiting the empire's need for liquid funds. In 1238 Baldwin mortgaged the marquisate of Namur to him in return for 50,000 livres with which to hire some 30,000 men. Two years later he depleted the relic bank of his empire by selling off the crown of thorns and the sponge and napkin of St Veronica for undisclosed amounts used to pay off his Venetian creditors. In 1257 those same creditors demanded the person of Baldwin's son Philip as surety, and in the last years of the empire plate and the lead from the palace roof was being sold off to raise cash. The empire was more talked about in western Europe in the 1240s than at any other time during its existence. The talk, however, was not about crusade but about a topic everyone could appreciate, namely the poverty of the Latin emperor and his pitiable state. Interestingly, Matthew Paris recorded a considerable amount concerning the visits of Baldwin to western Europe and particularly his visit to England in 1247.[75] This growing awareness of the Aegean might tie in well with the interest in Greek in the circle around Bishop Grosseteste of Lincoln.[76]

By 1261 the empire was bankrupt and had exhausted both the resources and the patience of its principal backers. The Venetians had been involved from 1204 and provided loans, transport, council and naval assistance. Indeed it was they who were responsible for the depleting of the Constantinople garrison in July 1261 in order to participate in the naval expedition to Daphnousa in the Black Sea. However, after their loss of Gallipoli to the Greeks in 1234 their enthusiasm for the empire seemed to wane. The same was true of the papacy. All Latin emperors had enjoyed the privilege of formal papal protection and the popes could not be accused of being ungenerous in proffering assistance to the Empire. In the 1230s and 1240s they had assigned clerical taxation from the Aegean for the defence of Constantinople. However, they had become involved in Aegean politics in the first place to recover the Holy Land and to promote the unity of the universal church. In 1204 these aims had been linked to the creation of the Latin Empire. However, those concerned with the vineyard of the lord of Sabaoth might well pluck out the infertile vine. As early as 1224, and even more seriously in 1234 and 1256, it was clear that the popes of the day were prepared to turn a blind eye to a Greek reoccupation of Constantinople in return for a commitment to church union. Even the Villehardouin of Achaia, unstinting in their financial and material support in the 1230s, seemed to be thinking of themselves as potential overlords in the Aegean by the mid-1250s.[77] If those intimately concerned with the empire were having

---

[75] Ibid., pp.54–5, 75–6, 295, 625–6.
[76] See p.300.
[77] See pp.89–90.

second thoughts, it is hardly surprising that the rulers of the west would commit themselves no further than small gifts and unwanted advice such as that proffered by Blanche of Castile to Baldwin II regarding the exclusion of Greeks from his councils.

In the 57 years of its existence the Latin empire was both a symptom and a casualty of changing west European interests and perceptions. The variety of crusading experiences were widening in the thirteenth century and the Latin empire was just one of a number of options worthy of special pleading, but lacking the religious and emotional cachet of virtually all its competitors. Papal taxation of the clergy in support of crusading activities roused resentment and opposition on grounds of the growing number of demands and inability to pay. Requests for the Latin empire seem to have attracted no specific opposition other than this. The thirtieth requested in 1239 for Pierre de Dreux's proposed expedition to Constantinople was uncollected. The subsidy for the Latin empire authorised in 1245 provoked opposition and arrears were still being collected in the 1260s, whilst a subsidy proposed in 1262 to finance Baldwin II's restoration to Constantinople seems never to have been collected.

Lacking both an imperial lineage and any traditions of kingship, the counts of Flanders and their relatives the de Courtenays from Namur had done well to establish a solid dynastic imperial base which they could pass on. In any hereditary system in which the character and dynamism of the ruler matter, there are bound to be differences in the quality of rulership. The Latin empire was no different in this request from any other medieval realm. The emperor Henry (1206–16), 'a second Ares' and the only emperor to attract a contemporary biographer, may be contrasted with Robert (1221–28), whom Alberic des Trois-Fontaines described as '*ille esset quasi rudis et idiota*'.[78] These were the extremes of dynamism and ineptitude. The other four Latin emperors fell somewhere in between. Personally brave and tenacious, they were adequate warriors and prudent strategists in the use of their exiguous forces. In the end they were overwhelmed by circumstances beyond their control.

After the loss of Thessalonika in 1225 the Latin empire was hemmed in on the west. In Asia Minor only Nicomedia remained in Latin hands by 1228. In 1234 the Gallipoli peninsula was lost and the following year whatever remained in Latin hands in Turkey was recovered by the Greeks of Nicaea. Even at this stage the Latins could still hold their own in a straight fight, such as the chevauchées sent out from the Latin base at Pegae in the years in 1233–35 and the land and sea fights before Constantinople in 1235. John de Brienne was credited with all these victories and even the Flemish

---

[78] *MGH, SS* XXIII (1874), p.910; for a Greek folk song on Henry see M.I. Manousakas, 'To Elleniko Demotiko Tragoudi yia to Vasilia Erriko tis Phlantras' *Laographia* 14 (1952), 3–52.

poet and chronicler Philip Mouskees, no friend of John's, compared him to Hector. But like Hector's victories before Troy, they were only of local significance and were in no sense decisive. It has been said that the Latins only retained control of Constantinople because of the division of their enemies. This was probably true, but it was an assessment not shared by the Latins and it does not diminish their originality and creativity both in exploiting these divisions and making the most of their resources. Even John II Asen's proud boast that the Latins only clung to their lands because of his benevolence, was set up in the Church of the Forty Martyrs in Old Tirnovo in 1230 where the Latins were most unlikely to see it or to dispute its veracity. It does say much for the repair of the walls and the mettle of the Latins that in July 1261 the troops of Strategopoulos could only enter Constantinople when it was completely stripped of its defenders, who were absent on an expedition to the island of Daphnousa in the Black Sea. The active days of the Latin empire were over on 27 July when Baldwin II left the city in a Venetian ship bound for Negroponte. Many lords either stayed in the Morea or entered Angevin service in Italy. Both Baldwin and his patriarch, Pantaleone Giustiniani, fled to Italy where they remained for the rest of their lives as papal pensioners, dying in 1273 and 1286 respectively.

Titular claimants

The loss of the empire in 1261 went virtually unnoticed in the west. Even the Roman curia was in the midst of a papal election in the months of May to late August 1261 and failed to register any firm reaction. However, even though it no longer had a territorial existence, the Latin empire did not disappear in 1261. Indeed with powerful claimants in the west it might be argued that the Latin empire exerted more political influence in the century after 1261 than it had ever done so before. Over the next century a series of titular emperors and empresses advanced their claims to the throne of Constantinople seeking to trade future commercial and political concessions in return for immediate military help. In May 1267 at Viterbo, Baldwin assigned his interests in the empire to Charles I of Naples and agreed to the marriage of his son and heir Philip de Courtenay to Charles's daughter Beatrice. On Baldwin's death in 1273 Philip inherited his father's titles. On his own death in 1301 Catherine, his daughter by Beatrice, became titular empress. She married Charles de Valois, a brother of the French king Philip IV, at a time that the French court entertained ambitions of Mediterranean domination as expressed in the work of Pierre Dubois. Catherine left a twelve-year-old daughter Catherine de Valois-Courtenay to inherit the title in 1308. Until his death in 1325 her father exercised her claim to the empire as did her husband Philip of Taranto whom she married in 1313. On her own death in 1346 her claim passed to her sons by Philip (d. 1331), first Robert (1346–64) and then his brother Philip, who died childless in 1378. The last claimant was Philip's nephew Jacques de Baux, on whose death in 1382 the line of the titular Latin emperors of Constantinople came to an end.

This catalogue of titular claims and diplomatic counters can be matched by those advanced for the kingdom of Thessalonika. As we have seen, Demetrius had passed his rights on to the emperor Frederick II in 1230. Apart from dangling his claim before the Epirote Greek rulers of Thessalonika in the years 1228 to 1231, Frederick was preoccupied with matters other than Aegean conquests, and in August 1239 ceded the title back to the house of Montferrat. The emperor Baldwin II, in his role as suzerain, also had a hand in the disposing of the title. In 1235 he had recognised the claim of William da Verona, a triarch of Euboea who had married Helena, possibly a niece of King Demetrius or more likely a daughter of Manuel Komnenos Doukas, the Greek ruler of the city at that time. In 1266 when this claim had withered away, Baldwin granted the title to Hugh IV, duke of Burgundy. This concession was made at the request of Charles of Anjou to console the Burgundian for his ruptured engagement with Isabelle de Villehardouin and to clear the path for her marriage with Philip of Anjou. The Burgundian claim continued on contemporaneously with that of the Montferrats until is was sold to Philip II of Taranto in 1331, after which it was heard of no more. Meanwhile, the Montferrat claim was taken sufficiently seriously in Constantinople for the Greek emperor Andronikos II to marry Yolande-Irene in 1284 and thereby extinguish the Montferrat claim. It was the diplomatic aspect of Angevin ambitions in the east Mediterranean which highlighted these dynastic politics in the fourteenth century. With the revival of Byzantine fortunes in the Aegean after 1261, the recovery of the Holy Land and the union of Christendom no longer seemed to be acceptable as credible motives for military action in that sphere. Title and the claims to property now set the agenda for the ambitions of western families in the Aegean and ironically Byzantine emperors were to open negotiations for church union in order to counter such schemes.

Both the Latin states of the north Aegean had short existences and assumed greater significance in the politics of the Mediterranean world as diplomatic bargaining points in the hands of west European dynasties with ambitions in the east. In truth, the anonymous annalist of the abbey of Santa Justina at Padua penned the epitaph for both these ephemeral states when he wrote of Baldwin's flight from Constantinople in 1262: '*Tunc imperator Balduinus, cui capta urbe remanserat tantum magni nominis umbra ...*'.[79]

---

[79] *MGH, SS* XIX, (1866), p.182.

The Latin States in Greece, 1204–1311

Central Greece, 1204

In October 1204 a Latin army under the command of Boniface of Montferrat embarked upon a campaign of conquest down the eastern side of the Greek peninsula. All the Frankish sources suggested that the initial conquest was rapid and encountered relatively light opposition. The informants of Nicetas Choniates were clearly of the same opinion since he described the Frankish campaign more in the manner of a progress than a war, and with some bitterness recorded the rapturous reception of Boniface at Thebes and the surrender of Greek landowners in the Thermopylae area without a fight. The archon Sgouros could not defend the pass of Thermopylae because '... The inhabitants of those parts submitted to the marquis [Boniface] readily in the base and despicable spirit which is ever disposed to side with the more powerful'. As a result central Greece lay open to the Latins and 'As the marquis led the army into Boeotia he was enthusiastically received by the Cadmeans [Thebans] as though he were returning home after a long absence'.[1] The Latin campaign was a surprisingly speedy one: 'The barbarians have outdistanced my narration, flying faster than the the quill of my history ... Despoiling Thebes, subduing Athens, and trampling on Euboea, they proceeded on their way'.[2] To Choniates's disgust the Latins were welcomed as liberators in many of the towns through which they passed. This suggests that they were seen as a force for stability by many influential Greeks in the former Byzantine provinces.

It is not clear just how long all this took, but certainly by February 1205, and possibly two or three months earlier, the main force of Boniface's

---

[1] Choniates, 609 (Magoulias trans., p.334) for this and preceding quotation.
[2] Choniates, 609–10 and 638 (Magoulias trans., pp.334, 350).

army was divided between the sieges of Corinth and Nauplion.[3] By contrast with the Latin armies in Thrace and Asia Minor, Boniface had had an easy time.

The conquest of central Greece had proceeded in orderly fashion from north to south, dictated by the topography of the area and the course of the single road running through Thermopylae. Boniface seems to have left only small garrisons behind him since he had Jacques d'Avesnes and his other commanders with him in the Argolid confronting Sgouros and his supporters. None of these territories had been assigned to Boniface in the partition arrangements of September 1204, but formed part of those lands east of the Pindos granted to the crusaders. Whether Boniface saw these lands as part of greater Thessalonika or himself as a crusading baron as entitled to conquer these lands as any other, is not clear but the acceptance of his leadership was obvious. Boniface avoided any involvement in the territory assigned to the Venetians in Epiros and the Morea. Whether this was deliberate policy or the accident of war and topography is unclear. Just how he would have tackled the conquest of the Peloponnese and handled any difficulties that might have arisen with Venice is unknown since he was never put to the test. Indeed, Boniface had been supported by the Venetians when he sought to obtain a free hand in Thessalonika from the emperor Baldwin and to fall out with them was not in his interest. It is perhaps too cynical to see this behind Boniface's welcome of the younger Geoffrey de Villehardouin to his camp at Nauplia in February 1205 and his quick and positive response to Geoffrey's proposals which involved William de Champlitte.

There is an air of opportunism about this deal with a comparatively obscure knight from Champagne who, despite being the nephew of the chronicler and marshal Villehardouin, had left the ranks of the crusaders around May 1203 to go to Syria. For all that, Geoffrey may have used his relationship to his uncle to approach Champlitte, who was the neighbour of the elder Villehardouin in Champagne. Geoffrey's report of a weak and divided Greek resistance can hardly have been news to Boniface in the light of his recent experience in central Greece. The fact that Greek resistance was talked about at all in the crusader camp may suggest that stiffer opposition was expected further to the south. Boniface needed to concentrate on the exploitation and defence of his lands around Thessalonika, and seems to have felt that he could weaken the force besieging Nauplion without too much risk. He had little to lose and much to gain if Champlitte and Villehardouin were successful. The details of the arrangements which he worked out with them are unknown, but they were given a fairly free hand in the conduct of the campaign, which seemed to justify Villehardouin's impression of the weakness of the opposition.

---

[3] Villehardouin, 324.

Leo Sgouros and the Byzantine opposition

The Byzantine opposition in Greece was divided in 1204. It was in the hands of ambitious members of the local aristocracy, who were motivated almost completely by family interest. Even the former emperor Alexios III had to work with one of these men, Leo Sgouros, when he and his suite arrived at Larissa in the summer of 1204. If he was looking for a base from which to oppose the Latins, he was to be disappointed. The best that he could do was to make Sgouros his son-in-law and to hope that the close kinship bonds thereby created would be remembered should Sgouros prevail against the Latins. There seems to have been no question of the former emperor actually leading the forces which Sgouros had at his disposal. Sgouros welcomed the prestige which the hand of an emperor's daughter, even a much-married one like Eudokia Angelina, could confer but not the continued presence of the discredited emperor. Alexios continued his wanderings in Thessaly until he was captured near Halmyros by the advancing Latin army and sent into captivity at Montferrat.[4] The vermilion boots and the imperial vestments captured with him were sent to the emperor Baldwin by Boniface in a generous and loyal gesture.[5] For some five years until Michael Doukas Komnenos securely established himself at Arta, there was to be no emperor or quasi-emperor amongst the Greeks of the west to coordinate resistance or act as a focus of loyalty.

In the late twelfth century the themes of Hellas and Peloponnesos were regarded as backwaters by those sent to administer them. These provinces enjoyed none of the prestige that was later to be associated with the despotate of Mistra. The metropolitan of Athens, Michael Choniates, recorded that the occasional visits of provincial governors from Constantinople were seen by them as an opportunity to compensate themselves, and by the inhabitants as a time of official extortion. No one liked paying taxes, but there was also a profound cultural divide between the centre and the localities. Constantinople sucked in resources from its empire, such that the difference in sophistication and cultural amenities was very tangible. Local bishops often saw their cure of souls as a virtual exile amongst barbarians. This attitude was more than just a literary topos. The historian Nicetas Choniates, despite having a brother who had been archbishop of Athens since 1182, only mentioned Attica when the Franks invaded it in 1204. With such a negative attitude amongst those who were responsible for maintaining links between the centre and the provinces, it is hardly surprising that ambitious local landowners should emerge as the

---

[4] Alexios was ransomed from Montferrat by Michael I Doukas in 1209 or 1210 and sent by him to Konya. He was rescued by Theodore I Laskaris in 1211 and placed in a monastery in Nicaea where he died in 1211 or 1212 (*ODB*, p.65).
[5] Choniates, 605–9; Villehardouin, 309.

patrons and protectors of their localities. Their family ties, clientage networks and economic resources gave them more effective power over the lives of their neighbours than the emperor and his administrators in Constantinople. They became the virtual rulers of their regions, prepared to counter by force any opposition and to use relatives to dominate localities and settlements. Here was a social and political reality based upon wealth and influence.

The local grandee often enjoyed some sort of recognition in Constantinople where the government appreciated the need for their quiescence and might be prepared to recognise their real local influence with honorary court titles. Thus the Chamaretos family were dubbed 'Paneutychestatos despotes' and their neighbours the Daimonoioannes 'Protopansebastohypertatos'. Such titles and favours were important adjuncts for a local power-broker, but none of the archontes concerned mistook the trappings of power for its reality. Leo Sgouros, himself a 'sebastohypertatos' and the husband of an imperial bride, adopted the military saint Theodore as his patron on his seal, as was fitting in one prepared to resort to massive violence towards those who would not do his bidding.

The advent of the Franks left such resistance as there was in the hands of these men, but what were they defending? It was certainly not a national defence. They had to consider carefully whether this new political influence coincided with their own interests or if they were too compromised by their lives in the pre-1204 world to come to terms with the Franks. 'Philotimo' or personal honour seems to have played an important part in all this. The local archons of Thermopylae clearly preferred the protection offered by Boniface to that of Sgouros. The latter's own decision to abandon the Pass of Thermoplyae in 1204 may have had as much to do with this rejection of his personal protection as with the difficulty of holding the pass without local support. His own dramatic suicide in 1208, which may be just a good story and which involved riding his horse off the heights of Akrocorinth, showed that he lacked neither self-awareness nor a sense of occasion.[6]

Within an extensive family group not all members might share the same interest with regard to the Franks. Of the Chamaretos family which controlled the south-west Peloponnese, only John held out against the Latins. Whether John was the son of Leo is not known. It was probably Leo Chamaretos, who was the tyrant of the Laconians, who approached Geoffrey de Villehardouin as he wintered at Modon in 1204. The two men respected each other and Leo proposed to unite his followers with Geoffrey's mounted warriors to their mutual territorial advantage. On his death early

---

[6] A. Savvides, 'A note on the death of Leo Sgouros in AD 1208' *Byzantine and Modern Greek Studies* 12 (1988), 289–95 also notes that Sgouros may have withdrawn to Nauplion and died in action against some Lombard knights in late 1208/early 1209.

in 1205 his son turned against Villehardouin and forced him to flee across the Peloponnese to the Frankish army at Nauplion. Both the Doxapatres family in the Skorta region and the (Eu)Daimonoiannes in the south-east around Monemvasia seem to have played a double game. They were in contact with the Greeks of Epiros and occasionally talked of revolting against the Latins, but nonetheless seem to have maintained fairly cordial relations with them. The Daimonoiannes would not or could not induce the town of Monemvasia to surrender to the Franks and it preserved its independence until 1249. If this family could not be totally relied upon by the Latins, they were also distrusted by the Greeks. A certain Gabriel Larnyx, on good terms with the Latins and at the same time a host to Epirote Greeks entering the Peloponnese, advised the latter against travelling on to the Daimonoiannes in case they were handed over to the Franks. Perhaps deletion had formed a new weapon in the armoury of Greek archons who had francised.[7]

Leo Sgouros, with some sort of private army, controlled the area from the Argolid to the Pass of Thermopylae. In terms of territory he was the most successful of the pre-1204 archontic leaders and unlike most of his fellows he resisted the Franks. His poor reputation derived mainly from the correspondence of Archbishop Michael of Athens who had defended his own interests against Sgouros's henchmen before 1204, and through him to his brother the chronicler Nicetas who, despite deploring the capitulation of most Greeks, did not praise Sgouros for the fight which he showed. Selfish, greedy, and violent Sgouros may have been but he did mount a credible resistance to the Franks. His decision to abandon Thermopylae accounted for the easy Frankish progress through central Greece. Although, lacking the support of the local landowners there, he could probably have done little else. However, he did hold Akrocorinth until his death in 1208 and so arranged matters after it that the fortress did not fall to the Latins until 1210. His Frankish opponents generally gave him a much better press than his fellow countrymen. Villehardouin described him as a '*halz hom … mult sage et enginous*' and the Greek chronicle of the Morea as 'a great man and formidable soldier'. Even the French version of the chronicle paid grudging tribute to his military achievement by casting him in a poor light as '*uns villains homs grex*' compared with '*tous les gentil hommes grex*' who had come to terms with the Franks.[8]

---

[7] P. Magdalino, 'A neglected authority ...' *BZ* 70 (1977), 316–23 for events discussed.
[8] Villehardouin, 310, 321; X t M, 1528; L de C, 94, 96.

Conquest of the Peloponnese, 1204–49

The army of Champlitte and Villehardouin consisted of 500 men of which 100 were knights and the rest mounted sergeants. Although there is some disagreement over details, the route followed by this force seems to have led from Nauplion via Corinth and the north coast of the Peloponnese to Patras, and thence down the west coast to the Byzantine fortress at Kyparissia, where it encountered its first substantial opposition.

The chronicler Villehardouin described the campaign as a '*chevauchée*' and concentrated on events in Messenia and Arkadia, especially the sieges of Coron and Kalamata. Modon was described as in ruins and Coron as still in Greek hands. Clearly the Venetians had done nothing to occupy these two harbours which were to become so important to their naval interests in later years. Villehardouin also mentioned the dispatch of a Greek army from Epiros, but gave no further details about it.[9] All versions of the *Chronicle of the Morea* agree on Patras and Andravida as being the opening targets of the campaign, with some consolidation going on in Elis.[10] The Greek version is somewhat muddled in its account at this point and placed the conquest within the context of Champlitte's passage from France to the siege of Corinth. It gives a graphic account of the use of trebuchets and mangonels on the walls of the lower town at Patras, after which the garrison in the citadel surrendered. It also emphasised that the battle at Koundoura was the only battle offered by the Greeks and that they were decisively defeated by the Latins. The Greek army was described as mustering in Lakonia and the initiative given to the Franks who sought it out with the aid of Greek scouts. The Franks, although outnumbered by almost six to one, were determined to bring the Greeks to battle.[11] The French version emphasised the concern of Champlitte and Villehardouin to capture coastal stations for the purpose of ensuring sea-borne supply lines and listed three sieges at Kyparissia, Coron and Kalamata.[12] The mention of ships and the value of harbours suggests that combined naval and military operations may have been of greater significance in the conquest than the sources specifically indicated, and if this was so it might account for the confusion in those sources regarding the precise route and chronology of the conquest of the Morea.[13]

Negotiation and reconciliation were resorted to whenever possible. The Franks were not sufficiently numerous to do anything else. In central Greece, according to Choniates, the Franks had been welcomed, but in the Morea the Greeks needed some persuading. After a show of force at Patras, Villehardouin addressed the archons of the Plain of the Morea at Andravida.

---

9 Villehardouin, 328–30.
10 L de C, 105; L de F, 107: X t M, 1390–504.
11 X t M, 1723–38.
12 L de C, 108.
13 X t M, 1650–70.

He played not only on their fears of Frankish military prowess but offered them a place within the Frankish settlement. This was original and creative. It guaranteed religious observances, ownership of patrimonial lands and the maintenance of the traditional system of inheritance which involved the division of property between all surviving children. Inheritance systems are fundamental to any culture and clearly this policy of live-and-let-live worked. Greek information and cooperation were essential to Latin success. Soon a commission of six Greeks and six Franks was made responsible for compiling a register of landholding. This policy of concession was not always understood by observers in western Latin Christendom. The difference between the agenda for church union set in Rome and the actions of those Latin lords campaigning in the Aegean is most marked. The existence of the one could not be inferred by the actions of the other. Greek collaboration with the Latins could be obtained in no other way and it was clearly vital. The *Chronicle of the Morea* noted at least seven incidents when Greek advice substantially influenced the course of this initial Frankish campaign.[14]

Despite the emphasis on accommodation in the pages of the chronicle, there were a number of Greeks who sought refuge in Epiros. The size and date of this population movement is far from clear. It seems to have been individuals with their immediate families and supporters rather than a substantial migration. Clearly those who saw no chance of a personal accommodation with the Frankish leadership thought it prudent to go to Epiros. Some must have fled early on, like the former empress Euphrosyne, the wife of Alexios III, whose estates in Thessaly were a specific target for confiscation by Boniface. Others like Constantine Melissenos from Volos would have found his kinship with Michael Doukas reason enough to leave.[15] Presumably what movement there was occurred after the collapse of Greek resistance in the Argolid and after Michael Doukas had established a credible haven in Arta and Ioannina. Michael was described as a second Noah rescuing men and their families from the Latin flood. Nonetheless their presence in Ioannina caused some tension with local residents, although it appears from the correspondence of Demetrios Chomatianos, bishop of Ochrid, that the refugees came from the wealthier spectrum of society.[16]

The general outline of the Latin conquest of mainland Greece is clear enough but there is much in the sources which is obscure and which makes the writing of a detailed narrative history impossible. The chronology of the conquest is vague, as is the role of seamen and mercenaries in the Frankish army. The relationship of the ruler of Thessalonika to the new rulers in the

---

[14] X t M, 1612–50, 1706.

[15] For Michael I Doukas see pp.37 and 182, n.45.

[16] D.M. Nicol, *The Despotate of Epiros* (Oxford, 1957), p.42; P. Magdalino, art. cit.

Morea is unknown. The chronology of the land apportionment in the Morea is unclear, as is the extent and process of land allotment in central Greece. Events north of the Isthmus of Corinth were very poorly recorded and this is particularly regrettable since Thebes had been the most important city in the former theme of Hellas and Peloponnesos. Even the role which castles played in the conquest, and when and how were they constructed, is left to supposition and not easy of proof or contradiction.

The role of castles

As in so many theatres of medieval conquest, the role of the castle is not as obvious as it was once assumed to be. It is certain that the *Chronicle of the Morea* offers us a rationalisation of events, but if the role of the castle was crucial in the initial conquest then this point escapes the reader of that chronicle.

In the available sources castles in Greece were described as beautiful rather than as awesome or strong. It seems only when sited near a frontier or perceived to be under threat were castles given the imagery of a key (*clavis*). But why a key and not a lock or a bar? Thus Siderokastron in southern Thessaly was described in 1367 as '*existens in fronteria ... clavis Athenarum ducatus noscitur*', whilst in 1454 the town of Negroponte (Chalkis in Euboea) was seen by members of the Venetian senate as '... *clavis et fundamentum rerum nostrarum...*'.[17] From all this we might conclude that the prime function of the castle was to consolidate conquest rather than achieve it. The castle as administrative centre, storehouse and statement of power was more significant than any purely military function. The complete absence of any castle building programme during the attempted Latin conquest of Thrace and Asia Minor in the years 1205–7 would seem to bear this out. The Latin troops in those areas were content to fortify churches, as at Nikomedia, or occupy former Byzantine fortifications, as at Stenimaka and Cyzikos.

In addition to the fortresses at Corinth, Argos and Nauplion which contained Greek garrisons until 1210/12, seven Byzantine fortifications or kastra were recorded by the Greek and Aragonese versions of the *Chronicle of the Morea*. At Patras, Pondikos, Coron and Kalamata serious fighting took place involving the construction of siege trains by the Franks. Arkadia (mod. Kyparissia) was deemed too strong for assault and had to be

---

[17] Document dated Thebes, 2 January 1367, in Francesco Guardione, *Sul dominio dei ducati d'Atene e Neopatria dei Re di Sicilia* (Palermo, 1895), p.22, cited K. Setton, *Catalan Domination of Athens* 2nd edn (London, 1975), p.83, n.17; Thiriet, 2982 (29 October 1454).

bypassed. Its garrison surrendered later only when there was no hope of relief, presumably some time after the battle of Koundoura. Kalamata was described as dilapidated, but nonetheless its defenders offered some slight resistance and then handed the fortress over to Villehardouin. Modon was deserted, having been destroyed some years previously by a Venetian flotilla making a sweep against pirates. It was nonetheless gratefully used as a refuge by the Franks. Of the fortress at Oreklovon we have but the name. It was called Bucelet by the Franks which might suggest that it was garrisoned by them immediately on gaining possession. This was the case, too, at Pondikos where Champlitte repaired the walls and renamed it Belveder or Beauvoir. All of these pre-existing Byzantine fortifications were recommissioned at some stage, but exactly when is unclear in the majority of cases.

The important centres of Nikli and Veligosti remain problematic. They seem to have been open towns, although the chronicle suggests that fortifications did exist at both places although it is unclear whether these were added by Frankish lords. No traces of these castles survive today. The existence of Byzantine defences is not mentioned in the sections actually dealing with the conquest of the areas concerned and the fact that the men of those towns joined up with the Greek army which fought at Koundoura might suggest that the towns were open. Given the Greek predilection for fighting from defensive positions, they would probably not have enlisted were defences constructed in their own towns, but this can be no more than a supposition.

The chronicle also recorded the building of four castles *de novo* and linked them with the period of conquest by citing the first lords as builders.[18] Gautier de Rosiere with 24 fees in the Mesara region built Akova (Matagrifon), Hugues de Bruyere in the 'Drongos' of Skorta with 22 fees built Karytaina, Guy de Nivelet in Tsakonia built Geraki, and Robert de Tremolay with 4 fees '... built Chalandritza and was called lord (aphendes)'. Yet we are also told that Geraki and Karytaina were built by the sons of the original grantees. This casts doubt over the date of these supposedly primary castles; perhaps they should be placed in the 1220s to 1260s context too. Only Akova, with its grisly bye-name of Matagriffon or 'Greek-killer', smacks of an aggressive role, yet this is purely subjective and could just as easily be associated with a defensive stance. For the other tenants-in-chief, that is Guillaume Aleman at Patras, Mathieu de Mons at Veligosti, Guillaume de Morley at Nikli, Othon de Tornay at Kalavryta, Hugues de Lille alias de Charpigny at Vostitza, Jean de Neuilly at Passava, Geoffrey de Villehardouin at Kalamata and Arkadia, and a certain Sir Luc at Gritsena, we cannot postulate primary castles either. The sites of Gritsena, Veligosti and Nikli are lost, although there was a castle at Nikli by 1262 when the

---

[18] L de F, 119–33; X t M, 1912–61.

Parlement des Dames was held there.[19] All the other places mentioned have castle remains, but of a late thirteenth century date.[20] There is an air of makeshift about the fortifications of the early days of the conquest. Later wealth display and status would have a more important part to play in castle building than strategy, and it was often these very features which drew Greek attacks upon these castles in the 1260s rather than any strategic role that they might be thought to have filled.

References to the strategic role of castles are distinctly limited in the sources. The reference to Chlemoutsi (Clermont), on its completion in 1223, as being built as a protection against the schismatic Greeks is far too vague to allow a military function to be assigned to it and does not disguise its real purpose as a princely stronghold at the centre of the Villehardouin lands in Elis, equidistant from the capital at Andravida and its port at Glarenza.[21] In the sources castles were not mentioned in any specifically strategic context until the 1250s with regard to the containment of the Slav tribes of the Taygetos. This was to be achieved by controlling any large-scale movement in the passes which gave them access to the plains to the north.[22] Mistra, Maina and Leutron (Beaufort) were listed as being built for this purpose and, by dint of its location in the Mani peninsula at the opposite end of a pass from Passava, the castle at Vardounia should be probably included in this group too.[23] The mechanism of control was probably more passive than active in that these castles could really only function against such marauders as they tried to return to their mountain fastness laden with booty and pursued by Frankish forces from the plains.

The second castle construction which was noted in the *Chronicle of the Morea* as strategically motivated was the building of Chastelneuf in the Val de Calamy by Isabelle de Villehardouin in 1297, in order to protect the surrounding villages from the Greeks of Mistra who in 1264 had erected a fortress at Gardiki.[24] The lapse of 30 years between the original Greek threat and the Frankish response suggests that the castle formed part of a plan for the long-term political recovery of the area rather than a military response. It was to achieve this by preventing the Greeks from exacting tribute from the villagers of the Arkadian Plain, a function that the garrison might well achieve using the new castle as a base for patrols.

---

[19] See p.305.
[20] BMF, pp.601–76.
[21] X t M, 2626–720.
[22] L de F, 215–16; X t M, 3004–7, 3035–7; BMF, pp. 501–5.
[23] J.M. Wagstaff, 'Further observations on the location of Grand Magne' *DOP* 45 (1991), 141–8; P. Burridge, 'The castle of Vardounia and the defence of the Southern Mani' in P. Lock & G. Sanders, eds, *Essays in the Archaeology of Medieval Greece* (forthcoming).
[24] L de F, 830. The Minnesotta Expedition has identified this structure with the ruined castle of Mila. It is not to be confused with another Castiello Nuevo, recorded in L de F, 471, built by Nicholas III de St Omer about the same time and which passed to the Teutonic Order about a century later.

It is difficult to escape from the impression that castles were built to be captured. In the Morea we often learn of castle sites for the first time when they fell to the Greeks in the campaigns of 1263–64, 1302 and 1320–25. From that it would appear that most of them were constructed between the 1220s and the 1260s, but why? Just what is meant by a castle controlling a region or an important line of communication is unclear and the mechanisms of this control do not really stand up to scrutiny. All the surviving castles were military buildings in that they were structures designed to resist attack, with cisterns, crenels, flanking towers and narrow window openings and arrow-slits much in evidence. Yet most of them were handed over to the Greeks in the late thirteenth and early fourteenth centuries as a result of negotiation or treachery and seldom by storm. The garrisons of most castles were probably tiny with a fair proportion of the personnel made up of Greeks who saw to the provisioning.

The castles were often built on inaccessible sites, as difficult to approach as they must have been to swoop out from and surprise an enemy. They consist of curtain walls forming one or two enclosures with a keep dominating the whole from its highest point. The function of these large enclosures is unclear; that at Livadhia in Boeotia was turned over to crop growing in the 1370s. Most attracted some form of settlement around them, although some like Navarino and the lost castle site of Sanctus Arcangelus also in Messenia did not and the reason for this is not clear.

With the exceptions of Chlemoutsi (Clermont) completed between 1220 and 1223,[25] the five castles of Androusa, Basilicata (Vassilika), Leutron (Beaufort), Maina and Mistra which the Chronicle assigned to the 1250s, the castle of Old Navarino (Avarinos) which Nicholas II de St Omer built for his nephew Nicholas III around 1278 and the castle at Thebes which he built for himself in 1287, the chronology of castle building in Greece is not securely fixed.[26] The chronicle mentions about 20 castles belonging to the thirteenth century. Many like Androusa, Geraki, Argos, and Akrocorinth continued in use long after the middle ages and later alterations are not always easy to spot. A list of fiefs compiled in 1377 mentions 51 castles. Some were very small indeed, but a comparison of the figures in these two documents would suggest that there was a proliferation of castle-building in the late thirteenth/early fourteenth centuries.

What castle building there was, then, in the thirteenth century seems to have fallen to the lot of the second and third generations of the Frankish baronial families in Greece. An examination of the military role of those castles with anything like a secure date suggests that they were prizes to be

---

[25] X t M, 2626–720. See Andrews, *Castles of the Morea* (Princeton, 1953), pp.146–7 for discussion of dating and the excommunication by Honorius III in 1220 for seizure of church property.

[26] L de F, 215–17; X t M, 2985–91, 3038–42, 8096; L de C, 564.

won rather than military objectives in their own right. The castle at Thebes constructed for Nicholas II de St Omer in 1287 was paid for out of the fortune of his wife, Princess Marie of Antioch. It was built in the centre of Thebes 50 years after a period of prolonged Greek attacks on the city in 1235–36 had come to an end and at a time when the Franks in central Greece were going over to the offensive once again in southern Thessaly. Display was clearly important. William Miller has described the building as large enough to house an emperor and his court. It was decorated with frescoes which depicted the conquest of the Holy Land by the warriors of the First Crusade. Yet in 1311 it took no part in the defence of Thebes which surrendered to the Catalans (see p.121) without a fight, whilst 30 years later in 1331 those same Catalans slighted the castle rather than let it fall into the hands of Gautier II de Brienne.[27] It was a prize rather than a strong-point. The same impression is given by the part played by the castles in Elis in 1315–16 in the struggle between Ferrando of Majorca and Louis of Burgundy for possession of the principality of Achaia (see p.127). Castles might serve for princely bivouacs but the issue was decided on the battlefields of Picotin and Manolada. The campaigns of the emperor Henry in Thessaly and Boeotia in 1209 reveal a similar picture. The castles at Larissa and Boudonitza surrendered as he approached, whilst the two Templar castles at Lamia and Ravennika did not bar his march on Thebes and were confiscated by him to reward his supporter Raoul of Tabarie. The Templars claimed that they had actually built castles at these places at great expense. Presumably construction had taken place since 1205 but sadly the two sites of these early Frankish castles are lost.[28] Rather than strategy it was display, administration and storage which brought forth the castles of Greece. Certainly defence as well, but ironically, as Tom McNeill has found in medieval Ireland, castles often invited attack because they were there and known to be places where resources were stored.

The castles of medieval Greece as a whole are numerous indeed. Some exist in texts only and their sites are not yet known. Others exist as physical remains without textual pedigree and cannot be dated from their masonry or plan alone.[29] The documentary sources tell us nothing of the time and cost of construction or of the size and make-up of the labour force. Certainly some re-used classical masonry is evident in the walls, but the bulk of the masonry must have been quarried and nothing is yet known of these quarries, let alone the masons engaged on these projects. All of this is pertinent, but it is perhaps steering us away from the early days of the conquest. Castles might have had a very limited strategic role in medieval

---

[27] S. Symeonoglou, *The Topography of Thebes* (Princeton, 1985), p.229; W. Miller, *Essays on the Latin Orient* (Cambridge, 1921), pp.76–7.
[28] PL, 216, 564.
[29] BMF, pp.601–76; K. Andrews, op. cit., pp.219–41.

Greece, but they could certainly slow up any re-conquest and to this use they were soon to be put.

Greek raids, resistance and recovery, 1210–64

The Frankish conquests were not secure conquests. At the outset they were quick and easy but they were not total. Greek resistance had not been warred down and no substantial leaders had been killed in battle. In the accounts of the fighting in 1205–9 no mention was made of Frankish penetration into Lakonia. In 1206–7 fighting with the Venetians in the Messenian Peninsula had held up the progress of conquest, which was largely confined to the northern and western sea-board of the Peloponnese. The clauses of the Treaty of Sapienza of June 1209 reveal that fighting was still going on in the centre of the Peloponnese. Villehardouin conceded the Venetian claims to the ports of Modon and Coron and also to one-quarter of the region of Lacedemonia when he had conquered it, but clearly little progress had been made when the treaty was signed.[30]

The account of Geoffrey de Villehardouin's avoidance of Champlitte's heir Robert may well be a fiction of the chronicler, but in geographic detail the story sheds some light on the extent of Frankish conquest in the Morea around 1209–10. William de Champlitte had been recognised as prince of Achaia in 1205. He returned to France in 1208 or 1209 leaving his nephew Hugh to protect his interests. On Hugh's own death soon afterwards, Geoffrey I de Villehardouin had assumed power, either on Champlitte's direction or by the choice of the barons in the Morea. On Champlitte's death in France in 1209 his cousin Robert was said to have come to the Morea to claim the principality. According to the story, Villehardouin kept moving around between Andravida, Kalamata, Nikli and Veligosti in order to avoid meeting Robert until the full period of a year and a day had elapsed since the death of Champlitte. This was the legal time limit for an inheritance claim on a fief to be lodged. It was longer for someone not resident in the Morea. Despite the implausability of it all and the idea that a term could be placed on a titular claim, it was only when the pursuit hotted up that Villehardouin moved off to Lacedemon, which was apparently not yet in his hands.[31]

Apart from Guy de Nivelet's holding of six knights' fees in Tsakonia and the construction of the castle at Geraki by his son Jean, we know nothing of Frankish penetration east of the Taygetos in these early years.

---

[30] *Urkunden* II, 96–9.
[31] L de F, 154–71; X t M, 2226–428. Champlitte's son Eudes succeeded to his lands in Champagne.

Monemvasia was not attacked in these years and its citizens managed to maintain a sort of armed neutrality. The presence of '*Monemvasios oinos*' or malmsey wine at a banquet at the Latin court in Constantinople in 1214 shows that trading relations with the Latins could be carried on whilst their more aggressive intentions could be resisted. There seems to have been no concentrated Frankish attack on the fortress at Monemvasia until 1246 when the town was subjected to a tight siege. After three years the Monemvasiots surrendered on peculiarly generous terms, and thereafter the Franks turned their attention to another unsubdued group, the Slavs of the southern Taygetos.[32]

The new conquests were far from secure and the society of Frankish Greece was both violent and unsettled, requiring a state of constant alert and a readiness to fight and to die. Nowhere was this more apparent than in southern Thessaly, a sort of debateable land between the Franks in Thebes and Boudonitza and the Lombards in Thessalonika. It was fiercely contested by the Greeks of Epiros too, who within six years of the initial conquest were recovering important towns from the Latins. In 1210 Amedée de Pofoy had been crucified by the troops of Michael Doukas and by 1215 Amedée's former lordship of Domokos, along with the town of Demetrias, were once again in Greek hands, signalled by the installation of Greek Orthodox bishops in both places. In 1210, according to the Chronicle of Galaxidhi, a Frankish army was routed near Salona and the lord of that town, Thomas I d'Autremoncourt, killed. The town passed once again into Greek hands and in 1218 an attempt to recapture it was successfully repulsed. For some time virtually all the harbours along the north shore of the Corinthian Gulf were in Epirote hands, facilitating communications with sympathetic Greeks in the Peloponnese and increasing the threat of a sea-borne assault on the Frankish Morea across the Gulf of Corinth.

Epirote pressure in northern Thessaly did not ease up. In 1212 Larissa was recaptured. The town had been under pressure from the Greeks since 1209 when its Latin archbishop had sought safety in Ferchikam, modern Pteleon. In 1212 he moved his residence to Thebes and was still there in 1222. By 1218 most of central Thessaly was back in Greek hands. Lamia, Neopatras and Platamon were lost by the Latins in that year and along with them the domains of some important lords like William of Larsa and Roland Piche. With the fall of Serres in 1221 and of Thessalonika in 1224 the Greek hold on northern Thessaly was secure. The army led by William of Montferrat had had to come by sea in 1225, disembarking at Halmyros.

By 1218 the lordship of Athens and Thebes was bounded on both the north and the west by a hostile Epirote neighbour who could raid more or less unopposed. The Latins abandoned the countryside and concentrated themselves in the towns and it was these centres which attracted Greek

---

[32] H.A. Kalligas, *Byzantine Monemvasia, The Sources* (Monemvasia, 1990), pp.71–9.

attack. However, the lure of Thessalonika and prizes in Macedonia and Thrace diverted the Epirotes from their southern neighbours until their defeat by the Bulgarians at Klokotnica closed off the prospect of expansion to the north. In July 1235 and again in June 1236 frequent Greek attacks on Thebes were referred to in the correspondance of Pope Gregory XI. The Franks had to rely upon the Byzantine walls around the Kadmea, strengthened by towers at each of the gates. The castle of Nicholas II de St Omer, co-seigneur 1258–94, was not built until 1287 and was a statement of worldly success rather than a response to Greek attacks.[33] In April 1244 Innocent IV had received a request from Guy de la Roche to remove a community of Greek monks in the village '... *quod Laragie vulgariter nuncupatur*', who were suspected of passing on information to his Greek enemies.[34] In 1246 Halmyros and Volos were occupied by the Greeks, and a Venetian force which had established a presence there in 1241 was driven out. Not only were two important Aegean ports lost, but the triarchy of Oreos in the north of the island of Euboea was now threatened by the Greeks of Epiros. Any landings on that island might well outflank the northern defences of the lordship of Athens and Thebes which hinged on the castle of Boudonitza. That fortress too came under attack as the key to the pass of Thermopylae and the whole northern part of the duchy. Its lord, Umberto Pallavicino, appealed for aid to the prince of Achaia.

In this unstable society even Greek monastic communities had become objects of suspicion. This was not solely the result of Latin paranoia since the Frankish leadership in central Greece clearly felt that its continued existence was in doubt and would not tolerate informers, monkish or otherwise. A more enduring symbol of an unstable society were the 80 or so great towers erected in the Attic and Boeotian countryside with another 50 across the Euripos in Euboea. Such massive structures had been a feature of southern French society in the twelfth century and probably of the Greek countryside too. As conditions had become more settled in France, so they had ceased to be built in this massive form. However, in thirteenth century Greece there clearly was a need for the continuance of these archontic structures, symbols at once of lordship and of external threat.[35]

Threats from the Greek rulers of Epiros subsided during the late 1240s and the loss of Thessalonika to the Greeks of Nicaea. Their drive on Constantinople was effectively at an end and their one chance of maintaining their own independence from their Nicene rivals was in alliance

---

[33] L. Auvray, *Les Registres de Gregoire IX* II (Paris, 1896), docs 2671, 3214; S. Symeonoglou, *The Topography of Thebes* (Princeton, 1985), pp.161, 229.

[34] E. Berger, *Les Registres d'Innocent IV* I (Paris, 1884), doc. 657, pp.112–13.

[35] P. Lock, 'The medieval towers of Greece: a problem in chronology and function', in B. Arbel et al., eds, *Latins and Greeks in the Eastern Mediterranean After 1204* (London, 1989), pp.129–45 and references; E. Vanderpool, 'A monument to the Battle of Marathon' *Hesperia* 35 (1966), 93–106.

with the Franks. One such alliance, celebrated in 1259 by the marriage of William de Villehardouin with Anna Komnene Doukaina, the daughter of Michael II of Epiros (1237–71), ended a little later that year with the disastrous defeat and capture of William at Pelagonia. In the aftermath of that battle Thebes was sacked by the victorious Nicene army lead by the sebastokrator John Palaeologos. Thereafter the despots of Epiros drew closer to their former adversaries, the Franks.

After 1259, and more especially after the cession of Mistra, Monemvasia and Maina to Michael VIII Palaeologos in 1262, the nature of the threat to Frankish Greece changed dramatically. From these bases the imperial troops pushed hard to reconquer the Morea. The fighting was fierce and casualties high. According to Marco Sanudo, '... one woman was married to seven husbands, one after the other, who were killed in this fighting'.[36]

For the campaign of 1263 the Greeks used Monemvasia as their point of entry. The initiative was clearly with them. Fifteen hundred Turkish mercenaries were brought over from Asia Minor and the Slavonic tribes of the Taygetos raised against the Franks. The loss of Mistra and Maina seems to have impugned the ability of the other Frankish fortresses in the Mani to control the Slavs. The area of Tsakonia was first secured and the garrison at Sparta (La Cremonie) besieged. With this castle effectively isolated, the Greeks could raid widely. They reached the coast of the Gulf of Corinth at Veligosti, which they burnt to the ground, although unable to capture the castle there. Prince William sought to rally his vassals from Athens and Euboea leaving Jean de Catavas in charge of the defence of Elis whilst he was away. Partly encouraged by Villehardouin's absence, the Greeks raided in the Alpheios valley where they burned the Cistercian house at Issova. Further destruction in Elis was averted by the victory of Catavas at Prinitza. However, lack of men prevented the exploitation of this victory and the Greek army was able to retire intact. Villehardouin laid the blame for this incomplete victory on the rulers of Athens and Euboea, none of whom had responded to his summons.[37] Greek attacks persisted and in May 1264 Urban IV ordered the preaching of a crusade against the Greek schismatics. This was the second crusade to be widely preached in the west specifically against the Greeks. Western European rulers had their own preoccupations and the response was as negative as to the similar appeal made in 1262. Western rulers had to be secure in their own realms before they would venture abroad to bolster up the throne of another.[38]

Meanwhile, warfare continued in the Morea. The scraps of information given in the *Chronicle of the Morea* show that it was a series of

---

[36] CGR, p.118.
[37] L de C, 331–8.
[38] J. Giraud, *Les Registres d'Urbain IV* II (Paris, 1901), docs 131–7, 577–9.

small-scale engagements, of raids and counter-raids in which the principality seems to have stood alone. Why the lords of central Greece were unwilling to participate on the side of their fellows is unclear. Whether it was suspicion of the ambitions of the Villehardouin (see pp.90–1) or pre-occupation with their own defence can only be matters for speculation. There was a significant pause in the fighting in the year or so after 1265 when serious negotiations for the unification of the churches was underway, but raiding seems to have been resumed by 1267. According to the correspondence of Michael VIII and Clement IV in early 1267 this amounted to daily hostilities, the destruction of towns, the depopulation of the countryside, the death of countless men cut down in their prime and the compulsive search for plunder.[39] As in the earlier contest between the Latin empire and its enemies, no side yet had sufficient advantage to defeat the other and thus bring about settled conditions. By the end of the 1260s the boundaries of the Frankish Morea were no longer intact and the whole area was deteriorating into one big battle-ground. The one hope of survival was direct western European assistance.

The Treaties of Viterbo, May 1267

To this end on 24 May 1267 at the papal court at Viterbo, Pope Clement IV summoned a meeting of the interested parties from Latin Christendom through which he sought both to secure the safety of the Franks in the Morea and to restore the Latin empire to Constantinople and with it to re-establish the stepping-stone for the liberation of the Holy Land. At the same time he hoped to occupy the energies of Charles of Anjou outside Italy which might serve to preserve papal freedom of action within it. The papal agenda represented just one interest at the conference.

The hopes and fears of William de Villehardouin can be gauged from the concessions that he made. The Greek offensive of 1263–64 had led to an abandonment of any ambitions which William may have harboured regarding hegemony over Frankish Greece. He surrendered his principality to Charles of Anjou acknowledging him as his suzerain. Charles was the brother of Louis IX of France and had been invested with the kingdom of Naples and Sicily by Pope Clement in June 1265. In January 1266 he had been crowned and one month later had defeated and killed his Hohenstaufen rival, Manfred, at Benevento. His willingness to be a party to these negotiations at Viterbo showed where his own ambitions lay and where immediate aid for the embattled Franks might be sought. In addition the two men were not strangers since they had both taken part in the Sixth Crusade led by Louis IX. William had joined the crusade at Cyprus in 1249

---

[39] Setton, p.101.

with a substantial contingent of 400 knights and a fleet of 28 ships. He remained with the force all through the Egyptian campaign until 1250. Villehardouin's change of suzerain was ratified by his former suzerain, the emperor Baldwin II, three days later in a second round of negotiations, also at Viterbo. This second treaty of Viterbo was mainly concerned with the recovery of the Latin empire and the Angevin role in that.

The preamble to the 24 May treaty graphically summarised the state of affairs in the Frankish Morea which had brought it about. The territory had been constantly attacked by the forces of the schismatic Michael VIII and was now in large part occupied by them. Appeals to various European princes and magnates had produced no active help, and so rather than lose all by standing alone '... we have recourse to your most serene prince, lord Charles, illustrious king of Sicily'. In return for unspecified military assistance, Villehardouin's principality was to pass to the house of Anjou, either to the descendants of Charles' second son Philip of Anjou and his future wife Isabelle de Villehardouin or, failing such heirs, to the direct rule of the Angevin king of Sicily. Even the rights of any future male heir which William might beget were signed away by this agreement. Should an heir be born, he was to receive just one-fifth of his father's lands as a fief from the Angevin rulers. This shows the straits to which the principality had been reduced by the Greek offensive since William had every hope of a male heir from his wife, Anna Doukaina, who was then pregnant. William regretted these concessions that military necessity had forced him to make. The claim put forward in 1311 by Margaret of Akova, his younger daughter and the child expected in May 1267, that he had made a secret will on his death-bed bequeathing the Morea to her, gained little credence at the time but must have been based on memories of family humiliation. However that may be, the rule of a minor was in any case undesirable in the military situation of the 1260s.

In the meantime William was to exercise all the authority and jurisdiction which he had before he became a signatory of the treaty, '... but with this exception that we cannot make enfeoffments which will remain in effect after our death, beyond 14, 000 hyperpera of land...'. There was to be no squandering of royal resources prior to a change of ruling house. Unlike the aid promised to the exiled emperor Baldwin II, that is of a force of 2, 000 mounted warriors within six years, no limit was placed on the aid which Charles might provide to William. The principality was to belong to the Angevins whilst they only had a one-third interest in the lands of the former empire which might be reconquered using the troops which they would provide. The Angevin claim on the Morea was clearly understood by all parties to the treaty to be absolute.[40]

---

[40] The two treaties of 1267 are published in Perrat & Longnon, pp.207–11 and discussed in Setton, pp.103–6, and D. Geanakoplos, *Michael Palaeologus and the West* (Harvard, 1959), pp.197–200.

Much hung on these Treaties of Viterbo in terms of Mediterranean politics and the crusade agenda conceived by Clement IV. It was a grand universalist scheme but it brought no immediate aid to the Franks of the Morea. Rather the immediate effect was to divert troops and William's attention from his beleaguered principality. William, as vassal of Charles, was summoned to fight with the latter against the last Hohenstaufen claimant of the Sicilian throne, the young Conradin. At the battle of Tagliacozzo fought on 23 August 1268, William together with 400 Moreot knights fought for their new suzerain. This Italian involvement demonstrated a realistic understanding on the part of the Franks that they could expect no substantial aid from southern Italy until Charles was firmly in control in his newly won kingdom. Certainly, none were in doubt that the Frankish Morea had ceased to be an independent crusader state and was now a province of the kingdom of Naples and intimately involved in the politics and fortunes of its new suzerain. From now on any response to events in the Morea was to be directly dictated by the power politics of the west.

It was not until 1269 that active Angevin involvement in Greece was forthcoming. In January William secured Avlona in Albania as an advance base for the disembarkation of Italian troops in continental Greece. In 1270 a commission sent out from Naples received formal recognition from the barons of the Morea for the agreements reached at Viterbo. In 1271 Charles sent Dreux de Beaumont, his marshal in Sicily, to the Morea as captain-general. An expedition lead jointly by Dreux and Prince William was mounted soon after to recover territory lost to the Greeks in Euboea, and as a result the fortress of La Cuppa near Avlonari in the east of the island was recaptured. The Greek troops on Euboea were led by Licario of Karystos, a gifted Latin commander with considerable ability for conducting combined naval and military operations. He had recently received the title of megadux from Michael VIII and was clearly at ease in the Byzantine court. Older history books sometimes dismiss him as a renegade but it is doubtful that this term had much significance in the late medieval Aegean. A growing Angevin involvement in Greece in the 1270s can thus be seen, and its success in bolstering the Franks of southern Greece may be measured in the attention placed by Michael VIII on other areas like Euboea and Thessaly. The forces from the Morea seem not to have acted in concert with the Franks from the duchy of Athens which had close interests in the island of Euboea. This at least is the impression which the chronicle gives, admittedly from a position of silence.

The lordship of Athens and Thebes

As yet the rulers of the lordship of Athens and Thebes, and the independent counties of Boudonitsa and Salona which surrounded it, remained states free from direct dependence on any specific west European monarchy. Unlike the Villehardouin, the de la Roche had not intermarried with the cadet branches of the French royal family or within the Latin imperial dynasty. In the mid-thirteenth century this was partly because the area lacked direct access to the Adriatic, other than through the roadsteads at Livadostro and Itea on the Corinthian Gulf. Furthermore, before they could be encompassed within the ambitious gaze of any south Italian monarch, Epiros would have to be conquered. Certainly the Angevins now had a bridgehead in Epiros through Avlona, but in the past potentates like Robert Guiscard (d. 1085) and Peter de Courtenay (d. 1217) had made little headway there. The rulers of the central Greek lands were thus in a measure isolated from the west in the thirteenth century and as such they were forced to shift for themselves, to cultivate relations with their Greek neighbours and hence to become more involved with political problems and aspirations of those neighbours than their southern brethren who had hitched their future with the kingdom of Naples.

This is not to say that the rulers of central Greece sought to divorce themselves from Europe. In familial, cultural and religious terms this would have been unthinkable. France was a source of military recruitment, financial assistance and honours. In return they sent back religious endowment and accorded the king of France some sort of quasi-suzerainty which had never been accorded to the Latin emperors from Flanders. As a result of a feudal dispute with the Villehardouin, Guy I de la Roche had visited the French court in the years 1259–60, at which time he may have been granted both the formal title of duke and the right to mint money modelled on the French denier tournois. However, there is no numismatic evidence to show that either the title or the right of minting were exercised before 1280.

Judging from the involvement of Duke Guy (d. 1263) and his successor Jean (d. 1280) in the politics and warfare of southern Thessaly and Euboea in the 1260s and 1270s, they were prepared to take over the mantle of the Villehardouin as the suzerains of Greece. In 1275 their forces assisted those of the self-appointed ruler of Neopatras, John, against their common foe the Greeks of Constantinople. Their victory at Neopatras was accompanied by the marriage of the sebastokrator's daughter Helene to the duke's brother William and the cession to the Franks of the towns of Lamia, Gardiki, Gravia and Siderokastron, which had been lost to them for nearly 60 years. In the following year the duke himself was captured at the battle of Vatonda in Euboea as he took an active part in resisting the inroads of Licario of Karystos. There was also an element of self-preservation about all this since Michael VIII's campaigns in Thessaly, Epiros and Euboea threatened to encircle the duchy of Athens. The sack of Thebes in 1259 in the aftermath of the battle of Pelagonia showed early on what could be expected from such encirclement. However, a willingness to assume new titles and new lands and generally to cut a figure in the Frankish politics of Greece was something new for these Burgundian rulers from central Greece.

The suzerainty which Duke Guy had exercised after his own return from France and whilst William de Villehardouin was still a prisoner in Constantinople was a mark of a new status for the rulers of Athens. They might have had to yield to the prince of Achaia in 1258 after their defeat at his hands at Karydi, but they had presented the Franks of central Greece with a credible alternative to an overweening potentate, and on William de Villehardouin's death in 1278 the ruler of Athens and Thebes was the most powerful lord in Frankish Greece and one of the few who could trace his ancestry back to the time of the conquest just 74 years previously. Indeed in 1280 William duke of Athens was to be appointed Angevin baili of the Morea. The calamitous defeat of William de Villehardouin at Pelagonia in 1259 had spelt the end for the independent Frankish principality of southern Greece. It had also caused the Villehardouin to lose face in the eyes of their neighbouring rulers and rivals. Just what had been the ambitions of the house of Villehardouin which had led to this change of fortune?

A Villehardouin hegemony?

By 1210 Geoffrey I de Villehardouin had been elected prince of Achaia by his fellow barons and acknowledged as such by Pope Innocent III and by the Latin emperor Henry. However dubious his relationship to William de Champlitte and his heirs appears to have been, Geoffrey was thus no *primus inter pares* but a ruler whose title had been constituted by a universal authority. He had taken the leading role in the distribution of lands in the Morea and as such had given the barons there a material interest in the establishment of his dynasty. His wife, Elizabeth des Chappes(?), was summoned to join him from France about 1210 and the whole family given material interests in southern Greece. In relation to the rest of Frankish Greece the desire for suzerainty is made clear by the *Chronicle of the Morea*, which asserts, somewhat anachronistically, that Boniface of Montferrat had invested William de Champlitte with the overlordship of Athens and Euripos (Euboea).[41] Whilst this was not the case in 1205, in 1212 Otho de la Roche, who had assisted Geoffrey in the long sieges of the three Argolid fortresses, was given two of them, Argos and Nauplion, as personal fiefs, saving his liege homage to the emperor. Otho, as lord of Athens and perhaps Thebes too by this time, was the most powerful ruler in Frankish Greece after the Villehardouin and the grant, although in the nature of a reward for services

---

[41] L de F, 102; X t M, 1550–66.

rendered, did imply some dependence on the house of Villehardouin. Judging from their marriage partners, the lords of Athens may not have been the social equals of the Villehardouin, but they were certainly deemed to be socially superior to the barons of the Morea, whose acknowledgement of their social insufficiency to judge them in 1259 had resulted in Guy's visit to the French court. Such grants reserving liege homage were not unusual in medieval Europe and perhaps too much should not be made of it, but wherever such grants were made there was an implicit act of subordination and the opportunity for meddling in the affairs of the vassal. The deliberate granting out of a fief was a totally different act than the acceptance of the claim of a vassal by marriage, such as the claim by Wiliam de la Roche to Damala and Veligosti made in the early 1260s in right of his wife, the daughter and heiress to Mathew II de Valaincourt. There the de la Roche were the innovators and presumably exercising some ambition in relation to lands in the principality. In 1212 the initiative seems to have come from Geoffrey de Villehardouin himself and was seen in the fourteenth century *Chronicle of the Morea* as tantamount to suzerainty.

In 1236 as a reward for the military aid brought by William de Villehardouin to Constantinople in person, the prince was granted the overlordship of the Archipelago (duchy of Naxos), Euboea and the possessions of the lord of Athens south of the Isthmus of Corinth. This last was a confirmation of the position with regard to Argos and Nauplion which had held since 1212. It was as vassals of William that the Lombard lords of Euboea or triarchs (tierciers or terzieri) were present at the siege of Monemvasia in 1247–49.[42]

In 1217 the Villehardouin family formed a link with the imperial house of de Courtenay. In that year Geoffrey I negotiated the marriage of his son and heir Geoffrey II (d. 1246) to Agnes de Courtenay, the daughter of the newly-crowned Latin emperor Peter. The marriage was duly celebrated at Andreville in the presence of the empress Yolande and signalled the pretentions of the Villehardouin. This imperial connection was kept up by family visits. Agnes's brother the emperor Robert died in the Peloponnese in 1228 whilst on a visit to his sister. During the 1230s Geoffrey aided the beleaguered Latin emperor, John de Brienne, with an annual cash subsidy said to be worth 22,000 hyperpera and in 1235 and 1236 raised naval expeditions which he sent to the Bosphorus to lift sieges of Constantinople. The princes of the Morea seem to have been alone amongst the rulers of Frankish Greece to furnish such aid on such a scale. Their suzerainty in the

---

[42] The term 'triarch' is an anachronism, but one that has become well-established. It originates in an article on Euboea written by J.B. Bury in 1886 (*JHS* 7, 314) and represents both an anglicisation and classicisation of Hopf's term 'Dreiherren' for the lords of the three fiefs established on Euboea by Boniface of Montferrat. These lords did not refer to themselves by this term nor were they so addressed by contemporaries. Subject to partiable inheritance the term 'hexarch' is also encountered.

peninsula to some extent rested upon it, since it was not really until after the demise of the empire in 1261 that the de la Roche were able to emerge as rivals of the Villehardouin in continental Greece. It is interesting that the last Latin emperor Baldwin did not seem to maintain the close links which his brother Robert and his co-emperor John de Brienne (d. 1239) had formed with the Villehardouin. Perhaps it was only the knowledge of the weakened state of the principality following the captivity of William de Villehardouin in 1259 that prevented him from seeking refuge and military support in the Morea in 1261. Perhaps, however, it was his fear of the imperial ambitions of Prince William that precluded this. Baldwin was certainly not disinclined to act out his role of suzerain of the principality at Viterbo in 1267, even if it was for the last time. Professor Geanakoplos has pondered the possible imperial ambitions of the Villehardouin. Regrettably it can only remain a conjecture.[43]

That apart, a projected overlordship in Greece was more accessible. Geoffrey I had sought to establish direct feudal ties with the lordship of Athens in 1212, ties that were restated by imperial grant to his son William in 1236 and also at that time extended to Naxos and Euboea. In 1255, following the death of his second wife Carintana dalle Carceri, William laid claim to the whole of northern Euboea in her name, calling himself a triarch and apparently prepared to upset the inheritance structure followed by the Lombard lords of the island since 1216. There was more behind this than just feudal dispute. It was an attempt to put landed resources behind the title of overlord and perhaps, too, assert his own claim as suzerain of Euboea in the face of a Venetian counter-claim which a fourteenth-century Venetian chronicler Dandolo pre-dated to the early days of the Frankish conquest. Whether greed or necessity was behind Villehardouin's claim, it provoked a widespread and hostile reaction amongst the Frankish lords of central Greece and led to a state of civil war in Frankish Greece. The Venetians, the triarchs of Euboea, Guy of Athens and, in 1258, even William's own nephew, Geoffrey de Briel, lord of Karytaina and reputedly the outstanding knight of the Morea, ended up defying William who was their lord for all or some of their landed possessions. This breakdown of the personal relationship involved in feudal landholding was serious. It must have seemed all the more so to William who was somewhat scrupulous over feudal ties when it suited his own interests. In 1256 and 1257 Euboea, Attica and parts of the Argolid were fought over by the opposing sides – anywhere where one of the combatants had lands and possessions which might be seized or ravaged by his enemies in an unguarded moment. Whatever this might reveal about the quiescence of the Greek population in these years, the material losses to the Franks must have been considerable. Frankish society in Greece was violent and unsettled, whether due to continuous conflict with

---

[43] Geanakoplos, op.cit., pp.54–9.

Greek opposition elements or because of disagreements amongst the Frankish lords themselves. In the spring of 1258 William invaded the lordship of Athens and Thebes, defeated an army sent against him at Karydi, on the road running from Eleusis to Thebes, and pressed on to besiege that city. Guy de la Roche was forced to surrender, to go to Nikli to make formal submission to William, and to face judgement by the barons of the Morea. These, although the vassals of Villehardouin like Guy himself, declared that they were not the peers of the lord of Athens and Thebes and that he should go to the court of Louis IX for judgement. This he duly did in the spring of 1259 and returned in 1260 apparently with increased honour and prestige. In this decision the barons of the Morea perhaps showed more tact than their lord had shown in his dealings with the lords of central Greece. It is perhaps unusual that the case was not referred to the emperor in Constantinople, the overlord of both Villehardouin and de la Roche. This omission was perhaps a comment both on the low esteem in which the Latin emperor was held in mainland Greece and upon the status of those still in Constantinople in these years.

In the next year, 1259, William became involved in the politics of Thessaly as one of the allies of Michael II, despot of Epiros, who had become his father-in-law when William took as his third wife the latter's daughter, Anna Komnena Doukaina. The alliance also included King Manfred of Sicily who sent over some 400 German knights to assist in the campaign. The allies were the aggressors and hoped to win territory controlled from Thessalonika by the Nicene Greeks. As in 1235–36 and 1255–58 William showed that his territorial ambitions extended far across the Isthmus of Corinth and embraced an overlordship of the Greek peninsula. The occasion for the attack was the death of the ruler of Nicaea, Theodore II Laskaris, and the accession of his young son, John IV Laskaris, in 1258. The troubled regency of the Mouzalon brothers, who were murdered in September when Michael Palaeologos usurped the regency, gave every encouragement that a weak response and easy gains could be expected from the campaign. Quarrels and disagreements between the allies, encouraged by an agent provocateur sent to the allied camp by Michael Palaeologos ensured that the Latin contingent stood almost alone at the decisive battle of Pelagonia.[44]

The battle was decisive since in the flight which followed many Frankish knights were captured, including William, who were led captive to Nicaea. The victorious Greek army swept into Boeotia to sack the city of Thebes whose lord was absent in France. This raid illustrated the extent to which a defeat by the Moreote Franks was seen in Greek eyes as a defeat for the Franks in general and to that extent a judgement on the success of the

---

[44] Geanakoplos, op.cit., pp.47–74; idem, 'Greco-Latin relations on the eve of the Byzantine restoration: the Battle of Pelagonia, 1259' *DOP* 7 (1953), 101–41.

Villehardouin's overlordship. For the first 60 years of Frankish Greece the princes of Achaia had set the agenda, but in 1259 their ambitions had ended in a haystack at Kastoria, where William was found hiding. The ignominy of Prince William's flight was lost sight of in the perils that now beset Frankish Greece, especially with the subsequent recapture of Constantinople by the Greeks of Nicaea in July 1261.

By 1260 it was clear that neither the Latin emperors nor the princes of Achaia could provide an acceptable or convincing leadership within the Frankish Aegean. By 1267 both the emperor Baldwin II and Prince William had been convinced of the need to subordinate their personal and familial ambitions to the rising fortunes of the house of Anjou. The Frankish states of the Aegean thus became virtual marcher lordships of the Angevin kingdom of Naples and no longer lordships in their own right. They become subsumed in the power politics of the Mediterranean as viewed from a Neapolitan perspective.

Angevin involvement in Greece

The death of William de Villehardouin at Kalamata on 1 May 1278 left the lord or megaskyr of Athens and Thebes as the leading ruler actually present in Frankish Greece and with ambitions to conquer territory in southern Thessaly to match this new prominence. However, a new overlord had inherited the position of both the Villehardouin and the Latin emperor, and the megaskyr would have to gauge just how effectively Charles of Anjou, now Charles I of Naples, would exploit his new position within Frankish Greece. Would he be so ineffectual in the Greek peninsula as the Latin emperors who had succeeded Henry in 1216? From the start it was clear that Angevin political ambitions in the Aegean were considerable. Indeed so had been those of the first Latin emperors. It was equally clear that, like the majority of the Latin emperors with regard to Greece, they would be absentee rulers.

By the terms of the Treaties of Viterbo the death of Philip of Anjou in 1277 had resulted in the bypassing of the interests of Isabelle de Villehardouin in the Morea, which now passed under the direct rule of Charles I of Naples. Lacking a spare son to take up the burden of these new lands, Charles, who could not absent himself from his Italian possessions, appointed regents to govern the principality in his name. These regents were noblemen from the kingdom of Naples with no background in the life and traditions of crusader Greece and they seemed more concerned with exploiting the rights of their master in Naples than in defending the principality from the Greeks.

It appeared that the Morea was indeed just a satellite of Naples since

Angevin troops were sent there unpaid and the prince's castles left unprovisioned. In this context in 1278, the duke of Athens was left in no doubt that he was to be involved with the Angevin scheme of things, when he was required to loan money to the regent, Galeran d'Ivray, for the payment of troops in order to limit some of the worst excesses of an unpaid soldiery living off the land. Although the loan was made to aid the megaskyr's overlord, the king of Naples, in the sensitive atmosphere amongst the barons of southern Greece it cannot have done his standing in the Morea any harm. Twelve years later, in 1290, when Florent de Hainault sought to exercise that suzerainty directly, he was met with a rebuff by the rulers of the duchy. It was, however, clear to all concerned that the suzerainty of the Villehardouin had passed to the rulers of Naples along with the rule of the Morea in 1267.

The Angevins were prepared to spend money on recapturing the city of Constantinople and restoring the Latin empire rather than on protecting what there was left of Frankish Greece. To be sure, that was a part of the empire but it was in the wrong place since the key to Constantinople for a land power was control of Epiros and the western end of the Via Egnatia. This was no new strategic appreciation, but earlier attempts to control the route had failed through under-resourcing and lack of local allies. The Angevins sought to remedy this by establishing a sound military presence and a system of local protectorates. Any spare Angevin resources were concentrated in consolidating and expanding the bridgehead around Avlona, which had first been secured for Charles by Villehardouin in 1269 with an attack on Byzantium in mind. The despots of Epiros had to be brought into alliance and here the fears of the despot Nikephoros, who lacked the forcefulness of his father Michael II who had died in 1267/8, were played upon. In 1265 he had been forced to take Anna Palaeologina, the niece of Michael VIII, as his bride and as a guarantee of the pro-Byzantine stance of the rulers of Epiros. Nikephoros hoped to use the Angevins to counter any ambitions his relative might harbour and in 1279 had ceded important ports in Albania to Charles and had acknowledged him as suzerain.[45]

The attack came in 1280, one year after Charles had appointed the Burgundian noble Hugues de Sully, known as 'le rousseau', as captain-general and vicar of Albania with the task of leading an overland expedition to Constantinople. The ease with which Angevin suzerainty had been accepted in Epiros perhaps lead to over-confidence in the leadership of the Angevin army. De Sully opened his campaign with the siege of Berat which gave access to the Via Egnatia. Here, in April 1281, a Byzantine relieving force succeeded in capturing him while he was out reconnoitering without a sufficient escort, and thereafter routing the Angevin army. At about the same time in July 1281 in Orvieto, Charles was cementing a grand alliance

[45] Nicol, op.cit., pp.9–33 for details on this and the next paragraph.

with the Venetians and possibly the despot of Epiros to put a combined naval and land assault on Constantinople in motion for the spring of 1283. The serious intent of this Angevin scheme was not lost on Michael VIII and most certainly would not have escaped the attention of Frankish rulers, who could see their own territorial interests sacrificed to the wider ambitions of the Angevins.

Angevin attentions were, however, diverted elsewhere in March 1282 by an uprising in Palermo which soon spread to the whole of the island of Sicily. Known since 1500 as the 'Sicilian Vespers', it was apparently engineered by Michael VIII in order to delay any further Angevin aggression in the Aegean.[46] For the next 20 years they fought Sicilian rebels and Aragonese invaders in order to maintain their throne. No Italian ruler could embark upon Aegean enterprises if not secure at home. Ironically the scheme of William de Villehardouin to save his possessions in Greece had resulted in the transfer of Moreote knights and resources to support the Angevins.[47]

Angevin ambitions for the control of the Aegean world did not evaporate in 1282 but were merely postponed. The tenacity with which the house of Anjou pursued its aims for the territorial acquisition of Greek lands and the possession of Constantinople shows just how beguiling was the prospect of a Latin emperor of Constantinople in the Mediterranean world, always provided that he had the right western lineage. This had been what the emperors from Flanders had lacked. Certainly their reception in the west in the years before 1261 would not have led anyone to suppose that a cadet branch of the French royal family would seek that sovereign title with such enthusiasm. It is unknown to what extent the opportunity to control of the routes from the Black Sea to western Europe occupied their thoughts, but they were following a long-standing tradition of Aegean expansion by the rulers of Sicily. After the battle of Benevento the Angevins had taken over not just the south Italian lands of the Normans and Hohenstaufen but also the dreams of its rulers like Robert Guiscard (d. 1085), Roger II (d. 1154) and Manfred (d. 1265).

As the war in Sicily commenced around 1283, serious attempts were made to reconcile the Franks in Greece to Angevin rule with the appointment of the first indigenous Frankish lord as baili of the Morea. This was Guy de Tremouille, lord of Chalandritsa who was followed in 1285 by William de la Roche, duke of Athens and Thebes, and in 1287 by Nicholas II de St Omer, lord of half Thebes and one of the wealthiest and most famous lords in Greece. Not only were indigenous lords felt to be essential but were lords of sufficient standing to compel respect where it was not given freely. Here was a tacit acknowledgement on the part of the Angevins

---

[46] S. Runciman, *The Sicilian Vespers* (Cambridge, 1958) where the wider issues of the Aegean and Mediterranean politics are discussed.
[47] Setton, pp.140–62.

both of the position of the dukes of Athens within Greece and of the thwarted ambitions of the de la Roche as heirs to the Villehardouin.

Then in 1289 a further change was made, this time with the agreement of the barons of the Morea. Isabelle de Villehardouin, the eldest daughter of William, had been a widow living in Naples since 1277 and kept away from the political life of the Morea. Now she was seen as a way of reconciling the Moreot barons to Angevin rule and was, provided a suitable husband could be found, no threat to that rule. A husband was found in the person of Florent de Hainault, a forty-year-old soldier of fortune who was fighting in the Sicilian wars. He was both of proven ability and highly-kinned, at least in terms of the Frankish Aegean, being the descendant of Baldwin of Flanders and the first lord of Negroponte, Jacques d'Avesnes. He was also distantly related to Charles II of Naples himself. Between June and September 1289, immediately before the marriage to Florent in Naples on 16 September, Isabelle was granted the lordships of Karytaina and Araklova and the title of princess of the Morea.[48] Charles made the grant for reasons 'of restitution and concessions', motivated by generosity and good will. However, whatever might be read into those words in terms of Angevin guilt at the treatment of Isabelle over the last twelve years, the Angevin monarch took care to limit the succession of the principality. The succession to the principality was to pass to the heirs of the body of Florent and Isabelle, saving the homage due to Charles. Any daughters were not to contract marriage without Charles's consent and approval and the same restriction applied to Isabelle herself should Florent predecease her.

Central Greece, Epiros and Thessaly, 1270–1309

The lords of Athens had in large part restored the prestige which they had lost to the Villehardouin in the aftermath of the battle of Karydi in 1258. Since the 1260s they had developed ambitions of their own and perhaps saw themselves as the only sure hope for the defence of Frankish Greece. We have already noted the efforts of Jean de la Roche (1263–80) in Euboea and southern Thessaly. His successor William (d. 1287) continued to expand Frankish control around Lamia and Gardiki in order to place lands between the Greeks in Thessaly and the heartland of his duchy around Thebes. In this he placed much reliance on his Greek father-in-law, John I Doukas, the sebastokrator of Thessaly, whose daughter, Helena, he had married sometime between 1273 and 1275.[49] In 1285, when he was invited to

---

[48] Perrat & Longnon, docs 1, 5–8, (pp.21–9).
[49] Nicol, op.cit., p.67.

become baili for the Angevin monarchy in the Morea, he began the construction of the castle at Dimatra, on the boundary between Skorta and Messenia. His successor as baili in 1287 was Nicholas II de St Omer, lord of one half of Thebes and the husband of Villehardouin's widow, Anna Doukaina. He too built castles in the south-west at Navarino and Maniatochori near Modon. The builders were both extremely rich men and these structures were as much about their status in Frankish Greece as about protecting the interest of their suzerain in Messenia from Greek and Venetian challenge.[50] In the appointment of indigenous Frankish bailies, the Angevin monarchy had had to acknowledge the standing of lords from central Greece and during the late 1280s had had to use them as their representatives in the Morea. During these years the dynamism of the old Villehardouin principality of the Morea seemed to be passing to the duchy of Athens and Thebes, where substantial indigenous Frankish lords could still be found. This made the next change in the devolution of Angevin authority in the Morea hard to endure in central Greece and was to lead to a bitter feudal wrangle in the 1290s.

By 1289 the aspirations of the house of de la Roche seemed at an end. Duke William had died two years before and was succeeded by his infant son Guy II or Guyot. The arrival of Isabelle and Florent in the Morea in November 1289 meant the arrival of a suzerain in fact as well as in name and with them the revival of the old Villehardouin claims. Between 1287 and 1294 the guardians of the young duke, that is his mother Helena Doukaina and after 1291 her second husband Hugues de Brienne as well, concentrated on preserving the ducal rights and avoiding military entanglements in Thessaly. They also avoided rendering homage to either Florent de Hainault or King Charles II and seemed intent on severing the feudal tie between the duchy and the principality of Achaia. They dodged the issue of the homage due for Argos and Nauplion, but were careful not to deny the general suzerainty of the kings of Naples which seemed acceptable so long as it remained distant and vague. In January and May both parties ignored summonses to the Angevin court, then in Provence. The whole dispute was concerned with the relative prestige of the contending parties within Frankish Greece, and dragged on until 1294 when it vanished from our sources. Whatever its eventual settlement, it did show just how shaky Angevin dominion really was in practice in the face of local interests and hauteur.[51]

The ambitions of the de la Roche and the claims of the Villehardouin seem set fair to be united in 1299 in defiance of the best laid Angevin schemes. On 23 January 1297 Florent de Hainault died at Andravida, leaving Isabelle to rule the Morea in her own right and a three-year-old

[50] L de C, 547, 554; X t M, 7987–92, 8093–8; BMF, p.159, 654.
[51] Setton, pp.433–40.

daughter Mathilde or Mahaut as the fruit of their union. Over the next eighteen months, apparently on the advice of Nicholas III of St Omer, marshal of the Morea and lord of half Thebes, a marriage alliance was proposed between Mahaut and Duke Guy II of Athens that would have the effect of uniting Frankish Greece under a ruler produced by the union of the two most important families going back to the days of the original conquest. Naturally the Angevins were unmoved by such a convenient arrangement and complained that the marriage had been agreed without the necessary consent. A canonical dispensation was required since the consenting parties were related in the third degree of consanguinity. This impediment was removed by papal dispensation given at Anagni on 9 August 1299 '... *pro bono pacis*'. After consultations with Pope Boniface VIII, Charles II also removed his objections and wrote to Duke Guy to this effect in April 1300.[52]

Other paper arrangements made in Naples also produced a reaction on the part of Frankish lords intent on protecting their own interests rather than acting as good Angevin vassals. In 1294 Charles II took advantage of the coming of age of his fourth and favourite son, Philip, to regularise the feudal dispute between the Villehardouin and the de la Roche, and to institute tighter control of the Angevin lands in Greece. He definitely granted the overlordship of the duchy of Athens to Florent, saving the homage now owed to Philip. Since 1291 when the marriage of Philip to Thamar, the daughter of Nikephoros, despot of Epiros, was first mooted, Charles II was forming a scheme to rationalise the Angevin claims to the Latin empire in the person of his favourite son. In February 1294 Philip was created prince of Taranto, a principality facing Greece across the Straits of Otranto with convenient harbours for access to the same. On 13 August he was granted the suzerainty of all Angevin possessions in Greece and given outright possession of Corfu and Butrinto. Soon after he was married to Thamar, who brought in her dowry a sum of 100,000 hyperpera a year and a string of fortresses – Naupaktos, Eulochos, Angelokastro, and Vonitsa – which ensured control of the Corinthian Gulf and the southern approaches to Epiros.[53] Some move in this area could clearly be expected.

Military interference in Epiros and Thessaly had always been a natural area of interest to the rulers of central Greece because of the integrity of its borders which that might entail. The marriage of William de la Roche and Helena Doukaina of Neopatras had brought not only substantial additions of territory to the duchy but also, by bringing the two rulers together, the prospect of peace on its northern frontier. However, Angevin interests in

---

[52] Perrat & Longnon, docs 21 (pp.181–2) and 237 (pp. 201–2); G. Digard, ed., *Les Registres de Boniface VIII* II, (Paris, 1890), no. 3175; Setton, pp.436–7.
[53] Nicol, op.cit., p.47.

Epiros and Thessaly were tending to cut across the interests of the dukes, especially with the build-up of Philip of Taranto's position in 1294.[54]

The relationship between the duke of Athens and his northern and western neighbour, the sebastokrator of Thessaly, labelled the duke of Neopatras by the Franks, became closer with the recovery of Constantinople by the Greeks of Nicaea in 1261. Both jealous of their independence they now shared a common aggressor. The despot of Arta Michael II had conferred the lands around Neopatras on his illegitimate son John Doukas sometime in the 1250s. Certainly at the battle of Pelagonia in 1259, Duke John, firmly in control in Neopatras, had changed sides at a critical moment in the battle leaving William de Villehardouin to defeat and capture. Inclined to the Byzantine cause by religion and culture, personal ambition inclined the rulers of Thessaly to side with the Franks. On the death of the despot Michael II in 1267/8 (or 1271?) this informal landed provision for an illegitimate offspring took on a more formal character. The legitimate heir, Nikephoros, ruled Old Epiros from Arta and, as we have noted, had sought to preserve his independence from Byzantine control by linking his house and his interests with those of the Angevins. As a constant reminder of the Byzantine threat to his despotate was his second wife, Anna. His father had offered military resistance to the Byzantines in the years 1261–63, but in 1264 had had to climb down in the face of a considerable military demonstration at Thessalonika led by Michael VIII himself. The emperor sought to keep a watchful eye on the despots and had forced Michael to agree to the marriage of his son and heir, Nikephoros, to his niece Anna Palaeologina. The marriage took place in 1265.[55]

Across the Pindos mountains in Neopatras, John I Doukas controlled the territory from the Gulf of Corinth at Galaxidhi right up to Thessalian Olympos. This territory thus formed the northern and western border of the lordship of Athens and Thebes and thus the two areas tended to be drawn closer together in the face of a common threat. An interesting measure of the feudal terminology infiltrating the Byzantine court in the late thirteenth century, and at the same time confirmation of the very real interests of the Byzantines in both Thessaly and Epiros, was recorded in the Papal Registers in 1280. Michael VIII Palaeologos explained to the envoys of Pope Nicholas III his difficulty in imposing religious union in all his lands, especially his westernmost dominions. This was due to the obstinacy of Nikephoros and John, both described as liege men of his empire.[56] In 1283, one year after his father's death, Andronikos II mounted a campaign aimed to bring the rulers of Arta and Neopatras to heel, and again in 1292 there were to be Byzantine

---

[54] P. Magdalino, 'Between Romaniae: Thessaly and Epiros in the Later Middle Ages', in B. Arbel et al., eds, op.cit., pp.87–110.
[55] Nicol, op.cit., pp.93–35 and 63–81.
[56] J. Gay, ed., *Les Registres de Nicolas III* (Paris, 1898–1938), 135A, discussed in Geanakoplos, op.cit., p.323.

attacks on Arta. This Byzantine policy of alternating blandishments with violence turned the rulers of Arta and Neopatras towards the Franks. In 1273 John seemed to incline towards an Angevin alliance. In a trade treaty of that year concerned with silk imports to Apulia he was addressed by Charles I as '*Ducis Patere Karrissimi amici nostri*'.[57] However, Angevin and Athenian interests could conflict in this area if the interests and ambitions of their Greek allies in Epiros/Thessaly should collide. Byzantine pressure kept the rulers of Epiros and Thessaly more or less in the same camp during the 1280s. Difficulties would appear when family interests and vendettas turned them against one another. This was likely given the web of dynastic and feudal ties being formed in the region by the competing Byzantine, Angevin and Frankish power blocks against a back-cloth of the political schizophrenia of the local Greek rulers.

During the 1270s the emperor Michael VIII sought to convince Popes Gregory X (1271–76), Innocent V (1276) and Nicholas III (1277–81) of the sincerity of his declared desire to bring about religious union and thereby protect his empire from the growing threat of an Angevin attack. He was prepared to bring force to bear on outspoken opponents of his uniate policy. It appears that most destruction to monastic property on Mount Athos, which has been traditionally blamed on the Latins, was done by the agents of Michael in these years.[58] One of these opponents, as we have seen, was John Doukas. John, motivated at least in part by sincere religious feelings, set himself up as the protector of Orthodoxy, encouraged ecclesiastical refugees from Constantinople to make a home in his lands, and through the agency of a church council composed of such exiled bishops secured the excommunication of Michael VIII and his patriarch.

In late 1296 Nikephoros of Arta died, leaving the regency for his six-year-old son Thomas in the hands of his widow, Anna Palaeologina, an able and ambitious woman who often acted against the decisions of her husband. Having failed to gain an imperial Byzantine groom for her daughter Thamar in 1291, she had had to acquiesce in her husband's decision to marry Thamar to Philip of Taranto and thus bring the despotate further under Angevin control. Earlier, in 1283, she had helped Andronikos II secure the person of Michael Doukas, the son and heir of John I Doukas, by luring him to Arta under pretence of arranging a marriage with one of her daughters. This successful abduction was followed up by a destructive raid on Arta by the disconsolate John which succeeded in destroying the property of some Venetian merchants there and a somewhat unsuccessful and under-financed campaign in Thessaly on the part of Andronikos. What might have led to Epirote control of Thessaly under Byzantine hegemony

---

[57] F. Carabellese, *Carlo d'Angio nei rapporti politici e commerciali con Venezia e l'Oriente* (Bari, 1911), pp. 36, 42–3, cited in Geanakoplos, op.cit., p.328,

[58] F.W. Hasluck, *Athos and its Monasteries* (London, 1924), pp.28–9. See p.226.

came to nothing. Relations were broken off between Arta and Constantinople soon after. The next Byzantine army to campaign in the area was aimed against Arta itself in 1292 and provoked the intervention of Florent of Hainault, the last incident recorded in the Greek version of the *Chronicle of the Morea*. Nonetheless, Anna was inclined towards a Byzantine alliance and the acquisition of land from the duchy of Neopatras, with whose ruling family a state of vendetta might be said to have existed since the abduction of Michael, who was to remain a captive in Constantinople until his death trying to escape in 1307.[59]

In Neopatras John I Doukas had died in 1289, leaving his eldest son Michael still a prisoner in Constantinople and two minors, Constantine and Theodore, to succeed him. Andronikos II tried to marry the captive Michael into the imperial family and thereby ensure the attachment of the Thessalian lands to Byzantium. Failing this, he seems to have stage-managed the retirement of John's widow to a nunnery. Certainly an imperial charter was readily granted in March 1289 to the convent which she founded at Lykosada near Phanari in Thessaly. The minors were granted the court titles of sebastokrator, but now without a guardian from their own immediate family they were placed under the protection of Anna Palaeologina, the aunt who had betrayed their elder brother six years before.

Constantine must soon have attained his majority since during the early 1290s he seems to have assisted his aunt Helena Doukaina, the regent of the duchy of Athens, in the evasion of her feudal duties as defined by the Angevins. In 1294 he and his brother, Theodore Angelos, occupied Demetrias on the Gulf of Volos, a possession of the Byzantine emperor, and the next year they mounted an attack on Arta in which they confounded the Angevin military adviser there, seized the towns of Angelokastro, Acheloos and Naupaktos and provoked a series of orders from Charles II to Florent de Hainault to assist the despot Nikephoros against the '… duke of Neopatras and [Theodore] Angelos, his brother'.[60] Peace was restored in 1296 and the towns, which had formed part of Thamar's dowry to Philip of Taranto, returned.

In the to and fro of Angevin/Aragonese fighting in Sicily, Philip of Taranto was captured in 1299 and remained a prisoner until released by the terms of the Treaty of Caltabellota in 1302. Angevin control and interference in Greek affairs was thus limited. Charles II had negotiated a general peace with Andronikos II in 1300 that was intended to cover the whole of Greece. However, events in Thessaly showed both the resentment of the Angevin dominance of the area and the extent to which the Aegean area and Frankish Greece in particular had become an appendage of western European power politics.

---

[59] Nicol, op.cit.
[60] Nicol, op.cit., p.49.

Anna Palaeologina needed Angevin support to maintain her six-year-old son Thomas as despot in Arta and had assisted her daughter Thamar in raising the ransom for the release of Philip of Taranto. In 1302 the sebastokrators of Neopatras had seized lands in Epiros and Charles had ordered the barons of Achaia and Athens to assist Anna. Soon after, Constantine of Neopatras died, leaving a minor to succeed him. For whatever family reasons, Constantine had secured the agreement of his cousin Duke Guy II to act as guardian for his infant son John, and Guy had appointed one Boutomites, labelled 'Vucomity' in the *Chronicle of the Morea*, as his baili in Neopatras.[61] Anna took advantage of this situation to occupy the fortress of Phanari and thus to challenge the control of the young duke of Athens in the lands on his northern frontier. Guy called on his vassals to provide warriors for an expedition against Ioannina in 1303. One of these, Nicholas III de St Omer, as well as being lord of half Thebes was also marshal of the Morea, and as such forbidden by the prince of Achaia to take part. He did anyway and his absence from the Morea in part contributed to the successful revolt of the archons of Skorta who destroyed the castles of St Helena and Crevecour in the Alpheios valley.[62]

In the meantime Guy led a glittering expedition to Thessaly which, allowing for the colourful and exaggerated description in the chronicle, intimidated the Epirotes sufficiently to force them to relinquish Phanari and pay an indemnity of 10,000 hyperpera to be shared by the duke and Nicholas de St Omer.[63] The florid language used in the French version of the chronicle has contributed much to the romantic perception of Frankish Greece. Nothing is further from the truth. The Thessalian archontes in the army were given the credit for negotiating the practical and profitable outcome to the campaign.[64] Honour had been maintained and any defiance of the Angevins implicit in attacking their vassal Anna Palaeologina had been avoided. The Thessalian archons now persuaded the expedition to raid towards Thessalonika to gain more plunder and to weaken the hand of the Byzantine emperor who threatened their own possessions. The expedition turned back before reaching Thessalonika, apparently not wishing to inconvenience Yolande-Eirene de Montferrat, who sent messengers to inform them that she was in the city. They gained a reputation for honour and *courtoisie* thereby but they were also at pains to send messengers to Andronikos II excusing their aggressive action and apparently blaming his advisers for threatening behaviour towards the archons of Thessaly.[65] Here, too, a tacit acknowledgement of Angevin suzerainty was operating. The Angevins had signed a peace treaty with Andronikos in 1300 which had

[61] L de C, 873–80.
[62] L de C, 920–51; BMF, p.178.
[63] L de C, 891–914.
[64] L de C, 904–7.
[65] L de C, 916.

brought a measure of stability to the Morea after nearly 30 years of war and this the duke of Athens dared not upset. However, it was made clear in the chronicle that he alone sent the '*ij chevaliers et ij arcondes grex de la Blaquie*' as envoys to the emperor. Guy had succeeded in asserting some sort of protectorate over Thessaly thereby and for the first time since 1259 a Frankish lord from mainland Greece was playing a role on an Aegean-wide scene.

Courtoisie need not mean the abandonment of practical politics. By the late thirteenth century notions of chivalry and epic were very influential in the thought world of the leading men of Frankish Greece. In his short account of the Franks in the Aegean, Professor Mayer devoted space to the cultivated taste of William de Villehardouin (1246–78) and his circle, one product of which was the richly illuminated *Manuscrit du Roi* (Bibliothèque Nationale, Paris, Franc. 844).[66] Villehardouin enjoyed some celebrity as a chansonier and the manuscript contains two of his songs.[67] The castle at Thebes contained rich frescoes depicting the crusades, which not only paid tribute to Nicholas II de St Omer's wife Marie of Antioch but also placed the Frankish states consciously within the crusade tradition. In that very castle Muntaner witnessed the elaborate knighting ceremonies of Duke Guy in 1296.

It is unclear whether the failure of the Angevins to intervene in 1303 in what was essentially a dispute between their vassals, Anna of Epiros and Guy of Athens, convinced Anna to follow her predilections and to seek out Byzantine protection for the interests of her son, Thomas. Whilst acknowledging the claims of her son-in-law, Philip of Taranto, to the towns in southern Epiros, which had formed part of Thamar's dowry, she refused to pay homage to him for the despotate itself. Early in 1304 Charles II reminded her of the terms of the marriage contract of 1294. The Angevin claim was a legal one but it had to be enforced, like all the legally-justifiable claims which were to be made on Frankish lands in Greece in the fourteenth century. The Angevins had more resources behind their claim than many later claimants and so in the summer of 1304 troops were sent from southern Italy and the prince of Achaia, Philip of Savoy, was ordered to meet up with them in Epiros, with a force from the Morea. The united force undertook two futile siege operations at Arta and at Rogoi and then withdrew.

A further campaign was set by the Angevins for the spring of 1305. The lords of Frankish Greece seemed unenthusiastic for another campaign of sieges, which cost them dear in the furtherance of Angevin interests. This lack of enthusiasm was shared by Philip of Savoy in particular. He had been forced upon Charles II as a suitable consort for Isabelle de Villehardouin by

---

[66] H.E. Mayer, *The Crusades* 2nd edn (Oxford, 1988), pp.196–213, esp. p.209.
[67] J. Longnon, 'Le Prince de Morée Chansonnier' *Romania* 257 (1939), 95–100.

Pope Boniface VIII in 1300. The return of Philip of Taranto to active political life in 1302 and Philip's own poor showing in the Epirote campaign of 1304 both induced Charles to declare his tenure of the principality of Achaia as forfeit on 9 October 1304.[68] Uncertain of his future in the Morea, if not of his feudal obligations, Philip of Savoy was the more open to a payment of 10,000 hyperpera from Anna not to participate in the forthcoming campaign in the spring of 1305. As a plausible excuse to offer Charles, and on the advice of Nicholas de St Omer, he summoned a parlement to meet at Corinth for May 1305. The baronage of Greece must also have welcomed this opportunity not to participate in the campaign. The tournaments that took place on the occasion of the parlement is the point at which the French version of the *Chronicle of the Morea* ended.[69]

The Angevins continued to make paper plans and dispositions for their lands in Greece. These schemes were both legalistic and dynastic in their inspiration and have a certain theoretical air about them. They not only overlooked the human failings of those involved but treated the Frankish territories in Greece as an Angevin appanage and gave scant attention to its governmental and military problems. The passing of the house of Villehardouin focused the attention of the chroniclers upon the legality of various claims to the title of prince of Achaia. Important as the personality of the ruler was in this era of personal monarchy, no ruler could achieve very much if he was always absent from the lands which he claimed as part of a wider European territorial estate. On 5 June 1306 the barons of the Morea were released from their allegiance to Philip of Savoy and Isabelle. One year later on 2 May 1307 the couple's claim to the principality was bought off by Charles II for the reversion on the county of Alba in Italy, now raised to the rank of a principality and an annuity of 600 gold onzi. Isabelle died in 1311. In 1312 Philip of Savoy married Catherine Dauphine de Viennois. The male descendants of this marriage continued to style themselves princes of Achaia until the line died out with Louis of Savoy in October 1418.

In 1307 Philip of Taranto became prince of Achaia. One year earlier in June 1306 he had crossed to the Morea with an army of 10,000 men campaigning to recover lost territory from the Greeks of Mistra in which he gained some success regaining the castle of Tripotamos. Leaving a certain Thomas de Marzano as his lieutenant to continue the war against the Greeks, he entered Epiros where his army was ravaged by disease and achieved nothing. He then returned to Italy to revisit Greece no more. On his departure he appointed Guy II de la Roche baili of Achaia, presumably to silence the claims which the duke and his thirteen-year-old wife Mahaut,

---

[68] Nicol, op.cit., p.60; R. Rodd, *The Princes of Achaia* ... II (London, 1907) pp.279–82.
[69] L de C, 1003–24.

the daughter of Isabelle and Florent, were making to the title of the principality.[70]

Just as the extinction of the Villehardouin had led to the subsuming of the Morea into the political aspirations of west Mediterranean rulers, the same fate awaited the duchy of Athens and Thebes when the line of the de la Roche failed in 1308. On 5 October 1308 Duke Guy II died childless at the age of 28, worn out by debauchery. Two of Guy's cousins came forward to dispute the title for the duchy. Gautier (or Walter) de Brienne was the son of Guy's aunt Isabelle and her second husband Hugues de Brienne. Isabelle had died in 1279 and in 1291 Hugues had married Guy's own mother Helena Doukaina, and as such had been baili and regent during the minority of Guy. Hugues had died in 1296. The other claimant was Eschiva de Ibelin, lady of Lapithos in Cyprus. She was the daughter of Alix or Alice de la Roche and John II de Ibelin, the lord of Beirut. The custom of the Morea laid down that in the case of a disputed claim between two relatives of equal degree but of different gender the male claim should be preferred. The court of peers thus decided in favour of Gautier. Gautier was to die fighting the Catalans on 15 March 1311. He left an infant son Gautier and a daughter Isabelle. The son became titular duke of Athens and as constable of France was killed fighting the English at Maupertuis in 1356. The title thereafter passed to the descendants of Isabelle, who had married Gautier III d'Enghien in 1320. The title remained in the house of Enghien until 1381.

The arrival of the Catalans in Greece

The duchy of Athens was wrested from the hands of its legitimist rulers by conquest. The conquerors were the Catalan Grand Company, themselves a force that the wars between Aragon and the Angevins in Sicily had brought into being and after the Peace of Caltabellota in August 1302 passed on to the Aegean world. The leadership, formation and movements of this company show how intertwined were the interests and the ambitions of rulers both in the Aegean and in the central Mediterranean, just how subordinate and dependant the former had become on the latter, and the sort of persons now seeking to improve their fortunes in the east in the late thirteenth and fourteenth centuries.

The Catalan Company had formed around Roger de Flor. He was the son of a German soldier who had been killed fighting for the Hohenstaufen at Tagliacozzo in 1265. Sometime in the early 1270s the eight-year-old Roger began his association with the Templars. In 1291 he rescued several

---

[70] L de F, 520–6; L de C, p.402; BMF, p.185.

nobles and considerable treasure from falling into Egyptian hands after the fall of Acre. At that time he was well-known as a Templar. The order accused him of purloining some of the treasure that he had saved, and thereafter he fled the order and set up on his own account. He made overtures to both sides in the Angevin–Aragonese war and eventually took service with Frederick II, the brother of James II of Aragon, when he became king of Sicily in 1296. According to the chronicler Ramon Muntaner, who served in the company, Roger formed a mercenary company composed of Catalans and Aragonese which rendered valuable service. The Peace of Caltabellota signed on 31 August 1302 brought an end to the wars in southern Italy and made the presence of large mercenary forces an expensive and unwonted liability. Roger was still wanted by the Templars and decided that approaches to the Byzantine empire might find profitable employment for his warriors and a refuge from the long arm of the Order of the Temple.

Accordingly, negotiations were successfully entered into with Andronikos II, who had use of the westerners in his conflict with the Turks. Angeliki Laiou has demonstrated that this was the first time that Andronikos had invited westerners into his empire and that he expected quick and decisive results. Although the Byzantine treasury lacked the resources to pay the mercenaries, Andronikos acted from desperation. The first time that the Osmanli or Ottoman Turks imposed themselves on Byzantine consciousness was their victory, recorded by Pachymeres, over a Byzantine army at Baphaeum (possibly mod. Koyunhisar) near Nicaea on 27 July 1301. Soon after they were on the coast of the Black Sea and the Sea of Marmara. Only a narrow strip of water separated the Turks from Constantinople. It was this situation that the Catalans were hired to deal with. In Sicily Frederick II was glad to see them go and provided the transport to enable them to start their new career.[71]

The Catalan army arrived in Constantinople in September 1303. According to Muntaner it numbered 1,500 cavalry, 4,000 Almogavers or lightly armed infantry and 1,000 foot soldiers together with their dependents. Ethnically it was composed of Catalans, Aragonese, south Italians and Sicilians.[72] Quartered at Cyzicus, they achieved some successes against the Turks in 1304. Roger de Flor was clearly sufficiently encouraged by this to contemplate the establishment of a principality in Asia Minor within the framework of the Byzantine empire. Other than that, their stay in Asia Minor was marked by violence and plundering from their hosts, provoked by frequent disagreements over pay as stipulated in the terms of their contract. During 1304 there was growing suspicion among both the Genoese

---

[71] For this and following paragraphs see A. Laiou, *Constantinople and the Latins, The Foreign Policy of Andronicus II, 1282–1328* (Harvard, 1972), pp. 128–242; Setton, p.441; Muntaner, *Cronica,* cc. 201–41.
[72] Muntaner, *Cronica,* c.201.

in Pera and from them in the imperial court itself that the Catalans might well join in a projected expedition against Byzantium planned by Frederick III of Sicily. During early 1305 the Catalans raided the area around Gallipoli, where they were now based, in order to force the emperor to pay their arrears. That apart, Roger de Flor seemed content to receive the title of caesar and a Greek wife, Maria. On 30 April 1305 he was murdered in the camp of Michael IX, apparently out of jealousy rather than any deeper diplomatic motive. From then on, relations between the Catalans and their employers deteriorated and the years 1305–8 were marked by raids in Thrace (Macedonia and Thessaly) in which the monasteries on Mount Athos were attacked.

During this time, from August 1307 until some time in 1310, the company was subsidised and retained by Charles of Valois, the brother of Philip IV le Bel of France, and since 1301 the husband of Catherine de Courtenay, the titular empress of Constantinople, who sought to use them to recapture Constantinople. He sent Thibaut de Cepoy as his representative. Neither Aragonese nor Capetian plans to use the Catalans to capture Constantinople came to anything. The Picard knight, Thibaut, could do nothing with the Catalans and returned home. They were then employed by Gautier de Brienne, the duke of Athens, to further his ambitions in Thessaly, where the ruler of Neopatras, the former ward of the late Duke Guy, was turning to Constantinople and Arta for support. The ambitions of the Catalans for territory and the problems caused by unpaid mercenaries had all been amply demonstrated in the years since 1303 when they had been in the Aegean. Operating from the duchy by 1310 they seem to have captured Domokos and Halmyros. In 1311 Gautier sought to dismiss the bulk of his Catalan troops retaining some in his service and sending the rest away. The Catalans, based on the port of Halmyros defied him and he had to resort to force to clear them out. The result was the annihilation of the Frankish army of over 700 knights somewhere near Halmyros on Monday 15 March 1311, a decisive battle which resulted in the control of the duchy passing to the Catalan Company.[73] Sometime in 1312 the Catalans in the duchy recognised the overlordship of the Aragonese crown of Sicily and adopted a new seal depicting the head of St George.

By the end of the thirteenth century the indigenous rulers of Frankish Greece had disappeared, at least on the mainland. Their territorial ambitions and their biological failure to produce male successors had linked the

---

[73] L de F, 551–3. This battle was thought to have been fought near Thurion in Boeotia and was dubbed the battle of Cephissus; see W. Miller, *The Latins in the Levant* (London, 1908), p.227, followed by N. Cheetham, *Medieval Greece* (Yale, 1981), pp.140–1. However, D. Jacoby has shown that the battle was fought at Halmyros in Thessaly, see 'Catalans, Turcs et Venitiens en Romanie (1305–1332) ...' *Studi medievali*, 3rd ser., 15 (1974), 223–30, reprinted in idem, *Recherches sur la Mediterranée orientale du XIIe au XVe siècle* (London, 1979).

fortunes of their territories to the power struggles between the royal families of France and Aragon for control of the Mediterranean. The background, instincts and necessities of the original conquerors had made the French royal family and French culture the dominating influence throughout the thirteenth century. The next century was to see the dominance of Italian influence and dynasts in the Aegean area.

Mainland Greece in the Fourteenth and Fifteenth Centuries

Ethos and influences

The political map of the Aegean became even more complex and intricate in the fourteenth and fifteenth centuries. At the very beginning of the fourteenth century both the Catalans and the Ottoman Turks made their appearance in the Aegean. At first each constituted what was basically a military presence, but within a decade they had set about state-building in their own right. The Catalans were to disappear from the record of Aegean history by 1388. The Ottoman Turks were eventually to destroy the Latin states in the Aegean and to restore that region once again into a centralised imperial system ruled from Constantinople.

New dynasties replaced the original Frankish families of the conquest period, most of which had become extinct by the early fourteenth century. Some, like the Acciaioli, the Briennes, the Foucherolles, the Misito and the le Maure, were new arrivals; others, like the Ghisi, the Tocci and the Zaccaria, rose to greater prominence.

The number of titular claimants to principalities in the region proliferated and in 1312 an additional suzerain from the west Mediterranean emerged in the person of Frederick II of Sicily (1295–1337). The female descendants of William de Villehardouin had little choice but to accept the provisions of the Treaty of Viterbo of 1267 with as much grace as they could muster. As long as they lived they presented a threat to the Angevin dynastic schemes in the Aegean. Any noble adventurer who was able to gain their hands in marriage could establish a claim to the principality of Achaia in right of his wife. This was no easy task in view of the strict supervision which the Angevins of Naples sought to exercise over the choice of marriage partners for the Villehardouin princesses, but the infante Ferrando of Majorca achieved such a marriage in 1315. Jacques de Savoy (d. 1367), the son of Philip of Savoy by his second wife Catherine the dauphine of Viennois, laid a claim to the principality of Achaia in the 1360s and thus started a claim which was only dropped when his descendants became kings of Italy in 1861. The descendants of Gautier I de Brienne, who was killed at the battle of Halmyros, actively maintained a claim on the duchy of Athens to the end of the fourteenth century, whilst Gautier's supplanters, the Catalan Company, acknowledged the suzerainty of the Aragonese king of Sicily in 1312. The Angevin–Aragonese rivalry in Sicily seemed set fair to enter the Aegean.

Less dramatic but really much more significant in its long-term implications for society in the southern tip of the Balkans was the infiltration of Albanian clan groups into Thessaly and Greece which begun sometime before 1348. The Venetian report of an Albanian raid on Pteleon in south-west Thessaly in 1350 is the first record of a group which can be securely identified as ethnic Albanians in Greece.[1] The Albanians were graziers and farmers. They soon began to leave off raiding and to establish new village communities in the area. It was not long before their aptitude and availability as agricultural colonists was recognised by the rulers of the Frankish states to the south of Thessaly. Faced with widespread rural depopulation, these Latin rulers chose to ignore the Albanian penchant for brigandage and vied with each other in offering incentives and tax concessions to clan chiefs in order to attract Albanian settlement. Sizeable Albanian communities still exist in Greece and the islands.[2]

Violence seemed on the increase or at least there were more groups prepared to achieve their interests by this means. By 1300 Greek reconquest had driven the Franks from the islands of Chios, Mytilene, Kos, Samos and Rhodes. In the Peloponnese the Greek despots of Mistra kept up military pressure on the Latins and were soon to confine them to the coastal plain of the north and west, and within a century to limit them to Glarenza and Patras. The Catalans raided into the Peloponnese, Euboea and Thessaly, whilst Turkish sea-borne raids across the Aegean were settling into an annual pattern by 1316. Within 30 years the Turks had replaced the Byzantines as the principal enemy of Latin Christendom in the Aegean. Pirates, slavers, and raiders of all ethnic backgrounds profited from this further fragmentation of political authority. The displacement of coastal and island populations caused by this raiding and slave-taking, together with the death-toll of the Black Death which swept through the Aegean in 1347–48, caused a depopulation of the countryside which no amount of Albanian settlement could offset. Military and naval pressure on the frontiers of Latin Romania had increased both in scale and quality. The Aegean was a much more dangerous place for its inhabitants in the fourteenth century.

---

[1] Thiriet, no.238 (14 March 1350).
[2] A.P. Kollias, *Arvanites Kai H Katagoge Ton Ellenon* (Athens, 1983); F.W. Hasluck, 'Albanians in the Islands' *ABSA* 15 (1908–9), 223–8.

In these disturbed conditions the Venetians and the Knights Hospitallers emerged as the only powers with the interest and the resources to counter the threat posed by the military and naval success of the Ottoman Turks and to a lesser extent the Catalans. By the end of the fourteenth century both Venetians and Hospitallers were to be invited by Latin and Greek rulers to occupy territory and to extend protectorates where their own local resources were inadequate to defend their subjects. This trend may be noted as early as 1321. This was a desperate time in the Angevin principality of the Morea. In September 1320 the Greeks of Mistra had captured the important baronial centres of Akova and Karytaina together with a number of lesser strongholds. John of Gravina, the absentee Angevin prince of Achaia, seemed powerless to send help. Jean de Baux, the preceptor of the Hospitallers acting for the Angevin baili, used the Franciscans in Achaia to sound out the Venetians regarding the possibility of their extending a protectorate over the Morea. Nothing came of these delicate approaches but they revealed a willingness to discard ineffective suzerains which was surprising.

A well-placed observer in about 1315 would have noticed a number of profound changes in the personnel and structure of medieval Greece. First, virtually all the noble founding-families of the early thirteenth century had died out. The male line of the Villehardouin had been extinguished with the death of Prince William in May 1278. Of his two daughters, Isabelle had died in retirement in Flanders in 1311 and her younger sister Margaret in 1315. Of his granddaughters, Mahaut had lost her husband, Louis of Burgundy, in 1315 and having disobliged the Angevins by refusing to marry John of Gravina, left the Morea in 1317 for imprisonment in Naples where she died in 1331. Isabelle of Sabran died in childbed in 1316. The line of the de la Roche dukes of Athens came to end with the death of Guy II in 1308 and the title passed to the family of de Brienne. Many Frankish families passed into extinction when their lords were killed at the battle of Halmyros in 1311. Two notable casualties were Renaud de la Roche, lord of Damala and the last male representative of the family, and Thomas III d'Autremencourt of Salona. Salona passed to the Catalans, Damala to the Zaccaria family through the heiress Jacqueline de la Roche. The St Omer family came to an end with the death of Nicholas III in 1314. For whatever reasons, environmental or military, the fertility of these Frankish families had not been good. The Venetian and Genoese rulers of the islands had a more successful record in this respect.

Greeks had always played some part in the councils of the Frankish conquerors, but in the early fourteenth century they were taking a much more prominent role. As we have seen, Greeks had virtually managed Guy II de la Roche's expedition into Thessaly in 1304. In the Morea, a representative of the Greek family of Misito was castellan of Kalamata in 1313 and by 1316 had established itself in the barony of Molines in

Messenia. The days when Blanche of Castile could caution the emperor Baldwin II against Greek advisers were long gone. There was a perceptible change too in those Greeks who opposed the Franks. Whereas the Greeks in 1205 had generally avoided pitched battles with the Latin armies and had retired instead to the defences of Akrocorinth and Argos, from the 1260s they sought out the Latins on the field of battle and on the sea.

The gap between principle and practice was increasing in the political world of the fourteenth century. In the Aegean the universalist ideology of the Roman church and the titles to empires and dukedoms put forward by various western families were acknowledged on paper and ignored in practice. Through most of the century the Catalan community in central Greece was under ban of interdict and its rulers excommunicated. This seemed to cause little inconvenience in the duchy of Athens where the ministrations of the Greek Orthodox Church seemed readily available to the Catalans. The political ambitions of the Angevins in the Aegean had carried much weight in the Mediterranean world in the late thirteenth century, but were much less prominent in the fourteenth. The materialisation of the Turkish threat produced a change from a crusade based around a powerful western potentate with ambitions in the Aegean, to a group response embodied in the Holy Leagues and their fleets in the 1330s and 1340s. Concomitant with this change in emphasis from the individual to the group, came a change from grand power politics to political settlement and from titular claims to real power on the ground. Possession was nine-tenths of the law in the valley and coastal politics of the Aegean. The Catalan chronicler Muntaner recorded his social misgivings about the Catalans who apportioned the lands and the widows of those whom they had slaughtered. He felt that they were not good enough to hold the finger-bowls of their new wives.[3] However, after due regard for these social niceties, it was the enterprise and good fortune of the company which struck Muntaner and that other sympathetic observer, James II of Aragon. A decisive battle and not the marriage bed was what had mattered, and nowhere was this to be seen more tellingly than in the Aegean in the fourteenth century. In 1314 the Catalans went on to promote their own brand of enterprise culture by granting the notional Latin kingdom of Thessalonika to a younger son of the dauphin of Viennois if he could capture and hold it: '... *acquirendo et suo dominio et jurisdictioni submittendo et subjiciendo ...*'.[4] The future lay with those who were actually present in the area.

A sound pedigree and a good marriage allied to hope and a deep pocket were the qualities shared by the various claimants to the Latin throne of Constantinople, the principality of Achaia, and the duchy of Athens. There was considerable difference between the resources devoted to these

---

[3] Ramon Muntaner, *Cronica*, c.CCXL. Setton, p.441. See p.291.
[4] DOC, no.LXX (p.88).

claims by the cadet branches of the French royal family, the Angevins and the Valois, and less wealthy claimants like the families of de Brienne and the counts of Savoy. The former could cause many waves in the papal curia and in diplomatic and noble circles. They could also keep representatives in the Aegean, like the succession of Angevin bailies and Thibaut de Cepoy, who met with the Catalans between 1307 and 1309 on behalf of Charles of Valois. The others had to campaign personally and could only set foot in Greece when financial and political conditions at home permitted. The Briennist claimants to the duchy of Athens could only afford two widely separated attempts to recover their ducal throne in 1330–31 and again in 1370–71. The climate and the terrain of Greece lent itself to the strategem of tactical withdrawal and delay, and this was just how the Catalans dealt with Gautier II de Brienne in 1331. His funds ran out and he was forced to give up. In between their projected expeditions to Greece these men made careers for themselves in the courts of western Europe. Gautier II de Brienne became tyrant of Florence in 1342–43 before his death on the field of Poitiers in 1356. The era of the titular ruler was passing. The claims might persist into the modern era, like the Savoyard claim to Achaia which was quietly dropped in the late nineteenth century, but they were more honoured in the breach after the fourteenth century.

It is ironic that as the age of realpolitik was dawning in the Aegean, none other than the Byzantine emperor Andronikos II should turn to noble western practices to better establish a title over territory he already possessed in fact. In 1284 he had married Yolande de Montferrat in order to extinguish the Montferrat claims to Thessalonika. The marriage was not a happy one and Thessalonika became the home of Yolande and, for the first time since 1224, free of any western claims. It is perhaps a measure of Byzantine decline on the Mediterranean stage that this marriage should have been performed to satisfy western notions of what constituted a title to real estate. Whatever his concern for a legally water-tight claim in western eyes, his troops did at least occupy the city which had been in Greek hands since 1224 and in possession of the legitimist emperors of Nicaea since 1246.[5] Even the Catalans had to acknowledge this, whatever they might think of the titular claims of western noble houses.

The Catalans in Greece, 1311–88

For the next 77 years following the battle of Halmyros in March 1311, the Catalans formed the dominant political group in central Greece.[6] In that

---

[5] A. Laiou, *Constantinople and the Latins* (Harvard, 1972), pp.45–6.
[6] For detailed accounts of the Catalan activities in the Aegean see K.M. Setton, *Catalan*

period of two generations the Catalans established themselves by violence and terror but failed either to reduce the number of their enemies or to endear themselves to their neighbours. Something of the violence and destruction caused by the Catalans is only now coming to light in excavations in Corinth which was sacked by the Catalans in 1312.[7] Strategically the area which they dominated was becoming increasingly important in western schemes to combat the Turks and to recover both Cilician Armenia and the Holy Land. This view of the Frankish states in Greece as an important area in the fight against Islam had had some currency since 1204, but received much greater emphasis in the fourteenth century. In 1304–5 Frederick II of Sicily had drawn attention to the value of the Aegean as a base for an attack on Egypt and Islamic lines of communications.[8] Six years later at a session of the Council of Vienne in November 1311, the strategic importance of central Greece and the potential role of the Catalans as crusaders was discussed.[9] Robert Burns has shown that these papal proposals to use the Catalans were not as preposterous as they might appear. The Catalans fought under a papal banner and displayed some crusading fervour in their attacks on the schismatic Greeks after 1305.[10] Seven years later the Catalans were unreceptive to these suggestions since, as Marino Sanudo observed in 1327, they had developed close ties with the Turks and Saracens.[11] Although they owed their introduction to the Aegean in 1302 to a contract with the Byzantines to fight the Ottoman Turks, they had soon established alliances on their own behalf with the emirates of Menteshe and Aydin. They recruited Turks into their army and had used them in their raids against the Christian states in Thrace and Boeotia in 1310–11, and in the years 1312–17 used them to ravage Angevin, Briennist and Venetian territory in the Morea and on Euboea.

During 1312 numerous complaints of Catalan slaughter and destruction were received in the papal curia and resulted in the excommunication of 'these senseless sons of damnation' and a threat of the use of the Knights Hospitallers against them. Certainly it was with a sense of

---

[6] *cont.*
Domination of Athens 1311–1388 revised edn (London, 1975); Setton, pp.441–68; DOC and A.E. Laiou, op.cit. For the repercussions of this east Mediterranean involvement on the court of Barcelona, see Placido de Jove y Heredia, 'Indagaciones acerca de los Ducados de Atenas y Neopatria en los coronas de Aragon y Sicilia' *Revista de Espana* 12 (1870), 230–68.
[7] C. Williams & O. Zervos, 'Frankish Corinth: 1991' *Hesperia* 61 (1992), 133–91.
[8] DOC, nos. XV and XV, cited R. Burns, 'The Catalan Company and the European Powers, 1305–1311' *Speculum* 29 (1954), 751–71, esp. 756.
[9] DOC, no. LIII, cited Setton, p.446.
[10] Burns, art.cit., 755–6.
[11] E.A. Zachariadou, 'The Catalans of Athens and the beginning of the Turkish Expansion' *Studi medievali* 21 (1980), 821–38.

disappointment and outrage that Pope Clement V, in a letter dated 14 January 1314, condemned those '... who once were believed to have gone to those parts to help the faithful and who, some were trusting, would defend the lands of those faithful ...',[12] and in particular their killing of Gautier I de Brienne in 1311, whom he described as an '... athlete of Christ and faithful boxer of the church against the Greek schismatics'.[13] Some, like James II of Aragon and the French *Chronicle of the Morea*, felt that the disaster at Halmyros was entirely the fault of Gautier and indeed, as Burns has suggested, Clement may well have seen the Catalans as a worthy replacement. Hence the three year gap between Gautier's death and this papal paean and the parallel demotion of those formerly '... beloved sons the Catalan Company in Romania'. Nonetheless, with the disinclination of the Catalans in Greece to participate in western crusading plans, Gautier had been the most powerful Latin ruler on the marches with Byzantium and was well-connected with the powerful families of the west to whom the pope would be turning to combat the growing Turkish menace. By 1313 his loss was evident whilst the destabilising effect that the Catalans were having in the region was clear. The countryside was being depopulated not just by their raids but by the flight of Greeks and Latins to the island of Euboea (Negroponte). Their indiscriminate use of Turks against Christians may well have persuaded many that they were themselves not Christian – certainly in the preliminaries to the battle of Halmyros, the Turkish contingents were surprised and relieved that the Catalans chose not to join with the Briennist army and turn upon them![14]

As a group the Catalans were never quite acceptable to their neighbours and to the west Mediterranean potentates with an interest in the Levant. Their violence and acquisitiveness certainly attracted general comment and many like the papacy and the Venetian authorities claimed to be outraged by their use of Turkish mercenaries. However, it was a violent age and the Aegean a particularly volatile area. The Catalans were not unique amongst the Christian groupings in the Aegean to employ Turkish troops. The Byzantines had used them in 1264 in their campaigns in the Morea and the Franks had been delighted to poach them into their own service. More recently neither Charles de Valois, through his emissary Thibaut de Cepoy, in 1307 nor the dukes of Athens in 1308–10 had baulked at enlisting the Catalans together with their Turkish allies for use against their Greek enemies.

By 1320 the Catalans seemed to be linked with the enemies of all the established Christian powers in Greece. In 1316 Catalans from the duchy

[12] Register Clement V, doc.10167, cited Burns, art.cit., 757.
[13] DOC, no. LXIV (pp.80–1): '... *tanquam Christi verus athleta et fidelis pugil ecclesie adversus Graecos scismaticos laborabat*'.
[14] Muntaner, c.CCXL (Goodenough, II, 577).

had helped Ferrando of Majorca gain his victory over Louis of Burgundy at Picotin, and thereafter reinforcements had been sent which landed at Vostitsa too late to avert Ferrando's defeat at Manolada and had to be re-embarked.[15] In that same year the commander of the Teutonic Order had been killed in Elis defending the principality against attacks from the Greeks of Mistra.[16] The Catalans had had no hand in that but their aggressive stance to the legitimate Frankish powers in the area made any accommodation with them difficult. Defence of the Morea was high on the agenda in Naples and provoked discussions with the pope in Avignon. In a letter to his vassals in the Morea written in Avignon in July 1321, King Robert of Naples lumped Catalans and Greeks together as enemies of his territories there.[17] Whilst in October 1323, writing to the archbishop of Patras, Pope John XXII singled out Catalan raids along the north coast of the Morea, and in particular their selling of captives to the Turks, as an especial misery of the inhabitants in that unsettled region.[18] No wonder there were doubts about the Christian affiliation of the company in the west.

Matters were no better 100 miles to the east. In the Aegean basin increased Turkish raids began to be regularly noted by Venetian officials there after 1318. Responsibility for some of these attacks, like those on Santorini and Karpathos in June 1318, were widely believed to have been instigated by Alfonso Fadrique, the Catalan vicar-general of Athens and Thebes.[19] This and the growing perception in Venetian circles of the Turkish potential to dominate the Aegean accounted for the deprecatory remarks about the Grand Company made by Sanudo and the Venetians in the 1320s. Somehow the disapproval of the Catalans went even deeper and was more entrenched. Muntaner ended his record of the mission of Berenguer de Entenza to Avignon to seek western assistance for the Catalans in their struggle with the Byzantines in 1305 as follows: 'But much might he labour; I do not believe that the pope nor the House of France wished that all the infidels of the world should be conquered by the followers of the lord king of Aragon'. Burns suggests that here was a Catalan attempt to play the crusader and that resentment evident in Muntaner's chronicle is apparent in modern Catalan historians like d'Olwer, who saw the papacy as opposed to Catalan mercantile expansion in the eastern Mediterranean.[20]

Certainly it went deeper than commercial rivalry since the Catalan Company in Greece made it clear to the Venetians in Negroponte (Chalkis) as soon as practicable that they did not intend to challenge their mercantile interests in the region. Nonetheless, as Professor Shneidman has pointed out,

---

15 L de F, 587–98; 610–23.
16 L de C, 404–5; L de F, 641–54.
17 DOC, no.CXIX (p.147).
18 DOC, no.CXX (p.148–9).
19 Zachariadou, art.cit., p.827.
20 Burns, art.cit., p.755 and n.16.

the capture of the duchy of Athens marked the easternmost extension of Catalan power in the Mediterranean and spelt an end to the Italian monopoly of long-distance commerce in those waters.[21] By the last decade of the thirteenth century Catalan merchants were extending their activities in the eastern Mediterranean and consulates had been established in Constantinople, Alexandria and Acre. It was in these centres that the real commercial challenge to the Venetians was mounted. After 1311 the occupation of central Greece would seem to place the Catalans on an equal footing with the Venetians and Genoese in the Aegean trade too. However, the realisation of this potential proved beyond the resources of the house of Barcelona. Its control of the duchy was weak and the Catalan Company in Romania was only nominally part of an Aragonese–Catalan empire. Whatever commercial hopes and expectations might have been harboured by the merchants of Barcelona, the ambitions of the Catalan Company were territorial. They would have to come to terms with the Venetians on Negroponte in order to further their own landed ambitions in continental Greece and this was precisely what they did in 1319, sacrificing prime harbour facilities in the Saronic Gulf in return for non-interference in their conquests in southern Thessaly.

In 1318 the Venetians had occupied Pteleon at the invitation of the Byzantine emperor Andronikos II, or at least with his consent, in order to defend it from the Catalans. Originally employed by the duke of Athens in 1310 to conquer southern Thessaly, the Catalans now took advantage of the confusion which followed the death of John II Doukas without heirs to grab as much territory in Thessaly as they could. This included the towns of Neopatras, Zeitounion and Gardiki and represented a substantial enlargement of the boundaries of the duchy of Athens.[22] Andronikos had much to fear. Not only was Thessaly slipping from any semblance of Byzantine control with Albanian, Serbian and Catalan aggression, but the Catalans had shown that they were not only the heirs of the dukes of Athens in their northern backyard but that they dared to threaten where Duke Guy had courteously withdrawn in 1302. The threat took the form of a resurrected Latin claim to Thessalonika which Andronikos had hoped he had laid to rest in 1284. In March 1314 the Catalans ceded the kingdom of Thessalonika to Guy de Montauban, the third son of Umbert of Viennois, on condition that he would conquer it and provide preferential land grants to any Catalans from the duchy who volunteered to assist in the enterprise.[23]

In 1317 when a Catalan force had arrived in Euboea, the Venetians

---

[21] J.L. Shneidman, *The Rise of the Aragonese-Catalan Empire, 1200–1350* 2 vols (New York, 1970), II, pp.347–8.

[22] D. Nicol, *The Despotate of Epiros, 1267–1479* (Cambridge, 1984), p.101.

[23] DOC, nos.LXX–LXXI (pp.88–9); R-J. Loenertz, *Byzantina et Franco-Graeca*, II (Roma, 1978), p.187.

tried to put together an offensive alliance against them to include the Angevins of Naples, supporters of the Briennist claim and the Hospitallers. Emissaries from Constantinople, from Mahaut de Hainault in Andravida and from the Briennist in Paris had come to Venice in that year to discuss the situation in central Greece.[24] The Venetians could cause much trouble for the Catalans and demonstrated this when they finally expelled their forces from Euboea in 1319 effectively ending the military phase of Fadrique's claim to Karystos and Larmena in right of his wife. With developing interests in southern Thessaly the Catalan leadership sought to safeguard their gains there by coming to terms with the Venetian baili of Negroponte on grounds of mutual self-interest. On 9 June 1319, Alfonso Fadrique and Francisco Dandolo agreed to a truce which proved sufficiently advantagous to both parties to be renewed in 1321 and again in 1331.[25] By the terms of the treaty all Catalan trade to or from the duchy was to be confined to the port of Livadostro on the Corinthian Gulf. In comparison with the Piraeus, the harbour facilities at Livadostro (Riva d'Ostro) were rudimentary. There was only a watchtower there and all cargoes would have to be rowed ashore. No Catalan trading vessel was to use the Saronic Gulf and any vessels there were to be decommissioned and their tackle stowed on the Acropolis (*in castro Athenarum*). Whatever the commercial ambitions of the house of Barcelona in the western Aegean, these had been given away by the Catalans in central Greece in return for a benevolent Venetian attitude to their territorial gains on the mainland.

If it is not too fanciful a descent into psycho-history, the real objection to the Catalan Company in western Europe was a social one. They certainly offended the hierarchical and monarchical principles of the day. They had seized lands from its rightful owners, the churches and nobles of Greece, and disposed of that property as their own. They ignored the commands of both the pope and their natural superior, James II of Aragon, who addressed them as his 'vassals and sons' (*fideles et naturales*) and urged them to return captured property to its rightful owners. For the company possession constituted the only right and this was made clear in their grant to Guy de Montaban. The papacy, too, tacitly acknowledged this political reality when it urged the master of the Hospital to occupy those territories which the Catalans had not yet managed to seize (presumably Briennist lands in the Argolid?).[26] The Catalans were condemned in moral terms by the rulers of the west – '*prava societas*', '*in devium ambulantes*' – whose occupation of the duchy was an insult to monarchs ('*ipsumque ducatum continuis*

---

[24] DOC. nos. LXXXVI (pp.105–6) and XCIII (pp.112–13); Setton, p.448, n.45.
[25] DOC, nos. CIX (pp.132–4), CXVI (pp.141–4), CLIII (pp.196–200); Setton, p.449.
[26] DOC, no. LXV (pp.81–2). The Hospitallers do not seem to have acted on this suggestion, but in any case the Argolid possessions of the former dukes were defended by the family of Foucherolles who had acquired an interest there through marriage into the de la Roche, see Luttrell, *PBSR* 24 (1966), 52.

insultibus invadentes') and a plague and pestilence to their subjects. To princes and property-owners they were judged as hydra-headed ('*coanimi ocupare*'), as commoners in arms, and as mercenaries out of control, who were upsetting the property nexus of the medieval world. Condemnation in these terms came from both ecclesiastical and lay dignitaries. According to the cardinal bishop of Ostia, they were self-seekers outside the bounds of society: '... *illa gentium disimilitudo que compagnia vocatur*'. To Mahaut de Hainaut they trampled on all the usual markers of social subordination: '*celle gens de la Compaigne ne tanront ne foi ne liaulte a vous ne a nous, ni a nelui de tout le monde*'. To the Venetians they were simply pirates.[27] It was, however, left to one of their own number, their chancellor, comrade, and chronicler Ramon Muntaner, to make a judgement as to their social unacceptability from the point of view of a landowner. His often quoted observation on the Catalan settlement in Attica and Boeotia ('... And so they divided amongst themselves the city of Thebes and all the towns and castles of the duchy and gave the ladies as wives to the men of the company, to each according to his importance, and to some they gave so distinguished a lady that he was not worthy to hand her her bowl to wash her hands ...')[28] was a social observation using the finger-bowl as its metaphor and equating the new Catalan landlords with servants at the table. He did not address in any way the tenurial and settlement implications of this act, let alone the fate of the wives and mistresses who made up a substantial part of the company and of whom he had made so much on the Catalan departure from Sicily in 1303. Fanciful Muntaner's observation may have been, but it certainly struck a chord with historians and novelists of a later age.

To R.J. Loenertz they smacked of the third estate. Certainly they had offended both church and nobility. As professional soldiers their skills were up for tender and it was fitting that they should serve under the direction of their betters. They were valued, but given the hierarchical and monarchical ideas current in the courts and curia of the west, there was no place for a state established by mercenaries out of control. There had been nothing like it since the Norman establishments in southern Italy in the early eleventh century and that was a long time ago when western society had not stabilised. Their only path towards political recognition was through acknowledging the suzerainty of the Aragonese king of Sicily. This satisfied western ruling-class susceptabliites but, as Shneidman has noted, muddied Aragonese diplomatic relations in Latin Christendom. It was almost with a sense of relief in official Latin circles that the duchy passed to Nerio

---

[27] Letter of Cardinal Bishop of Ostia, 4 September 1318, cited by Setton (1975), p.26, n.20; DOC, no.LXXXVI (p.106) and no.LXXIX (p.99).

[28] Muntaner, c.CCL (trans. Goodenough, II, 578). In 1331 when Orhan captured Nicaea he gave the Greek widows to his Turkish soldiers, who married them, see S. Vryonis, *The Decline of Medieval Hellenism in Asia Minor* ... (Berkeley, 1971), p.228, n.510.

Acciaioli in 1388. Nerio was the nephew and adoptive son of Niccolo Acciaioli, formerly the grand seneschal of Naples (d. 1365). For all his faults Nerio was at least a well-connected lord who could be fitted into western aristocratic perceptions. The Catalans seemed to fade away overnight. The Accaioli and the rulers of the west were content that this should be so. They left no monuments which can definitely be attributed to them and very few loan-words in the Greek language. This somewhat unlikely biological event and anachronistic sense of impermanence has perhaps been the more readily accepted because of the decisive and sudden way in which they had burst upon the Frankish political scene in 1311, and has been unconsciously packaged with that aura of romance which has come to surround the crusader states in the Aegean in modern Greek and Catalan novels.

There was much that was positive about the Catalan Company in Greece, in addition to their ferocity on the battlefield and their consummate skill in the use of the cross-bow. They showed a marked ability for state-building and administration which might not be expected from a band of freebooters and which was certainly not emulated by the Navaresse Company which captured Thebes and Livadhia in 1379–80. It may well have been that the unsuspected success at Halmyros and the possessions which fell into their lap as a consequence encouraged them to utilise their organisational skills. Certainly as a mercenary company which had fought together for a considerable period, often son following father in his profession, they had a developed sense of corporate identity expressed in a common seal, a patron saint in St George, and the three banners under which they fought. They had a developed historical identity which was evident in the desire to keep tripartite public records of important events like their defiance of Andronikos II in 1305, and which achieved literary expression in Muntaner's chronicle, written down in 1325–28. They possessed a rudimentary administration made up of a chancellor who kept the seal and oversaw a number of clerks, who amongst general writing duties kept a register of the company on the basis of which food and equipment were apportioned. Decisions seem to have been taken by all assembled in council, a procedure which left much room for powerful and influential men like Entenza and Rocaforte to get their way. The general council could delegate important or involved matters to a subcommittee of worthy men chosen by general consent from among themselves and by whose decision the company would be bound, as we see from the reception of Ferrando of Majorca. Dealing with such a republic of arms clearly perplexed western commentators.

Following their victory over Michael IX Palaeologos, the eldest son and co-emperor of Andronikos II, at Apros in June 1305, the company settled in Thrace around three centres – Maditos, Gallipoli, and Panedon – each group being under a leader, but with some sort of primacy retained by Gallipoli where a collective treasury and depot seems to have been maintained and a trading-post for Catalan merchants set up. None of this suggested permanent settlement. There was no recorded attempt to settle the land and at the same time Byzantine and Genoese pressure was maintained. Muntaner, writing over 20 years after the events that he witnessed, was perhaps struck by the difference between the Catalans in 1305 and what they were to become as landowners in Greece when he wrote of those years: '... We owed nothing nor ploughed nor dug over the vineyards nor pruned the vines, but took, every year, as much wine as we wanted and as much wheat and oats ... So we lived five years on after crops, and the most wonderful raids were made ...'.[29] In 1307 when they moved to Macedonia, Muntaner confirms that they raided and behaved as they had done before. Indeed, the reference to Charles of Valois being no more than the king of the hat and the wind may be as much a reference to the Catalans in their tented accommodation at Cassandrea as to the substance of Charles's claim to Constantinople.[30]

The victory at Halmyros changed all this. Muntaner's account is concerned more with drama than with historical accuracy, but it is all we have in terms of narrative.[31] It seems that the decision to settle was relatively sudden, since it did not suit the Turkish contingents in the Catalan army, who refused the offer of two or three areas for their own settlement and departed the duchy. In order of priority, Muntaner records that first the company sought a leader and then the settlements, rights and lands were divided amongst the victors. There is no suggestion of how lands were apportioned or by whom. The Turks were speeded on their way and a leader sought from outside the ranks of the company. Roger Deslaur, the new captain, received the widow of Thomas d'Autremencourt and the castle of Salona that went with her, but otherwise seemed to have played a purely passive role in the territorial distribution. This might be deemed prudent in one of the only two notable Frankish survivors from the recent battle, but suggests that he was not regarded as their suzerain for their lands. Rather, Muntaner emphasised the role of the widows of the Frankish lords in this transfer of property. We must assume that the slaughter at Halmyros was as considerable amongst Frankish landowners as Muntaner suggested, and that, therefore, fathers and sons of legal age died on the same field. Equally these widows and their finger-bowls were easily rounded up, presumably because they were town dwellers in Thebes or Athens. Maria da Verona, the widow of Alberto Pallavicino, escaped this Catalan marriage market and in 1312 married Andrea Cornaro, transferring to him a moiety of Boudonitza. It was not till 1318 with the northward expansion of the Catalans that military pressure was brought on both her territory and her husband's island

---

[29] Muntaner, c.CXXIII (trans. Goodenough, p.530).
[30] Muntaner, c.CCXXVI (trans. Goodenough, p.567).
[31] Muntaner, cc.CCXL–I (trans. Goodenough, II, p.578).

of Karpathos.[32] According to the Assizes of Romania (articles 31–35) the female succession to fiefs and the rights of widows to half of the fief or fiefs was recognised. The new Catalan spouses could thus become lords to this half by right of marriage and control the other half as guardians to any minors. It was more than just a good story since it provided some legal basis for the apportionment of the conquered lands, without the vassalic burdens that lay behind Frankish land-holding. The suzerainty of Charles II of Anjou was certainly not acknowledged, neither was the mediate lordship of Roger Deslaur, nor the ultimate suzerainty of James II of Aragon, the elder brother of Frederick of Sicily, who was seen as the natural lord of the Catalans by contemporary experts on the feudal hierarchy.[33] The suzerainty of Frederick II of Sicily was acknowledged and defined by contract (*Capitula et conventiones*) in 1312 with the important provision that he would not alter or interfere with property acquired in the duchy up to that time.[34] Frederick was to be a suzerain over men rather than lands, over an urban militia rather than knights' fees. Not only did the land allotment avoid the process of enfeoffment by a lord, but it also required no research in captured archives such as the crusaders of 1204 had had to undertake. In the Burgundian duchy the usual symbol of lordship was the free-standing tower with the fiefholder resident in a town. The process of '*cherchons la femme*' may well have been the most convenient way of sorting out the territorial complexities.[35]

The Catalans were conquerors but in this respect they followed legal niceties. Landed title seems to have been transferred with the widows and the free status of these women was not infringed. Here was an attempt by the Catalans to 'frankify' their activities and provide some sort of continuity with the immediate past. This would explain why these Frankish women were not just sold into slavery like many other unnamed Greek, Christian victims of Catalan raids in the Aegean. On a less legalistic level it might well demonstrate a Catalan preference for western women as much as for heiresses. In his chronicle Muntaner skated over any difficulties by claiming that there were only two male survivors from the battle, Roger Deslaur and Bonifacio da Verona. Nothing whatsoever is said of the 30 or more fiefs which Boniface had received from Duke Guyot in 1294. Whether the offer of the marriage of his daughter, Marulla, to Alfonso Fadrique in 1317 was intended to safeguard these possessions is just not known. Equally, Nicholas III de St Omer may not have fought at Halmyros, but he survived till 1314 and it is surely not just coincidental that it was not until March of that year that the company granted '*castrum nostrum Sanctus Adamanus iuxta ...*

---

32 Zachariadou, art.cit., 827; CGR, p.478.
33 DOC, nos. LXVI–LXVIII (pp.82–5).
34 DOC, no. LIII (pp.67–9).
35 P. Lock, 'The Frankish towers of central Greece' *ABSA* 81 (1986), 101–23.

Thebanum' to Guy de Montauban. Some, like Antoine le Flamenc, still alive in 1313, were also known to the Catalans because he had been involved in negotiations with Rocaforte in 1308 for a possible attack on Euboea. We can only guess how these lords and the Greek archontes of the duchy, who had occupied such an influential role in the councils of Duke Guy II, fitted into the new property arrangements. An unkown number fled to Euboea, sufficient to cause papal concern at '... *gravioris depopulationis iacturam*' and presumably providing ample room for the estimated 6,000 Catalan settlers.[36] There was room for those who wished to stay. Flamenc's presence in the area in 1313 and his rebuilding of the Church of St George at Karditza (mod. Akraiphnion) suggests that some at least continued to occupy their lands.[37] At any rate we hear little of land disputes between Catalans in the duchy. The seizure of Salona, Loidoriki and Veteranitza from the Fadrique family by Pedro de Pou in 1361 was the extension of a power struggle in the duchy into real estate.

Much more serious were the disputes about leadership: whence should a leader come – from the ranks of the company, from the royal house of Aragon or from outside – and how should he behave in respect of the *universitas*? The need for a leader was recognised practically in terms of the day-to-day conduct of affairs and strategy and, after the occupation of central Greece, in terms of representing the company in the courts of the west. Muntaner suggests that policy decisions were discussed in a general assembly of the company. The Catalans were not democrats, however, and power seemed to rest with an oligarchy made up of the heads of individual companies. It was they who devised the abduction of Rocaforte and his family in 1309, and in 1333 Pope John XXII had no difficulty in identifying some 28 of them including Fadrique, Nicholas Lancia and Odon de Novelles, albeit in new guises, for excommunication, which was eventually pronounced in 1335 by William Frangipani, the archbishop of Patras.[38] Any would-be leader had to steer a careful course between what might be interpreted as tyrannical behaviour and the requirements of neighbours and potential employers to deal with a ruler. Roger de Flor, the founder of the company which entered Aegean politics, seemed to have steered the company towards integration within the Byzantine political system, seeking by marriage and the court title of 'caesar' to create a place for the company. The Byzantine rejection of this scheme was signalled by his murder at Adrianople on the orders of the co-emperor Michael. Muntaner's reaction to this rejection was the so-called 'Catalan revenge', a period of violence

---

[36] DOC, no.LXIV (p.80), January 1314.

[37] W. Miller, *Essays on the Latin Orient* (Cambridge, 1921), pp.132–4. By 1365 one Pedro de Puigpardines was lord of Karditza, cf. CGR, p.478.

[38] Muntaner, c.CCXXXIX (trans. Goodenough, p.573); DOC, no.CLVIII (pp.206–9). Those excommunicated were listed by Ducange, see note to DOC, p.208.

towards Byzantines and general drift in terms of leadership and policy. To be sure, when the Catalans had divided into three groups in Thrace in 1305, each band had a leader: Ferran Ximeno de Arenos at Maditos, Berenguer de Rocaforte at Panedon, and Muntaner himself at Gallipoli. Each might vie for some sort of overlordship, but sought either a western suzerain in either Ferrando of Majorca or Charles de Valois or an employer in Guy de la Roche or Gautier de Brienne. A disinclination to deal with the house of Barcelona had manifested itself in 1307, when the infante Ferrando of Majorca had been sent east by his father Frederick II of Sicily. This opposition found expression behind one leader, Rocaforte, who was not only establishing himself as lord of the company, at least in the eyes of Thibaut de Cepoy, but was following up a variety of options to bolster his own position, namely service under Charles of Valois or employment in Thessaly with the duke of Athens. Rocaforte was high-handed in his treatment of the Catalans and was displaced by a coup led by the chiefs of the company.[39] Quite who led the company into the duchy is unclear. Roger Deslaur, a knight from the county of Rousillon and thus a Catalan-speaker, was the chief negotiator from the Briennist side, but who negotiated for the Catalans now that Rocaforte was removed and Ximenos dead?

Conquest and a land settlement highlighted the need for a recognised leader or suzerain to mediate with the rulers of the west and gain recognition. Certainly observers in the west were alarmed at the multi-headed nature of the company and, according to Muntaner, this observation of contemporary political wisdom was not lost on the Catalans who '... saw clearly that it was not well for them to be without a lord'.[40] The consensus seemed to be for a leader from outside the ranks of the company and the first choice had been from amongst the survivors of the battle at Halmyros, who enjoyed some standing in the immediate area of central Greece and were believed to have some sympathy with the company. Both Boniface of Verona, the son of a triarch of Euboea, and Roger Deslaur enjoyed some standing in the immediate area, but both were distinctly lightweight in terms of west European courtly politics. The second choice, Deslaur, was persuaded to become '*marescalcus et rector universitatis*', but in 1312 the company put aside its objections to the house of Barcelona, which had led to the rejection of Ferrando of Majorca's mission in 1307, and through the mediation of Deslaur acknowledged the suzerainty of Frederick of Sicily. Frederick appointed his second son, the infante Manfred, duke and appointed Berenguer Estanol as vicar-general. All together there were to be seven dukes of Athens from the house of Barcelona – the first four were the younger sons and a grandson of King Frederick himself, and thereafter

---

[39] Muntaner, c.CCXXX (trans. Goodenough, pp.549–51), CCXXXIII (p.556) and CCXXXIX (pp.572–3).
[40] Muntaner, c.242 (trans. Goodenough, p.580).

Frederick III of Sicily (1355–77) and Pedro IV of Aragon (1379–87). None of them visited the duchy, which they ruled through vicar-generals.[41]

The king and his infant son were to have '*dominium ... merum et mixtum imperium*' and the company and their newly conquered subjects were to be '*... fideles, subditos et vassallos suos*'. The feudo-vassalic nexus was weak since the king undertook to recognise all rights and lands (*in statu officio seu beneficio*) which members of the company had acquired since 1311, and seemed to have instituted no enquiries into military service owed to his predecessors, the Burgundian dukes. At first sight this lack of fief-holders bound to provide military service would seem to produce insurmountable problems for the defence of the duchy. However, in the first 20 years of their settlement the Catalans were not on the defensive but actually acquired key-points in southern Thessaly, including Gardiki which came into western hands for the first time. By 1350 the Serbs and Albanians had overrun Thessaly and Epiros, Catalan territory was contracting, and Siderokastro, somewhere between Lamia and Salona had become the key to the duchy.[42] Clearly towns and their associated fortresses were vital in the defence of the duchy. Setton has stressed the importance of the castellan in this respect, but probably the veguers and captains in the lower towns were as important in the moves to generalise military service which Philippe Contamine has noted in western Europe at this time and to which the Catalan Company by its very origins would seem to have been ideally suited.[43] There is no specific statement that military service was expected from all free subjects in the Catalan duchy, but it would fit with the wording of the contract of suzerainty of 1312 and the needs of defence. We do not know the exact nature of the limitations which individual towns sought to this service but limitations there were, as can be seen in the absence of a castellan at Thebes or the voice which the inhabitants of Livadhia sought to exercise in the appointment of their veguer. When local manpower resources proved inadequate, the Catalans like their Burgundian predecessors sought military help from outside the duchy. They could not turn to triarchs or Moreote lords but to the Turks of Menteshe.

A ducal domain had to be created or recreated from the former Burgundian lands which had been confiscated in the wake of 1311. The Burgundian dukes had created no great sub-vassals and based their power in the towns of Athens and Thebes. The Catalan dukes seem to have followed this policy too, appointing castellans, veguers and/or captains in the five

---

[41] Setton, *Catalan Domination of Athens* op.cit., pp.15–17. List of Catalan dukes of p.17, n.10 and CGR p.474 for the dukes and p.475 for the vicar-generals.
[42] Setton, *Catalan Domination of Athens* op.cit., p.63; the site of Siderokastro/Sideroporta in the Sperchios plain is not securely known, cf. Bon, *BCH* 61 (1937), 130–41. In 1275 it formed part of the dowry of Helena Angela-Komnene on her marriage with William de la Roche (L de C, 408, 413).
[43] P. Contamine, *War in the Middle Ages* (Oxford, 1984), pp.83–7, 248.

principal towns of Athens, Thebes, Neopatras, Livadhia and Lamia, with their associated castles. Just as most Frankish settlement in the thirteenth century had been in towns, so it was with the Catalans. Muntaner emphasised towns and castles in the allocation of 1311 and modern historians like Setton noted the survival of the corporate identity of the company in the municipal organisation of the towns. Certainly we read for the first time of the collective identity of the communes (universitates) of the duchy. Sometime in 1355 they presented a petition to Frederick of Randazzo to replace Raymond Bernard of Sarbou as vicar-general.[44] The ease with which the ducal domain was re-created in 1312 and the general lack of disputes over land allocation in 1311 both suggest Catalan urban settlement and Frankish survival in the countryside at Karditza and Bodonitza.

The king of Sicily appointed the vicar-general, and the various castellans (castella or alcaydus), veguers and captains.[45] The vicar-general was his viceroy and lieutenant. However, the king was careful to maintain all appointments and judicial appeals in his own hands. In terms of war and diplomacy, let alone political stability within the duchy, an effective vicar-general made all the difference. The apogee of the Catalan duchy has been generally dated to the years 1317 to 1330 when Alfonso Fadrique, the bastard son of King Frederick, was captain general. In those years the Fadrique family negotiated a number of prestigious marriages with the dalle Carceri and Ghisi families, threatened Venetian interests on Euboea and made substantial territorial gains in southern Thessaly. These were listed in 1325 by Marco Sanudo in a letter to Ingram, bishop of Capua as Neopatras, Loidoriki, Siderocastro, Zeitoun or Lamia, Gardiki, Domokos, Pharsala, Trikkala, and Kastoria. Many of these places had never been in Latin hands before and some only very briefly in the years before 1210. Greek rulers in the area and Albanian raiders were kept in check.[46] The destabilising effects of a tyrannical vicar-general were revealed during the governorship of Pedro de Pou in 1361–62 which ended in the murder of himself, his wife and a handful of supporters, including Michael Olwer, the dean of Thebes, in a coup in Thebes in April or May 1362, engineered by the ambitious and able marshal of the company, Roger de Lluria, who usurped the office and functions of the vicar-general.[47] The castellans guarded the principal fortresses of the realm, *die noctuque*, and maintained the arsenal and siege engines stored therein. There are references to castellans in Athens, Livadhia,

---

[44] DOC, no.CCXXV (pp.306–7) discussed in Loenertz, op.cit., p.195.
[45] Setton, *Catalan Domination of Athens* op.cit., pp.80–91; summarised in Setton, pp.443–5.
[46] DOC, no.CXXIX (pp.159–61). Loenertz, op.cit., p.189 noted that Pharsala, Domokos and Gardiki were presumably soon lost since they do not figure in Catalan documents relating to the duchy.
[47] DOC, no.CCXC (pp.377–9) and no.CCLII (p.335) cited in Setton, p.456, n.105.

Siderocastron, Neopatras, Salona and Veteranitza, of which the first four places were specifically mentioned as forming part of the *regium sacrum demanium*.[48] No castellan was ever recorded at Thebes. In some way it was the property of the company rather than the crown, since it was the company which granted '*castrum nostrum*' to Guy of Montauban in 1314 and the company which slighted the castle in 1331 to prevent its capture by Gautier II de Brienne. By whose authority it was granted to Bartolomeo II Ghisi in 1327 is unclear.[49] The duties of the castellans were primarily those of guardianship not just of the fabric but of the supplies and materials within the walls.[50]

The principal officers in the lower towns and for some unknown area around were the veguers and the captains. Their letters of appointment concentrated exclusively on their judicial functions – the criminal and civil jurisdiction of the one and the criminal jurisdiction of the latter.[51] Both were assisted by a staff of judges, notaries and councillors, and the judgements of both were open to appeal to the royal court in Sicily. All three offices might be held by one man like Galeran de Peralta who was '*castella, capita e veguer del castell e ciutat de Cetines*' throughout the 1370s.[52] Veguers and captains were to be found in Thebes, Athens and Livadhia, which were part of the royal domain and held for the king, but only captains were recorded in Siderocastro, Neopatras and Salona, towns which were held by others. This suggests that the royal dukes sought to monopolise high justice, and to that extent they were very much the heirs of the Burgundian dukes.

From the royal archives in Palermo and Barcelona we learn for the first time of towns, of the interplay of church and state, and of the administrative framework in the duchy. Just how much this can be extrapolated back into Burgundian times is an open question, but the Catalans took on the territorial ambitions, the property and many of the values of the Burgundians so why not much of their administration as well, albeit with different offices? The archives tend to stress system and order from a royal point of view, but really what is striking is the tension between the expectations of the absentee dukes and those of the Catalans in the duchy. In their seizure of church lands, their enactment of mortmain legislation and their acknowledgement of the letter if not the spirit of western inheritance

---

[48] DOC, no.CCLXXXIX (pp.374–5) and no.CCCXXXIV (p.42) cited Setton, p.444, n.19.

[49] DOC, no. LXXI (pp.89–90). By 1327 the castle had passed to Bartolomeo II Ghisi, presumably as the dowry of Fadrique's daughter Simona. According to the prologue of the French *Chronicle of the Morea* (L de C, p.1) the text as we have it was copied from a book in the possession of Ghisi 'en son chastel d'Estives'. See Setton, p.156, n.60. See L de C, 554 for its destruction by the Catalans.

[50] DOC, no.CCCXLIII (p.431) for castellan of Livadhia.

[51] DOC, nos CCLXII–CCLXIII (pp.345–7) for captain of Livadhia and no.CCXLVI (pp.443–4) for veguer of Athens.

[52] Setton, p.445.

practices, there are parallels between the Catalan conquest and that of the Franks a century earlier. Like the Franks whom they displaced they were to dominate the duchy for nearly three generations and in their turn to be displaced violently by unemployed mercenaries from western wars. Many were to return to Catalonia and Sicily, but the fate of those who stayed on remains as much a mystery as the fate of many dispossessed Franks in 1311. One point that all contemporaries were agreed upon was that it was the Catalans who gave the Turks a taste for Balkan conquests. Perhaps this was the ultimate Catalan vengeance on the Acciaioli, the last dukes of Athens, who ended their days as vassals of Mehemet II.

The Peloponnese, 1313–64

In the Morea there is evidence of increasing unease with the Angevin overlordship. The self-consciousness and pride of the Frankish barons had never sat well with Angevin bailies from Italy or with a series of princes politically approved in Naples. In the *Chronicle of the Morea* the reputation of Nicholas III de St Omer was based on his total commitment to the Frankish establishment and a proper concern for the honour and esteem of the local baronage as a whole. His defiance of Philip de Savoy in 1301 over the arbitrary imprisonment of Benjamin of Kalamata was portrayed as resistance to one who behaved '... *comment li tyrant de Lombardie*' by '*le plus gentil homme*' – the insider and the stranger.

The struggle between Louis of Burgundy, the Angevin-approved husband of Mahaut de Villehardouin, and Ferrando or Ferdinand of Majorca, husband of Isabelle of Sabran, the daughter of Margaret de Villehardouin, in 1315 brought the Angevin–Aragonese struggle from Sicily to the Morea. It exposed fissures in the Frankish noble community. The baili, Nicholas le Maure, remained loyal to the Angevins and resisted Ferrando, if somewhat half-heartedly, as did Nicolo Sanudo from the Archipelago, for which support he attracted Catalan raids on his island in 1317. Count John of Kephalonia changed sides to suit his own advantage. Originally supporting Ferrando, he also led the army which was defeated by Ferrando at the battle of Picotin near Palaeopolis on 22 February 1316. Stouter support was provided by Nicholas de Tremolay and Richolithi de Nivelet, the only surviving male representatives of the original twelve high barons of Achaia. Indeed Beverley Berg has made a plausible suggestion that the author of the Aragonese chronicle was a Moreote supporter of Ferrando's, who had joined up after the latter's capture of Glarenza in July 1315. Ferrando's precipitate action before reinforcements arrived from Majorca led to his defeat and death at the battle of Manolada, near Elis, on

5 July 1316.[53] The victor, Louis of Burgundy, was dead by October, possibly poisoned by the count of Kephalonia. Angevin plans for tighter control of its Moreote lands did not end here. Mahaut was now envisaged as the bride of John of Gravina (in Apulia), the younger brother of Robert I of Naples and Philip of Taranto. Pressure was brought to bear by both King Robert and Pope John XXII, but her secret marriage to Hugues de la Palisse upset these plans. She left the Morea in 1317 and spent the rest of her life imprisoned in Naples, dying in 1331 in Aversa. Her third husband was executed in 1322 for plotting against King Robert. But in the Morea the struggle of 1315/16 had involved both Greeks and Catalans, and threatened to involve the principality in a much wider conflict rather than to secure its survival in the face of Byzantine reconquest. There is some evidence that the barons of the Morea now became disillusioned with Angevin ambitions and paper schemes to save the principality.

Between 1316 and 1321 the Greeks operating from Mistra took the castle of Akova, occupied the mountain known as 'Messogalnica', reduced Karytaina and Matagriffon, and began the siege of the castle of St George in Skorta.[54] In June 1321, as Professor Bon has pointed out, a number of prominent Franks in the Morea wrote to the doge of Venice, drawing attention to the plight of the Morea and offering to hand over the bay of Navarino (Port des Joncs) in return for effective protection and arms supplies. Both the pope, John XXII, and Robert of Naples were to be approached to facilitate this transfer should the Venetians be interested. Those involved in this approach were Jean de Baux, preceptor of the Hospitallers in Romania and baili and captain-general of the principality, John, bishop of Olena, and Benjamin of Kalamata, the chancellor. Other approaches were made by Pietro Gradenigo, a Venetian and the minister of the Franciscans in Greece, who wrote from Glarenza on behalf of the barons of the Morea, and William Frangipani, the archbishop of Patras.[55] Some of these men had Venetian connections but they were all men in a position to take a wider view of events and their actions did not represent narrow sectional interests. There was very real concern and low morale amongst the Franks of the Morea. The Venetians did not act upon these approaches – they had much to occupy them with the Genoese – but it did prompt some action in Naples.

In 1322 and 1323 an ambitious joint expedition was planned. John of Gravina, who had been created prince of Achaia in January 1322 by his eldest brother Robert I of Naples, proposed to campaign in person in the Morea. His other brother, Philip of Taranto, was to mount a campaign in

---

[53] L de F, 555–623; Beverly Berg, 'The Moreote Expedition of Ferrando of Majorca' *Byzantion* 55 (1985), 69–90.
[54] L de F, pp.641–54; L de C, pp.404–5.
[55] BMF, pp.202–4: DOC, pp.144–6.

Epiros at the same time, and Gautier II de Brienne was to be approached to attack central Greece and thus occupy the Catalans. Armaments and supplies were sent to Glarenza during 1322. While these preparations dragged on, Catalan raids along the north coast of the Morea increased in intensity. Cash was a problem and loans were raised from the banking houses of Florence including the Acciaioli family, who loaned a sum equivalent to 40,000 gold onzi or unciae in 1323.[56] In the same year Acciaiolo Acciaioli was created royal chamberlain to Robert I of Naples as a reward for his efforts in this respect with his uncle Dardano, the head '*de societata Aczarellorum de Florentia, mercatores, familiares, et fideles nostros ...*'.[57] This was the first serious involvement of the Acciaioli in the affairs of Greece. Nothing came of the Epirote and Boeotian campaigns. However, in January 1325 John of Gravina arrived in Glarenza with a fleet of 25 galleys containing 4,000 knights and 1,000 foot-soldiers. As Kenneth Setton has recorded, John's expedition in 1325–26 was the last major campaign against the Greeks of Mistra.[58] It achieved nothing except huge costs, which John could only meet by granting Moreote lands to those creditors who would accept them. The Acciaioli accepted the fiefs of Lechaina and La Mandria, near Andravida.

In 1333 John sold his interest in the Morea to his nephew Robert, the son of Philip of Taranto (d. 1331) and Catherine de Valois-Courtenay, the titular empress of Constantinople, in return for cash, the duchy of Duras and the title to the kingdom of Albania. Two years later he was dead. Some of the funding for this purchase, 5,000 gold onzi, was raised by the Acciaioli. Robert held the principality until his death in 1364. Catalan, Turkish and Greek raids eroded his Moreote territory. There is nothing approximating to a year-by-year account of these depredations, but their gravity is attested in the writings of Marco Sanudo, then resident in Glarenza, and references in papal letters to attacks by schismatics and others, and of the tendencies of those Latins in Romania to seek the ministrations of Orthodox priests to the danger of their souls. Difficult times meant opportunities for venture capital and by 1335 the Acciaioli family had established a branch bank in Glarenza and were on the threshold of adding substantially to their properties in the Morea.

---

[56] Gold coins had ceased to be coined in Naples in the fourteenth century. Sums were expressed nominally in gold onzi, ounces or unciae each equivalent to 60 silver carlini. The sum involved was equivalent to over 2,400,000 silver coins. See P. Spufford, *Handbook of Medieval Exchange* (London, 1986), pp.62–5.
[57] J. Buchon, *Nouvelles Recherches historiques ...* (Paris, 1843), doc.1, pp.31–2.
[58] Setton, p.158.

The Acciaioli in Greece, 1338–94

The most famous member of the family was Niccolo Acciaioli (1310–1365/6), the son of Acciaiolo and Guiglielma de Pazzi, buried in the Carthusian Priory of St Laurence, known as La Certosa, near Florence which he had re-endowed and where a fresco depicting him may still be seen.[59] He was grand seneschal of Naples, a friend of Petrarch and Boccaccio, and was awarded la rosa d'oro by Innocent VI in 1360. His rise and ability fascinated contemporaries. In 1440 Matteo Palmieri wrote a short biographical study emphasising these very qualities.[60] But all this came after 1341 and the end of his personal involvement in the Morea. By 1335 he had passed from the family counter in Naples to the service of King Robert, where he was the adviser to the widowed Catherine de Valois (d. 1346) and tutor to her three sons including the new prince of Achaia, Robert. There was clearly much discussion of Moreote affairs and ambitious schemes to tighten control of the Angevin lands there. The personal presence of the new prince was seen as an advantage. Niccolo built up his possessions in the Morea by gift and by purchase, mainly in Elis, Arkadia, and around Kalamata.[61] Between October 1338 and June 1341 the titular empress and her suite were in the Morea. Niccolo was there too. He had made his first will on the eve of his departure and his safe return provoked a letter of congratulation from Boccaccio. It is to this visit that we may owe the writing down of the Assizes of Romania and possibly the extant text of the French version of the *Chronicle of the Morea*, but otherwise little was achieved and various Moreote barons made overtures to John Cantacuzenos, the grand domestic in Mistra, and later to James of Majorca offering them the suzerainty of their lands.[62] Robert did not return to the Morea but left a succession of bailies as his representatives, and Niccolo's attention was now given over to the affairs of the Neapolitan kingdom, but he financed much of his building activity at the Certosa from revenue from his Greek lands and in April 1358 received the grant of the lordship of Corinth. By the dispositions of his second will in 1359 he did create a Greek branch of the Acciaioli family, to which we must now turn.

Just as the Villehardouin were associated with the history of Frankish Greece at its height, so the Acciaioli in Athens and Thebes have come to represent the last days of the Frankokratia. It was a cadet branch of the Acciaioli family which made its way in Greece. These were the children and grandchildren of Giacomo Acciaioli and Bartolomea Ricasoli, distant

---

[59] G. Leoncini, *La Certosa Di Firenze* (Salzburg, 1980).
[60] G. Scaramella, ed., *Matthei Palmieri Vita Nicolai Acciaioli* Muratori, XIII, 2 (1934). This edition contains his wills written in 1338 and 1359.
[61] Listed in BMF, pp.210 and 230.
[62] L de C, pp.647–76; BMF, pp.208–14; Setton, pp.158–60.

cousins of Niccolo. The latter had failed to interest his own children in Greek possibilities and had adopted Rainerio or Nerio as his son in 1362. In 1365 he received the baronies of Vostitza and Nivelet by bequest, in 1366 he replaced his brother Donato as vicar of Corinth on behalf of Niccolo's son Angelo, and in 1371 he replaced him as lord. The castellany of Corinth was effectively made into an hereditary palatinate for Nerio in a ceremony which took place in Brindisi on 27 February 1371, and four years later all his titles and possessions in Greece were confirmed by Joanna of Naples in her capacity as princess of Achaia. In 1374–75 Nerio took advantage of a dispute between William de Almenara, the veguer of Thebes, and Galeran de Peralta, the veguer and castellan of Athens, to besiege and seize Megara from the Catalans. During the 1380s he devoted his energies to fighting the Navarrese and the Turks in the Argolid. In 1385 he started to call himself lord of the duchy of Athens, and between April 1387 and 2 May 1388 he besieged and captured the Acropolis. Thebes, which had been captured along with Livadhia by the Navarrese companies under John of Urturbia in 1379 and 1380–81 respectively, seems to have fallen to him in 1388, since he and his family were described as living there during the siege of Athens because of a plague which had broken out in the lower town there. In 1388 he sought to strengthen his position within Greece by a series of important marriages. His eldest daughter, Bartolomea, became the wife of Theodore Palaeologos, the despot of Mistra, and his other daughter, Francesca, was married to Carlo I Tocco, the duke of Leukadia. Neither seem to have rendered material assistance on his campaigns into Attica but at least their quiescence was assured. He was engaged in fighting both Catalans and Navarrese in his conquest of the duchy and was held a prisoner by the Navarrese in Patras for nearly a year in 1389–90. Neopatras in Thessaly was taken from the Catalans in 1390 only to be lost forever to the Turks in 1393. He failed to capture Salona from the Fadrique family or to secure Boudonitza. The lords of both these centres acknowledged the suzerainty of Bayezid I on his lightning campaign into central Greece in 1394. It is unclear precisely when Nerio gained control of Livadhia, but in his will he left it along with Thebes to his natural son Antonio.

Nerio died in Corinth on 25 September 1394. In his will he was at pains to restore church property seized during his campaigns and to re-embellish the cathedral church on the Acropolis at Athens. He is credited with the construction of the palace and its tower on the Acropolis. Apart from Thebes and Livadhia that went to Antonio, he left Corinth to his daughter Francesca and Athens to the Cathedral chapter under the military protection of Venice.

The last years of Frankish Greece, 1377–1460

The political situation in Frankish Greece both north and south of the Isthmus of Corinth was becoming very confused in these years. Thessalonika was in Turkish hands in 1395 and their first considerable campaign into Greece was conducted in 1393–94, while Navarrese, Catalans, and the Acciaioli with their Albanian armies were picking over the fragments that were left. It was no longer a contest for hegemony but each contestant seized opportunities whenever they came in order to carve out lands for themselves. Only the Venetians and the Hospitallers seemed to be engaged in salvaging what they could of the formal political structure of the area in order to mount an effective opposition to the Turks. The fragmentation of the Aegean polity had gone about as far as it could go since the centrifugalism evident in the Byzantine world in the late twelfth century. It was now left to the Ottomans to reimpose unity on that disunited region.

The work of Raymond Loenertz and Anthony Luttrell has done much to shed light on the entry of two institutional players in the southern Balkans in the 1370s.[63] These were the Hospitallers of Rhodes who had considered moving their headquarters from Rhodes to the Morea in 1356, and the four companies of Navarrese and Gascon mercenaries. In the summer of 1376 Joanna I, the queen regnant of Naples and since 1374 the princess of the Morea, leased the principality to the Knights Hopitallers for a period of five years at an annual rent of 4,000 ducats. The rent was small and presumably represented a desire on the part of Joanna to bolster the defences of her principality compromised by Albanian, Turkish and Catalan raids. Rural depopulation was the main result, the soil could not be tilled or rents collected. The Greeks from the despotate of Mistra apparently took a second place to these other threats, but they were by no means quiescent. By the summer of 1377 she appointed the Hospitaller Daniel del Carretto as baili responsible for overseeing the transfer of the Morea to the order. It is at this point that the Aragonese version of the *Chronicle of the Morea* ends. Coincidentally in the same year the able Aragonese warrior and papal servant Juan Fernandez de Heredia (1310–96) was nominated grand master of the Knights Hospitaller by Gregory XI.[64] His appointment was irregular in that it bypassed election by the chapter on Rhodes. He began a forward policy of reconquest which he planned in Rome and launched from Naples

---

[63] BMF, pp.254–61; R-J. Loenertz, 'Hospitaliers et Navarrais en Grece' *Orientalia christiana Periodica* 20 (1956), 316–60; A. Luttrell, papers in *BZ* 57 (1964), 340–5; *Speculum* 41 (1966), 30–48, and *PBSR* 26 (1958), 195–212; K. Setton, 'Simon Atumano and the fall of Thebes to the Navarrese' *Byzantinisch-neugriechische Jahrbucher* 18 (1945–49; published 1960), 105–22. The views of Antoni Rubio i Lluch in his classic work *Los Navarros en Grecia* (Barcelona, 1880) have been superseded by these works.
[64] H.J. Sire, *The Knights of Malta* (Yale, 1994), pp.41–9 for a well-illustrated account of Heredia.

in December 1377. From the Morea and with the support of the archbishop of Patras, Paul Foscari, he crossed into Akarnania and soon recovered Naupaktos (Lepanto) from the Albanians. At some point in 1378 he was captured by the Albanians who sold him to the Turks and it was not until May 1379 that he was back again in Glarenza. In the meantime Gaucher de la Bastide, the prior of the order in Toulouse and Heredia's lieutenant in the Morea, had hired two companies of the Navarrese mercenaries commanded by Jean d'Urtubia and Mahiot de Coquerel for service either in Epiros or central Greece.

The Navarrese companies, containing a high proportion of Gascon warriors, had been engaged in the struggles in the Pyrenees between the French, English and various Spanish rulers.[65] Thrown on the job market by a peace treaty between Charles II of Navarre and Charles V of France in 1366, these professional soldiers took service with Charles II's brother, Louis d'Evreux, who had acquired an interest in the port and duchy of Durazzo through his marriage in that year with Jeanne duchess of Duras, the granddaughter of John of Gravina. It was he who transported these troops to the Balkans in 1368 in order to recover Durazzo from the Albanians. On his death in 1372 they remained in Greece and took service with the Hospitallers in 1378 and were almost certainly encouraged by them to intervene in central Greece the following year. Others, in 1380, directed their attention into the Morea in the pay of Jacques de Baux, who decided to press his claim to the principality in opposition to that of Joanna of Naples. At various times they occupied Androusa, Navarino and Patras and fought with Nerio Acciaioli in the Corinthia and with Theodore Palaeologos, the despot of Mistra (1382–1407). Their support for de Baux was nominal and they took care to carve out lands for themselves both in the Morea and in central Greece. They were yet another group seeking to exploit the troubles of Frankish Greece to their own advantage.[66]

The events of the last years of the independent states in the Aegean is generally well-known and well-covered in most studies. Here they will be briefly summarised. The bequests made by Nerio Acciaioli in his will of September 1394 led to many disputes amongst the beneficiaries. Increased Turkish military pressure on the rulers of central Greece made the settlement of these differences more urgent than ever, especially since in 1397 for a short period the Turks occupied the lower town of Athens. In 1402 Duke Antonio, not content with his bequest of Thebes and Livadhia, attempted to take Athens from the Venetian castellan, Matthew of Moncada. This provoked reprisals from the Venetians on Euboea which took the form of an expedition against Thebes. Antonio defeated this army and successfully gained possession of the Acropolis in early 1403. He ruled as duke until his

---

[65] J. Hillgarth, *The Spanish Kingdoms, 1250–1516* I (Oxford, 1976), pp.347–407.
[66] Setton, *Catalan Domination of Athens* op.cit., pp.125–47.

death in 1435. The duchy was then divided between two distant cousins Nerio II (1435–51) and Antonio II (d. 1441). They squabbled over possession of the Acropolis and for two years prior to his brother's death Nerio II was forced to flee the duchy, retiring to Florence. He was succeeded by his infant son Francesco I who was in the guardianship of his mother and her lover, the Venetian Bartolomeo Contarini. It was Mehemet II who safeguarded Francesco's rights and installed him in Athens in 1455 from which he was pensioned off to Thebes the following year when the Turks occupied Athens for themselves. In 1460 he was murdered on the orders of the sultan and central Greece passed for ever from Frankish possession.

In the Morea the Angevin line of princes had died out in 1383 with the death of Jacques de Baux. By 1386 the Navarrese captain Pierre de Saint-Superan was styling himself vicar-general of the Morea and after 1396 prince of Achaia; force made up for any deficiencies in blood. Following his death in 1402 his wife Maria Zaccaria was regent. She was dispossessed along with her infant children in April 1404 by her nephew Centurione II Zaccaria, lord of Damala and Chalandritza. The principality was effectively confined to the south-west of the Peloponnese and Centurione spent his reign protecting these interests against Greeks and Venetians. In January 1430 the principality passed to the despot of Mistra, Thomas Palaeologos, as the dowry of his bride, Caterina, the daughter of Centurione. Apart from the Venetians in Messenia, Nauplia and Monemvasia Frankish rule in the Morea was at an end. In 1458 the Peloponnese passed under the control of the Ottomans. Modon and Coron held out until 1500 and Nauplia and Monemvasia until 1540.

Venice, Genoa and the Aegean

The four phases of involvement

Venetian involvement in the Aegean can be broadly divided into four phases. In the first phase Venice was one of a number of Italian merchant cities seeking to gain an edge in the trade of luxury commodities from the east for which there was a growing demand in western Europe. Her provision of naval support for the Byzantines and the crusader states helped provide her merchants with a privileged position in Constantinople and some of the commercial centres of the Aegean world. The privileges might be capriciously altered or withdrawn by the host government, occasionally resulting in considerable loss of life and property by her merchants. This seemed to end in the second phase when Constantinople passed under Latin control in 1204 and the Aegean seemed about to become a Venetian lake. The focus on the Venetians as the villains of the Fourth Crusade is not as sharp as it once was, but certainly the merchants of Venice gained a virtual monopoly in Constantinople and the Black Sea, possession of the ports and maritime cities, like Modon, Coron, Negroponte, Karystos and the island of Crete, which she required to protect and supply her shipping lanes to Egypt and Syria.[1] The recovery of Constantinople by the Greeks in 1261 and its successful occupation with considerable Genoese assistance meant the loss of this most-favoured-city status and a period of nearly 100 years of intense commercial rivalry with Genoa. Four wars were fought with the Genoese between 1258 and 1381 over the control of the Black Sea trade and its Aegean approaches. These wars provoked some major naval engagements

---

[1] C.M. Brand, 'The Fourth Crusade: some recent interpretations' *Medievalia et Humanistica* 12 (1984), 33–41; A.E. Laiou, 'Observations on the results of the Fourth Crusade ...', ibid., 43–60; L.B. Robbert, 'Venice and the Crusades', in N. Zacour and H.W. Hazard, eds, *A History of the Crusades* V (Madison, 1985), pp.379–451.

involving considerable fleets in the Aegean area. Such was the battle of Settipozzi (Spetsopoulos) off Nauplia in 1263, and that off Kastro near Negroponte in 1350. The years of peace were marked by state-sponsored piracy along the Aegean sea-lanes. Such was the value of the Aegean commercial zone and its position in the trade network of the Levant. Commodities brought to the west still included luxury items, but there was a growing demand for less costly goods at competitive prices, like alum, wax, salt, wine, olives, and wheat. The final phase was closely connected with the Turkish entry into the Aegean world, of which Venice was the first western power to take note, in the opening decades of the fourteenth century. From then on Venice virtually operated a protectorate of Christian powers in the Aegean, garrisoning cities like Athens, Argos, Nauplia, Navarino, Monemvasia, Naupaktos and Patras when their rulers could no longer maintain their defence. These protectorates were extended not solely with an eye to the Turk but also to prevent Genoese adventurers from tendering for their defence should the Venetians fail to respond.

Phase 1: pre-1204

Geographically and historically Italy had ties with the Byzantine empire going back at least to the emperor Justinian's wars of reconquest (533–55). Parts of Apulia in the south remained part of the Byzantine empire until 1071. By the tenth century conditions were right for some maritime towns like Amalfi and Venice to exploit their position as nominal parts of the Byzantine empire in order to enter the carrying trade between east and west, and in particular that part of the Italy–Egypt–Aegean triangle which lay under the control of their former suzerain and where long-distance trade was largely in the hands of Jewish merchants. The displacement of the Jews from commercial predominance was to take place during the twelfth century. In the next century Venice was to establish her mastery in the commercial life of the Aegean by the principal role which its sailors played in providing a navy for Byzantium and transport for the Fourth Crusade. After 1204 the Venetian state and some of its noble families were well-placed to gain colonial and patrimonial possessions, some of which, like Crete, remained in Latin hands until 1669. Not just commercially and territorially but in the religious life of the crusader states of Greece Venetians were to play a prominent part, as well as in extending a protectorate over what was left of Frankish and Byzantine territory in the face of the Turkish expansion of the fourteenth century. From the 1150s Genoa, too, sought to further her commercial interest in the Aegean. As a late entrant her naval commanders were to contest the Venetian naval supremacy in those waters and after 1261 sought to replace Venice as the principal naval ally to the restored Byzantine order.

Both Venetian and Amalfitan merchants were sailing to Constantinople in the tenth century with sufficient regularity to carry correspondence and ambassadors from Germany to the eastern capital. Yet despite the potential of its hinterland north of the Alps, it was not the merchants of Venice but those from the town of Amalfi on the Gulf of Salerno who first established a permanent presence in Constantinople.[2] Sheltered from Saracen raids and able to exploit the local wax, honey and olive oil in exchange for luxury items purchased in Egyptian ports, the Amalfitani were able to establish a triangular trade between Alexandria, Constantinople and the central Mediterranean. Its only rival in the Aegean in the eleventh century was Venice, but for a time the advantage lay with Amalfi. There seems to have been an Amalfitan commercial quarter in Constantinople by the late tenth century, and Amalfitan connections at the imperial court were sufficiently good for a Benedictine monastery to be founded on Mount Athos sometime after 985.[3] However, involvement with the Normans, first as allies and then after 1131 as part of the Norman kingdom of Sicily, lead to the reduction and then eclipse of the privileges of Amalfitan merchants in the Byzantine empire. It had been the Amalfitans in Durrazzo who had admitted the forces of Robert Guiscard in February 1082, eight months or so after a Venetian fleet had relieved the town, and in that same year in his chrysobull to the Venetians, Alexios I forced the Amalfitan community in Constantinople to pay an annual tribute of three hyperpera to St Mark's in Venice.[4] In 1147 Roger of Sicily sent his fleet to capture Corfu and Cephalonia and to raid the commercial centres of Corinth and Thebes. In that same year in a chrysobull and treaty, Manuel I granted the Venetians free trade throughout the empire and the right to establish trading-posts in many towns in Greece and the Aegean. At the same time all Amalfitan commercial quarters were closed down. For the next century Venice was to be without a rival in the Aegean trade.

The Chrysobull of 1082 was the foundation of Venetian power in the Aegean. It gave the Venetians enormous advantages over rivals and potential rivals for the next century and, like all later confirmations and extensions of Venetian privileges, was in return for naval assistance to Byzantium. The

---

[2] Heyd, *Histoire du Commerce du Levant au Moyen-Age* (Paris, 1885–6) I, pp.100–1,112 and 190–264 on relations between the Italian cities and Byzantium in the eleventh and twelfth centuries; R.S. Lopez, *The Commercial Revolution of the Middle Ages* (Cambridge, 1976), pp.63–5; M. Balard, 'Amalfi et Byzance (x–xii siecles)' *Travaux et Memoires* 6 (1976), 85–95.

[3] Leo Bonsall, 'The Benedictine Monastery of St Mary on Athos' *Eastern Churches Review* 2 (1969), 262–7.

[4] Heyd, op.cit., I, pp.105–8, 118; *Urkunden* I, 52, 109–24 esp p.118; D. Abulafia, *The Two Cities* (Cambridge, 1977), pp.54, 81.

Byzantines disliked the sea and were prepared to hire fleets in return for commercial concessions.[5] For the first time a permanent Venetian quarter in Constantinople was established with shops (*ergasteria*), three wharfs (*maritimas III scalas*), and the church of St Akindynos with its bakery (*mankipium*).[6] These elements were the essence of an embolon or commercial quarter. To the east there were the Amalfitans, joined in 1111 by Pisan and in 1155 Genoese quarters. The Venetian area was extended in 1147, presumably at the expense of the Almafitans. The Pisans and Genoese had concentrated upon trade in the west Mediterranean and were late-comers to the Aegean. From the start the Venetians saw the Genoese as their main rivals, and in 1162 combined with the Pisans to attack the new Genoese quarter and did so again on their own account in 1171.[7] This favoured nation status within the empire placed the Venetians in a fine position to assist in the partitioning of the empire after the fall of Constantinople to the Fourth Crusade.

In addition to the trade compound in Constantinople, the chrysobull granted the Venetians the right to trade free of duty in a number of important towns in Syria and Asia Minor and also at Durazzo, Avlona, Boudonitza, Corfu, Modon, Coron, Nauplion, Corinth, Athens, Thebes, Negroponte (Chalkis), Demetrias, Thessalonika, and the towns of Thrace. The Venetians were the most privileged traders in the empire after 1082; not even native merchants could compete on equal terms with them. However, it is now generally accepted that these trading concessions did not harm the Byzantine economy, which showed signs of rapid expansion throughout the eleventh and twelfth centuries and which only halted with the Fourth Crusade.[8] Indeed it was in the interest of local wholesalers to deal with the Venetians since those selling to Venetians were exempt from the kommerkion on that transaction. Nonetheless, the Venetians were not free of rivals either in Constantinople or continental Greece. Herrin cites examples of both Pisans and Genoese acting as ambassadors of Byzantium and providing shipping to the Byzantine state. In 1179 Baldovino Guercio of Genoa provided the ships which brought Agnes-Anna from France to be the bride of the future Alexios II, and in 1189 and 1192 two Pisans, Jacob and

---

[5] A. Kazdhan and G. Constable, *People and Power in Byzantium* (Washington, 1982), pp.42–3.

[6] H. Brown, 'The Venetians and the Venetian Quarter in Constantinople to the close of the twelfth century' *JHS* 40 (1920), 68–88; M. Martin, 'The Venetians in the Byzantine Empire Before 1204', in J. Howard-Johnston, ed., *Byzantium and the West c.850–c.1200* (Amsterdam, 1988), pp.201–14.

[7] G.W. Day, *Genoa's Responses to Byzantium, 1155–1204* (Urbana, 1988), pp.24–8; J.K. Fotheringham, 'Genoa and the Fourth Crusade' *EHR* 25 (1910), 26–57.

[8] M.F. Hendy, 'Byzantium, 1081–1204: an economic reappraisal' *TRHS* 5th ser., 20 (1970), 31–52; idem, 'Byzantium 1081–1204: the economy revisited', published for the first time as essay II in idem, *The Economy, Fiscal Administration and Coinage of Byzantium* (London, 1989) in which essay I is a reprint of the earlier study.

Pippino, were used as ambassadors to Germany and Cyprus respectively.[9] Indeed in late 1201 it was a Pisan vessel which brought Alexios Angelos from Constantinople to Ancona and thereby set in place one of the principle actors in the diversion of the Fourth Crusade to Constantinople. Around 1170 the Rabbi Benjamin of Tudela noted a substantial Jewish silk manufacturing and trading community in Thebes, merchants from many nations at Negroponte, and traders from Venice, Genoa and Pisa at Halmyros.[10] The Genoese were established at Thebes as early as 1169, where they were joined some time before 1185 by a colony of Venetian merchants. In March 1196 a Venetian fleet appeared at Abydos, presumably to attack Pisan merchant vessels, but also to intimidate the new emperor Alexios III should he wish to favour the merchants of Pisa at the expense of the Venetians.[11]

The privileged position of the Italian republics, especially that of the Venetians, had been built up at the will of the Byzantine emperors, and at his will the republics might be played off against one another or the privileges even terminated altogether should political or military conditions prove conducive. Although the chrysobull of 1082 had been granted in perpetuity, no emperor need be bound by the grants of his predecessor. In 1119 John II, on being approached by a Venetian embassy, refused to confirm his father's chrysobull of 1082. This attempt at ending Venetian privileges resulted in devastating Venetian attacks on Dalamatia and Corfu in 1122–23 and the destruction of Modon in 1125. The following year the chrysobull was confirmed. The lack of an effective navy showed both the necessity of Venetian support and the folly of resisting them.[12] Nicol has noted the delay on the part of Manuel in confirming the privileges of the Venetians in 1147. It came some four years after his accession and in the face of a Norman naval attack on the empire.[13] Again after 20 years of ruptured relations caused by the seizure of Venetian merchants and their goods in 1171, Isaac II Angelos confirmed all previous confirmations and extensions of the 1082 chrysobull in February 1187, two years after his elevation to the purple and the violent overthrow of Andronikos I. The immediate cause seems to have been the action of the Norman fleet under Tancred of Lecce in the Sea of Marmora and Astakenos Gulf in 1185,

---

[9] J. Herrin, 'The collapse of the Byzantine Empire in the twelfth century: a study of a medieval economy' *University of Birmingham History Journal* 12 (1970), 188–203, esp.193, n.2.

[10] M.N. Adler, ed., *The Itinerary of Benjamin of Tudela* (London, 1907), p.11.

[11] R. Morozzo della Rocca and A. Lombardo, *Documents del commercio veneziano nei secolo XI–XIII* 2 vols (Turin, 1940), I, 348; C.M. Brand, *Byzantium Confronts the West* (Cambridge, Mass., 1968), pp.196–200; S. Symeonoglou, *The Topography of Thebes* (Princeton, 1984), p.157.

[12] D. Nicol, *Byzantium and Venice* (Cambridge, 1988), pp.77–81; Herrin, art.cit., 191.

[13] Nicol, op.cit., pp.85–7.

subsequent to their seizure and sack of Thessalonika and the failure of a Byzantine fleet to recapture Cyprus from Isaac Komnenos and his Norman allies in the spring of 1187. The Norman occupation of Corfu (up to the peace between William II of Sicily and Isaac in 1188?) brought Byzantines and Venetians together as it had in 1082. The three chrysobulls of 1187 were largely concerned with the equipment of Venetian ships for service in the Byzantine fleet. Nicol has pointed out that this agreement was designed to restore the harmony of Veneto–Byzantine relations prior to the arrests and seizures of 1171, which had dominated and soured any commercial and naval cooperation between the two states. In November 1197, again two years after his seizure of power, Alexios III confirmed the 1187 agreement. The overthrow of Isaac might have been disastrous for Venetian interests, but for the first time all towns and districts in which Venetian merchants were exempt from the kommerkion were listed and this was to form the basis for the Venetian claims to one third of the empire in 1204.[14]

The Venetian commercial monopoly was thus an uncertain asset. Not only was it at the mercy of the diplomatic and political needs of the emperor, but the presence of a considerable body of merchants in Constantinople (the estimate of 10,000 is generally reckoned too high) and the provinces affected the life, opinions and actions of the native population. Brand has noted a difference in attitude between the artisans and merchants of the empire who were disadvantaged competitors of the Venetians and the great landowners who found ready buyers in the Venetians for their agricultural produce, especially wine and olive oil, bought and sold without payment of the kommerkion which local wholesalers would have to pay.[15] It was popular support that the regent Andronikos Komnenos was courting when he incited the massacre of the Latins in Constantinople in April 1182. There were then factions developing in Byzantine political life around a pro- and anti-Latin ticket.

The Byzantine writers Kinnamos, Eustathios of Thessalonika and Nicetas Choniates show that the Latins were far from popular in the towns of the empire with their proud and haughty demeanour, cocking a snook at any attempts to confine them to ghettoes and posing a problem of public order for the imperial authorities. Kinnamos emphasised their vulgarity, their boastfulness and their insulting behaviour to Greeks – treating 'the citizen like a slave, not merely one of the general commonalty, but even one who took pride in the rank of sebastos'. These insults were seen by Kinnamos as extending from physical violence and acts of piracy to the '...

---

[14] For the Latin texts of the chrysobulls of 1082, 1126, 1147, 1187 and 1196 see *Urkunden* I, 43–54, 95–8, 179–203, 246–80. The most recent text of the 1082 chrysobull is S. Borsari, 'Il crisobullo di Alessio I per Venezia' *Annali dell' Instituto Italiano per gli studi storici* 2 (1969–70), 111–31. See Nicol, op.cit., pp.60–2 and 84–103 for comment and summaries.

[15] Brand, *Byzantium Confronts the West*, op.cit., p.12.

taking for themselves Roman wives and dwelling like other Romans in their houses outside the residential area granted them by the emperor'.[16] The graecising tendency of these married Venetians was more than skin deep. They adopted Greek hairstyles, spoke Greek and were clearly sufficiently committed to their Greek families not to abandon them in either 1171 or again in the winter months of 1203/4 when xenophobic feeling was at its height in the city and there was no firm central authority to keep it in check. The Latins might be unpopular with the populace, the Greek clergy and the civil bureaucracy, but they were protected by imperial law and outrages against them, like the arrests of 1171 and the massacre of April 1182, were either officially provoked or carried out with official connivance. It says much for a weak emperor like Alexios III and the law-abiding tendency of the Constantinopolitan populace that few if any outrages were recorded against the foreign residents of the city in July 1203 when the fleet of the crusaders arrived off the city. It was only in August that a mob fired the Venetian, Pisan and Genoese quarters of the city and forced 15,000 Latins to flee to the crusader camp. Even then there were sufficient married Venetians left in the city to provide some protection for the refugee party of Nicetas Choniates in April 1204.[17]

The Venetian responsibility for the diversion of the Fourth Crusade is not proven and rests upon circumstantial evidence only. Both the reigning emperor Alexios III and his brother Isaac whom he he had displaced in 1195 had shown marked favour to the Venetians. Any increase in the privileges of the Pisans and Genoese, such as those granted in 1199, had happened before and had been accommodated. Some Pisans had manned the walls of Byzantium in July 1203. It must have been clear that a destabilised situation would benefit neither their trade nor the interests of their citizens. The decision to conquer the empire that was made by March 1204 came suddenly and after the collapse of authority in the city, the influx of refugees into the Latin camp and the removal of the western puppet emperor Alexios IV in January. As a result the crusaders could not proceed on their intended crusade and the future of Venetian commerce and citizens in Constantinople could not be guaranteed. It was these very practical concerns rather than any ultra-devious planning on the part of doge Dandolo which brought about the decision in March 1204 to attack Constantinople and to elect a Latin emperor. All of this could have been done in July 1203 if such had been the original intention of the crusader. Eight months later this new aggressive policy was adopted '... *ad honorem Dei et sancte Romane ecclesie et*

---

[16] Ioannes Kinnamos, *Epitome rerum ab Ioanne et Alexio Comnenis gestarum*, ed. A. Meineke (Bonn, 1836), pp. 280–2; English trans. by C.M. Brand, *Deeds of John and Manuel Comnenus by John Kinnamos* (New York, 1976), pp.210–11.
[17] Choniates, pp.553–6; Villehardouin, 203–5; D. Queller, *The Fourth Crusade* (Pennsylvania, 1977), pp.116–21; Nicol, op.cit., pp.136–9.

imperii' – presumably the empire as it had been in 1203 not what it had become since the arrival of the crusading army.[18] The agreement of March 1204 guaranteed the trading position of the Venetians within the empire as it had been established by the chrysobulls of the Komnenoi in the eleventh and twelfth centuries. Legally this did not represent an advance but might leave room to expel the Genoese and the Pisans, some of whom had actually fought in defence of the city in July. Yet would a Latin emperor be any more reliable? Much is made of Boniface of Montferrat's pro-Genoese stance and the effort by the electoral college to obtain an emperor acceptable to the Venetians, but their prime concern must have been stability. Too much then has been made of the wily doge and the conflict between the men of commerce and the men of war – the latter were by no means simpletons and the former, especially the doge, not ultra-devious. Indeed some interpretations using this model have little more to recommend them than the romantic accounts of Martin da Canale and the *Chronicle of the Morea* which they often hold up to ridicule.[19]

Phase 2: 1204–61

After the capture of the city, the Venetian interest in the Aegean changed radically. Apparently quite suddenly it changed from a commercial power seeking most-favoured-nation status to that of a colonial power in its own right. Historians of Venice link this change to the triumph of the commune in the last decade of the twelfth century.[20] Certainly many Venetian aristocratic families gained territories in Crete and the Aegean which they held either as vassals of the Latin emperor or of Venice.[21] Thiriet saw this colonial expansion as the natural corollary of the conquest of Constantinople but no such territorial expansion had followed the conquests in the Holy Land a century earlier. There was a climate of opinion which endorsed this overseas expansion evident not just in Venice but in the other maritime republics. Genoese pirates *cum* lords had established themselves in Cephalonia in 1203 and in Crete in 1204 from whence they were expelled. Opportunities had been missed in the Levant in the preceeding century; the Aegean frontier was all that was left. The immediate impetus for this territorial expansion may well have come from the Venetians resident in the city, who now had the doge himself as their head, actively protecting their

---

[18] *Urkunden* I, 450.
[19] Setton, p.10.
[20] F.C. Lane, *Venice, A Maritime Republic* (Baltimore, 1973), pp.86–101.
[21] F. Thiriet, *La Romanie Venitienne au moyen age* (Paris, 1959; re-issued 1975), pp.74–83.

interests on the councils of the crusading host. Enrico Dandolo showed no sign of returning to Venice where his son, Ranieri, was acting as vice-doge and who was later to be killed commanding the conquest of Crete.[22] Enrico sent the fleet home in August 1204, but he threw himself into establishing the Latin settlement, defusing the quarrel between Boniface and Baldwin in September,[23] buying the rights to the island of Crete from Boniface in order to forestall a Genoese offer[24] and, despite his age and poor eyesight, taking an active part in military expeditions into Thrace.[25] By 1 June 1205 he was dead but the *stato da mar* was created.[26]

It was in the first half dozen years of the empire's existence that the bulk of those territories to which the Venetians were to cling so tenaciously in the face of the Turkish threat in the fourteenth and fifteenth centuries were acquired. The gaining of some of them, like Crete, required nearly 50 years of colonial war, and the protection of others were to require annual naval expeditions and the acquisition of yet more lands like Pteleon and the strip of eastern Boeotia in order to protect Euboea. All this was in the future, but for Dandolo and his generation it represented a major change in attitude in the furtherance of overseas trade.

Circumstantial evidence would suggest that the Venetians of Constantinople and certain officers from the Venetian ships which took part in the crusade provided the impetus for territorial acquisitions. First, the terms of the March 1204 Pact itself, which assigned the Venetians nearly half of the city of Constantinople and gave them equal weight on the commissions to elect an emperor and to distribute lands in the empire, suggested an early stirring of territorial ambitions. Two months before this agreement was signed there had been a substantial influx into the crusader camp of Italians from Constantinople. Secondly, the retention by the Venetian community of such a prestigious artefact as the icon of the Virgin Hodegetria, alleged to have been painted by St Luke, suggests at the very least a developed community with a strong political identity. The icon was lodged in the church of the monastery of Pantokrator, now a part of the extended Venetian enclave, which encompassed three-eighths of the city. It appears that the icon had come into the hands of Henry of Flanders or his brother, the emperor Baldwin, during the sack of the city but that it may have come to Patriarch Morosini as the price for his agreement to Henry's coronation in August 1206.[27] Whether it was deference to the feelings of the

---

[22] Lane, op.cit., p.94 for an assessment of Ranieri's role.
[23] Villehardouin, 282–302; Clari, CIV–CV (McNeal trans., pp.120–1).
[24] *Urkunden* I, 512ff.
[25] Villehardouin, 361, 364–6, 375, 384.
[26] Villehardouin, 388. There is some doubt whether the tomb slab bearing his name in the south gallery of Haghia Sophia is the place of his burial or a nineteenth century addition.
[27] R.L. Wolff, 'Footnote to an incident of the Latin occupation of Constantinople: the church and the icon of the Hodegetria' *Traditio* 6 (1948), 319–28.

Greek populace or a desire to have a protecting emblem of their own, the relic was not sent to Venice as so many relics in the previous century had been. Certainly any dubious circumstances attending their acquisition had been ignored and it is difficult to see that circumstances would have been different with this relic. The Venetian community in Constantinople had political plans and a knowledge of local conditions.

Within a month of Dandolo's death they had elected a podesta and council of their own to administer their new enlarged quarter. The first podesta, Marino Zeno, took not just the title of '*Potestas*' but also that of '*quartae partis et dimidiae totius imperii Romanie Dominator*'. These developments alarmed the government in Venice, where, it appears, rumours were rife of a proposal to transfer the seat of government from Venice to Constantinople. This governmental preoccupation, which is only known from the chronicle of Daniele Barbaro who dated it to 1224, reflected the change in Venetian interests about this time – one which Venetians two or three generations later could better appreciate. The new doge, Pietro Ziani, and his councillors acted quickly to bring the new political entity under home control. Reports were requested from Zeno, who in October 1205 took an oath acknowledging the suzerainty of the doge and ceded lands along the Adriatic seaboard and the title of dominator to Ziani. Finally, the opportunity to acquire territories in the Aegean was thrown open to all Venetian citizens who could conquer and hold it.[28] It was at this point that the aristocratic families of Venice got their opportunity to share in Aegean real estate. It appears that Venice had been dragged into the acquisition of Aegean territory but that this change in direction reflected the mood both in Venice and amongst the Venetians in the east.

The Venetians were not the first Italians to acquire territory in the Aegean. This distinction seems to belong to various lone operators from Genoa and Pisa who had resorted to piracy following the slaughter of Italian merchants in Constantinople in 1182. These men occupied bases in the Aegean in the furtherance of their piratical activities some ten years before the Fourth Crusade reached Constantinople.[29] The ports which they occupied were temporary bases rather than colonies, but territory which had been occupied by westerners and to which some claim might be exerted tended to be more formally occupied. Thus in 1199 Leone Vetrano captured and garrisoned Cape Polacro in western Corfu, an island which had been conquered by William II of Sicily in 1185 and granted to Margaritone of Brindisi as a fief. The island had been subsequently recovered by Byzantium.

---

[28] R.L. Wolff, 'The oath of the Venetian podesta' *Annuaire de L'Institut de Philologie et d'Histoire Orientales et Slaves* 12 (1953), 539–73, reprinted as essay VI in *Studies in the Latin Empire of Constantinople* (London, 1976).

[29] This paragraph is based upon J.K. Fotheringham, 'Genoa and the Fourth Crusade' *EHR* 25 (1910), 26–57.

Until the mid-1190s the Aegean ports and islands were still regarded as Byzantine territory. However, in 1194 five Pisan galleys occupied Abydos and used it as a base to attack Venetian shipping. It was occupied in turn by the Venetians in 1196. The wars of the Italian commercial republics were spilling over onto the Aegean sea-lanes as well as onto the streets of Constantinople. Indeed in July 1203 Pisans helped to defend the city against the first assault of the crusading army with its Venetian allies. The Byzantine hosts could not control their Italian guests. Sometime after 1195 the Genoese Gafforio began a piratical career in the Archipelago, feeling himself cheated in commercial dealings with the Greeks. His death at Greek hands in 1199 is said to have been the reason for a Genoese fleet in the harbour of Fraschia in Crete. To the south of Corfu the islands of Kephalonia, Ithaka and Zakynthos were in the hands Count Maio Orsini, and a number of Genoese corsairs controlled that well-known pirates' nest, the harbour of Modon, where they relieved the Templar Barozzi of his treasures in late 1204. In 1206 Enrico Pescatore, count of Malta, arrived in Crete with a substantial fleet of 29 ships intent on the conquest of that island. It took four years from 1207 to 1211 for the Venetians to expel him, and in 1212 Jacopo Tiepolo was appointed the first governor or duke of Crete and 200 fiefs were designated for Venetian settlers. The trend towards territorial conquests was as evident in Genoa as in Venice. If anything Genoa set the pace and provoked a Venetian response.

Venice was slow to exploit its lands in Romania. The Partition Treaty of March 1204 had given it a claim to three-eighths of the former Byzantine territory, whilst the purchase of Crete from Boniface for 1,000 silver marks in August 1204 brought a title to the largest island of the region and one athwart the sea route to the eastern Mediterranean from Venice.[30] It was the security of the sea-lanes rather than any territorial imperative that dictated what lands from the considerable Venetian concession were to be occupied. This principle directed the spread of direct rule by Venice in the Aegean. Immediate Venetian action was concerned with the security of the Adriatic approaches to Venice itself. Thus the flotilla escorting the first Latin patriarch, Tommaso Morosini, from Venice to Constantinople in the spring of 1205 took advantage of its presence in Greek waters to reduce Durazzo, Corfu and the pirate bases of Modon and Coron. Yet a glance through Hopf's list of the Venetian governors in the Aegean shows that it was in the late fourteenth century and later that they were appointed in any number in response to the Turkish threat.[31] In the decade or so after 1204 only Modon and Coron received a castellan in the person of Rafaello Goro in 1209, Crete a duke in 1211, and Negroponte a baili in 1216, who resided in the city of that name rather than in the Venetian harbours of Oreos and

---

[30] *Urkunden* I, 464–73, 512–5.
[31] CGR, pp.371–413.

Karystos. Many of the territories nominally acquired in 1204 were neither immediately conquered nor, indeed, ever occupied. The harbours and centres of Thrace, like Rodosto and Gallipoli, seem never to have received Venetian garrisons, whilst Adrianople on the Via Egnatia was granted by the Latin emperor to Theodore Branas in 1206 in the interest of security.[32]

From the start the Venetian government adopted a minimalist approach to its overseas possessions. It sought to exploit the self-interests of territorial magnates in the protection of its own possessions. Thus in August 1204 by the so-called Treaty of Adrianople with Boniface of Montferrat which secured the purchase of Crete, Venice also secured his benevolence towards the dignity and possessions of Venice in Romania – so much for Boniface's links with Genoa. In June 1209 diplomacy was again resorted to. The Treaty of Sapienza with Geoffrey de Villehardouin not only limited the ambitions of that leader in Messenia but secured his benevolence towards Venetian interests in Romania. The vagueness with which the boundaries of Modon/Coron and Achaia were set out shows that at this time Venice was more concerned with the harbours than with their hinterland.

For the occupation of the remainder of the territories assigned to it in September 1204, more especially the islands of the Archipelago (Egeon pelagos) where a number of Genoese outposts were scattered as at Apalire on Naxos, it relied on the self-interest of territorial ambition once again. In this case the personal initiative of its noble citizen families with spare sons and capital to invest in Aegean real estate. There were clearly sufficient takers in Venice for the government to leave colonial conquests and exploitation to its citizens. Corfu was leased to ten Venetian nobles in 1207, and in 1208 Count Maio was recognised as a vassal of the Venetian Republic.

The relationship of the various potentates to Venice reserved the suzerainty of the Latin emperor of Constantinople. Franks like Boniface and Geoffrey de Villehardouin were granted Venetian citizenship and their links were the loosest. On Euboea the baili residing in Negroponte (Chalkis) slowly expanded Venetian influence as the honest broker in the succession disputes to the dalle Carceri inheritance after 1216, and latterly as the surest defence against Turkish raids in the fifteenth century, but those like Sanudo and his colleagues were expected to give very direct material support to Venice. Thus in 1212 the duke of Crete sought military help from Marco Sanudo in the suppression of a rising by the Hagiostephanitai family in eastern Crete.

---

[32] Villehardouin, 423, 441.

Phase 2: the islands of the Aegean

The sources for the conquests of the Aegean islands are both late in date and vague in content. We have no details of the campaign or of the extent of Italian settlement in the islands in this first decade, let alone the proportion of state to private investment in the expeditions. In the absence of such evidence, discussion and speculation has concerned itself with the leadership of the expedition or expeditions and not unnaturally been confined in its discussion by the trammels imposed by the late Venetian chroniclers recording the conquest. The main source is the chronicle of the doge Andrea Dandolo (*c*. 1309–54) who was concerned with the titles acquired in the Aegean rather than the thoroughness of Venetian penetration of the Archipelago. He gave no details of the size, composition or course of the expeditions which acquired them.[33] He implied that there was one leader, Marco Sanudo, and hence one expedition, but that he and his compatriots, Marino Dandolo and the brothers Andrea and Geremia Ghisi had '*segregatim navigantes*' which presumably means minimal coordination and diverse objectives. He also lists Ravano dalle Carceri, the lord of Negroponte (Euboea), and Philocalo Navigaioso, lord of Stalimene (Lemnos), as members of the expedition. These last had received their territories quite independently of Marco Sanudo, the former in some way from Jacques d'Avesnes, the original conqueror of the island in 1205, and the latter by grant from the emperor Henry who also created him mega dux. The chronicler Daniele Barbaro (1511–70) provided further names of expedition members but drew a distinction between Sanudo's expedition to Naxos, which he placed in the winter of 1204–5 with the backing of Enrico Dandolo in Constantinople, and the more general conquest of the Archipelago in 1206–7 in the time of Pietro Ziani.[34] Both these late medieval chroniclers assumed that the island lords of their own day could trace their lordships back to the the initial conquest in the early thirteenth century. However, the process of death and marriage had introduced much new blood, in the intervening two centuries, from Negroponte. Thus the Quirini, usually described as lords of Astypalaia from 1207 or from 1310, in fact acquired that island in 1413 and held it until their displacement by the Turks in 1537.

Around 1212 there were six Venetian families ruling in the Archipelago. Marco Sanudo (d. 1227), duke of the Archipelago, occupied the islands of Naxos, Paros, Antiparos, Melos, Siphnos, Cythnos (Thermia), Ios (Nio), Amorgos, Cimilos, Sicinos, Syra and Pholegandros. Marino Dandolo received Andros; the Ghisi brothers received Tinos, Mykonos,

---

[33] Relevant text translated in J.K. Fotheringham, *Marco Sanudo, Conqueror of the Archipelago* (Oxford, 1915), p.57.
[34] Text in ibid., pp.105–8.

Skyros, Skopelos, Seriphos and Keos (Zia); Jacopo Barozzi received Thera (Santorini); Leonardo Foscolo received Anaphe; Marco Venier received Kythera (Cerigo); and Jacopo Viaro received Cerigotto.[35] All these families were expected to rule in the Venetian interest. For example, the Venier family on Kythera followed an overtly conciliatory policy towards the Greek archons of the island, certainly by contrast with that of the Venetians on nearby Crete. On two occasions Venier sons took brides from Greek families, in 1238 and c.1295/1300. Their philhellenic stance was noted by Professor Thiriet. However, it was not this but their support of a revolt of Venetian settlers in Crete in 1363 which lost them their island, which passed under direct Venetian rule.[36] Occurrences like this, intermarriage and the leasing out of islands, like the proposal to lease Tinos and Mykonos to Stefano Delilofordozi in 1432, meant that in the course of time these founding families were supplemented or replaced by other members of the Venetian nobility.[37]

In the third generation the Sanudi created island lordships for its younger sons on Melos, Nio, Paros and Syra. In 1376 Fiorenza, the daughter of Marcelino, lord of Melos, brought the title to that island to one Franceso Crispo, a minor lord from Euboea. The direct male line of the Sanudi died out in 1362 with the death of Giovanni I. The title passed to his daughter, another Fiorenza, who in 1349 had married Giovanni dalle Carcere, the leading triarch of Euboea. Since 1358 she had been a widow and as duchess of Naxos and regent of Negroponte was a very desirable match, and one over which the Venetian senate was determined to keep control. The approaches of Pietro Raccanelli, the leading Genoese mahonese of Chios, were rejected in 1361, as were those of Giovanni Acciaiuoli, the archbishop of Patras (1360–63) on behalf of his brother Nerio, the future duke of Athens (d. 1394).[38] On her own death in 1371 the dukedom passed to her son, Niccolo dalle Carceri. He was murdered by Francesco Crispo in 1388 and the fortunes of the Archipelago along with the inheritance customs of the Sanudi passed to the Crispi family. Likewise the family of Sommipara acquired the lordship of Andros and Paros in 1390 on the marriage of Gasparo to Maria Sanudo, the daughter of Fiorenza and her second husband, Niccolo Spezzabanda, whom she had married in 1364.

According to Dandolo's chronicle, Greek assistance was offered to the

[35] Ibid., p.59; *Cambridge Medieval History* IV, i (Cambridge, 1967), p.425. The most recent account is C. and K. Frazee, *The Island Princes of Greece, The Dukes of the Archipelago* (Amsterdam, 1988).
[36] Chryssa Maltezou, 'The historical geography of Kythira', in A.E. Laiou-Thomadakis, ed., *Charanis Studies, Essays in Honor of Peter Charanis* (New Brunswick, 1980), pp.151–75; F. Thiriet, 'A propos de la seigneurie des Venier sur Cerigo' *Studi veneziani* 12 (1970), pp.199–210.
[37] Thiriet, no. 2273 (24 March 1432).
[38] Setton, p.247, n.114.

conquerors as a means of bringing some stability to the island economies. However, Greeks also fought alongside the Genoese garrison at Apalire in 1206. Perhaps we can distinguish a divide between legitimist and pragmatist Greeks in their reaction to the Latins. Presumably an arrangement similar to that reached with the Greeks of the mainland regarding freedom to exercise their religion was arrived at. Certainly Michael Choniates, the former metropolitan of Athens, was left undisturbed in his exile on Keos (1205–17), whilst the rights of the monks of Patmos were respected.

The limited population of the islands, together with scarce natural resources and communications restricted by tides and wind, did not intensify rivalry and aggression between Greeks and Latins. Latin settlement was limited to the the towns of the larger islands, leaving the countryside to the Greeks. Sanudo and his fellow conquerors were probably able to leave local landowners undisturbed, expropriating only absentee landlords, and generally the Latins constituted less than 10 per cent of the population of these larger islands. Anthony Luttrell has given some figures. In 1395 Chios contained some 10,000 Greeks and less than 1,000 Latins. Whilst in 1500 about 20 per cent of Cycladic islanders followed the Latin rite. Some of these were converted Greeks, like the predominantly female inhabitants of Siphnos who, according to the Florentine priest and traveller Cristoforo Buondelmonti in the Aegean (1414–20), followed the Roman rite although they knew no Latin. The increase in piratical activity in the late twelfth century following the run-down of the Byzantine navy had caused settlement to relocate inland and such towers and fortifications that the conquerors built were designed to protect the inhabitants rather than to overawe them. Politics tended to be familial feuds rather than nationalist uprisings, whilst the tiny populations of some islands made such risings a remote possibility. Some islands close to Asia Minor remained in Greek hands – Chios until 1304, Rhodes until 1306, Kos until 1337, and Lesbos until 1337. Increased Turkish piratical and naval activity after the first decade of the fourteenth century led to the positive seeking out of Venetian protection by island rulers and the Byzantine emperor. The response was the plethora of Venetian governors noted by Hopf in the decades after 1350. However, the larger islands provided a contrast to the smaller Cycladic islands. These were visited by western traders.[39] The contrast between the Venetian penetration of Negroponte and the costly military campaigns in Crete, coupled with religious persecution there in the 1359, is most marked and worthy of attention.

---

[39] For further discussion of material in this paragraph see A. Luttrell, 'The Latins and life on the smaller Aegean islands, 1204–1453' *Mediterranean History Review* 4 (1989), 146–57, and Ben Slot, 'The Frankish Archipelago' *ByzF* 16 (1991), 196–205.

Phase 2: Euboea (Negroponte)

After the conquest of Euboea by Jacques d'Avesnes in the summer of 1205, his suzerain Boniface of Montferrat had created three large fiefs centred on Karystos, Negroponte (Chalkis), and Oreos. The southern fief of Karystos was granted to Ravanno dalle Carceri of Verona. By 1209 Ravanno had secured possession of the whole island through a combination of the death and disinterest of his fellow Veronese lords. On the death of his suzerain Boniface in September 1207 he had become one of the main supporters of the Lombard legitimist party in Thessalonika, which by the spring of 1209 had collapsed in the face of military and diplomatic pressure from the emperor Henry (see pp.58–9) leaving some of its supporters like Biandrate, the Canossa brothers and the Templars subject to loss of lands. To protect himself through the good offices of his brother Henry, the bishop of Mantua, Ravanno sought the suzerainty of the doge. The representatives of both parties met in Negroponte in March 1209. Ravanno undertook to protect Venetian interests, to provide the Venetian merchant community in Negroponte with a church, a warehouse and customs concessions, to enforce the judgements of such Venetian judges as should be chosen to adjudicate in cases in which Venetian subjects were involved, and to pay an annuity of 2,100 gold hyperpera and a robe of samite to the doge, as well as an altar cloth for the church of St Mark in Venice. This was the first official Venetian involvement with the island, although they had a claim to the ports of Oreos and Karystos by the 1204 partition. This had been conveniently ignored by Boniface in his granting out of the island and Venice had done nothing about it until now. However, in return for guaranteeing the dalle Carceri interests, the republic had gained all that it appeared to want on the island. An interesting clause in the privilegium and promissio also protected the interests of the Greek landowners who were to to occupy the condition which they held '... *Emanuelis tempore*', that is before 1180. By 1216 the Venetian community on the island was organised with a baili of its own. In November that year the baili organised and underwrote the distributed of landed property between the six heirs of Ravanno and in each new property distributed amongst the Lombard lords the privileges of the Venetians on the island increased. However, Negroponte was never to be a Venetian colony in the sense that Crete, Modon and Coron were. Its citizens enjoyed most-favoured-nation status in the capital of the island, which was the resort of the principal landowners, both Greek and Latin. The influence of its baili was paramount, especially when external dangers threatened as in 1258 with Geoffrey II de Villehardouin, the 1270s with the virtual conquest of the island by Licario of Karystos in the name of his employer Michael VIII, and throughout most of the fourteenth century with the raids of Turkish fleets from Anatolia. The baili organised what there was of island defence, sought reinforcements and munitions from the duke of Crete, and took over more and more fiscal privileges in order to pay for this protection. In 1388 an arsenal was built in Negroponte recognising the island's growing importance in the fight against the Turks. In 1415 Venice spent 10,000 hyperpera a year more than it received in income from the island. Economies in that year, in the form of the disbandment of mercenary companies and the abandonment of outposts in the east of the island, coincided with the heaviest Turkish raids. Greek landowners sent petitions not to the Lombard triarchs but to the doge to restore some of the island's defences. Venice might be the protector and the greatest influence in the island but it was not the suzerain and its bailies were instructed to respect the rights of the triarchs and not to come between them and their Greek tenants. Those same Greeks in 1451 had petitioned for the application of the Assizes of Romania. Venice responded positively. What a difference in Veneto–Greek relations. Greeks had not been disposed, Franks or Lombard influences were present, and Venice was seen as an asset rather than as a conqueror.[40]

Phase 2: Crete

The reluctance of the Venetian government to commit troops to the acquisition of colonial territory was well-founded. In Crete, where purchase gave it the title and the presence of the Genoese commanded by Pescatore the impetus to intervene, the signoria and its representatives created the conditions and suffered the consequences which it had been careful to avoid in its dealings with the nascent commune in Constantinople in 1205 and in its treatment of the Greek populace on Negroponte. Crete is the third largest island in the Mediterranean and an important watering place between Italy and the Levant. St Paul had stopped at Kallilimenia (Fair Haven) in the first century at the spot where Venetian troops were to disembark in 1214, whilst Arab raids in the Aegean from 828 until their expulsion in 961 not only slowed the development of the western pilgrim traffic to the Holy Land but provided a base from which to raid the Aegean. The immense booty acquired by Nikephoros Phokas in 961 showed how profitable this endeavour was, whilst the use made by the Venetians of the island as their eastern arsenal in the thirteenth and fourteenth centuries showed that its strategic significance was not lost on them either. Pescatore had to be expelled and the island conquered. This was achieved by 1211, a duke, Jacopo Tiepolo, appointed to replace the Byzanine doux or katapan, and

---

[40] *Urkunden* II, 89–96, 176–8; III, 14–15. J.B. Bury, 'The Lombards and Venetians in Euboia' *JHS* 7 (1886), 309–52; 8 (1887); 194–213; 9 (1888), 91–117; L. de Mas Latrie, 'Les Seigneurs tierciers de Negreponte' *Revue de l'Orient Latin* I (1893), 413–32; R.J. Loenertz, 'Les seigneurs tierciers de Negreponte ...' *Byzantion* 35 (1965), 235–71.

200 fiefs created for settlers from Venice. A little Venice was to be created halfway to Africa and the Levant, not only useful for long-distance commerce but a bread-basket for the home republic. Professor Laiou has charted the commercialisation of Cretan agriculture, which provided grain, olive oil, wine, cheese and timber for the serenissima as well as supplementing the needs of its citizens in Negroponte and the Archipelago. Crete was to be directly exploited in a way which the other Greek areas occupied by Venetians never were. There was no room in the early calculations of the Venetian planners for Greeks on the island, yet in about 1204 its population was something like 500,000. It was much larger and enjoyed far better maritime communications than any of the islands of the Archipelago.[41]

In September 1212 the lands of Crete, with the exception of some territory around Candia (Megalo Kastro) and Temeno, were divided up into 200 fiefs or casals in six blocks such that enterprising volunteers from the six sestieri or wards of Venice might hold their new lands near former but equally enterprising neighbours. Hopf has pointed out that colonists from the ward of Santi Apostoli held Sitia, Hierapetra, Lassithi and Mirabello in the east of the island, those from San Marco the south-west around Pediada, and those from Santa Croce the Mesarea or central plateau.[42] The names of some of the original male colonists are listed by sestieri at the end of the 1212 decree. The preponderance of knights' fees and sergeants' fees to those of foot-soldiers, in the order of 12:1, has been taken to show that enthusiasm for this first Venetian colonial enterprise was most fervent amongst the scions of the noble families.[43]

Unlike the other islands of the Aegean, Crete did not form part of the Latin empire. The doge was the suzerain and the new land grants could only be alienated with his consent and even then only to another Venetian. The colonists were to protect the interests and share the enemies of the mother city, and after the elapse of four years pay an annual tribute of 500 hyperpera to the republic. Whether the land division was drawn up in Venice or in Crete, like the division of the empire in 1204, it bears testimony to western geographic knowledge of the island and presumably to the use of Greek tax records. The actual apportionment of property, that is of farmsteads and town houses, was to be done by the duke of Crete. It is unclear what was to happen to the Greeks. They received mention in only one paragraph in the decree of 1212, namely that their persons and their chattels were under the protection of the duke of Crete. Whilst the poor had merely exchanged landlords, the archontic families of the islands had fallen

---

[41] Robert Pashley, *Travels in Crete* II (London, 1837), p.326.
[42] C. Hopf in Ersch Gruerber, *Enkyklopedie*, vol. 85, p.241; Flaminius Cornelius in *Creta Sacra* II, 237 lists the principal settlements in each colonial sexteri together with the noble captains of each division. This is reprinted with a Latin translation in *Urkunden* II, 143–5.
[43] Text of 1212 decree in *Urkunden* II, 129–36. See also F.C. Hodgson, *Venice in the Thirteenth and Fourteenth Centuries* (London, 1910), pp.47ff.

from landlords to, at best, unfree tenants. This one paragraph was headed '*De facta laycorum Grecorum*'. This implied that all Greeks were now regarded as laymen since the preceding paragraph had assigned all churches to the Venetians to be assigned by the duke of Crete.

Tight Venetian control of its first colony alienated first the Greek landowning families on the island, who on paper at least were excluded from any part in local government or from the rank of esquire, and second, within a generation, some of the Venetian colonists as well.[44] Not surprisingly the first to resist were some of the archontes families with property and status to lose, like the Hagiostephanai in the east of the island and the Scordilli and Melissini in the west. The resistance which manifested itself in 1212 clearly both surprised the Venetian authorities and placed them in considerable difficulties. Reinforcements were not available and help was sought from Marco I Sanudo of the Archipelago in 1213, who attempted to exploit this situation to gain lands and strong-points for himself.[45] The initial trouble in Crete concerned the loss of status and influence felt by the Greek landed families. In 1219 the Melissini were granted knights' fees in the Mussela valley.[46] The Venetian authorities did not learn their lesson from this. Their brand of conquest was on paper at least to be more thoroughgoing than that of the Franks on the mainland. The prudence of both the Franks and the Sanudi in their dealings with their Greek subjects is most marked and leads one to speculate on the imperial idea and its effect upon those responsible for its implementation. The Venetians had much to offer in terms of military and naval protection, but they exacted their price and took a number of generations to emerge as the protector of Christendom against the Turk. In the meantime repression and tardy concessions continued in Crete. In 1299 the Kallergis family were granted similar privileges in order to end their revolt which had lasted since 1282/3 and for some time had confined the Venetians to the harbour towns of the north. The concessions worked and the Kallergis family not only sold grain to the Venetians in bulk orders, but in 1334 and 1342 remained loyal to the Venetian regime during other revolts on the island.

There were many revolts in Crete during the Venetian occupation. They generally took the form of archontic families seeking recognition and privileges from the Venetians. In general the Greeks controlled the countryside and the Venetians held on to the coastal towns. The latter sought outside help from Venice, Naxos and Euboea but were unable to

---

[44] For an outline summary see M. Llewwellyn Smith, *The Great Island* (London, 1965), pp.24–33; Hodgson, op.cit., pp.49, 52; R.W. Dawkins, ed., *Leontios Makhairas, Recital concerning the Sweet Land of Cyprus entitled 'Chronicle'* II (Oxford, 1932), pp.94–5; F.J. Boehlke, *Pierre de Thomas* (Pennsylvania, 1966), pp.169–72.

[45] *Urkunden* II, 159–68.

[46] *Urkunden* II, 210–13. The pact coincided with the end of hostilities with Genoa and the empire of Nicaea.

prevent military assistance reaching the Greeks from both the Genoese and from the empire of Nicaea which kept troops on the island at San Nicolo from about 1230 acting as a stiffener in any revolt by the Greeks. From 1341 the Turks of western Anatolia were a possible source of aid. It was said in 1666 in the bitter sieges of Candia (Heraklion) and Chanea that the countryside was firmly for the Turks. The duke of Candia sought to control the Greeks not just by grudging concessions but by the practice of divide and rule, of supporting one family against another. This could have dire results when that support left the law courts for the mountains of the interior. In 1275 the duke of Crete, Marino Zeno, was killed in an ambush as he proceeded against the Curtacio family. The Venetian attempt to create a Cretan underclass left much bitterness and resentment. As a colonial enterprise it was no worse nor more successful than many. Control of the harbours eased trade links with the sultans of Menteshe and Aydin and with Beirut and Alexandria, but any Venetian attempt to replace the emperors of Byzantium as the bulwark of Christendom in the fifteenth century was not well received by the Cretans or by Greeks anywhere else.

The situation was further complicated by Venetian settlers wishing to loosen their ties with the mother city. Troubles within the Venetian community not only stirred up the Greeks in the interior to revolt in support, but if the trouble reached high enough up in the Venetian colonial administration it might also affect the control over the sea-lanes to the Levant. The first such revolt came in 1268. However, a far more serious crisis developed in 1359 when the duke of Crete seems both to have exacted heavy taxation on the island and to have dabbled in some unspecified heretical practices, such as to bring the papal legate Pierre de Thomas to the island in 1359. Professor Dawkins linked this legatine visit with the persecution of Orthodox christians but Thomas's biographer Boehlke demonstrated that the visit was concerned with the duke and his family. Their treatment of Thomas was far from courteous and the troubles contributed to the delay of the 1365 crusade gathering on Cyprus.

Phase 2: Modon (Methone) and Coron (Korone)

The ports of Modon and Coron were also colonies in the sense that they too were administered by officials appointed in and sent out from Venice. There was a succession of castellani of Modon and Coron from 1209 when Rafaelo Goro and Lorenzo Polani were appointed right down to 1500 when the fortresses fell to the Ottomans. After 1287 the appointments were for regular two-year periods and probably so before that, but the records are not extant to confirm this point. The harbours became known as the eyes and ears of the republic; not only were they a regular stopping-place for ships bound east and homeward, but those returning to the waters of the Adriatic were obliged to report any intelligence of events in the Aegean and the Levant which might be of assistance to captains sailing east. The territory around the harbours which the Venetians controlled is not securely known. It appears that no records on these matters were kept by the home government. If this is correct then it illustrates the preoccupation of the Venetians with the naval bases rather than with landward aspects. The extent of the lands controlled by Venice around the harbours is not clear. For the thirteenth century there is just the Treaty of Sapienza of June 1209, by which Geoffrey de Villehardouin recognised the Venetian right to the Messenian ports. Rivers seem to have been used as boundaries.[47] The situation became fluid in the fourteenth century when the struggle between the Palaeologi and Centurione Zaccaria threatened to engulf the hinterland of the ports. Venice was at pains to extend its boundaries and the purchase of Navarino from Centurione Zaccaria in 1427 gave an opportunity to extend its territories northwards as far as Navarino and Androusa to keep the raids of Theodore Palaeologos at bay.

Venetian interests in the Aegean were concerned with the protection of sea-lanes and merchant shipping. Its colonial territories did indeed form an empire of naval bases, as Frederic Lane has dubbed them. The arrival of the Catalans in central Greece in 1311 provoked both a refugee problem on Negroponte and increased raids by the Catalans across the Euripos. Later in the century the Venetians would welcome such refugees on Negroponte, whose population was to be depleted by Turkish corsairs in search of slaves, but in 1311 before the Turkish raids started in earnest the refugees seem to have brought pressure on the island resources. The Catalans were confined in their naval operations to the Corinthian Gulf and to the roadstead of Livadostro with its tower on the beach. The abandonment of the harbour facilities at the Piraeus for this bay shows a Catalan awareness of the importance of Venice to their own continued interest in the Aegean.

Phase 3: 1261–1388

The third phase was ushered in by the fall of Constantinople to Michael Palaeologos in July 1261.[48] The defences of the city had been denuded at the

---

[47] *Urkunden* II, 96–100; C. Hodgetts, 'The colonies of Coron and Modon under Venetian administration, 1204–1400', unpublished PhD thesis, London, 1974, p. 465ff. Dr Hodgetts is currently writing a book on this topic.
[48] On this phase see Lane, op.cit., pp.74–84, 170–96; D.J. Geanakoplos, *Emperor Michael Palaeologus and the West* (Harvard, 1959), pp.145–54, 161–71, 214–18; A.E. Laiou, *Constantinople and the Latins* (Harvard, 1972), pp.101–13, 147–57, 183–4; D.M. Nicol, op.cit., pp.212–27; W. Miller, *Essays on the Latin Orient* (Cambridge, 1921), pp.283–353.

behest of the Venetians in order to capture the island of Daphnousia, seventy miles east of the point where the Bosporus entered the Black Sea.[49] As well as providing the occasion for the loss of the city, it pointed the way into this third phase with emphasis being placed on the control of sea-lanes to and from that area. The port of Negroponte leap-frogged in importance in 1261. It was the first port of call for the emperor Baldwin and other refugees rescued from the city by Venetian ships, and thereafter it became the terminus for the annual flotta di Romania with its escort of fifteen or so galleys. Venetian naval activities in the Aegean were to hinge on this port with its arsenal, and in the succeeding century there were to be many calls on its resources. This third phase was connected with the challenge mounted by the Genoese.

As we have seen Genoa had been a relative late-comer to the Aegean trade, entering into treaty arrangements with the Byzantine government in 1155. To a greater extent than the Venetians the city relied upon the enterprise of individual citizens formed into companies or mahonnas. This sometimes led to embarrassment for the home government or to lack of support at a critical juncture in individual overseas enterprises. Thus the fortuitous seizure of the ship bearing Brother Barozzi, the emissary of Baldwin I, in the Adriatic in late 1204 had led to an interdict against the city until the jewels and other precious gifts bound for Innocent III were recovered. Equally the attacks by Vetrano on Corfu and that of Enrico Pescatore on Crete in 1210–11 were totally under-resourced and turned into little more than piratical raids. After 1204 the Genoese were effectively excluded from the Aegean and Black Sea trade. However, it also had its strengths and these were amply to appear in the late thirteenth century, following the Treaty of Nymphaeum (Ninfio) negotiated on 13 March 1261 and ratified in Genoa four months later on 10 July.[50]

By that treaty, in return for a fleet of 50 ships to support a proposed Greek attack on Constantinople, the Genoese received trade quarters on Chios, Lesbos and in Smyrna, together with free trade concessions throughout the empire. The treaty was obviously anti-Venetian in its intentions since the Venetians were to be banned from trading in the Byzantine empire, and their commercial quarter in Constantinople handed over to the Genoese, so the monopoly which they had enjoyed since 1204 was thus effectively given to their rivals from Genoa. In return for such concessions the Genoese honoured the treaty, sent most of the ships and weathered the ban of excommunication and interdict which was placed on their city in late 1261. More immediately the Venetians seem to have feared revolt in their Greek possessions and were active both in the Roman curia in

[49] W. Ramsay, *The Historical Geography of Asia Minor* (London, 1890), p.182.
[50] See C. Manfroni, 'La Relazioni fra Genova, l'impero bizantino e i Turchi' *Atti della Societa ligure di Storio Patria* 28 (1896–1902), 791–809 for the Latin text of the treaty, cited Setton, p.91.

promoting a crusade against the Greeks in support of Baldwin II, and in Romania in forming an alliance with William de Villehardouin and in encouraging naval raids from Negroponte on Greek and Genoese shipping. That apart, the years 1261–62 were relatively quiet in terms of naval operations in the Aegean. The Venetians did not attack Constantinople, nor did the Genoese attempt to seize Venetian territory. Indeed, in 1262 a Greco–Genoese fleet retired into Thessalonika rather than give battle to a Venetian squadron.

In the longer term the Genoese found the Byzantine government no less ambivalent in its dealings with them than their rivals had in the twelfth century. Fear of first a Hohenstaufen-backed and later an Angevin-backed crusade induced Michael VIII to appease the Venetians and play them off against his new Genoese allies. The commitment of the latter to the Greek cause came under scrutiny in 1264 when they were accused of plotting with Manfred of Sicily to overthrow Michael. The Genoese colony was removed from Constantinople to Heraklea on the Thracian coast of the Sea of Marmara. Negotiations were opened with the Venetians in 1265 and in 1268 a truce was negotiated which readmitted the Venetians to Constantinople and to the Black Sea trade. In 1267 the Genoese were granted Galata, known as Pera in the west, on the northern shore of the Golden Horn, as their commercial quarter. In spite of this tendency to play one city off against the other the Genoese certainly basked in Michael's favour in 1275 when the Treaty of Nymphaeum was ratified by the Greeks. In that year a young German merchant, Manuale Zaccaria, was granted the monopoly of the alum mines around Phocaea. Alum was the main fixing agent used in the west in the dyeing of cloth. The quality of alum used was of prime importance and according to Peggalotti the product of Phocaea was very nearly the best available outside the Black Sea. The monopoly was extended to the Genoese in general in 1304 but not before the Zaccaria family had made a fortune in its exploitation. They had built a new town, Foglia Nouova, to house the Greek workforce and installed expensive equipment to process the alum, like the two large vats which were damaged by Venetian raiders in 1302. In 1278 a certain Genoese captain, Giovanni de la Covo, was granted the title megadux along with lands in Rhodes and Nymphaeum. The favoured treatment received by the Genoese provoked reprisals at the hands of the Venetians.

The rivalry of Genoa and Venice over the Aegean trade deteriorated into four hot wars in this period: 1258–70; 1294–99; 1350–51; and the fourth Veneto–Genoese War, or War of Chioggia, 1375–81. Much destruction was caused in the Aegean, and the advance of the Turk and the different turn of events dictated the policy of the competing powers in the wider world of Aegean politics. The Venetian naval expedition of 1296 resulted in the seizure of several Aegean islands which the Venetians held on to in the Treaty signed with Andronikos II in March 1302. Rights were conceded to various leading Venetian families which now appeared in the Aegean for the first time: the Barozzi on Amorgos and Santorini, the Guistiniani on Seriphos, and the Michaele on Zea. That same expedition went on to attack the Genoese settlements at Kaffa in the Crimea, Phocaea and Galata. Two great vats were destroyed at Phocaea and other direct results of this raid were the decision to fortify the Genoese quarter and the construction of a wall around Galata, begun in 1302. The famous tower which is all that remains to be seen today was erected in 1348.

The beginning of the fourteenth century saw the beginning of Turkish control of the western Anatolian coast. In 1300 the Turks seized Smyrna from the Genoese and used it as a base to raid the Aegean islands. In 1303 severe attacks on Carpathos, Chios, Rhodes, Samos and Tenedos were noted by Pachymeres. In the next year Benedetto Zaccaria seized Chios both to protect his investments in Phocaea and to safeguard the mastic gardens from destruction. The revenue from the latter was to be applied to the island's protection. Chios was the only known source of mastic, the favoured toothpaste of the wealthy in the west. The Catalans operating in Asia Minor in the early fourteenth century were also used by the Zaccaria family in their inheritance disputes. On the death of Benedetto in 1307 Tedisio appealed to them for help against his uncle Nicino. The chronicler Muntaner took part in an attack on Fuylla in which he tells us that 3,000 Greeks lived there occupied in alum production. Neither the Genoese nor the Venetians were sufficiently strong to wipe out the competition of the other. A very similar situation was developing as held in the political competition amongst the various states in mainland Greece – too many evenly-matched players causing enormous damage to the local economy, whilst the arena in which they competed was becoming ever more dangerous with the advent of the Turks.

Around the middle of the fourteenth century two Genoese adventurers made considerable insular acquisitions in the Aegean. The first was the recovery of Chios which had reverted to Byzantine rule in 1329. In the week following the 15 June 1346 a Genoese fleet of 29 vessels commanded by Simone Vignoso stole a march on the smaller fleet of Umberto the dauphin of Viennois, who proposed to secure Chios and follow up the seizure of Smyrna by the forces of the Holy League in 1344. In the week following the 15 June 1346 Vignoso reduced the whole of the island of Chios. The Genoese government, unable to repay the cost of the expedition, passed the government and exploitation of the island to a company composed of those who had paid for and equiped the 29 galleys which had been levied in the first place for an attack on Monaco. The island remained in Genoese hands till 1566. As Miller has pointed out, this was perhaps the earliest example of a chartered company administering colonial possessions.[51] The

---

[51] Miller, *loc.cit.*; P. Argenti, *The Genoese Occupation of Chios, 1346–1566* 3 vols (Cambridge, 1958); M. Ballard, 'Les grecs de Chio sous la domination genoise' *ByzF* 5 (1977), 5–16.

other adventurer was Francesco I Gattalusio, who in return for helping John V Palaeologos to enter Constantinople in November 1354 was rewarded with the island of Lesbos and an imperial marriage with the emperor's sister Irene. The family succeeded in establishing a north Aegean dynasty based on Lesbos which it held until 1462. It made much of the Byzantine symbol, the double-headed eagle, particularly on the iconography of its tombs, many of which may still be seen on the northern Sporades. From the late fourteenth century, the Gattalusi acquired other islands as grants or purchases from the Byzantine government: Aenos in 1384, Thasos in 1419, Samothrace in 1431, and Imbros and Lemnos in 1453.[52]

Two excellent and detailed studies of the administration of the Genoese and Venetian possessions have appeared in recent years and the reader should refer to them for further information. All that can be done here is to draw attention to the Genoese propensity to leave the exploitation and the administration of their Aegean lands in the hands of individual families and groups, as compared with what Frederic Lane has described as the more cohesive approach of the Venetians relying on bailies, castellans and proveditori, regularly appointed for short terms of office and accountable to the home government.[53]

Phase 4: 1377–1718

The fourth and final phase of the Venetian presence in the Aegean in the middle ages was not clearly demarcated from the preceding phase. Often protectorates were extended over towns to prevent them being offered to Genoese adventurers should the Venetians decline. However, Venice was perceived as the only power in the Aegean area capable of mounting any serious opposition to the Turks. Throughout the fourteenth century they were engaged in locating and containing Turkish raids on their island territories, and from the opening of the fifteenth century in the Peloponnese in general. The latter clearly posed the problem of intelligence. In 1411 the podesta of Nauplion was proposing to set aside 100 hyperpera a year in order to hire scouts (*exploratores*) to locate and report the position of Turkish marauding bands.[54] Professor Housley has drawn attention not only

---

[52] Miller, *loc.cit.*; A. Luttrell, 'John V's daughter: a Palaeologan puzzle' *DOP* 40 (1986), 103–12; E. Ivison, 'Funerary monuments of the Gattalusi at Mytilene' *ABSA* 87 (1992), 423–37.
[53] F. Thiriet, *La Romanie Venitienne au Moyen Age*, op.cit.; M. Balard, *La Romanie Genoise* 2 vols (Genoa and Rome, 1978).
[54] Thiriet, nos 15 and 30 for first negotiations in 1332 regarding the naval league; no.1413 for the scouts, and passim from no.86 onwards for Turko-Venetian conflicts in general.

to the initiative of the Venetians behind the various naval leagues from the 1330s onwards, but also to the very new form of crusading which they ushered in and which achieved its greatest success on 7 October 1571 at the battle of Lepanto.[55] There were Venetian vessels present with Umberto de Viennois in Negroponte in 1346 when Vignoso sailed off to pre-empt them in Chios.

In 1377 the castles of Nauplia and Argos were placed under Venetian control by the guardians of Marie d'Enghien, in order to protect them from capture by the Greeks of Mistra or the Acciaioli in Corinth. The heiress was found a suitable Venetian husband in Pietro Cornaro, but on his death in 1388 she was persuaded to sell the two castles to the republic. In that same year they were lost to the Greeks of Mistra. Fear of the Turks induced Carlo II Tocco of Epiros to sell Naupaktos (Lepanto) to the Venetians in 1407, and the archbishop of Patras to lease the castle of Patras to them in 1408. Forced to return Patras in 1419 the town was lost to the Greeks in 1430, and Naupaktos became the Venetian entrepot for trade with the region until it too was lost to the Turks in 1499. Navarino was purchased from Centurione II Zaccaria in 1423 to stop the Greeks from capturing it or the Genoese from purchasing it in their own right. It remained in Venetian hands until 1500. In 1446 the Turks stormed the Hexamilion Wall which had been refurbished and recommissioned in 1415. The town of Monemvasia was ceded to Venice in 1463 and that held out till 1540. In the Veneto–Turkish war of 1463–79 some 26 fortresses in the Peloponnese passed at one time or another into Venetian hands.[56] These were listed by the chronicler Stefano Magno, but were relinquished in 1479 with the exception of the Messenian fortresses and Monemvasia noted above. The Venetian occupation of Crete lasted until 1669 and the eve of that last crusade when, in 1685, the army of the Holy League led by the Venetian general Francesco Morosini attacked the Turks in Greece. Between then and 1715, sixteen of the larger castles of the Peloponnese were garrisoned by western troops.[57] In 1715 the Turks reconquered the Peloponnese with apparently little resistance from the small garrisons in these forts. Only Corfu remained in Venetian hands. At the battle off Cape Matapan early in 1718 the Venetian fleet was worsted but the Turkish fleet was prevented from sailing to Corfu. In the Treaty of Passarowitz signed on 21 July 1718, the Turks kept possession of the Morea and Venetian involvement in the Aegean was effectively at an end.

---

[55] N. Housley, *The Later Crusades* (Oxford, 1992), pp.59–63.
[56] 'Estratto degli Annali Veneti di Stefano Magni' in CGR, p.206.
[57] K. Andrews, *Castles of the Morea* (Princeton, 1953; reprinted Amsterdam, 1978), pp.7–10, 29, 40, 91, 117, 198.

Chapter 7 ....

Lordship and Government

Problems and perspectives

The lordship and government of the Latin emperor and of the various territorial rulers who acknowledged his suzerainty has to be approached in very broad and very general terms. The sources are just too few, too late and too unsophisticated to permit any detailed and sustained account of the personnel of the various households and entourages, of income and expenditure, of any administrative developments or of the personal and material factors which affected them. For example, we do not know if there were any local revenue officials accountable to the imperial exchequer, or indeed if there was an imperial exchequer at all. The best that can be done is to present a model anchored in the first half of the fourteenth century and extrapolate from that. The case in point comes in the discussion of the sources of income available to a ruler in the Frankish Aegean. We have to rely on the Assizes of Romania written down in the form in which we have them between 1331 and 1346 and to make generalisations from it not just for the whole period but for the whole area as well. The picture that results is a static one with none of the dynamics and subtleties evident in studies of French and English government in the same period and with none of that mixture of continuity and change observable in Byzantine government. Any generalisations that may be advanced can be taken as provisional only and as a sort of working hypotheses. The first such statement is that the Franks of the Aegean lagged a long away behind the Byzantines in the collection and referencing of administrative documentation.

Be that as it may, there are grounds for thinking that this unilateral approach to the separate Frankish administrations in the Aegean is justified. First, western household government is observable in almost all these states and may be surmised for the Duchy of Athens, where documentary evidence is lacking. The traditional offices of seneschal, marshal, chamberlain, butler and chancellor were all to be found as in Capetian France and Plantagenet England. Originating from parts of Flanders, France and north-west Italy where social subordination and monarchical power were well-established, these rulers would share not just the gamut of household offices but the presuppositions that went with them regarding the duties and authority of a prince, something of princely rights and income and the necessity of a peripatetic monarchy.

The Frankish lands in the Aegean were termed an empire, the *imperium Romanie*. It was not an integrated state, other than in terms of French ethnic and cultural dominion based on land resources which had been seized by force and the possession of which was legally underpinned by the Latin emperors. Interestingly, despite a considerable amount of allusion to the good old laws of the classical Greeks and to the Trojan stemma of the Franks who had returned to avenge the Greek victory at Troy, there was no reference at the time to the Latin conquest as a *'renovatio imperii Romani'*.[1] The new Latin imperium carried little weight as such in the courts of western Europe. Rather Romania was seen by many contemporaries as much in cultural as in political terms. In 1224 Pope Honorius III chose to characterise it culturally by describing it as *'Nova Francia'* rather than in terms of the person of its emperor or other rulers.[2] This cultural imperialism was designed to flatter the French court and to elicit some support for the Latin empire. However, within the Aegean world it clearly went further than mere rhetoric and was seen by both Greeks and westerners as a political statement. The generic term 'Frank', applied to westerners by the Greeks, showed the preponderance of French culture amongst the holders of power in the Latin Aegean and should warn us not to expect too much of an emerging Franco-Greek culture in the Frankish Aegean. Likewise the degree of courtoisie and French linguistic purity consciously fostered by those leaders was recorded approvingly by Muntaner in the fourteenth century and became one of the enduring images of Frankish Greece.

The suzerainty of the Latin emperor

The Latin states in the Aegean are often dealt with as if they were completely separate entities from the Latin empire of which they formed a part.[3] This convenient division overlooks the significance of the empire and

---

[1] '... *quatenus justis legibus, privilegiis ac consuetudinibus Atheniensium et Graecorum, ut olim, quum Graecia florebat, ...*', *Urkunden*, I, p.302; Clari, CVI/29–37 (McNeal trans., p.122) for Troy.

[2] Pressutti, 5006 (20 May, 1224).

[3] For the institutions of the Latin empire see the articles by Benjamin Hendrickx contained in *Byzantina* 1 (1969), 59–80; 6 (1974), 85–154; 9 (1977), 187–217; 14 (1988),

the idea of empire in the history of the region. The emperor was the ultimate overlord of a collection of lordships varying considerably from vavassories and sergeanties to principalities, dukedoms and counties. How did he exercise this suzerainty?

Neither the Latin emperor nor his followers saw the imperial office in terms of the prerogatives of the Byzantine autokrator or basileus.[4] As we have seen, when the Byzantine empire was divided in September 1204 once the endowment of the emperor had been settled, territory was distributed amongst the interested groups defined in terms of community – Venetian or crusader – along geographical lines and with the idea of a standard fief as the yardstick for any grants.[5] There was no state structure to replace the would-be centralised Byzantine empire. The emperor would live from the income derived from his own lands, supplemented in times of crisis by the military assistance of the vassals of the empire. Such rights like the levying of tolls and customs duties, and feudal dues and services which western European rulers enjoyed could only be exacted from his own condominium. He might try to enforce his rights in former imperial monasteries but any rights that he took over from his Greek predecessor effectively only applied to the lands directly assigned to him in the partition treaty and not to the whole territorial empire of which he was suzerain. Everything depended upon the force of his personality.

Potentially a major problem for the political and military cohesion of the empire of Romania was the fact that not all lands, indeed it was but a tiny proportion, were to be granted directly by the emperor himself. On paper he was entitled to call upon the military service of the knights, both Venetian and Frankish, who had received lands in Romania. However, if the ties of self-interest did not mobilise this military help then the emperor had no means of exacting it since he had no direct material links with three-quarters of the imperial territories and could not threaten confiscation of fiefs for services unfulfilled. That role was reserved for the immediate lord of the vassals concerned.

In practice this seems to have caused few problems. The partition committee of 1204 had assigned spheres of influence rather than precise grants and left it to the community of interest to whom particular territories were allotted to control them as they could or as they saw fit. In both the Venetian and crusader condominia ambitious and enterprising lords rapidly took the initiative, organised the conquests and assigned the land to

---

[3] *cont*

7–221, and in *Acta Classica* 17 (1974), 105–19; 19 (1976), 123–31, and A. Carile, 'La Cancellaria Sovrana dell'Imperio Latino di Constantinopli' *Studi Venziani* 2 (1978), 37–73.

[4] P. Lock, 'The Latin emperors as heirs to Byzantium', in P. Magdalino, ed., *New Constantines* (London, 1994), pp.295–304.

[5] See chapter 2.

individuals. Boniface granted lands in Greece to his major supporters, from whom the rulers of central Greece and Achaia were to emerge by 1209 when they secured recognition for their territories from the emperor Henry. Likewise in the Aegean, the various Venetian nobility that secured land sought confirmation from the emperor saving their fealty to the republic. Those who were successful in the scramble for lands clearly sought out imperial confirmation of their acquisitions.

It was this legitimising of the states thus carved out from the former Byzantine empire which gave the emperors their main role in the Frankish Aegean. They were recognised by the papacy and the emperor of the west, by the courts of England and France, and as such represented the public face of the Latin Aegean to western Christendom. Even when the empire had ceased to exist as a territorial entity, this imperial role continued. In Naples the titular Angevin emperor of Constantinople sought to centralise control over his scattered possessions in Greece by emphasising that the Assizes of Romania applied to the whole Latin Aegean because they derived from the Latin empire and by limiting final appeals to the Latin emperor. These provisions must be later additions to any thirteenth-century imperial law code which might have existed. The use of this imperial ideology by the Angevins over 60 years after the loss of Constantinople by the Latins in 1261, shows that the Frankish settlement in the Aegean was perceived by those within it as part of an empire and that it remained a potent idea.[6] That this empire and its dependencies had some form of political cohesion is seen by the confidence with which Baldwin II could dispose of overlordship within it either to the rulers of the Morea in the 1240s or to the Angevins in 1267, and also in the assurance with which the Angevin rulers of Naples could make dynastic dispositions for the area, especially in the series of marriages performed in 1313.[7] Ironically, the Latin empire of Constantinople exercised greater influence on the Mediterranean world after 1261 when it existed largely as an idea. After 1267, and more especially after 1301 and 1313, the titular emperors and empresses were related to the French and Neapolitan royal families with considerable military and financial potential at their disposal.[8]

In the years 1207 to 1209 the would-be rulers of the Aegean actively sought to legitimise their position and territorial acquisitions by acknowledging the suzerainty of the Latin emperor. The first to gain such recognition was the Venetian Marco Sanudo possibly as early as 1207 but certainly by 1213. In 1206 he had put together a small flotilla and used it to

---

[6] P. Topping, 'The formation of the Assize of Romania' *Byzantion* 18 (1944–5), 304–14, reprinted as essay II in *Studies in Latin Greece* (London, 1977). See the prologue and articles I, 117, and 136 of the law code as it has come down to us.

[7] See pp.66, 93–5 and Appendix 1.

[8] See p.108.

persuade the inhabitants of the Archipelago to recognise him as their ruler, which took a year according to one source, and then sought and received imperial recognition for his achievement in the form of a grant of a dukedom to himself and his heirs even though some of his new dominions might have been within the Venetian land allotment. In January 1209 Margaret of Hungary had asked the emperor to crown her son Demetrius king of Thessalonika in return for homage and sureties and the confirmation of her regency, whilst in the following May Geoffrey I de Villehardouin was confirmed as prince of Achaia, having master-minded the conquest of southern Greece and effectively supplanted the interests of the family of Champlitte.[9] The value of this latter submission to the emperor was acknowledged by his appointment of Geoffrey as seneschal of the empire at the same time.[10] We see in these transactions a marked change from those initial grants of dukedoms in 1204, a change from an assertion of what ought to be, to one of legitimising and establishing what was. Whatever the ambitions of these adventurers, they realised that legal possession and European acknowledgement of their new patrimonies rested with imperial confirmation. The position of the new Latin emperors was secure and indeed considered essential, at least as far as their Frankish subjects were concerned.

This state of affairs, so good for the position of the new emperors, would not have been possible without the intervention of the emperors themselves. The first two emperors were acutely conscious of this need to exert control and to be seen to do so. In general they got their way. Baldwin gained Boniface's recognition of his overlordship in 1204 by swift and decisive action, pushing Boniface to the brink of civil war. It had been Boniface who had soothed the difficult relationship that had resulted by the marriage of his daughter Agnes to the new emperor Henry in 1207, and he used the occasion of a conference at Ipsala in September 1207 to renew the homage due to the new emperor for his lands in Thessalonika. In 1209 Henry had got his way in the re-ordering of the kingdom of Thessalonika and brought pressure on the rulers of central and southern Greece to acknowledge his suzerainty. Henry exercised his overlordship by creating Geoffrey seneschal of the empire through whom he might hope to exercise imperial authority in Greece. Certainly he provided two of his own trusted followers, Conon de Bethune and Guy d'Henruel, to return to Achaia with Villehardouin to advise on the conclusion of the Treaty of Sapienza with the Venetians. He himself stayed with Otho de la Roche in Athens and

---

[9] Valenciennes, 602–5; 668 for Villehardouin's attendance at the parliament of Ravennika on 1–2 May 1209. Whether he was acknowledged Prince of Achaia here or assumed the title later, he was addressed as such by Innocent III on 22 March 1210 (PL, 216:221–222).

[10] J.K. Fotheringham, *Marco Sanudo, Conqueror of the Archipelago* (Oxford, 1910), pp.60–1; Valenciennes, 605 and 670.

confirmed that lord's dominance in central Greece. A theoretical hierarchy had thus been made an actuality. Its smooth operation would depend upon the personalities of the principal actors and their responses to events. At the top of that hierarchy was the emperor.

The powers of the emperor

The Latin emperor, like all medieval monarchs, was expected to rule as well as reign. He was more than just a figurehead of the Frankish conquest of the Aegean. The absence of an adult emperor in 1228 led to discussion of the feasibility of maintaining the city of Constantinople as an imperial capital in the face of Greek aggression. As we shall see, the principate began as elective but became hereditary. There was no automatic succession and the coronation began each principate, although during the Angevin tenure of the titular emperorship between 1313 and 1331 imperial authority was exercised without such sacral backing. The novelty of the Latin imperium in the Aegean and the circumstances of its creation by the contracting parties to the Fourth Crusade meant that its sacramental basis was weak and led to an attempt to define the imperial powers. Against the background of contemporary west European constitutional developments – in England in 1216 and the late 1250s, in France during the minority of Louis IX, and in Hungary (1221), Germany (1231) and the Spains – it is not improbable that the barons of the crusade had political ideas of their own about the limitation of monarchical powers.[11] After all the Fourth Crusade had been organised and carried through by barons and not by kings. Some of them, like Baldwin of Flanders himself, had experienced the authoritarianism of Philip Augustus (1180–1223) and the arrangements for the new empire reflected their concerns as vassals. They had no wish to see in one of their number an elected and anointed emperor, a reduplication of west European sovereignty let alone Byzantine theocracy.

The crusaders were monarchical by tradition. In the context of the imperial elections of May 1204, Robert de Clari saw the ideal candidate as one '... who is right well able to maintain the law, a man of gentle birth and a high man'. Justice was one of the main duties of a monarch but beyond that Clari seemed to leave little scope for the exercise of royal power, even omitting defence.[12] Clari placed this observation on the lips of Nivelon de Cherissy, one of the episcopal electors. Perhaps in this context this omission was explicable. The imperial duties as defined in the confirmation oath of

---

[11] M. Prestwich, *English Politics in the Thirteenth Century* (London, 1990), p.148; A. MacKay, *Spain in the Middle Ages* (London, 1977), pp.95–117.
[12] Clari, XCV/20–4 (McNeal trans., p.115).

the regent Henry in October 1205 were more businesslike and emphasised defence and the role of emperor as commander-in-chief. He was to maintain and defend the empire from his own imperial resources and to act as a court of appeal together with a committee of Venetian and Frankish judges. The convention of April 1229 by which John de Brienne was offered the throne of Constantinople did not enlarge upon these duties which were to defend and maintain the empire, its laws and customs.[13] The emperor could not create law. Indeed he could not even play the role of royal Solomon. Imperial justice did not encroach on baronial courts, although under Angevin influence an appeals procedure was developed in the fourteenth century.[14] Disobedience to the emperor did not amount to treason in the thirteenth century. The count of Biandrate was not dubbed a traitor for his refusal to pay homage to the emperor in 1207 and even his abortive plot to kill the emperor in Negroponte in 1209 did not attract this charge. Again it seems to have been Angevin influence in the fourteenth century which led to the beginnings of a definition of treason. The case of Nicolas de Tremolay in 1315 and the punishment of disinheritance was the first definite step in this direction.[15] The emperor was an important figurehead and symbol of Frankish settlement and property rights in the Aegean. In such a disturbed military situation which followed the initial conquest, his defined duties were onerous and he was not sufficiently endowed with revenues to meet those demands.

Coronation and election in the making of the emperor

Coronations are always important events; those designed to legitimise a new dynasty even more so. The crowning of the first Latin emperor had to provide religious backing for a western baron in the eyes of his followers, many of whom had apparently considered themselves as equally worthy of the imperial dignity. At the same time the ceremony had to demonstrate the finality of the Latin victory and to reconcile Greeks to Latin rule.

The coronation robes of the emperor-elect were certainly more Byzantine than French but whether this could be said of the ceremonial itself is much less easy to decide. Most of the French crusaders, even the leading ones, would have been too young to have witnessed the coronation of Philip Augustus in the cathedral of Reims on 1 November 1179, although Count Baldwin's maternal uncle, Philip count of Flanders (d. 1191), had taken a prominent role in that event. However, there would have been some Latin

---

13 *Urkunden* I, 572; II, 269. See p.82 for the circumstances of John's election.
14 Assizes of Romania, article 143.
15 Valenciennes, 683, 687; Assizes of Romania, article 18.

bishops present who might have been able to advise from experience. One of these was Nivelon de Cherissy who not only took a leading role in the coronation of 16 May 1204, but had been consecrated bishop of Soissons in 1176 and as such may have attended at Reims. On the other hand the propensity of the Franks to learn from their surroundings must not be overlooked. The information which Robert de Clari gleaned from his tours of Constantinople in the spring of 1204 was impressive as, some months later, was the willingness of both Geoffrey I de Villehardouin and Henry d'Angres to quiz and utilise local informants in the Morea and in the Troad. This might suggest that the first coronation of a Latin emperor was modelled on that of Alexios IV on 1 August 1203, which all the leaders of the crusading host had witnessed. The ceremonial was a political act intended to demonstrate visually to both Greek and Latin spectators the transference of imperial power.

The imitation, if such it really was, would have been external rather than of much greater significance. The use of terms like the imperial throne of Constantinople by Villehardouin and the throne of Constantine by Clari were statements of fact rather than an awareness of the Latin emperors as the successors of the basileus or of the Latins as renewers of the Byzantine empire. Renewal was part of the Byzantine imperial tradition.

The only account of an imperial coronation service approaching anything like a description was that written by Robert de Clari of Baldwin I's coronation on 16 May 1204. The emperor was brought to Hagia Sophia where he was divested of his own clothes and was robed as an emperor in Byzantine fashion. Clearly Alexios III had not made off with all the regalia and loroi kept in the church.

> ... [the clergy and high barons] put on him chausses of vermilion samite and shoes all covered with rich stones. Then they put on him a very rich coat all fastened with gold buttons in front and behind from the shoulders clear to the girdle. And then they put on him the palle, a kind of cloak which fell to the top of the shoes in front and was so long behind that he wound it about his middle and then brought it back over his left arm like the maniple of a priest ... Then over this they put a very rich mantle, which was all covered with precious stones, and the eagles on it were made of precious stones ...[16]

He was anointed before the altar, crowned and then sat on a throne holding a sceptre and an orb while high mass was sung. There is no mention of a coronation oath. However, all subsequent emperors were required to swear to uphold the Pact of 1204 as a condition of their election and prior to their coronation. After the service in Hagia Sophia there was a procession

---

[16] Clari, XCVI/13–20 (McNeal trans., p.116).

back to the palace of the Bukoleon where the emperor sat upon the throne of Constantine and received, amongst others, some of his new Greek subjects. Whether the distribution of the plunder seized in the sacking of the city, which was given away soon after the coronation, was in any sense an imitation of the Byzantine donatio is debatable. The inspiration came from the barons and was probably only linked to the coronation by Clari as a chronological marker.

Only in externals like the wearing of the loros and the use of Byzantine regalia should this ceremony be seen as a Byzantine ceremony, although clearly Greek witnesses to the coronation were in no doubt that an emperor had been made and, in the words of Clari, '... bowed down before him as the sacred emperor'. Acclamation, anointing and crowning were probably common or at least similar enough in both traditions. The Latins wished to stress some sort of continuity by the use of Byzantine regalia, but they were not constitutional historians nor inclined to take their conciliatory moves towards the Greeks too far, as was shown by their contempt for the Byzantine civil and military bureacracy in the city which they dismissed without even an interview.

Most discussion about the coronation has stemmed from the suggestion made by Georg Ostrogorsky in 1955 that the ritual of anointing was introduced into Byzantine coronations as a direct imitation of this particular coronation. The question must remain open but it does seem strange that the Greeks in Constantinople accepted the ceremony as nothing particularly innovative. Although no rite of anointing is specifically mentioned before the thirteenth century in Byzantine ceremonial, there were many allusive references to it and Michael Choniates appears to suggest that it was traditional. The whole debate, as Ruth Macrides has pointed out, is bedevilled by the tendency of most Byzantine writers to use the language of anointing metaphorically.[17]

It is not clear whether the coronation of 1204 established an ordo for the making of Latin emperors of Constantinople. Certainly an oath to observe the partition arrangements of 1204 was exacted before coronation, since this underpinned all property rights within the new state. Peter de Courtenay took this oath before his coronation in the church of San Lorenzo fuori le Mura, by Honorius III on 9 April 1217. What coronation ordo was followed on that occasion, particularly with regard to the material (holy oil or chrism) and the method of anointing (on head or hands) is unknown to us, nor do we know if he would have had to undergo a second coronation in

---

[17] G. Ostrogorsky, 'Zur Kaiseralbung und Schilderhebung im spätbyzantischen Krönungszeremoniell' *Historia* 4 (1955), 246–56; Michael Choniates, *Michael Akominatou tou Choniatou ta sozomena*, ed. S. Lampros (Athens, 1879–80), II, pp.258, 20–4, 336–7; and discussion by M. Angold, *A Byzantine Government in Exile* (Oxford, 1975), pp.43–5; R. Macrides, 'Bad historian or good lawyer? Demetrios Chomatenos and Novel 131' *DOP* 46 (1992), 187–96, esp. 188; see also p.45.

Constantinople should he have arrived there. Certainly Honorius's hesitation over the ceremony and his decision to stage it outside the walls of Rome in the church of San Lorenzo fuori le Mura to avoid any offence or prejudice to the Staufen emperor, Frederick II, clearly demonstrated that the Latin emperors from the Bosphorus were not regarded as serious emperors on the western model.

The Latin emperor derived his power both upwards from the people by election and downwards from God at his coronation (*a Deo coronatus*). In the circumstances attending the capture of Constantinople the election formed the legal basis of Baldwin's power and, perhaps incidently, because of the role played by clerical electors on 9 May 1204, provided some sort of ecclesiastical approbation of it. However, with no hereditary claim the coronation, and one suspects especially the anointing, were essential to mark the public transfer of imperial power and to provide a religious sanction of it.[18] We must not assume that the parties to the Fourth Crusade, Franks and Venetians, shared a common view of the nature of political power. The leaders of the crusade were not kings but barons, most of them liege vassals of the king of France. They would have subscribed to the view that all power derived from God and that seigneurial power as well as property should be passed on by primogeniture. Surely only the doge, Enrico Dandolo, had the necessary experience and background to propose the means of disposing and legitimising power in the new conquest which was enshrined in article 5 of the Pact of March 1204, namely election and coronation.

Baldwin became emperor because of the Latin victory over the Greeks at Constantinople in April 1204 and because of his selection from a number of candidates by the electoral college of French and Venetian priests on 9 May. The emperors who followed him were elected too, although the choice of the electors was influenced by hereditary considerations. This first election was thus far more critical than any subsequent ones since it selected a dynasty as much as an emperor. This explains the fortnight spent in bitter argument as to who should form the electoral body. The ambitions of Boniface of Montferrat emerged clearly in his desire to gain electors who would vote for him. The clerical college that eventually emerged seems to have been a compromise. Thereafter no formal attempts were made to define the electoral college for the selection of emperor in order to reduce the undue influence that Nicetas Choniates felt had been exercised by the Venetians. Indeed the role of election in the creation of the Latin emperors thereafter diminished. Never again was there to be a formal electoral college. Later emperors were to be selected from a list of blood relatives by a group of leading magnates and Venetians chaired by the baili of the empire. The

---

[18] For a general discussion of these issues see Fritz Kern, *Kingship and Law in the Middle Ages* (Oxford, 1939), pp.27–50.

unexpected deaths of many emperors in their prime away from the imperial city suggest that they exerted little influence in the choice of their successors. The hereditary principle, however, was strong amongst the westerners and seems to have guided or limited their choice. Baldwin died mysteriously in captivity, Henry died unexpectedly in Thessalonika, Peter disappeared in Epiros, and Robert died while on a visit to the Morea. The election of the successors of both Baldwin I and Peter was thus attended by a delay until the death of the emperor could be confirmed or not reasonably doubted. Baldwin, having no children, was succeeded by his brother, who was followed in 1216 by their brother-in-law, Peter de Courtenay, the husband of their sister Yolande, and from 1219 by the younger sons of Peter and Yolande, Robert (d. 1228) and the young Baldwin II (b. 1217). The Latins found it difficult to cope with heirs apparent. It would appear from the price of the icon of the Hodgeteria demanded by the Venetians from Henry in 1205 that he had not been singled out by Baldwin as his heir, although after the death of Mary of Champagne at Acre in 1204 it is difficult to see where an heir of the blood would come from if not from Baldwin's brothers.[19] Equally the young Baldwin absented himself from Constantinople through most of the 1230s whilst his father-in-law, Jean de Brienne, was emperor.[20]

Both for Greeks and Latins the coronation seems to have been the decisive act in the creation of an emperor. This had been the substance of the advice given to Boniface at Adrianople in 1204 when he tried to set up his stepson as a counter-emperor to Baldwin I. Villehardouin was explicit in stating that Baldwin only began to discuss imperial affairs after his coronation on 16 May and not after his election one week before, whilst his grandson Baldwin II dated his reign from his coronation in the spring of 1240 and not from the death of Jean de Brienne in 1237. Nonetheless, the elective nature of the Latin emperorship could not be ignored, as was shown in 1229 with the choice and offer of the co-emperorship to John de Brienne, the former king of Jerusalem. The betrothal of his daughter Mary with the young Baldwin II harmonised this action with the hereditary principle. The Latin emperors successfully played down the elective side of their power and reverted to the blood line that was in their western background. Lacking imperial lineage, they were in some ways successful in establishing an imperial dynasty when their empire was snatched from them in 1261.

Imperial election phased out entirely after the loss of the empire in 1261. Baldwin II passed his title and his interests to the Angevins of Naples

---

[19] Clari, CXIV (McNeal trans., p.126); PL, 215:1077; but see R.L. Wolff, 'Footnote to an incident of the Latin occupation of Constantinople: the church and the icon of the Hodegetria' *Traditio* 6 (1948), 319–28, which suggests that the icon incident was not connected with Henry's coronation at all and that this is a confusion on the part of Robert of Clari, then returned to the west.

[20] See pp.62–3 for the circumstances of John de Brienne's election as emperor.

at Viterbo in 1267, and after 1285 the various heirs and heiresses were titular rulers without benefit of choice, presumably a state of affairs that would have to be regularised should Constantinople ever be recaptured.

Latin emperors and the west

The Latin emperorship was a very localised phenomenon. In the west it was not fitted into the imperial model which had been worked out since 800. Baldwin sought papal confirmation of his imperial status. The letter that he sent in May together with some splendid gifts never reached the pope. Pope Innocent III was aware of the coronation by November 1204. He was happy to confirm the title which Baldwin had chosen, a latinised version of that of his Byzantine predecessors: *Balduinus, Dei Gratia Fidelissimus in Christo Imperator, a deo Coronatus, Romanie Moderator et Semper Augustus*, but he had no intention of making Baldwin into a basileus. Baldwin, both as a westerner and as one who had been taken under the protection of St Peter since 1199 for his lands in Flanders, was expected to conform to behaviour consonant with a vassal of the pope. Innocent now took the emperor and his new empire under the protection of the Holy See. He certainly had no intention of conceding to Baldwin the caesaropapal powers which, judging from his correspondence with Alexios III in 1202–3, he clearly felt that the basileus exercised. For his part Baldwin never claimed them or even seemed aware that they had existed. He and his successors were deferential in their correspondence with the pope, invited him to call a general council at Constantinople to settle the matter of the union of the churches, and did not raise objections to papal interference with the appointment of the Latin patriarchs, the rights of imperial monasteries, or the advowson of the conventual churches of Constantinople. They did not behave like basileoi in terms of the church and many western imperialist writers would have considered them to have forfeited the title by their close relationship with the pope.

The papacy supported and legitimised the new imperial authority in western Europe. Beyond that it kept its options open to see if the new empire would become a serious power in international politics. Clearly by 1217 this was not to be the case. Honorius III was more concerned not to prejudice the rights of the Roman emperor Frederick when presented with a request for a coronation in Rome by Peter de Courtenay. For his part the Hohenstaufen emperor Frederick II, frequently at odds with the papacy, did not accord the Latin emperors imperial status. He did not recognise the Latin emperor as his suzerain for the kingdom of Thessalonika which had been made over to him in 1230 by the titular king Demetrius, conducted diplomatic relations with the emperor's enemies in Nicaea with no regard to

Latin imperial policy, and in 1239 had delayed military reinforcement passing through his territory to the Latin empire. There is little to suggest that the papacy ever considered the new imperial authority as an alternative to the Holy Roman emperors of the west. Only at the First Council of Lyons in 1245 when Baldwin II sat at the pope's right hand and Innocent IV declared Frederick II deposed was there any hint of this. Indeed in 1233–34 Pope Gregory IX entertained the idea of restoring Constantinople to the Greeks in return for the union of the Greek and Latin churches. In France, Italy, and England the poverty of the empire advertised during the 1240s by the begging missions of Baldwin II and his empress Marie de Brienne to the courts of the west led to a patronising assessment of the empire in court and cloister alike, as exhibited in the writings of Blanche of Castile, Matthew Paris and the anonymous annalist of Santa Justina in Padua.[21]

Latin emperors and the Aegean world

In Romania the emperor was taken more seriously, ironically by the new emperor's Greek subjects who equated him with his theocratic Greek predecessor and during the coronation ceremony of 1204 had performed proskynesis before him. The Greeks under Latin rule seemed to have no doubts that coronation could indeed create an emperor. The subject Greek response to later coronations is not recorded, although the emperor Henry was to be greeted by Greek citizens of Thebes in 1209 and by Greeks in Constantinople as the properly constituted emperor whom they were prepared to obey. The emperor's Frankish subjects had taken pains to circumscribe imperial powers in 1204 and throughout the thirteenth century did not question the emperor's ability to bestow honours and overlordships. Even Charles I of Naples considered that Baldwin's ratification of the Treaty of Viterbo was necessary to a proper legal transfer of suzerainty over the Morea in 1267. By 1209 imperial overlordship was accepted by Franks in Greece and the Aegean islands, and by the the 1260s in the court of Naples also.

Within the Aegean this overlordship was an active institution, even in the 1240s when the financial and military weakness of the imperial lands and capital was plain to see. In 1243 Baldwin invested William of Verona with the kingdom of Thessalonika despite the grant made some thirteen years before by the titular king Demetrius apparently without imperial approval, and in 1246 or thereabouts he granted his suzerainty over Negroponte to Geoffrey II de Villehardouin. Geoffrey's son William could

---

21 *Cambridge Medieval History* IV, i (Cambridge, 1967), pp.311–12.

force his overlordship over the lords of Athens in the 1250s using the same justification of an imperial grant. Whilst at Viterbo in 1267 the emperor Baldwin's confirmation of the concessions made by William de Villehardouin on 24 May was deemed necessary for a properly binding deed. There was no repeat here of the backstairs procedure of Frederick and Demetrius in 1230. Whatever the ambitions of the Villehardouin to the domination of Greece, it was a domination to be exercised under the Latin empire and possibly leading to possession of the imperial crown itself.[22]

Emperors might vary in the direct control that they sought or were able to exercise over the lands held from them. Under Baldwin I and Henry there had been some attempt to make imperial control a reality, as shown by the dispute over the occupation and granting out of Thessalonika in September 1204 and in the campaign of the Emperor Henry in central Greece in May 1209. The clergy and rulers of Greece were regularly called upon by both pope and emperor to provide military and financial assistance in the 1230s, whilst in 1267 at Viterbo, Baldwin II exercised his role as suzerain in assigning rights over his notional Greek empire to the Angevins.[23] Imperial suzerainty, notional or otherwise, was acknowledged by the Frankish rulers of Greece. The delay in the production of their own coinage, until the 1260s and the 1280s by the prince of Achaia and the duke of Athens respectively, quite possibly has as much to do with the end of Baldwin's suzerainty as with other economic factors with regard to this important regalian right.

The imperial council

One of the main imperial duties was to consult and to seek advice from council and in the case of the Latin emperors there was some precedent for following a consensus. In general the Latin emperors seldom broke away from this procedure. On the occasions when they did, it lead to humiliation and retreat. In September 1204 Baldwin had to abandon his attempt to exert control over Boniface by force given a considerable amount of sympathy for Boniface's cause amongst the leading barons in Constantinople. The new emperor's chosen councillors were overruled and the position of his natural councillors, the great men, reiterated.

According to the regent Henry's confirmation of the 1204 Pact, the emperor was to act in consultation with the podesta of the Venetian community in Constantinople and his council together with the less formal

---

[22] See p.88ff.
[23] Villehardouin, 272–99; Valenciennes, 600; see p.66.

group composed of the leading French barons.[24] This was the newly constituted imperial council of late 1205. It was to remain the core of the imperial advisory body until 1261. It represented a considerable refinement on the position which had been allowed to develop in 1204 almost as a continuation of the decision-making machinery of the crusade itself and evident at the baronial councils held at Soissons and Compiegne in 1200. The deaths of Baldwin of Flanders, Enrico Dandolo, and Hugues of St Pol by October 1205 probably made a radical reappraisal easier.

Alongside this council both Baldwin and Boniface had their own councils to which they turned for advice and support. The names of Boniface's council are known because the chronicler Villehardouin approved of them personally and chose to list them. They were Jacques d'Avesnes, William de Champlitte, Hugues de Coligny and Otho de la Roche. Of Baldwin's advisers we know nothing beyond their existence separate from the imperial council and their sense of shame at being overruled by the great men in September 1204. Villehardouin did not choose to name them, perhaps out of contempt since he blamed them for fomenting the rift between Baldwin and Boniface. Thus the existence of three advisory bodies led to disputes and a lack of coordinated policy. The 1205 rationalisation of the council showed that the crusade leadership was both adaptable and creative. These qualities must have some contribution to make to the survival of the Latin empire for which the disunity of its enemies is usually given all the credit.

The council of great men was part of the organisation of the crusade. Following the capture of Constantinople it had quickly restored order and brought an end to looting. It appointed the committee to elect the emperor, arranged the coronation ceremony, selected the committee to oversee the division of lands, and reconciled Boniface and Baldwin in September 1204. In so far as its membership can be established, it consisted of the chronicler Villehardouin, the doge, Louis of Blois, Conon de Bethune, Milon le Brabant and Manasser de l'Isle. Almost certainly Hugues de St Pol was a member too. He had signed the 1204 Pact and had taken a prominent role in suppressing looting by hanging one of his own knights. With the exception of Dandolo, who had much Levantine experience in his own right as a merchant, all of these men had taken part in the Third Crusade and had distinguished themselves in some way at the siege of Acre in 1190. All came from crusading families with a background of involvement going back to the 1090s. They were also men of wealth and status at home. The leading decisionmakers and early creators of the Latin empire were all familiar with the crusader kingdom of Jerusalem.

The first emperor had failed to establish his independence of the

---

[24] *Urkunden* I, 571–4.

council of great men. The troubadour Raimbaut de Vaquieras lamented that Baldwin was incapable of a generous action:

> ... since he conducts all his affairs by council, and would do nor more nor less than his councillors would have him say and do. And I counsel him, if he aims at excellence, to give henceforth without counsel; and, without consulting the barons' council, let him hearken to the counsel of the worthiest man [Boniface of Montferrat], for such is a counsel befitting an emperor.[25]

The reconstituted council of 1205 bore superficial resemblance to the haut court of the kingdom of Jerusalem as it was in the late twelfth century, made up of all the tenants-in-chief. It is possible that the new imperial council was to be attended by only the most important barons, the magnates Francigenarum, but this was an open term and perhaps too much should not be read into it. There was no indication of what constituted a quorum. There does seem to have been scope for the emperor to nominate his own advisers. Such was Pierre de Douai who spent a year in the Aegean in 1208/9 and became a familiar of the emperor Henry. Later there were the Greek advisers of Baldwin II, which so incensed Blanche of Castile and whose existence he denied in August 1243.[26]

Unlike the haut court in Jerusalem, however, provision was made for representatives of the Venetian commune in Constantinople to have a direct voice in imperial policy. The emperor had to consult with the Podesta and his council before going to war. The 21 judges and wisemen who made up this council were listed for the first time as witnesses to a charter issued by Marino Zeno on 29 June 1205. Zeno was elected by the commune in Constantinople.[27] Whatever aspirations for an independent hand the commune cherished in 1205, the home government had exerted tighter control by 1207 when it sent out Ottaviano Quirino as podesta. Venetian concerns and those of the emperor were not always the same, yet the better-organised part of the emperor's council was drawing its instructions from Venice.

The conciliar government of the Latin empire was of more than purely regional significance in that it could be seen to fit in with other baronial

---

[25] Lyric poem XX/1–10 in J. Linskill, *The Poems of the Troubadour Raimbaut de Vaquieras* (Paris, 1964), p. 227.

[26] Valenciennes, 512, 574–84, 689–93; Alex Teulet, *Lavettes du Tresor des Chartes* II (Paris, 1866), doc.3123, p.519, cited Setton, p.66, n.92.

[27] *Urkunden* I, 558–61; on Zeno's possible election see *Urkunden* I, 566–9 and for discussion see D. Nicol, *Byzantium and Venice* (Cambridge, 1988), p.153, and R.L. Wolff, 'A new document from the period of the Latin Empire of Constantinople: the oath of the Venetian podesta' *Pankarpia Mélanges Henri Grégoire IV (Annuaire de l'Institut d Philologie et d'Histoire Orientales et Slaves XII (1953)),* 539–73, reprinted as essay VI in idem, *Essays on the Latin Empire of Constantinople* (London, 1976).

movements to circumscribe increasingly authoritarian rulership in western Europe in the thirteenth century. However, the means by which the empire was set up meant that the council had a deliberative as well as a purely advisory function and that the emperor could not lightly ignore the counsels of his councillors.

In 1227 there occurred one of the most bizarre incidents not just in the history of the Latin empire but in the history of medieval monarchy. Certain knights forced themselves into the imperial bedchamber where the emperor Robert (1221–28) was sleeping with his wife, whom he had married in a secret ceremony and whose name is not known. Both the secrecy of the marriage and the ill-treatment of the lady in question suggest that she was not deemed emperor-worthy. The marriage of an emperor was a political act and one to be decided in consultation with the imperial council. The woman was the daughter of Baudouin de Neuville, a knight from Artois, who had been killed at the battle of Adrianople in 1205. It is possible that she was a widow, but it is certain that she was attended by her mother. The animus shown to the latter may suggest undue influence in imperial affairs or an unacceptable sexual liaison. The mother was thrown from the palace window to a waiting boat whose crew took her out into the Bosphoros and drowned her. The face of the emperor's wife was mutilated whilst he was restrained by the conspirators. The only parallel for such treatment of a monarch was the case of the tenth-century west Saxon king of England, Edwy (955–59). The conspirators were not named in any of the sources but clearly they had access to the imperial suite. Robert did not exact revenge but quit the capital and journeyed to Rome to lay his complaint before the pope. These were not the actions of a strong and resourceful ruler. Certainly, judging from the comment of Alberic of Trois-Fontaines, Robert, whom he described as '*quasi rudis et idiota*' had forfeited the respect of his advisers. We are not told why or how this came about. However, it must surely have had something to do with this secret marriage and his earlier disinclination to marry Eudokia, the daughter of Theodore Laskaris, which in 1221 would have brought territorial concessions and cash to the hard-pressed Latins.[28]

Imperial rights and revenues

We know very little indeed of the revenues of the Latin emperors. No source specifically informs us of what they were or how they were collected, and no accounts survive to allow any quantification of receipts or expenditure. As a

---

[28] Alberic of Trois-Fontaines, *MGH,SS* XXIII (1874), p.910/42–43, sub anno 1220; J. Longnon, *LEmpire Latin* ... (Paris, 1949), 157–9, 162–3.

result we have to rely upon conjecture and circumstantial evidence. In the first place the imperial revenues seem to have been no different in kind than those enjoyed by other Frankish seigneurs in the Aegean. The one big difference was that rather than being on a grander scale than that of other lords, the emperors were unable to exploit their resources to the full due the state of continuous warfare in their lands. By the 1230s these territories were confined to the city of Constantinople itself. In such circumstances the emperors were pleased to receive financial assistance from any source. The first of these aid packages seems to have been a levy on Greek rural priests granted to Robert by Gregory IX in April 1227.[29] More assured and even more welcome was the annual subvention of 22,000 hyperpera '... *ad conducendos auxiliarios*' contributed by Geoffrey II de Villehardouin from 1236 onwards.[30] This sum may show the aid given by a vassal to his suzerain in times of crisis but it certainly shows the surplus revenue of a successful ruler.

Landed estate formed the basis of imperial and princely revenue. Baldwin I had received a landed endowment of one-quarter of the lands of the empire, which Gunther of Pairis in the *Historia Constantiopolitana* records was formed into a royal fisc to finance the government of the empire.[31] The main settlements in these lands were listed in the Partitio Regni Graeci.[32] However most of this land had to be conquered and remained little more than a name in a register since the empire never enjoyed the peaceful conditions which would have allowed the exploitation of these resources outside the walls of Constantinople. The princes of the Morea too reserved a royal fisc for their use. From this land in 1261 Prince William made grants in Arkadia to Villain d'Aulnay, the former marshal of Romania and a refugee from Constantinople, and to this fisc land confiscated for treason or other reasons was added.[33] In the Morea the protovestarius and various treasurers ran the fisc and were accountable to the prince. Failure to account satisfactorily could result in imprisonment, as in the case of Benjamin of Kalamata in 1301, although the reaction of the Moreote barons on that occasion showed that they considered this high-handed treatment of a liege vassal typical of 'Lombard tyranny'. There must have been similar functionaries in the Latin empire. From the landed estate derived all the rights of the ruler. Lacking any direct evidence for the Latin emperors and their exploitation of their demesne lands, two assumptions are made here. First, that he exploited his lands like any other lord. Second, that the Assizes of Romania can be used to provide a model for this, although its

---

[29] L. Auvray, *Les Registres de Gregoire IX*, I (Paris, 1896), no. 47.
[30] Alberic of Trois-Fontaines, *MGH, SS XXIII*, p. 939.
[31] *Urkunden* I, 457: '*Provinciae ... in tres parts divisae sunt: unam, quae ad fiscum Regis specialiter pertineret ...*'.
[32] *Urkunden* I, 473–9.
[33] X t M, 1326–7; Assizes of Romania, article 171.

fourteenth-century date must always be borne in mind. The following paragraphs provide a qualitative guide only for imperial revenues, in the absence of any other source.

The emperor, prince or duke had the right of taxation. It would appear that many features of the late Byzantine tax system were continued. This is certainly no surprise if Professor Oikonomides is right in his suggestion that fiscal documents from the reign of Alexios IV were used as the basis for the partition of the empire. Certainly the kommerkion or commerclum, an import-export tax, continued to be levied. This does seem to have been an impost reserved for the ruler, since article 84 of the Assizes of Romania reserved fiscal rights at ports and saltworks to them. Treasure trove too was reserved to the ruler (article 155), no mean right in a land full of antiquities. All free peasants paid the cens, whilst all unfree peasants paid a poll tax and their possessions were deemed those of the lord.[34] Although the emperor or other ruler enjoyed those revenues as a lord of land, he did not enjoy them from the state as a whole once lands and rights had been granted out to his vassals. Here we have a continuation of Byzantine state taxation within a western feudal context.

The difficulties of exploiting the imperial demesne did not allow the emperors to live of their own. As far as is known the Latin emperors were the only rulers of the Aegean to exploit home resources to bolster their position in the Aegean in the thirteenth century, that is after the initial expenses of going on crusade had been met. Back in the Low Countries the various emperors possessed family estates which they seemed prepared to use to finance military help for their new empire. The imperial seal was well-known in Flanders and used to authenticate land sales by the former counts. The false Baldwin active in Flanders from March to September 1225 produced a number of charters whose contents are not known, but judging from Alberic of Trois-Fontaines' account of his activities he made no attempt to sell land on the pretext of raising money for the empire.[35] In the 1220s such use of comital resources was unfamiliar. It was in 1239 and later that Flemish comital lands were being sold outright or mortgaged on a large scale in order to raise cash for the hire of mercenaries. It is noteworthy that we know more about the estate officials and the accounting of the sums raised in Flanders than we do of similar procedures in Thrace. There, Greek tenants would presumably have paid the akrosticon and rendered other dues if circumstances rendered their collection feasible. Primarily, however, these lands were used to endow knights with a view to increasing the military base of the empire. The importance of land in this context resulted in one of the earliest pieces of Mortmain legislation known in the middle ages. Although

---

[34] Assizes of Romania, articles 142, 183, 185, 190 and 192.
[35] *MGH, SS* XXIII, p.915; R.L. Wolff, 'Baldwin of Flanders and Hainaut …' *Speculum* 27 (1952), 281–322.

the emperors made grants to religious institutions, these grants were to the military orders and date from before 1209.[36]

The right of coinage was one fully reserved to rulers. Regrettably we know little of the mint policy and the profits derived therefrom by the Frankish rulers in the Aegean. Until recently it was not even certain if the Latin emperors produced a regular coinage at all. This has proved difficult to identify and must have imitated the Byzantine coinage. It is known that they did not rely upon the specie in circulation. Peggalotti listed '*perperi latini*' and Choniates noted the melting down of bronze statues by the Latins in 1204 to produce coins, but what were these coins? Were they straight imitations? Presumably Byzantine dies for the copper trachea were used to produce this small change for the soldiery in the city in 1204.[37] However, the Latins had some skills in mint operation. Akropolites noted that the Latin emperors were refining gold, apparently for private individuals, in the former Byzantine mint.[38] The Latin rulers of Greece did not coin money until the latter half of the thirteenth century, after the end of the Latin empire's active existence.[39]

Profits of justice seemed to derive primarily from land forfeitures consequent upon conviction of a liege vassal for homicide, the non-performance of service, desertion on the battlefield or for treason.[40] Treason was as yet not clearly defined. Article 3 makes it clear that it was an action like fighting against the ruler, having sexual relations with his wife, raping his daughter or refusing to serve as hostage for the lord. It did not encompass plots against the ruler and was very similar to the treason legislation which emerged in England in 1352.

Rulers enjoyed a variety of feudal dues and services. In the land of the fisc they enjoyed the rights of any seigneur. Land was cultivated by unfree peasants or *paroikoi* as part of their *dispoticaria* or labour services. In return they received a *staxia* or peasant holding for which a small payment or *acrostico/crustilio* was due in acknowledgement of the lord's status. They were obliged to use the community oven, mill, and olive and wine presses provided by the lord and for which payment was required. The goods of the unfree peasantry was at the lord's disposal. If a peasant died without heirs the lord inherited and if necessary he could take all the peasant's possessions as his own and evict him from his staxia provided he left him enough to live.[41] In return for this minimal subsistence right the peasant paid a poll

---

[36] PL, 216:296; E. Gibbon, *The Decline and Fall of the Roman Empire* c.LXI, vol.VI, p.429 in the J.B. Bury edn (London, 1898).
[37] Choniates, 649 (Magoulias trans., p.358); M. Hendy, *Studies in the Byzantine Monetary Economy, c.300–1450* (Cambridge, 1985), pp.520–1.
[38] Akropolites I, c.78, p.163; P. Grierson, *Byzantine Coins* (London, 1982), pp.269–70.
[39] See p.174.
[40] Assizes of Romania, articles 69 and 167.
[41] Ibid., articles 183, 185, 190, 197, 205 and 215; see p.245ff.

tax. With regard to lands which had been granted out they could levy a relief or inheritance tax from the heir of a vassal (article 34). Greeks too presumably paid a relief although article 138 made allowance for the practice of partiable inheritance amongst the Greeks. The size of the relief is nowhere stipulated, although the widow of a liege vassal on choosing to marry again at her own discretion could do so on paying a relief to the value of one-third the annual revenue of the fief concerned (article 31). Peter Topping has suggested that here was a Champenoise custom brought east by the Villehardouin and therefore one of the original clauses of the Assizes. The right of wardship was a valued right since the guardian could enjoy the produce and revenues of the land in question until the minor was invested at the age of fifteen (thirteen for girls). It was of course subject to abuse since the Assizes of Romania contained numerous articles designed to protect the interests of the ward from too grasping a guardian (article 83). Purveyance or hospitality for the ruler and his household at a fixed rate provided he paid for it was enjoyed by the ruler. However, on the three occasions – 1209, 1228, 1261 – when a Latin emperor visited Greece he was well received and entertained by the rulers there apparently free of charge. It is, however, difficult to discern the reality of payments from the narrative sources that record these visits.

The ruler enjoyed certain financial rights with regard to the church. By the right of regale the revenues of bishoprics reverted to the ruler during vacancy as did that of other church dignitaries whose appointment was in their hands. Thus there was the dispute in 1208 between emperor and patriarch over the advowson of the prebendal churches in Constantinople.[42] It was concern over the loss of regalian rights to the Venetians which prompted the emperor's protest to Innocent III in November 1209. It appears that the patriarch had united two bishoprics in Thrace and the problem was that one of them was located in imperial territory whilst the other was in part of the Venetian condominum.[43] Equally, imperial protection for so-called imperial monasteries brought revenue in the form of exploitation of the monastic estates during an abatial vacancy. In 1209 the emperor Henry tried to get papal acknowledgement for the rights of the Latin emperor to former Byzantine imperial monasteries.[44] The size of income generated is unknown but clearly it was a right worth protecting and presumably exploited. In addition the clergy of the Aegean owed an oath of fealty to the emperor and in times of difficulty could be urged by the pope to contribute part of their income to aid the emperor.

Finally, there was the right to demand military service and aids. In western Europe these latter involved payments on the marriage of the ruler's

---

[42] PL, 215:1349.
[43] PL, 216:148–9.
[44] PL, 216:147.

daughter for the first time, and the knighting of his eldest son and the raising of a ransom for the ruler. Article 24 allows for the first and the last aid. The knighting of the eldest son is not specifically listed in the Assizes of Romania. Articles 3 and 15 stipulate that a vassal may be sent as a hostage in place of his lord. This was perhaps the most famous aid in Frankish Greece since the sending of Margaret of Passavant to Constantinople in place of Prince William in 1262 resulted in the forfeiture of her inheritance and the famous lawsuit of 1276.

The military expenditure of the empire soon outstripped its income. A large amount was expended in the hiring of troops and the provision of war material. Ready cash with which to pay troops was a major problem. The emperors were unable to turn their landed resources in the east into ready cash. This seems to have been a problem from the early days of the empire, but it became critical in the late 1230s with the accession of Baldwin II. Various ways round this dilemma were sought. From the first the emperors had sought to economise in the rates of pay. As a result they had lost western soldiers to the Greeks of Epiros and Nicaea whose leadership seemed more able to pay the rates required by these troops and in 1205 had provoked a rebuke from Innocent III who urged the payment of more on the recruitment of western soldiers.[45] Both Baldwin and Henry seemed content to employ cheaper native troops and to make substantial grants of frontier territory to their Greek commanders. The services of Ponce de Charpigny (alias de Lyon) were utilised to sell or pawn relics in the west and probably to perform other financial services as well, since in the period up to 1221 he is found making regular trips to western Europe and back. His sale of relics to the chapter at Lyons in April 1208 was the first recorded selling off of Byzantine relics to raise money for the defence of the Latin empire.[46] He seems too to have been a member of the imperial council since in December 1221 he is the second witness to the confirmation of the privileges of the Venetians by the emperor Robert.

Increasingly, financial aid was sought from the west. In Constantinople itself rather desperate measures seem to have been resorted to. Lead was stripped from the roofs of the two imperial palaces for coinage and their timbers used for firewood. It is possible that the emperor Baldwin was forced to reside in the monastery of the Pantokrator, but on this point the

---

[45] PL, 216:353–4 (7 December 1210). Innocent stated that westerners who fought with Michael Doukas did so because they were '*cupiditate caecati*' (blinded by greed). He urged the emperor through the patriarch to raise rates of pay to staunch the loss of troops to the Greeks – '*commonens nihilominus imperatorem eumdem ut ipsis congrua stipendia subministret, ne se ad Graecos transferre prae inopia compellantur ...*'

[46] Henrickx, *Byzantina* 14 (1988), p.66, no.86; J. Longnon, *Les Compagnons de Villehardouin* (Paris, 1978), p.219.

sources are divided.[47] The reference in Akropolites to the Latin emperors refining gold may well refer to one of these desperate measures rather than any industrial minting process as such. The lack of mention of any revenue collecting officers raises the question of whether there were any revenues to collect outside of the city in the 1240s. It is therefore not surprising that Baldwin II should risk the reputation of his monarchy in order to raise loans, and that before returning to Constantinople, Baldwin, who since March 1237 had been emperor in his own right, sought to raise cash and troops in the west to reinvigorate his empire. Was this a policy initiative of Baldwin? John de Brienne seems to have been content with loans from the Villehardouin of the Morea and equally content to let his successor pick up the bills in the forms of grants of suzerainty. Baldwin must have realised that desperate measures were required and set about pawning the most precious relics and alienating ancestral property in the Low Countries.

During 1238 cash was raised in the west by selling or mortgaging the ancestral lands of the emperors in Flanders. In April 1239 the forests at Tettefolz and Rovroit were sold to various monasteries and before his departure for Constantinople on 15 May 1239 he mortgaged the county of Namur to Louis IX for 50,000 livres. Meanwhile, in the east around March 1238, the regency council had handed over the crown of thorns to the Venetian podesta to hold as a surety for a loan of 13,134 hyperpera from a consortium of creditors. In the following September Baldwin sold this most precious of relics to Louis IX in return for 10,000 livres cash and the payment of the loan.[48] However, from the early days of the empire the large number of relics that had fallen into imperial hands in 1204 were used as pious gifts to gain diplomatic and ecclesiastical favours and, at least once as we have seen, to purchase provisions and war material.[49] The hidden 'interest' which a Constantinopolitan relic had in the west lay in the donations from increased numbers of pilgrims. A portion of the true cross financed the re-building programme at Bromholm Priory in Norfolk in the 1230s whilst an arm of St Stephen brought back by bishop Nivelon de Cherissy paid for the erection of a bridge at Chalons-sur-Marne in 1217.[50]

---

[47] Nikephoros Gregoras, *Bizantina historia* 3 vols, eds L. Schopen and I. Bekker (Bonn, 1830–45), I, 85/24 refers to the Pantokrator Monastery as the palace of the Latins, but L. de C, 84 and Pachymeres 144/11–13 write of Baldwin fleeing from the Blachernae Palace. The monastery had become the headquarters of the Venetians in Constantinople after 1204 (*Urkunden* II, 284) and it was there that the icon Hodgetria was kept. See D.J. Geanakoplos, *Emperor Michael Palaeologus and the West* (Harvard, 1959), pp.110–11 and A. Van Milligen, *Byzantine Constantinople* (London, 1889), p.269 for discussion.
[48] Hendrickx, *Byzantina* 14, pp.131–54; R.L. Wolff, 'Mortgage and redemption of an Emperor's Son ...' *Speculum* 29 (1954), 45–84.
[49] Valenciennes, 666.
[50] F. Wormald, 'The Holy Rood of Bromholm' *Journal of the Warburg Institute* 1 (1937), 31–45; V. Mortet and P. Deschamps, eds, *Recueil de textes relatifs à l'histoire de architecture et à la condition des architects en France au moyen âge* 2 vols (Paris, 1911–29), II, pp.199–210, cited M. Barber, *The Two Cities* (London, 1992), p.15.

Household government

In so far as we can glimpse it, the administration of the empire and of the various domains that composed it was modelled on contemporary western household government. A trained professional civil service was outside the experience of the crusading leadership and as such dismissed. We should not take Choniates's deprecatory record of this dismissal as the last word on Frankish governmental practice. The crusading leadership was not composed of administrative pygmies abashed by a highly centralised and bureaucratised empire. All of them had had some experience of estate administration in western Europe. Many ruled counties and marquisates and, like Boniface of Montferrat, were not slow in mobilising their new resources even if it meant unpopularity with their new Greek subjects. Indeed Baldwin of Flanders hailed from one of the most administratively advanced parts of western Europe where a central fiscal system had been in place as early as 1089. Administrative duties may not have been their predilection but they were not inexperienced at them and were not slow to appreciate the value of Byzantine archives in the exploitation of their new dominions.

Prominent noblemen and clerics were preferred to professional civil servants. Many of these participated in the government as messengers, financial advisers, military commanders and the like as the need arose without any formal institutional post. Article 17 of the Assizes of Romania stipulated that the ruler could send any liegeman outside his dominions on a matter of governmental concern providing his expenses were paid. Such was Ponce de Charpigny.

The list of witnesses to Henry's confirmation of the March 1204 Pact in October 1205 consisted of Conon of Bethune, the protovestarius of the empire, Manassis de l'Isle, the chief cook, Macaire of Ste Menehould, the baker, and Milon le Brabant, the butler.[51] In addition we know from the pages of Villehardouin that John of Noyen was chancellor, Thierry de Termonde constable and the chronicler himself marshal of the empire.[52] In 1209 his nephew Geoffrey was to become seneschal of Romania.[53] All of them were household officials. The protovestarius was the equivalent of chamberlain and from his prominence both in this witness list and later in the affairs of the empire during the regency of the empress Yolande, it can be said that his headship of the privy chamber placed him at the head of the administration. It was very much household government. In 1238 the baili of the empire, Anseau de Cayeaux and his close advisers, Geoffrey de Mery, the constable, Villain d'Aunay, the marshal, and Narjot de Toucy, a former

---

[51] *Urkunden* I, 574.
[52] Villehardouin, 290, 404–5, 430.
[53] L de C, 185: Valenciennes, 669–70.

baili in 1228, sealed the box containing the crown of thorns with their personal seals as a guarantee of its authenticity.[54] The great men in the empire no longer bear the purely household titles of their forebears a generation before. The evidence is scanty in the extreme, but does this prominence of the military side of the household not reflect the concerns of the empire in its hour of need? Admittedly the emperor Baldwin was in the west and such officers of the chamber and the hall might have been with him. If they were, they have left little mark on the record of his activities there. Certainly it was the man that made the office rather than vice versa.

Both in the kingdom of Thessalonika and in the principality of the Morea the same pattern of household officers is evident. Although we have nothing like full establishment lists but only the names and titles of certain office-holders, they are enough to demonstrate the presence of western household government. Thus we find Amedée Pofoy doubling as constable of Thessalonika as well as of the empire, and Renier de Tabarie as chancellor in the years before 1209. In the Morea virtually all our information comes from the 1270s and after. There was a hereditary marshal (Jean I de Neuilly), a constable (such as Jean de Chauderon, in whose family the office was hereditary, and Engilbert de Leiderkerke), a chancellor (Leonard de Veroli and Benjamin of Kalamata), but interestingly no seneschal, although since 1209 the Villehardouin princes themselves were hereditary seneschals of Romania.[55] There was also a protovestarius, an office which Benjamin had held before his appointment as chancellor and in which he was succeeded by Quir (Kyrios) Vasylopule. The protoficier was concerned with safeguarding the feudal dues and the revenues of the prince. He oversaw the tax farm whilst the actual receipt and storage of revenue was in the hands of the treasurer (articles 169 and 171). The Moreote protovestarius was more of an official than the imperial protovestarius Conon de Bethune. In the Morea in 1301 Benjamin was called to account for the revenues of the Morea from his period as protovestarius by Philip of Savoy and imprisoned as a result. This high-handed action on Philip's part resulted in a protest from Nicholas II de St Omer, the former baili. This action does show, however tantalisingly, the outlines of political alignments which such officers might adopt.[56]

The sources reveal little of the functioning of these officers and force us to draw a composite picture based upon the several states in the Aegean. All of them were advisers of the ruler apparently exercising duties as circumstances dictated rather than having specifically defined functions as were evident in the Byzantine bureaucracy. The new Latin administration, although finding the Byzantine archives convenient sources of information

---

[54] P. Riant, ed., *Exuviae sacrae Constantinopolitanae* II (Paris, 1877), pp.122–3.

[55] L de C, 182, 328, 662, 829.

[56] L de C, 856–69.

for conquerors, do not seem to have imitated the keeping of records in triplicate. Records of court cases, copies of legal decisions and charters, and registers of fiefs formed the main administrative documents which have come down to us or which are noted in passing in the Assizes of Romania. For example, article 168 states that a litigant may have an official copy of a sentence or judgement under the seals of the judges, whilst article 191 allows for copies of testimonies in civil actions to be provided to litigants on demand. Court records were clearly kept and referred to. In the case concerning Margaret of Passavant and her claim to the barony of Akova in 1276, before making some restitution the protovestarius Colinet was ordered to produce the court minutes and eventually Margaret received a charter or Frankish privilege.[57] The written word in the form of charters was clearly the preferred method of showing title but oral testimony was not ruled out either for individuals or communities like the Venetians in Constantinople in 1204. From the fourteenth century a number of estate accounts and surveys survive, often in fragmentary condition. The Franks were certainly not strangers to such procedures. It is to our great loss that so few have survived to flesh out the bones of the picture here provided.

The chancellor was concerned with the writing of official documents. It was a post that could develop important political powers in the hands of the right men. Chancelleries existed in the Venetian possessions as well as in the other Frankish states of the day. The general anonymity of the holders of this office in the Aegean would suggest that in general most chancellors were content to fulfil their notarial function. We know the names of four chancellors from Romania as a whole in the thirteenth century. These were ambitious able men often absent from the courts which employed them and often busy on political and diplomatic matters. It is because of this other significance that we know their names. Those from the Latin empire in the early part of the thirteenth century were clergymen of some status and ability. Those from the Morea from later in the same century were laymen. Does this illustrate the laicisation of the administration as evidenced in western Europe at this time, or does it show a difference between the empire and one of its component states?

John of Noyen, bishop-elect of Acre, came east apparently as the personal chancellor of Baldwin of Flanders, who had left Gerard, provost of Bruges, as chancellor of Flanders. John, who was described as learned and inspiring, was presumably the man who dealt with Baldwin's correspondence. He did, however, preach to the crusaders before the assault on Constantinople and took part in the electoral college which chose Baldwin as first Latin emperor. After the elevation of Baldwin to the imperial throne, John became chancellor of the empire. He died in the late summer of 1204

---

[57] L de C, 501–31; X t M, 7301–752.

and is credited with the letters of Baldwin before that date. However, he spent considerable time away from his master on diplomatic missions to the papal curia in 1203.[58] The next chancellor, Warin, was elected archbishop of Thessalonika in 1208 and entrusted with the running of that city on the emperor's behalf after the Lombard revolt. By 1216 he was chancellor of Romania but seemed to live in Thessalonika away from the imperial court. On the fall of Thessalonika in 1222 he left Romania for Flanders (where he was still alive in 1239) to return east with the emperor Baldwin II.[59]

In the Morea we have the names of Leonard of Veroli (d. 1281), Angelo de Mauro, his successor (d. 1297), and Benjamin of Kalamata (still in post in 1324), as three long-serving chancellors in the period 1260 to 1320, the period that marked the change-over from direct rule by the Villehardouin to absentee rule from Naples. The former, originally from the papal states, was an intimate adviser of William de Villehardouin, a diplomat and the drafter of the important Treaty of Viterbo in 1267.[60] He certainly was a writer of documents, as shown by his part in the Akova affair in 1276. He drew up the charter as ordered and authenticated it with his own seal. Again when producing charters granting the remaining two-thirds of Akova to Villehardouin's younger daughter Margaret, the chancellor drafted the document and sealed it with his own seal. In both cases it was the bestowing of the document and investiture by the prince which the Greek chronicler focused upon as the main act. The chancellor does not seem to have kept the prince's seal or to have deemed it necessary to authenticate documents drawn up by him in the prince's name. Leonard was termed logothete by the Greek chronicler and chancelier in the French version, where he was also described as 'le maistre conseiller'.[61] Both socially and politically he was much more than the head of a writing office. His successor, Benjamin, was a Frank despite his unusual name. He had served as protovestiary before his appointment as chancellor, and as we have seen he was imprisoned in 1301 until he produced satisfactory accounts of his dealings in his former post. His release was secured by Nicholas III de St Omer, presumably because of past favours owed to Benjamin. Indeed it is due to their political rather than their administrative activities that we know the names of these four chancellors. The office was what an individual chose to make it and did not confer greatness because of its rank. Outside of the principality and the empire local chancelleries existed in the Venetian possessions and in the Duchy of Naxos, where we have the name of Giovanni Jordoano who we know because he subscribed an extract he had copied from the Assizes of Romania in 1494. He was a legal and secretarial

---

[58] Longnon, *op.cit.*, pp.163–6.
[59] Hendrickx, *art.cit.*, pp.132–3, no.202.
[60] Perrat & Longnon, p.211.
[61] L de C, 517.

official. The Assizes of Romania inform us that Latin lords were not always literate men and would need someone to write for them. Seals were in use and someone to keep these would be required. This man was the chancellor, and how he used his contact with the ruler and his technical knowledge was up to him.

The Assizes of Romania record that the protovestiary and the Treasurer were responsible for the collection and farming out of the prince's revenues in the principality of Achaia. The protovestiary recorded the fiefs and the services owed to the prince and oversaw the management of the prince's farms and vineyards. He was expected to give advice before grants were made and was consulted in lawsuits arising from such matters. The post was no sinecure and involved an active knowledge of the estates and geography of the Peloponnese. In 1276 the protovestiary was involved in the restitution of one-third of her barony to Margaret of Passava, and in 1293 in investing Geoffrey d'Aunoy with the barony of Arkadia.[62] The title itself was a Greek one and was early adopted by the Latins. Conon de Bethune was so dubbed in 1206, although in his case it seems that it was his role as close confidant of the emperor which was important rather than any revenue duties. It is also possible that in Conon's case the adoption of this title was a personal matter since the title did not appear to be used in the Latin imperial council after his death in 1219. In Naples it was sometimes seen as the equivalent of the post of chamberlain in western Europe. Thus in 1283 Charles of Salerno sent Ricardo de Pando de Scala to the Morea as his chamberlain or protovestiary of the principality of Achaia.[63] He combined the post with that of mint-master at Glarenza. Greeks like *'Quir Vasylopoule'* (L. de C. para. 829) were employed in this post as well as Franks like Colinet and Benjamin of Kalamata and Italians like Ricardo.[64] It is probable that Greeks were employed in this office from the early days of the conquest and hence the ease with which the title was used in the Moreote administration.[65] In general, though, the debt of the incoming Latin rulers to the Aegean was considerably less than that of the Normans to the Anglo-Saxons in eleventh-century England.

Constables and marshals are found in Achaia as in the Latin empire. Both offices were hereditary within the male line in Achaia and probably, although we have no evidence, in the empire. Their role was primarily a military one, although they might well take on diplomatic and adminis-trative responsibilities as the need arose, as with the Chauderon family, the

---

[62] L de C, 526 and 752.

[63] Camillo Minieri Riccio, *Saggio di codice diplomatico* ... 2 vols in 3 (Naples, 1878–83), I, pp.204–5, cited by P. Topping, *Studies on Latin Greece* (London, 1975), p.124, no.5.

[64] L de C, 829.

[65] L de C, 526, 752, 829; P. Topping, *Feudal Institutions As Revealed in the Assizes of Romania* ... (Pennsylvania, 1949), p.124, no.1.

hereditary constables of the Morea. The first grand constable Geoffrey, lord of Estamirra, took an active role in negotiating the marriage of Geoffrey II de Villehardouin with Agnes de Courtenay in 1218, whilst his son Jean was active as a negotiator in the marriage of Isabelle de Villehardouin and Florent of Hainault in 1289 and four years later was sent to the court of Andronikos II to negotiate the return of Kalamata to the Franks after its seizure by the Greeks of Skorta.[66] Seneschals, panterers and butlers were recorded within the court of the early Latin emperor but not in the Morea. The perceived status of a suzerain may have dictated whether such officials were appointed. Arguments from silence are, however, dangerous since on those grounds we would have to conclude that the lordship of Athens and Thebes had no writing office, treasury or any other sort of officials at all, which cannot have been the case.

Local government

Local government was in the hands of castellans who, if the castellany of Kalamata is any guide, were assisted by a constable and a number of sergeants.[67] The former summoned the local vassals to perform their military service to the ruler providing fifteen days' notice when applicable and exercised some sort of appeal jurisdiction from local courts. It was the sergeants and vavasours who would have been most familiar to the Greek peasantry, exercising control of their agricultural and social lives, and in theory too able to direct their religious lives in the general responsibility which a lord had for the good behaviour and spiritual well-being of his serfs. According to the crisis of 1301 in the Morea, there seemed to exist in the towns of the principality a system of bailies, some of them Greeks, responsible for rendering the farm or dues from the towns to the prince. A similar system may well have existed in central Greece where the Catalans installed veguers or bailies in the towns after 1311. We can hardly suppose that this system was entirely new to the inhabitants.

Byzantine office titles

The use of Greek official titles such as protovestarius and logothete, and within the imperial lands honorifics like sebastokrator and caesar, does not necessarily imply that the reconciliation of Greeks was intended or that any

---

[66] L de C, 182, 328, 699.
[67] L de C, 753.

Byzantinisation of western household government was in progress. The usage can be explained in part by the personal predilections of certain individuals, by the need to preserve Byzantine forms in the exploitation of the Greek peasantry on estates, and the close identification of Byzantine offices with Latin equivalents in the perception of the writer of the Greek version of the *Chronicle of the Morea*. The Latins were aware of certain Greek official titles from the Byzantine court such as megadux, caesar, protoallagatoras and the like, and that the Greek bureaucracy wore customs and possessed seals which expressed those ranks. The use of Greek titles was very limited amongst Latins. In Constantinople it seemed to have been limited to just two men, Conon de Bethune, protovestarios in 1205 and sebastokrator in 1219, and Philip de Toucy, whose relative Anselin was described as 'brother of the caesar' in 1248.[68] Both men had long association with the Aegean and the courts of Byzantine and Cuman rulers, and may well have had a personal predilection for such titles. The *Chronicle of the Morea* usually emphasises when a member of the Frankish aristocracy had a knowledge of Greek manners and language, as in the case of Geoffrey d'Aulnay and Anselin de Toucy.[69] They were usually men born in Romania and the infrequency of occurrences of such knowledge suggest that linguistic skills and an interest in Greek institutions may not have been pronounced amongst the majority of the Frankish ruling class. Where Greeks were employed in the Latin administration, then Greek titles might well be maintained. Thus in the Morea the office of prothoficier was frequently held by Greeks. It does seem to be a term adopted from the Byzantine administration by the Franks and does not appear in the twelfth-century Sicilian kingdom. One wonders what dealings and understanding of the original Byzantine office the Greeks of the Morea would have had, since it was a Byzantine court post and not one involved in provincial government. Under the Franks the post entailed keeping the register of fiefs and duties and required a knowledge both of the country and possibly the (Byzantine) records on which the land division was based. This was much more in line with the western seneschal's task and, as we have noted, there was no evidence for a seneschal in the Morea. This is perhaps why. However, as we have also seen, the Angevins identified the office with that of chamberlain, much more in line with its original Byzantine function. It was probably a pivotal office in the accommodating of Greek archons within the Frankish territorial and social structure, and its role came to be accepted by the Greeks as much as by the Latins. Despite the antiquity of the term, which went back to the fifth century, it was probably an office as new to the Moreote Greeks as to their Latin masters.

Equally, those individuals for whom a Byzantine title had some

---

[68] X t M, 1308.
[69] L de C, 357, 702.

significance or use were given one. In 1208 the emperor Henry bestowed the title caesar on his new son-in-law, the Bulgarian prince Alexios Slav, who was still using it in 1220, a sign of the value which he personally placed upon it. Two years previously the emperor Henry had granted the title of megadux or commander of the fleet to the Genoese Philocalus Navigaioso, along with rule of the island of Lemnos, on the sea-route between Constantinople and Thessalonika. It is possible that Henry issued a golden bull for the grant but unclear if a title or an office was involved.[70] In the late twelfth century honorific titles such as caesar had been bestowed on westerners like Conrad of Montferrat who had a close relationship to the imperial family. This practice was still used in Byzantine circles in the fourteenth century when Roger de Flor, the Catalan mercenary leader, received the title on his betrothal to a Byzantine princess from the imperial family in the spring of 1305. The Catalan chronicler Muntaner saw the office as second only to that of the emperor and one with almost equivalent powers which had been in abeyance for four hundred years. He wrote of the title in terms of the Roman principate of the first century and not as a Byzantine honorific.[71] Such misunderstanding was not evident amongst the Frankish and Venetian leadership a century before. Muntaner translated Byzantine titles literally into presumed western equivalents. In 1302 when Roger had received the title of megadux, Muntaner interpreted this as grand duke and assumed that Roger had been exalted to a social status commensurate with that of a western duke.[72] Was this just a personal foible or did it represent a closing of western minds to Byzantium and a distancing of Greeks and Latins, at least in the north Aegean world since 1204?

Parliament

As in western Europe in the late thirteenth/early fourteenth century parliament was an act of government and not a specific institution. It was distinguished from the high court of liegemen by a wider body of participants. Judging from the regulations governing tallage in article 23 of the Assizes, it appears that all liegemen, vassals and freemen could attend, although with the powers to speak for and bind themselves only. There was no hint of them speaking as representatives. Parliaments were not mentioned once in the Assizes of Romania and this shows that they were regarded as a princely prerogative summoned by the ruler or his representative. The parliaments summoned in Romania either by the emperor in 1209, 1210

---

[70] Hendrickx, *Byzantina* 14, p.55, no.68; pp. 87–8, no.88.
[71] Muntaner *Cronica*, CCXII (Goodenough trans., II, p.507)
[72] Muntaner, *Cronica*, CXCIX, (Goodenough trans., II, p.480).

and 1219 or by the prince of Achaia or his representative in 1261 and 1305, all had some specific purpose and significance. The parliament of women which met at Nikli in 1261 was properly convened but nothing like it could have been found anywhere else in Europe in the thirteenth century.[73]

The government of Frankish Greece was almost totally western in its inspiration and offices. It was household government, but in creative and adaptable hands. Greek titles, personnel, and archives were not spurned and the institutions were used to fit the political needs of the day. Indeed some features like mortmain, tight conciliar government and women in parliament may have been brought about by political and military necessity, but they were in the forefront of the developments of their day. There was nothing ossifying about the rulership of Romania. It was not a pale imitation of Byzantium or Paris but an original and creative response to a set of unique circumstances.

---

[73] See p.305.

Chapter 8 ....

The Latin Secular Church[1]

The replacement of the Greek higher clergy, from patriarch to bishops, by Latin incumbents and the grafting on to that basic structure of a Latin cathedral clergy was one of the unforeseen results of the diversion of the Fourth Crusade to Constantinople in 1204. Within a year there existed two patriarchs of Constantinople: the Greek incumbent, John X Kamateros (1198–1206), who lived ignored in the city suburbs, and Thomas Morosini, a Venetian noble in minor orders, whose uncanonical appointment by the Venetian clergy on crusade had given the pope little option but to confirm it. In 1208 Michael IV Autoreianos was chosen in Nicaea as the legitimate successor to Kamateros and recognised as such in the Orthodox world. The schism had physically arrived. It was exported around the Aegean in the succeeding decade by the haphazard Latin appropriation of the Greek church. The schism between pope and patriarch had been potentially present since the fourth century with the debate over the primacy of the patriarch of Rome and his relationship to the other patriarchates of the Roman empire. At the beginning of the thirteenth century an aggressive papacy was naming patriarchs of its own and able to install them because of the Latin occupation of Constantinople.

---

[1] Parts of this chapter have been previously published in 'The Latin secular church in mainland Greece, 1204–1220' *Medieval History* 1 (1991), 93–105. The best general accounts are G. Fedalto, *La Chiesa latina in Oriente* I 2nd edn (Verona, 1981), pp.219–415, and Walter Norden, *Das Papsttum und Byzanz*, (Berlin, 1903) supplemented by two articles by R.L. Wolff, 'The organization of the Latin patriarchate of Constantinople, 1204–1261' *Traditio* 6 (1948), 33–60 and 'Politics in the Latin patriarchate of Constantinople' *DOP* 8 (1954), 228–303, and C.A. Frazee, 'The Catholic Church in Constantinople, 1204–1453' *Balkan Studies* 19 (1978), 33–49. See also J. Hussey, *The Orthodox Church in the Byzantine Empire* (Oxford, 1986), pp.184–206 and K.M. Setton, *The Papacy and the Levant* I (Philadelphia, 1976), pp.1–68, 405–40, and B. Hamilton *The Latin Church in the Crusader States* (London, 1980).

Greek and Latin Christians

The designation *Latinoi* or Latins seemed to go back to the eighth century and the competition of western and eastern missionaries in the lands of the Slavs. Physical proximity had led to ready comparisons of the liturgical languages of the rival missionaries and the term for the followers of the western Latin rite coined. It was adopted proudly by western Christians themselves. Eustathios of Thessalonika commented on '… the stupid and discordant cries of a Latin service … disturbing good order and holy harmony.' When forced to live alongside Latins, their mixing of suet and lard with oil led to an infringement of Orthodox fasting rules, whilst there was the danger that religion would be mocked as well as the unintentional pollution through the provision of Latin dishes to the hungry. Clearly it was easier to be charitable at a distance. Neither the wordy controversy between Pope Nicholas I (858–67) and Patriarch Photios (858–67, 877–86) over the proposed addition of the words 'filioque' to the Nicene Creed in the ninth century, nor the reciprocal excommunication of Pope Leo IX (1049–55) and Patriarch Michael I Keroularios (1043–58) on the 16 July 1054, had brought about a permanent rift. The former was put down to linguistic misunderstanding and the latter was seen by the clergy of both sides as a temporary rupture in cordial relations and a personality clash between the patriarch and the papal legate Cardinal Humbert rather than a point of no return.[2] There was no foreboding that the anathemas then uttered would not be repealed until 7 December 1965. Indeed the occasion for these anathemas had been a synod summoned to discuss the various liturgical differences which had grown up between the two rites. These involved clerical celibacy, then being enforced on the Greek clergy of southern Italy, the use of unleavened bread (*azymon*) by the Latins, the formal addition of filioque to the creed in 1014, and apparently less important matters like clerical hairstyles, western tonsure v. eastern beards, and the mode of making the sign of the cross. Indeed, for those who were not scholastic theologians the doctrinal implications of much of this and even of the papal primacy were obscure. It was the concrete and visible signs that mattered the most to ordinary worshippers and represented traditions to which they had become attached in their daily battle with evil. Eustathios makes this clear and illustrated that it was equally true for the Norman soldiery in Thessalonika who were incensed by the bearded priests and the semantra of the Greeks.[3]

Good fences made good neighbours. The legalistic and systematising tendency of the western church was a product of its immediate post-Roman

---

[2] F. Dvornik, *The Photian Schism* (Cambridge, 1948); S. Runciman, *The Eastern Schism* (Oxford, 1953).

[3] J.R. Melville Jones, *Eustathios of Thessaloniki: The Capture of Thessaloniki* (Canberra, 1988), pp.127, 133, 135.

past. Latins tended to be aggressive in propagating their religious institutions as the minimum expression of the unity of Christendom. Direct political control or the promise of military aid was often the excuse for the imposition of such religious unity. In the west it had been the church which had inherited the Roman concept of universality and the pope as the successor of St Peter was accorded the headship of the church not just a primacy of honour. Spiritual authority was held to be superior to temporal authority. Such grand claims meant little when the political power of the papacy was weak, but following the eleventh-century reform movement, papal elections were freed from lay control in 1059, and 40 years later the First Crusade under papal leadership recaptured Jerusalem and led to an important extension of western Christendom in the Levant. A new and considerable problem of the role of the church in society moved eastwards with the crusading army. The emperor of Byzantium, as head of the oikumene and the viceroy of God on earth, embodied many of the functions which the pope exercised or claimed to exercise in the west. This conflict of lay and spiritual authority was unfamiliar to the east, where acceptance of the God-protected emperor made political theorising a specious activity. Western '*auctorititas*' and Byzantine '*oikonomia*' did not sit well together.[4]

The Greeks were regarded as fellow Christians and the same ideals had been appealed to by the leaders of the First Crusade, but there seems to have been an objection to the Greekness of the eastern church rather than to its ideas. The Greek fathers were seen as 'Father' rather than as Greeks, whilst the persistence of Greek congregations in their traditional practices was seen as wilful rather than as cultural.[5] When Latins formed a minority group religious co-existence seems to have been the norm. There were numerous examples of Latins attending Orthodox services in the twelfth century in Constantinople. This occasionally provoked papal reprimand to the Latins concerned as back-door byzantinisation.[6] Respect and harmony was what mattered from the Greek side and any minor liturgical differences could be overlooked provided that they were not forced upon the host congregation. Priests ministering to westerners could console themselves with the thought of the poverty of Latin as a theological language, whilst both they and the laity could rest secure in the superiority of their own tradition hallowed by

---

[4] For more information on this cursory summary see J.H. Burns, ed., *The Cambridge History of Medieval Political Thought* (Cambridge, 1988), pp.21–36, 51–82, 211–305; B. Hamilton, *Religion in the Medieval West* (London, 1986), pp.7–25, 38–9; F. Dvornik, *Byzantium and the Roman Primacy* (New York, 1966); S. Runciman, *The Great Church in Captivity* (Cambridge, 1968), pp.3–17, 81–111.

[5] M.V. Anastos, 'Some aspects of Byzantine influence on Latin thought', in M. Claggett, et al., eds, *Twelfth Century Europe and the Foundation of Modern Society* (1961; reprinted NY, 1980), pp.137–88; W. Daly, 'Christian fraternity, the crusades and the security of Constantinople' *Medieval Studies* 12 (1960), 43–91, esp. p.56.

[6] G. Every, *The Byzantine Patriarchate* (London, 1947), pp.165–8.

the gospels and the pronouncements of the seven ecumenical councils. For all that, daily observances of hair, leavened bread (*artos*), the administration of both bread and wine to the laity, and the fingers and direction of the hand in signing with the cross, were not to be betrayed. At the official level these cultural and ecclesiological differences which time and geography had brought about were ignored. There was a general acceptance that the liturgical differences could be harmonised and this accounts for the many negotiations over union before and after the Fourth Crusade. Everything would depend upon charity and a willingness to compromise and accommodate. The developing papal monarchy and expanding Latin Christendom were marked by aggressiveness and in 1204, when Constantinople was sacked, this was all too evident in the Aegean.

The phoney union, 1204

The Latin church in the Aegean had no planned beginning, certainly not in Rome. From the start of his pontificate Pope Innocent III (1198–1216) had concentrated upon the organisation of a crusade to liberate the Holy Land. In order to assist this venture materially and to prepare Christendom spiritually he sent two priests from the curia, Albert and Albertinus, to seek support from the emperor and the patriarch. He took advantage of the occasion to re-open negotiations for the unification of the Greek and Latin churches, whose continued separation he saw as an affront to the Christian faith, due largely to the negligence of his own and the patriarch's predecessors.[7] The pope was clear that the Greeks were misguided and wilful in their refusal to acknowledge the papal primacy in the universal church and that complete submission must be made. In the battery of biblical citations that filled the two letters the Greeks were cast in the subordinate role as daughter, spouse and sheep to the western mother, husband and shepherd – submission and not negotiation was envisaged. The pivotal role of the emperor was appreciated in the west but no practical details could be discerned in this plethora of biblical imagery as to just how one man was to surrender the traditions of his culture. Judging from a letter of November 1202 to Alexios III, the papacy regarded this as a problem for the emperor himself, and asked for detailed plans for the promotion of the union of the two churches.[8]

The turn of political events seemed to give the pope just what he had demanded. In December 1202 or January 1203 the envoys of the refugee Prince Alexios had concluded the Treaty of Zara with the crusading

[7] PL, 214:325–9 (1198).
[8] PL, 214:1123–5.

196

leadership. One of the concessions was the return of the Greek church to obedience to Rome in the person of the emperor once placed on the throne. No practical details seem to have been discussed.[9] The first practical hitch came in July with an interview with Alexios's father, Isaac II, who pointed out the difficulties of fulfilling the Treaty of Zara, both financially and religiously. He, however, had no choice but to confirm his son's actions. By the end of the month both he and his son and the patriarch had acknowledged the primacy of Rome in a letter to the pope but had not made the fact public. In August 1203 Innocent wrote to acknowledge their action, but in accompanying letters to the crusading leadership and to the bishops of Soissons and Trier, congratulating them on what they had achieved in terms of church unity and aid for the Holy Land, he emphasised the need for publicity – oaths, open letters and the receipt by the patriarch of his pallium in Rome – before he could exercise the patriarchal office.[10] Whatever might be thought about the lack of analysis and reality in Rome, the Greek church was seen as on the path of reunification and there were no plans at the end of 1203 for the appointment of a Latin patriarch or a Latin clergy in Constantinople. The crusade, both in the camp at Estanor and in the papal curia, was still on its way to the east.

One year later in early November 1204, when news reached Rome that Constantinople had been captured by the crusaders and that a western emperor had been elected, there was still no indication that Innocent contemplated the appointment of a Latin patriarch. He did not follow up the enthusiastic suggestion of the new emperor Baldwin, written probably in May 1204, that he should summon and attend a general church council in Constantinople and thereby inherit the Byzantine conciliar tradition and advertise the reconciliation of the old and the new Romes. Greek schismatics were to be invited to the proposed council.[11] Innocent's letters to Baldwin and to the bishops and abbots in the crusading army dwelt instead on divine intervention in human affairs as displayed by the transfer of the empire of Constantinople from the proud to the meek, from the disobedient to the devout, from the schismatics to the Catholics. He did not enquire about the fate of the Greek patriarch, John X Kamateros, who had retired to Selymbria, virtually a suburb of Constantinople,[12] nor did he offer any practical suggestions for the organisation of a Latin church or the rapprochement with the Greeks. The conquest was the just judgement of God on the Greeks, who presumably now realised the errors of their ways. A battery of biblical quotations pointed to the common ground of Greek

---

[9] Villehardouin, 90–4: Choniates, 539, 550–1; and see p.41.

[10] Villehardouin, 187–8; PL, 215:259–62.

[11] PL, 215:447–54.

[12] John later moved to Demotika (Didymotichon) in Thrace where he died in June 1206. This town was controlled by the Latinophile Theodore Branas and was destroyed by Kalojan in September 1206.

and Latin beliefs and the Latins were exhorted to work towards the reconciliation of the '*regnum Graecorum*'. Only two practical orders were contained in this correspondence, namely to defend the empire of Constantinople for the better succouring of the Holy Land and to preserve church property intact until further consideration could be taken.[13] There was nothing here to indicate that Innocent III yet thought in terms of the establishment of a Latin church or even of a permanent crusader presence in former Byzantine territory.

The same was true of the first use of Greek churches by Latin clerics. The papal authorisation for this came in a letter written on 7 December 1204 addressed to the bishops and abbots in the crusading army who were presumably to make the arrangements by personal inspection or knowledge.[14] Churches which had been abandoned by the Greeks were to be used for the celebration of the sacraments. Emphasis was placed upon the need to use empty churches both for the honour of God and, presumably, to avoid incidents of counter-services as noted by Archbishop Eustathios in Thessalonika in 1185. There was to be no appropriation of benefices by Latin clerics. Furthermore, the Latin clergy were asked to select a rector or provisor from their number to supervise their activities until a papal legate was sent out. During November Innocent seems to have accepted that there would be a delay, at least until the spring of 1205, in the departure of the crusading army and that some temporary arrangements would need to be made amongst the clergy present. It is debateable whether this provisor was a Latin patriarch in waiting, but this was unlikely since both Innocent and some of the crusading leadership still thought of the crusade proceeding to the Holy Land. Whether it was meant to be understood in the general exhortation of November 1204 to preserve church property, Innocent wrote nothing specific about the plundering of pious relics, and this form of asset-stripping continued. Perhaps the allusion to the return of Israel to Judah after the destruction of the golden calf in that same letter might indicate that such sacred spoils were thought fair gain from those whom God had deserted, and certainly does not point to Latin interest in staffing the churches of the former Byzantine empire. Papal attempts to play for time were outstripped by events. The churches of the Holy Apostles and St George of Mangana were already being used for the burial of noble crusaders who died about this time.[15] More seriously, a body of fifteen Venetian clerics, including four illiterates, had been appointed by the Venetian leadership on the crusade to nominate a Venetian patriarch. This had been part of the agreement made in the crusader camp in March 1204

---

[13] PL, 215:454–61.
[14] PL, 215:471–2.
[15] Villehardouin, 262, 334.

as they prepared for the assault on the city and formed an important omission from Baldwin's letter to Innocent in the preceding May.[16]

There was a significant time-lag of some eight to fifteen weeks between events on the Bosphorus and cognisance of them in Rome, even without the additional delay caused by pirates in the Adriatic and Ionian Seas which had held Father Barozzi's mission up from May to November in 1204. This was further compounded by the need to consult, form a policy and relay it back to Constantinople. Misinformation was a problem of which the pope became acutely aware in January 1205 when Baldwin asked him to confirm the Pact of March 1204 between the Venetians and the crusaders.[17] In May he despatched Benedict, cardinal-priest of Santa Susanna, as his legate to the Greeks with the tasks of consolidating the union of the churches and keeping him impartially informed of events.[18] In the meantime, between October 1204 and March 1205 small expeditions were mounted into Thrace, Greece and north-west Turkey to occupy lands which had been granted out by Baldwin to the crusading leaders. Naturally the Latins required the ministrations of Latin priests. In 1205 there was no Latin diocesan or parochial structure in the conquered lands nor apparently any proposals for such. No priests were mentioned by name or by inference in the conquering bands, which suggests that the bishops and abbots stayed behind in Constantinople.[19]

It is almost as if the new lands in the Aegean were seen as a re-endowment for the crusaders before proceeding on their crusade. The Fourth Crusade was underfunded from the start and had involved much creative financial operation on the part of the crusaders. The response to the proclamation of crusade in August 1198 had produced little money and so the crusaders themselves had provided the bulk of the funding. This had proved woefully inadequate in the summer of 1202 in Venice, whilst the generous promises of re-endowment made by Alexios in 1203 had only been partly fulfilled. Certainly, both Baldwin I and Boniface of Montferrat, who were both major beneficiaries of the partition of the Byzantine empire, publicly expressed their resolve to continue to the Holy Land. Some time after his coronation Baldwin wrote to the bishops of Cambrai, Artois, Therouanne and Tournai confirming his intention of leading the crusade to the Holy Land.[20] In mid-1205 Boniface, now self-styled king of Thessalonika, still protested his intention of proceeding to the Holy Land and it was not until 30 March 1207 that Innocent himself last used the

---

[16] PL, 215:516.
[17] PL, 215:510–11.
[18] PL, 215:622–4.
[19] Villehardouin, 302–32.
[20] Hendrickx, 'Régestes des Empereurs Latins de Constantinople (1204–1261/1272)' *Byzantina* 14 (1988) p.34, no.37.

address 'Universis ... crucesignatis in Romania'.[21] These were more than pious platitudes. If no permanent settlement of Latins was envisaged in 1205, then there was clearly no perceived need for a Latin church in Greece.

The movement of relics from Constantinople to the west would also seem to bear this out. First Paul Riant in the nineteenth century and more recently Alphonse Frolow have shown the importance of relics in the thought-world of the thirteenth century. Relics were objects venerated by both eastern and western Christians, yet little or no regard seems to have been shown for the feelings of the Greeks in this matter. The pious thefts of men like abbot Martin of Pairis and of bishop Conrad of Halberstadt in 1204 were inspired by the desire to secure relics for more worthy hands and through them to acquire powerful links with the saints and association with the passion of Christ.[22] There is no inventory of the relics which passed to the west at this time, but in view of the varied social backgrounds of those making pious benefactions to their home churches and monasteries, it is generally reckoned that the traffic was considerable.[23] Apart from the famous sale of the crown of thorns, the holy lance and sponge together with the napkin of St Veronica to Louis IX in 1240, most relics from Constantinople seem to have made their journey west within a few years of the capture of the city.[24] Cult objects were not kept for the new Latin church since neither robbers cum pious donors nor clerical recipients in the west had any notion of establishing a Latin church in the Aegean.

The Latin patriarchate

During 1205 the Latin church in Constantinople was organised. There was no indication that Innocent contemplated the creation of any other Latin church outside of the queen city until November 1205 when he approved the establishment of the archdiocese of Patras.[25] He was clearly concerned at the unsettled situation in the new conquests, since on a number of occasions in 1205 he wrote of the '*totius terrae turbationem*' and seemed resigned to

---

[21] PL, 215:710–14, 1131 (doc.XXXVIII).

[22] A. Frolow, *Recherches sur la déviation de la IVe croisade vers Constantinople* (Paris, 1955), pp.28–9, 47–83; for discussion see D.E. Queller & S.J. Stratton, 'A century of controversy on the Fourth Crusade' *Studies in Medieval and Renaissance History* 6 (1969), 235–77, esp. 270ff.

[23] P. Riant, *Des dépouilles religeuses enlevées à Constantinople au XIIIe siècle et des documents historiques nés de leur transport en Occident*, Mémoires de la Société nationales des Antiquaires de France, VI, (Paris, 1875).

[24] See pp.20 and 183; H.R. Luard, ed., *Matthei Parisiensi Chronica majora* IV (London, 1877), pp.75–6, 90–2; Hendrickx, 'Régestes des Empereurs Latins', pp.35, 46, 56, 57, 59, 66.

[25] PL, 215:727–9.

wait on events.[26] As regards the '*Regia civitas*' he could no longer do this and once again was forced to react to a situation caused by elements of his crusading army. As we have seen, by 21 January 1205 he had learned of the partition treaty of March 1204. Two provisions were especially alarming since they effectively instituted lay control of the church in Constantinople, limited papal jurisdiction over that church and constrained his options regarding the form which that church might take both in terms of relations with the Greek clergy and of its economic foundations. One provision handed control of the church in Constantinople to the Venetians since '... The clergy who are of the party from which the emperor shall not have been chosen shall have the power to ordain to the Church of St Sophia and to elect a patriarch ...'.[27] In the same month Innocent learned that the Venetians had proceeded to arrange this and had chosen Thomas Morosini, a son of one of the most distinguished Venetian families and a papal subdeacon who was then resident in Ravenna. Doge Dandolo may well have been behind this unexpected choice since in March 1205 Innocent informed Dandolo's son Raineri that he had confirmed the choice of Morosini to please his father.[28] There was nothing amiss in Morosini's record from an ecclesiastical point of view, other than its modesty, whilst those who advised the electors had every reason to hope that such a noble scion would serve Venetian interests well. Neither party took any cognisance of Greek sensibilities, or the fact that the eighty-first patriarch was still alive and that real schism would result, or of the positive qualities desired in a candidate for such an important post in making a reality of the religious union which was now assumed. The second proposition set aside a potential endowment for the maintenance of churches and clerics; whether a Greek or Latin clergy was envisaged was not made clear, but it was felt that there was a considerable number of both buildings and bodies to sustain. Church property was to be divided up like the rest of the land and moveables in the city, but from it a sufficient sum was to be devoted to the upkeep of the clergy '... *quo honorifice possint vivere et substentari*'.[29] There was to be no protection of Greek ecclesiastical property as Innocent had ordered in his letter of 7 November 1204. In early 1205 it looked as if any church organisation that would emerge in Constantinople, be it Latin or unionist, would be poorer than the former Greek church and would be subject to lay control, since the conquerors held the purse-strings and had already disposed of the patriarchate.

In the past Innocent had generally adapted himself to situations which he could not change, in the interest of the greater good of the crusade. The

---

26 PL, 215:577, 624, 698–9.
27 PL, 215:518. The treaty is printed in full in cols 517–19 and in *Urkunden* I, 444–51.
28 *Urkunden* I, 538.
29 PL, 215:518.

election of the patriarch was one issue that he could and must affect and this he did but at the expense of the new patriarch and his successors.[30] If there was going to be a Latin patriarch in Constantinople, it was important that the pope should choose the first incumbent. The patriarch-elect was actually resident in Italy and one of his own subdeacons. The original election of Morosini was annulled in open consistory and immediately thereafter Innocent exercised his right of electing and ordaining him to the see of Constantinople. Between 5 and 20 March he personally consecrated him deacon, priest, and bishop and invested him with the archbishop's pallium.[31] In addition to standard metropolitan powers Morosini was conceded the right to anoint kings and, in view of the disturbed state of his new province, the privilege of alienating church property and of continuing to draw income from benefices which he held in Italy.[32] Once matters of precedence and jurisdiction had been settled Innocent built up the status of the patriarchate within the Latin communion, expounding for the first time the idea of the five patriarchates of which Constantinople was second to Rome, pledging no further interference in patriarchal elections and recommending the new patriarch to the emperor and the doge.[33] A policy of drift and reaction had created a new metropolitical office in the hierarchy of western Christendom and had totally failed to accommodate the Greek clergy or to discover their inclinations. Innocent may have been prepared to accept a reformed Greek clergy but had allowed his attention to be side-tracked to the issues of lay control and canonical election. In the first three months of 1205 he showed that he had no understanding of the religious issues involved nor of the effect of appointing a patriarch without reference to the Greek situation. He confused his aim with the means – negotiation meant complete subjection, a Latin patriarch the union of churches. Regrettably the new patriarch was irascible and temperamently ill-equipped to play the role of reconciliator of the Greeks; all too easily his attention was diverted from the obligations of his new office to its implications in terms of precedence, patronage, and rewards.

Morosini's failure to win over Greek clerics to the union church was beyond the scope of any Latin, even the popular Emperor Henry. However, Morosini proceeded to quarrel with virtually all sections of the Latin community – with the emperor over his coronation in August 1206 and later over appointments to the conventual churches of the capital, with the French community over the same issue and his alleged fraudulent receipt of large sums from the treasury of St Sophia, with the Venetian podesta over the

---

[30] Wolff, 'Politics in the Latin patriarchate of Constantinople, 1204–1261', art.cit., 228–303.
[31] PL, 214: CXLIII (Gesta Innocentii, c.98).
[32] PL, 215:576–7.
[33] PL, 215:512–13.

possession of the Hodegetria, with the prior of the Pisan church over the supply of chrism, and with the archbishop of Patras and other Latin diocesans in Greece over patriarchal monasteries.[34] In August 1206 he banned all Greek services in Constantinople when he learned that his name was omitted from their prayers.[35] He was a petulant and irascible man, whose appearance and behaviour lent themselves to mockery amongst the Greeks as the archetypical bad Latin priest.[36] His death in June or July 1211 in Thessalonika was followed by a four year interregnum, the legacy of the partisan dispute over the canonries of St Sophia and their role in the canonical election of the patriarch as laid down by the pope. Papal relations with the church in Constantinople were more flattering to papal self-esteem than conducive to Christian unity. The appellate jurisdiction of Rome had been stressed by Innocent and he was to use this to regulate patriarchal elections and the college of electors.

To rid the new church of lay control Innocent had to break the Venetian monopoly of the canonries of St Sophia and hence the patriarchate which the Pact of March 1204 had created. If combatting lay control was the pope's concern then he reckoned without the Venetian agenda which very deliberately sought to retain it. It was sometime after Morosini's departure for the east that Innocent learned of the extent of Venetian desire to maintain its clerical position in Constantinople. In May 1205 when he was instructing cardinal Benedict preparatory to his departure as legate to the Greeks, he urged him to monitor the new patriarch's appointments to prebendal stalls and to ensure, by making his own appointments if necessary, that they were distributed amongst suitable men of all nations.[37] By 21 June 1206 Innocent learned of the oath taken by Morosini to exclude all except Venetians from prebends in Constantinople and between then and 1210 he actively appointed six French canons. In April 1208 he commanded Morosini to publicly adjure this oath and to suspend the canons of St Sophia until they should do the same. In December 1208 the patriarch complied.[38] However, by November 1209 Innocent learned of another oath extracted from Morosini when he had been organising transport east in the summer of 1205, namely his confirmation of the possessions and privileges of the Venetian patriarch of Grado within his patriarchate. Morosini was again

---

[34] PL, 215:1387, 1395; Wolff, 'Politics in the Latin patriarchate of Constantinople, 1204–1261', art.cit., 232; idem, 'Footnote to an incident of the Latin occupation of Constantinople: the Church and the Icon of the Hodegetria' *Traditio* 6 (1949), 319–28; *ODB* sub 'Thomas Morosini'.

[35] C. Frazee, 'The Catholic Church in Constantinople, 1204–1453' *Balkan Studies* 19 (1978), 33–49, esp. p.35.

[36] Choniates, 623/73–79, 647/8–14.

[37] PL, 215:628, 715, 946, 951.

[38] PL, 215:1392 and 216:118. See *Urkunden* II, 61, 75 for oaths of Venetian canons to exclude non-Venetians taken in 1207 and 1208.

ordered to repudiate this oath.[39] By 1210 the Venetian hold over the church of Constantinople had been contained if not removed.

There still remained the problem of limiting Venetian influence in patriarchal elections. In May 1205 Innocent had enlarged the body of electors to the patriarchal office to include not just the canons of St Sophia but also the heads (*praepositi*) of the 32 conventual churches in the city.[40] In effect these were all the churches which had been taken over by Latin clergy and were generally thought to be the wealthiest.[41] A simple majority from this body of electors was to secure election. Over the succeeding years this led to intense competition to secure appointments of these praepositi and to a certain amount of competitive creations of canons well beyond the fixed number of prebends at St Sophia by both patriarch and papal legates. No patriarchal election was to take place without direct papal interference. This followed on the precedent set in 1205, reinforced in the protracted vacancy of 1211–15. By the end of 1205 the principal prelate of the Latin empire was in office and the richest churches in the city were staffed by Latin clergy. The start had not been an elevating one. The lack of a firm papal policy, Venetian ambitions and conflicting and changing agendas in which church unity had slipped in priority were to dog the Latin patriarchate for the remaining 57 years of its active existence.

In 1261 the Latin patriarch Panteleon Guistiniani fled to Italy where he died in 1286. He was succeeded by Pietro Correr on whose death in 1302 the patriarchal rights were reserved to the pope and the patriarchal residence officially transferred to Venetian territory. In 1302 the patriarchal office was united with the archdiocese of Crete and in 1314 transferred again this time to the diocese of Negroponte. By the late fifteenth century the patriarchal residence was in Venice itself and the title was usually reserved for one of the college of Cardinals. In the aftermath of the Council of Florence the title was conferred on three prominent Greek uniate prelates in succession. They were Gregory Melissenos or Mammas (1453–59), Isidore of Kiev (1459–63) and Bessarion of Trebizond (1463–72). Late in the day and for a brief period of 20 years the Latin patriarchate of Constantinople might be said to have fulfilled something of the original hopes of Innocent III, but by that time there was no empire of Constantinople, either Greek or Latin, in existence.[42] The titular Latin patriarchate of Constantinople continued in existence until 1965 with its residence in Rome, although during the last years of its existence the post was kept vacant.[43]

---

[39] PL, 216:162.
[40] PL, 215:628; Pressutti, 1174, Appendix II; *Urkunden* I, 558.
[41] R. Janin, 'Les sanctuaires de byzance sous la domination latine (1204–1261)' *Etudes byzantines* 2 (1944), 134–84.
[42] L. de Mas-Latrie, 'Patriarches Latins de Constantinople' *Revue de l'Orient Latin* 3 (1895), 433–56.
[43] *Annuario Pontificio*, 1960, 1967.

Latin diocesan structure

There was nothing inevitable about the establishment of the Latin church in Greece as some scholars have asserted.[44] The creation of an archdiocese at Damietta in 1219 during the Fifth Crusade (1217–21) is not evidence that crusaders established churches wherever they went, since it was territory newly conquered from Islam where a place of Christian worship was necessary. The attachment of the see to the province of Jerusalem was both natural and politically convenient. The Byzantine empire, however, was a Christian state amply provided with dioceses and churches. It is not known just what information was available in Rome regarding the Greek diocesan structure. The last substantial Roman involvement with Balkan dioceses had been in 521 when Rome had asserted its claim to jurisdiction over the vicariate of Illyricum.[45] It is inconceivable that the papal legate did not forward to Rome a taktika or precedence list of the higher clergy of the Byzantine empire, yet there is no evidence of any such list being forwarded to Rome and certainly nothing on the part of the church authorities to match the fiscal research carried on in Constantinople in late 1204. In 1228 a revised version of Cencius Sabelli's *Liber Censuum*, a list of archbishoprics subject to Rome originally compiled in 1192, contained a conspectus of the Latin hierarchy in Greece as it was at its fullest extent around 1211/12 after the creation of the bishoprics.[46] The general impression is of haphazard creations with the momentum coming from the Latins in Greece rather than in response to a formulated plan for a Latin diocesan structure. There were vague references in the papal correspondence to the maintenance of the boundaries of Greek dioceses, but these seem to have been virtually unknown in Rome and only imperfectly established by the Latin authorities in Greece, where some of the bishops of Achaia were squabbling over their jurisdictions in 1210.[47] It was only after 1205 with a certain amount of Latin settlement in the towns and countryside of Greece that the creation of ecclesiastical provinces and dioceses became desirable. Two waves of diocesan creation may be distinguished in these early years – the first in 1206 and the second in 1207–9. The impetus for the first group came not from any missionising zeal on the part of Latin clerics but in response to Latin lay rulers wishing to bolster their status in their new states.

[44] A. Luchaire, *Innocent III, La Question D'Orient* (Paris, 1907), 149ff; G. Every, op.cit., p.191; J. Hussey, op.cit., p.186.
[45] A.H. Jones, *The Later Roman Empire* II (1964), pp.887–9; G.D.Y. Mansi, *Sacronum concilionum nova et amplissima collectio* VIII (Leipzig, 1901–27), 749–72 for documents cited in 521 regarding the vicariate of Illrycum.
[46] P. Fabre & L. Duchesne, *Le Liber Censuum de l'Eglise Romaine* II (Paris, 1910), 3ff. Abstracted and compared to Byzantine taktika by Wolff, 'The organization of the Latin patriarchate of Constantinople, 1204–1261', art.cit., pp.51–6.
[47] PL, 216:223.

The first province to be created outside Constantinople was the archdiocese of Patras sanctioned by Innocent on 19 November 1205 at the request of William de Champlitte, '*princeps totius Achaiae*'. The canons of the church of St Andrew in Patras had unanimously elected Antelmus, who had then proceeded to Rome. There was no mention of the installation of the canons and the patriarch was instructed to proceed with the consecration.[48] A year later Nivelon de Cherissy was elected archbishop of Thessalonika with the backing of Boniface of Montferrat, '*qui in terra illa obtinet principatum*'.[49] Two of the leaders of the new states in Greece had thus secured Latin archbishops for their territories. It is likely that the third, Otho de la Roche, lord of Athens, did the same. On 27 November 1206 Innocent granted the archbishop-elect of Athens, Berard, the same jurisdiction as his Greek predecessor, that is Michael Choniates who had fled to the island of Keos.[50] This appeal to precedent naively assumed a uniformity of function and aspiration between western and eastern prelates and ignored the fact that little was actually known of what this jurisdiction was composed. No heed was given to the consecrated Greek bishops now in hiding, nor to the visible fact of schism that the consecration of a second strand of bishops would bring about. The following March Berard and the archbishop-elect of Thebes, now mentioned for the first time, were reported as on their way to Syria to be consecrated due to the dearth of other archbishops in Greece.[51] Thebes was a larger and far more important town than Athens yet relatively little was recorded about the establishment of the archbishopric and de la Roche's role in it, if any. Although he was lord of Thebes by 1210, it is far from clear if he held this distinction in 1206. Thebes may well have been created with the support of the Canossa brothers and the silence in terms of their role was a reflection of their relative status among the new lords of Greece. The support of the Latin lord would have been essential to secure possession of the cathedral church. The influence that the regent Margaret of Hungary had in moderating the impact of the Latin clergy on the local Orthodox is an example of the establishment of the territorial lord in the imposition or otherwise of the Latin church.[52] Yet nothing is known of the procedure of these appropriations. Were there any negotiations with the Greek dignitaries of these cathedral churches? Were they offered continuance in office if they acknowledged Roman primacy? Were there any attempts to reconcile Greek cathedral posts with the Latin chapters? The general impression is that none of these activities took place

---

[48] PL, 215:727–9.

[49] PL, 215:1037–8.

[50] PL, 215:1031; J. Longnon, 'L'organisation de l'eglise d'Athènes par Innocent III', in *Archives de L'Orient Chrétien I: Mémorial Louis Petit* (Bucharest, 1948), pp.336–46.

[51] PL, 215:1130.

[52] PL, 215:1467 (October 1208).

and that the Greek clergy may well have fled their cities like most of their bishops. Yet who or what determined the size of these chapters in the early days and thus determined the body of electors for the first Latin dignitaries? Lay support and influence must have been strong, yet nothing is said of it in Innocent's letters of confirmation. Greek dignitaries and their functions seem simply to have been ignored.

The second wave of creations seems to have been organised by the church itself and very consciously based on existing Greek dioceses.[53] Since the eleventh century there was a body of precedent available in Rome on the treatment of Greek clergy in southern Italy. In Greece, however, the prime concern was with the Greek hierarchy and the policy was worked out in response to practical problems. In 1206 Morosini had requested guidance on ethnically-directed episcopal appointments. Innocent replied that in wholly Greek dioceses Greek bishops were to be preferred provided that they had personally acknowledged the primacy of Rome, whilst in areas of mixed population Latins were to be appointed. Before any such new appointments were to be made the Greek incumbent had to have abandoned his diocese or refused to recognise papal supremacy.[54] In 1210 on the eve of the fall of Akrocorinth to the Latins, Innocent proposed that the Greek archbishop of Corinth should be confirmed in his office if he would acknowledge the pope.[55] Provision was made for those bishops prepared to latinise and the advice to Morosini in March 1208 to make the whole process as uncomplicated as possible showed a growing awareness in Rome that Greek bishops were not going to flock into the Latin church and needed to be enticed.[56] In fact only four Greek incumbents, John of Rodosto, Benedict of Kephalonia, Theodore of Negroponte and the Bishop of Neopatras, were prepared to acknowledge papal supremacy and continue in their dioceses.[57] This small group, together with the circle of Greek clergy in Thessalonika who in 1210 made exploratory enquiries regarding the confirmation of the privileges and income of their churches in return for canonical obedience, and the unknown number of proponents of a dual patriarchate on the lines of that established in Antioch in 1100 which emerged in discussion with the legate Benedict in 1206, showed that there were Greeks prepared to compromise, but that concessions from Rome were required in order for their numbers to grow.[58] The lack of response to what he might well have regarded as generous terms must have been discouraging for Innocent and

---

[53] PL, 215:1130.
[54] PL, 215:963.
[55] PL, 216:201.
[56] PL, 215:1353, 1468. T. Haluscinskyi, ed., *Acta Innocentii PP III* (Rome, 1944), pp.317–20.
[57] PL, 215:1030, 1129, 1492; 216:460, 647.
[58] PL, 216:229; Hussey, op.cit., pp.190–2.

may well have seemed inexplicable in the face of God's judgement on the Greeks delivered in April 1204.

There is a certain geographical pattern observable in the chronology of the second wave of Latin episcopal appointments, radiating outwards from Constantinople: Verissa, Selymbria, Panidos, Gallipoli, Nicomedia, and Heraklea, all had a Latin hierarchy by the end of 1207. In the last half of 1208 the diocesan map of Thessaly between Thessalonika and Thebes was filled up: Larissa, Domokos, Pydna, Zeitoun, Kastoria, Thermopylae, Neopatras and Daulia. At some point before 1211 bishoprics were set up in Salona and Megara too. These, like Thermopylae, were not former Greek dioceses but entirely new Latin creations presumably serving Latin population concentrations or the ambitions of the lords of the castles of Salona and Boudonitsa. Apart from the installation of a Latin chapter at Modon and the creation of a diocese at Andravida in 1206/7 there were no major additions to the principality of Achaia until the capture of Corinth in 1210 and Argos in 1212. In the same year the bishops of Coron and Amyclae were mentioned for the first time, as was the bishop of Olena in 1211.

With the exception of the four new dioceses of Thermopylae, Salona, Megara and Andravida, the new Latin church initially attempted to base itself on existing Greek dioceses, providing a Latin bishop wherever there had been a Greek diocesan and maintaining the boundaries of the Greek dioceses. The former policy was questioned by Morosini in 1206 who pointed out that the Greek dioceses were both too numerous and, often, too poor to be adequately staffed and that a more flexible policy which would permit diocesan amalgamation was desirable. Innocent conceded the point but reiterated the principle that Greek diocesan boundaries must be maintained.[59] In mainland Greece south of the River Strymon at the end of the first decade of the Latin occupation, there were nine provinces and some twenty-seven dioceses. Naturally there were variations in size and prosperity, the one not always reflecting the other. For example, in central Greece the province of Athens extended from Megara and Salona in the south to Thermopylae and Daulia in the north and included the islands of Aegina and Euboea. It contained eight suffragan sees and surrounded the relatively small archdiocese of Thebes with only two suffragans at Kastoria and Zaratoriensis (Askra?). Yet in the fifteenth century, according to Eubel's figures, papal assessors considered the archdiocese of Thebes (500 florins) worth four times that of Athens (120 florins). Outside Constantinople the richest provinces seem to have been Patras and Corinth. Like provinces dioceses varied in size and wealth, although in this context small meant poor. The ecclesiastical map was a Mediterranean one more familiar to an Italian priest than to one from north of the Alps. However, there was a

---

[59] PL, 215:959; 216:223.

cultural difference too in that some Greek dioceses just could not support a western bishop in the style which his church expected and, as more information became available to the western authorities, such dioceses were amalgamated. Thus in July 1208, during the second phase of diocesan establishment, the diocese of Calidoniensis (location unknown) was united with Domokos and that of Platamon with Pydna.[60] Two years later the diocese of Medensis (unknown) was conferred on the archbishop of Verissa and the bishoprics of Demetrias and Gardiki amalgamated.[61] There were to be other amalgamations over the next 20 years. Most notably in March 1222 when Honorius III confirmed many of the recommendations made by the papal legate John Colonna who sought both to streamline Latin diocesan organisation by transferring suffragans to provinces more geographically proximate and to make official provision for redundant Greek dioceses that had never received Latin bishops or entered into communion with Rome and were effectively unadministered. The former Greek cathedral church of Geminensis was united with Corinth, that of Quenicensis with Patras, those of Abilonensis, Calistensis, and Lorotensis on Euboea with Negroponte and that at Damala joined with Argos '… *qui Latinorum tempore nunquam extit ordinatus nec Latini habitant in eodem*'.[62]

The Latin episcopate

Papal correspondence, the main source for the Latin church in Greece, tends to draw attention to the sensational and the anecdotal, but alongside disputes over the electoral college for the patriarchate and the financial basis of the new church, there was much that smacked of the routine. Bishops were normally resident in their dioceses. Their main business seems to have been researching the rights and resources of their new sees in Byzantine archives and establishing and protecting those rights against lay appropriation or the encroachment of neighbouring bishops.[63] When they were not plaintiffs themselves they might well sit on one of the local tribunals appointed by the pope to investigate the disputes and grievances of their episcopal colleagues. This emphasis upon the material was to be expected in the economic and jurisdictional chaos that confronted the new church in the aftermath of the conquest. Even the bishops of poor sees like Zaratoriensis, which could scarcely support one canon, resided in a house in their diocese while the great like the archbishop of Patras built castles for

---

[60] PL, 215:1433.
[61] PL, 216:355, 596.
[62] Pressutti, 3833–4 and 3844. See 536 for Colonna's commission of April 1217 to order the Greek diocesan situation.
[63] PL, 216:339–40, 581–2.

their abode.[64] In October 1210 there was a spate of commissions of enquiry concerned with the property claims of the Templars. Virtually all the diocesans of central Greece were involved in one way or another with these commissions, all of them in residence and able to investigate personally.[65] Conforming Greek bishops were not normally involved in such commissions but confined to the pastoral role of convincing their fellow Greek clergy to acknowledge Roman primacy and to join the new church.[66] Permission for absence on personal grounds like pilgrimage to Compostella were sought from the pope and irregular absenteeism, like that of the bishop of Domokos who in July 1210 was to be forced back to his diocese which he had left three days after his consecration some three years before, was regarded as outrageous.[67] No evidence of provincial synods survives, nor do any episcopal registers appear to have been kept, at least none have come down to us. The confirmation of the Latin laity may well have been a problem. In the west it was a rite reserved to bishops, but in the Orthodox Church it was part of the baptismal ceremony and was performed by priests. It was probably this fundamental difference which troubled the papacy. In 1336 it was noted in Rome that Latin parents on Euboea were attending Orthodox churches for the confirmation of their children, due to the scarcity of Latin bishops.[68] Provincial organisation was rudimentary and confined to establishing the endowment of canons' prebends, reducing suffragans to obedience and seeking economic support for essential visits to Rome. Occasionally these relationships deteriorated into violence, as when the archbishop of Patras lost control of his cathedral chapter in 1210 or when relations were too cooperative and resulted in pillage and gangsterism in the province of Thebes in 1212 in which the archbishop and chapter had a hand.[69] If pastoral care and provincial organisation were virtually non-existent, at least at the level at which they can be glimpsed, metropolitans and their suffragans seem to have worked conscientiously for their church and its endowments.

During the fourteenth century the Latin hierarchy in Greece became markedly more Italian in its ethnic composition. It also tended to be recruited from one or other of the two great mendicant orders, but seldom from those serving in Greece. There seems too to have been a continuing if tiny number of Greeks gaining preferment within the Latin church. In 1299 one Demetrius secured election to the archdiocese of Corfu, whilst Kenneth Setton has pointed out that the enemies of the scholar-prelate Simon Atumanno, who was transferred from the diocese of Gerace in Calabria to

---

[64] PL, 216:342, 565–6.
[65] PL, 216:327–37.
[66] PL, 216:647.
[67] PL, 216:299–300, 576.
[68] A.L. Tautu, ed., *Acta Benedicti XII (1334–1342)* (Rome, 1958), pp.18–19, no. 11.
[69] PL, 216:564–6.

the archdiocese of Thebes by Pope Urban V in 1366, did not hesitate to draw attention to his mixed parentage, possibly Greek and Turkish, and his need to flee to Italy when a young monk in order to establish a good reputation. Whether true or not, Atumano held on to his see, despite royal opposition, until at least late 1382.[70]

Latin secular clergy

The Latin clergy in Greece was almost entirely a cathedral or conventual clergy. This reflected the limited pattern of Latin settlement and the very real dangers of isolated minority groups in a hostile land. During 1212 Michael Doukas, the despot of Epiros, was beheading Latin clergy wherever he found them, assisted in this by western mercenaries who seem to have experienced no ethnic or religious qualms.[71] The pope's concern for the housing of the canons of the adjacent dioceses of Larissa and Daulia '*in loco tuto*' in 1209 was thus much more than a polite commonplace. Perhaps this safe place was Ferchikam, modern Pteleon, whence the archbishop of Larissa had previously been granted permission to withdraw should the deteriorating political situation warrant it.[72]

All the cathedral chapters were secular, although that at Patras was handed over to regular canons from St Ruff near Avignon in October 1210 because of absenteeism and fraud on the part of the original secular canons. The difficulty of changing the prebendal structure of the cathedral was to defeat the archbishops of Patras, who in March 1222 were ordered to install secular canons again. Outside Patras and, of course, Constantinople, which was affected by the struggle to create a canonical college of electors to the patriarchate, the number of prebends attached to each chapter seemed to have remained fixed from the days of its institution. New bishops seemed disinclined to re-order the chapters which had elected them and occasional lay pressure to increase the body of canons to reward clerical servants seems to have been resisted, as at Andravida in 1212.[73] By no means all the chapter sizes are known. Judging from those which are, they varied considerably in size from four at Andravida, twelve each at Athens and Thebes, the former consciously modelled on the chapter in Paris, to sixteen, and once even twenty-four, at Constantinople.

Of the cathedral officers the papal correspondence gives but a sketchy impression. Greek cathedral officers and functionaries seem to have been

---

[70] Perrat & Longnon, doc. 213 (pp.183–5); K. Setton, *Catalan Domination of Athens* 2nd edn (London, 1975), pp.140–3.
[71] PL, 216:353–4.
[72] PL, 215:1471, 1557.
[73] PL, 216:560–1.

ignored or dismissed and Latin capitular organisation installed. All that can be said is that a dean, a treasurer and a cantor were regularly found. No chancellor was mentioned in the papal correspondence in any chapter, whilst archdeacons are attested in six chapters only. They seem not to have confined their attentions to Latin priests, who must have been virtually non-existent in the countryside, but to have assumed some responsibility for the Greek parish clergy as well. This would have involved visits to Greek communities and it was presumably from such men that information on the status of the papates and their children, which took up some time at the parliament of Ravannika in 1209, was derived. Their attentions were not always welcomed judging from the assault on Hugh, archdeacon of Daulia, by certain Greeks from Gravia in April 1212.[74] There is no indication whatsoever as to which of these cathedral officers headed the chapter or whether there was any uniformity about this matter in the Latin church in Greece. Just what arrangements were made by Greek bishops who had latinised are likewise unknown. Judging from an obscure incident in January 1224, some of them employed Greek cathedral staff. Theodore of Negroponte employed a Greek vicar who in 1224 had sought to restore one of the redundant Greek dioceses, Loretos (Oreos?), which the papal legate John Colonna had merged into Negroponte in 1222.[75]

The non-residence of canons seems to have been a widespread and persistent problem outside of Constantinople and one which in the years after 1209 received regular attention in papal correspondence. The only definite action was taken in Patras in 1210 with the replacement of a secular chapter by a regular one. The latter were allotted a communal endowment instead of individual prebends and this seems to have been the only practical distinction between regular and secular canons in this period. The displaced seculars did not leave the province but remained as an unofficial chapter, drawing revenue from their former prebends and organising a number of violent attacks on the incoming regulars.[76] Prebends were most certainly valued by their recipients. In Greece it was not unusual for a high proportion of grantees to seek papal confirmation of their canonries. In the mid-fourteenth century the practice of papal provision or nomination to a vacant benefice developed. This led both to a general improvement in the quality of priests so nominated and to an increase in the number of non-resident Italian priests holding benefices in Greece. If Eubel's figures are to be believed, it also led to an increase in the number of provinces and suffragan bishoprics, virtually all titular. The number rose to eleven and forty respectively, an increase of some 20 to 30 per cent on the early

---

[74] PL, 216:564, 968–72.
[75] See p.61 and Pressutti, 3843, 4730.
[76] PL, 216:336–8, 559–60; Pressutti, 1601.

thirteenth century figures at a time when Latin Greece was diminishing in area.[77]

The ordinary Latin priest ministering in Greece after 1204 is as elusive as is the representation of his Byzantine counterpart in a fresco. Paradoxically more is known about those 'simple priests' in the Italian concessions in twelfth-century Constantinople who were warned against obtaining chrism from Greek bishops and following Greek practices of confirmation.[76] No Latin parochial structure developed in Greece and this reflects the failure of the Latins to colonise the countryside. Very few Latins must have lived more than ten miles from a cathedral church and many of those with rural property maintained town houses to which they could easily resort.[79] In March 1210 Otho de la Roche had asked the pope that communities of twelve or more Latin households should have the ministrations of a Latin priest.[80] His letter is unique and did not represent a major problem for the Latin church; certainly no steps were taken to implement his proposal. In the early days of the conquest there seems to have been an apprehension that Latin priests would be in short supply and that priests with a dubious background or not even canonically ordained would head for Greece to fill the gap. The archbishop of Patras, as the provincial nearest to Italy, was warned against such people in April 1207, whilst the anonymous clerk credited with bringing the rood of Broomholm to England seems to have gained casual employment in the chapel of the emperor Baldwin and just as easily left bringing one of its treasures with him.[81] Certainly by 1217 and the legateship of Cardinal Colonna, the principle that Latin cathedral clergy would be sufficient to minister to the needs of Latin communities seems to have been accepted and by 1222 acted upon.

In a church which lacked seminaries for the training for its own clergy, it would be idle to expect any formal re-training schemes for Greek clergy. However, the pope did not lack confidence in the means at his disposal and provided or proposed a number of opportunities for the Greek clergy to be influenced by direct contact with Latin spirituality and scholarship. In June 1205 Innocent wrote two letters to the clergy of France citing the Emperor Baldwin I as the inspiration.[82] The first was addressed to all the archbishops of France and asked them to put forward men '*de singulis ordinibus*' recommended by their life and learning to go to Greece to strengthen the

---

[77] K. Eubel, *Hierarchia Catholica Medii Aevi* I (Regensburg, 1913), pp.543–4.

[78] G. Every, op.cit., pp.165–8.

[79] PL, 216:564. See Hamilton, *The Latin Church in the Crusader States*, op.cit., pp.86–112 for comparative material for Syria–Palestine.

[80] PL, 216:216.

[81] PL, 215:1142; F. Wormald, 'The Holyrood of Broomholm' *Journal of the Warburg Institute* 1 (1931), 31–45.

[82] PL, 215:636–7.

Christian religion. Whether Latin monastic foundations were envisaged at this early stage by anyone other than Baldwin is not clear. The second letter was addressed to the masters and scholars of the University of Paris and invited them in the emperor's name '... to come to Greece and work for the reform of the study of letters there, where it is known to have had its first beginning ...'. Whether this was an invitation to found a new university or not, the scholars would provide an orthodox Latin intellectual framework for the united church. Those responding to the call could expect preferment in a land '... filled with silver and gold and gems, furnished with corn, wine and oil, and abounding in all good things ...'. Nothing seems to have come of these proposals, whatever their precise import may have been. However, both proposals were directed at the persuasion of Greeks rather than the pastoral needs of the Latins. The role of the emperor Baldwin in all this is worthy of note since he perceived himself as having a role in the union of the churches and was so seen by the pope.[83] The legate Benedict was appointed to discuss religious issues with the Greek clergy and to this end held seminars in Constantinople, whilst enthusiastic latinised Greeks like John of Rodosto were similarly employed.[84]

Ecclesiastical revenues

To appropriate the revenues of the former Greek church was no easy task. In late 1204 Innocent had proposed that the assets of the Greek church simply be frozen thus allowing the Latin church authorities a free hand in their dealings with the Greeks, either to reward latinisation by a confirmation of income and privileges or, should there be individuals not prepared to swear canonical obedience, to transfer those same rights and revenues to a Latin incumbent who would discover for himself their nature and extent. As events turned out, a Latin church was created and its clergy found itself in competition both with the former Greek incumbents who often continued to draw income from their former lands relying on the unfamiliarity of the incoming Latin bishops with their new lands and, much more seriously, with the lay conquerors themselves on whom they depended for protection and support. The Pact of March 1204 had sanctioned the seizure of all Greek property, regardless of whether it was secular or ecclesiastical, and left clergy remuneration at the discretion of the conquerors themselves provided it met a seemly style and livelihood could be maintained. This arrangement was intended to cover churches in Constantinople during the period of the crusader occupation, which was

---

83 PL, 215:1352.
84 PL, 216:647.

regarded as temporary, certainly in 1204, and its implications for the church were vague in the extreme.

Both in Byzantium and the west church property was regarded as inalienable, but in both regions extraordinary circumstances had been used as an excuse for lay encroachment. In January 1205, some four months after the Byzantine territories had been partitioned, Innocent first became aware of the March 1204 Pact. Immediately he wrote to all the lay authorities concerned and pointed out the illegal and injurious nature of the proposal and its insult to God and the papal office.[85] The best that could now be arranged was an indemnity. It took nearly 20 years for the proportion of territory to be assigned to the church to be agreed. There are no details of the negotiations themselves or the manner in which the discussions involving the pope, the emperor, the patriarch and the papal legate actually took effect in the locality. On paper at least the new church clawed back first (1205) a fifteenth, then (1209) a twelfth, and finally by 1223 an eleventh of all conquered territory.[86] However, in the unsettled military situation, Latin rulers often ignored the various agreements and found it necessary to implement some of the earliest mortmain provision and forbid bequests of land to the church. Virtually all dioceses in the Aegean were taken under papal protection in these years of protracted negotiations – what was regarded as a privilege in the west was a necessity in Greek lands.

It has been estimated that by 1200 something like one-fifth of the land of western Europe was in the hands of the church.[87] By these standards the new church was a poor one and its hierarchy clearly felt the pinch. As we have seen smaller bishoprics became economically unviable in the years after 1210, whilst the competition for resources in the Theban archdiocese deteriorated into armed raids organised by the Theban chapter into a suffragan see.[88] Even essential business was affected and official visits to Rome could only be afforded by contracting debts; the archbishops of Patras and Thessalonika raised loans and contributions from their suffragans, whilst the archbishop of Thebes had debts that he could not meet.[89] The resources of the new church were just not adequate and its laity were disinclined to endow it.

In both east and west provision for the maintenance of clergy had followed broadly similar lines. There was acceptance that the laity should pay for its clergy and that a standard proportion of produce, to be paid annually by all Christians, should be established to replace voluntary gifts. In the west it was the tithe, one-tenth of all natural produce; in the east the

---

85 PL, 215:519, 521: *Urkunden* I, 534.
86 J. Gill, *Byzantium and the Papacy, 1198–1400* (New Brunswick, 1979), pp.30–1; Wolff, *Politics in the Latin Patriarchate of Constantinople*, op.cit., pp. 255–74.
87 C. Morris, *The Papal Monarchy* (Oxford, 1989), p.388.
88 PL, 216:564–5, 897.
89 PL, 215:598, 1082, 1141.

kanonikon, a payment of one gold and two silver coins, one goat, eighteen bushels of wheat and barley, six measures of wine and thirty fowls from each community of thirty hearths. In the east the payment was made to the bishop, whilst in the west the principle that tithe was payable to the parish was only just emerging and its collection and distribution were still very much in episcopal hands. In both areas there had been resistance to this tax and the attitude continued when the tithe was introduced by the Latin church. It was certainly no revolutionary proposal but it provoked much opposition both from Latin rulers and from the Greek laity. Margaret of Hungary was not the only ruler to forbid her subjects to pay it. Her attitude has often been linked to a pro-Greek stance, but it is just possible that it had more to do with her Lombard links, since in July 1208 Innocent wrote five letters concerning the non-payment of tithes. These were addressed to the Canossa brothers as lord of Thebes, the triarchs of Euboea, the lord of Thermopylae, the constable of Thessalonika, Otho de la Roche, and Rolando Pissa, all former supporters and vassals of the late Boniface of Montferrat.[90] An assent to the payment of tithes was usually extracted from a Latin ruler when an agreement was reached over the indemnity of church lands. Priests were obliged to pay the acrosticon or land-tax on any lands which they occupied which traditionally paid that impost. The non-payment of tithes by Greeks was also acknowledged and their incorporation within the system seen as a challenge.[91]

Heresy

The Inquisition did not operate in Frankish Greece and heresy does not seem to have been a problem for the authorities of the Latin Church in Greece. However, to assume that Latin heretics did not exist there would be a mistake. For young men without family eager to escape the attentions of the Inquisition in France or Italy, employment as a mercenary in either a Greek or a Latin army may well have been attractive.[92] Greece was not the only area of Europe where the Inquisition did not function, but surely a major reason for this in the case of Greece was the presence of a majority Orthodox population and the can of worms which any such investigations might have opened up. This is not to say that the Greeks were regarded as heretics. From the Roman point of view they were schismatics who went their own way whilst the Latin church existed in their midst. The attitude of

---

[90] PL, 215:1434–5.
[91] PL, 215:967, 1348–9; Pressutti, 1816, 4059–60.
[92] B. Hamilton, *The Medieval Inquisition* (London, 1981), p.56, and pp.13 and 88–91 for other aspects of the Inquisition in this paragraph.

Orthodox theologians to heresy was less legalistic than that of the west. They regarded it as a sin and not as a crime to be punished. No Albigensians (Cathars) appear in the records such as they exist at all. This is not to deny that some sought refuge in the Aegean. There was a concern among the bishops of the Latin church in Greece that undesirables might venture east. In the early days it had been felt that caution should be exercised regarding priests who presented themselves without credentials. However, this seems to have been concerned with canonical ordination rather than with any refugee heretics, and since the Latin clergy in Greece soon settled down as a capitular clergy this problem seems to have solved itself. Only some Spiritual Franciscans or Bisoci who had fled to Greece in 1299 threatened the orthodoxy of the Latin church in Greece. Their presence provoked an order to the Latin patriarch and the archbishops of Patras and Athens to seek them out and punish them. Angevin officials were instructed to help the clerical arm if required.[93]

Monuments of the Latin church in the Aegean

Archaeologically the Latin church in Greece has left little trace. This must reflect both a lack of resources and a certain lack of confidence in its own identity. Certainly it lacked the associations of the Holy Land, and although there were local saints and relics there was little promotion of any particular saint's cult by the new Latin lords. Apart from the chapel on the bridge near the castle at Karytaina, only at Isova, Andravida and Zaraka were there complete Gothic churches and these were all constructed within a monastic context in the 1220s or after. The slighting of the town of Glarenza in 1429 and the passage of time have not dealt kindly with the churches of this discrete Frankish site. Only the ruins of one church remain above ground and its dedication is unknown. Its plan belongs to the thirteenth century and so it cannot be the church of San Marco built after 1340 by a Venetian consul.[94] For the rest there are Gothic decorative additions to existing structures like the facade at Daphne, and the corbels at Hagia Paraskevi, Chalkis.[95] Latin ecclesiastical architecture is no more evident in Thessalonika or in Istanbul. The churches of the capital seem to have received no identifiable Latin alterations. Even the flying buttresses and the porch on the south-east side of Hagia Sophia, which were once attributed to

---

[93] Perrat & Longnon, docs 230–1 (pp.197–200); Setton, p.151.
[94] BMF, pp.537–77.
[95] B.K. Panagopoulos, *Cistercian and Mendicant Monasteries in Medieval Greece* (Chicago, 1979), esp. bibliography, pp.170–88.

the Latins, have been called into question, and only a small belfry which was removed in the nineteenth century has been vouchsafed to them.[96]

There is a further group of churches displaying mixed Byzantine–Gothic styles where it is almost impossible to distinguish Gothic addition from Gothic influence. They represent some of the most interesting structures of Frankish Greece. The monastery church of the Blachernai near Glarenza, the Katholikon at Gastouni and the two churches in Chalandritza, Aghios Athanasios and the Koimesis, all have earlier Byzantine structures with seemingly western structural additions like a square apse, a south porch, and the use of ashlar without brick. The church of St Nicholas at Isova, some 20 metres south of the ruined Cistercian monastery, was built in the fifteenth century, possibly 150 years after the destruction of the monastery in 1263. Yet on a site associated with east-west conflict and the destruction of Gothic architecture, the church of St Nicholas contains a real mixture of Byzantine and Gothic styles which perhaps suggests a lingering western architectural influence after the passing of Frankish domination.[97] It must not be forgotten, however, that these churches claim our attention precisely because they were unusual; the normal practice of the Frankish clergy was to reuse and not to remodel existing Byzantine churches.

One thing all this shows is that the Latins could recognise the sanctity of Greek churches and tombs and use them. The picture is one of the re-use of Greek churches with apparently minimal structural adaptation, which is perhaps surprising since the bulk of them were not really well-suited to Latin ritual and processions. They did, however, suit small congregations. What seems to have been important was the dedication of the church and there is some evidence that these were changed by the Latins. The church of Hagia Fotini in Thebes became the church of Santa Lucia, some regard being paid here to the meaning of the original dedication. The church of Hagia Paraskevi in Negroponte became San Marco and a church in Andravida of unknown Greek dedication was rededicated jointly to Saint James and Saint Stephen.

There was no campaign of church building to rival the 400 or so churches built or re-built in Palestine by the crusaders during the 200 years of their occupation.[98] Some churches were built or repaired but using Greek craftsmen working in a Greek style. There is the Church of St George at Akraiphnion (Karditsa) in Boeotia with an inscription recording its repair in 1311 by Antoine le Flamenc in pursuance of a vow, and then there is the

---

[96] E.H. Swift, 'The Latins at Hagia Sophia' *AJA* 39 (1935), 458–74; R.J. Mainstone, *Hagia Sophia, Architecture, Structure and Liturgy of Justinian's Great Church* (London, 1988), pp.104–5, 113.

[97] R. Traquair, 'Frankish Architecture in Greece' *Journal of the Royal Institute of British Architects* 3rd ser., 31 (1923–4), 33–48, 73–86.

[98] D. Pringle, *The Churches of the Crusader Kingdom of Jerusalem* I (Cambridge, 1993), p.1.

church of St John, later St Pantelemon, at Galaxidhi, which was built by the Hospitallers for the Greek community in 1404 and renamed on their departure from the region. There is some indication that the church in the so-called Frankish complex recently discovered in Corinth may have been built at this time too.[99] The chronicler Villehardouin noted the re-use of aristocratic tombs in Constantinople for the burial of members of the crusading leadership in 1204.[100] In June of the following year Enrico Dandolo was buried in Santa Sophia. It is debateable whether the tomb-slab visible in the south gallery today is of medieval date or a feature of the nineteenth-century heritage industry. There is the tomb-chest of a Frankish archbishop in the Parthenon whilst the tomb-chest at Akraiphnion is often associated with Antoine le Flamenc but equally might be a Byzantine arcosolium.[101] Where were all the Franks buried and can their tombs be distinguished from their Greek neighbours? Amongst the well-born or wealthy there seems to have been a preference for internment in a religious house. Rennell Rodd has suggested the Franciscan church of the Blachernae near Glarentza as the last resting place of the emperor Robert in 1228. The Franciscans were favoured, too, by the emperor John de Brienne who joined the order on his death-bed in 1237. Sigrid Dull has noted a number of Genoese funerary monuments in the Dominican church of Galata belonging to the fourteenth century, and from the same area, but about 1220, the monks of the Cistercian house of St Angelus in Pera refused to move the site of their monastery across the Bosporus because it contained the remains of certain noble Latins. Sadly its site is now lost and can add nothing at present to this debate.[102]

Armorials and inscribed stones are also extremely rare in the Latin states of the Aegean, either in churches or castles.[103] Whether this surprising paucity is an accident of survival or evidence of knightly attitudes to their involvement in the Aegean is not at all clear. The survival of five exceptionally fine tombs built for the Genoese family of Gattelusi on the island of Mytilene (Lesbos) together with a mortuary church permits a

---

[99] W. Miller, 'The Frankish Inscription at Karditza', in idem, *Essays on the Latin Orient* (Cambridge, 1921), pp.132–4; J. Rosser in P. Lock & G. Sanders, eds, *Essays in the Archaeology of Medieval Greece* (Oxford, forthcoming), citing the Chronicle of Galaxidhi; C. Williams and O. Zervos, 'Corinth, 1990: southeast corner of Temenos E' *Hesperia* 60 (1991), 1–58, see pp.19–24 for a description of the church.

[100] Villehardouin, 200, 262, 334, 388.

[101] Villehardouin, paras 334, 388; Eric Ivison for verbal information on the Parthenon burial, see his unpublished 1993 Birmingham PhD thesis on Byzantine arcosolia and their social influence, *c.* 1100–1453.

[102] R. Rodd, *The Princes of Achaia...* I (London, 1907), pp.141–2; S. Düll, 'Unbekannte Denkmaler der Genuesen aus Galata' *Istanbuler Mitteilungen* 33 (1983), 225–38; R.L. Wolff, 'The Latin Empire ... and the Franciscans' *Traditio* 2 (1943–4), 215–18, and see p.230 below.

[103] Antoine Bon, 'Pierres inscrites ou armoriées de la Morée franque' *Deltion tis Christianikes Archaiologikes Etaireias* 4 (1964–5), 89–102.

glimpse at the iconography and heraldic display to which wealthy western lords might aspire in the fourteenth century.[104]

In fresco and icon-painting the current state of knowledge would suggest that Latin influence was virtually non-existent, if not deliberately resisted. Inability to fund or attract artists from the west would partly account for this. Certainly the corpus in the Aegean is small, but growing. There were the secular frescoes depicting events of the First Crusade in the castle at Thebes executed after 1287 and lost in 1332. Another cycle depicting the capture of Troy was recorded in the castle at Patras by the traveller Niccolo da Martoni in 1395. As Dr Van Der Vin has noted, without Martoni's chance reference nothing would be known today of this Trojan cycle.[105] It would seem that loss rather than absence is at stake here and this is borne out by recent work in Istanbul. In the 1970s during restoration work at Kalenderhane Camii in Istanbul, formerly the mid-ninth century church of the Kyriotissa, Lee Striker discovered the first frescoes belonging to the period of Latin rule in the city. Coincidentally they were also the earliest cycle of frescoes depicting the life of St Francis. They were executed soon after the saint's death in 1226 and have been identified as the work of a court painter from the kingdom of Jerusalem.[106] Fragments of other frescoes, probably from the fourteenth century, have been noted recently in Arup Camii, the former Dominican church of SS Paolo e Domenico in Galata.[107] Doom-paintings were almost non-existent in eastern Christendom and none appeared in the thirteenth century. However, at that time some Greek artists were busy constructing the mosaic of judgement on the west wall of the cathedral of Santa Maria dell'Assunta on the island of Torcello in Venice. Appropriate patronage could fund work by Greek craftsmen to western taste; perhaps such patronage was not available in the Latin Aegean.

The Latin church in Greece was not a missionising church. The Greeks were not pagans to be converted but Christians of long-standing, indeed, even longer standing than the Latins. It disappointed Innocent that not only did the Greeks fail to learn the lesson which he felt that the capture of Constantinople should have taught them, but that they clung to their own traditions even more closely and saw the Latins as polluters. They associated them with unclean animals like pigs and dogs, washed altars used by Latin priests and re-baptized children in their own rite.[108] With no spontaneous

---

[104] F.W. Hasluck, 'Monuments of the Gattelusi' *ABSA* 15 (1908–9), 248–69; E.A. Ivison, 'Funerary Monuments of the Gattelusi at Mytilene' *ABSA* 87 (1992), 423–37.
[105] J.P. Van Der Vin, *Travellers to Greece and Constantinople* I (Leiden, 1980), pp.215–16.
[106] C.L. Striker & Y. Dogan Kuban, 'Work at Kalenderhane Camii in Istanbul' *DOP* 21 (1967), 267–71; 22 (1968), 185–93; 25 (1971), 251–58.
[107] Düll, art.cit.
[108] PL, 215:699; Mansi, *Sacrorum conciliorum* XXII, c. 990.

response to the divine call to unity and only problems in the wake of the policy of gentle persuasion, the Latin church came into existence as a sort of consolation prize. It ministered neither to the indigenous population nor to mass Latin settlement which did not materialise. Its prime function seemed to be its own survival. With its Latin missals and scriptures it was linguistically separated from the Greek community, with the filioque and the azymaton doctrinally distinct and with its dress and tonsure visibly different. It was the church of the conquerors rather than the church of God.[109]

---

[109] As this book was in press, excavators at the Taxiarchs–Ermitsas site near Panaitolion in Aitolia reported what may be a discreet Frankish cemetary. Finds include 356 coins of Guy II de la Roche and a gold ring with the inscription AVE MARIA. See *Archaiologikon Deltion*, 42, *Chronika*, 330.

Chapter 9 ....

The Religious Orders[1]

The western religious orders which were to be found in the Frankish Aegean may be summarily listed. They were the Cistercians, the two new mendicant orders, the Dominicans and the Franciscans, the three great international military orders and two groups of canons regular, the Premonstratensians and the Augustinians. They represented the full spectrum of the religious life of the contemporary medieval west and embraced both male and female religious. Their particular ministry, contemplative or pastoral, conditioned the time and place of their first establishment, but all were present in the Aegean by the 1230s. The inspiration for their spread along with the necessary endowments to support it came equally from lay rulers and from Latin metropolitans. The Cistercians and the Templars were present from the start and had received endowments soon after 1204, primarily in rural areas. The canons regular appeared in 1210 – the Augustinians of St Ruff who came to serve the cathedral chapter of Patras and the Premonstratensians who received lands at Thespiae in Boeotia. The mendicant orders established themselves first in Constantinople in the 1220s and 1230s, and thereafter spread out into the urban centres of the Aegean.

---

[1] This chapter is based upon the following: Beata Panagopoulos, *Cistercian and Mendicant Monasteries in Medieval Greece* (Chicago, 1979); E.A.R. Brown, 'The Cistercians in the Latin Empire of Constantinople and Greece, 1201–1276' *Traditio* 14 (1958), 63–120; Brenda Bolton, 'A Mission to the Orthodox? The Cistercians in Romania', in D. Baker, ed., *Studies in Church History, 13: The Orthodox Churches and the West* (Oxford, 1976), 169–81; Berthold Altaner, *Die Dominikanermissionen des 13 Jahrhunderts* (Habelschwerdt, 1924), pp.1–72, 225–39; R.L. Wolff, 'The Latin Empire of Constantinople and the Franciscans' *Traditio* 2 (1943–4), 213–37; P.W. Lock, 'The Military Orders in Crusader Greece', in M. Barber, ed., *Fighting for the Faith and Caring for the Sick* (London, 1994), pp.333–9.

The Cistercians

The Cistercian order had been involved with the Fourth Crusade from its inception or at least from mid-1201. Initially it had ignored a papal appeal to contribute funds for the crusade. Relations eased in July 1201 when the General Chapter promised a sum of 2,000 marks. Thereafter the order put its considerable weight behind the expedition. Abbots from Rievaulx to Lake Constance were urged to preach the crusade and some, like Luke of Sambucina, were clearly effective in doing so. The General Chapter at Citeaux in September 1201 forwarded the crusade. Boniface of Montferrat was in attendance and a number of abbots were appointed to accompany the crusade. Of these, four took a prominent part in the events of the crusade. Guy de Vaux-de-Cernay, was a supporter of Simon de Montfort and opposed to any attacks on Christian cities. He left the crusade before the attack on Zara and proceeded to Syria with de Montfort. Martin of Pairis was in Rome after the Zara attack. He rejoined the crusade before Constantinople in early 1204, having visited the Holy Land on the way. Thereafter his main concern was with relic hunting and his return to his house in Alsace with his sacred booty. Simon of Loos preached to the crusaders before the second attack on Constantinple. He died in the city in July 1204 and not in 1203 as Villehardouin had noted. Finally Peter of Locedio in Piedmont was a supporter of Boniface of Montferrat. He was one of the college of electors to the principate in May 1204 and the following year, having reconciled Margaret of Hungary to the church of Rome, was given the monastery of Chortaiton by Boniface as a daughter house for Locedio.[2]

In a letter addressed to the archbishops and bishops of France and dated 25 May 1205, Pope Innocent passed on the request of the emperor Baldwin for '*viros religiosos ... de ordini Cisterciensi, Cluniacensi, canonicorum Regularium, aliarumque religionum, ad fundandam fidei catholicae veritatem perpetuoque firmandam ...*'.[3] Whatever his motive in making this request and whether he intended these new settlers for Constantinople or elsewhere, Baldwin appeared to be casting his net wide. Yet in May 1204 he had written an account of the achievements of the crusaders to the abbot of Citeaux and the the other abbots of the Cistercian order.[4] No other religious order was so favoured and it is difficult to avoid the impression that the Cistercians were his preferred order. Indeed on his way to Venice in 1202 he and his contingent had stopped off at Clairvaux and Citeaux.[5]

[2] Brown, art.cit., 67–78.
[3] PL, 215:636–7.
[4] Hendrickx, 'Régestes des Empereurs Latins de Constantinople (1204–1261/72)' *Byzantina* 14 (1988), p.15, no. 5.
[5] D.E. Queller, *The Fourth Crusade* (Pennsylvania, 1977), p.37.

Elizabeth Brown has succeeded in tracing a total of twelve Cistercian monasteries and nunneries in Romania in the thirteenth century. Most of their sites are now lost and the nunneries barely have a recorded history at all. After 1273 only the Cistercian house at Daphni seems to have survived.[6] Often houses which were deserted by their Greek monks were given to the Cistercians, although in the case of Daphni the Greeks seem to have been expelled. The first foundation was the Chortaiton near Thessalonika given by Boniface to Peter of Locedio in July 1205. A certain Geoffrey was brought from Locedio in Piedmont as its first abbot. In 1207 Otho de la Roche granted Daphni to the monastery of Bellevaux, a Burgundian house to which his family was attached. It became the most important Cistercian house in Greece and the burial place of the dukes of Athens. In 1208 or soon after the Venetian community in Constantinople through its podesta granted the monastery of St Stephen near the city to the community of St Thomas of Torsello as a daughter house. The site of St Stephen has not been identified from the numerous houses of this dedication in and around Constantinople. On Crete the order received the monastery of Gergeri in 1217 and that of St Mary Varangorum in 1230. In Constantinople it received the house of St Angelus in Pera in 1213/14 which received as a daughter house the monastery of Rufiniani in Bithynia one year later. In 1210 Geoffrey de Villehardouin had offered the monks of Hautecombe near Geneva a house in Patras. There is no evidence that this was ever founded, although a tantalising reference in 1212 to a monk of Hautecombe as '*qoundam abbate in Graecia*' may just suggest otherwise.[7] In 1225 Geoffrey summoned monks from Hautecombe to Achaia to found the house at Zaraka on Lake Stymphalia in the archdiocese of Corinth. The Greek name for this house, Saracez, would suggest that it took over the site from an existing Greek community, yet it is one of the few Cistercian houses whose site is known and where Gothic arcitecture may be seen. Finally, there was the house at Isova, architecturally the most complete of Gothic monasteries in Greece. It was not mentioned in any Cistercian records and was once thought by Buchon and others to have been a Benedictine house. Its Cistercian credentials have been established both by its dedication to the Virgin and architecturally by comparison with the Italian houses of Fossanova and Casamara. Be that as it may, it seems to have had a short existence. It was burnt to the ground in 1263, the perpetrators being said to have been chased from Skorta in the following year by a lady on a white horse.[8] As lands were lost to the Greeks so it seems that the Cistercians were expelled. Apart from the destruction of Isova there is only the expulsion of some Cistercian nuns near Modon and those of a Constantinopolitan nunnery in the 1260s to

---

[6] Brown, art.cit., 78–96.

[7] See Brown, art.cit., 86 for the problems in this interpretation associated with Cistercian practice on the residence of former abbots.

[8] L de C, 338; X t M, 4671–2.

indicate something of Greek attitudes to these religious immigrants. After 1276, only the house at Daphni remained in Cistercian hands in mainland Greece and that was occupied down to 1458.[9] The abbey received its greatest privilege and largest notice in the records of the General Chapter in 1263. In that year Othon de Cicon, lord of Karystos, gained possession of the right arm of John the Baptist from the Boukoleon palace chapel. In return for his part in transporting this most glorious relic to Citeaux, the abbot de Dalphino was personally excused from attending the General Chapter except in every seventh year, a privilege usually reserved for houses in the Holy Land.[10]

The Cistercian nunneries are poorly documented and their sites unknown. This reflects the ambivalent, not to say hostile, attitude of the religious orders towards women. It was not until 1213 that the Cistercians officially recognised the existence of nunneries following the Cistercian rule and sought thereafter to limit the foundation of new Cistercian nunneries. In the Aegean they were clearly unsuccessful in this. By 1221 nuns had established themselves in the former Greek monastery of St Mary of Percheio in or near Constantinople and were placed under the supervision of the abbot of St Angelus. It was a rich house with possessions in Acre and in 1238 lent the emperor Baldwin II the sum of 4,300 hyperpera.[11] Nothing is known of the nunnery of Laurus established between 1212 and 1256; even its approximate site is variously given as Constantinople or Achaia. The same is true of the nunnery of De Nicenal in the diocese of Corinth and to a lesser extent of that of De viridario beate Marie or St Mary de Verge in the diocese of Modon. All that is known of the latter house are the circumstances of its demise in 1267, when the convent was destroyed by the Greeks and the community under its abbess, Demeta Palaeologina, fled to Italy where it was re-housed at Conversano. The visitor for the house in Italy was the abbot of Daphni, since in 1271 the General Chapter decided that he was nearer than the abbot of Citeaux, an arresting illustration of the ease of traffic between Greece and southern Italy.

Of these houses only the sites at Daphni, Zaraka and Isova are known at the present day.[12] Archaeologically and historically the Cistercians in the Aegean are not well-covered. However, the number of their houses and the patronage which they enjoyed showed that they were a popular order amongst the Frankish ruling class. Sometime before 1221 the monks of St Angelus had objected to a possible transfer of their house to Rufiniani

---

9   Panagopoulos, op.cit., pp.55–7.
10 J. Canivez, ed., *Statuta Capitulorum Generalium Ordinis Cisterciensis* III (Louvain, 1935), pp.12, 18; Brown, art.cit., 112, 115; Bolton, art.cit., 180.
11 Brown, art.cit., p.92–3; Pressutti, 4487; *Urkunden* II, p.346–9.
12 BMF, pp.537–44, 553–59; A.K. Orlandos, 'Neotera Evremata eis tin Monen Dafniou' *Archeion Byzantinon Mneemeion tis Ellados* 8 (1955–6).

because of the bodies of many noble Latins buried at St Angelus.[13] Brenda Bolton has pondered the apparent gap between Cistercian theory and practice in Romania. They were neither great builders nor great colonisers of the waste in the Aegean. They seemed more concerned with the acquisition of relics and the exploitation of resources than in any mission to the Orthodox.[14] Yet the name of Demeta Palaeologina as abbess of the house near Modon is suggestive if nothing else of some Greek recruitment into the order. The fate of the order in the Aegean in many ways reflected the political fortunes of their patrons. By 1276 all their houses had fallen into Greek hands with the exception of Daphni and possibly the two Cretan houses.

Greek communities

Within a claustral context, there seems to have been no overt move against Greek monks. Certainly the monks of Daphni were expelled but of the other houses handed over to the Cistercians the former monks had fled their cloister. It is not clear whether this happened as a result of the conquests of 1204 or had happened some time previously. Only at Rufiniani in Bithynia and at Chortaiton near Thessalonika did Greek communities seem to maintain their existence under Cistercian rule. At Rufiniani they eventually decamped on being asked to acknowledge papal supremacy, but at Chortaiton they seem to have resisted the depredations of Abbot Gregory and in 1207 the monastery of St Maria de Chortaitis was restored to the Greek monks by the emperor Henry. It was in seriously depleted condition but in 1212 the monks of Locedio tried to regain the monastery by personal presence in Thrace and in 1213 the Greeks were confirmed in their possession and taken under papal protection.[15]

This action of protection and a measure of tolerance was fairly typical of the papal stance towards Greek monasticism. As Patricia McNulty and Bernard Hamilton have shown, eastern monks had played a significant role in the development of western monasticism in Italy in the tenth century and Greek spirituality was held in high esteem in the west.[16] Administratively, too, the hierarchy of the Latin church had gained much experience in dealing with Greek priests and monks in southern Italy since the eleventh century. With regard to Greek priests and clerical celibacy this had not

---

[13] Brown, art.cit., 89.

[14] Bolton, art.cit.

[15] Brown, art.cit., 80–1: PL, 216:594–5, 951–2.

[16] P. McNulty and B. Hamilton, 'Orientale Lumen et Magistra Latinitas: Greek influences on Western monasticism (900–1000)', in *Le Millennaire du Mont Athos, 963–1963: Etudes et Melanges* I (Chevetogne, 1963), pp.181–216.

always been a happy experience but with regard to monastic communities the Latin church was not uninformed in its approach to Greek monasticism in the Aegean.

Greek communities were allowed to function, apparently under the direct oversight of the pope or his legate. We have already noted the appeal of Guy de la Roche to Innocent IV in April 1244 concerning the movement of a community of Greek monks from the village of 'Laragie' because they were passing on information to the Epirote Greeks.[17] What is noteworthy in this context is that it was to the pope that the appeal was made and any action regarding the monks was apparently left to him and his legate. So long as the the pall of suspicion did not fall over a Greek monastic community, it was free to receive endowments and conduct its affairs as it saw fit. The wealthy monastery of Sagmatas on Mount Kithaeron with its associations with the life of Hosios Meletios (c. 1035–1105) continued to function and to maintain its lands and flocks, as did another important monastery in the area associated with Meletios. This was the monastery of Myoupolis where Meletios had died in 1105. It lay near Aigosthena, midway between Thebes and Megara in the lordship of Athens and Thebes. In September 1218 all its customs and privileges as a monastery of the Greek rite were confirmed by Pope Honorius.[18] Both William Miller and Kenneth Setton have noted the inscription at Stavros dated to 1238 (= AM. 6746) which recorded the construction or repair of a road leading to the monastery of St John the Hunter on Mount Hymettos, and this at a time when Thebes was suffering numerous attacks from the Greeks of Epiros.[19] The policy of tolerance was applied to the monasteries on Mount Athos too. However, there it got off to a shaky start due to the depredations of the representatives of the bishop of Samaria. The diocese of Samaria or Sebaste was a suffragan see of Caesarea in the Holy Land and the reputed burial place of John the Baptist. On 27 November 1206 Innocent III confirmed a grant made to the bishop of Samaria by Boniface de Montferrat possibly on the prompting and certainly with the support of the papal legate Benedict.[20]

Until well into the twentieth century 'the pope' was still credited with destruction and pillage in connection with Mount Athos.[21] This reputation was totally undeserved. Certainly Athonite estates like all church lands would have suffered in the plundering which accompanied the Frankish

---

[17] See above p.82; E. Berger, ed., *Les Registres d'Innocence IV* 4 vols (Paris, 1884–1919), doc. 657, pp.112–13.

[18] A.K. Orlandos, 'I Moni tou Osiou Meletiou ...' *Archeion tou Byzantinon Mnemeion tis Ellados* 5 (1939–40), 34–118; J. Koder and F. Hild, *T.I.B.1: Hellas und Thessalia* (Vienna, 1976), pp. 252–3; Pressutti, 1627.

[19] *Corpus inscriptionum graecarum* IV (Berlin, 1856–9), no. 8752, p.345, cited Setton, pp.65 and 419 and W. Miller, *Latins in the Levant* (London, 1908), p.93.

[20] PL, 215:1030.

[21] E. Amand de Mendieta, *La Presqu'ile des Caloyers, Le Mont Athos* (Bruges, 1955), p.30.

conquests. Whatever strong-arm tactics the representatives of the bishops of Samaria were involved in, they were as nothing compared with the destruction of the officials of Michael VIII in the late 1270s and seem to have been easily checked, at least if the silence of the papal archives is any guide.[22] To his credit, Innocent took measures to stop any undue exploitation by his subordinates as soon as he was convinced of it. Hasluck, as well as defending Innocent's reputation, has suggested that the monastery of Iveron formally subscribed to Roman tenets at this time. Certainly Athos was known in the west and, as we have seen, a Benedictine monastery of Amalfitans had been set up soon after 985. This was one of the oldest Athonite houses and had an independent existence down to 1393.[23] Whatever Boniface or Innocent had intended by the *concessionem Monti Sancti*, the bishop clearly took it as a licence to plunder. On 17 January 1214 Innocent acknowledged the receipt of a letter from various communities on Athos complaining of the theft of precious objects by the henchmen of the bishop who had constructed a tower, Frangokastro, on the neck of the peninsula for this purpose. Innocent seems to have put an end to the plundering. He restored the privileges and status of the monasteries and placed them under papal protection. In a letter announcing his decision he painted an informed word-picture of the Holy Mountain. He knew that it was surrounded by the sea and by sheer cliffs, that it contained some 30 houses and numerous monks, and that it attracted many benefactions and visitors. He juxtaposed a description of the arid soil with the spiritual fecundity of the mountain.[24] It is not clear when the Holy Mountain passed out of Latin control, but it cannot have been long after 1224 and the loss of Thessalonika.

Canons regular

Before passing on to the mendicant orders, note should be taken of the establishment of the other regular orders in the Aegean. There is little to say and the picture can only be a provisional one, which will be filled out in part by archaeological fieldwork. As we have seen the Augustinians of Saint Ruff near Avignon served the cathedral church of Patras from 1210 until 1222, when secular canons were again installed and the regulars returned to their

---

[22] L. Petit, *Actes de l'Athos, I: Actes de Xenophon* (St Petersburg, 1903, reprinted Amsterdam, 1964), pp.7–8.
[23] F. Hasluck, *Athos and its Monasteries* (London, 1924), pp.27–8; R. Dawkins, *The Monks of Athos* (London, 1936), p.144, and see p.137.
[24] PL, 216:956–7; '... *licet aridus sit et asper de temporalis fertilitatis gratia destitutus, et tamen inter alios mundi montes maxima speritualium ubertate mirabiliter fecundatus* ...'.

mother house.[25] In 1209 a certain Simon de Lagny had granted the monastery of 'Safadin' dedicated to the Holy Saviour in Messenia to the Augustinians from the house of Saint-Loup in Troyes.[26] Of the Premonstratensians, there are but two recorded endowments in Greece. On 23 May 1212 Innocent confirmed a grant made to the abbot and brothers of Saint Mary's de Parvo Ponte in Brindisi by Nicholas I de St Omer. Besides some houses in Thebes they acquired the '*casale quod dicitur Hermocastro*'.[27] Hermocastro or Eremocastro is modern Thespiae. Whatever the manner of the canons' occupation, it has left no recognisable trace today. Indeed no house as such may ever have been built but some arrangement would have been necessary for the exploitation of the estate. Sometime before 1228 the Premonstratensians were granted an abbey at Kalavryta in the diocese of Patras. It had ceased to be occupied by them by 1320. Its site is not securely known but Bon and others have suggested Hagia Lavra.[28] No Premonstratensian nuns seem to have been active in Greece.

The Benedictines

As far as I am aware, there was very little Benedictine involvement in the Aegean. Other than the Amalfitan establishment of the house on Athos in the tenth century there are just three notices of Benedictine foundations in Greece, none of which may have progressed being the planning stage. Possession of the monastery of Gerokomion near Patras, said to be worth 2,618 hyperpera, was in dispute between the archbishop and the Templars throughout 1210 and 1211. The archbishop offered it to the monks of Cluny, but nothing seemed to come of this offer.[29] Karl Hopf has noted a reference to a possible Benedictine foundation in 1273, that of Santa Maria de Camina in the diocese of Olena, but details are lacking.[30] Finally, Niccolo Acciaioli in his will of 1359 left property to the order for the founding of a house in or near Kalamata but it seems never to have been established.[31] Whatever Baldwin had intended in his letter of 1204 regarding the sure

---

[25] PL, 216:336–8; Pressutti, 3842 (10 March 1222); see p.211.

[26] BMF, pp.71, 100.

[27] PL, 216:591 (doc.LXVIII).

[28] N. Backmund, *Monasticon Premonstratense* (1949), pp.403–4, 611; BMF, pp.100, 469.

[29] PL, 216:330–1, 471; BMF, p.100, n.6. For an alternative view see L. de Mas-Latrie, 'Donation a l'abbaye due monastere de Hiero Komio pres de Patras en 1210' *Bibliotheque de l'Ecole des Chartes 5* (1848–9), 311ff., cited by A. Ilieva, *Frankish Morea* – (Athens, 1991), p.214.

[30] K. Hopf, *Geschichte Griechenlands ... I* (Leipzig, 1867), p.227.

[31] Published as an appendix in G. Scaramilla, ed., *Mathei Palmerii Vita Nicolai Acciaioli* (Milan, 1934).

foundation of the truth of the catholic faith in the Latin empire, that task was to be left to the new mendicant orders, the Franciscans and Dominicans, which lay more than a decade in the future when the Latin empire was created.

The mendicant orders

There was no gap between the western theory and the eastern practice of the two great mendicant orders in their Aegean provinces. Their missionary work in the Aegean often involved them in didactic, polemical, and diplomatic roles as spokesmen for the western church at the Nicene and Constantinopolitan courts. This work naturally brought them into complex intellectual and political situations which required a high degree of theological and linguistic training. Some spoke Greek fluently. The English Franciscan, Haymo of Faversham, who was sent to Nicaea by Gregory IX in 1234 to discuss the union of churches, is often credited as being one of the first to have the necessary linguistic skill. His theology he certainly acquired at Paris and perhaps also, but less certainly, his Greek. There were native recruits to the order and one of these, John Parastron, accepted the profession of faith from Michael VIII before the Council of Lyons in 1274 and went on to attend it as translator for the Greek delegation.[32] Not surprisingly Constantinople was the focus of both these orders. The two Franciscans, John de Piano Carpini and William of Rubruck, who extended the horizons of western Christendom by their separate journeys to Karakorum in the Mongolia in 1247–49 and 1253–55 were both familiar with Constantinople and its geographic relationship to the lands beyond the Black Sea.[33] Our concern, however, is with the mendicants in the Aegean.

The Franciscans, variously known as friars minor, minorites, and to the Greeks as '*phrerioi*', were founded in 1209 originally with a non-clerical, lay bias. The order grew rapidly in its first ten years, numbering some 3,000 recruits by 1220 when members of the order first arrived in Constantinople. Preaching and caring was their raison d'etre and the town their environment. Ironically their use within the Aegean rose in the late 1220s with the abandonment of the ideal of absolute poverty and a tendency to shun the learned and the clerical. The order was highjacked by the university-trained wing of friars and turned into a dynamic, educated missionising force. It was Haymo of Faversham who was foremost in the attack on Francis's successor Brother Elias.[34]

There was a Franciscan presence in Constantinople by December 1220

---

[32] *ODB*, p.802.

[33] C. Dawson, ed., *The Mission to Asia* (London, 1955, reprinted, 1980).

[34] C.H. Lawrence, *Medieval Monasticism* (London, 1984), pp.192–203.

when a certain Brother Luke, '*ministro de fratrum Minorum de partibus Romanie*', was cited as a witness in a dispute between the papal legate John of Colonna and the provost of the church of the Holy Apostles.[35] The Franciscans became influential at the Latin court when John de Brienne became co-emperor. He had a Franciscan confessor and as the former king of Jerusalem during the minority of his daughter Maria, may well have had a hand in obtaining the painter to produce the frescoes in the Franciscan church of the Kyriotissa.[36] Most of the Franciscans who played a prominent part in the later attempts to reunite the Greek and Latin churches were not members of the province of Romania but like Haymo of Faversham in 1234, Dominic of Aragon in 1246, and the general of the order, John of Parma in 1249, were sent from Rome as part of an official legation.[37] Wolff has shown that their knowledge and use of Greek scriptures in debates with the Nicaeans was good and has suggested that the knowledge of Greek amongst westerners may have been better than is generally thought to have been the case.[38] Others like John Parastron were recruited from the province. The order abandoned its house in Constantinople in 1261, returning briefly between 1296 and 1307. It maintained its friary in Galata throughout the fourteenth century.

By 1260 the general assembly of the order in Narbonne noted that the province of Romania with its 20 convents ranked thirtieth amongst the provinces of the order. Apparently the Franciscans had expanded in continental Greece under the direction of Benedict of Arezzo, the former provincial of the March of Ancona. They were certainly there by 1223 and playing an active role in the political life of the principality. In that year they formed part of a deputation with two knights sent by Geoffrey I de Villehardouin to end the dispute between himself and the pope over the seizure of church endowments to pay for the construction of the castle at Chlemoutsi.[39] In 1277 part of the legal proceedings over Margaret de Neuilly's Akova inheritance were heard in the church of St Francis in Glarenza.[40] By 1260 they were grouped into three custodiae based on Negroponte, Thebes and Glarenza.[41] According to A.K. Orlandos, there was a Franciscan presence in Greece up to the seventeenth century as on Crete. The best preserved remains of their convents are in the Peloponnese at Blachernes near Glarenza where they seem to have occupied and extended a twelfth-century Byzantine church.[42]

---

[35] Pressutti, 2845, 3105.
[36] Wolff, art.cit., pp.214, 220.
[37] Wolff, art.cit., pp.228–9.
[38] Wolff, art.cit., p.230.
[39] X t M, 2659.
[40] L de C, 516; X t M, 7518.
[41] BMF, p.102.
[42] Panagopoulos, op.cit., pp.77–85.

The Dominicans, or friars preacher, were founded in 1215, a product of the work of St Dominic in preaching against the Albigensian heresy in the Languedoc. From its inception it was much more clerical and learned than the Franciscans. It had been rivalry with the Dominicans which had caused the Franciscans to shift their emphases in this direction and which had made them such a prominent missionary force in the east. The Dominicans seem to have entered the Aegean field later than the Franciscans and were established in Constantinople by 1228. However, it was for the Franciscans that the appellation '*phrerioi*' was reserved which suggests that the appeal of the Dominicans was to the more intellectual Greeks considering joining the Roman church. The brothers Andrew, Theodore and Maximos Chrysoberges and Manuel Kalekas joined the order in the early fifteenth century.[43]

The new Dominican province of Greece was created in 1228 but not specifically mentioned as such until 1241. Four convents were listed in 1228 at Thebes, Glarenza, Negroponte and Candia in Crete. By 1277 the number of houses had risen to seven with the additions of convents at Athens, Andravida and Modon. It was in the house of the friars preachers at Andravida in 1264 that Geoffrey I de Bruyeres came to accept the judgement of his peers regarding his elopement with the wife of Jean de Catavas, the victor of the battle of Prinitza.[44] The house in Constantinople was first mentioned in 1233 but was founded earlier. With the return of the Greeks to the city in 1261 it was closed. However, its members had played a significant part in the events of the Latin empire. In 1238 its prior, Jacobus, was responsible for actually transporting the crown of thorns to France and in return a number of French Dominicans were sent out to bolster the numbers in the house. In 1252 a certain brother Bartholomew wrote a treatise *Adversus errores Graecorum*. In 1299 the convent of SS Paolo e Domenico was opened in Galata, the new Genoese colony across the Golden Horn from Constantinople. A Dominican presence was thereafter maintained at various locations in Galata until the late seventeenth century.[45] The church of Santa Sophia at Andravida is the finest remains of a Dominican church in the Aegean. It is completely western in style and bears comparison with other Dominican churches of the west. This, however, is more than can be said for the grave-slab of Agnes de Courtenay (d. 1286) which it contains. The inscription is in Latin and in gothic script but it surrounds a field rich in Byzantine imagery.[46]

Other orders receive an occasional record in the sources. The prior and

---

[43] Lawrence, op.cit., pp.203–7; *ODB*, p.648.

[44] L de C, 410.

[45] Altaner, op.cit., pp.9–19; R-J. Loenertz, 'Les établissements dominicains de Pera-Constantinople', in *Byzantina et Franco-Graeca* (Rome, 1970), pp.209–26.

[46] Panagopoulos, op.cit., pp.65–77.

brothers of the Hospital of St Samson were established in Constantinople by early 1210 when a grant to them of the '*castellum quod Garelis vulgariter appellatum*' was confirmed by the pope.[47] The French and Aragonese versions of the *Chronicle of the Morea* also record the presence of the brothers of St Nicholas-de-Carmel at Andravida in 1264.[48] The crutched friars, another order of mendicants established in Italy by 1169, also had a house in Negroponte by 1256.[49]

The military orders

Material and documentary evidence for the deeds of the three great international military orders in mainland Greece is not abundant for the thirteenth and fourteenth centuries.[50] It is, however, sufficient for certain models to be advanced. The Templars took an active role in the conquest of central Greece in 1205–10. The Hospitallers tried in vain to stem the Turkish advance around 1400 as allies and rivals of the Venetians. Paradoxically the Teutonic order has left the best documented and most elusive sites for archaeological fieldwork.

During the thirteenth century the orders seemed content to use their Greek estates as sources of endowment. In the fourteenth century, the Teutonic order and, more especially, the Hospitallers took an active role against the Greeks of Mistra and then the Turks and their involvement became more overtly political. In both these activities they received considerable backing from popes and publicists in the west. Their mode of operation was not dissimilar to the activities of the Venetians in protecting their colonial possessions in the Aegean. Not only were Frankish and Greek potentates prepared to make considerable concessions to both the Hospitallers and the Venetians, but both were selective in what territories they took over and concerned to mount a common Christian front with the Greeks. In this both groups failed and by 1500 the whole Balkan peninsula was in Turkish hands. The material remains of the orders quickly disappeared – the names of their churches were changed, whilst their casals and castles have left few traces today.

On the face of it the three military orders seem to have played little role in the planning and execution of the Fourth Crusade. Villehardouin ignored the orders and Robert de Clari mentioned them only once but in connection with the story of Conrad of Montferrat and events in Jerusalem

---

[47] PL, 216:217 (doc.XVII).
[48] L de C, 410; L de F, 346.
[49] *Urkunden* III, pp.13–14.
[50] In the paragraphs which follow I have used my paper 'The Military Orders in Crusader Greece', in M. Barber, ed., *Fighting for the Faith and Caring for the Sick* (London, 1994) with kind permission of the publishers variorum (Ashgate Publishing Ltd.).

in 1185.[51] Not surprisingly this silence extends to modern historical works on the crusade, none of which mention the military orders.[52] Whilst this absence of evidence need not amount to evidence of absence, it does permit two models to be considered.

The first is that the orders took no hand in the crusade and such endowments as they received in Greece between 1206 and 1210 came as pious gifts in support of their work in the Holy Land, with such members as were present in the new Latin states arriving with the influx of Latins from the Holy Land in or soon after November 1204. Yet this is unlikely judging from the strong Lombard connections evident in the early days of the orders in Latin Greece. There is strong circumstantial evidence that the military orders, especially the Templars, played a considerable role in the conquest of Greece and that they hailed mainly from northern Italy. Quite apart from Clari's narrative aside which linked the orders with the interests of the house of Montferrat, three other points must be considered: namely the presence of Barozzi, a Venetian and the Master of the Temple, in Lombardy in Constantinople in May 1204, to whom the task of announcing the coronation of Baldwin of Flanders and presenting precious gifts to Innocent III was entrusted;[53] the support which the Templars were to give to the legitimist Lombard faction in Thessaly in 1208–9;[54] and above all the active acquisition of estates in central Greece and Thessaly, the very areas over which Boniface of Montferrat as ruler of Thessalonika claimed suzerainty.

The source for these land grants is the registers of Innocent III. In the middle of September 1210 the Templars sought papal confirmation of various grants that had been made to them since 1205. This action was brought about because of the political embarrassment caused by their unsuccessful support of the Lombard faction in Thessalonika in 1207–8. In early 1209 they lost both Ravennika, where there seems to have been some sort of repaired Byzantine fortification, and 'Sydonius', or Lamia, where they had spent heavily on the construction of a castle.[55] Ravennika had been granted to the order by Boniface himself and Lamia had been a joint grant by his constable Amedée de Pofoy and Guido Pellavicino, both landowners with a need for help against the Greeks of Epiros as Pofoy's crucifixion in 1210 was to demonstrate. The emperor Henry, who did the confiscating, seems to have asserted his rights as overlord and perhaps chose to make an

---

[51] Clari, XXXIII (McNeal trans. p.62).
[52] See for example Queller, op.cit; J. Godfrey, *1204 The Unholy Crusade* (Oxford, 1980); J. Longnon, *Les Compagnons de Villehardouin* (Paris, 1978); and E.H. McNeal and R.L. Wolff in K. Setton, general ed., *A History of the Crusaders* II 2nd edn (Wisconsin, 1969), pp. 153–85.
[53] PL, 215:cols 447–54.
[54] Valenciennes, 671 strongly identified the Templar strongholds with the Lombard cause.
[55] PL, 216:323–4.

example of a military order to make this point more widely. No doubt he was spurred on by the presence of fortifications in these places, but whatever his fears the Templars resorted to appeals to the papal curia rather than to arms. With this example before her and with imperial backing, Margaret of Hungary disputed certain unnamed rights and possessions in the kingdom of Thessalonika granted to the Templars by her dead husband before September 1207.[56] These grants belonged to the very early days of the conquest and the same was true for the other grants for which confirmation was sought in September 1210. The papal legate, Benedict of Santa Susana, had granted them the house of Philokalia in Thessalonika and the church of Fota or Fotini outside the walls of Thebes.[57] This church had been renamed Santa Lucia – an example of a Latin name encapsulating the meaning of the Greek dedication. Rolandino and Albertino da Canossa had granted them '*de Rupo*', presumably Sykamino near Oropos on the Attic coast, where a Templar castle was taken over by the Hospitallers in 1314.[58] The late archbishop of Thebes had given them a garden in Thebes 'when he had been archbishop elect', that is in August 1206, and Jacques d'Avesnes, who was dead by 1210, had conceded various estates and rights on Euboea.[59] Some of these grants, like the house of Lagnan and the casal of Oizparis, had been confirmed by the new ruler of the island, Ravanno dalle Carceri, but other rights he sought to retain for himself and were now a matter of dispute. It would appear that the initial grants to the Templars were considered over-generous by the second generation of settlers who perhaps did not look to Templar support as their immediate predecessors had done.

In the Peloponnese the Templars received the casal of Pasalin from William de Resi, the casal of Palaiopolin from Hugh of Bezanson and that of Luffestan from William de Champlitte; all of these grants were confirmed by Geoffrey de Villehardouin in 1210, who at that time or fairly soon after granted them four knights' fees as he did the Teutonic knights and the Hospitallers.[60] In Achaia there were disputes with the Archbishop of Patras over the monastery of Provata and the house of Gerocomita.[61]

The fortifying of some of these sites suggests that the Templars were actively involved in the subjugation of Greece. Given the state of the evidence this can be no more than an hypothesis but it seems to hold good. In 1206 the Latin emperor had granted Satalia to the Templars.[62] On the strength of the concentration of Templar lands in central Greece, Dr Hendrickx has identified this with the area of Satalia near Chalkis in

---

[56] PL, 216:230–1.
[57] PL, 216:327–8 (docs CXLIII, CXLV).
[58] PL, 216:328 (doc. CXLIV); *Revue de l'Orient Latin* III, 655.
[59] PL, 216:329, 331.
[60] PL, 216:329–30; L de C, 121; L de F, 131; X t M, 1951–3.
[61] PL, 216:331–2.
[62] PL, 216:1019.

Euboea. However, it is more likely to have been Satalia in western Turkey and to have formed one with the ambitious grants of yet unconquered lands which had been made to Renier de Trit, Louis de Blois and Étienne du Perche as dukes of Philippopolis, Nicaea, and Philadelphia respectively and to the Hospitallers at Pergamum.[63] If this identification is correct it certainly places the Templars in the context of conquest.

The same can be said on a limited scale for both the Hospitallers and the Teutonic knights, although the latter as a relatively new and poor order played a more constrained role. In 1210 the Knights of St John had seized the castle of Gardiki from the Latin diocesan. Gardiki in the Pindos Mountains was a precarious outpost of Latin rule and the town must have been lost by June 1212 when Larissa was reoccupied by the Greeks.[64] The Teutonic order did not enjoy the same freedom of action for many decades. Certainly it received four fees in Messenia soon after 1210, but as late as 1237 its resources were considered only sufficient to defend Chlemoutsi castle.[65]

After the first four years of conquest, the sources suggest a passive role for the orders in Greece. In the *Chronicle of the Morea* they appear to have played no significant part in the defence of either Thebes or Constantinople in the mid-1230s nor to have participated in the Pelagonia campaign of 1259. The specific locations of the properties of the orders in the Peloponnese are not securely known.[66] They seem to have been either in north-west Messenia around Kalamata or in Elis.[67] One thing that is certain is that they were not in Skorta which was the area in which conquests were to be made up to 1249. Indeed the Greek version of the chronicle, in explaining the conflict between Villehardouin and the Church in 1219, suggests that neither the Templars nor the Hospitallers were prepared to help in any way in the subjection of the area.[68] The three orders do not seem to have offered much hope of assistance to the Latin empire either. In 1246 the emperor Baldwin II approached the Spanish order of Santiago to provide a force of 1,500 warriors for two years in return for land in Constantinople and 40,000 marks.[69] The scheme never materialised but it does show a

---

[63] B. Hendrickx, 'Régestes des Empereurs Latins de Constantinople (1204–1261/72)' *Byzantina* 14 (1985), 37; Villehardouin, 304–5, 311, 316; R. Rodd, *The Princes of Achaia and the Chronicles of the Morea* 2 vols (London, 1908), I, p.65.

[64] PL, 216:304, 307–8; D.M. Nicol, *The Despotate of Epiros* (Oxford, 1957), pp.36–7.

[65] E. Strehlke, *Tabulae ordinis Theutonici* (Berlin, 1860), p.134, doc. 133; Alan Forey, *The Military Orders* (London, 1992), p.39.

[66] BMF, p.100.

[67] W. Miller, *The Latins in the Levant* (London, 1908), p.52; C. Hodgetts and P. Lock, 'The topography of Venetian Messenia', in P. Lock and G. Sanders, eds, *Essays on the Medieval Archaeology of Greece* (Oxford, forthcoming). I owe information on the German investigations near Olympia regarding Mostenitsa to verbal communication from Col. Erhard P. Opsahl.

[68] X t M, 2631–720; BMF, p.95.

[69] Forey, op.cit., p.39.

disinclination on the part of the orders to become involved militarily in the Aegean in the mid-thirteenth century.

After 1312 the Hospitallers became the most powerful order in Greece when they acquired all former Templar property in Achaia and Crete. Lands seem to have changed hands whilst enquiries into Templar activities, begun in August 1308, were still in progress. The Hospitallers received charge of the hospital of Saint Sampson in Corinth in 1309 together with the casal of Palaiopolis,[70] and in November 1310 all proceeds from the Templar lands in central Greece were to be handed over to Duke Gautier I de Brienne to resist the frequent incursions '... *a graecis scismaticis de imperio Romanie ...*'.[71] In 1310 and 1311 the inquisition and torture of the Templars proceeded only in Achaia and Crete.[72] Presumably the disturbed nature of central Greece made it difficult to gain custody of the Templars and their lands there, but what about Euboea where the Venetian baili exercised reasonable control? The actual fate of the Templars in Greece is unknown. Presumably it was no different than that of Templars elsewhere. However, they were probably few in number and the opportunities to avoid detention much greater than in western Europe.

In 1314 the former Templar lands in central Greece did not pass directly to the Hospitallers as did those lands in the Morea and Crete. Instead they were assigned to Gautier de Châtillon, the constable of France and grandfather and guardian of Gautier II de Brienne, the infant lord of Athens whose father had been killed by the Catalan Company near Halmyros in March 1311. Nonetheless, the Hospitallers acquired the former Templar stronghold at Sykomino in Attica, perhaps by agreement with Gautier to give the order a material interest in the Briennist cause.[73]

During the fourteenth century the attitude of the orders in Greece changed from one of economic exploitation to one of active military participation.[74] The brethren are recorded as taking part in battles. For example the *Libros de los Fechos* noted the death of the preceptor of the Teutonic order during the defence of the castle of St George in Elis about 1320.[75] The campaigns of Andronikos Asen in the Alpheios valley after 1316 seemed to have provoked a reaction amongst the Teutonic knights which previous Greek campaigns in the same valley in 1262–63 had not.[76]

---

[70] Register Clement V, III, 3401, 3415, 3515; IV, 1000; L de F, 588, see Innocent III, PL, 216:329–30 for Templar possessions at Picotin near Palaiopolis.
[71] Register Clement V, V, 5768.
[72] Register Clement V, VI, 7597, 7600, 7606.
[73] DOC, no. LXIII, (pp.78–9); J. Delaville le Roulx, *Les Hospitaliers à Rhodes* ... (Paris, 1913), p.201 attests the existence of two commanders, one for the Morea and one for the Duchy of Athens in late 1330. See also BMF, p.243, n.6 and Miller, op.cit., p.239.
[74] A. Luttrell, 'The crusade in the Fourteenth Century', in J.R. Hale et al., eds, *Europe in the Late Middle Ages* (London, 1965), pp.129, 139–44.
[75] L de F, 652.
[76] Note the silence of L de C, 320–46.

The loss of Acre in 1291 may have increased their interest in their Greek lands at a time when Greek raids threatened those interests and inclined them to shoulder their feudal obligations to the princes of Achaia and their bailis. In June and July 1324 Nicholas, the preceptor of the Teutonic knights at Mostenitsa, and Jean de Baux, the commander of the Hospitalliers in Greece, were ordered, along with fourteen other liege vassals of the principality, to appear at Glarenza ready for a campaign against the Greeks of Mistra.[77]

Just as warfare had removed the Templar properties in central Greece as a source of re-endowment after 1311, so ten years later endemic raids and official wars threatened the substance and the safety of the orders and their neighbours in the Morea. In addition to Greek campaigns from Mistra, the Catalans and their Turkish auxiliaries raided for slaves along the Corinthian Gulf. Prior to the 1370s the Hospitallers, preoccupied with Rhodes, seemed disinclined to follow up the numerous papal directives to move against the Catalans and were content to leave the defence of the Morea to the Venetians. Indeed one of the principals in the negotiations in 1321 to turn the Morea into a Venetian protectorate was Jean de Baux.[78] However, the advance of the Turks in the southern Balkans brought the frontier to the Morea and from the early 1340s, as Norman Housley has noted, the Turk became the main foe of crusading activity, the naval league its main expression and Romania the front line.[79]

Within Greece the task of defence fell to the Hospitallers and the Venetians. Both parties took a more active role in the diplomacy and administration of Romania and were prepared to create protectorates over territories no longer governable or defensible by their rulers.[80] Dr Luttrell has examined the chronology and the pitfalls of the leasing of the principality of Achaia by the Hospital in 1377.[81] In 1399 the Greek governor of the Morea ceded Corinth and Mistra to the knights for a year because of the invasion of Yakoub Pasha.[82] The *Chronicle of Galaxeidi* written in 1703 gives an account of an abortive three-month naval operation in the Gulf of Itea in 1404 mounted by the knights from three galeotes and intended to capture Salona.[83] The knights provided funding to the inhabitants of Galaxeidi for a church of St John of Jerusalem which was built and renamed Panteleimon on their evacuation, and substantial

---

[77] Rodd, op.cit., II, p.157.

[78] Register Clement V, VII, 72–3, 125, 338; VIII, 14, 131–2; IX, 44–7; Rodd, op.cit., II, 157.

[79] N. Housley, *The Later Crusades* (Oxford, 1992), p.59.

[80] R.J. Loenertz, *Byzantina et Franco-Graeca* I (Roma, 1970), pp.21–2 and 329–69.

[81] A. Luttrell, *Byzantinische Zeitschrift* 57 (1964), 342–7.

[82] Loenertz, op.cit., pp.21–2.

[83] C.N. Sathas, *Chronikon anekdoton Galaxeidiou* (Athens, 1865), pp.208–9. See John Rosser in Lock and Sanders, eds, op.cit.

financial aid to the villagers of Loidoriki and Vitrinitsa to revolt against the Turks. Church construction by the Hospitallers for Greek communities specifically as a means of cementing a Latino-Greek front against the Turks in the late fourteenth century might well have extended beyond Galaxeidi. It might also explain the reconstruction of the church recently found in 1990 at the west end of the former Roman forum in Corinth. It appears that its rebuilding as a free-standing church after its destruction by the Catalans in 1312 may well belong to the period when the Hospitallers occupied the city at the end of the fourteenth century.[84]

The archaeological record of the military orders in Greece is elusive.[85] We really know nothing of the whereabouts of the fiefs granted at various times to the three orders. Even a relatively well-documented site such as the headquarters of the Teutonic order at Mostenitsa has been sought in Messenia and in Elis and may point to relocation of the order between 1220 and 1320.[86] Toponyms are rare and sherding can only point to a period rather than to a century. Even the much mentioned 'German House' at Modon lies unrecognised in the grid of streets awaiting excavation.[87]

[84] *Hesperia* 61 (1992), 133–91; ibid., 62 (1993), 1–52.
[85] Panagopoulos, op.cit., p.66; S. Symeonoglou, *The Topography of Thebes* (Princeton, 1985), p.167; W. Leake, *Travels in the Morea* II (London, 1830), pp. 103–5; Rodd, op.cit., I, pp.163–4 for some of the problems.
[86] X t M, 1955; article 48 of the Assizes of Romania; Miller, op.cit., pp.52, 392; BMF, p.243.
[87] Miller, op.cit., pp.344, 495.

Chapter 10 ....

Economic Aspects of the Frankish Aegean

Sources and variables

In western Europe the possession of Romania by the Franks was perceived to have been a good thing. Both popes and merchants saw it as a land of wealth and opportunity, whilst the Genoese and Venetians fought a series of wars in the fourteenth century in order to gain the monopoly of its exploitation. The crusading leadership saw wealth in terms of land, as did the church authorities. For the first 20 years of the Frankish occupation they too were locked in dispute over the proportion of the land of the Aegean to be assigned to the church. There was, then, not just a perception of Aegean wealth but a very real move to exploit it. Such opinions and activities cannot be ignored. Yet it is difficult to see in what this agricultural wealth actually consisted and the mechanisms for its exploitation, and impossible to attempt any quantification of either agricultural production or commercial trans-actions.

Two major problems confront the student of the Aegean economy in the later middle ages. First, the sources are scanty indeed for any demographic or economic study. All the evidence is indirect. It is either circumstantial, much of it derived by implication from narrative sources, or it is comparable but derived from territories no longer in western hands or from too late or too early a period. The direct evidence of travellers is undoubtedly useful in gaining an impression of a particular area, but they are usually late in date and limited in the generality of their observations. Like travel writers in any age they emphasised the positive. This tendency is evident as early as 1191 in the observations on the area around Monemvasia recorded by Benedict of Peterborough who wrote that '... *in toto mundo non est locus ubi sit tanta copia olii olivarum ...*', and three centuries later observations in a similar vane were written by Cristofero Buondelmonti concerning the large plains on Naxos covered with vines and

240

fruit trees.[1] A less subjective view might be provided by the investigations of archaeological pathologists and palaeobotanists. These certainly can provide information regarding sex ratios, aging and disease as well as diet. However, practitioners are thin on the ground and the paucity of cemetery excavation in western Europe as a whole, let alone in the Aegean in particular, means that it will be some time before any considerable information is available. It appears that indicators so beloved by modern economic commentators are all that we have. Thus we are well-informed on the commodities traded within the Aegean and exported from it, but we have few reliable clues as to the size of any particular trade or of its periodic fluctuations, of agricultural productivity or demesne organisation.

Agricultural productivity was fundamental to all other activities in the middle ages: a truism applicable everywhere. We accept it for the Aegean, yet do we get much further when we seek for data in its support? In agriculture it is just not possible to quantify populations, agricultural yields, the proportion of demesne to rented land, incomes or revenues. The size and legal position of the peasantry is a matter of controversy, leaving aside any data regarding their standard of living. British medievalists used to the relative abundance and sophistication of evidence pertaining to medieval English estate administration, cannot expect the same level of comment on the baronial estates in the Aegean, where the evidence is simply lacking. Indeed in the English-speaking world we have long been prepared for this, by being presented as undegraduates with large tomes on particular English medieval estates and much thinner volumes on the economic history of medieval Europe.

The result is a picture in which change for better or worse can be subjectively viewed but not conclusively known. Where hard evidence is lacking, we must beware of sweeping statements. For example, the effect of the Black Death in Greece in 1348 is not known.[2] It is generally assumed that something like one-third of the population succumbed. Yet Greece was always a much more rural country than England, with the bulk of its population living in villages or hamlets. The concentrations of poor urban dwellers, the main victims of plague in England, were not present in the Aegean, outside Constantinople and Thessalonika, and even there they are postulated rather than recorded. Indeed from mainland Greece there are just two notices of labour shortages, widely spaced in time and perhaps only in part attributable to the plague. The scale of activity and change is lacking. The problems are well explained by Aglaia Kasdagli in her article on Naxos.[3]

---

[1] W. Stubbs, ed., *Benedict of Peterborough, Vita et Gesta Henrici II Angliae Regis* II (London, 1867), p.200; E. Legrand, ed., *Christophe Buondelmonti, Description des îles de l'Archipel* (Paris, 1897), pp.56–8.

[2] A.E. Laiou-Thomadakis, *Peasant Society in the Late Byzantine Empire* (Princeton, 1977), p.7.

[3] A.E. Kasdagli, 'Peasant and lord in fifteenth century Naxos' *ByzF* 11 (1987), 347–55.

This introduces the second problem, that of substantial regional variations. Naxos was one of the largest, well-watered and most fertile of the two hundred or so Aegean islands. After 1207 it was the centre of the duchy of the Archipelago and remained in western hands until 1564. For the Venetians it was a major source for the abrasive mineral corundum, which the Greeks called '*smeridion*' and which word entered Venetian Italian as '*smeriglio*' in the thirteenth century.[4] It is also the most mountainous island of the Cyclades and this has created a variety of micro-economies just within its small area of 442 square kilometres. On the uplands there are marble quarries and pasture; cutting into it are many fertile valleys which produce olives, citrus fruits and vegetables and also containing many towers, a mark of agricultural prosperity. If one island has so many differences, let alone contrasts, with the other seventeen islands in the Cycladic group, the difficulty in writing of the Aegean economy can be envisaged. The disparity of documentary survival, both with regard to time and place, can make this summary highly provisional only.

The manifestations of trade and industry in towns is equally elusive. It is only in the 1380s with the Navarrese assault on the towns of central Greece, that some glimpse is afforded of the organisation of the urban community in that region. The archaeological manifestations of urbanism are scant too in the high medieval period. In a region in which the town was the earliest recorded unit of settlement and the city-state the arena for political activity, focus has been placed on the survival of towns from antiquity. In the absence of evidence opinion has not been slow in coming forward and this has led to a diversity of models being advanced. In general the field has been held by those who would paint a muted picture with apparently little agricultural colonisation and no urban revival. The plaints of papal letters pointing to destruction in the towns and countryside with concomitant rural depopulation have been taken to support this view. Only very recently has the view from the west been supplemented by the study of the Byzantine economy in terms of the expansion evident in the west in the twelfth century. This setting of Byzantium within a broader medieval European framework has served to replace the traditional model of a declining Byzantine economy with one of growth and renewal. We still may not know a great deal about the Frankish economy in Greece but we do at least have some reliable comparative material by which to measure what we have. The most hopeful historical sources yet to be tapped are the notarial documents in the archives of Venice, Genoa and Malta. Most of these await study and certainly publication. It is from the transcription and study of the lists of property, commercial and personal contracts and the like which they contain that most light will be shed on this currently intractable area.

---

[4] H. and R. Kahane, 'Byzantium's impact on the west: the linguistic evidence' *Illinois Classical Studies* 6 (1981), 389–415, esp. p.401.

Population

In a pre-industrial society in which the sources of energy were natural and renewable, namely wind and water power and animal and human muscle, the size of the agrarian population provided both the stimulus for and the only means by which agrarian productivity could be increased. For Frankish Greece the sources do not exist for demographic analysis to be carried out. However, recent work on the Byzantine agrarian economy by Alan Harvey and others has suggested that the twelfth century was a period of economic expansion and of consequent population growth, and that this growth continued into the early fourteenth century. Death was ever present and life-expectancy of around 35 was comparable with figures for the west. The impact of war and epidemics is not certainly known, although the burning of fields and slaughter of livestock cannot have made a hard life any easier. Some Byzantine praktika of the fourteenth century dealing with southern Macedonia together with material from estates of the Athonite monasteries of Lavra and Iveron at Gomatou in Chalkidiki have been used in this respect.[5]

In 1047 the monastery of Iveron had a domain extending to 10,800 acres containing some 246 families of paroikoi. Within 50 years the number of families had risen to 294 and by the early fourteenth century to 460. The trend upwards is unmistakeable. In central Greece too in the area between Thebes and Chalkis described in the portion of the so-called Thebes cadaster surviving from the sale of klasmatic land (land abandoned by its cultivators) has been taken to show the expansion of the area under cultivation rather than an indicator of decline as previously. Angeliki Laiou has undertaken an analysis of the population of Gomatou as revealed in praktika surviving from 1300–1, 1316–17, 1321 and 1347. Allowing for all the biases and adjustments necessary in using material from praktika, especially the lack of age definitions and the under-registering of women who were not heads of households, a picture of a rural society not markedly backward in pre-industrial terms does emerge. This picture does not conflict with population increase and bears comparison in terms of life expectancy with figures for England produced by Russell: a figure of 22 per 1,000 net births per year, a sex-ratio of around 105 males per 100 females and a life expectancy at birth of 25 years, compared with 30 for England in the early fourteenth century.[6] It would appear that at the beginning of the thirteenth century the Franks took possession of a settled and flourishing land in which the population was growing. Just how that translated into material terms we must now attempt to see.

---

[5] A. Harvey, 'Economic expansion in central Greece in the eleventh century' *Byzantine & Modern Greek Studies* 8 (1982–3), 21–8 for discussion of this material and the debate on demographic trends.
[6] Laiou-Thomadakis, op.cit., pp.267–98.

Frankish Greece, like the rest of medieval Europe, was predominantly rural and agrarian. The rate of agricultural production underpinned any urban and industrial development. Judging from what we know of the size of towns in the thirteenth century and the reports, almost certainly exaggerated, of the people taken by Catalan and Turkish slavers, it can be said that like the rest of medieval Europe the bulk of the population lived in the countryside in hamlets and villages. Just how large this population was is impossible to say. We are afforded a glimpse of this rural economy in the surveys of the Acciaioli estates in the south-west Peloponnese in the middle of the fourteenth century.[7] These are inventories rather than accounts, and late in date.

From the point of view of demography information is given on five Messenian villages in the years 1354 and 1357. Following Peter Topping, who used a hearth-multiplier of four for each of the peasant households recorded, the following figures emerge from the five settlements: Kremmidhi (Ano and Kato Kremmidhi) contained 228 persons and 21 deserted hearths, equivalent to 84 persons; Grizi (Akritochori), 268 hearths and no desertions; Kosmina (site lost but near Longa) 312 persons and 17 deserted hearths; Voulkano (site unknown, but perhaps Ithome) 244 persons, 14 deserted hearths and a further 3 deserted holdings which had been planted with vines for the lord; and Petoni (unknown) with 304 persons and 14 deserted households. It must be stressed that these figures are estimates and for guidance only. All the settlements are large by south Balkan standards, but they cannot be used to ascertain either settlement density or even a guess at the population of the area. Two of the villages, Kosmina and Petoni, were in the hands of two or more Frankish lords. Rents from the tenants being the main, if not the only, form of income for some of these lesser knights.

The high proportion of deserted hearths, some 30 per cent, must be in part explicable by the plague, although the process of desertion was underway in the 1330s. The Venetian senate noted the ravages of the plague in Coron and Modon in February 1348 and sent out one hundred mercenaries and artisans to make up the losses of which four caulkers, four masons, four carpenters and two joiners were specifically listed to be part of the reinforcements. The losses seem to have been urban and Italian. On Crete the toll was more severe and scarcely an estate was reported to have sufficient labour to bring in the harvest of grape and grain. Yet in 1363 Negroponte was reported as being sufficiently repopulated, presumably by immigration.[8] The commutation of the angaria, or services owed to the lord, for cash payments seemed to have caused substantial flights of peasant cultivators. First in Modon and Coron when it was levied at 58½ sterlings

---

[7] Longnon & Topping. For discussion see P. Topping in W. McDonald & G. Rapp, eds, *The Minnesota Messenia Expedition* (Minneapolis, 1972), pp.66–9.
[8] Thiriet, 209, 214.

per year in 1347, and again in 1402 on Negroponte more than 1,000 families left the island rather than pay an angaria of 50 sous, dubbed '*el capanicho*' at 50 sous. The demand for coin both prompted the exodus and showed that the use of coinage was becoming foreign to the peasantry of Frankish Greece. It is not possible to assign a priority of purpose behind village desertion. It is no new phenomenon in Greece, caused today by the influx of the younger generation to Athens. Security was an important factor. As we have seen the refugee problem does not seem to have been a serious one in 1204. Indeed Choniates complained of the welcome accorded the Franks in central Greece. Yet in 1311 there was a flow of refugees from Boeotia into Negroponte with the arrival of the Catalans, and again in 1435 with a succession dispute which involved the Turks.[9] The Aegean was more dangerous in the fourteenth century. Those not prepared to migrate resorted to fortifying their villages by means of planting barriers of prinari or prickly oak (Quercus coccifera) around them. The sites of villages too might relocate. The motive behind this is not always clear where inland sites are concerned. Sometimes there are strong oral traditions of village movement as from old Mavrommation between Halyartos and Panaghia in Boeotia to the present site in the foothills near Vayia. This tradition seems to have something to do with the influx of Albanians into the region in the mid-fourteenth century and may have more to do with discovering the amenities of a site through trial and error than the search for security. Nonetheless, the village does have its prickly hedge surround. At Leukosia on the Boeotian side of the south Euripos channel the present village is in the inland foothills, whereas the former site was on the coast. The loss of sites since the Acciaioli surveys were completed would be in part due to this movement of settlement, both from one inland site to another and more especially from the coast to an inland site which should alert us to the role of the search for security in the face of warfare and piratical raids in this process. Migration seems to have been unstoppable and could be used, as in the case of the Albanian migrants into central Greece, to settle areas depopulated by plague or migration of the former inhabitants. There are some but very, very few laments on labour shortages. It would appear that despite razzias and wars, the population continued to increase and the losses to have been made up in part by natural means and in part by immigration from Epiros.

Latin estate farming

The nobles and their armies that moved into continental Greece reckoned wealth and status in terms of land. There is some indication that agricultural

---

[9] DOC, no.CCCLXXXIV; Thiriet, 2396.

profits were increasing in the 1220s and 1230s. In 1217 Geoffrey I de Villehardouin had had to use the revenues of the church in order to pay for the construction of the castle at Chlemoutsi, a situation that would suggest that his own revenues were insufficient. Within 20 years his successors were making substantial annual payments of 22,000 hyperpera to the emperor in Constantinople and hiring armies for campaigns in Euboea and Thessaly in 1258 and 1259. He was not alone in this. There were other rich men whose income derived from their estates. As we have seen Jean de la Roche could indulge in castle building and in military campaigns in Thessaly. Othon de Cicon, lord of Karystos, had loaned the emperor Baldwin 5,000 hyperpera of gold, which was repaid in October 1261 by the gift of the right hand of John the Baptist, the very hand which had baptised Christ in the Jordan and which Othon passed to Citeaux via the abbot of Daphni.[10] Finally, bankers like the Acciaioli were prepared to accept estates around Kalamata as full payment for the debts of various members of the Angevin family in the 1330s. How did they exploit their lands and were they in any sense colonisers or improvers?

Information on the exploitation of estates in Greece by western lords comes almost entirely from the twelve documents published by Jean Longnon and Peter Topping in 1969.[11] Virtually all of these documents deal with the lands of the Acciaioli in the Peloponnese and, with the exception of two short accounts of receipts, are surveys of potential rather than of actual production. South Italian practices seem to have been used in the organisation of the properties, and perhaps this had always been the case, but we must be careful not to assume that what we read in these documents typifies Frankish agricultural exploitation or may be used to characterise the thirteenth century. However, it does provide some guidance and, until the discovery of more evidence, a provisional view of casal exploitation.

An important man like Niccolo Acciaioli who owned many estates or casals was represented by a vicar in the Peloponnese. In the mid-1350s the vicar was a certain Jacopo Buzuti of Brindisi. He fulfilled all Niccolo's responsibilities as liegeman in the principality of Achaia and it was he who oversaw the repair and refurbishment of Nicclo's splendid tower at Christiana (Krestena) in 1354.[12] The tower had a gilded roof and private apartments. Sadly it no longer survives and its precise location is as yet unknown. It was clearly a tower for an important lord and possessed many amenities not found in the towerhouses of lesser vassals.

Leaving aside the vassals who owed knight service, the various casals or estates farmed by the lord were divided into demesne land and peasant holdings or stasia. The former was known as messaria after the Neapolitan

---

[10] Setton, p.95; see p.225.
[11] Longnon & Topping.
[12] Ibid., p.71.

practice. The messariae seemed to have been united in regional groupings under a magister masserie; in 1365 a certain Teodoro or Thedore was magister for those lands in the castellany of Corinth. Certain towers and castles had garrisons of archers, who judging from the Krestena list of 1354 were all Greeks. Their legal status is unknown but in the unsettled conditions of the time they were probably kept for use rather than display. There were nineteen of them at Krestena, presumably lodged in the tower which has since disappeared. None seem to have had any family relationship with the paroikoi of that casal, although the surname of four of them, Stasino, might suggest a paroikos background. At Voulkano all the archers were paroikoi and rendered the acrosticon and the grape tax; in the castle of Arcangeli there were 36 archers commanded by a Greek comestabulus argeriorum, one Costa Chosalinos.[13]

Much of the lord's revenue came from the rents and other Byzantine state taxes, now classed as customary dues payable to the lord by his paroikoi. Neither the income of any Latin lord nor the proportions of peasant dues to agricultural profits derived from the messariae is known. Much of the latter, with the notable exception of surplus wine, figs and raisins, seems to have been stored in the castles and towers of his estates for local consumption rather than for wholesale or export. In these Acciaioli records each casal is listed separately and its peasant farmers assessed to the acrosticon casal by casal. It is assumed from this that each estate was centred around a village community and that each estate was both self-contained and self-sufficient.

The peasant paid an acrosticon reckoned on the size of his stasia holding and the number of his animals. The amounts rendered by the head of each family varied. At Krestena in 1354 the total payment of fifteen households was 80 hyperpera and 15 sterlings. Sixteen stasia were recorded as deserted (stasia apora, stasia deserta or eremustasi), five of which were in the hands of the lord. This high rate of abandonment for whatever reason was not good for the lord's income. The large numbers of archers, usually agriculturally unproductive, might suggest that Turkish raids were responsible.

Exceeding the acrosticon and the servicio in value were the variety of payments or banalities to be made 'pro aliis juribus'. Perhaps the most important was the gemorum or payment of one-tenth of the crops of those who held land from the lord, free and unfree alike.[14] So important was this due that a special class of servants, the gienmoratori, cienmoratori or zemoratori were employed in its collection. In 1365 in the Corinth region three Latins were listed as holding this office, whilst in Grebeni in 1354, a paroikos, Theodore Mabrudi, was exempt from paying the acrosticon and

---

[13] Ibid., pp.72, 88, 99.
[14] Ibid., pp.61/39, 60/20, 100/23, 164/12, 190/27, 269.

labour services in return for overseeing the receipt of the gemorum.[15] The relationship of the gemorum to the ycomedium and ycometrum or mostoforia, which seem to be payments on natural products and grape-pressing by the community to the lord, is unclear. The arico or larico was a fine levied on the damage caused by wandering sheep and pigs. Pigs figured prominently on the estates of Kosmina where a decima porcorum raised 24 hyperpera 18 sterlings. Were pigs sold on to the Venetians in Messenia for ship supplies? There was certainly a bakery for ship's biscuit at Modon and pork was to be produced by Moslem farmers in the area in the late fifteenth century for the very purpose of nautical provisions for non-Moslems.[16] The preda was an impost on grazing animals.[17] This and the decima porcorum might often have been included in the acrosticon payment. In the 1354 account for Petoni these animal charges were singled out as they were occasionally in the accounts of Aldobrando Baroncelli for his master Angelo Acciaioli in 1379.[18] The commerclum was of uncertain import in an estate context but an impost regularly exacted,[19] and the ius limbrosii a charge on the use of steeping-tanks for retting flax.[20] The ius salinorum of 3 sterlings for each modius or load of salt brought from the lords salines was recorded at Kosmina in 1336. There was also profit to be made on the use of the lord's mill both for the grinding of corn and the pressing of olives. The ius carpeci of 1½ hyperpera per measure of oil produced at the tarpetum or olive press was recorded twice in 1336/7 at Kosmina. Some 30 mills are mentioned in the surveys. To refer to just three, a one-quarter share of the mill at Amacona was worth 6 hyperpera, a half-share in that at Kalyvia 15 hyperpera, whilst the mill at Kothiki brought an annual return of 20 hyperpera.[21] The assigning of monetary values to the various services and dues would suggest that a process of commutation was in progress. Judging from the reaction of the paroikoi in the Venetian colonies noted above, the impetus for this came from above and was not popular. It is noteworthy that only one payment totally in kind was actually recorded in these documents as being made. That was in June 1336 when 'Stammati presbiter Catuzopulus pro suo annuo redditu yperperum unum et libram unam, gallinas quinque, ova triginta et, omnibus in pecunia computatis, yperperum unum sterl. sedecim et medium'.[22] Even then he fell slightly short in his payment. From the inventory of 1338, many of those

---

[15] Ibid., pp.127/21, 170/6, 171/24, 176/3, 270.
[16] Ibid., p.78/21, 80/13, 81/7, 275; P. Topping, 'Le Regime agraire dans le Peloponnese latin au XIVe siecle' *L'Helenisme contemporain* 10 (1956), 255–95, reprinted idem, *Studies on Latin Greece* (London, 1977).
[17] Longnon & Topping, pp.38/12, 201/3, 210/15, 275.
[18] Ibid., pp.103, 200ff.
[19] Ibid., pp.139/36, 146/20, 162/1, 275–5.
[20] Ibid., pp.38/13, 275.
[21] Ibid., pp.25/38, 38/8, 78/18.
[22] Ibid., p.26/33–5; see Topping, art.cit., pp.265–6 for discussion.

listed in Krestena as having left their stasie were recorded as those who also paid in kind.[23] The grant of estates to Niccolo Acciaioli in June 1338 listed virtually every household in Petoni as paying partly in kind and partly in cash.[24] Wax seems to have continued to be an acceptable form of payment for small amounts. Was there a decline in the status of the poorer paroikoi going on here? Certainly in his accounts of November 1379 Aldobrando Baroncelli made frequent mention of having received cash payments.[25]

The inventories give us a somewhat static picture but they do reveal that the chief crops from the Acciaioli estates were wine, olives, olive oil, and grain. The grain products were wheat, barley, oats, millet and a type of vetch called rovi. This last together with the oats and millet may have constituted animal feedstuffs. Mainland Greece does not seem to have been self-sufficient as regards wheat. During the 1290s Florent de Hainault had arranged for the importation of wheat from southern Italy, whilst the Cretan wheat-fields were used as a source of imports into Messenia and Negroponte by the Venetian authorities during the early fourteenth century. Other products included honey, wax, raisins, figs, nuts, oranges, cotton, flax, linen, carobs and valonia. As we shall see roving Venetian merchants operating mainly from Modon and Negroponte bought up wax, figs, wine, cotton and valonia and were encouraged by their government to take these products to Negroponte for transport to Venice on the galley of Romania. Just how much of these products were so sold is unclear. Wine was a major surplus product and seems to have been sent by boat from Corinth to Glarenza and hence the figuring of '*labboraggio*', the lading of boats with wine, in the castellany of Corinth in October 1365, just after the grape harvest in late August/early September.[26] The sale of figs and raisins seems to have been an important cash crop for the Greek smallholder. In 1360 there were serious riots outside the castles of Argos and Nauplion when Averardo de'Medici, the baili of Guy d'Enghien, tried to restrict the sale of these commodities.[27]

The Acciaioli also exploited the forests on their estates. Article 159 of the Assizes of Romania set aside the forests for the supply of castles, which suggests some form of forest management on many Latin estates. Forest dwellers could use trees which bore no fruit to build houses and to make fire. Acorns which lay on the ground were available as mast for pigs, but the rest were harvested for dyeing. A distinction was drawn between forest belonging to lords and the wild forest which was common to all. Interestingly no mention was made of sheep and goats, the great browsers and deforesters of the modern Greek landscape. The Acciaioli owned two

---

[23] Longnon & Topping, pp.65/22–66/6.
[24] Ibid., pp.59/8–61/23.
[25] Ibid., pp.204/9, 21, 205/20, 28.
[26] Ibid., pp.162/17, 277.
[27] A. Luttrell, 'The Latins of Argos and Nauplia' *PBSR* 21 (1966), 34–55, esp. p.39.

forests of Aleppo pines known as the '*arveri de rasa*' at Blemma and at Capicianu which Topping has suggested lay along the Agoulinitsa Lagoon near Krestena.[28] As well as a source of wood, resin and pitch used for ship construction, pine was the favoured building timber in its area of distribution south of the Kithairon Range in Boeotia.[29] The resinous wood was also used to make tapers for household lighting and the cones were used to flavour wine.[30] In 1354 unspecified timbers, presumably pine, were used in the construction of the roof and drawbridge for the tower at Krestena.[31] Many of these timber products were presumably used within the local economy, but there must have been some demand for the export of timbers and pitch to Venice. Although there is mention of some silk production on the Acciaioli estates, no mention was made of mulberry plantations.

Agricultural productivity measured in terms of cereal yields was low by modern standards but a yield of four to five times the seed sown on the most fertile estates was comparable in proportions to that on the estates of the bishop of Winchester in England at about the same time.[32] From the 1379 account, the harvest at Krestena brought in 40 measures of wheat less 8 for seed, 9 measures of oats less 7½ for seed and 20 measures of barley less 12 for seed. At nearby Kremmidhi the wheat yield was 35½ measures less 8 for seed. The wheat yield from the casals of Sperone and Machona was significantly worse, the proportions of wheat yield to seed sown being 40:26 and 13:8 respectively. Behind these figures lay the usual reasons cited – poor estate management resulting in lack of manure, too many weeds and over-cropping, together with lack of peasant motivation. War and the disturbed military situation in general cannot have helped. The soil was too poor for good grain yields and vines were the favoured crop.[33]

From these few accounts and other sparse fragments from the thirteenth century, it is of course impossible to assess to what extent the Franks as landowners invested any of their receipts in making permanent improvements to their estates. Although we have virtually no data from village studies to indicate the peasant standard of living in medieval Greece, it is generally assumed that at the tenant level there was a preoccupation with subsistence farming and the production of a surplus for seed and to pay the fairly substantial dues to their lord. From the lord's point of view a

---

[28] Ibid., p.71/12–13; Topping in McDonald and Rapp, eds, op.cit., p.67.

[29] O. Rackham, 'Observations on the historical ecology of Boeotia' *ABSA* 78 (1983), 291–352.

[30] E. Slatter, *Xanthus* (London, 1994), pp.77–8 for these domestic uses of the pine in the nineteenth century.

[31] Longnon & Topping, p.71/2–6.

[32] D.L. Farmer, 'Grain yields on the Winchester manors in the latter Middle Ages' *Economic History Review* 30 (1977), 560.

[33] Ibid., 201–7; C. Dyer, *Standards of Living in the Latter Middle Ages* (Cambridge, 1989), p.127.

proportion of income was invested in storage and security such as the repair and construction of castles and towers and the support of archers in the case of the Acciaioli estates. Whatever military function a castle or tower might have, it was certainly a place of storage for the vintage and other crops. There was a certain amount of investment in infrastructure as attested by the maintenance of fish-ponds and salines, the construction of the bridge at Karytaina some time in the thirteenth century, and of course the number of free-standing towers in the countryside. In terms of tools and equipment little can be said and even less is known for certain. Of the mills recorded in the mid-fourteenth century inventories it is not recorded whether they were driven by animal, water or wind power. Certainly, none were identified as windmills, despite their supposed introduction of the post-mill to the Levant from the west at the time of the Third Crusade. The windmills which began to make their appearance in Byzantine records in the fourteenth century, first on the estates of Lavra in 1304, seemed to be an independent development which owed nothing to Frankish technological innovation.[34] Whether for status or security the bulk of investment in building seems to have been in the military sphere.

The Acciaioli of the early fourteenth century were comparable more with their Angevin masters in having interests in Italy rather than in Greece and as such they were interested in taking their profits out of the Morea, as indeed would have been the significant number of absentee Italian clerics with prebends there. The disturbed conditions of the peninsula married with ignorance and unfamiliarity with the conditions there made such long-distance realisation of assets no easy task. In late 1360 one Nicolas de Boiano was sent by Marie de Bourbon, the titular empress of Constantinople, on a revenue raising trip to her Moreote estates. Turkish raids caused many peasant cultivators to flee the empress's estates and bad weather had significantly hampered the grain and grape harvests. Nicolas succeeded in gathering together the equivalent of 2,000 ducats in cash which on arrival at Glarenza he could not change into gold for transportation. It would apear that abseentee Frankish landlords derived no substantial profits from their agricultural operations in the Morea. Of resident lords from the thirteenth century we have no information whatsoever.[35]

The products of the Aegean

One major result of the Fourth Crusade was that the Aegean became fully a part of the Mediterranean trade system, as much as the Adriatic and the

---

[34] J. Gimpel, *The Medieval Machine* 2nd edn (London, 1992), p.24; G. Demetrokalles, 'Hoi anemomyloi ton Byzantinon' *Parnassos* 20 (1978), 141–4.
[35] Ibid., 144–55, discussed by Topping in McDonald and Rapp, eds, op.cit., p.67.

Tyrrhenian Seas. As Professor Laiou has emphasised, after 1204 and more especially after the 1320s Byzantium and the Aegean became a hinterland to Italian-dominated markets. In terms of medieval economic history the Aegean and its offshoot the Black Sea had little meaning except in terms of the broader economy of the Mediterranean.[36] Venetian merchants became legally established in the new Latin empire of Romania and were able to expand their network of agents and consuls around the twice-yearly sailings of its merchant ships to and from Constantinople. Local maritime trade between Crete, Negroponte, Modon and Nauplion began to develop, and room was made in this carrying trade for Greek vessels. For the exploitation of the local economy and the gathering of products from the Aegean for transport west it was important that the dates of sailing of Venetian merchant shipping were fixed. The sailing season was known as the '*muda*'. The voyage took approximately eight weeks and took place in the spring and autumn of each year with shipping heading both east and west during these times, hence the importance of the naval intelligence gathered at Modon and Coron, the so-called chief eyes of the republic. In 1328 the dates of the muda for ships coming from Romania were fixed at 15 March – 15 April and 15 September – 31 October for vessels from Constantinople and 15–30 April for those from Lower Romania, with the autumn sailing being the same as for Constantinople. Merchant vessels were easily adaptable to fighting ships and were not required to sail in convoy except in time of extreme danger or risk.[37] So influential were the Italian merchants at the Latin and Byzantine courts in Constantinople and elsewhere that they frequently succeeded in regulating and forcing Aegean trade into fixed channels, far more ambitious than the contemporary staple system emerging in English overseas trade with the Low Countries.

It has been well-observed that during the fourteenth century at a time of great political disunity the Aegean displayed an amazing economic unity.[38] Much of this was due to the application of Italian commercial practices and procedures to the economic life of the area, procedures which Greek families like the Kalleigis on Crete were quick to adopt. Credit operations, contracts, currency, weights and measures, and shipping were all either produced in Italy or modelled on Venetian and Genoese practice. Certainly the idea of contract was not alien to the Byzantines. In the seventh

---

[36] In the paragraphs which follow I have relied upon A.E. Laiou, 'The Byzantine economy in the mediterranean trade system; thirteenth–fifteenth centuries' *DOP* 34/5 (1980–1), 177–222, reprinted in idem, *Gender, Society and Economic Life in Byzantium* (London, 1992).

[37] F.C. Lane, 'Fleets and fairs' and 'Maritime law and administration' in *Venice and History. The Collected Papers of Frederic C. Lane* (Baltimore, 1966), pp. 128–41 and 227–52; D. Nicol, *Byzantium and Venice* (Cambridge, 1988), pp.283–95.

[38] E. Zacharidou, 'Prix et marchés des céréales en Romanie (1343–1405)' *Nuova Rivista Storica* 61 (1977), 291–306, see esp. pp.291–2.

or eighth centuries the compilers of the Nomos Nautikos had built upon the ancient Rhodian sea law to spread the risk and profits of sea voyages, but from the thirteenth century the colleganza and the commenda could be found from one end of the Mediterranean to the other.[39]

Perhaps more important for the home economy of the Venetians and the Genoese than the products of Romania was the role of the Aegean as a transit centre for the products of the East. The Aegean was no more useful in this than the eastern Mediterranean in general, but its significance rose with time, especially with the loss of Acre in 1291 and the Mongol conquests of the early thirteenth century, which put a premium on the bypassing of Moslem lands and focused attention on the Black Sea ports of Kaffa and Tana and, of course, the Aegean sea-lanes leading to the Black Sea. Just as the Venetians used Modon, Negroponte and Crete as stopping-places in their long-distance routes to the Black Sea and Egypt, so did the Genoese use Chios.

Figures in non-standard forms like tons and measures should not lull us into thinking that we have anything approaching statistics regarding the volume of the trade to and from Romania. However, the commodities are generally well-known and the best description of them is still the study of Wilhelm Heyd.[40] Leaving aside the high-priced luxury items from the east like spices from camphor to cinnamon, and from mace and pepper to rhubarb, porcelain, gem-stones and silks, which passed through the Aegean in its role of entrepot, to concentrate upon the area's own import-export trade. In general raw materials were exported from the area and manufactured goods imported.

In terms of bulk the principal exports were foodstuffs, particularly grain from Crete and Thrace. Wine was widely available and bought up from the vineyard, *in tabernam*, for export. It seems to have been the vendor's task to convey it to a suitable shipping point. The wines of Chios, famous since antiquity, and so-called malmsey wine from Monemvasia seem to have been particularly in demand. Other important consumables included olive oil, oranges, which remained a luxury in northern Europe until the late sixteenth century, apricots, figs, raisins, cheeses, honey and nuts, particularly almonds and walnuts, and from the confines of the region, sugar from Cyprus.[41] Important raw materials were those concerned with the manufacture and dyeing of cloth and the tanning of leather. Cotton

---

[39] R.S. Lopez, *The Commercial Revolution of the Middle Ages* (Cambridge, 1976), pp.73–9; *ODB*, p.1792.

[40] W. Heyd, *Histoire du Commerce du Levant au Moyen-Age* 2 vols, ed. Furcy Raynaud (Paris, 1885–6; reprinted Amsterdam, 1959), II, pp.555–787.

[41] Fruits like the almond, fig and raisin were obtained by north Europeans from Spain. Almonds figure prominently in thirteenth century recipes and the English royal household consumed something in excess of 28,000 lbs of them in 1286. Italy was the principal market for these Aegean products.

(bombacinus), linen, raw silk from the Peloponnese and a medium/poor quality wool from Crete formed the main textiles exported. Furs were also recorded, presumably from Thrace. Cochineal or grana, the base for a red dye, was sold in the markets of Corinth. The fixing agent for dyes used in the west was alum, which was not so used in the Aegean. It could be found in the Peloponnese from where it was exported by the Venetians, but the best quality alum came from the Black Sea region and the second best from Phokaea or Foggia near Smyrna. Gall-nuts from Chios and valonia from the Peloponnese were both exported for use in the tanning of leather. A certain amount of lead and tin came from Palatia (ancient Miletos) on the Turkish coast opposite Chios. Pitch derived from pine resin was exported for all forms of weather-proofing from ships to roofs, and another bulkier product was turpentine distilled from the resin of the terebinth or turpentine tree (*Pistacia terebinthus*). Commodities concerned with personal hygiene for the wealthy were also sold in the region, especially the gum mastic of which the southern part of the island of Chios was the only source known in medieval Europe. From the resin of the mastic tree (*Pistacia lentiscus*) a sort of chewing gum was produced much in demand in the medieval west for sweetening the breath and promoting healthy gums. The island of Chios was the only source of mastic and it was this which had attracted the Genoese to the island. Soap too seems to have been exported, although the Venetians had an important import trade of soap into the region in their own right. Slaves too were taken in the region and sold either in the west or in Egypt.

Slaves

The political fragmentation of the Aegean, the relative ease of communication by sea and the existence of markets in Crete and Alexandria meant that slave-taking was a profitable activity for large-scale raids and small-scale piracy alike. Slaves were a crop which could be harvested with little labour and very little risk. The classic work on medieval slavery is that by Charles Verlinden and that has been followed here.[42] The main slave-takers were the Catalans, whose raids were militarily motivated, that is they took slaves from the lands of their opponents, and the Turks who raided for similar reasons but usually on religious and ethnic lines. The bulk of their commerce could therefore be said to be made up of prisoners of war who thus provided an early example of total war from the medieval period. The Venetians and the Genoese were generally slave-traders rather than slave-takers, although they too might indulge in small-scale raiding activities

---

[42] C. Verlinden, *L'Esclavage dans L'Europe Médiévale* II (Ghent, 1977), pp.800–84, 964–77.

amongst the Aegean islands, but these had more the appearance of kidnappings for ransom rather than large-scale razzias since the victims' families had the opportunity to buy them back before they were sold off. They bought their slaves from the Turks, the Catalans and from the potentates of the Black Sea region and traded them at most harbours in the Aegean but principally in the slave-markets of Crete. The ethnic make-up of the slave body was broad – Bulgarians, Cumans, Turks, but with a high preponderance of Greeks after 1300, lifted from the Aegean islands and the Anatolian coast, Corinthia and Thessaly by the Catalans and Turks, both of whom were establishing their presence in the Aegean at that time. Some of these slave-taking operations were on a very large scale with figures of 20,000 being occasionally cited as the haul in an extended razzia on a large island like Negroponte, and with whole islands being left depopulated. There was a demand for slaves in the Moslem lands of the east and many found their way to the slave-markets of the Islamic Levant, but for those being sold within Romania or for transhipment to the west, Crete was the great slave market.

Attitudes to slaves and slavery were ambivalent. It was not considered appropriate to enslave co-religionists. However, this seemed to leave Latins free to enslave Greeks. This caused much bitterness and suspicion. As Professor Zachariadou has pointed out, in 1339 the monk Barlaam was sent as ambassador to Pope Benedict XII in Avignon. The monk stressed that one of the great hindrances to church union and to a united action against the Turks was the fact of Latin slave-trading and slave-owning at the expense of Orthodox Christians.[43] Slaves were both a human commodity and a social grouping lacking all but a very few legal rights. As chattels themselves they could not bear testimony in a law court but they were indictable for homicide. They were about the only group which could not own a slave but they could acquire some belongings and occasionally save money to buy their freedom. This ambivalence comes through in the variety of master-slave relationships. Manumission on the death of an owner, marriage with a slave, and even freedom after a period of seven years, very like indentured labour, could all be found in the Mediterranean. Restrictions still attached to manumitted slaves and possibly some stigma too. Whatever kindnesses and relationships grew up between owner and his human chattel, it did not serve to excuse but only to palliate yet another example of man's inhumanity to man.

It must not be thought that because slavery existed here were slave economies in the sense of the ante-bellum southern states of America. Slaves were bought for domestic work as servants, cooks, gardeners and house-keepers, as unskilled labourers in a a variety of manual occupations

---

[43] E.A. Zachariadou, *Trade and Crusade, Venetian Crete and the Emirates and Menteshe and Aydin (1300–1415)* (Venice, 1983), pp.159–63, esp. p.159. See note 45 below.

like carpenters, caulkers, builders, and less often for agricultural work. The price of women slaves was generally much higher than that of males. Prices rose throughout the fourteenth century. An initial glut worked its way through the system whilst the ravages of the plague increased the value of the slave. On average the price ratio of male:female expressed in hyperpera was 8:17 (1317), 30:43 (1330s), and 64:96 (1380s) . With the advance of the Ottoman power around the Aegean, the supply of slaves to the west tended to dry up. Captives were now sent to the markets of the east.

Wheat

Considerable fortunes could be made on commodities particularly in demand in the west. Despite the poor yields of wheat in Greece and the Aegean islands, the peripheries of Romania, namely Crete, Thrace and the north coast of the Black Sea, made the area an important net corn exporter. On Crete the harvest was frequently sold in advance. In February 1333 Joannes Kallergis, the son of Alexios who had led the revolt on Crete in 1282–99, offered 47,000 measures of wheat to the Venetian authorities in Canea which he offered to deliver at his own expense. The wheat was to be delivered in annual loads of 6,000 measures, the price being fixed at 15 hyperpera per 100 measures. Three years later another Kallergis, George, received a payment of 8,000 hyperpera in return for 44,000 measures of wheat to be delivered over the next five years at a fixed price of 18 hyperpera per 100 measures. The price of corn generally rose through the fourteenth century and clearly a bulk contract like this could safeguard against such price increases. The corn was sent around the Aegean to Negroponte and Messenia and was also exported to Venice itself.[44]

Mastic and alum

On Chios the Genoese mahonna kept the price of mastic artificially high by limiting the annual production, and quotas were earmarked for the west, for the Black Sea and for those parts beyond Cyprus and Rhodes. Representatives of the mahonna were kept in these areas to oversee the selling of the mastic crop. The 'usual price' seems to have been 40 lire a quintal. Dr Argenti has estimated that around 1407 this represented a profit in the region of 7 per cent.[45] If this was not a clear profit it certainly

[44] Thiriet, 27, 28, 66.
[45] P. Argenti, *The Occupation of Chios by the Genoese* I (Cambridge, 1958), pp.484–8.

represented a generous interpretation of the idea of the just price. Also in Genoese hands were the alum mines and market at Foggia. Around 1330 the annual production was 700 tons of refined alum worth in excess of 50,000 Genoese lire. This represented an enormous sum in the hands of one family, the descendants of Benedetto Zaccaria (d. 1307). They provided a delivery service for their bulky commodity replete with an armed escort.[46]

The Aegean emporium

The products imported from the west included fine cloth from Flanders, Brabant and northern Italy, areas which would only buy the best quality alums in order to produce the best-finished and therefore more expensive cloth. These were luxury items and by no means to be compared with the cheap, so-called new draperies manufactured for the Mediterranean market in northern Europe in the sixteenth century. Armaments and mercenaries were also available for purchase and hire to all-comers, Franks, Greeks or Turks, and had been since the twelfth century. From archaeological sites in southern and central Greece finds of proto-majolica from southern Italy shows that there was an import of ceramics for specific, perhaps western, tastes. Given the current state of knowledge, this is to imply too much since, sadly, chance finds are not a good indicator of either the size or the intended market of such imports. There was also a considerable soap trade, although just who was buying it was unclear. Soap in the form of nitron mixed with oil was readily available in the Aegean, presumably the Venetian product was a superior one. it was certainly preferred by a Venetian on Crete, who, as Professor Laiou has noted, ordered soap, cloth and locks from home rather than use the local products.[47]

Being a merchant in the Aegean was no easy life. Bandits and pirates were to be found in both northern and south-eastern Europe. However, the Turks and Catalans seemed to inspire a particularly unsavoury reputation and the scale of piracy seems to have been both more widespread and more profitable than that practised in the English channel, at least judging from the Venetian claims commission of 1278. There were not the irksome rivalries between the merchant guilds of various towns to contend with which bedevilled the commercial life of northern Europe, but there were the even more irksome restraints provoked by the arbitrary actions of local rulers and their subordinates. Thus in 1336 the Genoese were attempting to set the standard of weights and measures in Pera and beyond to the disadvantage of the Venetians. In 1343 Marino Viadro suffered physical

---

[46] Lopez, op.cit., pp.139–41; see p.157.
[47] Laiou, art.cit., pp.179–80.

violence at the hands of imperial officials as he toured the despotate of the Morea in search of corn and vallonia. In the same year in Constantinople the houses of a certain Filippo Donusdeo were forcibly occupied by the megadux Apokaukos and the injured party left uncompensated.[48] Travel was probably no more difficult than at home and possibly in the dry climate and with a Roman heritage of road building may have been slightly better. Profits to be gained by advancing money to rulers were always risky but possibly slightly less so in the Aegean, where threats of retribution could be made by the Venetians and Genoese with a fair chance of being taken very seriously indeed by the threatened party. During the third decade of the fourteenth century some of the very real advantages of the integration of the Aegean economy into that of the Italian world became noticeable. There was sufficient system observable for the production of handbooks for merchants to be both useful and profitable. The best-known handbook was that of Francesco Balducci Pegolotti.[49] This gave information on exchange rates prevalent in the Aegean and listed the commodities obtainable in various markets. Money exchanges existed in most centres, the Acciaioli setting up a counter in Glarenza by 1331. Finally, changing money was not a problem unless large sums in gold were demanded at short notice, as we have seen in Glarenza in 1354.

Piracy was a fact of life in the late medieval Aegean.[50] The 200 or so Aegean islands provided ready refuges for pirate vessels and trade routes were never far away. As Frederic Cheyette has shown, piracy was always violent but the pirates were not always treated as criminals. It was all a matter of perception varied by the scale of operations and the nature of the employer and the circumstances.[51] For the gasmouloi laid off from the Byzantine fleet in 1283, enrollment in pirate crews was a respectable alternative employment. Small-scale operations by Aegean islanders turned pirate as a by-occupation to fishing were limited in scope and always deplored. So too was the employment of privateers by the Byzantine authorities, perhaps because they claimed some responsibility for protection of the Aegean sea-lanes. In the years after 1261 Michael VIII had recruited over 90 pirate groups, mainly operating from west Mediterranean harbours, to attack Venetian shipping in the Aegean. Western captains like Licario of Karystos and Giovanni della Covo from Genoa were both granted lands and the title of megadux by Michael for their services. This had clearly been a

---

[48] Thiriet, 71, 75, 156.

[49] A. Evans, ed., *Francesco Pegalotti, La practica della mercatura* (Cambridge, Mass., 1936).

[50] P. Charanis, 'Piracy in the Aegean during the reign of Michael VIII Palaeologus' *Annuaire de l'Institut de Philologie et d'histoire orientals et slaves* 10 (1950), 127–36; reprinted in idem, *Social, Economic and Political Life in the Byzantine Empire* (London, 1973).

[51] F.L. Cheyette, 'The sovereign and the pirates, 1332' *Speculum* 45 (1970), 40–68.

successful operation since in 1285 Michael's successor Andronikos had agreed to pay 24,000 hyperpera to the Venetians as an indemnity for lost goods and shipping, but at the same time he relinquished any formal Byzantine responsibility for all piratical acts committed in the Aegean. On the other hand the piratical activities of the various admirals in the Veneto–Genoese conflicts in the Aegean in the late thirteenth and fourteenth centuries achieved some sort of respectability, as did those Venetian island dynasties so long as they raided Catalan and Turkish shipping. Francesco Crispo and Niccolo Sanudo both operated personal pirate fleets in the 1370s and 1380s. The latter was so notorious that he acquired the nickname of '*Spezzabanda*' or 'Army destroyer', the mark of a successful pirate in any age.[52]

Elizabeth Zachariadou has studied the Venetian mercantile policy in relation to the emirates of Menteshe and Aydin, which established control of western Asia Minor around 1300 and maintained authority and restored prosperity there in the century or so until 1424, when their territories were absorbed into the Ottoman dominions by the sultan Murad II.[53] Early contacts with the emirates from Crete suggest that the trade was in slaves, provisions and horses. The only commodity going into the emirates was a large consignment of soap. Relations with the emirates were entrusted to the duke of Crete (duca di Candia) to arrange on a local basis and were not substantially hindered by Turkish raids into the Aegean or Venetian promotion of the Holy League. Eleven treaties between the duke and the emirs survive from the years between 1331 and 1414 and are reproduced in Elizabeth Zachariadou's study.[54] Venetian possessions in the Aegean in general were usually included in the treaties. They reveal that the principal items to be purchased from the emirates were slaves, mainly Greeks from Asia Minor, corn, domestic animals, particularly horses, skins, wax and alum. From Crete brightly coloured cloth, turquoise and greenish hues apparently being favoured, which originated in Florence, Narbonne, Perpignan and Toulouse, were exported as luxury draperies to supplement the native cloth industry. Wine, presumably from Greek vineyards, and soap manufactured in Venice formed the other exports into the region from the west.[55] The usual vagaries over weights and measures do not permit anything like a quantification of trade to be made. The number of treaties, however, suggests that this trading relationship was very important. The Genoese and the Hospitallers from Rhodes also maintained trade relations with the emirates. In spite of crusade and djihad it was business as usual for the Latin merchants of the Aegean.

---

[52] W. Miller, *Essays on the Latin Orient* (Cambridge, 1921), pp.168–9; C. & K. Frazee, *The Island Princes of Greece...* (Amsterdam, 1988), pp.41–2.
[53] E. Zachariadou, op.cit.
[54] Zachariadou, op.cit., pp.187–242.
[55] Zacharidou, op.cit., pp.159–73.

The domestic economy of farm, vineyard and textiles delivered its surpluses to the collecting centres of Negroponte, Pera, Chios, Candia and Modon for transport west in Venetian or Genoese ships. This is of course a simple statement of a complex intermeshing. Greek archons, merchants and sailors were active in the mechanisms of this local trade, although we have no idea of the proportions of natives to aliens. Most voyages within the Aegean and Black Sea of other than purely local significance were undertaken in Genoese or Venetian vessels, but local coastal traffic was probably very much in Greek hands.

The local economy would have been largely run by Greeks. Certainly they provided the vast majority of the labour force in agriculture and in haulage work associated with the construction of castles. Archons took a prominent part in the supply of agricultural provisions and many entered into commercial contracts with Latin sons-in-law. The building trade seems to have been largely in the hands of Greek masons. The masonry styles evident in churches and towers of the period would indicate this, whilst building contracts for the construction of towers on the island of Chios, albeit dating to 1516/17, were drawn up between the mahonese and Greek builders.[56] It seems to have been the religious orders that brought their own architects and masons with them, as evidenced by the keystone and capitals from Zaraka and the St Francis cycle frescoes in Kalenderhane Camii. The glass-makers of Corinth were probably Greeks.[57] Equally, the supply of pottery must have relied upon Greek potters working within a broad Aegean tradition in their localities. Fabric analysis might serve to identify local workshops and their markets, whilst form analysis might serve to establish to what extent they catered for the needs of their Frankish masters or whether the latter conformed to Greek ceramic forms and styles. One would expect a difference but I am not aware that any has yet been observed. Tanning was traditionally an occupation reserved for Jews but the butchery and sale of meat and fish as well as peddling would have remained firmly in Greek hands. The economic infrastructure of the Frankish Aegean was Greek.

Towns

In the history of the Frankish Aegean a great deal has been said about social evolution and ethnic co-existence, but very little indeed about the town. The Aegean was an area where the town as a settlement unit had developed as early as the Bronze Age and had maintained its significance and vitality into

---

[56] Argenti, op.cit., pp.111–12.
[57] R. Davidson, 'A medieval glassfactory at Corinth' *AJA* 44 (1940), 297–324.

at least the seventh century AD. Towns like Athens, Thebes, Patras and Corinth, even if they were Roman foundations or re-foundations, continued to be the resorts of local aristocracies and governors, the abode of the higher clergy, and for the generality of country-dwellers places of refuge in times of disturbance.[58] The survival of smaller towns like Thespiae, Askra and Koronea had some form of existence into the early medieval period but thereafter their fate is still the subject of some speculation. That apart, this urban world into which the crusaders of 1204 emerged was distinctly different from what they had known at home. They were not strangers to the town but in 1201–2 they had chosen to hold their planning sessions for the forthcoming crusade at monasteries or at fairs. Both Villehardouin and Clari had been astounded by the size and amenities of Constantinople. Their colleagues venturing into Thrace and Greece left no such record of their impressions of the towns which they found there. Presumably they were much more on a par with the towns of Lombardy and France.

The Franks as the minority population tended to concentrate in the towns and in part to take on the role of an urban aristocracy. Their clergy was a capitular clergy which functioned from the most important urban centres. What capital investment in buildings within the traditional towns of Greece took place we do not know. It might be expected to have been more than negligible, since the Frankish landowners resident in towns would have been the very people with the spare capital needed for just such investment. There were of course the grand statements like the palace on the Acropolis at Athens built up by the Acciaioli and the palace in Thebes built by Nicholas II de St Omer in 1287, yet of ordinary houses we know nothing except for an allusion to 'certain houses constructed in the city of Thebes' contained in a grant of an annuity to a certain Ferdinand de Zaguda on 22 June 1361. As Kenneth Setton has pointed out, this is the only known reference to any new buildings in the duchy of Athens throughout the whole of the Catalan occupation.[59] Giambattista Ubaldini, the sixteenth century biographer of the Acciaioli, claimed that Antonio I also adorned the city of Athens with streets and buildings.[60] However, it would appear that in the towns the Franks were content with the Greek building stock. Sadly, urban renewal in Greece in the 1960s has not dealt kindly with the remains of the medieval past.

There were, however, some striking new town foundations. The town of Glarenza was founded by Geoffrey I de Villehardouin on the site of ancient Kyllene near the chapel of St Zacharias which was the only building

---

[58] T. Gregory, 'Cities and social evolution in Roman and Byzantine south east Europe', in J. Bintliffe, ed., *European Social Evolution* (Bradford, 1984), pp. 267–76; J.H. Finlay, 'Corinth in the Middle Ages' *Speculum* 7 (1932), 477–99.

[59] DOC, no.CCXLVI (p.328); Setton, p.445, n.25.

[60] G. Ubaldini, *Istoria della casa degli Ubaldini* (Florence, 1588), p.176, cited in K. Setton, *Catalan Domination of Athens* 2nd edn (London, 1975), p.245.

on the site in 1204; whilst the Venetians re-founded Modon, which was ruined and deserted in 1205. Both there and later at Negroponte they invested considerably in providing town walls and an aqueduct system to bring water into the towns. Both towns fulfilled the functions of ports. The Venetians had occupied many Byzantine harbour towns in the partition of 1204 and had subsequently built them up and used them, but their Frankish colleagues seemed slower to develop such facilities. The harbour for Salona was Itea, whilst the principal harbour for the duchy of Athens seems always to have been Livadostro (Rivadostro), also on the Corinthian Gulf. Both were little more than roadsteads guarded in each case by a tower. Trade through them must have been limited and quick access with the ports of southern Italy seems to have been their chief recommendation. The Piraeus, of course, had harbour facilities of a more developed kind to which a harbour tower was added at some point before the middle of the fifteenth century. The port served the Aegean and seems to have become much more significant in terms of the duchy of Athens in the fourteenth century. The Venetians were at pains to limit Catalan naval activity there and it is Antonio I Acciaioli who is credited with setting up the two marble lions there from which it acquired the name of Porto Leone.

Of the privileges and immunities of the towns in this period we know little. Certain residents in Livadhia were granted the Catalan franchise in 1311 for negotiating the surrender of the town. It is not after 1367 in the various petitions for better governance that we read of the '*sindichs, prohomens e consell*' of the municipalities of Athens, Thebes and Livadhia.[61] Presumably these were the leading merchants in those towns but we have no names or trades to help us get behind the titles. They represented their towns in the Catalan parliament and when authority broke down organised affairs within those towns. Thus in January 1398 the community of Athens sent two ambassadors to negotiate with the Venetian senate to request a garrison for Athens in the face of incursions by Antonio Acciaioli and the Turks. In May 1399 the garrison was supplemented by ten crossbowmen and fifteen cavalrymen because of the approaching grain and grape harvests, incidentally illustrating the close links between town and country which must not be ignored.[62]

Coins and the monetary economy

Whilst there is probably little to be said for counting up the recognisable Latin coinage of the Aegean as an indicator of economic vitality, it can be

---

[61] DOC, no.CCCXCI (pp.473–9). Rubio i Lluch dubbed these petitions Articles (capitols) by which name they are generally known today.
[62] Thiriet, 938, 962.

said that the range and diversity of the coinage used in the Aegean reflects the area's significance as an international trading zone. Gold coins from various Italian mints, the ducats and florins, were used interchangeably. Gigliati or carlini, a silver coin from Naples, was of such purity that it took a leading role as one of the international currencies of the Aegean, and it was probably this coin that was referred to by the Greeks as stavrata and not the gold stavraton minted by the Palaeologoi in the 1370s.[63] The Venetians minted the tornosello at Venice for use in the Aegean trade. These base coins tended to displace the other west European currencies imported into Greece in the thirteenth century.[64] Alongside all these the Byzantine and Turkish coinages also circulated. Three hyperpera was the equivalent of one ducat as were 23 akce or aspra from the emirates of Menteshe and Aydin.

Certainly within the coastal cities of Greece the monetary economy was well-established. Loans could be raised and money changed from one currency to another. The inventoried coins from the recent excavations in Corinth show the variety of coins in circulation: tournois minted in Glarenza, Corinth and Thebes, Byzantine coins, imitative Latin and Bulgarian issues of the same, tornaselli, soldi and grossi from Venice, deniers from the Angevin despotate of Epiros established in 1294 and a variety of jettons from Pisan and Lombard banking houses.65 The extent to which the money economy extended into the countryside is more questionable. By the middle of the fourteenth century payments of rents and taxes in coin seem to have been introduced. D.M. Metcalf has suggested that during the thirteenth century the duchy of Athens, due to the lack of a local Frankish aristocracy and the commercial activities in Thebes, led the field in the maintenance of a petty currency. At first this was made up by the continued circulation of bronze Byzantine currency issued by Manuel I (1143–80) and his successors and importations of debased denier tournois from France, some of them seigneurial issues, and sterlings from England. The mechanism of these imports is not understood. Around 1250 a billon or copper coinage was minted in Corinth by the duke of Athens. The demand which prompted the issue of such a low value coin is unknown. After 1280 a denier tournois was produced in Thebes.[66]

The Latins minted coins in their own right. Those of the Latin empire are attested in the documentation but not readily recognisable as artefacts.

---

[63] Zachariadou, op.cit., pp.140–3.

[64] A.M. Stahl, 'The mint of Venice in the thirteenth century', in N. Mayhew and P. Spufford, eds, *Later Medieval Mints* (Oxford, 1988), pp.97–127; idem, *The Venetian Tornosello* (New York, 1935).

[65] C. Williams and O. Zervos, 'Frankish Corinth: 1991' *Hesperia* 61 (1992), 133–91, esp. 179ff.; idem, 'Frankish Corinth: 1992' *Hesperia* 62 (1993), 1–52, esp. 36ff.

[66] D.M. Metcalf, 'The currency of deniers tournois in Frankish Greece' *ABSA* 55 (1960), 38–59; idem, 'Frankish petty currency from the Areopagus at Athens' *Hesperia* 34 (1965), 203–23.

Choniates wrote of small denominations (*kermata*) being produced in 1204 and Pegalotti wrote of '*iperperi latini*'. Michael Hendy has recently advanced an identification of some of the coins of these north Aegean states based on coin hoards from known Latin sites like Kalendarehane Camii in Constantinople.[67] These coins had a lower silver content than their Byzantine counterparts but were otherwise imitative of Byzantine coinage. The states in Greece did not issue a coinage of their own until after the end of the Latin empire. Byzantine coinage continued to circulate after 1204. The concave trachy coinage was often hammered flat and coins were often halved to make lower denominations. The date for the first issues from Glarenza (De Clarentia) is a matter of dispute. Some, like David Metcalf, advance 1260 as a possibility; others, like Antoine Bon, hold to the last years of William de Villehardouin. The denier tournois coinage of Thebes and Glarenza was modelled on the contemporary French petty currency.[68] It is not known why the Latin rulers of Greece only minted low value coins and why so late in the thirteenth century. It would be too convenient and too circular to conclude that the payment of mercenaries and the collection of agricultural rents prompted their coinage policy. Small change is very much an urban phenomenon for regular small purchases. Commerce was very much in Italian hands and the relevant city republics seem to have taken care to issue their own 'dollars' for the Aegean to replace the debased Byzantine nomismata.

Archaeology and the medieval Aegean economy

Medieval archaeology has far to go in Greek lands, especially in regard to urban development and the rural economy. The study of deserted settlements has barely advanced beyond the stage of site discovery and recognition. The geology which has favoured the preservation of high sherd densities on the surface of the ground has not preserved village layouts in fossilised form in which they appear in northern Europe. Village morphology can still be retrieved, but the chronological framework of desertion is patchy in the extreme and the perceived tendency for villages to relocate rather than to re-align about one site further complicates the task of deciding which village community moved where and why. The picture of village movement and abandonment was a clearly complex one and its

---

[67] M. Hendy, *Studies in the Byzantine Monetary Economy* (Cambridge, 1985), pp.520–1.
[68] D.M. Metcalf, *Coinage in South-Eastern Europe, 820–1396* (London, 1979), pp.132–8, 234–67 where the author's articles in *ABSA* are summarised; idem, *Coinage of the Crusades and the Latin East in the Ashmolean Museum, Oxford* (London, 1983) for photographs of the Latin coinage of the Aegean.

economic, ethnic, and political motors are but barely perceived. In the scramble to unravel classical and prehistoric city sites medieval urban archaeology has yet to be born. Where it occurs at all it is largely confined to the study of standing structures. Field survey has produced some interesting interpretations of sherd scatters on former town sites and fared well in plotting the shrinking of urban areas in the late Roman period, but the problems associated with the dating of medieval ceramics from the Aegean, means that at present it is severely handicapped in this respect. Classical and Roman Thespiae are becoming reasonably well-known but the site of the Norbertians of Erimokastro, that is medieval Thespiae, remains as elusive as ever. There is still much that can be done in a more conventional field-work role. The infrastructure of roads and bridges is barely known at all. Yet a glimpse at the records of the secretary of the Venetian commander Sigismondo Malatesta reveals that the roads by which he travelled in Messenia in 1465 lay in the foothills, higher up and further inland from the modern road pattern.[69] Work along these lines would reveal much that is tended to be taken for granted in the medieval archaeology of much of northern Europe.

---

[69] K.N. Sathas, ed., *Mnemeia tis Ellenikes Istorias* IV (Paris, 1885), p.25. See C. Hodgetts and P. Lock, 'The topography of Venetian Messenia', in Lock and Sanders, eds, *Essays in the Archaeology of Medieval Greece* (Oxford, forthcoming).

Symbiosis and Segregation

A Franco–Greek culture?

The most interesting and most elusive question of the period of Frankish rule in the Aegean area is the affect which it had upon Greek society and the extent to which a hybrid Franco–Greek culture may be said to have emerged. The diverse groups of Frankish settlers were too small and their control too brief and too limited geographically for anything other than a curdling, rather than a true intermingling, to take place – what Professor Jacoby has termed 'an encounter between two societies' rather than an acculturation.[1]

Comparison is invited with those other crusader states in the Levant. The late R. C. Smail has shown that the interests, loyalties, and thought world of the crusaders in Syria were too bound up with Christendom for a Franco–Syrian nation to result from crusader settlement.[2] The same was true of crusader Greece. Crusader occupation was even briefer there than in Syria and their dependence on the courts of western Europe much more direct. The Latin emperor Baldwin II sought loans by personal visits to western courts, and the rulers of central Greece and the Morea participated in western crusades and power struggles in southern Italy as well as referring difficult feudal law suits to the French court. From the outset the papal curia looked to the new states to heal the schism between western and eastern Christians and justified the capture of Constantinople in terms of the

---

[1] D. Jacoby, 'The encounter of two societies: western conquerors and Byzantines in the Peloponnesus after the Fourth Crusade' *AHR* 78 (1973), 873–906, reprinted in *Recherches sur la Mediterranée orientale du XIIe au XVe siècle* (London, 1979). For an extreme view which minimises the Latin influence in the Aegean, see Franz Dölger, 'Die Kreuzfahrerstaaten auf dem Balkan und Byzanz' *Südost-Forschungen* 15 (1956), 141–59.
[2] R.C. Smail, *The Crusaders in Syria and the Holy Land* (London, 1973), pp.182–6.

liberation of the Holy Land. This made a total commitment to the interests of their new lands even less possible. This and their inability to free themselves from their western thought world prevented any but the very basic moves towards a hybrid culture unlikely.

The capture of Constantinople was a cataclysm from the point of view of the Byzantine ruling classes. This has served to highlight the Frankish conquest and to suggest comparisons with that other cataclysm of the middle ages, the Norman conquest of England, where the survival of the old and sophisticated Anglo–Saxon state was decided on the field of Hastings on 14 October 1066. However, the cataclysm apparent to Choniates, Acropolites and others was not so apparent to the farmers and traders in the suburbs and countryside around Constantinople or even revenue clerks in the civil service within the city. These could accommodate and cooperate with the westerners with certainly no greater animadversion than they felt for the rich, the powerful, and the urban. For them the capture of Constantinople had much of continuity about it. The Frankish arrival merely accentuated home-grown trends which have led the period from 1000 to 1261 to be dubbed the period of westernisation by modern Byzantinists. On the mainland a highly feudalised nobility took over the empire but largely ignored the institutions and traditions of an old and established culture. Most of the new men at the top were proud of their pure French ancestry, whilst life for the majority of the agricultural classes went on much as before. It is in the middle ranks of society that any fusion of race and culture was discernible and much of this, at least at an intimate family level, was already qualitatively present in those children of mixed Venetian and Greek parentage in the Venetian quarter of Constantinople.

It is important to get behind the labels '*Frankoi*' and '*Latinoi*'. These were Greek terms for westerners and were used indiscriminately for Burgundians, Catalans, Champagnards, Florentines, Genoese, Navarrese, Normans and Venetians. Quite apart from the chronological distinction of their respective involvements in the Aegean they were culturally and institutionally quite different from each other. At a glance it can be seen that there was not the cultural and assumptive homogeneity amongst the Frankish settlers in Greece which was present by and large with the Normans. Both in their homelands and in the Aegean the various Frankish elements remained culturally distinct. Yet the term Frank was a perceptual one, used by their Greek subjects or opponents. What did it mean to be a Frank in Greek eyes?

This chapter will be concerned with the sources available to study cultural symbiosis: the impact of the Franks on the institutional structure of the Byzantines and the influence of the Greeks upon the Latins. There was no steady progression or liberalising of attitudes. Political conditions and the nature of external threats changed in the two centuries of the Frankokratia and with it official and legal attitudes of the two groups were modified in areas under their respective control. In Frankish Greece there seems to have been a hardening of attitude through time. The conquerors of 1205 were prepared to concede much whereas their descendants and successors a century later were eager to distance themselves from the Greeks. Whatever we might learn about institutions, it is really at the personal level both in terms of perception and in terms of bilingualism that the true basis for any coming-together of two cultures must lie. What had been achieved by the waning of the Frankokratia in, say, 1400?

The sources

The traditional literary sources have been known for a long time. They were written for the ruling Latin elite and reflect their cultural interests. They have come down to us in fourteenth century versions and are really too little too late for anything other than a fragmentary view of Frankish society in Greece. Nonetheless they are virtually all that we have and are therefore of enormous import. These scraps of circumstantial evidence were used by William Miller in 1921 to provide a social model of Frankish Greece. He wrote before the influence of the Annales School and the impact of feminist history had made themselves felt. He tended to emphasise the institutional over the perceptual, and the individual over the sociological, but for all that he certainly pointed out broad lines of enquiry and drew attention to differences between the various states of Frankish Greece. However, no historian can be better than his sources and he, like his contemporary Rennell Rodd, emphasised the romantic and chivalrous qualities of the Franks which were precisely the topics which interested the Frankish elite of fourteenth-century Greece. He also suggested a cultural homogeneity of the Franks and tended to omit any sense of social evolution. For all that, the essay's readable style and its general availability meant that it held the field for a long time and exerted an influence which its author never intended. The Franks emerged as caricatures of chivalric romance, their pragmatism and realism submerged beneath feats of arms and pageantry. Since the 1970s Frankish Greece has emerged from this realm of impression to attempts to make some assessment of quantity and quality. Although by no means alone in this field, the scholar most responsible for this rigorist approach is David Jacoby of the Hebrew University, Jerusalem. In what follows, the extent to which his work has influenced and changed perceptions of problems will be obvious.

The literary sources present a particular and generally late view of the conquest and its social outcomes. They cannot be dismissed but they have been well-worked over. Archive material is exiguous in the extreme. The barrel has to be scraped to the bottom to reveal any dynamic picture of social evolution in Frankish Greece. Before dealing with this task what other avenues of approach are available?

The philological approach with its emphasis upon place names and loan-words is not a new one but it is fraught with difficulties for any but the expert.[3] It bears out the impression from papal letters from the early thirteenth to the mid-fourteenth century that the numbers of westerners settled in Greece were few. Too few, in fact, to have much effect on the language of the Aegean or its place names. Frankish toponyms are known to us only from western-inspired sources which would suggest that they did not enjoy a wide currency outside the western community and did not long survive the displacement of the Franks as the political elite. The exceptions seem to be personal names like Kerpini (Charpigny) and Santameri (St Omer), perhaps further emphasising the importance of individuals and personality in any cross-cultural dealings. On the other hand they most certainly do not represent any attempt by the Franks to stamp their culture on the countryside. They were not a process in cultural imperialism but one feature of a polyglot society which must have sprung up in the very early days of the conquest. Usually they were straight transcriptions of Greek names like Malvasie for Monemvasia, le Daffenis for Daphni, la Glisiere for Vliseri and la Veternicie for Vitrinitsa, often using the definite article like Greek. In some texts from the beginning of the thirteenth century the Greek article was even used untranslated: I Kydonea, To Lotro, etc; more often it was translated as in la Bondonice, la Vostice, etc. Some names derived from an aural misunderstanding, thus La Crémonie for Lakadaimon, and those names indicating motion towards by the use of the Greek prepositions '*eis*' and '*se*' together with the accusative of the article. Thus the oft-cited examples of Estives for '*eis tas Thebas*' and Satines or Sathimes for '*eis tas Athenas*'. Much less often French names were derived from a direct translation of the Greek. In this small category Longnon has singled out l'Ille or l'Isle for Nisi in the Pamisos delta near Kalamata, les Boveries for Voukolia in Attica, la Closure for Klissura and Castel-de-Fer for Siderocastro near Patras.[4] Place names originating with the Franks were usually connected with the construction or repair of a fortification and may well not be an alternative for the Greek name of the nearest settlement. These names might be descriptive of a perceived or imagined quality, often warlike such as Bucelet (Araklavon), Crèvecouer (Andritsaina) and Matagriffon (Akova), or physical like the less intimidating Beauvoir (Katakolo), Clermont (Chlemoutsi), and Port du Jonc (Pylos). The distinction between these aggressive and pacific toponyms certainly represent a change in outlook and might well reflect the changing fortunes

---

[3] Otto Markl, *Ortsnammen Griechenlands in Fränkischer Zeit* (Graz-Koln, 1966) for sources and listing; Jean Longnon, 'Les Noms de Lieu de la Grèce Franque' *Journal des Savants* (July–Sept. 1960) 97–110 for discussion.
[4] Longnon, art.cit.

of the Frankish Morea. Clearly both Greeks and Latins could live with a double nomenclature. It would be most interesting to know what name or names the adventurer Geoffrey II de Bruyere (Briel) gave to Bucelet when he threatened to hand it over to the Greek governor of Mistra when Nicholas II de St Omer was baili in 1287–89. Whatever each side called it, no-one was in any doubt as to its strategic significance for the control of Skorta. Geoffrey gained an heiress and lands for himself near Chalandritza in return for keeping it in Frankish hands.[5] A unique example is provided by the Frankish castle at Amphissa called Salona or La Sola by the Franks, a name said to be derived from the kingdom of Salonika.[6] There is nothing in any of this to suggest centres of Frankish settlement or concentrations of western landed estates. The Franks seemed content with the place names they found and had a purely practical outlook on the exploitation of land. There was no distinctive Frankish attitude to the countryside and its features, beyond a very slight tendency to describe some sites with reference to the view enjoyed from them rather than in terms of the shape of the feature on which they stood, which seems to have been a tendency amongst the Greeks.

The work of Henry and Renée Kahane is both the most recent and the most convenient study of the linguistic impact of the eastern and western cultures on each other.[7] It was a two-way process anchored in the common Latin heritage of both Byzantium and the west. The 200 or so borrowings of Byzantine terms in the west generally pre-date the high middle ages and reflect the western perception of an advanced and wealthy Byzantine empire. In reverse apart from the Latinisms that went back to the days of the Roman empire and were to be found in ecclesiastical, military and legal terminology, most loan-words appeared at the time of the Frankokratia. Italianisms were mainly sea-borne and relevant to an enduring nautical and commercial life. By contrast with this and with the Latinisms, the French impact was the least enduring. It was confined to social and cultural descriptions, largely concerned with feudal institutions and the chivalric code.

The newest and most hopeful source is archaeology – hopeful in that it generates its own new material.[8] It does have a number of serious drawbacks for the historian. Its findings are largely anonymous, whilst its emphasis on processual change does not compensate for this nor fit easily into historical analysis. Its dating to within 50 years or so is just not precise enough for historical purposes. All this apart there is a notorious backlog in publication. The student in search of information on medieval ceramics is

---

[5] W. Miller, *Latins in the Levant* (London, 1908), pp.167–8; X t M, 8387–455; L de C, 563–86; L de F, 442–4.

[6] Miller, op.cit., p.34.

[7] H. and R. Kahane, 'Byzantium's impact on the west: the linguistic evidence' *Illinois Classical Studies* 6 (1981), 389–415; idem, 'The western impact on Byzantium: the linguistic evidence' *DOP* 36 (1982), 127–53. See p.242.

[8] See p.32ff.

forced to rely upon data gathered and published in the 1930s and 1940s. However, on a more hopeful note the last two years have seen a number of important articles discussing and publicising the closer dating of thirteenth century ceramics from Corinth.[9] This problem is compounded by the emphasis upon non-excavational fieldwork in Greek lands in the last decade or so. Its findings depend upon the dating of surface finds of pottery, that is non-stratified material that depends upon good date sequences published in excavation reports of well-stratified habitation sites. Currently Morgan's study of Corinthian material published in 1942 is the vademecum. However the 1988–93 excavations at Corinth, which are as yet only available in interim reports, have unearthed stratified Frankish material found in association with coins. The opportunity for dating which this presents may well change entirely present concepts of the chronology of Frankish ceramic material.[10]

Finally, there is a problem of terminology. It must be realised that the term 'Frankish', when applied to sites which depend upon ceramics for their attribution, is a chronological and not an ethnic nor a cultural description, embracing the thirteenth to the fifteenth centuries. It is easier to say this than to comprehend it. It would be both clearer and at the same time form a better basis for discussion between the two disciplines of history and archaeology if a chronological terminology rather than an ethnic one were to be adopted. Thus a site which surface field survey reveals as being a discreet collection of Frankish pottery does not mean that the settlement was one exclusively of Franks, but that the settlement existed during the thirteenth to fifteenth centuries. The implications of a distinctive Frankish pottery or production for the Frankish market, let alone the identification of Frankish rural settlement, would add a new dimension to our understanding of crusader settlement in Greece. Equally the dating of pottery, except for imported wares, is not yet tight enough to aid historians who require dates within at least a 50-year span. As yet there are no good date sequences of Frankish finds, especially from habitation sites. We cannot say whether there is a noticeable ranking of pottery in terms of forms and wares such as has been noted in the crusader states in Palestine with regard to proto-maiolica and thus we cannot identify a Frankish site in the ethnic sense from a Greek settlement of the Frankish period. Clearly it would be of enormous import if the archaeologist could reveal whether the Frankish elite bought their pottery from local craftsmen, as we assume, or whether their tastes were so idiosyncratic as to demand imported craftsmen, or if there was a penchant

---

[9] G.D.R. Sanders, 'An assemblage of Frankish pottery at Corinth' *Hesperia* 56 (1987), 159–95; idem, 'Excavations at Sparta: the Roman Stoa, medieval pottery' *ABSA* 88 (1993), 251–93.

[10] C.H. Morgan, *Corinth XI: The Byzantine Pottery* (Cambridge, Mass., 1942); C.K. Williams and O. Zervos, 'Frankish Corinth: 1991' *Hesperia* 61 (1992), 133–91; idem, 'Frankish Corinth: 1992' *Hesperia* 62 (1993), 1–52.

for imported Italian or North African wares amongst the Franks not shared by the Greeks, or if the cooking habits and dietary preferences of the Franks of Constantinople were evidenced in the archaeological register of the forms and therefore the functions of pottery of the Frankish period. The state of our knowledge at present sheds little light on these problems but it remains the most hopeful of our sources.

The western contribution to Aegean society

The pure western contribution to Aegean society is very difficult to isolate. There has been much controversy as to whether the crusaders of 1204 introduced feudalism and a hierarchical feudal society into the Byzantine world. As John Critchley has shown, there was nothing unique to western crusading society either about military service tenures or about social subordination.[11] The pronoia was a grant of imperial land to an aristocrat for the term of his life and in return for services, usually military, to the emperor. These grants were not hereditary and they had no element of sub-infeudation. Nonetheless the crusaders in 1204 had no difficulty in identifying the pronoia with the fief, even if, as we shall see, they were careful to preserve Byzantine law in respect of the inheritance of patrimonial lands of their Greek subjects. With regard to social subordination, since the tenth century at least Byzantine emperors had tried to prevent the free peasantry from seeking the patronage or prostasia of great landowners. By becoming a part of a great estate they shared in the tax immunity of that estate. These paroikoi tied to the soil were seen as parallels to the western serf. There was much that smacked of feudalism in the Aegean in 1204. If feudalism is set to one side the few direct western influences were limited in the extreme and mostly confined to court society. First, the office of konostaulos, derived from cométable, was created in the reign of John III Vatatzes (1222–54) for the commander of Frankish mercenaries in the Nicaean army. Its first holder was the future emperor Michael Palaeologos and applied by him in the 1270s to foreign mercenary leaders like Licario of Karystos. Then there were western chilvalric institutions like the tornemen and the dzoustra, transliterations of the tournament and the joust. In this context Manuel I was believed by some in the west to be familiar with the ceremony of dubbing a knight, a ritual of which even Saladin was deemed ignorant.[12] In 1146 St Bernard sent Henry, son of the count of Champagne, to Manuel I that he might dub him a knight and so honour Henry by the

---

[11] J. Critchley, *Feudalism* (London, 1978), pp.24–5, 150–1. For what follows see also *ODB* sub 'Feudalism' (p.784) and 'Pronoia' (pp.1733–4).
[12] M. Keen, *Chivalry* (Yale, 1984), pp.7, 69.

imperial association.[13] The term kavallarios entered official Byzantine language in the mid-thirteenth century, apparently from the demotic Greek for a Latin mounted warrior, equivalent to the Greek stratiotes. By the fourteenth century it had changed in meaning to something very like the late-medieval western meaning of 'miles' as a title marking a minor noble. Bartusis has plotted this change in usage and the appropriation by Byzantium of this western usage.[14] Finally there was trial by ordeal first recorded in Epiros in 1224. When it was offered to Michael Palaeologos at Philippi in 1252 as a means of disproving certain rumours which impugned his loyalty to the emperor, it was rejected by him as a barbarian practice and on no account to be used in place of Roman laws and written tradition. With the probable exception of the latter, all of these direct contributions may well have entered Byzantium from the crusader states or northern Italy. If anything the period of the Frankokratia accelerated and accentuated a process of social and political change which was present in the Aegean world before 1204 and had its origins more in Byzantine politics and society that in Western ambitions and drive.[15]

During the twelfth century Greeks and Latins were no strangers to each other. As Anthony Bryer has emphasised, the contacts were local and individual involving little of high culture.[16] The emphasis has been placed on military, political and commercial relations, namely the service of Greeks and Latins as mercenary troops in each other's armies, on the commercial privileges of the Italian republics in the Byzantine empire physically marked by ships at quays and resident merchants, and upon the reception and treatment of western nobles and kings at the Byzantine court as advisers, mercenaries or transient crusaders.[17] It was the merchants who came to stay and to form a sizeable commercial colony of some 10–20,000 persons. In response the host government encouraged marriages between Greek women and these new residents. The tenth-century Book of Ceremonies had

---

[13] RHGF 15, 607–8 (letter LXXXI).

[14] Mark Bartusis, 'The Kavallarioi of Byzantium' *Speculum* 63 (1988), 343–50.

[15] A.P. Kazhdan and A.W. Epstein, *Change in Byzantine Culture in the Eleventh and Twelfth Centuries* (Berkeley, 1985), pp.167–96; *ODB*, sub 'Foreigners' (pp.796–7), 'Konostaulos' (p.1147) and 'Sports' (p.1939); M. Bartusis, 'The Kavallarioi of Byzantium' *Speculum* 63 (1988), 343–50, who cites Pseudo-Kodinos' treatise on offices for the megas konostavlos; D.J. Geanakoplos, *Interaction of the Sibling Byzantine and Western Cultures* (New Haven, 1976), pp.146–55, and M. Angold, 'The interaction of Latins and Byzantines during the period of the Latin Empire: the case of the ordeal' *Actes du Xve Congrès international d'études byzantines* 4 (Athens, 1980), 1–10; both summarised in R. Bartlett, *Trial by Fire and Water* (Oxford, 1986), p.131.

[16] A. Bryer, 'Cultural relations between east and west in the twelfth century', in D. Baker, ed., *Relations Between East and West in the Middle Ages* (Edinburgh, 1973), pp.71–94.

[17] C. Brand, *Byzantium Confronts the West* (Cambridge, Mass., 1968), pp.18–20, 34–7, 80–4 for the involvement of the brothers Conrad and Renier of Montferrat in Byzantine politics.

discouraged mixed marriages but not with westerners.[18] Nonetheless this policy of encouragement represented some modification in official attitude. There was also a marked increase in the number of imperial marriages with western princesses in the twelfth century – rising from two during the rule of the Macedonian dynasty (867–1056) to fourteen under the Komneni (1081–1185).[19] Much less work has been done on influences going the other way in the twelfth century. Marriages of Byzantine princesses to western rulers ceased after the three betrothals/marriages arranged by Basil II (976–1025).[20] This seems a complete reversal of Macedonian policy, at least until the late 1170s when Manuel I expended a number of daughters of the imperial family in order to attract north Italian support. In 1170 his niece Eudokia was married to a staunch papalist, Odo Frangipani de Veroli, and in 1179 another niece, also called Eudokia, was given in marriage to William of Montpelier. In the following year Renier de Montferrat married Maria Porphyrygenita, Manuel's daughter, and received the title caesar and rights over Thessalonika. This policy of courting the Montferrat was continued by Isaac II Angelos who married his sister Theodora to Conrad, again with the title of caesar.[21] The so-called Monza Vocabulary, a list of 65 Latin or Italian words with their Greek equivalents written in the Roman alphabet on the last page of a tenth-century manuscript, shows an elementary knowledge of Greek on the part of some north Italian cleric.[22] Greek styles of dress and behaviour seem to have filtered westwards at least as far as Venice where there may well have been a small Greek merchant colony at this time.[23] All this shows that in the century before the Fourth Crusade, despite incidents of official violence perpetrated by both sides in 1147, 1182 and 1185, there was a degree of toleration and trust by individuals on both sides, and that the respective diatribes of Greek and Latin writers regarding the regrettable characterisitics and reprehensible religious practices of the other should not be taken at face value.[24] As soon as individuals met face to face and a caricature became a person with a face and a name, cooperation, friendship and conjugal fidelity were thought possible. Nonetheless, political and cultural identities were maintained.

---

[18] R. Macrides, 'Dynastic marriages and political kinship', in J. Shepard and S. Franklin, eds, *Byzantine Diplomacy* (London, 1992), pp.263–80.

[19] *ODB*, sub 'Latins' (p.1187) based on V. Grumel, *La Chronologie* (Paris, 1958), 363f.

[20] The three marriages were Theophano to Otto II in 972, the betrothal of the Porphyrgenita Zoe to Otto III in 1002, and Maria Argyrou to the doge John Urseolo in 1004. The latter is sometimes credited with introducing the fork to western Europe.

[21] C. Brand, op.cit., pp.18–21, 80. On the political significance of these marriages see P. Magdalino, *The Empire of Manuel I Komnenos* (Cambridge, 1993), pp.100–2.

[22] *ODB*, p.1408.

[23] Kazdhan and Warton, op.cit., pp.177–80; D.J. Geanakoplos, *Byzantine East and Latin West* (Oxford, 1966), pp.112–38; A. Fotheringham, 'Byzantine art and culture in Rome and Italy' *AJA* 10 (1895), 160ff.

[24] P. Magdalino, *The Empire of Manuel I Komnenos, 1143–1180* (Cambridge, 1993), pp.27–108 for the most recent discussion of westernisation in general.

The otherness of the Franks had been established in the tenth century. They were barbarians because they lived outside the empire and were therefore not Romans, but they were Christians, they had once formed part of the empire and they were credited with providing at least one emperor, Constantine the Great, and so were regarded as having a special relationship with the Byzantines.[25] They were characterised by Anna Komnene in her account of the First Crusade written in the late 1140s as ambitious, brave, contentious, greedy, hot-headed, uncontrollable and untrustworthy. They were barbarians because they lived '... between the further side of the Adriatic and the pillars of Heracles'.[26] Nicetas Choniates and Eustathios of Thessalonika both echoed this stereotype but stressed appearance and language. They were robust and swarthy, fierce and quick to anger. They did not understand Greek – Eustathios described them as babbling and shrieking. They were suspicious of both Greek church services and the beating of the semantra. They deliberately disrupted the one and put a stop to the latter by force. Hair was an important ethnic marker. The Latins were beardless and wore their hair cropped short. They cut the beards and long hair of any Greek who came into their hands in 1185 and made them go bare-headed. They were still categorised as barbarians but less so because of their place of origin, more in terms of their behaviour in capturing and sacking the cities of the Balkan parts of the empire and in terms of mocking the Orthodox religion.[27] These observations were made in times of pronounced violence and stress. With the coming of Latin settlers and a modicum of political control in the early thirteenth century, there was a shift in emphasis from comments about appearance and behaviour to the perception of Latins as polluters and as unclean. Altars were washed after Latin use, they were labelled dogs, their cooking was dirty and to be exposed too long to their company was an abomination. It is noteworthy that all these negative connotations were written by Constantinopolitan Greeks. At the time of the second crusade Odo of Deuil had noted that Greek priests washed down altars used by the Latins. Sixty years later, with a Latin hierarchy established in the Aegean, this behaviour could not be tolerated by the Latin church.[28]

---

[25] Constantine Porphyrogenitos, *De Administrando Imperio*, ed. G. Moravcsik and R. Jenkins (Washington, 1967), pp.13/116–122 (p.71). Constantine was born at Naissos (mod. Nis in former Yugoslavia) in 273/4 but had been proclaimed Augustus at York in 306.

[26] B. Lieb, ed., *Anne Komnene, Alexiade* II (Paris, 1943) book X, pp.206–7. Trans. E.A.S. Dawes (London, 1928), vols 2–4, pp.248–9 and E.R.A. Sewter (Penguin, 1969), pp.308–9.

[27] J.R. Melville Jones, *Eustathios of Thessaloniki, The Capture of Thessaloniki* (Canberra, 1988), pp.61, 121, 123, 135, 147. Choniates, 565–95, (Magoulias trans., pp.311–27).

[28] Odo of Deuil, *De profectione Ludovici VII in orientem*, V.G. Berry, ed., (New York, 1938), p.55; Choniates, 557 (Magoulias trans. p.305); PL, 215:701 (July 1205) and PL 216:351 (December 1210); Mansi, ed., *Sacrorum conciliarum ...* (Venice, 1778, reprinted

The perception of difference should not be taken as either indifference or as a mark of subordination. Reading between the lines of the chroniclers who gave voice to the ethnic stereotypes, the positive and optimistic side of personal contacts can be seen at all levels. Alexios Angelos was treated well on his arrival in the crusader camp at Corfu in May 1203. At a less exalted level Nicetas Choniates had at least one close Venetian friend by whom he was saved in April 1204 and Robert de Clari formed a very favourable impression of the Greek tour guides in Constantinople in late 1203. These were perhaps the epitome of the east–west relationship of the twelfth century when contacts had been individual, temporary and often at long distance. Latins, often recruited in Venice, were eager to serve as mercenaries in the armies of Epiros and Nicaea. Attracted by favourable rates of pay, they put up with papal disapproval and excommunication to render signal service to their Greek employers. Western mounted warriors of the sergeant class seem to have harboured few reservations based on racial stereotyping, religious differences or national identity. In the summer of 1210 in Thessaly they did not baulk at decapitating Latin priests, crucifying Amedée de Pofoy and three companions, or in burning Latin property in the service of their employer Michael Angelos of Epiros.[29] Others in the service of Theodore Laskaris formed the bulk of his army at the battle of Antioch-on-the-Maiander in 1211 when they perished almost to a man gaining him a victory over the Seljuks.[30] In the campaign of 1214 which rid Paphlagonia of the Komnene of Trebizond, western mercenaries, including Latins from Constantinople, were again prominent in the Nicene army.[31] Pirate crews too were of mixed race and did not necessarily direct their attacks along ethnic lines. This disregard of cultural and religious divisions was no less true of those more intimate contacts between Greek women and the various merchants of the Italian mercantile republics resident in Constantinople. On the strength of Nicetas Choniates these have generally been taken to have involved greater familiarity on a day-to-day basis as lodgers with Greek families and as the partners of Greek women, all of which would have involved a spoken if not a written knowledge of Greek. It

---

[28] *cont.*
Leipzig, 1903) XXII, col.990 (1215); Pachymeres, 156, 161/7–11; Nikephoros Gregoras, *Bizantina Historia*, L. Schoper and I. Bekker, eds, I (Bonn, 1830), p.87/20–23; A. Dmitrievski, ed., *Typikon for St Michael* (Kiev, 1895), p.771, cited D.J. Geanakoplos, *Emperor Michael Palaeologus and the West* (Harvard, 1959), p.137, see pp.92–137 for treatment of the Latins in Constantinople in 1261 and the apparent absence of reprisals.
[29] PL, 216:353–4 (December 1210).
[30] Akropolites I, 16/6–9; Gregoras, op.cit., I, 18/16–19 and 19/24–25. For discussion see M. Angold, *A Byzantine Government in Exile* (Oxford, 1975), p.184, and M. Bartusis, 'The Kavallarioi of Byzantium' *Speculum* 63 (1988), 343, n.1.
[31] M. Angold, op.cit., p.182.

was a Venetian friend and former lodger who came to the aid of Nicetas and his family in the dangers which threatened both in April 1204.[32]

The military conquests following the Fourth Crusade led to much greater physical contact between a small number of westerners and the non-Constantinopolitan Greeks. These last were largely unused to a Latin presence of any kind unless they lived near the Via Egnatia or some of the commercial centres of the land where concessions had been granted to Venetian merchants. Those living in the Strymon valley were inundated each autumn by a large number of western merchants attending the St Demetrios fair at Thessalonika, but for the rest contacts would be limited to a handful of merchants attending the small merchant colonies such as that set up in Thebes by 1185.[33] Their other contact might be aural rather than direct and would have been based on fear and suspicion engendered by accounts of Norman attacks on the Peloponnesus and Thebes in 1147, Norman fleets on the Bosphorus and in the Aegean in 1149 and 1157, and the more recent sack of Thessalonika in 1185. Nonetheless a very marked difference can be distinguished during the Frankokratia between urban, that is Constantino-politan, and rural attitudes to the Franks, almost the reverse of what might be expected from the twelfth century background. Tolerance marked by an absence of large-scale destruction and the mass dispossession of landowners is noticeable in the Greek mainland and on the islands.

New bridges could be built in provincial Greece where class and economic self-interest led to accommodations between Latin lords and the traditional Greek landowners. The former needed the support of the archontic class in order to control the majority Greek population. To this end they were prepared to forego rights over the Greek church and not impose the Catholic religion on their new subjects. The archontes wished to maintain their patrimonial lands and their status as local dignitaries. In this they were encouraged by the small number of the Latins, who in the Morea seemed able to be settled on land surplus to Greek requirements.[34] Both groups were aided by their identity of interests and their similarity of background. Both were of the middle rank on the social scale and had never passed into the upper ranks of either western or Byzantine aristocratic society. Their sense of otherness was as strong with regard to court society as it was to the ethnic backgrounds of each other and their cooperation was aided by a recognition of their common economic and class interests and aspirations. The two groups, by whatever means they acquired or held their

---

[32] Choniates, 588 (Magoulias trans. p.323).
[33] Barry Baldwin, trans., *Timarion* (Detroit, 1984), pp.44–5. See discussion by Spyros Vyronis in Sergei Hackel, ed., *The Byzantine Saint* (London, 1981), pp.202–4. For Thebes see C.M. Brand, *Byzantium Confronts the West* (Harvard, 1968), p.196 citing R. Morozzo della Rocca and A. Lombardo, ed., *Documenti del commercio veneziano nei secoli XI–XIII* I (Turin, 1940), p.348 (dated 13 Feb. 1185).
[34] L de C, 106.

lands, saw that they had more in common as landlords and as men than either the feudal system or the upholding of the Roman primacy. This materialism might be thought all too provincial.

In Constantinople cross-cultural relationships were founded upon the ambitions of the middle ranks of the Greek population for whom the beginning of the Latin empire might hold promise of the lands and positions which had been denied them under the convention-bound society of the Komnenoi. Not all the Greek clerks who assisted in the transition from Byzantium to the Latin empire wished to slip away from Latin service like the father of George Akropolites.[35] The outs of the previous regime like Michael Doukas and Theodore Branas did not hesitate to seek service with the Latins. Branas clearly received the recognition which he craved, whilst Doukas's departure from the service of Boniface of Montferrat may have had as much to do with lack of prospects as with nationalist fervour.

Although Latin writers coined no metaphors for the city of Constantinople, its very occupation by a Latin emperor and a Latin patriarch were the most potent symbols of western triumph and rule and a source of shame and reproach to the former Greek ruling class. Byzantine aristocrats and bureaucrats were too closely identified with the patronage and ideology of the toppled regime to wish to stay or to be invited to do so by the Latin conquerors. As the successful supporters of the old order the signs of their former material success in terms of palaces, villas and fine artefacts made them targets of western looting, whilst their ideological commitment made it impossible for them to remain in the queen city controlled by barbarians. Constantinople became a symbol of the triumphant papal monarchy, of western interference with Greek life and of the continuing crusade. As such it attracted the attention and the advice of the papal curia, the French royal family and the presence of aggressive legates like cardinal Pelagius. Nonetheless, at a middling level of society, between the aristocrats who fled in 1204 and the lower classes who jeered them as they went, a hybrid culture was beginning to emerge even in these unfavourable surroundings. Both in city and country in the early thirteenth century there seems to have been room for accommodation, yet what of social and economic organisation? Did the Frankish elite introduce anything new?

Since the 1950s scholarly debate has raged over the issue of the feudalisation of Byzantium and the role of the western conquerors in it either as originators or intensifiers of institutional change. The ambivalence noted by Kazdhan and Constable has extended from the Byzantines

---

[35] Akropolites, *Chronike Syngraphe*, c.30, II, p.46; N. Oikonomides, 'La Décomposition de L'empire byzantin à la veille de 1204 ...' *XVe Congrès International d'études Byzantines, Rapports et co-rapports 1/1*, Athènes, 1976, 3–28, reprinted in idem, *Byzantium from the Ninth Century to the Fourth Crusade* (London, 1992). See p.48.

themselves to the Byzantinists. Some, following Ostrogorsky, have argued that the extension of the pronoia in the twelfth century marked the arrival of fully-fledged feudalism in Byzantium, others have denied the validity of the term in a Byzantine context, whilst still others urge the abandonment of the term 'feudalism' altogether as a subjective and reductionist construct which hinders rather than clarifies any understanding of the social and political organisation of medieval Europe.[36] There clearly is a problem here stemming from the subjectivism involved in defining the term. Too narrow or too broad a definition would permit feudalism to be seen everywhere or only in Normandy as the case might be. Economic historians prefer a broader, processual definition treating feudalism as a mode of production which can encompass all those people living in a feudal society, not just that small proportion of the feudal nobility. This approach has been shown to be justified and helpful for drawing comparisons between the Byzantine agrarian economy and that of the medieval west in the tenth and eleventh centuries.[37] However, it does not take us far in terms of social analysis and the impact of western conquerors on Byzantine society.

Generally a narrower more legalistic definition of feudalism in its developed western form has been retained by historians like Professor Jacoby and others. This has drawn attention to the differing degrees of feudalism in the western European homelands of the conquerors and attempted to see their broadly similar treatment of the Greeks in terms of a common feudal ethos. It has also tended to produce a somewhat mechanistic social model divorced from the lives of people in the real world. For example, the Catalan conquerors of central Greece were not feudalised, yet they are credited with taking over the fiefs of their dead feudalised Frankish foes and presumably exploiting them. In 1317 they were feudalised when they acknowledged the king of Aragon as their overlord. There are parallels here with the debate over the effect of the Norman conquest of England which occupied the first half of this century and was clearly on the mind of William Miller in 1908 when he somewhat inappropriately dubbed the battle of Koundoura the Hastings of the Morea. Were the Normans highly feudalised before or after 1066? Did they introduce feudalism or develop a feudal plan as they went along? One thing is clear: the Norman aristocracy occupied a land with a tradition of strong central authority which was not totally unfamiliar with social subordination and military service. To some extent Byzantium was in a comparable condition, although the emperor was unable to levy taxation in substantial parts of the empire. It is then not altogether surprising that, as Jonathan Shepard and Paul Magdalino have

---

[36] G. Ostrogorsky, *Pour l'histoire de la féodalité byzantine* (Brussels, 1954), p.26ff, summarised in *Cambridge Economic History of Europe* I 2nd edn (1966), pp.222–34. P. Lamerle, *Cinq études ...* (Paris, 1977), pp.186–7 Elizabeth Brown, 'The tyranny of a construct: feudalism and historians of medieval Europe' *AHR* 79 (1974), 1063–88.

[37] A. Harvey, *Economic Expansion in the Byzantine Empire* (Cambridge, 1989), pp.6–13.

shown, rulers like Alexios Komnenos and Manuel I Komnenos were fully aware of western feudal practice by the early twelfth century.[38] Ostrogorsky's identification of the pronoia with the fief has not fared well. Any similarities between the pronoia and the western fief were superficial. But he was not the first to see these similarities. It is not surprising that the Frankish conquerors, no legal historians themselves, could see the pronoia as the equivalent of the fief. This identification certainly does not mean that there was feudalism in Byzantium but that the Franks could relate in their own terms to certain realities of their new lands, namely land and its peasant cultivators. After all, landed wealth and the extraction of taxes and dues from the peasantry were features of pre-industrial societies and as such the empire was not exempt from these phenomena.[39]

The Latin ascendancy in Greece and the Aegean islands was made possible by the military capability of mounted knights and by their relatively small number which made mass appropriation of Greek lands unnecessary. There was enough former imperial territory and ecclesiastical land to allow them to settle without encroaching on the patrimonial lands of the archontes. The prime concern of the Franks was survival as a minority group and the exploitation and possession of their new estates. Most indeed took their title from these new lands. However, the further the Franks moved from Constantinople the more they moved into areas where local power groups had disputed for control and influence. Social differentiation in these areas was discussed in terms of the powerful (*dunatoi*) and the poor and therefore weak and lacking in influence (*ptochoi*). These were loose terms describing a fluid reality in which land, kinship and client networks defined status and power. Well before the crusaders had reached Constantinople in 1203 and certainly before they had entered the Peloponnese, the violent behaviour of Leon Sgouros described by Archbishop Michael of Athens and the proposals of the archon of the Messenia region with regard to using Geoffrey de Villehardouin and his companions in 1204 attest both the competitive nature of this society and its possibilities. The construction of free-standing towers in the countryside bear witness to the unstable situation. The value of knight service in such a situation was not lost on the western leadership, since an effective field force could be raised at very little cost.

On their arrival the Franks had the military advantage, being a unified force composed of neighbours and kinsmen from Burgundy, Champagne and northern Italy. Their settlement increased the number of factors in an already multi-faceted and fluid situation. To preserve their advantage it was essential to maintain their unity and their prowess as mounted warriors. In

[38] J. Shepard, 'When Greek meets Greek: Alexius Comnenus and Bohemond in 1097–98' *Byzantine and Modern Greek Studies* 12 (1988), 185–277; P. Magdalino, *The Empire of Manuel I Komnenos* (Cambridge, 1992), pp.32–3. See also *ODB*, sub 'lizios' (p.1243).
[39] Critchley, op.cit., pp.25–8, 39, 150–1.

response to almost constant warfare, not always against Greeks but sometimes against Latin neighbours, the land made available was apportioned in return for knight service. The great barons received between 24 and 4 fiefs, whilst the bulk of the 170 knight fiefs listed in 1225 went to knights with one fief and sergeants with a half of one fief. It is often remarked that this is not an impressive number, even when the number of fiefs listed had risen to 1,000 recorded in 1338.[40] However, as Professor Bartlett has reminded us, a fief was intended to provide sufficient revenue to support a knight, his mount and equipment, and therefore regional agronomy could not be ignored in the creation of fiefs.[41] Mounted service was frequently summoned in the thirteenth century. Both its length – eight months in the year – and the number of widows, shows that the military situation was far from settled. The Franks in Greece seemed not to have favoured the employment of mercenaries. Presumably as small players in a small field they lacked the finance to compete at recruitment fairs with the Latin emperor and the Greek rulers of Epiros and Nicaea. The Catalans in 1309 had presented themselves to Duke Guy II of Athens and the disastrous dispute of 1311 was over payment. Major campaigns outside the Morea required Greek troops either as allies in the case of the Pelagonia campaign in 1259 or as levies, presumably summoned in some way different to that of vassals. At some point there was clearly an inconclusive discussion as to whether Greek archontes could be summoned to provide knight service on the same terms as Latins.[42] This debate might have happened in 1268 before Moreote involvement in the Tagliacozzo campaign in support of Charles of Anjou or perhaps in 1304. Whenever it took place it was an important moment for the integration of the archontic class in Latin society.

Frankish Greece was a frontier society throughout its existence. As such the conquerors sought to maintain effective control by means of institutions imported from their homelands. Their ascendancy had been achieved by force or by the effective threat of force. To some degree this relied upon the myth of the Franks which had been current in Byzantine literary circles through most of the twelfth century and which during the Frankokratia was fostered by the Franks themselves in their literature and their wall-paintings. They also attempted to preserve a racial, linguistic, and territorial distinctiveness from their Greek subjects. The framework for this was consciously provided by various articles in the Assizes of Romania which evolved during the thirteenth century and has survived in a text written down in the 1330s, about the time that increasing military pressure

---

[40] L de F, 117–32 for list of 1225; see also D. Jacoby, 'Les états latins en Romanie ...' *XVe congrès international d'études Byzantines, Athènes, 1976, Rapports et co-rapport, 1/3* (Athens, 1976), pp.1–51, esp. pp.20–1, reprinted in idem, *Recherches sur la Méditerranée orientale* (London, 1979).

[41] R. Bartlett, *The Making of Europe* (Harmondsworth, 1992), p.51.

[42] Assizes of Romania, articles 70, 71.

evident since 1262 was making it impossible to prevent a measure of integration of the archontic class as mounted warriors and vassals in the Frankish army.

A top rung of foreign immigrants could not just be attached to Greek society without any account being taken of the social structures of the people whom it hoped to exploit and whose compliance was essential. In return for privileges the Greek landowners, both great (archons) and small (archontopoules), submitted and brought an end to resistance in the Morea. The privileges were not inconsiderable. From the start religious toleration was practically conceded, certainly for rural areas, although it was never given any legal sanction by inclusion in the Assizes of Romania. This would have been impossible in the light of papal intentions for the latinisation of the Orthodox as they evolved in late 1204 and after. They were legally free and could exercise jurisdiction over their serfs but they could not grant them freedom. The archons were confirmed in the possession of their patrimonial lands together with the peasants settled there. In return the archons prostrated (*proskunisan*) themselves before Champlitte as a sign of submission and subordination, equivalent to homage, and agreed to provide the homage (grecised very literally as anthropean) and military service consonant with their rank, that is knight service.[43] Either then or later their inheritance structures, so fundamental to any society, were preserved and kept separate from the primogeniture of the Latins. The landowners by their actions became the vassals of the prince. There is no means of knowing if these archons who had thus 'frankised' became abominations to their fellow Greeks as the late Alexios IV had become in late 1203. They presumably still exercised jurisdiction over their paroikoi. The words 'acquiescence' and 'co-existence' which are commonly used to describe the Frankish settlement with the Greeks conceal a multiplicity of details which cannot be known. For most Greeks who had the leisure to reflect after they had secured the survival of themselves and their families what mattered was who was their lord, their aphendiko, to whom they paid ther dues and to whom they looked for protection.

The social organisation of the Franks and the apparent ease with which the archons accepted their place in it attests to adaptability of both feudal law and the Greeks themselves. Those parts of it which impinged upon the Greeks did not appear to turn their world upside down.[44] As noted above, much western chivalric terminology had already entered the Greek vocabulary in the twelfth century. Acts of subordination were recognisable in both east and west but described differently. The chroniclers of the First Crusade interpreted the oaths sworn by the crusading leaders to Alexios I in early 1097 in terms of homage and fealty, whilst the Treaty of Devol in

---

[43] X t M, 1631–50; Assizes of Romania, articles 25, 47, 71.
[44] Assizes of Romania, articles 71, 138, 178, 194.

1108 was certainly regarded in crusading circles as establishing an imperial overlordship over the principality of Antioch. Nearly a century later in August 1204 Prince Bohemond IV, 'le Borgne', performed homage to Marie of Champagne at Acre in right of her husband, the Latin emperor Baldwin.[45]

Soon new words were to enter the demotic language, words like '*anthropea*' or '*homantzo*' for hommage, '*kourte*' for the high court, '*mparounia*' for barony, and '*phie*' or '*phe*' alongside '*pronoia*' for fief.[46] The existence of the pronoia from the late eleventh century showed that the holding of land in return for military service was not unique to western Europe, although its extension in the twelfth century to imperial soldiery may well have been influenced by Manuel I Komnenos's knowledge of western practice and his need for troops. It was certainly very like the fief. The pronoia was property, usually land, granted for a fixed term, usually the life of the pronoetes, and inalienable by him. In return for military service in the imperial army the pronoetes would maintain himself from the revenues from the lands granted to him. From this Georg Ostrogorsky and others have assumed that the grantee would have his own administrative devices for the exploitation of his rights and have thus predicated some devolution of central authority. Unlike western practice, however, there was no subinfeudation and consequently no hierarchy of vassals. All pronoia were granted by the emperor, they were not confined to the upper ranks of society and they were certainly not as widespread as the fief in the west. In Greek territory Michael VIII was the first emperor to make pronoia hereditary and to spell out unequivocally their military implications. It is likely but not proven that western influences were at work here.[47] The emperor and his advisers, some of whom were westerners, had an understanding of western feudal conventions and were not adverse to using them in their relations with westerners. The word '*lizios*' was mainly used to describe those westerners who, either individually or collectively, had sworn an oath of loyalty or fealty to the emperor, but it could be applied to subjects of the emperor as well. As early as 1170 it had been applied to a Greek subject, the diplomat Theorianos, and it was also applied to hellenised Latins like the pronoetes Syrgares with estates near Smyrna who was titled '*lizios kai kaballeros*' in 1251, and to John Doukas and his brother Nikephoros of Neopatras who were both described in an imperial letter of 1280 written in Latin as men bound to the emperor by an oath '... *fidelitatis et ligii homagii*'.[48] The emperor may have been acting as something other than a

---

45 Alberic of Trois-Fontaines, *MGH,SS* XXIII, 884. Alexios I had used the term '*lizios*' with reference to Bohemond I of Antioch in the Peace of Devol.

46 X t M, 1646, 1554/8, 2587, 1929, 1914/34/40 and 1920. See Jacoby, *TM* 3 (1967), 432–8 for a discussion of the dual usage of '*phie*' amd '*pronoia*'.

47 D.J. Geanakoplos, *Emperor Michael Paleologus and the West* (Cambridge, Mass., 1959), pp.212–13.

48 *ODB*, sub '*lizios*' (p.1243); Magdalino, op.cit., pp.106–7; P. Charanis, *Byzantinoslavica* 12 (1951), 96–9; Geanakoplos, op.cit., p.323.

feudal lord in these latter instances, but such actions were no more idiosyncratic than the action of William the Conqueror in 1086 when he demanded an oath of fealty from many who were not his vassals. William de Villehardouin had found it necessary to explain feudal tenure to Michael VIII in 1262 when the latter suggested he sell the Morea to him, but there is much to suggest that Byzantine feudalism had a development of its own.[49]

The Franks and Greek society

The Latin conquerors did not profoundly alter the society which they found in place in mainland Greece. There was no attempt to remove the topmost rungs of landlords as had taken place in Constantinople in April 1204. This was perhaps the single most important factor in the comparative stability of the Frankish states in Greece in contrast to the lands of the Latin empire in Thrace and Bithynia. Geography and the very small number of the Frankish army in the Morea, somewhere between 700 and 1,000 knights, made this both impossible and unnecessary. Greek landlords were confirmed in their patrimonial lands and the remaining territory, made up of former imperial and ecclesiastical estates and the lands of those archons who had sought refuge in Epiros, together with the towns and kastra placed in Frankish hands. Lack of friction seems to have characterised this process.

There was much cooperation between native Greeks and the invading Latins. On their arrival in central Greece the Franks were welcomed, capricious behaviour according to Choniates, whilst the reception given to the emperor Henry on his visits to Thebes and Negroponte in 1209, which included the town musicians and expressions of '*grant joie*' by the archons of town and country, showed that Frankish popularity had not yet dimmed.[50] Byzantine fiscal archives were made available for consultation together with the linguistic and technical skills necessary for their comprehension. Five Greek landowners were even included on the committee of twelve responsible for land allotments in the Morea and much local advice and guidance was freely available.[51] In the absence of guide books and maps this last was essential if the Frankish occupation was to take effect. For many people in the provinces not closely connected with the Byzantine court or the Orthodox hierarchy, the Franks were not seen as a threat.

---

[49] L de C, 314; X t M, 4271–301.
[50] Choniates, 609–10 (Magoulias trans. p.334); Valenciennes, 672, 683. See Clari XCIX/24–28 (McNeal trans. p.118) for pacific reception of the emperor Baldwin in the towns of Thrace in September 1204.
[51] L de C, 107.

A new rung of a Latin elite with estates for which they owed military service to the local lord was created and many of the fiscal and judicial functions of the former Byzantine provincial administration passed into their hands. They seem to have adapted easily enough to the local taxes of Byzantium and to the system of partiable inheritance followed by their Greek subjects. Far more is known of the feudal structure in the Morea than in any other of the Frankish states. In Boeotia/Attika and on the island of Euboea there seems to have been a large social and economic gap between the lord and his Latin vassals, whose standard of living may well have had more in common with their Greek neighbours than that of the megaskyr in Thebes or the triarchs in Negroponte. Certainly, according to Muntaner, Duke Guy II had to look outside the duchy for social equals to grace the festivities associated with his being dubbed a knight in 1296. The Burgundian vassals of central Greece seem to have consisted of men who might be classed as sergeants, although some of them were called 'miles', whatever that title might have meant.[52] Over 100 free-standing towers dot the central Greek countryside and seem to have been the mark of their lordship there, whilst the town was the site of their main residence. If Professor Vanderpool is correct in his dating of the Marathon tower to the twelfth century, then in adopting this building-type they seem to have followed the practice of local archons.[53]

In the Morea, where the conquest was incomplete, there was a need for more warriors and a continuing emphasis on ethnic unity. The Villehardouin seem to have been ambitious to distinguish their lordship within the Latin empire. This took the form of aiding the Latin emperor, placing neighbouring lords like the de la Roche under vassilic obligation, patronising religious orders and, of course, recruiting vassals. The first step was to retain the services of kinsmen, friends and followers. Their rewards necessitated a wider use of subinfeudation. There were the twelve great barons or tenants-in-chief, a strand of liegemen and others who held directly from the prince, many with vassals of their own, and at the bottom were the sergeants and the Greek archontes. For the twelve great baronies the quota of knights which they were due to provide to the princely army was listed in the chronicles of the Conquest. However, the obligations of the other feudatories are not listed. Possibly they were subject to an understanding based upon the practices of the Champagne, the region from which the majority of the Moreote Franks came.

It is clear that Byzantine tenures could be described in Frankish terms. It is unclear to what extent the pronoia system was diffused in the twelfth

---

[52] Muntaner, *Cronica*, c.244 (Hakluyt Society trans. 1921, pp.585–6); PL, 216:564–5 (doc.XXVIII) for O. miles, a knight resident in Thebes but with property in the diocese of Zaratoriensis, a region of free-standing towers.

[53] E. Vanderpool, 'A monument to the Battle of Marathon' *Hesperia* 35 (1966), 93–6: P. Lock, 'The Frankish towers of central Greece' *ABSA* 81 (1986), 101–23.

century empire. Professor Jacoby has shown that there is no direct evidence for the existence of pronoia before 1204 in territories conquered by the Latins. This may be due to the lack of specific references to Greece or, more likely but unprovable, the absorption of pronoia into patrimonial estates. The impression from the Assizes of Romania is that Greek pronoia dubbed fiefs abounded in the Frankish period. Not only that, the archons succeeded in preserving their inheritance customs and gained an extension of their terms to embrace the lands of a Greek female vassal married to a Frank, presumably the proportion of lands in Greek hands was not to be diminished by matrimony. Equally lands granted to an archon could not be revoked in the same way as they could for a grant to a paroikos. It would appear that the revenue from some lands were shared between Greeks and Latins and even by the relatives of some Greeks in Latin territory who were men of the emperor. The French chronicle an incident in the 1290s concerning the so-called casaux de parcons in the Corinthia.[54] Greek landowers were keen to be assimilated into the Frankish social organisations. Greek revolts in Crete were usually terminated with some grant of Latin titles to the erstwhile rebels, whilst article 71, which may well be a late addition referring as it does to the earlier lack of definition of Greek military obligations, shows that the Greeks were trusted to perform significant military service and that they were generally equated with the sergeant class, an identification which observations of their homes and lifestyle might well have prompted.

There are a number of accounts of princely and baronial armies in action in the thirteenth century. The campaigns range from major expeditions outside of Latin territory, namely the Pelagonia campaign of 1259 and the campaign of Guyot and Nicholas de St Omer into Thessaly in 1304, to smaller actions directed against the Greeks of Mistra, like the campaign of Geoffrey I de Bruyere in 1264. In all these armies we find mercenary soldiers and Greek feudatories fighting alongside the Franks and even taking a prominent and honoured part in the war councils of Guyot and Nicholas de St Omer.[55] At a time when the legitimate Byzantine power was being restored on the Bosphoros and in the Peloponnese, significant numbers of Greeks chose to remain loyal to the Latin domination with which after two generations their self-interests were clearly connected.

In central Greece following the Catalan conquest of 1311 and the end of Burgundian rule, the legal position of the archondes deteriorated. The absence of any grant of Frankish citizenship during the whole century of Burgundian rule noted by Professor Setton was not the indictment that he took it to be. As a territory in which the Assizes of Romania was acknowledged, the position of the archons as freemen who could acquire

---

[54] L de C, 663–70.
[55] L de C, 263, 881–908; L de F, 311–21.

and dispose of property was guaranteed. However, the ascendancy of the Catalans resulted in the abrogation of the Assizes and with it the cancellation of all privileges to the archons. Now freedom and privilege came with Catalan status and this had to be earned. Thus in 1311 certain archons living in Livadhia were to have the privileges of the Franks for themselves and their heirs for ever. Other such grants were to be made for signal service and loyalty, but the gulf between Greeks and Latins in this area widened permanently. Under the Acciaioli dukes of Florence two grants of such privileges were recorded. These two grants were probably not the sum total but they do indicate that the practice of the Catalans persisted long after their displacement in 1388.[56]

The majority group, the Greek peasantry, seem to have acquiesced passively in Latin rule. It seems that their legal status might well have been diminished in Latin-held territory. The Assizes of Romania has some twenty clauses dealing with serfs, that is unfree, dependent peasants. Most of those clauses which dealt with the stasis, staxia, or peasant holding and the taxes and services incumbent upon it preserved Byzantine legal provisions but substituted the western term '*villanus*', usually translated as serf, for the Byzantine '*paroikos*'. As with the term pronoia/fief we are back to that grey area where westerners could describe property and status in their own terms, which were apparently, but not exactly, similar to their own social and economic organisation in the west. For the peasantry prosperity and survival were more important than legal status. It might be that in lands under Latin rule the heritable status of serfdom was a western innovation not found in Byzantine territory until the fourteenth century and where only the heir to a peasant holding or staxia took on the services and status involved.[57] Within Latin-controlled territory it cannot be said whether there was any difference in the treatment of peasants on the lands of Greek archontes and those on fiefs held by Latin lords. Against the unfamiliarity of a new foreign lord with his Greek lands has to be set the appeals to such a lord by the Latin church to exert his position as the lord of serfs to regulate their religious life. We have already noted the attack by various Greeks from Gravia on Hugh, the archdeacon of Daulia, sometime in late 1211 or early 1212. What concerns us here is the letter from Innocent III to the lord of Gravia asking him to seek out and punish the malefactors.[58] It would be no use appealing to a

---

[56] DOC, no.CCLXVIII, pp.352–3, (1362 rather than 1366). K. Setton, 'Catalan Society in Greece in the Fourteenth Century', in L. Laourdes, ed., *Essays in Memory of Basil Laourdes* (Thessaloniki, 1975), pp.241–84, esp. pp.243–5; R.J. Loenertz, 'Athènes et Néopatras: Regestes et notices pour servir a l'histoire des duchés catalans' *Archivum Fratum Praedicatorum* 25 (1955), 100–212, 428–31, see especially pp.117, 194, 199–200, reprinted in *Byzantina et Franco-Graeca* (Rome, 1978), p.183ff.

[57] A. Laiou-Thomadakis, *Peasant Society in the Late Byzantine Empire* (Princeton, 1977), pp.142–58; D. Jacoby, in H. Hazard and N. Zacour, eds, *A History of the Crusades* VI (Madison, 1989), pp.185–9.

[58] PL, 216:564, doc.XXVIII. See p.212.

Greek lord in the same terms. Thus it might be that only in matters of religion might the serfs of a Latin lord be brought under occasional more direct and inconvenient pressure to conform to Latin religious practice than those on the estates of an archon. Although it is generally agreed that before 1204 the subjugation of the paroikos to his lord had become very tight, there were considerable legal differences between the paroikos in imperial territory and his fellow in lands ruled by the Franks.

The serf was tied to his lord and no superior lord could intervene in the relations of this vassal and his serfs (articles 162, 176, 181, 188, and 203).[59] The bond was a personal one which did not depend upon the cultivation of a staxia or temporary leases of holdings on the land of other lords. The bond could not be broken either by running away or by the staxia being confiscated or its revenue granted to another lord (183, 197). Article 183 deals with the inheritance and payments of a '*zurado*' or staxia granted to the church by the lord. The grantor continued to receive the acrosticon whilst the grantee derived the revenue of the land and decided which of any sons should take over the working of the land on the father's decease. The other sons, if there were any, reverted to the original lord. Such a grant was a usufruct, jurisdiction over the serfs incidentally involved remained with the lord and the zurado, who derived his new title from the status of his land, remained a part of the village community.

The visible signs of dependence were the rendering of taxes and services to the lord. The payment of the acrosticon in wax, fowls or eggs was the actual acknowledgement of lordship (183, 190). The profits that a lord derived came from labour services or dispoticaria (190) for the performance of which each peasant household had to maintain a pair of oxen and an ass (187, 215), the receipt of a portion of the crops of his peasantry, known as the zemuro (214), and the profits of justice from civil offences (43, 162 and 177). There was occasional income to be derived from treasure trove (155) and in emergencies the right to take all the movable goods of his serfs (197). From the lord's point of view, he had to ensure the sustenance of his serfs '... so that the fief to which the serf belongs is not diminished. ' (197). This involved the minimal provision of bread and water during imprisonment and some protection against the forcible taking of straw, poultry or any other thing (23). The bond worked both ways if somewhat unequally.

Many clauses in the Assizes emphasise again and again that servile status was hereditary. If a free woman, even if she were a vassal, married a serf she forfeited her free condition and joined him in serfdom. Should she

---

[59] P. Topping, *Feudal Institutions as Revealed in the Assizes of Romania: The Law Code of Frankish Greece* (Pennsylvania, 1949), reprinted as essay I in *Studies in Latin Greece* (London, 1977). The numbers given in brackets in the following paragraphs correspond to the numbering of the articles in this edition.

survive her husband she regained her free status as a widow but any of her children born of the servile union remained serfs and had no claim on their mother's fief (78, 180). Illegitimate children received the status and the lord of the mother, whilst legitimate children followed the status of the father (174, 179). For a female serf marriage to a free man brought freedom (125). Only the prince could free a serf (25) and any grants made to such a free man had to be written down and were valid for the term of the grantor's life.

The serf was a piece of property with a notional value. If he were accidentally killed by a liegeman he was to be replaced by a serf of equal value (151). Serfs could also be used as a form of currency provided that those given in payment did not exceed one-fifth the value of the fief (107). A serf could form no contractual relations of his own without his lord's consent. Without his lord's permission the serf could not contract himself or his daughters in marriage (174) ; he could not engage in trade, other than the selling of surplus animals and crops, since he could not contract any loan or debts on his landholding (187, 215); nor could he make a will and devise his property without his lord's permission (185). He could not be called as a witness in criminal proceedings involving the loss of life or limb (198) nor in any matter concerning an entire fief, although he could give information regarding parts of a fief like boundaries and occupancy of vineyards and parcels of land and about his fellow serfs (175). Should he find any treasure hidden in the ground his right to treasure-trove passed to his lord (155).

There were various categories of peasant, although the Assizes and the mid-fourteenth century documents from the Acciaioli estates published by Peter Topping and Jean Longnon made virtually no economic distinctions within the broad group of serfs, except between those who occupied a staxia and those who did not.[60] There could have been little difference in the wealth of those poorer archons with little land and few serfs mentioned in article 71 and richer serfs, some of whom may have been those Greek vassals who were serfs and apparently were obliged to seek investiture within a year. Just who were these servile vassals mentionned in article 138? Did they reproduce in Latin territory the Klazomenites or soldier-peasants stationed at Serres in 1342?[61] Just as perplexing, articles 142 and 192 seem to suggest that there were free peasants in the Morea who held vineyards and fields which they could devise by will in return for the payment of an annual rent or cens; like the acrosticon of the unfree it was an acknowledgement of the lord's superior right to the land. The majority of the unfree inhabitants of a casal held a staxia and paid the taxes and services due for it. Presumably what there was of a village hierarchy would be formed by those who could produce a surplus over and above their own

---

[60] Longnon & Topping.
[61] Laiou-Thomadakis, op.cit., p.142.

needs and the demands of their lord. At the bottom were those who had deserted their holding or as relative newcomers lacked any status or background within the casal. Such was the nicario, ennicarius or nicarius, an unfree peasant whose economic status is not made clear in the Assizes (181, 182, 184 and 214).[62] It is possible he was a rural labourer who grew crops on a share-cropping basis, with half the produce going to the lord. He did not hold a staxia and did not enjoy the full rights of the serf. Finally was there such a category as western serf in Latin Romania? At first sight it seems unlikely, but there was provision made for those placing themselves under a lord who came in from outside the principality, why not from the west? Article 198 seems to place an emphasis upon 'Greek' and to imply a distinction between the testimony of Greek serfs and that of other, presumably non-Greek, serfs.

The military conquest of the Aegean by the Franks and the establishment of a small number of westerners as a political, religious and legal elite led to a number of contractual accommodations between members of the old and the new elites. The Greek populace, whether they welcomed the Latins or not, seemed resigned to their Latin lords since clearly any mass resistance or non-cooperation would have made Latin rule and economic exploitation impossible. More than just capitulation and acquiescence would be necessary if a hybrid society were to develop. Changes in self-perception as well as changes in the perception of the other, Frank or Greek, must take place. This could not be brought about by edict but only by evolution through time. It is in the personnel of a ruler's councils, his estate management, and most of all in the marriage-bed and in ethnically mixed households that we should look for evidence of a new society.

Mixed marriages

Material regarding mixed marriages or extra-marital relations is patchy. Limited as it is to law-codes, the occasional papal letter and Venetian grants of citizenship in the fourteeenth century, it lacks any real personal ingredient or family dynamic. Since both Franks and Greeks were Christians there was no canonical impediment to intermarriage. However, as the thirteenth century wore on there was a hardening of attitude, certainly at the papal court. It was accepted that rulers had to marry for matters of state, despite religious or social preference, but even they, according to Gregoras, were expected to seek papal permission before contracting marriages with Greeks. Donald Nicol has noted that eight out of eleven female members of Greek ruling families in the thirteenth century married either French or Italian

---

[62] Longnon & Topping, pp.264–6.

husbands but that not one male member married outside the Orthodox world. Daughters might be expendable in the interest of Greek diplomacy but there seems to have been some reluctance amongst the Latins of the thirteenth century to marry their daughters to Greeks.

The late twelfth century had witnessed the marriages of Agnes of France and of Margaret of Hungary into the Byzantine imperial family. Both had married young and had been so successfully hellenised that in 1203–4 both required interpreters, presumably to translate the French of the crusaders into Greek.[63] After 1204 there is only the marriage of Maria de Courtenay to Theodore Laskaris in 1219. What might be termed diplomatic marriages came increasingly under papal ban. One reason for the emperor Frederick II's excommunication in 1245 was his giving of his daughter Constance to John Vatatzes in 1244. The courtship of Catherine de Courtenay, heiress to the Latin empire of Constantinople, by Andronikos II on behalf of his son came up against papal ban whilst Andronikos's own marriage to Yolande de Montferrat in 1284 was carried through without papal permission. Gregoras recorded that it was the custom of the Latin nobility not to contract marriages with Greeks without first seeking papal permission.[64] The Catalan chronicler Ramon Muntaner observed that the wealthy and the knightly classes in Frankish Greece took their wives from the best French houses and did not marry any lady who did not descend from French knights. From the Greek side Pachymeres noted that the Franks were very haughty.[65] It would appear that the upper levels of Latin society sought to maintain racial and linguistic purity as well as social exclusiveness as a mark of their dominance. With the single exception of Demetrius, the son of Boniface of Montferrat and Margaret of Hungary, born in 1206, the Latin aristocracy did not favour Greek personal or saints' names for their children. Just what the practice was in the mixed households of lower social groups we are not in a position to say. There does seem to have been a real fear of western settlers going native.

Marriage was a means of conveying property and status. Those in authority seem to have wished to prevent Greek blood entering the landholding classes. By the early fourteenth century if not earlier the Assizes of Romania contained a variety of clauses designed to discourage licit and illicit relationships with Greeks. The illegitimate children of a Latin with an unfree Greek woman retained the unfree status of the mother, whilst any free woman marrying a Greek adopted his status as did any children who had no rights with regard to their mother's landed property. In their first years as masters of central Greece the Catalan Company forbade the

---

[63] Clari, LIII (McNeal trans. p.79); PL, 216:222.
[64] D. Nicol, 'Mixed marriages in Byzantium in the thirteenth century', in C.W. Dugmore and C. Duggan (eds) *Studies in Church History* I (London, 1964), pp.160–72.
[65] Muntaner, ch. CCLXI (trans. Goodenough p.627).

marriage of Greeks with Latin women and backed this up with a ban on Greeks acquiring landed property.[66]

Marriage and family was a natural corollary of the acquisition of land. Westerners of modest origins or slender resources who through their enterprise and luck in moving into the Aegean, either as retainers or mercenaries, had ceased to be landless would have followed their instincts and sought a wife. It is not until the fourteenth century that papal letters mention the marriage of non-noble westerners with Greeks. Western women were in short supply in Greece. The temption to marry local women must always have been present for those like sergeants who lacked the resources to tempt a western bride to Greece. The rush to snap up Frankish widows in 1311 showed a predilection amongst the Catalans for western women, but once the supply had run out they loved where it was convenient to do so and they were clearly not alone amongst the western settlers in central Greece. If Pope Benedict XII is to be believed, by 1336 Italians and other Catholics on the island of Euboea were marrying Greek women and attending Orthodox services because of the lack of Catholic partners due, he believed, to the unstable military situation.[67] No statistics can be given but in Constantinople mixed mariages between Italian merchants and Greek women had been taking place since the early twelfth century without attracting undue attention from Greek or Latin writers except in times of political upheaval as in 1204 or 1261 when their loyalty might be brought into question.

Latins in town and country

Both in town and country the Latins were in a minority. This certainly explains their tendency towards ethnic solidarity. There are no sure guides to the population of Frankish Greece. The invaders of the Morea in 1204/5 numbered between 700 and 1,000 men. We have no idea of the number of women present with the army. Certainly the high men tended to bring their womenfolk eastwards after the conquests had been made. Professor Rubio y Lluch has made a number of estimates of the Latin population in central Greece in the fourteenth century. He estimated the Catalan population of Athens to be about 3,000 out of a total of some 10,000. His proportion of about one-third Latin population in towns has been generally accepted. In central Greece as a whole he reckoned that there were no more than 5–6,000 persons. Even in a group which seems to have moved around the

---

[66] *DOC*, nos.268–9 (pp.352–4); K. Setton, *Catalan Domination of Athens* (Cambridge, Mass. 1975), p.252.
[67] A.L. Tautu, ed., *Acta Benedicti XII (1324–1342)* (Rome, 1958) XI, pp.18–19, discussed in Jacoby, art.cit., 21.

Aegean complete with womenfolk and children this was not large. Under-population was always a problem with the Latin establishment in Greece. As early as 1212 there were insufficient priests for the small Latin settlement, Otho de la Roche's attempt to encourage the pope to establish a Latin parochial structure around a minimum of twelve resident Latins seems to have met with little success, whilst a century later Latins in central Greece and Euboea were attending Orthodox services. The '*raritatem et paucitatem*' of Latins was emphasised by Benedict XII in 1336.

The Latin minority, whatever their political and economic back-ground, tended to live in the towns. The countryside was left to the Greeks. Thus we see in the case of O. 'miles', an otherwise unknown Latin knight or sergeant, resident in Thebes but with landed property in the diocese of Zaratoriensis. The cathedral church of Zaratoriensis is probably identifiable with the large church on the south-western edge of the site of ancient Askra and known locally as 'Episkopi'. The boundaries of the diocese are not securely known. There is a free-standing tower some 500 metres from the church but whether this was the property of the offending knight is not known. However, the bulk of the diocese must have extended to the north-east, since to have done otherwise it would encroach upon the diocese of Nezerocensis, generally accepted to have been Thisbe. Zarartoriensis was an area containing many such towers and contained O.miles, a Latin landholder who lived in Thebes. Here he was attending mass whilst under ban of excommunication from the bishop.[68] Of the 200 Catalan family names known to us, the great majority lived in Athens, Thebes, Livadhia and Neopatras. The others lived in smaller urban complexes at Salona, Karditza and Kapraina. The countryside was given over largely to the Greeks and for a Latin priest to venture into it might invite violence. In the same year, 1212, the archdeacon of Daulia was beaten up near Gravia for interfering in a Greek wedding. At this incident, as well as the early accommodations of the Franks and the Greeks in the Morea, as well as in the ordinances and legislation discussed above, the divide between Greeks and Latins was a religious one. This together with the legal measures and unconscious attitude behind this legislation tended to lead to the social segregation of Greeks and Latins, an attitude that tended to harden through time.

Gasmouloi, the children of mixed parentage

Like the union of their parents, the children of mixed marriages escaped official notice until political change highlighted their existence in terms of a

---

[68] PL, 216:564–5.

question of loyalty. Legitimate children followed the status and religion of their father and would have been baptised by the Latin rite. Stable relationships with close bonds between husband and wife certainly did exist and resulted in many families being evacuated from Constantinople by the Venetian fleet returning from the Daphnousa expedition in July 1261 when the Latins on board saw their homes burning and their wives and families sheltering on the waterfront.[69] There is a hint of illegitimacy attached to this group, although those with Venetian fathers and grandfathers seemed conscious of their patrilineal descent in the discussions between the Venetian and Byzantine governments over their acquisition of Venetian citizenship in the half century after 1280. They seemed to have had considerable freedom to choose whether to be Greek or Latin and to change their minds as the situation suited their personal advantage. According to Tafrali they could pass themselves off easily as Latins. The first mention of these gasmouloi, as they were termed in Greek, occurred in the pages of Acroplites and Pachymeres in connection with the reconquest of Constantinople in 1261. They were deemed to have '... the discretion and cautious spirit of the Greeks with the ardour and pride of the Franks' and were used as marines and rowers in the imperial fleet.[70] With the Greek re-establishment in the Morea after 1262 many of them seem to have been recruited there along with the Tzakones. Certainly, in 1263 numbers of them served along with the Tzakonians in the naval squadron which ravaged Euboea, the Archipelago and the coast of the Morea.[71] If they were particularly valued as sailors they were hard hit as a group by the laying up of ships as an economy measure in 1285. Many found alternative employment as pirates serving in either Greek or Latin vessels. Their sentiments seem to have been towards their mothers' people; whether this was the result of broken homes or expediency cannot be known, although it is interesting that the Byzantine writers did not make something of this apparent rejection of Latin blood. The western chroniclers dealing with the Frankish states were silent about them; presumably like the poulaines or pulani in the kingdom of Jerusalem they were beneath their social interest.[72]

---

[69] Pachymeres, 146–7; Gregoras, 85; Akropolites, 182–3.

[70] Pachymeres, 1888/11–12; Gregoras, 98/8–10; D.J. Geanakoplos, *The Emperor Michael Paleologous and the West* (Harvard, 1959), p.127 and notes; A.E. Laiou, *Constantinople and the Latins* (Harvard, 1972), pp.65, 74–5, 270–1; D. Jacoby, 'Les Vénitiens naturalisés dans l'empire byzantin' *TM* 8 (1980), 221–4; O. Tafrali, *Théssalonique au quatorzième siècle* (Paris, 1913), p.44.

[71] Pachymeres, IV, 26 (CSHB, I, 309).

[72] Only Joinville, *Histoire de Saint Louis*, para 434 and Jacques de Vitry, *Historia Orientalis* I, c.67, have short mentions of this racially mixed group. J. Prawer, *The Latin Kingdom of Jerusalem* (London, 1972), pp.68, 529.

The language barrier

How did Greeks and Latins communicate with each other? Any transaction, commercial, legal, military or sexual, soon exhausts the bounds of body language and rudimentary vocabulary and requires a linguistic knowledge on the part of someone. The terms Latins and Franks, as used by both westerners and Greeks, were linguistic markers as much as anything else. Certainly the former was a religious label too. It referred to those who followed the usage of Rome with its emphasis upon Latin as a liturgical language.[73] Frankoi on the other hand was a straight linguistic description. Clause 145 of the Assizes of Romania suggests that the Franks as a body were not noted for their skill in acquiring languages. This clause may belong to the early days of the settlement, yet, judging from the pages of the chronicles of Villehardouin and Clari there seems to have been little problem in oral contacts. At first sight, deals were made and broken with Prince Alexios, lunch-time conversation with the bishop on Corfu, tours around Constantinople enjoyed and the figures presented by fiscal clerks in 1204 digested. However, when Louis of Blois tried to identify himself to his cousin Agnes-Anna in 1203, she required an interpreter, '*un latimier*'. Whatever Louis's lack of such an assistant might suggest about his own attitudes to non-Francophones, it can be seen that a situation in which body language might be thought to have been useful broke down completely without the assistance of a translator. Margaret-Maria took her interpreter Emmanual with her to her new home in Thessalonika as the wife of Boniface of Montferrat. Her own hellenophilia and her long residence at Constantinople makes it likely that Emmanual was there to translate French or Italian for this former Hungarian princess and Byzantine empress. Certainly the emperor Henry thought it advisable to have Emmanuel on his side in his dealings in Thessalonika in 1209 and made over to him some houses in Stagonicaria in 1210.[74]

Interpreters played a vital role in the Latin conquest and must have accompanied the Latin armies into Thrace, Thessaly and the Morea. We do not know how Geoffrey I de Villehardouin made himself understood or understood the offer of the local archons when he landed in Messenia in the winter of 1204. Did he have an interpreter with him acquired in the Levant or were bilingual skills available in Coron? There had always been interpreters at the imperial court responsible for diplomatic correspondence and occasional service with foreign embassies. In 1204 these were pressed into the service of the Latins. Choniates tells the story of Theodore Tornikes, the logothetes tou dromou or head of the interpreters, who unsuccessfully sought refuge with the Bulgarians on the defeat of the emperor Baldwin in

[73] Clari, XVIII/61/63/74; XXXIII/43/47/51 (McNeal trans. pp.48, 60).
[74] Clari, LIII/3–4 (McNeal trans., p.79); PL, 216:227.

1205. In the late thirteenth century the Angevin court in Naples seemed to rely upon the services of bilingual Greek priests fron southern Italy when they required a translation or authentication of a document in Greek.[75] This was all right for occasional translation but this policy of make-do would have been totally inadequate in crusader Greece. With the settlement of the Latins in the Aegean bilingual skills would be much more in demand and by a wider section of society. This may well have induced many Greeks of the middling rank to gain proficiency in the languages of the Mediterranean. There is circumstantial evidence for such knowledge. For example, in 1380 John Boyl, bishop of Megara, raised 20 ducats on the security of a box of books from a Greek money-lender Peter Moscho. This transaction took place in Phokis, not a centre of the book trade, and presumably Peter thought that he could cover the debt should Boyl default on his repayment.[76] Certainly in commercial centres these were skills which it was either prudent or directly rewarding to possess. Anthony Luttrell has drawn attention to the numbers of Greeks in Constantinople under John Cantacuzenos (1344–55) who knew Catalan, which was as widely used in the fourteenth century commercial world of the Mediterranean as Italian.[77] The Venetians seem to have preferred their own citizens as translators. This policy is evident from the records of the senate in the mid-fourteenth century. In 1341 Leonardo Zuliani, the interpreter to the podesta in Constantinople, was allowed leave of absence to return to Venice on personal business. His services were so highly regarded that he was allowed part payment during his period of leave. The scribe-interpreter to serve with the rector of Pteleon in the same year was to receive an annual salary of 60 hyperpera, some 20 hyperpera less than his master. Long periods of residence and service in its Aegean chancery seems to have been looked upon as essential for these interpreters. In 1413 the interpreter in the chancery at Negroponte was not to be replaced annually like the other executive officers there.[78]

Robert Browning has written of the complex effect of the Latin conquest on the Greek language. Since classical education was difficult to obtain in Greek lands under Latin control and advancement no longer depended upon a correct Atticistic style, one incentive was unconsciously provided for the development of vernacular Greek writing. The author of the *Chronicle of the Morea* was certainly a man little influenced by the

---

[75] Perrat and Longnon, p.82; R. Weiss, 'The translators from the Greek of the Angevin Court of Naples' *Rinascemento* l (1950), 195–225.

[76] *DOC*, no.CDIII (10 September 1380). For discussion of books see Setton, op.cit., pp.220–2.

[77] Setton, op.cit., p.251, citing A. Luttrell, 'John Cantacuzenus and the Catalans at Constantinople', *Martinez Ferrando, Archivero: Miscelanea de estudios dedicados a su memoria* (1968), 265–77, reprinted in *Latin Greece, the Hospitallers and the Crusades 1291–1440* (London, 1982).

[78] Thiriet, 119, 130, 1475.

Byzantine literary tradition of his day.[79] Some Greeks of the second and third generation after the conquest were closely involved with Latin neighbours and clearly could make themselves understood. In 1295 the archon Foty clubbed Guy de Charpigny to death mistaking him for Gautier de Liedekirke who had arrested and maltreated him. Foty or Photios was the cousin of Jacob Zassy or Tzausios and as such a member of the dominant family of Kalavryta after its recovery by the Greeks in the early 1270s. His words of vengeance were chosen to leave his victim in no doubt as to the motive for the attack and were clearly understood by the squires in attendance on Guy who made clear to Foty his mistake. It is not known what language Foty used in his ill-directed attack.[80] Other revenge incidents involving verbal abuse and physical insult offered to Greeks by Latins about this time seem to have resulted in appeals by the offended party to the Greeks of Mistra who used the allies thus thrown up to recover land from the Latins. Two cases, one of the merchant Corcondille (Chalcocondoules) insulted at the Vervena Fair by Gerard de Remy and the seizure of the castle of St George at Arakhova, and the parallel incident of certain unnamed Greeks insulted outside the Church at Nikli and the subsequent destruction of the castle there,[81] show that Latins and Greeks could understand each other when necessary and that the establishment of the Greeks at Mistra did provide an alternative to Frankish rule and a revival of self-esteem on the part of the Greeks in Latin territory. There is, however, very little hard evidence for there being much incentive outside Constantinople for Greeks to learn western languages and so make a career in the service of the Franks in government, notarial offices and estate management. To be sure there are individual examples, which, like those of Latins who we know were proficient in Greek, may represent the tip of an iceberg. The office of protovestarios or prothoficier in the Morea was often held by a Greek: the names of Quir Vasypoule, Stephen Cuttrullus, Johannes Murmurus and possibly Colinet (Kollinetos) have come down to us in this context.[82] Anino, the son-in-law of Corcondille, was the cellarer at the castle of St George and was in a position to hand it over to the Greeks.[83] Both this and the next example point to family traditions of dealing with the Latins and perhaps of bilingualism. There were the notaries, father and son, Nicholas and Constantine de Mauro. The latter received the public notariate of Livadhia in 1381 and clearly knew both Latin and Catalan, since in April 1380 he

---

[79] Robert Browning, *Medieval and Modern Greek* (London, 1969), pp.75–91.

[80] L de C, 664–78.

[81] L de C, 806–16; L de F, 474–85. Did these two stories which have many common features demonstrate a topos for Franco-Greek relations in the 1290s?

[82] L de C, 829; Longnon & Topping, pp.21/11 and 33/8. For the office of protovestarios/prothoficier see X t M, 7680–1, 7936, 8656; L de C, 526, 752; and the Assizes, article 171.

[83] L de C, 804–7.

had issued a notarial certification in Catalan of a document written in Latin.[84] Greek and Italian or Catalan notaries functioned almost in parallel existences in the Latin territories, with Greeks using their fellow countrymen and so on. Those who crossed the linguistic and cultural divide in the provinces were exceptional, essential and highly rewarded as we have seen.

Franks who learned Greek

On the Frankish side a number of notables of the second generation seem to have learned Greek. We are specifically told about some of them. Marino Sanudo Torsello recorded the conversation in Greek between John de la Roche and John Doukas at Neopatras in 1271, notable because of his apparent quotation from Herodotus.[85] William de Villehardouin spoke Greek like his native tongue as did Geoffrey d'Aulnay who shared his prison in Constantinople in 1262.[86] Equally both Philip de Toucy and his brother Anselin knew the language and customs of the Greeks because they were born and brought up in Romania.[87] Their father had come east with Peter de Courtenay in 1217 and their mother was the daughter of Agnes-Anna of France by her second husband Theodore Branas. Women took an important part in this language acquisition either as mothers or as wet-nurses for the first two or three years of their charge's life. Whilst a Greek mistress seemed to have provided some first generation westerners in Greece with more than the rudiments of the language, as was the case of Roneo de Bellarbre, the Catalan castellan of Athens in 1379 who had a mistress named Zoe, and of Nerio Acciaioli. The Toucy brothers seem to have entered into the flavour of Byzantium. Anselin had a Cuman squire named Perrin, whilst Philip dined out in Caesarea in 1252 on stories of the wedding ceremony of his father, Narjot, with a Cuman princess.[88] The Assizes of Romania, in presenting a general picture of Frankish linguistic incompetence, may have done a disservice to the many Franks who knew Greek. Such knowledge certainly went further down the social scale, although names are lacking. The Italian agent who compiled the various estate surveys for Niccolo Acciaioli in 1350s clearly knew sufficient spoken Greek to question and understand the answers of village elders on payments and services of rural communities in

---

[84] Setton, op.cit., pp.250–1 citing *DOC*, no.CCCXCIII, (p.484).

[85] CGR, pp.120–1. The quotation *'pollus laos, oligoi anthropoi'* comes from Herodotus, VII, 210.

[86] X t M, 4130; L de C, 702.

[87] L de C, 357, 646–66.

[88] L de C, 374; N. de Wailly, ed., *Jean sire de Joinville, Histoire de Saint-Louis* (Paris, 1874), paras 495–8 (trans. M.R.B. Shaw, *Chronicles of the Crusades*, Penguin, 1963, p.289–90).

the south-west Peloponnese, but could also read and check Greek fiscal documents and typika.[89] Professor Laiou has drawn attention to the bilingualism of Venetian notaries on Crete, able to translate Greek wills into Latin and transact business with Greek families. Some, like Stefano Bon, married a Greek wife, left bequests to both Latin and Greek monasteries and chose to be buried in the latter where he noted that he had learned Greek.[90] For all that, a certain cachet was attached to bilingualism in noble circles and at the Angevin court there was almost a casual air to the way in which documents in Greek were translated or verified by suitably qualified Greek priests from southern Italy, who swore on the Gospels that their translation was correct.[91] The difference may well be a class one – just as the great employed clerks to write for them, they did the same when they required translations. Only in the late fourteenth century was there a certain prestige attached to writing Greek in the west and hence the survival of a few letters written in Greek by the Acciaioli dukes of Athens in the archives of the family in Florence. For the less grand the acquisition of Greek was a fact of survival and as such seems scarcely to have warranted official attention.

The practical nature of linguistic contact comes through in M. Triantaphyllides's work on direct lexical borrowings published in 1909 which still dominates the field.[92] He has shown that loan-words from French were concerned primarily with feudal law and landholding, whilst the larger number of words borrowed from Italian were concerned almost exclusively with commerce and shipping. All this would suggest urban contacts limited to legal and commercial matters. Much of this already existed between the Greeks of Constantinople and the merchants from the Italian city republics. In the Peloponnese new links were clearly being formed at the landowning level, whilst the majority of people who did not commit their thoughts to writing must remain outside the field of analysis.

The Latin Aegean and the classics

Surprisingly the Latin occupation of Constantinople and the Aegean did not contribute significantly to the knowledge of the classics in the west. There were signs of an interest in Greek manuscripts on the part of a few exceptional scholars like William, a monk of St Denys who brought codices from Constantinople in 1167, but teachers and manuscripts in Greek were

---

[89] Longnon & Topping, pp.52/14–17, 164/6.
[90] A. Laiou, *Medievalia et Humanistica* 12 (1984), 49–50.
[91] Perrat and Longnon (1967), doc.79 (April 1294), pp.82–3.
[92] M. Triantaphyllides, *Die Lehnworter der mittelgriechischen Vulgarliteratur* (Strassburg, 1909, reprinted in his collected works, Thessalonika, 1963). I have used the summary of his work in Browning, op.cit.

in short supply in the west in the twelfth century. Those involved in the sack of Constantinople in 1204 were not classical scholars; their concern was for precious metals and reliquaries and clearly libraries were not spared in their search for loot. Byzantine scholars of the late twelfth century like Eustathios of Thessalonika, Michael Choniates and John Tzetzes, a schoolmaster from Constantinople, had all read texts which disappeared forever in 1204, like works by Callimachus and Hipponax.[93] Manuscript hunters from Italy did not tour the Aegean until the fifteenth century, but a modest start was made from a quite unexpected quarter, namely the diocese of Lincoln in England. When he became bishop in 1235 Robert Grosseteste (*c.* 1168–1253) was just getting into his stride as a Greek scholar. Both the chronicler Matthew Paris and the friar Roger Bacon described how the bishop gathered scholars and texts around him to assist in his translations of Greek theological works and, later, Aristotle's *Nichomachaean Ethics*. John of Basingstoke (d. 1252), who had visited Athens in the early thirteenth century, was made archdeacon of Leicester within months of his election. It may well have been he who stimulated the sending to foreign parts for scholars. Bacon stated that there were many Greeks in England and France at this time but only a very few who taught Greek correctly. Two of these '*veri Graeci*' were in the Grosseteste circle – Robert Grecus and a magister Nicholas Grecus who seems to have been a clerk connected with the Abbey of St Albans which presented him to the church of Datchet (Bucks.) in 1239 and who in 1246 became a canon in Lincoln. Apart from the translation work, the '*Parcioarium*', a Graeco–Latin lexicon, which made much use of the *Suda* in the bishop's translation, might also be attributed to this circle. It survives today in the College of Arms and was described by the late M.R. James as a monument to the study of Greek in thirteenth century England. Grosseteste did something to remedy the lack of teachers and books and his coincidence in time with the Latin occupation of the Aegean should not be dismissed lightly. He certainly inspired Roger Bacon (*c.* 1214–92), who regarded him as a pioneer in Greek studies, to produce a Greek grammar in the 1270s and to emphasise the importance of the Greek Fathers to theological studies, but both men were ahead of their times.[94]

Of the ranks of the Latin episcopate in Greece only one man can be securely assigned an interest in the language and literature of classical Greece. This was the Flemish Dominican William of Moerbeke (*c.* 1220–86) who set out to translate the whole Aristotelian corpus together with some of

---

[93] L.D. Reynolds and N.G. Wilson, *Scribes and Scholars* 2nd edn (Oxford, 1974), pp.63–9.

[94] K. Hill, 'Robert Grosseteste and his work of Greek translation', in D. Baker, ed., *Studies in Church History 13: The Orthodox Churches and the West* (Oxford, 1976), pp.213–22; R.W. Southern, *Robert Grosseteste, The Growth of an English Mind in Medieval Europe* (Oxford, 1986), pp.17–18, 181–6; E. Nolan, ed., *The Greek Grammar of Roger Bacon* (Cambridge, 1902).

the later Greek commentators into Latin. His interests and knowledge were clearly formed before 1260 when he visited Constantinople, Nicaea and Thebes. In April at Nicaea he completed the translation of Alexander of Aphrodisias and the following December in Thebes he finished translating Aristotle's *De Partibus Animalium*. He was active in the negotiations for church union at the Second Council of Lyons in 1274 and in April 1278 he was made the Latin archbishop of Corinth. On his return to Italy in 1274 he brought many Greek manuscripts with him, leaving in Greece only a vague toponymic association with the village of Merbaka (mod. Ayia Triada) in the Argolid.[95]

If knowledge of the classical Greek language was confined to the eccentric few in the west, there was much greater awareness of some of the major events of ancient Greek history. They were seen as inspirational and perhaps here lay the seeds of the Fallermayer thesis developed in the nineteenth century, when once again a western dynasty was imposed upon the Greeks. We have already noted John de La Roche citing Herodotus in an inspirational context, but there were other and earlier examples. In the first months after the conquest Innocent III alluded to Greece as the well-spring of education, the emperor Baldwin I was aware of the great age of Athenian democracy as contrasted with the period of the tyrants and used it as a guide for the conduct of newly dubbed knights, whilst both Pierre de Brachiaux and Robert de Clari knew something of the Trojan Wars and justified the capture of Constantinople as a revenge on the Greeks.[96] This interest did not extend to the preservation of ancient statuary about which attitudes were ambivalent. The magnificent group of gilded bronze horses were brought back to grace the facade of the basilica of San Marco but the bronze statues of pagan deities were melted down for small change.[97] As Professor Setton has emphasised, the first aesthetic eulogy of a classical site from a western pen was written by Pedro IV of Aragon in 1388 when he described the Acropolis as 'the most precious jewel there is in the world' (*la plus richa joya qui al mont sia*). The king had never seen the Acropolis but was clearly moved by the accounts of those of his subjects like John Boyl who had.[98]

---

[95] M. Grabmann, *Guglielmo di Moerbeke, OP., il traduttore delle opere di Aristotele* (Rome, 1946); *ODB*, p.2197.
[96] PL, 215:637; *Urkunden* I, p.302; Clari, XL/6, CVI/30.
[97] Choniates, 649; G. Perocco, ed., *The Horses of San Marco, Venice* (London, 1979). The Venetians took other pieces of sculpture and built them into St Marks. They also took ecclesiastical vessels of great age, value and beauty. The Franks on the other hand seemed to have been more interested in relics. Whether this was due to problems of transportation for the latter or whether it constituted a significant cultural difference is a moot point.
[98] K. Setton, op.cit., pp.188–9.

Women

An examination of the role of women in this frontier society is hampered because the sources only provide details concerning women of the topmost ranks and even that information is always within a political context. Margaret de Neuilly, la dame de Morena, was the daughter of Jean II de Neuilly of Passava, the hereditary marshal of the Morea, and through her mother, a daughter of Gautier de Rosiere, heiress to Akova or Matagriffon, the largest barony in the Morea. She was married three times to members of the Frankish nobility and in 1262 was sent as a hostage to Constantinople, together with the unnamed sister of Jean de Chauderon, the high constable, to secure the release of William de Villehardouin. During this time the barony of Akova passed to her, but due to her detention in Constantinople she was unable to claim within the legal period of a year and a day. Her second husband, Guglielmo II da Verona, seemed unable to bring any pressure to bear and on his death in 1275 she was advised to marry a strong man who could assist in her claim. Her choice fell on Jean de St Omer, joint lord of Thebes, and through his influence William compensated her with a grant by charter of one-third of the barony. She showed much persistence and determination, but we are left with the impression that she was ultimately successful only through the standing of her husband. She could read since she realised the import of the writ to the chancellor which Prince William asked her to pick up from under his counter-pain.[99] Despite legal protection for liegewomen in regard to the inheritance of a fief or the non-feudal (bourgeois) property of her husband, the backing of a powerful man made all the difference. In 1304 Margaret de Villehardouin found the support of Nicholas III de St Omer, '... the most puissant ... and feared man of the entire country', decisive in her appeal before the high court to regain the movable property of her late husband Richard of Cephalonia, which her stepson John hoped to keep.[100]

The chroniclers reflect male attitudes. However, they did not deny that women could exercise political power as ably and with as much determination as their husbands, nor did they assume that this led inevitably to a baleful result. Two Epirote Greek women who had married into the Frankish ruling class exercised regencies for their infant sons with marked success. Anna Angela Komnene had married first William de Villehardouin in 1259 and in 1280 Nicholas II de St Omer. Her niece, Helena Angela Komnene, married William de la Roche in 1275, by whom she had Guy II or Guyot. She was regent for her son between 1287 and 1294, aided by her second husband Hugh de Brienne. Both women were Greeks, respectively the sister and the niece of Nikephoros I, despot of Epiros (1267–96). Both

---

[99] X t M, 7301–752; L de C, 501–31.
[100] L de C, 955–72.

exercised power in their own right while their husbands were either dead or captive, and like Anna's sister-in-law, Anna Palaeologina Kantakouzene, and other aristocratic women of Byzantium, they played a prominent role in the politics of their day. The same was true of Anna's daughter Isabelle de Villehardouin and her granddaughter Mahaut, who in 1305 married Helena's son, Guyot (d. 1308).

Of the 219 articles in the Assizes of Romania as written down in the 1330s, 41 dealt with the legal position of women in Romania, 35 with free women, the wives of knights.[101] Women emerge as means of passing property, rights and status. The actions of a group of aristocratic women at the parliament of Nikli in 1262 could not be guessed from the legal status assigned to them in the Assizes. A distinction was made between liegewomen and the widows of simple vassals with regard to remarriage, but that apart, within the bounds of primogeniture women could inherit fiefs, do hommage, although it was customary for a man to speak for her, and be invested with a fief in their own right or in the right of their husbands should the latter be prevented from claiming the fief in person – a situation which did not work in reverse as we have seen in the case of Margaret de Neuilly. Women were regarded as in the guardianship of their husbands with regard to matters military. The husband was responsible for providing a substitute to perform military service on his wife's behalf should she hold a fief in another castellany to his own. On the death of a husband the widow received as her dower the profits from half of the fief or fiefs which he held at the time of their marriage. The dot or dower which the bride brought to the marriage passed under the husband's control. Should she predecease him without giving birth to a living child the dower should be returned to her family.

Most of these complex regulations were necessary to maintain the integrity of the fief and military service, and at the same time to protect the interests of heirs and widows in the tangle which might result from remarriage. Second and third marriages were not uncommon for women due to the high rate of attrition amongst the knightly class and the great imbalance between male and female in this immigrant warrior society.[102] No woman could be forced to remarry against her will. Decisions were taken in consultation with friends and mother, and love was often found where political influence and prestige already resided. Judging from Margaret de Neuilly's action in 1275, the choice of a partner often rested with them, was not taken lightly but not too tardily either. The Assizes contained a number of articles which sought to discourage marriage with Greeks. Some chose landless knights and thereby reduced the pressure amongst that group for

---

[101] Articles 31, 32, 34, 35, 37–41, 44–46, 56, 58, 64, 73–76, 78, 85, 109–10, 113–14, 119, 121, 125, 134, 137–8, 140–1, 154, 156, 174, 179–80, 189, 194, and 217. Articles 174 up to 194 deal with unfree women and marriages with Greeks.
[102] See p.83.

fiefs, but far and away the best option seems to have been an established man of power and prestige.

Both Isabelle de Villehardouin and her great niece, Isabelle de Sabran (1297–1316), sought to maintain or regain the Villehardouin influence in the Morea through their husbands, in both these cases with melancholic results. Due to their background, as possible but specious claimants to the former Villehardouin principality, and their residence and marital involvement in western courts, they lacked the opportunities to assert themselves in their own right such as their Doukana relatives enjoyed within the world of Frankish Greece. Isabelle's marriage to Florent de Hainault, a great grandson of the first Latin emperor Baldwin, in September 1289, was clearly acceptable to Charles II of Anjou who granted the principality of Achaia to the couple. Florent, an active and popular ruler, died in 1297 at the age of 47, leaving Isabelle with a title and a daughter but a tightly circumscribed sphere of action. Isabelle's second marriage to the egotistical Philip of Savoy in 1301 may have been a love match but it led to the eventual loss of the principality in 1305 due to Philip's aggressive attitude to the Moreot baronage and his lack of support at the Angevin court. He was bought off and the principality passed to Charles's favourite son, Philip I of Taranto. Isabelle strove in vain to assert her rights to the principality and eventually retired to Hainault where she died in 1311. In 1313 Isabelle's daughter Matilda (usually called Mahaut) was used to facilitate the marriage of Philip of Taranto with Catherine de Courtenay, the titular empress of Constantinople. Previously, Catherine had been betrothed to Hugues of Burgundy and now Mahaut was to be married to his brother Louis, and through her the title to the principality of Achaia was to pass to the Burgundians. There were advantages to both Mahaut and Louis in this arrangement. In the meantime, Margaret de Villehardouin, Isabelle's sister and Mahaut's aunt, went to Naples to request the principality in her own right as her father's heir. Her specious request was ignored but whilst at the Neapolitan court she sought the help of King Robert's wife, Queen Sancha, to speak to her brother, the king of Majorca regarding the marriage of his son Ferrando with her daughter Isabelle de Sabran, and thereby pass the Villehardouin claim to the principality to one who had connections with the Catalan Company and thus might well be in a position to upset the grand diplomatic designs of the Angevins in so far as they affected the Morea. The marriage took place at Messina in 1314. In July 1316 Ferrando was killed at Manolada in the reckless support of his claim in a conflict that prudence might have won.[103] Clearly there was a divide between the political power that a woman could exercise in Frankish Greece and that which she could exert across the Adriatic at the Neapolitan and Sicilian courts. Influence was the most that could be conceded there. Nowhere is this difference more

---

[103] L de F, 555–621.

strikingly brought out than in the parliament convened at Nikli in 1261 to discuss the fate of the Frankish prisoners taken at the battle of Pelagonia in 1259 and since then held in Constantinople.

Nowhere in Europe in the thirteenth century could there be found anything to parallel the parliament summoned to meet in the castle of Nikli in 1261. It was not quite the 'parlement de dames' which late-nineteenth-century writers liked to make out, but it was no less remarkable for that.[104] The baili of the Morea, Guy I de la Roche, summoned prelates, barons and knights to the parliament or council. Since most of those who owed personal military service were either dead or in prison with William de Villehardouin, the Greek chronicle informs us that the archontesses their wives were with the princess in the castle holding a parliament (parlama). It must have been expected that they would turn up to represent their husbands. There were, however, more men present than the four usually named – Leonard da Veroli, Pierre de Vaux, Geoffrey de Karytaina and Guy de la Roche. In the French chronicle these latter are depicted as presenting the cases for and against surrendering the three castles to the Greeks. It would probably be mistaken to read into this an implied contrast between the rational males and the emotional females. This gender stereotyping belongs more to this century than the thirteenth. Anna Doukaina seems to have represented her absent husband since duke Guy addressed his observations to her '... and you other lords, prelates and knights'. The women were treated formally, on a par with their absent husbands. The Greek terms were agreed and hostages chosen at the parliament to go to Constantinople.[105] These, as we have seen, were the daughters of the hereditary marshal and the constable; women again represented men, in this case their fathers, presumably because the offices which the latter held were hereditary. Margaret de Neuilly's husband, Guilielmo da Verona, was presumably present since he had recently been released from prison along with Narjot dalle Carceri by the baili Guy de la Roche in the light of the emergency. The military exigencies of a frontier society had produced a remarkable situation. The decision was a crucial one since it led to the re-establishment of Byzantine government in the Morea and to a worsening relationship between Latins and the Greeks living in Latin territory. No blame for this was attached to the women, but its effect can be measured by contrasting the relative quiescence of the Greek population in 1262 in the absence of the bulk of the Frankish forces with the disputes of the 1290s.

---

[104] Marquis Terrier de Loray, 'Un parlement de dames au XIIIe siecle', *Acad. des Sciences, Belles-Lettres et Arts de Besancon* (1881) pp.205–11; W. Miller, *The Latins in the Levant* (London, 1908), pp.116–17; R. Rodd, *The Princes of Achaia ...* I (London, 1907), pp.213–15.
[105] L de C, 323–8; L de F, 300–5; X t M, 4418–24; Sanudo and the Italian Chronicle in CGR, pp.108 and 447–8 respectively.

The Jewish community

Finally, mention must be made of the Jews in Frankish Greece. There is a total lack of material dealing directly with them under the Frankokratia and therefore nothing to inform as to the fate of those Jewish communities visited by the Rabbi Benjamin of Tudela in the 1160s. Even the Catalan documents have not one mention of Jewry or of the large Jewish community at Thebes, which was there in 1160 and there again in the post-medieval period. With the exception of the Jewish quarter or Stenon noted by the chronicler Villehardouin in Galata, which was subsequently burnt by the crusaders in fighting around the Galata tower in 1203, the impression from circumstantial evidence from Jewish sources suggests continuity. It is not definitely known when and where the Jews of Constantinople were relocated after 1203. Under the Palaeologi they occupied the Vlanka quarter of the city but that this occurred before 1261 is probable but unprovable.

Indirect evidence suggests the continuity of Jewish settlements in the Aegean. In 1218 Judah al Harizi visited Thebes and was impressed by the wine and the conversation of his co-religionists, whilst an unpublished letter of John Apokaukos written about 1210 listed Jews as one of the groups engaged in the cloth industry and trade at Halmyros. There is the mention of a solitary Jew at Salona, but the presence of medieval tanneries north of the castle has been taken to point to a Jewish community there. It has been argued that in the Aegean tanning was an occupation reserved almost exclusively to Jews. An anonymous letter of the early fourteenth century listed seven towns where Jews were to be found: Negroponte (Egrippon), Thebes, Corinth, Adro (Andros), Salona, Constantinople and Khrimini (La Cremonie). Jews were also settled at Patras and in the Venetian possessions of Romania. Jewish merchants from southern Italy seem to have frequented Glarenza without hindrance and Jewish travellers from western Europe to the Holy Land were glad to tarry in Greece.[106]

There is very little evidence to suggest that the Jews suffered any particular anti-semitic attitudes imported from the west in the wake of the Third and Fourth Lateran Councils. Certainly they owned property within Patras and its suburbs, a town owned by the archbishops after 1266.[107] In 1314 the Dominican Andreas Doto was appointed inquisitor in the province of Greece. His attention was directed mainly against the Orthodox Christians of Crete but he did prosecute a certain Sambeti or Sambetay who

---

[106] Steven Bowman, *The Jews of Byzantium, 1204–1453* (Alabama, 1985), pp.49–88, docs 12, 16, 22, 26, 30; J. Starr, *Romania, the Jewries of the Levant after the Fourth Crusade* (Paris, 1949), pp.70–82.

[107] L de F, 398. Guillaume Aleman sold the barony for 16,000 hyperpera (perperas de Morea).

was collector of the massetaria or tax on all commercial and, after 1338, property transactions.[108]

It was unusual for Jews to hold public offices, although it has been suggested that Sabbatay and a certain David of Negroponte were given privileges because of financial services rendered to the Venetians. Benjamin of Kalamata, the protovestarius of the Morea and after 1300 its long-serving chancellor, was a Frank, despite his suggestive name. He was granted the status of a Venetian citizen in 1320 and was still holding the office of chancellor in 1324. Although his career cannot be cited as that of a Jew holding high public office in the Morea, it should warn us from assigning ethnic attributions on the strength of a name and a toponymic alone.

There seem to be striking parallels with the treatment of the Jews in the Latin kingdom of Jerusalem. The capture of Constantinople and the conquest of the Aegean was not regarded as a disaster Jewish settlements were left undisturbed, apart from the Galata settlement burnt as an exigency of war in 1203, and Jews could hold public office. They were a tolerated minority.[109]

The Latin space in the Aegean

We have no information which will allow a quantification of the number of Greek let alone Latin inhabitants of the Aegean area in the thirteenth century. We therefore do not know the proportion of Greeks to Latins, or the relative proportions of social and economic groups within the two communities. The Black Death of 1348 and subsequent epidemics certainly put an end to any previous population growth as it did in western Europe. Whilst we have a solitary piece of indirect evidence in the letter of Peter IV of Aragon in 1380 that the Greek population of the countryside of central Greece was in serious need of supplementation by immigrant Albanians, we have no information of the effect of the plague on the Latins.[110] Those below the archontic class and the vast majority of those Latins outside the rank of liege lord have left scant literary and archaeological monuments to their existence. We are forced to rely upon impressions derived from sparse and chronologically diverse scraps of information. We are better informed on the ideal rather than the everyday, and it is this last which we must attempt to plumb in order to glimpse something of Greco–Latin life.

---

[108] D. Jacoby, 'Venice, the Inquisition and the Jewish communities of Crete in the early fourteenth century' *Studi veneziani* 12 (1970), 127–44; idem, 'Les Juifs vénitiens de Constantinople' *Revue des études juives* 121 (1972), 397–410, both reprinted in *Recherches sur la Méditerranée orientale* (London, 1979).
[109] J. Prawer, *The History of the Jews in the Latin Kingdom of Jerusalem* (Oxford, 1988).
[110] *DOC*, no.DXXXVI, p.587 (31 Dec. 1382).

Latins were a tiny minority. After the influx to Constantinople in late 1204 from the Levant, there was no large-scale immigration. Only the city of Constantinople exerted any attractions to would-be settlers. What there was was individual and small-scale. One effect of this was to ease pressure on landed resources and allow for accommodation with Greek landowners without wholesale dispossession. This was possibly the single most important factor which allowed the Latins to maintain their foothold in Greece. In Cyprus the Greek landed classes had been disappropriated and a vigorous policy of attracting western knights was put in hand by Guy I de Lusignan, who advertised in Armenia, Antioch and Acre, and as the continuator of William of Tyre wrote '... and I tell you, if the emperor Baldwin had settled Constantinople as king Guy did the island of Cyprus, he would never have lost it'.[111] The problem was not as clear cut as the anonymous chronicler might have thought. The Latins of the Aegean had advertised too, both in Syria and in the West, but Cyprus was clearly more attractive than the Aegean for western settlement. As an island it could be dominated and it could provide certain security from external aggressors. The rugged land frontiers of the Aegean were all too susceptible to the threat of Bulgarian, Epirote and Byzantine attack, whilst any aura of the Latin Holy Land in exile which might attach itself to Cyprus was missing in the Aegean.

Byzantine writers from Anna Komnene to Nicetas Choniates saw the westerners as barbarians with little to teach, whilst western writers were aware of their cultural insufficiency except in matters of war. Both these juxtapositions went back to classical antiquity: civilised Romans and uncivilised barbarians on the one hand, warlike Romans and unwarlike Greeks on the other, or even avenging Trojans and untrustwothy Greeks. Each culture perceived the positive qualities of the other but in the twelfth century chose to express them in a negative way. By the end of the thirteenth century there is some evidence for perceptual change. The gasmouloi were perceived as possessing the strength and valour of the Latins together with the cunning and intelligence of the Greeks. An anonymous Greek could translate the *Chronicle of the Morea* for his fellow Greeks in pro-Latin terms. These observations were confined to the Greek tradition. Within a century the Greeks of Galaxadhi congratulated themselves on duping the Hospitallers who were stupid like all Franks. Clearly in personal and perceptual terms there was a real change on the part of the majority Greek population to the Latins which they hosted. No such familiarity has come down to us on the Latin side. It would seem that what there was of Franco–Greek society did not develop much beyond what had already been

---

[111] Peter Edbury, *The Kingdom of Cyprus and the Crusades, 1191–1374* (Cambridge, 1992), pp.13–22; M.R. Morgan, ed., *La continuation de Guillaume de Tyr* (Paris, 1982), pp.138–9, cited by Robert Bartlett, *The Making of Europe* (Harmondsworth, 1993), p.53.

in place before the coming of the crusaders and that was largely due to Italian merchants domiciled in Constantinople. This is not surprising, since the estimates of the Venetian population domiciled there in the twelfth century may well have exceeded that of the number of Franks dispersed about the Aegean during the thirteenth century and certainly during subsequent centuries. There was no iron curtain between Greeks and Latins but there was a fairly broad chasm which could be crossed at some peril.

Chronological Summary

1204   *March*, Pact of Crusader and Venetian leadership regarding division of booty, lands and offices on capture of Constantinople.

12 April, Constantinople stormed followed by three days of sacking.

9 May, election of count Baldwin of Flanders as first Latin emperor.

16 May, coronation of Baldwin by Nivelon de Cherissy in Hagia Sophia.

June–Aug., Baldwin subdues Thrace as far as Adrianople and captures Thessalonika.

Dispute with Boniface regarding Thessalonika.

Theodore Laskaris continues resistance to Latins from Brusa.

'Empire of Trebizond' established by Alexios I Komnenos and his brother David, grandsons of Andronikos I (1183–85).

August, Boniface sells Crete to Venetians for 1,000 marks.

Sept–Oct., Committee of 24 partition Byzantine empire along lines of the March Pact.

Sept? Geoffrey de Villehardouin the younger travelling from Syria to Constantinople forced by weather to winter at Modon in Messenia.

Sept–Nov., many Latins from Syria arrive in Constantinople including a papal legate.

1 Oct, 600 men knighted and enfeoffed by the emperor Baldwin I.

Late Oct/early Nov., Boniface of Montferrat conquers Boeotia and Attica.

Michael Doukas leaves army of Boniface and sets up as governor of Nikopolis (Epiros).

1 Nov., Pierre de Bracieux campaigns in Brusa region.

11 Nov., Henry of Flanders begins campaign between Abydos and Adramyteion.

Renier de Trit occupies Philippopolis.

Baldwin's troops occupy Nicomedia.

Nov/Dec., Jacques d'Avesnes conquers Euboea.

Boniface begins siege of Akrocorinth and Nauplia.

6 Dec., Pierre de Bracieux defeated at Battle of Poemanenon by Greeks from Brusa.

1205   *21 Jan.*, Thomas Morosini confirmed as Latin patriarch by Innocent III.

Early, Villehardouin the younger fights his way to Nauplia where he acknowledges William de Champlitte as his lord in return for military assistance to conquer the Morea.

Theodore Laskaris moves headquarters from Brusa to Nicaea.

Spring, the Champlitte/Villehardouin expedition of 100 knights and 400 sergeants leaves Nauplia via Corinth, Patras and Andravida for Messenia. First check at Kyparissia but otherwise north and west coasts of Morea in Frankish hands.

19 March, Henry of Flanders defeats Nicene Greeks at Battle of Adramyttion.

30 March, Morosini consecrated patriarch in Rome.

April, Louis of Blois killed and Baldwin captured by Kalojan near Adrianople.

Latin conquests in Thrace and Asia Minor abandoned.

Henry of Flanders regent or baili of the empire.

Exodus of Latins from Constantinople.

May, Battle of Koundoura in north-west Messenia. Franks defeat army of 4,000 Greeks, some sent from Epiros by Michael Doukas who is now forced to abandon claim as governor of the Peloponnese.

15 May, Benedict of Santa Susana appointed papal legate to the Latin empire.

May, regulations for election of future Latin patriarchs published by the pope.

1 June, death of Doge Enrico Dandolo.

June, Venetians in Constantinople elect Marino Zeno as their podesta and dominator in Romania.

Papal appeals for clerics and scholars to proceed from west to Constantinople.

Late June, Morosini arrives in Constantinople.

August, Euboea divided into triarchies by Boniface.

19 Nov., William de Champlitte first mentioned as

'princeps totius Achaiae' in a papal letter acknowledging election of the first Latin archbishop of Patras.

Compilation of the feudal register of the Morea begins?

1206   Venetian fleet occupies Modon and Coron.

17 March, the regent and church authorities agree that 1/15th of territory to be ceded to the church.

July, death of Baldwin I in captivity in Bulgaria confirmed in Constantinople.

12 Aug., first mention of archbishop elect of Thebes.

20 Aug., coronation of Henry of Flanders by Thomas Morosini.

27 Nov., first mention of Latin archbishop elect of Athens.

Dec., Latin archbishop of Thessalonika appointed.

1207

Marco Sanudo conquers the Archipelago which he holds as a vassal of the Latin emperor.

Marco Dandolo seizes Andros which he holds from Sanudo.

Marco Venier captures Cerigo and Jacopo Viaro captures Cerigotto, both acknowledging the suzerainty of Venice.

4 Sept., Boniface killed by Bulgarians near Mosynopolis.

Lombard breakaway movement lead by Umberto de Biandrate emerges in Thessalonika.

Death of Kalojan of Bulgaria.

1208

March, coronation of Theodore I Laskaris at Nicaea.

Death of Leon Sgouros at Akrocorinth (or Nauplion?).

July, Latin episcopal structure extended into Thessaly.

Dispute over payment of tithes between Latin clergy and Frankish lords develops.

Latin rite to be used in all episcopal consecrations in Romania.

Sept., Battle of Voulae near Philippopolis, Henry defeats Greeks.

15 Dec., Morosini renounces pledge to appoint only Venetian canons to Hagia Sophia.

Dec., Emperor Henry marches to Thessalonika and places Boniface's son Demetrius on the throne.

William de Champlitte returns to France.

1209

Early, on death of Champlitte's nephew Geoffrey de Villehardouin assumes princedom in the Morea.

March, Emperor Henry captures Larissa.

Ravano dalle Carceri acknowledges suzerainty of Venice for his lands in Euboea.

1–2 May, Parliament of Ravennika near Lamia attended by 60 barons including Otho de la Roche and Geoffrey de Villehardouin.

8 May, Emperor Henry enters Thebes.

Templars lose castles at Ravennika and Sydonius for supporting the Lombards.

June, Treaty of Sapienza between Villehardouin and the Venetians: boundaries of Modon and Coron defined and suzerainty of Venice over the Morea recognised.

1210

Feb., Corinth falls to Villehardouin.

4 March, church at Corinth to be organised on western lines.

22 March, Villehardouin first addressed as 'Princeps Achaiae' in a papal letter.

His wife Elizabeth des Chappes arrives from Champagne with his son and heir Geoffrey.

2 May, Second Parliament of Ravennika sought to regulate relations with the church: all priests to be exempt from secular jurisdiction and exactions except the akrostikon or land-tax. Tithes and mortmain legislation remain in dispute. Geoffrey de Villehardouin did not attend.

Oct., archbishop of Patras in Rome with plans to turn his chapter over to regular canons. Castle at Patras under construction.

Dec., Amedée de Pofoy crucified on the orders of Michael of Epiros. Reports of decapitation of Latin priests in Thessaly reach Rome.

Battle of Salona results in temporary loss of Salona to Michael Doukas and the death of Thomas I d'Autremencourt.

1211	Venetians begin colonisation of Crete. *June/July*, Morosini dies at Thessalonika. Nicene Greeks defeat the Seljuks at Antioch-on-the-Maeander. *15 Oct.*, Nicene Greeks defeated at Hellespontine Pegae by the Latins who now claim to control lands from Poemanenon to Pergamum.
1212	*Jan.*, Emperor Henry at Pergamum. *Early*, Argos captured by the Franks. *May/June*, Larissa recaptured by the Epirote Greeks. *June*, Cistercians and Premonstratensians first mentioned in Greece. Dispute over treasures of the Corinthian church recovered by Villehardouin and de la Roche at Argos. *July*, John of Rodosto, a Greek uniate bishop, in Rome. *Sept.*, a papal notary Maximus sent to oversee election of a new patriarch.
1213	Durazzo recaptured from Venetians by Michael of Epiros. Marco Sanudo sends help to the duke of Crete to suppress revolt of the Agiostephanai family. Emperor Henry marries Mary, daughter of Boril of Bulgaria.
1214	*Jan.*, monks of Mount Athos placed under papal protection. Cardinal Pelagius offends moderate orthodox opinion in Constantinople. Corfu incorporated in despotate of Epiros.
1215	Fourth Lateran Council. Demetrias and Domokos in Thessaly recovered by the Greeks. Michael Doukas of Epiros murdered at Berat in Albania. Succeeded by his half-brother Theodore Komnenos Doukas. *11 Nov.*, consecration of Gervase as second Latin patriarch of Constantinople. Excommunication of Geoffrey de Villehardouin and Otho de la Roche by Gervase for ignoring the Concordat of Ravennika of 1210.
1216	*11 June*, death of Emperor Henry at Thessalonika. *16 July*, death of Pope Innocent III. *24 July*, coronation of Pope Honorius III. Death of Ravano dalle Carceri, lord of Euboea.

Nov., Pietro Bembo, the Venetian baili of Negroponte, arranges succession to the triarchies of Euboea.

Ochrid and Prilep captured by the despot of Epiros; the Via Egnatia effectively closed to Latins.

1217   *11 Feb.*, Pope Honorius orders relaxation of the sentence of excommunication against Villehardouin and de la Roche.

9 April, Peter de Courtenay crowned Latin emperor in San Lorenzo, Rome.

14 April, John Colonna appointed papal legate with powers to rationalise Latin dioceses in the Aegean.

17 April, Peter, with a force of 160 knights and 5,500 infantry, sets out to recapture Durazzo and reopen the Via Egnatia.

April–June, Peter de Courtenay and the legate John Colonna captured by Theodore Doukas. Peter dies in captivity.

1218   Epirotes capture Lamia, Neopatras, Platamon and Prosek.

Franks attempt to recapture Salona and the Epirotes fortify Naupaktos.

Geoffrey de Villehardouin and Otho de la Roche excommunicated again and lands placed under interdict for appropriating church revenues for the construction of the castle at Clermont (Chlemoutsi), which was completed by 1223.

1219   Maria de Courtenay given in marriage to Theodore I Laskaris.

Epirotes sack the monastery of Hosios Meletios between Athens and Thebes.

August, commercial treaty between Venice and Nicene Greeks.

Sept., Empress Yolande dies in Constantinople.

Oct., Parliament at Rodosto summoned by regency council headed by Conon de Bethune and the legate John Colonna.

8 Nov., death of patriarch Gervase in Constantinople.

1221   *31 Jan.*, Matthew, bishop of Jesolo consecrated patriarch.

25 March, Robert de Courtenay, second son of Peter and Yolande, crowned emperor in Constantinople.

Late, Serres occupied by the Epirotes.

Nov., Theodore I Laskaris dies at Nicaea, the emperor Robert supports his brothers in the succession dispute.

Demetrius of Thessalonika at Montferrat arranging aid for his kingdom.

1223   *March*, Margaret of Hungary quits Thessalonika for her native land as Epirotes begin the siege of Thessalonika.

August, John III Vatatazes crowned at Nicaea.

Sept., excommunication of Villehardouin and de la Roche rescinded and accord reached regarding the church in the Morea.

1224   *March*, William of Montferrat's troops assemble at Brindisi for relief of Thessalonika.
April, Latin army from Constantinople attacks Serres as part of the relief operations.
Nicene Greeks defeat Latins at Battle of Poemanenon in Asia Minor leading to the aborting of the Serres expedition.
Nov., Montferrat ill in Brindisi and crusade postponed.
Dec., garrison in Thessalonika under Guido Pallavicino surrenders to Epirotes.

1225   Chios and Lesbos recovered from Latin empire by Nicene Greeks.
Otho de la Roche returns to Burgundy leaving the lordship of Athens and Thebes to his nephew Guy.
Epirotes control Thrace right up to Constantinople and take over Adrianople from its Nicene garrison.
Montferratine crusade peters out in Thessaly.

1227   *18 March*, death of Pope Honorius III.
21 March, coronation of Pope Gregory IX.
April, Emperor Robert travels to Rome with proposals to abandon Constantinople.
Late 1227/early 1228, death of Geoffrey I de Villehardouin.

1228   *Jan.*, death of the Emperor Robert at Glarenza.
Feb., Maria de Courtenay regent for her brother the emperor Baldwin II.
2 July, Emperor Frederick II sailing to Jerusalem stops in Cephalonia to meet representatives of Theodore Doukas.
Dec., one-year truce between Latins of Constantinople and the Epirotes guaranteeing possession of three towns in Thrace to the Latins.

1229   *9 April*, at Perugia John de Brienne agrees to become co-emperor of Constantinople jointly with the 12-year-old Baldwin II who will become his son-in-law.

1230   *Spring*, Frederick II contributed troops to the Epirote army as a blow against John de Brienne whom he had defeated in Apulia the previous year.
April, Epirote army directed against Bulgaria decisively defeated at Klokotnica in the Marica valley near Philippopolis by John Asen II.
Subsequently the Epirote empire of Thessalonika begins to disintegrate and the threat to both Constantinople and Nicaea from that quarter is removed.
Death of Demetrius, titular king of Thessalonika, at Amalfi, bequeathing his claim to the emperor Frederick II.

1231   *Late July*, arrival of John de Brienne as emperor elect in Constantinople.

Geoffrey II de Villehardouin makes first annual payment of 22,000 hyperpera to John de Brienne.

Michael II Doukas establishes himself as despot of Arta.

1233   John de Brienne conducts campaign for four months in Asia Minor capturing Lampsakos and Pegae.

Nicene fleet recovers Rhodes from Leo Gabalas.

Construction of the Church of the Forty Martyrs begins at Veliko in Bulgaria to commemmorate the victory of Klokotnitza.

1234   Pope Gregory IX sends a mission of Franciscan and Dominican friars to Nicaea and Nymphaeum to discuss church union in return for the cession of Constantinople to the Greeks.

1235   *Early*, marriage of Helen Asen and Theodore Laskaris at Lampsakos to cement alliance between Bulgarians and Nicene Greeks.

New coalition attacks Constantinople.

Nicene Greeks capture Gallipoli from the Venetians, their first territorial acquisition in Europe.

July, frequent Greek raids on Thebes recorded.

1236   *Winter*, Geoffrey II de Villehardouin with fleet of 120 ships relieves Constantinople from Greek attack.

1237   *July*, Epirote Greek raids on Thebes continue.

March, death of John de Brienne in Constantinople.

Latins in Constantinople conclude a treaty with the Cumans, with whom they had been fostering closer relations since 1230.

1238   *18 Jan.*, first papal levy on hierarchy in Greece to aid Latin empire.

Early, Baldwin II visits English court.

Sept., Baldwin sells the crown of thorns to Louis IX for 10,000 marks and assumption of debts owed to the Quirini.

Late summer, Baldwin II returns to Constantinople with an army of 30,000 men.

Moreote fleet again in action against Nicene Greeks.

1240   Crown of thorns brought to France.

1241   *March*, Sainte Chapelle begun to house the crown of thorns.

June, death of John Asen II.

22 Aug., death of Pope Gregory IX.

27 Oct., coronation of Pope Celestine IV.

10 Nov., death of Pope Celestine IV.

Baldwin concludes a two-year truce with Nicaea.

1243   *28 June*, coronation of Innocent IV.

2 July, Mongols defeat the Seljuks at Kose Dagh making them vassals and increasing their reliance on the Nicene Greeks.

Greek rulers of Trebizond acknowledge the Mongols as their overlords.

1244
Marriage of Constance of Hohenstaufen, illegitimate daughter of Frederick II, to John III Vatatzes.
Truce with the Latins extended for one year.

1245
June–July, First Council of Lyons, Baldwin II in attendance.

1246
Spring, Epirote army drives Venetians from Volos and Halmyros and attacks Boudonitza and the duchy of Athens. Repulsed at Larissa with the help of William de Villehardouin.
Early summer, death of Geoffrey II de Villehardouin in the Morea; succeeded by his brother William.
Dec., Nicene army captures Thessalonika from the Epirotes.
Late, William de Villehardouin begins the siege of Monemvasia.

1247
Baldwin II visits London and Paris.
Nicene troops drive the Latins from Tzurulum and Vizye (Bizoë) in Thrace.

1248
Oct., Baldwin II returns to Constantinople from western Europe.
Monemvasia falls to William de Villehardouin who begins a programme of castle building at Mistra and Maina.

1249
May, William de Villehardouin joins Louis IX on Cyprus with 24 ships and 400 knights and proceeds on the Seventh Crusade to Damietta (Egypt).
He attacks Rhodes on his way to Cyprus.

1250
13 Dec., death of Frederick II at Castel Fiorentino near Foggia.

1251
Vatatzes campaigns in the Vardar valley to contain Epirote ambitions in Macedonia.

1254
3 Nov., death of John III Vatatzes in Nicaea, succeeded by his son Theodore II Laskaris.
7 Dec., death of Pope Innocent IV.
20 Dec., coronation of Pope Alexander IV.

1255–58
War of the Eubeote Succession: virtual civil war in Frankish Greece with Villehardouin and the Genoese fighting against the Venetians and the Frankish lords of central Greece, who fear the ambitions of the Villehardouin.

1256
Papal delegation sent to Nicaea to offer Constantinople in return for church union turned back in Macedonia by the Nicene Greeks.

317

1257	Prilep, the Vardar valley and most of western Macedonia captured by Michael II of Epiros from the Nicene Greeks.
1258	*May*, Villehardouin wins the battle of Karydi, bringing an end to the civil war in Frankish Greece.
	Guy of Athens sent to the French court for judgement. Absent from Greece until 1261.
	William de Villeharduin takes as third wife, Anna Doukaina (Agnes), daughter of Michael II of Epiros, and thereby cements an alliance against the Nicene Greeks.
	16 Aug., death of Theodore II Laskaris at Nymphaeum.
	25 Dec., double coronation of John IV Laskaris and his guardian Michael VIII Palaeologos.
1259	*Summer*, battle of Pelagonia in Macedonia. Villehardouin decisively defeated and captured by the Nicene Greeks.
1261	*13 March*, Treaty of Nymphaeum secures Genoese naval support for the Nicene Greeks.
	25 May, death of Pope Alexander IV.
	July, Latin naval expedition to Daphnousa in the Black Sea.
	25 July, Constantinople recaptured by the Nicene Greeks bringing the effective end of the Latin empire.
	Baldwin II flees to Negroponte and thence to Italy.
	15 Aug., coronation of Michael VIII Palaeologos in Hagia Sophia.
	Parliament of Nikli presided over by Anna Doukaina.
	Release of William de Villehardouin in return for the cession of the fortresses of Maina, Mistra and Monemvasia.
	4 Sept., coronation of Pope Urban IV.
1263	Death of Guy de la Roche, megaskyr of Athens and Thebes.
1263–64	War in Morea with Greeks of Mistra. Loss of the barony of Geraki to the Greeks.
1264	*2 Oct.*, death of Pope Urban IV.
1265	*15 Feb.*, coronation of Pope Clement IV.
1266	Baldwin II grants title to the kingdom of Thessalonika to Hugh IV of Burgundy.
1267	*24 May*, Treaty of Viterbo; William de Villehardouin becomes the vassal of Charles of Anjou.
	Marriage of Philip de Courtenay, son of Baldwin II, and Beatrice, daughter of Charles of Anjou.
1268	*25 Aug.*, William de Villehardouin in the army of Charles of Anjou which defeated Conradin at Tagliacozzo.

	29 Nov., death of Pope Clement IV followed by a three-year interregnum.
1270	Build-up of Greek troops in the Morea for new campaign following 1263–64. *June*, delegation sent by Charles of Anjou to the Morea to receive oaths of loyalty.
1271	Licario of Karystos begins sea-borne campaign against the Latins in the western Aegean. *28 May*, marriage of Isabelle de Villehardouin and Philip of Anjou, eldest son of Charles at Trani.
1272	*21 Feb.*, Charles of Anjou elected king of Albania. 700 troops sent from Sicily to the Morea under Dreux de Beaumont. *27 March*, coronation of Pope Gregory X.
1273	*15 Oct.*, death of Baldwin II at Bari, passing the title of Latin emperor to his son Philip.
1274	*6 July*, Second Council of Lyons secures union of the Greek and Latin Churches.
1275	*Spring/summer*, Guy of Athens repulses Byzantine attack on John of Neopatras. Naval battle at Demetrias won by the Greeks; William of Verona killed. Alum mines at Phokaea granted to Manuele Zaccaria.
1276	*10 Jan.*, death of Pope Gregory X followed by three short pontificates. Case between William de Villehardouin and Margaret de Passava over the barony of Akova (Matagriffon). Battle of Vatonda on Euboea in which Licario of Karystos gained control of much of the island and captured Jean de la Roche and Gilbert of Verona. Monastery at Daphni mentioned as the only Cistercian house left in Greece.
1277	*Jan–March*, death of Philip of Anjou without offspring. Loss of Kalavryta to the Greeks. *20 May*, death of Pope John XXI. *26 Dec.*, coronation of Pope Nicholas III.
1278	*1 May*, death of William de Villehardouin. The title to the principality of Achaia passes to Charles of Anjou by the terms of the Treaty of Viterbo.

Venetian claims commission set up to assess damages to Venetian shipping by Greek pirates.

Giovanni della Covo of Genoa granted Rhodes and Nanfio by Michael VIII with the title of Megadux.

1280   Death of Jean I of Athens and Thebes succeeded by his brother William.

22 Aug., death of Pope Nicholas III.

1281   *23 March*, coronation of Pope Martin IV.

3 July, Treaty of Orvieto; under papal patronage a Veneto-Angevin coalition to be formed to recover the Latin empire.

1282   *30 March*, Sicilian vespers, Angevin garrison expelled from Sicily which by the end of the year had passed to Pedro III of Aragon.

11 Dec., death of Michael VIII; succeeded by his son Andronikos II who repeals the Union of Lyon.

1284   Marriage of Andronikos II and Yolande de Montferrat, with whom passed one of the Latin claims to the kingdom of Thessalonika.

1285   *7 Jan.*, death of Charles of Anjou; succeeded by his son Charles II.

28 March, death of Pope Martin IV.

20 May, coronation of Pope Honorius IV.

15 June, indemity of 24,000 hyperpera paid by Andronikos II to the Venetians. The Byzantine government relinquished any formal responsibility for piratical acts in the Aegean.

1287   Death of William de la Roche; succeeded by his son Guy II (Guyot) under guardianship of his mother and Hugues de Brienne.

3 April, death of Pope Honorius IV.

1288   *22 Feb.*, coronation of Pope Nicholas IV.

22 April, death of Manuele Zaccaria. The alum mines at Phokaea pass to his brother Beneditto.

1289   *16 Sept.*, Florent of Hainault marries Isabelle de Villehardouin and becomes ruler of Achaia.

1292   *4 April*, death of Pope Nicholas IV followed by an interregnum of two years.

1294   Second Veneto–Genoese War breaks out marked by naval actions at Lajazzo, Candia and Modon.

24 June, knighting of Duke Guy II (Guyot) by Boniface of Verona at Thebes.

August, Charles II transfers suzerainty of the Morea to his son Philip of Taranto who marries Thamar (Catherine) of Arta, the daughter of the despot Nikephoros.

Catherine de Courtenay, the titular Latin empress of Constantinople, confirms the Treaty of Viterbo.
29 Aug., coronation of Pope Celestine V.
13 Dec., resignation of Pope Celestine V.

1295	*23 Jan.*, coronation of Pope Boniface VIII.
1296	Venetians attack the Genoese quarter at Galata and burn the alum works at Phokaea.
1297	*23 Jan.*, death of Florent of Hainault.
1299	*25 May*, peace between Venetians and Genoese.
1300	*22 Feb.*, Boniface VIII proclaims the first Jubilee Year in Rome which is attended by Isabelle de Villehardouin. Turks capture Smyrna from the Genoese.
1301	*18 Jan.*, marriage of Catherine de Courtenay and Charles of Valois, the brother of Philip IV of France. *12 Feb.*, Philip of Savoy marries Isabelle de Villehardouin and rules Achaia in the name of Charles II. *Nov.*, arrival of Philip and Isabelle in the Morea. Death of Philip de Courtenay; title to the Latin empire passes to his daughter, Catherine de Courtenay.
1302	*June*, Nicholas de St Omer and Guyot campaign in Thessaly. Revolt of the Greeks of Skorta in Nicholas' absence. *27 July*, Battle of Bapheon in Bithynia, the first encounter between Byzantine troops and the Ottoman Turks. *31 Aug.*, Peace of Caltabellota, ends the Angevin-Aragonese war in Sicily. Genoese begin the construction of the wall around Galata.
1303	Turkish raids on Aegean islands begin. *June*, Frankish vassals of Charles II ordered to attack Arta. *18 Aug.*, Catalans sack Keos en route to Constantinople. *Sept.*, Catalan Company from Sicily under Roger de Flor arrive in Constantinople. *11 Oct.*, death of Pope Boniface VIII. *27 Oct.*, coronation of Pope Benedict XI. *Winter–late summer 1304* Catalans campaign against Turks in Bithynia.
1304	Genoese leased Chios as part of their alliance with Byzantines against the Catalan Company. Benedict XI warns Andronikos II that Byzantine territory will be seized to mount an effective Latin resistance to the Turks.

May, parliament and tournament at Corinth.
7 July, death of Pope Benedict XI.
August, Catalan Company occupy Gallipoli.

1305   Marriage of Guy de la Roche and Mahaut de Hainault, heiress to the principality of Achaia.
30 April, murder of Roger de Flor in Constantinople.
10 July, Catalans defeat Byzantines at the battle of Apros.
14 Nov., coronation of Pope Clement V.

1306   *5 June*, Charles II removes Philip of Savoy.
June, Philip of Taranto makes his only visit to Greece to campaign against Mistra.

1307   *Easter*, Catalan sea-borne attack on Phokaea.
3 June, Clement V excommunicates Andronikos II.
Summer, Catalans move west into Macedonia.
Charles of Valois sends Thibaut de Cepoy to Macedonia via Euboea to negotiate for Catalan support against the Byzantines.

1308   *Early*, death of Catherine de Courtenay, titular empress of Constantinople. Her rights passed to her daughter, Catherine de Valois Courtenay.
27 March, Treaty of Lys, an alliance against Byzantium agreed by Charles of Valois and Stephen Uros of Hungary.
Spring, Catalans attack Thessalonika.
5 Oct., death of Guy II de la Roche; succeeded by his cousin Gautier I de Brienne.

1309   *6 May*, death of Charles II of Anjou; succeeded by his son Robert the Wise as king of Naples.
May/June, Catalans move into Thessaly.
15 Aug., Hospitallers capture Rhodes and begin to move their headquarters there from Cyprus.
Clement V moves papal residence to Avignon.

1310   *Spring*, Gautier de Brienne campaigns in Thessaly with Catalan mercenaries and captures more than 30 towns.
11 Nov., Venice signs non-aggression pact with Andronikos II on collapse of Charles of Valois's plans for an attack on Constantinople.
11 Nov., Templar properties in Attica and Boeotia transferred to Gautier de Brienne by Pope Clement.

1311   *15 March*, Battle of Halmyros; Catalans destroy Frankish army sent against them and win control of the duchy of Athens and Thebes.
Isabelle de Villehardouin dies in Hainault.

1312   *22 March*, Templars suppressed by the papal bull 'Vox in excelsis'.
Catalans sack Corinth.

22 Nov., Gautier de Chatillon, constable of France, constituted baili of Briennist possessions in Greece.
Catalans in central Greece acknowledge Frederick III of Sicily as their suzerain.

1313   *29 July*, Philip of Taranto marries Catherine de Valois Courtenay at Fontainebleau and acquires title to the Latin empire.
29 July, Louis of Burgundy marries Mahaut de Hainault and acquires rights to the principality of Achaia.
Hugh V of Burgundy cedes rights to the kingdom of Thessalonika to Louis (see 1266).

1314   *8 Feb.*, Titular Latin patriarchate of Constantinople united with the bishopric of Negroponte.
Feb., marriage of Ferrando of Majorca and Isabelle de Sabran, daughter of Margaret de Villehardouin at Messina.
20 April, death of Pope Clement V followed by a two-year interregnum.

1315   *Summer*, the infante Ferrando of Majorca lands at Glarenza to claim the principality of Achaia in right of his wife.

1316   *Early*, Louis of Burgundy arrives in the Morea to take up the principality.
22 Feb., battle of Picotin; Louis defeated by Ferrando with Catalan support.
5 July, battle of Manolada; Louis victorious, Ferrando killed.
August, death of Louis of Burgundy.
5 Sept., coronation of Pope John XXII.

1317–30   Don Alfonso Fadrique vicar-general of the duchy of Athens and Thebes.

1317   *March–Nov.*, Catalans in Euboea disputing possession of Karystos and Larmena.
9 Nov., Manfred, duke of Athens, dies at Trani.

1318–19   Don Alfonso Fadrique, vicar-general of Athens and Thebes, invades Thessaly capturing Neopatras, Siderokastro, Domokos and Pharsala.

1318   Venetians occupy Pteleon with Byzantine approval to defend it from Catalans.
Turks raid Santorini and Karpathos.
Venetian officials note Turkish depredations for first time.

1319   *9 June*, Treaty between Venice and the Catalans. Catalan shipping confined to the Corinthian Gulf and the port of Livadostro.

1320   *Sept.*, Greeks of Mistra capture castles at Akova, Karytaina, Polyphengos and St George. Only Chalandritsa, Patras and Vostitsa of the twelve original baronies remain in Frankish hands.

1321   *May*, Veneto-Catalan treaty of 1319 renewed.
             Mahaut de Hainault imprisoned in the Castel dell'Ovo by Robert of Naples. She dies at Aversa in 1331.

1325   *Jan.–Oct.*, campaign of John of Gravina in the Morea fails to recapture Karytaina.

1327   Turks raid Aegina and Damala.

1329   *Autumn*, Byzantine force recovers Chios from the Zaccaria family.
             Turkish mercenaries in Catalan employ sack Athens(?).

1330   *June–Oct.*, crusade preached against the Catalans of central Greece.

1331   *April*, Veneto–Catalan treaty of 1321 renewed.
             Autumn–late summer 1332, Gautier II de Brienne crosses from Taranto to Leukas for attack on Catalans. Despite some conquests in Epiros, nothing achieved in Boeotia.
             Catalans slight the castle of Thebes.
             Turkish raids on Greek coast and islands intensify.
             26 Dec., death of Philip of Taranto.

1332–34   First anti-Turkish naval league composed of Venice, Cyprus, Hospitallers and Byzantines.

1332   *Late summer*, Gautier II de Brienne returns to Taranto with enormous debts.
             17 Dec., John of Gravina exchanges the principality of Achaia with the titular Latin Empress Catherine in return for Durazzo and the kingdom of Albania.

1333–46   Assizes of Romania written down.

1334   *4 Dec.*, death of Pope John XXII.

1335   *8 Jan.*, coronation of Pope Benedict XII.

1336   *1 Feb.*, Niccolo Acciaioli received as a vassal of the principality of Achaia.

1338–41   *Nov. 1338–June 1341*, Catherine de Valois as princess of Achaia, her son Robert of Taranto and Niccolo Acciaioli visit the Morea.

1342   *25 April*, death of Pope Benedict XII.
             19 May, coronation of Pope Clement VI.

1343	*20 Jan.*, Robert I of Naples dies; succeeded by his granddaughter Joanna. *31 Aug.*, Clement VI forms Holy League of Venice, Cyprus and Hospitallers.
1344	*28 Oct.*, Holy League captures Smyrna. Turks occupy Naxos; population flees to Crete.
1346	*5 Oct.*, Catherine de Valois dies; succeeded as titular emperor of Constantinople and prince of Achaia by her son, Robert of Taranto. Genoese recapture Chios from the Byzantines.
1347–48	*Late 1347–spring 1348*, Black Death spreads through Aegean area from Kaffa in the Crimea.
1348	Serbs and Albanians overrun Thessaly and Epiros. Catalans lose control of Domokos, Gardiki and Pharsala.
1350–55	Third Veneto–Genoese War.
1350	*March*, Catalan and Albanian raids on Pteleon. *April*, Turkish and Albanian raids on Boudonitza.
1352	Tenedos handed over to Venetians by Byzantines. *6 Dec.*, death of Pope Clement VI. *30 Dec.*, coronation of Pope Innocent VI.
1354	Turks occupy Gallipoli. Roger de Lluria appointed marshal of Athens and Neopatras. *1 Dec.*, envoy sent from Aragon to remove the head of St George from the castle at Livadhia.
1356	*19 Sept.*, Gautier II de Brienne killed at the battle of Poitiers (Maupertuis).
1358	*23 April*, Corinth granted to Niccolo Acciaioli by Robert of Taranto.
1359	*May*, Pierre de Thomas appointed apostolic legate 'in partibus ultramarinis'. *June*, Turkish archers requested from central Greece as a bodyguard for Pedro IV of Aragon. *Oct.*, Venetians purchase Karystos from Fadrique family. Luke the Catalan raids the coasts of Cyprus.
1362–64	Conflict between Catalans and Venetians of Euboea.
1362	*May*, Roger de Lluria seizes Thebes and kills the tyrannical vicar-general Pedro de Pou, occupying the post himself until 1366.

	12 Sept., death of Pope Innocent VI.

12 Sept., death of Pope Innocent VI.
6 Nov., coronation of Pope Urban V.

1363   Crusade in the Aegean planned for March 1365. Pressure brought on Catalans to dismiss Turkish mercenaries.

1364   *Early summer*, Turkish fleet defeated off Megara by a force of Venetians, Greeks and Hospitallers. Turkish survivors take refuge at Thebes.
10 Sept., death of Robert of Taranto; succeeded by his brother Philip as Latin emperor and prince of Achaia.

1365   *July*, peace between Catalans and Venetians; Turks forced to leave duchy of Athens.
8 Nov., Niccolo Acciaioli dies in Naples.

1366   *Aug.–Dec.*, crusade of Amadeo VI of Savoy to recover Gallipoli, which he had offered to the Venetians, succeeds in restoring two towns to the Byzantines.

1367   *2 Jan.*, The Articles of Thebes.

1370–71   The Enghien brothers, nephews of Gautier II de Brienne, fail to recover the duchy of Athens from the Catalans

1370   *19 Dec.*, death of Pope Urban V.

1371   *5 Jan.*, coronation of Pope Gregory XI.

1372   *Nov.*, Gregory XI recognises Nerio Acciaioli as lord of Corinth.
Pope proposes an international conference at Thebes for Oct. 1373 to discuss the Turkish threat.

1373   *25 Nov.*, Philip of Taranto dies, leaving his title of titular Latin emperor to his nephew Jacques de Baux and the principality of Achaia to Joanna of Naples.

1376–81   Fourth Veneto–Genoese War.

1377–81   Principality of Achaia leased to the Hospitallers.

1377   *27 July*, Robert de Juilly, grandmaster of the Hospitallers dies.
24 Oct., Gregory XI appoints Juan Fernandez de Heredia grandmaster without consultation of the Chapter on Rhodes.

1378   *27 March*, death of Pope Gregory XI at Rome.
August, Heredia captured whilst campaigning in Epiros.

1378–1417	Great Schism between popes of Avignon and Rome.
1379	*May*, Heredia released from captivity. *May/June*, Navarrese Company capture Thebes.
1380	*20 May*, Articles of Athens. *31 May*, Articles of Salona. *1 June*, Articles of Livadhia. *Late*, Livadhia captured by the Navarrese.
1381	*Spring*, Government of the Morea formally handed back to representatives of Joanna of Naples by Hospitallers. *16 July-26 Aug.*, Joanna besieged in Naples by Charles of Anjou-Durazzo and supporters of Jacques de Baux as prince of Achaia. Joanna captured (murdered 22 May 1382). *8 Aug.*, Treaty of Turin ends Fourth Veneto–Genoese war known as the War of Tenedos or War of Chioggia. *Nov.*, Jacques de Baux flies banners of Romania and Achaia from his castle at Taranto.
1383	*7 July*, Jacques de Baux, last titular Latin emperor, dies at Taranto.
1386–91	Attempt by Amadeo VII of Savoy to gain principality of Achaia, backed by the Avignonese pope, Clement VII (1387–94). The Roman pope, Urban VI (1387–89) claimed the principality for the Holy See. Real power lay with the Navarrese led by Pierre Bordo de St Superan.
1388	*2 May*, Nerio Acciaioli seizes the Acropolis at Athens.
1389	*15 June*, Battle of Kossovo; Serbs crushed by Murad I.
1391–1403	Thessalonika occupied by the Turks.
1392–94	Thessaly conquered by the Turks.
1394	*Early*, Turks capture Neopatras, Livadhia and Salona. *25 Sept.*, death of Nerio Acciaioli at Corinth. In his will he left Corinth to his daughter Francesca, Athens to the cathedral chapter under Venetian protection, and Thebes and Livadhia to his bastard son, Antonio.
1394–1403	Venetian garrison installed on the Acropolis at Athens by the terms of Nerio's will.
1396	*25 Sept.*, slaughter of Burgundian and Hungarian crusaders by Bayezid I at Nicopolis.
1397	*3 June*, Argos razed by the Turks.

1399–1402	Manuel II Palaeologos tours Europe to seek aid against the Turks.
1402	*Summer*, Antonio I Acciaioli captures lower town of Athens. *28 July*, Battle of Ankara; Ottoman Turks defeated by hordes of Tamerlane. Bayezid I a prisoner and a temporary check placed on Ottoman expansion. *Nov.*, death of Pierre Bordo de St Superan, leaving principality to his widow Maria Zaccaria. *Dec.*, Tamerlane expels Hospitallers from Smyrna.
1403	*Jan/Feb.*, Antonio I Acciaioli seizes the Athenian Acropolis from Venetian garrison.
1404	*20 April*, Centurione II Zaccaria purchased investiture as prince of Achaia from Ladislas, king of Naples. Hospitallers attempt to raise revolt against the Turks in Salona area. Duke of Naxos visits England to seek help against the Turks.
1414	*20 June*, Boudonitza captured by the Turks.
1415	Greeks of Mistra rebuild the fifth century Hexamilion Wall across the Isthmus of Corinth.
1417–18	Elis captured from the Franks by the Greeks of Mistra. Principality of Achaia effectually reduced to Glarenza and Patras.
1423	*May*, Turks breach the Hexamilion Wall.
1423–30	Venetian garrison installed in Thessalonika with Byzantine consent.
1430	Glarenza captured by the Greeks of Mistra and used as a base to attack Patras.
1430	*29 March*, Thessalonika captured by the Turks. Patras captured by the Greeks, Centurione Zaccaria dispossessed.
1432	Death of Centurione II Zaccaria, the last Latin prince of Achaia.
1434	Death of Antonio I Acciaioli.
1439	*6 July*, Union of Greek and Latin churches agreed at the Council of Florence.
1443	Hexamilion Wall rebuilt again.
1444	*10 Nov.*, Hungarian and Slav crusaders annihilated at Varna by Murad II.

1446	Turks ravage the Morea and retain control of the Hexamilion Wall.
1451	*3 Feb.*, death of Murad II, succeeded by his son Mehemet II.
1453	*29 May*, Mehemet II takes Constantinople, ending the Byzantine empire.
1456	*4 June*, Athens annexed by the Turks bringing an end to Latin rule in central Greece.
1460	Conquest of the Morea by the Turks. Venice retains control of Modon, Coron, Nauplia, Argos and Euboea. Monemvasia placed under papal control.
1463–79	First Turko–Venetian War.
1463	Argos, Kalamata and Monemvasia receive a Venetian garrison.
1464	Campaign of Sigismondo Malatesta from Messenia to Mistra.
1470	*12 July*, Turks capture Negroponte. Venice surrenders Euboea and Argos.
1499–1500	Second Turko–Venetian War.
1500	Modon, Coron, and Old Navarino lost to the Turks.
1537–40	Third Turko–Venetian War.
1540	Monemvasia and Nauplia lost to the Turks.
1566	Turks capture Chios.
1571	*7 Oct.*, Battle of Lepanto (Naupaktos).
1645–69	War of Candia.
1669	*Sept.*, Crete passes under Ottoman control.
1684–1715	War of the Holy League with the Turks in the Morea.
1718	*21 July*, Peace of Passarowitz restores Morea and Aegean Islands to Turkish rule. Venice retains Kythera, Cerigotto, Leukas.

Appendix 2 ....

Lists of Rulers

Latin Emperors of Constantinople

Baldwin I	1204–5
Henry	1206–16
Peter de Courtenay	1216–17
Yolande de Courtenay	1217–19
Robert de Courtenay	1221–28
Baldwin II	1228–61
John de Brienne	1231–37

Titular Latin Emperors of Constantinople

Baldwin II	1261–73
Philip de Courtenay	1273–1301
Catherine de Courtenay	1301–8
Catherine de Valois	1308–46
Robert of Taranto	1346–64
Philip of Taranto	1364–73
Jacques des Baux	1373–83

Kings of Thessalonika

Boniface of Montferrat	1204–7
Demetrius	1207–25

Titular Rulers of Thessalonika

Demetrius	1225–30
Frederick II Hohenstaufen	1230–39
Boniface II of Montferrat	1239–53
William IV of Montferrat*	1253–84

title relinquished on marriage of Yolande and Andronikos II

Hugh IV of Burgundy	1266–73
Robert II of Burgundy	1273–1305
Hugh V of Burgundy	1305–13
Louis of Burgundy	1313–16

Dukes of Athens

Otho de la Roche	1205–25
Guy I	1225–63
Jean	1263–80
William	1280–87
Guy II (Guyot)	1287–1308
Gautier I de Brienne	1308–11
Manfred of Aragon	1312–17
William of Randazzo	1317–38
John of Randazzo	1338–48
Frederick of Randazzo	1348–55
Frederick III of Sicily	1355–77
Maria of Sicily	1377–81
Pedro IV of Aragon	1381–88
Nerio I Acciaioli	1388–94
Antonio I	1402–35
Nerio II	1435–39
Antonio II	1439–41
Nerio II (again)	1441–51
Francesco	1451–55
Franco*	1455–60

*Thebes only after 1456

Claimants to the Duchy of Athens

Gautier II de Brienne	1311–56
Sohier d'Enghien	1356–67
Gautier III d'Enghien	1367–81

Princes of Achaia

William I de Champlitte	1205–9
Geoffrey I de Villehardouin	1209–28
Geoffrey II	1228–46
William II	1246–78
Charles I of Naples	1278–85
Charles II of Naples	1285–89
Isabelle de Villehardouin	1289–1307
Florent de Hainault	1289–97
Philip of Savoy	1301–6
Philip of Taranto	1307–13
Mahaut de Hainault	1313–18
Louis of Burgundy	1313–16
Robert I of Naples	1318–22
John of Gravina	1322–32
Catherine of Valois	1332–46
Robert of Taranto	1346–64
Philip of Taranto	1364–73
Joanna I of Naples	1373–81
Jacques des Baux	1381–83
Pierre de St Superan	1396–1402
Centurione II Zaccaria	1404–30

Dukes of the Archipelago (Egeo Pelagos)

Marco I Sanudo	1207–27
Angelo	1227–62
Marco II	1262–1303
Guglielmo I	1303–23
Niccol I	1323–41
Giovanni I	1341–61
Fiorenza	1361–71
Niccolo	1364–71
Niccolo III dalle Carceri	1371–83
Francesco I Crispo	1383–97
Giacomo I	1397–1418
Giovanni II	1418–33
Giacomo II	1433–47
Gian Giacomo	1447–53
Guglielmo II	1453–63
Francesco II	1463
Giacomo III	1463–80
Giovanni III	1480–94
Francesco III	1500–11

Giovanni IV	1517–64
Giacomo IV	1564–66
Joseph Nasi	1566–79

Asen Dynasty (Bulgaria)

Asen I	1187–96
Peter	1196–97
Kalojan	1197–1207
Boril	1207–18
John Asen II	1218–41
Kaloman	1241–46
Michael Asen	1246–57
Constantine Tich	1257–77
Ivalo	1277–79
John Asen III	1279–80

Emperors at Nicaea

Theodore I Laskaris	1204–22
John III Vatatzes	1222–54
Theodore II Laskaris	1254–58
John IV	1258–61
Michael VIII Palaeologos	1259–(1261)

The Palaeologoi

Michael VIII (of Nicaea)	1261–82
Andronikos II	1282–1328
Michael IX	1295–1320
Andronikos III	1328–41
John V	1341–91
John VI Cantacuzene	1347–54
Andronikos IV	1376–79
John VII	1390
Manuel II	1391–1425
John VII (again)	1399–1402
John VIII	1425–48
Constantine IX	1448–53

Despots of Epiros

Michael Komnenos Doukas	1204–14
Theodore*	1214–25
*Emperor of Thessalonika, 1225–30	
Constantine	1225–36
Michael II	1236–71
Nikephoros I	1271–96
Thomas	1296–1318
Niccolo Orsini of Kephalonia	1318–23
Giovanni Orsini	1323–35
Nikephoros II	1335–37 and 1356–59

Kings of France

Philip II Augustus	1180–1223
Louis VIII	1223–26
Louis IX	1226–70
Philip III	1270–85
Philip IV	1285–1314

Angevin Rulers of Naples

Charles I*	1266–85
*Sicily lost 1282	
Charles II	1285–1309
Robert the Wise	1309–43
Joanna I	1343–82
Charles III	1382–86
Ladislas	1386–1414
Joanna II	1414–35

Kings of Aragon

Pedro II	1196–1213
James I	1213–76
Pedro III (of Sicily)	1276–85
Alfonso III	1285–91
James II (of Sicily)	1291–1327

Alfonso IV	1327–36
Pedro IV	1336–87

Aragonese Dynasty of Sicily until 1458

Pedro I (III of Aragon)	1282–85
James II of Aragon	1285–95
Frederick II	1295–1337
Pedro II	1337–42
Louis	1342–55
Frederick III	1355–77
Maria	1377–1402
Martin I	1391–1409
Martin II (of Aragon)	1409–10
Ferdinand (I of Aragon)	1412–16
Alfonso I (V of Aragon; Naples)	1416–58

Ottoman Sultans to 1566

Osman	d.1326
Orkhan	1326–62
Murad I	1362–89
Bayezid I	1389–1403
Mehemet I	1413–21
Murad II	1421–51
Mehemet II	1451–81
Bayezid II	1481–1512
Selim I	1512–20
Suleyman I	1520–66

Latin Patriarchs of Constantinople to 1261

(Dates refer to nomination by the Pope and death.)

Thomas Morosini	1205–11
Vacancy	1211–15
Gervase	1215–19
Vacancy	1219–21
Mathew	1221–26
Jean Halgrin	1226–27

Simon of Tyre	1227–32
Vacancy	1232–34
Nicholas de Castro Arquato	1235–51
Vacancy	1251–53
Pantaleone Guistiniani	1253–86

Titular appointments continued until 1965.

Popes, 1198–1503

(First date that of election; A(vignonese), P(isan) and R(oman) obedience in years 1378–1417.)

Innocent III	1198–1216
Honorius III	1216–27
Gregory IX	1227–41
Celestine IV	1241
Innocent IV	1243–54
Alexander IV	1254–61
Urban IV	1261–64
Clement IV	1265–68
Gregory X	1271–76
Innocent V	1276
Adrian V	1276
John XXI	1276–77
Nicholas III	1277–80
Martin IV	1281–85
Honorius IV	1285–87
Nicholas IV	1288–92
Celestine V	1294
Boniface VIII	1294–1303
Benedict XI	1303–4
Clement V	1305–14
John XXII	1316–34
Nicholas V (antipope)	1328–33
Benedict XII	1334–42
Clement VI	1342–52
Innocent VI	1352–62
Urban V	1362–70
Gregory XI	1370–78
Urban VI (R)	1378–89
Boniface IX (R)	1389–1404
Innocent VII (R)	1404–6
Gregory XII (R)	1406–15
Clement VII (A)	1378–94
Benedict XIII (A)	1394–1423

Alexander V (P)	1409–10
John XXIII (P)	1410–15
Martin V	1417–31
Eugenius IV	1413–47
Felix V (antipope)	1439–49
Nicholas V	1447–55
Calixtus III	1455–58
Pius II	1458–64
Paul II	1464–71
Sixtus IV	1471–84
Innocent VIII	1484–92
Alexander VI	1492–1503

Select Bibliography

In such a broad field which touches upon Mediterranean history in general and Byzantine and crusading history and archaeology in particular, any bibliography could be potentially immense and at the same time daunting in its linguistic demands. I have therefore tried to confine these suggestions and recommendations to secondary works mainly from the last thirty years, and mainly in English and French. This is not to suggest that contributions in other languages are in any way less important or less worthy of the reader's attention, but I indicate books and articles which an undergraduate readership might realistically obtain and study. The notes to each of the preceding chapters are intended both as the place to seek out the primary source material used and as a bibliography in their own right, repaying to some extent my own scholarly debts. Unless otherwise stated the place of publication is London.

Ahrweiler, H., (1975), 'L'expérience nicéene', *DOP*, 29:21–40.

Alexander, P., (1962), 'The struggle for empire and capital as seen through Byzantine eyes', *Speculum*, 37:339–52.

Andrews, K., (1953), *Castles of the Morea*, (Princeton, 1953, reprinted Amsterdam, 1978).

Angold, M., (1975), *A Byzantine Government in Exile, ... 1204–1261*, (Oxford).

Angold, M., ed., (1980), 'The interaction of Latins and Byzantines during the period of the Latin Empire: the case of the ordeal', *Actes du XVe Congrès international des Etudes byzantines*, (Athens), 4:1–10.

Angold, M., ed., (1984), *The Byzantine Aristocracy, IX to XIII Centuries*, (BAR, Oxford).

Angold, M., (1984), *The Byzantine Empire, 1025–1204*.

Arbel, B., et al., eds., (1989), *Latins and Greeks in the Eastern Mediterranean after 1204*.

Argenti, P., (1958), *The Occupation of Chios by the Genoese and their Administration of the Island*, 3 vols, (Cambridge).

Argenti, P., (1979), 'The Mahonna of the Guistiniani', *ByzF*, 6:1–36.

Ashtor, E., (1983), *The Levant Trade in the Later Middle Ages*, (Princeton).

Baker, D., (1973), *Relations Between East and West in the Middle Ages*, (Edinburgh).

Baker, D., ed., (1976), *The Orthodox Churches and the West*, (Oxford).

Balard, M., (1976), 'Amalfi et Byzance', *TM*, 6:69–98.

Balard, M., (1977), 'Les Grecs de Chio sous la domination génoise au xive siècle', *ByzF*, 5:5–16.

Balard, M., (1978), *La Romanie Génoise*, 2 vols, (Rome).

Balard, M., (1989), 'The Genoese in the Aegean, (1204–1566)', in B. Arbel, et al., eds, *Latins and Greeks in the Eastern Mediterranean after 1204*, 158–74.

Barber, M., (1989), 'Western attitudes to Frankish Greece in the thirteenth century' in B. Arbel, et al., eds, *Latins and Greeks in the Eastern Mediterranean after 1204*, 111–28.

Bartusis, M., (1988), 'The Kavallarioi of Byzantium', *Speculum*, 63:343–50.

Bartusis, M., (1992), *The Late Byzantine Army, Arms and Society, 1204–1453*, (Philadelphia).

Bent, J., (1889), 'The Lords of Chios', *EHR*, 4:467–80.

Berg, B., (1985), 'The Moreote Expedition of Ferrando of Majorca in the *Aragonese Chronicle of the Morea*', *Byzantion*, 55:69–90.

Bolton, B., (1976), 'A mission to the Orthodox: Cistercians in the Latin Empire', in D. Baker, ed., *The Orthodox Churches and the West*, 169–81.

Bon, A., (1937), 'Fortéresses médiévales de la Grèce centrale', *BCH*, 61:136–208.

Bon, A., (1951), *Le Péloponnèse Byzantin jusqu'en 1204*, (Paris).

Bon, A., (1964), 'Pierres inscrites ou armoriées de la Morée franque', *Deltion tis Christianikes Archaiologikes Etaireias*, IV:89–102.

Bon, A., (1969), *La Morée franque: Recherches historiques, topographiques et archéologiques sur la Principauté d'Achaie (1205–1430)*, 2 vols, (Paris).

Bonsall, L., (1969), 'The Benedictine Monastery of St Mary on Athos', *Eastern Churches Review*, 2:262–67.

Borsari, S., (1951), 'Federico II e l'Oriente bizantino', *Rivista storica italiana*, 63: 279–91.

Borsari, S., (1963), *Il Dominio veneziano a Creta nel XIII secolo*, (Naples).

Bowman, S., (1985), *The Jews of Byzantium, 1204–1453*, (Alabama).

Brand, C., (1962), 'The Byzantines and Saladin, 1185–1192: opponents of the Third Crusade', *Speculum*, 37:167–81.

Brand, C., (1968), *Byzantium Confronts the West, 1180–1204*, (Cambridge, Mass.).

Brand, C., (1968), 'A Byzantine plan for the Fourth Crusade', *Speculum*, 43:462–75.

Brand, C., (1984), 'The Fourth Crusade: some recent interpretations', *Medievalia et Humanistica*, 12:33–45.

Bratianu, G., (1929), *Recherches sur le commerce génois dans la Mer Noire au XIIIe siècle*, (Paris).

Brezeanu, S., (1974), 'Le Premier traité économique entre Venise et Nicée', *Revue des Etudes Sud-est Européenes*, 12:143–6.

Brightman, E., (1901), 'Byzantine Imperial Coronations', *Journal of Theological Studies*, 2:359–92.

Brown, E., (1958), 'The Cistercians in the Latin Empire of Constantinople and Greece, 1204–76', *Traditio*, 14:63–120.

Brown, E., (1974), 'The tyranny of a construct: feudalism and historians of medieval Europe', *AHR*, 79:1063–88.

Brown, H., (1920), 'The Venetians and the Venetian quarter in Constantinople to the close of the twelfth century', *JHS*, 40:68–88.

Browning, R., (1969), *Medieval and Modern Greek*.

Browning, R., (1975), *Bulgaria and Byzantium*.

Bryer, A., (1971), 'The first encounter with the West, AD 1050–1204', in P. Whitting, ed., *Byzantium, An Introduction*, (Oxford).

Bryer, A., (1973), 'Cultural relations between east and west in the twelfth century', in D. Baker, ed., *The Orthodox Churches and the West*, 77–94.

Bury, J., (1886–8), 'The Lombards and Venetians in Euboea (1205–1470)', *JHS*, 7:309–52; 8:194–213; 9:91–117.

Buchon, J.A.C., (1840), *Recherches et Materiaux pour servir a une Histoire de la Domination Francaise ... dans les Provins démembrés de l'Empire Grec...*, (Paris).

Buchon, J.A.C., (1843), *Nouvelles Recherches Historiques sur la Principauté Francaises de Morée et ses Hautes Baronnies ... (1334–1470)*, (Paris).

Buchon, J.A.C., (1846), *Recherches Historiques sur la Principauté de Morée et ses Hautes Baronnies ... (1204–1334)*, (Paris).

Buchon, J.A.C., (n.d.=1846?), *Atlas de Nouvelles Recherches Historiques sur la Principauté de Morée...*, (Paris).

Buckley, J., (1957), 'The problematical octogenarianism of John de Brienne', *Speculum*, 32:315–22.

Burns, R., 'The Catalan Company and the European Powers, 1305–1311', *Speculum*, 29:751–77.

Burridge, P., (1995), 'The Castle of Vardouniia and the defence of the Southern Taygetos' in P. Lock and G. Sanders, eds, *Essays in the Archaeology of Medieval Greece*.

Carile, A., (1965), 'Partitio Terrarum Imperii Romanie', *Studi veneziani*, 7:125–305.

Carile, A., (1972), *Per una storia dell'Imperio latino di Constantinopoli (1204–1261)*, (Bologna).

Carile, A., (1978), 'La cancellaria sovrana dell'Imperio latino di Constantinopoli', *Studi veneziani*, 2:37–73.

Carpenter, R. and Bon, A., (1936), *Corinth III: The Defences of Akrocorinth and the Lower Town*, (Cambridge, Mass.).

Charanis, P., (1941), 'Internal strife in Byzantium during the fourteenth century', *Byzantion*, 15:208–30, reprinted Charanis (1973).

Charanis, P., (1950), 'Piracy in the Aegean during the reign of Michael VIII Palaeologus', *Annuaire de L'Institut de Philologie et d'histoire Orientales et Slaves*, 10: 127–36, reprinted in P. Charanis, *Social, Economic and Political Life in the Byzantine Empire: Collected Studies*, (1973).

Charanis, P., (1951), 'On the social structure and economic organization of the Byzantine Empire in the 13th century and later', *Byzantinoslavica*, 12:94–153, reprinted in P. Charanis, *Social, Economic and Political Life in the Byzantine Empire: Collected Studies*, (1973).

Charanis, P., (1973), *Social, Economic and Political Life in the Byzantine Empire: Collected Studies*.

Cheetham, N., (1981), *Medieval Greece*.

Chrysostomides, J., ed. (1988), *Kathegetria: Essays Presented to Joan Hussey*.

Chrystomides, J., (1988), 'Was Nerio Acciaiuoli ever lord of Vostitsa and Nivelet?', in J. Chrysotomides, ed., *Kathegetria: Essays Presented to Joan Hussey*, 501–14.

Cook, M., ed., (1970), *Studies in the Economic History of the Middle East from the Rise of Islam to the Present Day*.

Cramer, J. and Düll, S., (1985), 'Arup Camii, Istanbul', *Istanbuler Mitteilungen*, 35:295–391.

Cutler, A., (1968), 'The *De Signis* of Nicetas Choniates: a reappraisal', *AJA*, 72:113–18.

Daly, W., (1960), 'Christian fraternity, the crusades and the security of Constantinople', *Medieval Studies*, 22:43–91.

Davidson, R., (1940), 'A medieval glassfactory at Corinth', *AJA*, 44:297–324.

Day, G. (1983), *Genoa's Response to Byzantium 1155–1204*, (Illinois).

Delaville Le Roux, J., (1913), *Les Hospitaliers à Rhodes jusqu'a la mort de Philibert de Naillac:1310–1421*, (Paris, reprinted 1974)

Dennis, G. (1960), 'The capture of Thebes by the Navaresse', *Orientalia Christiana Periodica*, 26:4–50.

Dolger, F., ed., (1932–65), *Regesten der Kaiserkunden des Ostromischen Reiches von 565–1453*, vols 3–5 (Munich).

Dolger, F., (1956), 'Die Kreuzfahrerstaaten auf dem Balkan und Byzanz', *Südöst Forschungen*, 15:141–59.

Du Cange, C., (1657), *Histoire de l'Empire de Constantinople sous les empereurs francais*, 2 vols, (Paris, reprinted Paris, 1826 and New York, 1971).

Düll, S., (1983), 'Unbekannte Denkmäler der Genuesen aus Galata', *Istanbuler Mitteilungen*, 33:225–38.

Dvornik, F., (1948), *The Photian Schism*, (Cambridge).

Edbury P. and Metcalf, D., eds, (1977), *Coinage in the Latin East*, (Oxford).

Edwards, K. (1932), *Corinth VI: Coins, 1896–1929*, (Cambridge, Mass.)

Eubel, C., (1913–14), *Hierarchia Catholica Medii Aevi*, (Regensburg).

Every, G., (1947), *The Byzantine Patriarchate, 451–1204*.

Fabre, P., ed., (1889–1952), *Le Liber censuum de l'Eglise romane*, (Paris).

Fedalto, G., (1981–2), *La Chiesa Latina in Oriente* 2 vols, (Verona).

Ferrard, C., (1971), 'The amount of Constantinopolitan booty in 1204', *Studi veneziani*, 13:95–104.

Fine, J., (1987), *The Late Medieval Balkans*, (Ann Arbor).

Finlay, G. (1877), *History of Greece, BC 146 to AD 1864*, 7 vols, ed. H.F.Tozer, (Oxford).

Force, Marquis de la, (1936), 'Les Conseillers latins du basileus Alexis Comnène', *Byzantion*, 11:153–65.

Fotheringham, J.K., (1910), 'Genoa and the Fourth Crusade', *EHR*, 25:26–57.

Fotheringham, J.K., (1915), *Marco Sanudo, Conqueror of the Archipelago*, (Oxford).

France, E., (1954), 'Sur la conquête de Constantinople par les Latins', *Byzantinoslavica*, 15:21–26.

Frantz, A., (1938) 'Middle Byzantine pottery in Athens', *Hesperia*, 7:429–467.

Frantz, A., (1961), *The Middle Ages in the Athenian Agora*, (Princeton).

Frazee, C., (1978), 'The Catholic Church in Constantinople, 1204–1453', *Balkan Studies*, 19:33–49.

Frazee, C. and K., (1988), *The Island Princes of Greece, The Dukes of the Archipelago*, (Amsterdam).

Frolow, A., (1959), *Recherches sur la déviation de la IVe Croisade vers Constantinople*, (Paris).

Gardner, A., (1912), *The Lascarids of Nicaea*, (reprinted Amsterdam, 1964).

Gautier, J., (1880), 'Othon de la Roche, conquerant d'Athènes et sa famille', *Academie des Sciences et Belles-Lettres et Arts de Besancon, Annee 1880*, 139–55.

Geanakoplos, D., (1953), 'Greco-Latin relations on the eve of the Byzantine restoration: the Battle of Pelagonia, 1259', *DOP*, 7:101–41.

Geanakoplos, D., (1959), *Emperor Michael Palaeologus and the West*, (Harvard).

Geanakoplos, D., (1968), *Medieval Western Civilization and the Byzantine and Islamic Worlds. Interaction of Three Cultures*, (Boston, Mass.).

Gerland, E., (1899), 'Bericht über Carl Hopfs litterarischen Nachlass und die dann vorhandene fränkisch-griechische Regestensammlung', *BZ*, 8:347–86.

Gerland, E., (1905), *Geschichte des Latinischen Kaiserreiches von Konstantinopel*, (Hamburg).

Gerland, E., (1905), 'Histoire de la Noblesse crétoise au moyen-age', *Revue de l'Orient latin*, XI:50–6, 67–79.

Gill, J., (1979), *Byzantium and the Papacy, 1198–1400*, (New Brunswick).

Gill, J., (1985), 'Venice, Genoa and Byzantium', *ByzF*, 10:57–74.

Goodenough, Lady, *The Chronicle of Muntaner Translated from the Catalan*, 2 vols, (Hakluyt Society, London, 1920–1).

Granstrem, E., et al., (1976), 'Fragment d'un Praktikon de la Région d'Athènes avant 1204', *Revue des Etudes byzantines*, 34:5–44.

Gregorvius, F., (1889), *Geschichte der Stadt Athen im Mittelalter*, 2 vols (Leipzig, reprinted as 1 vol, Munich, 1980).

Gregorovius, F., (1890–1), 'Briefe aus der Correspondenza Acciajoli in der Laurenziana zu Florenz', *Sitzungs berichte der philos-philol und hist. Klasse der K.Bayern. Akademie der Wissenschaft zu Munchen*, II:285–311.

Grierson, P., (1982), *Byzantine Coins*.

Gusta, M., ed. (1979) *Ramon Muntaner, Cronica*, (Barcelona).

Harvey, A., (1982–3), 'Economic expansion in central Greece in the eleventh century', *Byzantine and Modern Greek Studies*, 8:21–28.

Harvey, A., (1989), *Economic Expansion in the Byzantine Empire, 900–1200*, (Cambridge).

Haskins, C., (1910), 'A Canterbury Monk at Constantinople', *EHR*, 25:293–5.

Haskins, C., (1920), 'The Greek element in the Renaissance of the twelfth century', *AHR*, 25: 603–15.

Hasluck, F., (1910), 'The Latin monuments of Chios', *ABSA*, 16: 137–84.

Hasluck, F. (1913), 'Contributions to the history of Levant currencies', *ABSA*, 19:174–81.

Heers, J., (1961), *Gênes au XVe siècle activité économique et problèmes sociaux*, (Paris).

Heisenberg, H., (1922), *Neue Quellen zur geschichte des latiniischen Kaisertums und der Kirchenunion*, (Munich).

Hendrickx, B., (1969), 'Les Chartes de Baudoin de Flandre comme source pour l'histoire de Byzance', *Byzantina*, I:59–80.

Hendrickx, B., (1970), 'Recherches sur les documents diplomatiques non conservés concernant la Quatrième Croisade et l'Empire Latin de Constantinople pendant les premiéres années de son existence (1200–1206)', *Byzantina*, 2:107–84.

Hendrickx, B., (1972), 'Quelques problems à la conquête de la Morée par les Francs', *Byzantina*, 4:373–88.

Hendrickx, B., (1974), 'Les Institutions de l'Empire Latin de Constantinople: la diplomatie', *Acta Classica*, 17:105–19.

Hendrickx, B., (1974), 'The main problems of the history of the Latin Empire of Constantinople', *Revue Belge de Philologie et d'Histoire*, 52:787–99.

Hendrickx, B., (1974), 'Les Institutions de l'Empire Latin de Constantinople:le pouvoir imperial', *Byzantina*, 6:85–154.

Hendrickx, B., (1976), 'Les Institutions de l'Empire Latin de Constantinople: la chancellerie', *Acta Classica*, 19:123–31.

Hendrickx, B., (1977), 'Les Institutions de l'Empire Latin de Constantinople: la cour et les dignitaires', *Byzantina*, 9:187–217.

Hendrickx, B., (1980–2), 'L'Eglise grecque de Constantinople ... (1204–1216): status quaestionis et problematique', *Ecclesiastikos Pharos*, 62–4:129–54.

Hendrickx, B., (1988), 'Regestes des Empereurs latins de Constantinople (1204–1261/72)', *Byzantina*, 14:7–221.

Hendrickx, B. and Matzukis, C., (1979), 'Alexios V Doukas Mourtzouphlos: his life, reign and death (?–1204)', *Hellenika*, 31:108–32.

Hendy, M., (1969), *Coinage and Money in the Byzantine Empire, 1081–1261*, (Washington, DC.).

Hendy, M., (1970), 'Byzantium, 1081–1204: an economic reappraisal', *TRHS*, 5 ser., 20:31–52.

Hendy, M., (1988), *Studies in the Byzantine Monetary Economy*, (Cambridge).

Herrin, J., (1970), 'The collapse of the Byzantine Empire in the twelfth century: a study of medieval economy', *Univ of Birmingham Historical Journal*, 12:188–203.

Herrin, J., (1976), 'Realities of Byzantine provincial government: Hellas and Peloponnesos, 1180–1205', *DOP*, 29:253–84.

Hess, A., (1972), 'The battle of Lepanto and its place in Mediterranean history', *Past and Present*, 57:53–73.

Heyd, W., (1885–6), *Histoire du Commerce du Levant au moyen-age*, ed. F.Raynaud, (Paris, reprinted Amsterdam, 1959).

Hill, K., (1976), 'Robert Grosseteste and his work of Greek translation', in D. Baker, ed., *The Orthodox Churches and the West*, 213–22.

Hill. R., (1976), 'Pure air and portentious heresy', in D. Baker, ed., *The Orthodox Church and the West*, 135–40.

Hodgetts, C., (1983), 'Land problems in Coron, 1293–1347', *Byzantina*, 12:137–57.

Hodgetts, C., (1988), 'Venetian officials and Greek peasantry in the Fourteenth Century' in J. Chrysostomedes, ed., *Kathegelvia: Essays presented to Joan Hussey*, 481–500.

Hodgetts, C. and Lock, P., (1995), 'Topography of Venetian Messenia', in P. Lock and G. Sanders, eds, *Essays in the Archaeology of Medieval Greece*.

Hodgson, F., (1910), *Venice in the Thirteenth and Fourteenth Centuries*.

Hopf, K., (1867–8), *Geschichte Griechenlands vom Beginn des Mittelalters bis auf unsere Zeit*, in J. Ersch and J. Gruber, eds, *Allgemeine Encyklopädie...*, vols 85–86 (Leipzig, reprinted New York, 1960).

Hopf, C., ed., (1873), *Chroniques Gréco-Romanes Inédites ou Peu Connues*, (Berlin, reprinted Brussels, 1966).

Hopf, K., (1877), *Bonifaz von Montferrat und der Troubador Rambaut von Vaqueras*, (Berlin).

Houseley, N., (1992), *The Later Crusades, 1274–1580*, (Oxford).

Howard-Johnston, J., ed., (1988), *Byzantium and the West, c.850–c.1200*, (Amsterdam).

Hussey, J., (1962), 'Byzantium and the crusades, 1081–1204', in K. Setton, gen. ed., *A History of the Crusades*, II:123–52.

Hussey, J., (1986), *The Orthodox Church in the Byzantine Empire*, (Oxford).

Ilieva, A., (1991), *Frankish Morea (1205–62): Socio-cultural Interactions between the Franks and the Local Population*, (Athens).

Ivison, E., (1992), 'Funerary monuments of the Gattelusi at Mytilene', *ABSA*, 87:423–37.

Ivison, E., (1995), 'Some observations on Frankish mortuary practice in the Latin Levant', in P. Lock and G. Sanders, eds, *Essays in the Archaeology of Medieval Greece*.

Jacoby, D., (1966), 'La Compagnie catalane et l'état catalan de Grèce', *Journal des Savants*, 78–103, reprinted in D. Jacoby, *Societé et Démographie à Byzance et en Romanie Latine*.

Jacoby, D., (1967), 'Les Archontes grecs et la féodalité en Morée franque', *TM*, 2:421–81, reprinted in D. Jacoby, *Societé et Démographie à Byzance et en Romanie Latine*.

Jacoby, D., (1968), 'Quelques considérations sur les versions de la Chroniques de Morée', *Journal des Savants*, 133–89, reprinted in D. Jacoby, *Societé et Démographie à Byzance et en Romanie Latine*.

Jacoby, D., (1971), *La Féodalité en Grèce médiévale: Les Assises de Romanie, application et diffusion*, (Paris).

Jacoby, D., (1973), 'An encounter of two societies: western conquerors and Byzantines in the Peloponnese after the Fourth Crusade', *AHR*, 78:873–906, reprinted in D. Jacoby, *Recherches sur la Méditerranée orientale du XIIe au XVe siècle*.

Jacoby, D., (1974), 'Catalans, Turcs et Vénitiens en Romanie (1305–1332): un noveau témoignage de Marino Sanudo Torsello', *Studi Medievali*, 15:217–61, reprinted in D. Jacoby, *Recherches sur la Méditerranée orientale du XIIe au XVe siècle*.

Jacoby, D. (1975), 'Une classe fiscale à Byzance et en Romanie latine: les inconnus du fisc, éleuthères et étrangers', *Actes du XIVe Congrès internationales des études byzantines*, (Bucarest), II:139–52, reprinted in D. Jacoby, *Recherches sur la Méditerranée orientale du XIIe au XVe siècle*.

Jacoby, D., (1975), *Société et Démographie à Byzance et en Romanie Latine*.

Jacoby, D., (1976), 'Les états latins en Romanie: phénomènes sociaux et économiques', *Actes du XVe Congrès international d'études byzantines* (Athens), II:1–51, reprinted in D. Jacoby, *Recherches sur la Méditerranée orientale du XIIe au XVe siècle.*

Jacoby, D., (1979), *Recherches sur la Méditerranée orientale du XIIe au XVe siècle.*

Jacoby, D., (1981), 'Les Vénitiens naturalisés dans l'empire byzantin: un aspect de l'expansion de Venise en Romanie du XIIIe au milieu du Xve siècle', *TM*, 8:217–35.

Jacoby, D., (1989), 'Social evolution in Latin Greece', in K. Setton, gen. ed., *A History of the Crusades*, VI:175–221.

Jacoby, D., (1989), 'From Byzantium to Latin Romania' in B. Arbel, ed., *Latins and Greeks in the Eastern Mediterranean after 1204*, 1–44.

Janin, R., (1930), 'Les Francs au service des Byzantins', *Echos de l'orient*, 29:61–72.

Janin, R., (1945), 'Les sanctuaires de byzance sous la domination latine', *Etudes byzantines*, 2:134–84.

Janin, R., (1946), 'Les sanctuaires des colonies latins a Constantinople', *Etudes byzantines*, 4:168–77.

Janin, R., (1958), 'L'eglise latine a Thessalonique de 1204 a la conqueste Turque', *Etudes byzantines*, 16:206–16.

Jefferys, E., (1984), 'Western infiltration of the Byzantine aristrocracy', in M. Angold, ed., *The Byzantine Aristocracy, IX to XIII Centuries*, 2202ff.

Jefferys, M., (1973), 'Formualae in the Chronicle of the Morea', *DOP*, 27:165–95.

Jefferys, M., (1975), 'The Chronicle of the Morea: priority of the Greek version', *BZ*, 68:304–50.

Jelavich, B., (1981–3), *History of the Balkans*, 2 vols, (Cambridge).

Jeppesen, K., ed., (1981–6), *The Maussolleion at Hallikarnossos...* 2 vols, (Aarhus).

Kahane, H. and R., (1981), 'Byzantium's impact on the west: the linguistic evidence', *Illinois Classical Studies*, 6:389–415.

Kahane, H. and R., (1982), 'The western impact on Byzantium: the linguistic evidence', *DOP*, 36:127–53.

Kasdagli, A., (1987), 'Peasant and lord in 15th century Naxos', *ByzF*, 11:347–56.

Kazdhan, A., ed., (1991), *The Oxford Dictionary of Byzantium*, 3 vols, (New York).

Kazdhan, A. and Constable, G., (1982), *People and Power in Byzantium*, (Washington, DC).

Kazdhan, A. and Epstein, A.W., (1985), *Change in Byzantine Culture in the Eleventh and Twelfth Centuries*, (Berkeley).

Koder, J., (1971), 'Hellas' in K. Wessel, ed., *Reallexikon zur Byzantinischen Kunst*, (Stuttgart), II:1099–1189.

Koder, J., (1973), *Negroponte: Unterschungen zur Topographie und Sidlungsgeschechte der Insel Euboia wahrend der Zeit der Venizianerherrschaft*, (Wien).

Koder, J. and Hild, F., (1976), *Tabula Imperii Byzantina I: Hellas und Thessalia*, (Wien).

Laiou, A., (1967), 'The Provisioning of Constantinople during the Winter of 1306-7', *Byzantina*, 37:91–113.

Laiou, A., (1968), 'A Byzantine prince latinized: Theodore Palaiologus Marquis of Montferrat', *Byzantina*, 38:386–410.

Laiou, A., (1970), 'Marino Sanudo Torsello, Byzantium and the Turks: the background to the Anti-Turkish League of 1332–1334', *Speculum*, 45:374–392.

Laiou, A., (1972), *Constantinople and the Latins: The Foreign Policy of Andronicus II, 1282–1328*, (Cambridge, Mass.).

Laiou (-Thomadakis), A., (1977), *Peasant Society in the Late Byzantine Empire*, (Princeton).

Laiou (-Thomadakis), A., (1980–1), 'The Byzantine economy in the Mediterranean trade system; 13th–15th centuries', *DOP*, 34–5:177–222, reprinted in Laiou (1992).

Laiou, A., (1981), 'The Role of Women in Byzantine Society', *Jahrbuch des Osterriechischen Byzantinistik* 31:233–60 reprinted in A. Laiou, *Gender, Society and Economic Life in Byzantium*.

Laiou, A., (1982) 'The Greek merchant of the Palaiologan Period: a collective portrait', *Praktika of the Academy of Athens*, 57:96–139, reprinted in A. Laiou, *Gender, Society and Economic Life in Byzantium*.

Laiou, A., (1984), 'Observations on the results of the Fourth Crusade: Greeks and Latins in ports and markets', *Medievalia et Humanistica*, 12:43–60.

Laiou, A., (1992), *Gender, Society and Economic Life in Byzantium*.

Lanz, K., ed., (1846), *Chronik des edlin en Roman Muntaner*, (Stuttgart).

Lenormant, F., (1872), 'Le monastere de Daphni pres d'Athenes sous la domination des princes croises', *Revue archeologiques*, 24: 232–45, 278–84.

Linskill, J., (1964), *The Poems of the Troubadour Raimbaut de Vaqueiras*, (Paris).

Lock, P. (1986), 'The Frankish towers of central Greece', *ABSA*, 81:101–23.

Lock, P. (1989), 'The medieval towers of Greece: a problem in chronology and function', in B. Arbel, ed., *Latins and Greeks in the Eastern Mediterranean after 1204*, 129–45.

Lock, P. (1991), 'The Latin Secular Church in mainland Greece, 1204–20', *Medieval History*, 1:93–105.

Lock, P. (1994), 'The Latin Emperors as Heirs to Byzantium', in P. Magdalino, ed., *New Constantines*, 294–305.

Lock, P., (1994), 'The military orders in mainland Greece', in M. Barber, ed., *The Military Orders: Fighting for the Faith and Caring for the Sick*, 333–39.

Lock, P. (1995), 'The medieval towers of Euboea, Venetian or Lombard, agrarian or strategic?', in P. Lock and G. Sanders, eds, *Essays in the Archaeology of Medieval Greece*.

Lock, P. and Sanders, G., eds., (1995) *Essays in the Archaeology of Medieval Greece*, (Oxford).

Loenertz, R-J., (1943), 'Pour l'histoire de Péloponnèse au XIVe siècle (1382–1404)', *Etudes byzantines*, 1:152–96, reprinted in R-J. Loenertz, *Byzantina et Franco-Graeca*, I.

Loenertz, R-J., (1955), 'Athènes et Néopatras: Regestes et Notice pur servir a l'Histoire des Duchés Catalans (1311–94)', *AFP*, 25:100–212, 428–31, reprinted in R-J. Loenertz, *Byzantina et Franco-Graeca*, II.

Loenertz, R-J., (1956), 'Hospitaliers et navarrais en Grèce (1376–1383): regestes et documents', *OCP*, 22:319–60, reprinted in R-J. Loenertz, *Byzantina et Franco-Graeca*, I.

Loenertz, R-J., (1958), 'Athènes et Néopatras ... II', *AFP*, 28:5–91, reprinted in R-J. Loenertz, *Byzantina et Franco-Graeca*, II.

Loenertz, R-J., (1962), 'Généalogie des Ghisi, dynastes vénitiens dans l'Archipel (1207–1390)', *OCP*, 28:121–72, 322–35.

Loenertz, R-J., (1964), 'Les Quirini, comtes d'Astypalée (1413–1537)', *OCP*, 30:385–97, reprinted in R-J. Loenertz, *Byzantina et Franco-Graeca*, I.

Loenertz, R-J., (1965), 'Les seigneurs tierciers de Négropont de 1205 à 1280, Regestes et Documents', *Byzantion*, 35:235–76, reprinted in R-J. Loenertz, *Byzantina et Franco-Graeca*, II.

Loenertz, R-J., (1970), *Byzantina et Franco-Graeca*, I (ed. Peter Schreiner, Roma).

Loenertz, R-J., (1978), *Byzantina et Franco-Graeca*, II (ed. Peter Schriener, Roma).

Longnon, J., (1929), *Les Francais d'Outre-mer au moyen-age: Essai sur l'Expansion francaise dans le basin de la Méditerranée*, (Paris).

Longnon, J., (1937), 'Les Autremencourt, Seigneurs de Salona en Grèce', *Bulletin de la Société de Haute Picardie*, 15:15–48.

Longnon, J., (1939), *Recherches sur la vie de Geoffrey de Villehardouin*, (Paris).

Longnon, J., (1942), 'Le Rattachement de la Principauté de Morée au royaume de Sicile en 1267', *Journal des Savants*, 134–43.

Longnon, J., (1948), 'L'organisation de l'eglise d'Athènes par Innocent III', *Archives de l'Orient Chrétien, I: Mémorial Louis Petit*, 336–46.

Longnon, J., (1949), *L'Empire latin du Constantinople et la Principauté de Morée*, (Paris).

Longnon, J., (1960), 'Les noms de lieu de la Grèce franque', *Journal des Savants*, 97–110.

Longnon, J., (1965), 'La vie rurale dans la Grèce franque', *Journal des Savants*, 343–57.

Longnon, J., (1969), 'The Frankish states in Greece, 1204–1311', in K. Setton, gen. ed., *A History of the Crusades*, II:235–76.

Longnon, J., (1978), *Les Compagnons de Villehardouin...*, (Geneva).

Longnon, J. and Topping, P., eds., (1969), *Documents sur le régime des terres dans la principauté de Morée au XIVe siècle*, (Paris).

Lurier, H.E., (1964), *Crusaders as Conquerors, The Chronicle of Morea*, (New York).

Luttrell, A., (1958), 'Venice and the Knights Hospitallers of Rhodes in the fourteenth century', *PBSR*, 26:195–212, reprinted in A. Luttrell, *The Hospitallers in Cyprus, Rhodes, Greece and the West*.

Luttrell, A., (1964), 'The Principality of Achaia in 1377', *BZ*, 57:340–5, reprinted in A. Luttrell, *The Hospitallers in Cyprus, Rhodes, Greece and the West*.

Luttrell, A., (1969), 'La Corona de Aragon y la Grecia catalana, 1379–1394', *Anuario de Estudias Medievales*, 6:219–52, reprinted in A. Luttrell, *Latin Greece, the Hospitallers and the Crusades*.

Luttrell, A., (1970), 'Aldobrando Baroncelli in Greece, 1378–1382', *OCP*, 36:273–300, reprinted in A. Luttrell, *Latin Greece, the Hospitallers and the Crusades*.

Luttrell, A., (1970), 'Feudal tenure and Latin colonization at Rhodes, 1306–1415', *EHR*, 85:755–75, reprinted in A. Luttrell, *The Hospitallers in Cyprus, Rhodes, Greece and the West*.

Luttrell, A., (1974), 'Crete and Rhodes, 1340–1360', *Acts of the III International Congress of Cretological Studies*, (Athens), II:167–75, reprinted in A. Luttrell, *The Hospitallers in Cyprus, Rhodes, Greece and the West*.

Luttrell, A., (1975), 'The Hospitallers at Rhodes, 1306–1421', in K. Setton, gen. ed., *A History of the Crusades*, III:278–313.

Luttrell, A., (1978), *The Hospitallers in Cyprus, Rhodes, Greece and the West*, 24 collected studies.

Luttrell, A., (1982), *Latin Greece, the Hospitallers and the Crusades*, 16 collected studies.

Luttrell, A., (1986), 'Dalle Carceri', *Dizionario Biografico degli Italiani*, 33:73–7.

Luttrell, A., (1989), 'The Latins and life in the smaller Aegean islands', in B. Arbel, ed., *Latins and Greeks in the Eastern Mediterranean after 1204*, 146–57.

Luttrell, A., (1992), *The Hospitallers of Rhodes and their Mediterranean World*, 18 collected studies.

McDonald, W. and Rapp, G., eds, (1972), *The Minnesota Messenia Expedition*, (Minneapolis).

Macrides, R., (1992), 'Dynastic marriages and political kinship', in J. Shepard and S. Franklin, eds, *Byzantine Diplomacy*, 263–280.

Macrides, R., (1992), 'Bad historian or good lawyer? Demetrios Chomatenos and Novel 131', *DOP*, 46:187–96.

Madden, T., (1991–2), 'The fires of the Fourth Crusade in Constantinople 1203–1204: a damage assessment', *BZ*, 84–5:72–93.

Magdalino, P., (1977), 'A neglected authority for the history of the Peloponnese in the early thirteenth century: Demetrios Chomatianos', *BZ*, 70:316–32.

Magdalino, P., (1984), 'Byzantine snobbery', in M. Angold, ed., *The Byzantine Aristocracy IV to VIII Centuries*, 58–78, reprinted in P. Magdalino, *Tradition and Transformation in Medieval Byzantium*.

Magdalino, P., (1988), 'The phenomenon of Manuel I Komnenos', *ByzF*, 13:171–200, reprinted in P. Magdalino, *Tradition and Transformation in Medieval Byzantium*.

Magdalino, P., (1989), 'Between Romaniae: Thessaly and Epirus in the later Middle Ages', in B. Arbel, ed., *Latins and Greeks in the Eastern Mediterranean after 1204*, 87–110, reprinted in P. Magdalino, *Tradition and Transformation in Medieval Byzantium*.

Magdalino, P., (1991), 'Hellenism and Nationalism in Byzantium', first published in P. Magdalino, *Tradition and Transformation in Medieval Byzantium*.

Magdalino, P., (1991), *Tradition and Transformation in Medieval Byzantium*.

Magdalino, P., (1993), *The Empire of Manuel I Komnenos*, (Cambridge).

Manousakas, M., (1952), 'To Elleniko Demotiko Tragoudi: yia to Vasilia Erriko tis Phlantras', *Laographia*, 14:3–52.

Martin, M., (1988), 'The Venetians in the Byzantine Empire before 1204', in J. Howard-Johnston, ed., *Byzantium and the West, c.850–c.1200*, 201–14.

Mas-Latrie, L. de, (1893), 'Les Seigneurs Tierciers de Negroponte', *Revue de l'Orient latin*, 1:413–32.

Mas-Latrie, L. de, 'Patriarches latins de Constantinople', *Revue de l'Orient latin*, 3:433–56.

Metcalf, D., (1960), 'The currency of denier tournois in Frankish Greece', *ABSA*, 55:38–59.

Metcalf, D., (1964), 'The Brauron Hoard and the petty currency of Frankish Greece', *Numismatic Chronicle*, 4:251–9.

Metcalf, D., (1965), 'Frankish petty Currency from the Areopagus at Athens', *Hesperia*, 34:202–23.

Metcalf, D., (1974), 'The Berbati Hoard, 1953: deniers tournois and sterlings from the Frankish Morea', *Numismatic Chronicle*, 14:19–24.

Metcalf, D., (1979), *Coinage in South-Eastern Europe, 820–1396*.

Metcalf, D., (1983), *Coinage of the Crusades and the Latin East in the Ashmolean Museum, Oxford*.

Miller, W., (1908), *The Latins in the Levant; A History of Frankish Greece (1204–1566)*, (London, reprinted Cambridge, 1964).

Miller, W., (1921), *Essays on the Latin Orient*, (Cambridge).

Miller, W., (1923), *Cambridge Medieval History*, IV:432–77.

Morgan, C., (1942), *Corinth XI: The Byzantine Pottery*, (Cambridge, Mass.).

Morgan, M., (1973), *The Chronicle of Ernoul and the Continuations of William of Tyre*, (Oxford).

Morris, C., (1968), 'Geoffrey de Villhardouin and the conquest of Constantinople', *History*, 53:24–34.

Morris, C., (1989), *The Papal Monarchy*, (Oxford).

Moutsopoulos, N. and Demetrokalles, G., (1968), 'Bibliographie principale des châteaux-forts de la Grèce', *Technika Chronika*, 37:145–8.

Nicol, D., (1957), *The Despotate of Epiros*, (Oxford).

Nicol, D., (1962), 'Byzantium and the papacy in the eleventh century', *Journal of Ecclesiastical History*, 13:1–20, reprinted in D. Nicol, *Byzantium, its Ecclesiastical History and Relations with the Western World*.

Nicol, D., (1964), 'Mixed marriages in Byzantium in the thirteenth century', in C. Dugmore and C. Duggan eds., *Studies in Church History*, 1:160–72, reprinted in D. Nicol, *Byzantium, its Ecclesiastical History and Relations with the Western World*.

Nicol, D., (1966), *Cambridge Medieval History*, IV, i:275–330.

Nicol, D., (1967), 'The Byzantine view of Western Europe', *Greek, Roman and Byzantine Studies*, 8:315–39, reprinted in D. Nicol, *Byzantium, its Ecclesiastical History and Relations with the Western World*.

Nicol, D., (1972), *Byzantium, its Ecclesiastical History and Relations with the Western World*.

Nicol, D., (1972), 'The relations of Charles of Anjou with Nikephoros of Epiros', *ByzF*, 4:170–94, reprinted in D. Nicol, *Studies in Late Byzantine History and Prosopography*.

Nicol, D., (1976), 'Kaiseralbung: the unction of emperors in late Byzantine coronation ritual', *Byzantine and Modern Greek Studies*, 2:37–52, reprinted in D. Nicol, *Studies in Late Byzantine History and Prosopography*.

Nicol, D., (1976), 'Refugees, mixed population and local patriotism in Epiros and Western Macedonia after the Fourth Crusade', *Actes du XVe Congrès international d'études byzantines*, (Athens), I:3–33, reprinted in D. Nicol, *Studies in Late Byzantine History and Prosopography*.

Nicol, D., (1979), 'Symbiosis and integration. Some Greco-Latin families in Byzantium in the 11th to 13th Centuries', *ByzF*, 7:113–36, reprinted in D. Nicol, *Studies in Late Byzantine History and Prosopography*.

Nicol, D., (1984), *The Despotate of Epiros, 1267–1479*, (Cambridge).

Nicol, D., (1986), *Studies in Late Byzantine History and Prosopography*.

Nicol, D., (1987), 'The end of the Livre de la Conqueste: a chronological note', *ByzF*, 12:211–22.

Nicol, D., (1988), 'The fate of Peter of Courtenay ... and a treaty that never was', in J. Chrysostomides, ed., *Kathegetria: Essays Presented to Joan Hussey*, 377–84.

Nicol, D., (1988), *Byzantium and Venice: A Study in Diplomatic and Cultural Relations*, (Cambridge).

Norden, W., (1903), *Das Pasttum und Byzanz...*, (Berlin, reprinted New York, 1959).

Oikonomides, N., (1976), 'La décomposition de l'empire byzantin à la veille de 1204 et les origines de l'empire de Nicée a propos de la Partitio Romaniae', *Actes du XVe Congrès international d'études byzantines*, (Athens), I:3–28.

Oiknomides, N., (1979), *Hommes d'Affaires Grecs et latins a Constantinople (xiiie-xv siècles)*, (Paris).

Oikonomides, N., (1988), 'Byzantium and the western powers in the thirteenth to fifteenth centuries', in J. Howard-Johnson, ed., *Byzantium and the West c.850–c.1200*, 319–331.

Ostrogorsky, G., (1955), 'Zur Kaiseralbung und Schilderhebung im spätbyzantinischen Krönungszeremoniall', *Historia*, 4:246–56.

Panagopoulos, B., (1979), *Cistercian and Mendicant Monasteries in Medieval Greece*, (Chicago).

Papadopoulos-Kerameus, A., (1893), 'Documents Grecs pour servir a l'histoire de la 4me Croisade (Liturgie et reliques)', *Revue de l'Orient latin*, 1:540–55.

Perrat, C. and Longnon, J., eds., (1967), *Actes relatifs à la principauté de Morée, 1289–1300*, (Paris).

Pertusi, A., (1979), 'Venezia e Bisanzio, 1000–1204', *DOP*, 33:3–2.

Petit, J., (1897), 'Un capitaine du regne de Philippe le bel, Thibaut de Cepoy', *Le Moyen Age*, 1:231–36.

Prinzing, G., (1973), 'Der Brief Kaiser Heinrichs von Konstantinopel vom 13 Januar 1212', *Byzantion*, 43:395–431.

Prinzing, G., (1982–3), 'Studien zur Provinz- und zentral Verwaltung im Machtbereich der Epirotischen Herrscher Michael I und Theodoros Dukas', *Epeirotika Chronika*, 24:73–120 and 25:37–112.

Queller, D. and Stratton, S., (1969), 'A century of controversy on the Fourth Crusade', *Studies in Medieval and Renaissance History*, 6:235–77.

Queller, D. and Day, G., (1976), 'Some arguments in defence of the Venetians on the Fourth Crusade', *AHR*, 81:717–37.

Queller, D., (1977), *The Fourth Crusade*, (Pennsylvania).

Queller, D. and Katele, I., (1982), 'Attitudes towards the Venetians in the Fourth Crusade: the western sources', *International History Review*, 4:1–36.

Rackham, O., (1983), 'Observations on the historical ecology of Boeotia', *ABSA*, 78:291–352.

Richard, J., (1989), 'The establishment of the Latin Church in the Empire of

Constantinople (1204–27)', in B. Arbel, ed., *Latins and Greeks in the Eastern Mediterranean after 1204*, 45–62.

Richard, J., (1992), *Saint Louis Crusader King of France*, (Cambridge).

Runciman, S., (1955), *The Eastern Schism*, (Oxford).

Runciman, S., (1958), *The Sicilian Vespers. A History of the Mediterranean World in the Later Thirteenth Century*, (Cambridge).

Sanders, G., (1987), 'An assemblage of Frankish pottery from Corinth', *Hesperia*, 56:159–96.

Sanders, G., (1993), 'Medieval pottery from the Roman Stoa at Sparta', *ABSA*, 88:251–86.

Sanders, G., (1995), 'Two Kastra on Melos and their relations in the Archipelago', in P. Lock and G. Sanders, eds, *Essays in the Archaeology of Medieval Greece*.

Savvides, A., (1988), 'A note on the death of Leo Sgouros in AD 1208', *Byzantine and Modern Greek Studies*, 12: 289–95.

Setton, K., (1944–5), 'The Avignonese Papacy and the Catalan Duchy of Athens', *Byzantion*, 17:281–303.

Setton, K., (1945), 'The Archbishop Simon Atumano and the fall of Thebes to the Navarese in 1379', *Byzantinisch-Neugriechische Jahrbucher*, 18:105–22, reprinted in K. Setton, *Athens in the Middle Ages, Collected Studies*.

Setton, K., (1966), *Cambridge Medieval History*, IV, i: 389–430.

Setton, K., gen.ed., (1969–89), *A History of the Crusades*, 6 vols (Madison).

Setton, K., (1973), 'Saint George's Head', *Speculum*, 48: 1–12.

Setton, K., (1975), 'Catalan society in Greece in the fourteenth century', in L. Laourdas, ed., *Essays to the memory of Basil Laourdas*, (Thessaloniki), 241–84, reprinted in K. Setton *Athens in the Middle Ages, Collected Studies*.

Setton, K., (1975), *Athens in the Middle Ages, Collected Studies*.

Setton, K., (1975), *Catalan Domination of Athens, 1311–1388*, 2nd edn.

Setton, K., (1976–84), *The Papacy and the Levant (1204–1571)*, 4 vols (Philadelphia).

Shepard, J., (1988), 'Aspects of Byzantine attitudes and policy towards the west in the tenth and eleventh centuries', in J. Howard-Johnston, ed., *Byzantium and the West, c.850–c.1200*, 67–118.

Shepard, J., (1988), 'When Greek meets Greek: Alexius Comnenus and Bohemond in 1097–98', *Byzantine & Modern Greek Studies*, 12:185–277.

Shepard, J. and Franklin, S., eds, (1992), *Byzantine Diplomacy*.

Simon, D., (1987), 'Die Bußbscheide des Erzbischofs Chomatian von Ochrid', *Jahrbuch der Österreichischen Byzantinistik*, 37:235–76.

Slot, B., (1991), 'The Frankish Archipelago', *ByzF*, 19:195–203.

Spufford, P., (1986), *Handbook of Medieval Exchange*.

Spufford, P., (1988), *Money and its Use in Medieval Europe*, (Cambridge).

Stahl, A., (1985), *The Venetian Tornosello* (New York).

Starr, J., (1949), *Romania: the Jeweries of the Levant after the Fourth Crusade*, (Paris).

Tanoulas, T., (1987), 'The Propylaea of the Acropolis at Athens since the seventh century', *Jahrbuch des Deutschen Archaologischen Instituts*, 102:413–83.

Thiriet, F., (1959), *La Romanie vénitienne au moyen age. Le Développement et l'exploitation du domaine colonial vénitien*, (Paris).

Thiriet, F., (1976), 'La symbiose dans les états latins formés sur les territoires de la Romania byzantine (1202 à 1261): phénomènes religieux,' *Actes du XVe Congrès international d'études byzantines*, (Athens), I/3: 1–35.

Topping, P., (1977), *Studies on Latin Greece, AD.1205–1715*, 11 collected studies.

Van Andel, T. and Runnels, C., (1987), *Beyond the Acropolis: A Rural Greek Past*, (Stanford).

Vanderpool, E., (1966), 'A monument to the battle of Marathon', *Hesperia*, 35:93–106.

Van Der Vin, J., (1980), *Travellers in Greece and Constantinople. Ancient monuments and Old Traditions in Medieval Travellers' Tales*, 2 vols (Leiden).

Verlinden, C., (1977), *L'Esclavage dans l'Europe médiévale*, II, (Ghent).

Wagstaff, J., (1991), 'Further observations on the location of Grand Magne', *DOP*, 45: 141–8.

Wilkinson, H.R., (1951), *Maps and Politics: A Review of the Ethnographic Cartography of Macedonia*, (Liverpool).

Williams, C.K. and Zervos, O., (1992), 'Frankish Corinth: 1991', *Hesperia*, 61:133–91.

Williams, C.K. and Zervos, O., (1993), 'Frankish Corinth: 1992', *Hesperia*, 62:1–52.

Wolff, R., (1944), 'The Latin Empire of Constantinople and the Franciscans', *Traditio*, 2:213–37, reprinted R. Wolff, *Studies in the Latin Empire of Constantinople*.

Wolff, R., (1947), 'The Latin Empire of Constantinople (1204–1261)', unpubd. PhD dissertation, Harvard, (available on photostat).

Wolff, R., (1948), 'Romania: the Latin Empire of Constantinople', *Speculum*, 23:1–34, reprinted in R. Wolff, *Studies in the Latin Empire of Constantinople*.

Wolff, R., (1948), 'The organization of the Latin Patriarchate of Constantinople', *Traditio*, 6:33–60, reprinted in R. Wolff, *Studies in the Latin Empire of Constantinople*.

Wolff, R., (1948), 'Footnote to an incident of the Latin occupation of Constantinople: the church and the icon of the Hodgetria', *Traditio*, 6:319–28.

Wolff, R., (1949), 'The Second Bulgarian Empire: its origin and history to

1204', *Speculum*, 24:167–206, reprinted in R. Wolff, *Studies in the Latin Empire of Constantinople*.

Wolff, R., (1952), 'Baldwin of Flanders and Hainaut, first latin Emperor of Constantinople...', *Speculum*, 27:281–322, reprinted in R. Wolff, *Studies in the Latin Empire of Constantinople*.

Wolff, R., (1952), 'A new document from the period of the Latin Empire of Constantinople: the oath of the Venetian Podesta', *Annuaire de l'Institut de Philologie et d'Histoire orientales et Slaves*, 12:539–73, reprinted in R. Wolff, *Studies in the Latin Empire of Constantinople*.

Wolff, R., (1954), 'Politics in the Latin Patriarchate of Constantinople, 1204–1261', *DOP*, 8:225–304.

Wolff, R., (1954), 'Mortgage and redemption of an Emperor's son: Castile and the Latin Empire of Constantinople', *Speculum*, 29:45–84, reprinted in R. Wolff, *Studies in the Latin Empire of Constantinople*.

Wolff, R., (1957), 'Greeks and Latins before and after 1204', *Ricerche di storia religiosa*, 1:320–34.

Wolff, R., (1959), 'The Three Romes: the migration of an idelogy and the making of an autocrat', *Daedalus*, 88:291–311.

Wolff, R., (1969), in K. Setton, gen. ed., *A History of the Crusades*, II:187–234, reprinted in R. Wolff, *Studies in the Latin Empire of Constantinople*.

Wolff, R., (1976), *Studies in the Latin Empire of Constantinople*.

Wormald, F., (1937), 'The Holyrood of Bromholm', *Journal of the Warburg Institute*, 1:31–45.

Genealogical Tables

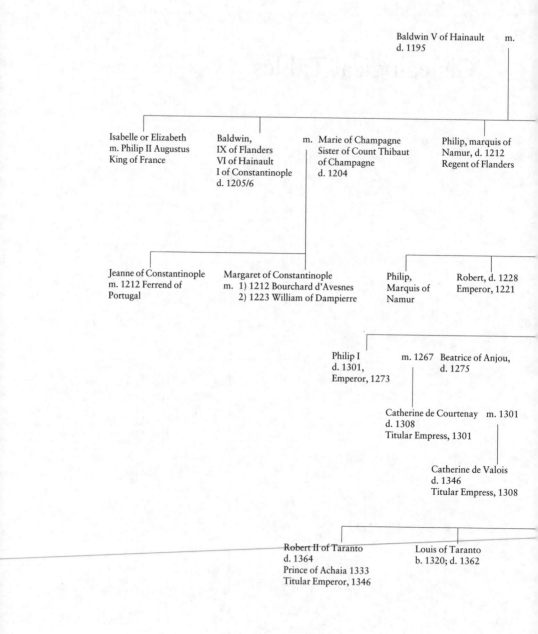

Table 1 The Latin Emperors of Constantinople

Margaret of Alsace, d. 1194.
Sister & heiress of Philip of Flanders

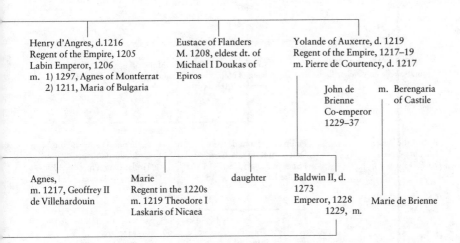

Henry d'Angres, d.1216
Regent of the Empire, 1205
Labin Emperor, 1206
m. 1) 1297, Agnes of Montferrat
   2) 1211, Maria of Bulgaria

Eustace of Flanders
M. 1208, eldest dt. of
Michael I Doukas of
Epiros

Yolande of Auxerre, d. 1219
Regent of the Empire, 1217–19
m. Pierre de Courtency, d. 1217

John de   m. Berengaria
Brienne   of Castile
Co-emperor
1229–37

Agnes,
m. 1217, Geoffrey II
de Villehardouin

Marie
Regent in the 1220s
m. 1219 Theodore I
Laskaris of Nicaea

daughter

Baldwin II, d.
1273
Emperor, 1228   Marie de Brienne
      1229, m.

Charles of Valois, d. 1325

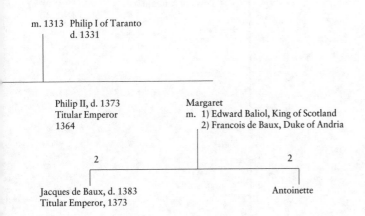

m. 1313 Philip I of Taranto
         d. 1331

Philip II, d. 1373
Titular Emperor
1364

Margaret
m. 1) Edward Baliol, King of Scotland
    2) Francois de Baux, Duke of Andria

2

Jacques de Baux, d. 1383
Titular Emperor, 1373

2

Antoinette

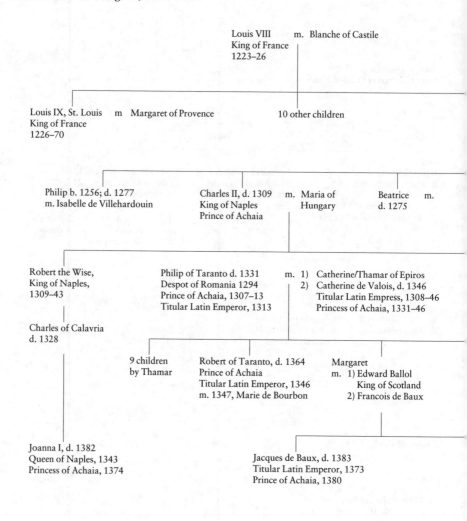

Louis VIII m. Blanche of Castile
King of France
1223–26

Louis IX, St. Louis m Margaret of Provence
King of France
1226–70

10 other children

Philip b. 1256; d. 1277
m. Isabelle de Villehardouin

Charles II, d. 1309 m. Maria of
King of Naples Hungary
Prince of Achaia

Beatrice m.
d. 1275

Robert the Wise,
King of Naples,
1309–43

Philip of Taranto d. 1331 m. 1) Catherine/Thamar of Epiros
Despot of Romania 1294 2) Catherine de Valois, d. 1346
Prince of Achaia, 1307–13 Titular Latin Empress, 1308–46
Titular Latin Emperor, 1313 Princess of Achaia, 1331–46

Charles of Calavria
d. 1328

9 children
by Thamar

Robert of Taranto, d. 1364
Prince of Achaia
Titular Latin Emperor, 1346
m. 1347, Marie de Bourbon

Margaret
m. 1) Edward Ballol
King of Scotland
2) Francois de Baux

Joanna I, d. 1382
Queen of Naples, 1343
Princess of Achaia, 1374

Jacques de Baux, d. 1383
Titular Latin Emperor, 1373
Prince of Achaia, 1380

Table 2 The Angevins or Naples House of Anjou

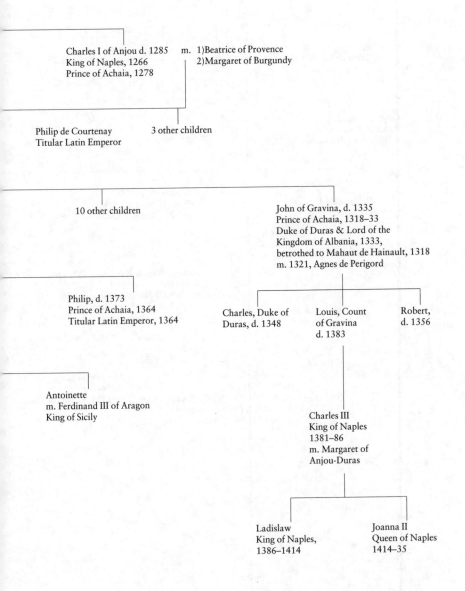

Charles I of Anjou d. 1285   m.   1)Beatrice of Provence
King of Naples, 1266   2)Margaret of Burgundy
Prince of Achaia, 1278

Philip de Courtenay   3 other children
Titular Latin Emperor

10 other children   John of Gravina, d. 1335
                                     Prince of Achaia, 1318–33
                                     Duke of Duras & Lord of the
                                     Kingdom of Albania, 1333,
                                     betrothed to Mahaut de Hainault, 1318
                                     m. 1321, Agnes de Perigord

Philip, d. 1373
Prince of Achaia, 1364   Charles, Duke of   Louis, Count   Robert,
Titular Latin Emperor, 1364   Duras, d. 1348   of Gravina   d. 1356
                                                    d. 1383

Antoinette
m. Ferdinand III of Aragon
King of Sicily   Charles III
                                                    King of Naples
                                                    1381–86
                                                    m. Margaret of
                                                    Anjou-Duras

                                          Ladislaw   Joanna II
                                          King of Naples,   Queen of Naples
                                          1386–1414   1414–35

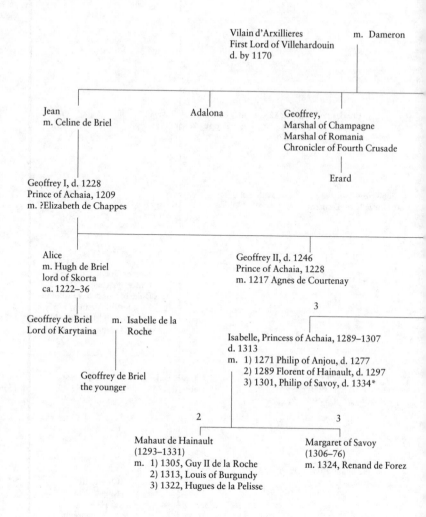

Table 3 The Villehardouin

Guy

William, d. 1278   m. 1) a daughter of Narjot de Toucy
Prince of Achaia   2) Carintana dalle Carceri, d. 1255
1246   3) Anna Doukaina of Epiros, d. 1286

3

Margaret, lady of Akova
m. 1) Isnard de Sabran
    2) 1299, Richard of Kephalonia

Isabel de Sabran (1297–1315)
m. Ferrando of Majorca (d. 1316)

Jaimes II of Majorca, 1324–44
Claimant to Achaia, 1338

* 1312, Philip of Savoy   m. Catherine dauphine of Viennois

Jacques de Savoy, d. 1367
Claimant to Achaia

Philip, d. 1368   Amadeo, d. 1402   Louis, d. 1418
                         Claimant to   Claimant,
                         Achaia,   1402–18
                         1367–1402

Otho de la Roche

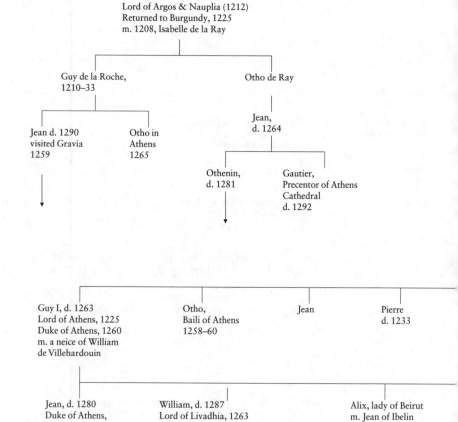

Otho de la Roche,
Lord of Athens (1205) & Thebes
(1209)
Lord of Argos & Nauplia (1212)
Returned to Burgundy, 1225
m. 1208, Isabelle de la Ray

Guy de la Roche,
1210–33

Otho de Ray

Jean d. 1290
visited Gravia
1259

Otho in
Athens
1265

Jean,
d. 1264

Othenin,
d. 1281

Gautier,
Precentor of Athens
Cathedral
d. 1292

Guy I, d. 1263
Lord of Athens, 1225
Duke of Athens, 1260
m. a neice of William
de Villehardouin

Otho,
Baili of Athens
1258–60

Jean

Pierre
d. 1233

Jean, d. 1280
Duke of Athens,
1263

William, d. 1287
Lord of Livadhia, 1263
Duke of Athens, 1280
m. 1275, Helena Angela Komnene

Alix, lady of Beirut
m. Jean of Ibelin

Guy II (Guyot) d. 1308
Duke of Athens, 1287
m. 1305 Mahaut de Hainault

Table 4 The de la Roche

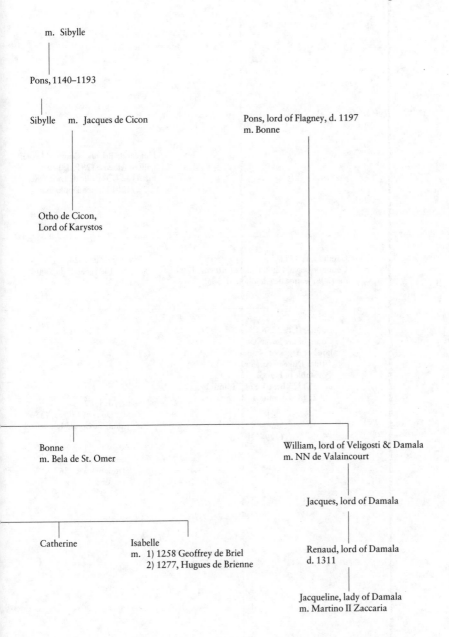

m. Sibylle

Pons, 1140–1193

Sibylle   m. Jacques de Cicon

Otho de Cicon,
Lord of Karystos

Pons, lord of Flagney, d. 1197
m. Bonne

Bonne
m. Bela de St. Omer

William, lord of Veligosti & Damala
m. NN de Valaincourt

Jacques, lord of Damala

Catherine   Isabelle
m. 1) 1258 Geoffrey de Briel
    2) 1277, Hugues de Brienne

Renaud, lord of Damala
d. 1311

Jacqueline, lady of Damala
m. Martino II Zaccaria

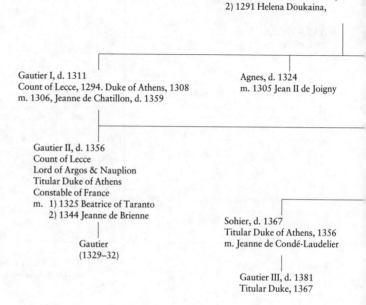

Hugues de Brienne, Count of Lecce,
baili of Athens, 1291, d. 1294
m. 1) 1277 Isabelle de La Roche,
    2) 1291 Helena Doukaina,

Gautier I, d. 1311
Count of Lecce, 1294. Duke of Athens, 1308
m. 1306, Jeanne de Chatillon, d. 1359

Agnes, d. 1324
m. 1305 Jean II de Joigny

Gautier II, d. 1356
Count of Lecce
Lord of Argos & Nauplion
Titular Duke of Athens
Constable of France
m. 1) 1325 Beatrice of Taranto
    2) 1344 Jeanne de Brienne

Gautier
(1329–32)

Sohier, d. 1367
Titular Duke of Athens, 1356
m. Jeanne de Condé-Laudelier

Gautier III, d. 1381
Titular Duke, 1367

Table 5 The Brienne

Co-lord of Karytaina

widow of Geoffrey of Karytaina
widow of William de la Roche

Jeannette, d. 1341
m. Niccolo I Sanudo
Duke of the Archipelago

Isabelle
m. 1320, Gautier d'Enghien

8 other children

Louis Count of
Conversano 1356–94
Titular Duke 1381
m. Jeanne de Sanseverino

Guy lord of Argos & Nauplion
1356–77
m. Bonne de Foucherolles

Marie (1364–93), lady of Argos & Nauplion
ceded towns to Venice in 1388
m. 1) 1377 Peter Cornaro
     2) 1388 Pascale Zane

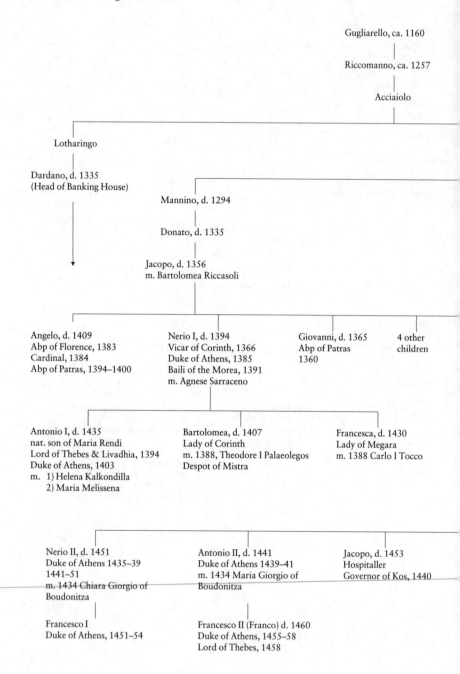

Gugliarello, ca. 1160
|
Riccomanno, ca. 1257
|
Acciaiolo

Lotharingo
|
Dardano, d. 1335
(Head of Banking House)

Mannino, d. 1294
|
Donato, d. 1335
|
Jacopo, d. 1356
m. Bartolomea Riccasoli

Angelo, d. 1409
Abp of Florence, 1383
Cardinal, 1384
Abp of Patras, 1394–1400

Nerio I, d. 1394
Vicar of Corinth, 1366
Duke of Athens, 1385
Baili of the Morea, 1391
m. Agnese Sarraceno

Giovanni, d. 1365
Abp of Patras
1360

4 other children

Antonio I, d. 1435
nat. son of Maria Rendi
Lord of Thebes & Livadhia, 1394
Duke of Athens, 1403
m. 1) Helena Kalkondilla
    2) Maria Melissena

Bartolomea, d. 1407
Lady of Corinth
m. 1388, Theodore I Palaeologos
Despot of Mistra

Francesca, d. 1430
Lady of Megara
m. 1388 Carlo I Tocco

Nerio II, d. 1451
Duke of Athens 1435–39
1441–51
m. 1434 Chiara Giorgio of
Boudonitza

Antonio II, d. 1441
Duke of Athens 1439–41
m. 1434 Maria Giorgio of
Boudonitza

Jacopo, d. 1453
Hospitaller
Governor of Kos, 1440

Francesco I
Duke of Athens, 1451–54

Francesco II (Franco) d. 1460
Duke of Athens, 1455–58
Lord of Thebes, 1458

Table 6 The Acciaioli

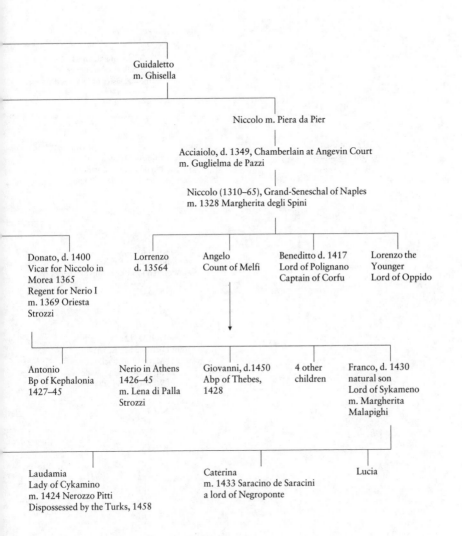

Guidaletto
m. Ghisella

Niccolo m. Piera da Pier

Acciaiolo, d. 1349, Chamberlain at Angevin Court
m. Guglielma de Pazzi

Niccolo (1310–65), Grand-Seneschal of Naples
m. 1328 Margherita degli Spini

Donato, d. 1400
Vicar for Niccolo in
Morea 1365
Regent for Nerio I
m. 1369 Oriesta
Strozzi

Lorrenzo
d. 13564

Angelo
Count of Melfi

Beneditto d. 1417
Lord of Polignano
Captain of Corfu

Lorenzo the
Younger
Lord of Oppido

Antonio
Bp of Kephalonia
1427–45

Nerio in Athens
1426–45
m. Lena di Palla
Strozzi

Giovanni, d.1450
Abp of Thebes,
1428

4 other
children

Franco, d. 1430
natural son
Lord of Sykameno
m. Margherita
Malapighi

Laudamia
Lady of Cykamino
m. 1424 Nerozzo Pitti
Dispossessed by the Turks, 1458

Caterina
m. 1433 Saracino de Saracini
a lord of Negroponte

Lucia

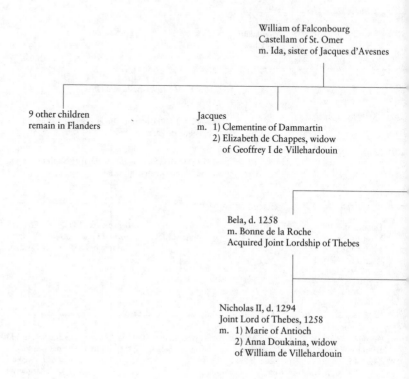

Table 7 The St Omer

Nicholas I
m. ?Maria, a widowed Hungarian
     Princess (not Margaret, widow of
     Boniface of Montferrat)

William
returned to Flanders

Othon, d. 1299
Joint Lord of Thebes,
1294

Jean
m. 1276, Margaret de Neuilly
Lady of Passava, widow of Guibert
de Cors and William of Verona

Nicholas III, d. 1314
Lord of Passava, 1290
Hereditary Marshal of Achaia, 1290
Joint Lord of Thebes, 1299
baili of the Morea, 1300–2; 1305–6
m. Guillerma of Kephalonia,
widow of Jean Chauderon, hereditary
Constable of the Morea

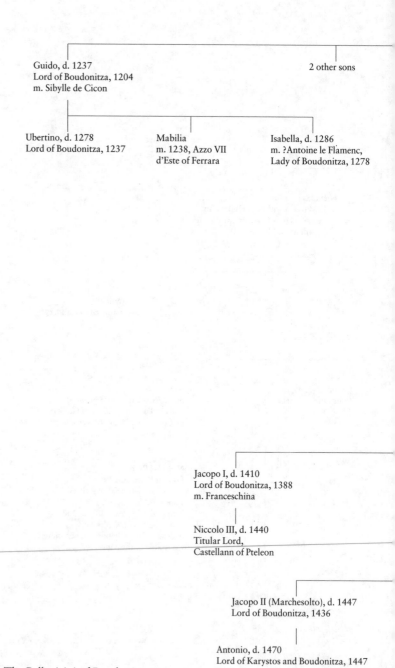

Guido, d. 1237
Lord of Boudonitza, 1204
m. Sibylle de Cicon

2 other sons

Ubertino, d. 1278
Lord of Boudonitza, 1237

Mabilia
m. 1238, Azzo VII
d'Este of Ferrara

Isabella, d. 1286
m. ?Antoine le Flamenc,
Lady of Boudonitza, 1278

Jacopo I, d. 1410
Lord of Boudonitza, 1388
m. Franceschina

Niccolo III, d. 1440
Titular Lord,
Castellann of Pteleon

Jacopo II (Marchesolto), d. 1447
Lord of Boudonitza, 1436

Antonio, d. 1470
Lord of Karystos and Boudonitza, 1447

Table 8 The Pallavicini of Boudonitza

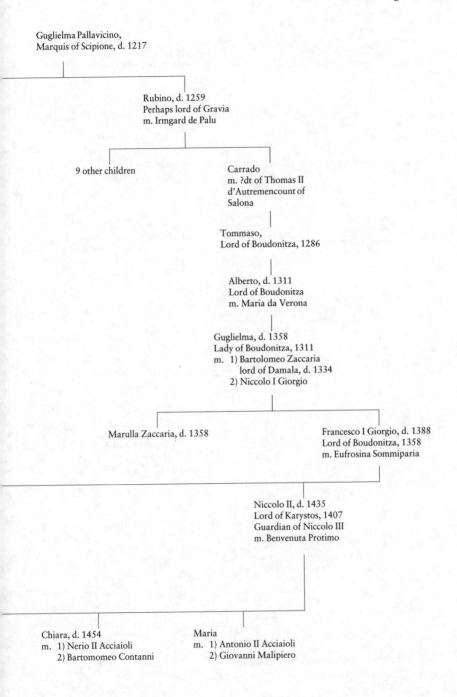

Guglielma Pallavicino,
Marquis of Scipione, d. 1217

Rubino, d. 1259
Perhaps lord of Gravia
m. Irmgard de Palu

9 other children

Carrado
m. ?dt of Thomas II
d'Autremencount of
Salona

Tommaso,
Lord of Boudonitza, 1286

Alberto, d. 1311
Lord of Boudonitza
m. Maria da Verona

Guglielma, d. 1358
Lady of Boudonitza, 1311
m. 1) Bartolomeo Zaccaria
       lord of Damala, d. 1334
    2) Niccolo I Giorgio

Marulla Zaccaria, d. 1358

Francesco I Giorgio, d. 1388
Lord of Boudonitza, 1358
m. Eufrosina Sommiparia

Niccolo II, d. 1435
Lord of Karystos, 1407
Guardian of Niccolo III
m. Benvenuta Protimo

Chiara, d. 1454
m. 1) Nerio II Acciaioli
    2) Bartomomeo Contanni

Maria
m. 1) Antonio II Acciaioli
    2) Giovanni Malipiero

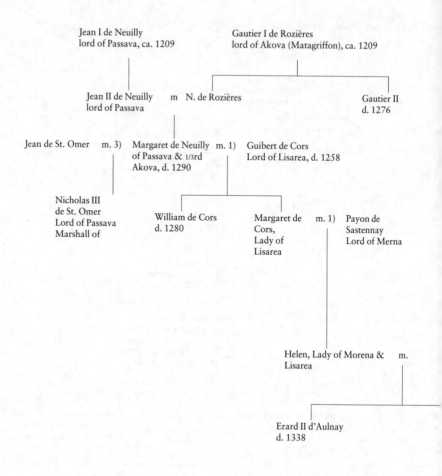

Table 9 Some baronial families of the Morea
Note: Aulnay = Aunoy
       Briel = Bruyere

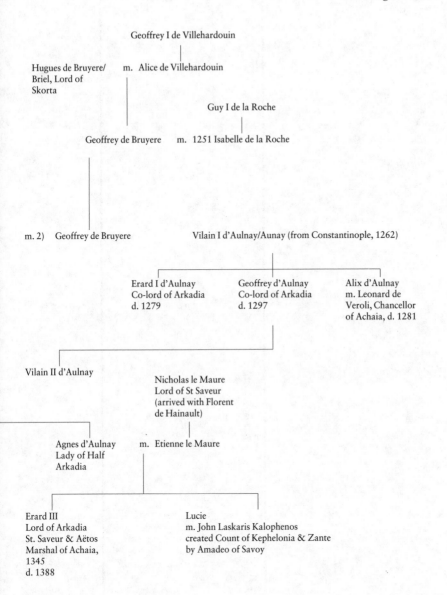

Geoffrey I de Villehardouin

Hugues de Bruyere/   m. Alice de Villehardouin
Briel, Lord of
Skorta

Guy I de la Roche

Geoffrey de Bruyere   m. 1251 Isabelle de la Roche

m. 2)   Geoffrey de Bruyere   Vilain I d'Aulnay/Aunay (from Constantinople, 1262)

Erard I d'Aulnay   Geoffrey d'Aulnay   Alix d'Aulnay
Co-lord of Arkadia   Co-lord of Arkadia   m. Leonard de
d. 1279   d. 1297   Veroli, Chancellor
                                         of Achaia, d. 1281

Vilain II d'Aulnay

Nicholas le Maure
Lord of St Saveur
(arrived with Florent
de Hainault)

Agnes d'Aulnay   m. Etienne le Maure
Lady of Half
Arkadia

Erard III   Lucie
Lord of Arkadia   m. John Laskaris Kalophenos
St. Saveur & Aëtos   created Count of Kephelonia & Zante
Marshal of Achaia,   by Amadeo of Savoy
1345
d. 1388

Maps

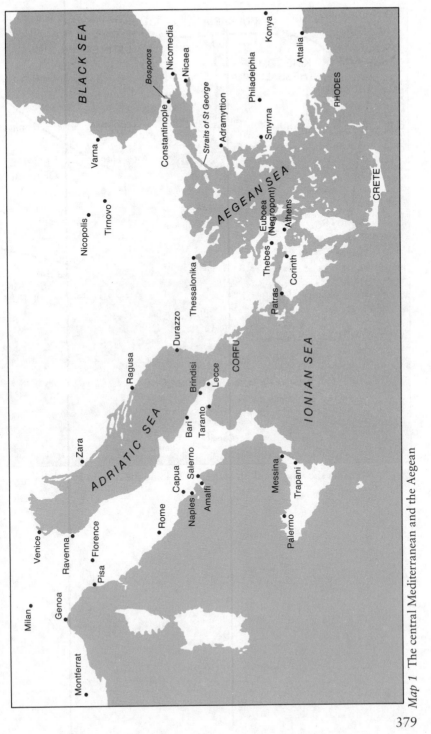

Map 1 The central Mediterranean and the Aegean

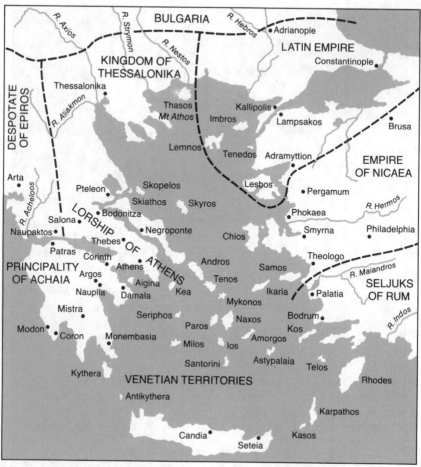

Map 2 Romania showing Frankish States, *c.*1214 and the Aegean Islands

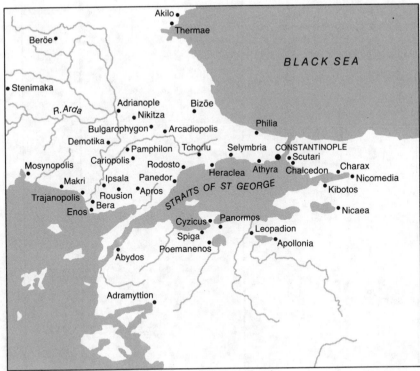

Map 3 Thrace, Bythynia and Pontus – the Latin Empire

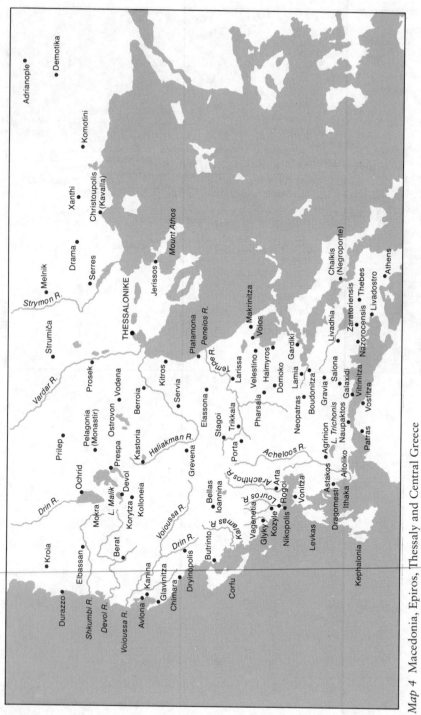

Map 4 Macedonia, Epiros, Thessaly and Central Greece

Patras
Vostitza
Gerokomeion
Glisaria
Chalandritsa
Zemena
Megara
Manolada
Kalavryta
Sicyon
Hexamilion
Wall
Salamis
Glarenza
Andravida
Corinth
Mostenitsa
Gastouni
Akrokorinth
Polyphengos
Chlemoutsi
Olena
Akova
Argyrokastro
Angelokastro
Aegina
Krestena
Argos
Merbaka
Isova
Mantinea
Nauplion
Andritsana
Karytaina
Troezen
(Damala)
St George
Vervena
Herimione
Veligosti
Siderokastro
Hydra
Kyparissia
Gardiki
Androusa
Gardiri
Spetsiai/
Sette Pozze
Avramiou
Mistra
Lakadaimon
Old Navarino
Kalamata
Nikli
Pylos
Zarnata
Geraki
Modon
Leuctron
Coron
Passava
Monemvasia
Vardounia
Maina

Map 5 The Principality of Achaia

Index